Sy— —n

Contents

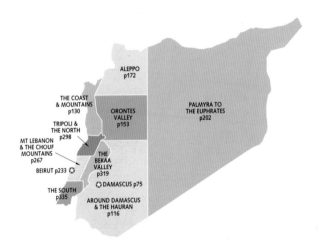

ALEPPO
p172

THE COAST
& MOUNTAINS
p130

ORONTES
VALLEY
p153

TRIPOLI &
THE NORTH
p298

PALMYRA TO
THE EUPHRATES
p202

MT LEBANON
& THE CHOUF
MOUNTAINS
p267

THE
BEKAA
VALLEY
p319

BEIRUT p233

DAMASCUS p75

THE SOUTH
p335

AROUND DAMASCUS
& THE HAURAN
p116

Destination: Syria & Lebanon

Discovering the myriad charms of these countries is an endless pleasure. Excellent food, breathtaking scenery, magnificent historical monuments and some of the friendliest people in the world await the traveller, just as they have for centuries. And centuries are a short span of time to these ancient lands, where evidence of the last few thousand years of civilisation can be seen in the museums or at the numerous significant archaeological sites. From the ancient snowcapped Cedars of Lebanon to the golden haze of the Syrian deserts, the journey to the sites is as fascinating as the sights themselves. You'll crane your neck to get a glimpse of a Bedouin camp, the black goat-hair tents standing out against the desert landscape. You'll pass small villages, orchards heavy with fruit and rich, red-soiled vineyards. But nothing can prepare you for the awesome scale, preservation and setting of the monumental ancient sites, the eerie, abandoned Dead Cities, or sublime sunsets over Crusader castles by the sea.

Between explorations of majestic archaeological ruins, such as Palmyra and Baalbek, you can enjoy the buzzy cosmopolitan nightlife and sophisticated designer shopping of Beirut, or wander the atmospheric alleyways and labyrinthine souqs of Damascus, Aleppo or Tripoli. A trip into these souqs is a trip back in time, with aromas emanating from sacks of herbs and spices blending with the sweet smell of frankincense and strong Turkish coffee, the sounds of the muezzin calls to prayer competing with the latest Arabic pop CD.

Surprisingly, considering the wealth of history on offer, the strongest memory of your trip to these ancient lands might not lie in your photo album. It could very well be the memory of the warmest of welcomes from the down-to-earth locals living among the Bosra ruins, or the offer of *chai* and a chat in the Tyre souq.

WAYNE WALTON

ALEPPO (p172)
Get lost in the labyrinthine souq and dine on Syria's best mezze

APAMEA (p167)
Stroll down the colonnaded main street of these impressive Roman ruins in a picturesque setting

DEAD CITIES (p200)
Tip-toe around the eerie remains of abandoned Byzantine towns, which remain empty, unexplored and largely undocumented

KRAK DES CHEVALIERS (p132)
Spend a complete day exploring what is simply *the* finest Crusader castle in the world

BAALBEK (p327)
Transport yourself back to the 'Sun City' of the ancient world, including one of Rome's most lavish temples, and study its debauched past

TRIPOLI (p300)
Sample Tripoli's famous sweets and then walk off the calories exploring the bustling medieval souqs

BYBLOS (p280)
Wander the impressive archaeological remains knowing that a seafood feast awaits at a charming ancient harbour

BEIRUT (p233)
Explore the Corniche, and discover the clubs of Beirut, and find out why it's the Middle East's most vibrant capital

AANJAR (p325)
Amble down the main street of the majestic remains of the Middle East's only Umayyad fortified city

BEITEDDINE (p294)
Stroll around the grounds of this magnificent Ottoman-era palace and marvel at the beautiful mosaics

DAMASCUS (p75)
Put down that map and just wander the Old City discovering the wonderful old Damascene houses and hidden restaurants

TYRE (p345)
Swim at one of its wonderful beaches after making a lap of the world's largest Roman hippodrome

BOSRA (p122)
Take a seat in this extraordinary Roman theatre, cocooned by an Arab Fortress

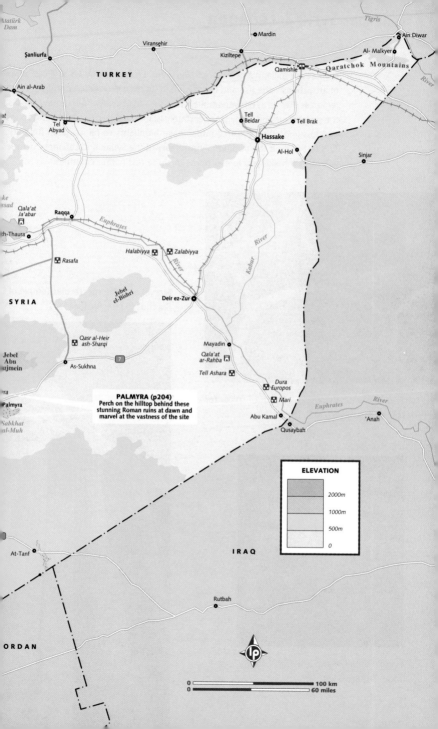

Tigris

Atatürk
Dam

● Mardin

● Ain Diwar

Viranşehir ●

Şanliurfa ●

Kiziltepe ●

Al- Malkyer ●

Qamishle ●

Qaratchok Mountains

River

TURKEY

Ain al-Arab ●

Tel
Abyad ●

Tell
Beidar ●

● Tell Brak

Hassake ●

Al-Hol ●

● Sinjar

Qala'at
Ja'abar 🏰

Raqqa ●

Euphrates

-Thaura ●

Kabur

River

Rasafa

Halabiyya ● ● Zalabiyya

River

SYRIA

Jebel
el-Bishri

Deir ez-Zur ●

Qasr al-Heir
ash-Sharqi 🏰

Mayadin ●

Jebel
Abu
ajmein

As-Sukhna ●

7

Qala'at
ar-Rahba 🏰

Tell Ashara 🏰

Palmyra

Dura
Europos

Mari 🏰

Euphrates

River

'Anah ●

Sabkhat
al-Muh

Abu Kamal ●

Qusaybah ●

ELEVATION

At-Tanf ●

2000m

1000m

500m

0

IRAQ

PALMYRA (p204)
Perch on the hilltop behind these
stunning Roman ruins at dawn and
marvel at the vastness of the site

Rutbah ●

ORDAN

0   100 km
0   60 miles

Over seven millennia of history in Syria and Lebanon adds up to a vast array of attractions – the rise and fall of numerous civilisations has contributed to a region as diverse as it is venerable. With a wealth of ancient ruins, snowy peaks, the sear desert and stony steppe, stately Islamic architecture, humming souqs and bustling cities, both countries have highlights to fill many an itinerary. And to top it off the traditional hospitality of the Syrian and Lebanese people will quickly make you feel at home in these fascinating countries.

BETHUNE CARMICHAEL

Take in the heady aromas of bags of spices for sale at a market (p302), Tripoli

Marvel over the spectacular Temple of Bacchus (p330), Baalbek

BETHUNE CAI

JOHN ELK III

Haggle for a bargain in a 13th-century souq (p178), Aleppo

Stroll through the impressive symbols of 19th-century architecture at Beiteddine Palace (p294), Beiteddine

BETHUNE CARMICHAEL

CHRISTOPHER WOOD

Visit one of the most notable decorative wonders of Islam, the Umayyad Mosque (p86), Damascus

Experience the glory of Palmyra (p204)

JOHN ELK III

Enjoy a local ritual, a leisurely afternoon stroll along the Corniche (p246), Beirut

Enjoy a few hours sampling a favourite Damascene pastime, take a nargileh break (p107), Damascus

Accept an offer to share a coffee with the desert nomads, the Bedouin (p216)

View the spectacular Pigeon Rocks (p247), Beirut

Getting Started

With ancient ruins from many great civilisations, medieval souqs, fascinating cities, and beautiful mountains and valleys all located in a reasonably compact area, you can cover a lot of territory in a small amount of time in Syria and Lebanon. For advice see our suggested Itineraries (p13).

In general terms, both countries suit all budgets, but there are cities and towns that some travellers would prefer to visit on a day trip where there's no suitable accommodation. While getting around these destinations may appear a little challenging at first – often because of the myriad methods of getting from A to B – you'll soon find yourself travelling like a local! Having mastered this, you're well on the way to getting to know these intriguing destinations.

WHEN TO GO

The best time of year to visit Lebanon and Syria is spring (March to May) when the weather is mild and wildflowers are in bloom. During May the weather can be warm enough for swimming and the mountains are carpeted with colour. In Beirut and Damascus, the winter rains would have cleared the haze that obscures the cities for some of the year. The rains would have swollen the rivers, so the wooden norias (waterwheels) in Hama are turning and fresh, clean water flows through Damascus. If your timing is just right, you may be able to live the Lebanese cliché and, at the end of the snow season, ski in the mountains in the morning and swim on the coast in the afternoon. If you can't make the spring, aim for autumn (September to November), between the intense heat of summer and the cloud of winter.

See Climate Charts (p359) for more information.

For sunworshippers, temperatures soar from June to the middle of September, although summers can be uncomfortably hot. Coastal areas, such as Tripoli and Lattakia, can get extremely humid, while the interiors will be very hot and dry. This may be fine if you want to lie on a Mediterranean beach but is not ideal for exploring the large exposed ruins at Palmyra, Apamea, Bosra or Baalbek. Travel in the northeast of the region and through the desert can become real endurance tests. Heading out early and returning to the hotel for an afternoon siesta is necessary to avoid heat stroke and exhaustion (for more advice see also p400). The winter rains can make sightseeing difficult, but if you're lucky enough a blanket of snow may cover Damascus and the high altitudes of both countries. Bear in mind

DON'T LEAVE HOME WITHOUT...

- Checking the latest travel advisory warnings.
- Getting a new passport if your current one contains an Israeli stamp.
- Ensuring you have proof of the relevant vaccinations (see p396) for the region.
- Applying for a Syrian visa and checking the current visa status for Lebanon (see p375).
- Making copies of important documents – main passport pages, travel insurance details and original receipt for travellers cheques.
- Carrying an Arabic phrasebook – a 'salaam 'alaykum' (peace be upon you) will get you far and bring smiles to faces!
- Packing that little black dress or a going-out shirt, and good shoes – if you're planning a night out in Beirut.

that the cheaper hotels may not have heating. Lebanon, on the other hand, is becoming increasingly popular as a winter sports destination. There are many ski resorts in the Mt Lebanon range (see p267 for details) and the season extends from early December to early April.

Like anywhere, if you are heading to Lebanon or Syria during school holidays, you should book accommodation well in advance. Religious and state holidays should not seriously disrupt any travel plans – some services may be cut back, but transport, hotels, restaurants and many businesses function as normal. The Muslim fasting month of Ramadan may require a bit more planning: make sure you eat breakfast at your hotel as some cafés and restaurants close during the day, and some offices operate reduced and erratic hours. Ramadan nights, particularly during the final three days of the Eid al-Fitr can be particularly lively. You may wish to schedule your trip around annual festivals, such as those at Baalbek, Byblos, Palmyra and Bosra. For details on these and other special events, see p363 and for more information on holidays across the two countries, see p365.

COSTS & MONEY

Lebanon and Syria are great value destinations. Although Lebanon's best restaurants and hotels are comparable in price to Europe, North America o Australia, you can live it up at elegant restaurants and top-end hotels in Syria for far less. At the finest Damascene restaurants, a feast with wine for two will cost around US$30, while a night on the executive floor of the Cham Palace, the city's best hotel, can be bargained down to US$130 in the low season. At the other extreme, a delicious shwarma and fresh fruit juice can be had for US$3 for two! You can spend as little as US$5 to US$10 at a decent sit-down restaurant.

At the lower-cost end, staying in dorms in hostels and living on shwarma, you could scrape by on US$25 per day in Lebanon, even less in Syria. A more comfortable budget – staying in hotels as opposed to pensions or hostels and eating in restaurants as opposed to street food – would be US$70 to US$80 (per person, travelling as a couple). You can live very well in either country for US$100 a day. Travel is also inexpensive, with a bus ride from Aleppo to Damascus S£150 and from Tripoli to Beirut LL2000. Once you get out of the cities in either country, prices are even lower.

TRAVEL LITERATURE

As there are very few travelogues focused solely on Syria and Lebanon, you may find yourself selectively reading chapters from foreigner's accounts of travels through the Middle East.

Paul Theroux wittily writes about his travels to Aleppo, Tartus, Lattakia, Krak des Chevaliers, Damascus and Maalula in *The Pillars of Hercules* (1996). From his one perceptive chapter on Syria you will learn more than you might from reading whole novels by other authors. Theroux's serendipitous style of travelling is truly inspiring – you'll glimpse a beautiful view or something interesting and find yourself jumping off buses and trains well before your intended destination!

Robert D Kaplan eruditely writes about his journeys in Syria and Lebanon in *Eastward to Tartary* (2001), cleverly weaving together historical and contemporary characters and stories as he did in *Balkan Ghosts* (1993).

A bittersweet, evocative and quirky account of travel in Syria can be found in Robert Tewdwr Moss' *Cleopatra's Wedding Present* (2003). Moss, who documents his affair with a Palestinian refugee, was murdered the day after he finished the book.

HOW MUCH?

Postcard
S£30/LL500

Newspaper
S£10/LL2000

Fresh fruit-juice cocktail
S£50/LL3000

Bottle of local wine
S£100/LL10,000

Short taxi ride
S£40/LL5000

LONELY PLANET INDEX

Litre of petrol
S£6.85/LL1100

Litre of bottled water
S£30/LL500

Beer – bottle of Barada/Al Maaza
S£50/LL500

Souvenir T-shirt
You'll be lucky to find one!/LL5000

Street snack – shwarma
S£75/LL3000

TOP TENS
BEST OF THE FESTIVALS

One of the great things about festivals in Syria and Lebanon is the location; most of these festivals are held amid evocative ancient ruins. Also see our comprehensive listing of Festivals & Events (p363).

- Al Bustan Festival
  February, Lebanon (p269)

- Spring Flower Festival
  April, Syria (p363)

- Palmyra Festival
  April/May, Syria (p211)

- Baalbek Festival
  July & August, Lebanon (p363)

- Beiteddine Festival
  July & August, Lebanon (p363)

- Byblos International Festival
  August, Lebanon (p363)

- Silk Road Festival
  September, Syria (p363)

- Bosra Festival
  September (odd years), Syria (p363)

- Mid East Film Festival Beirut
  October, Lebanon (p253)

- Damascus International Film Festival
  November & December, Syria (p102)

MUST-SEE MOVIES

Pre-departure dreaming can be done from the comfort of your sofa. If you can't find the following movies in your local video store, art-house cinema, or foreign movie channel, you can probably find them at www.arabfilm.com. See p51 for more details, including reviews of some of these films.

Syria

- *Under the Sky of Damascus* (1931)
  Director: Ismail Anzur

- *Dreams of the City* (1984)
  Director: Mohamed Malas

- *The Nights of the Jackal* (1989)
  Director: Abdulatif Abdulhamid

- *The Night* (1992)
  Director: Mohamed Malas

- *The Events of the Coming Year* (1986)
  Director: Samir Zikra

Lebanon

- *Towards the Unknown* (1957)
  Director: Georges Nasser

- *West Beirut* (1998)
  Director: Ziad Duweyri

- *The Little Wars* (1982)
  Director: Maroun Baghdadi

- *The Broken Wings* (1962)
  Director: Yousef Malouf

- *In the Shadows of the City* (2000)
  Director: Jean Chamoun

TOP READS

Perusing these titles are a short-cut to understanding the hopes, dreams and observations of life and love in Syria and Lebanon. For more details on literature in the region, see p49.

Syria

- *On Entering the Sea: The Erotic and Other Poetry* (1996)
  Nizar Qabbani

- *Just Like a River: from Syria* (2003)
  Muhammed Kamil Al-Khatib

- *Damascus Nights* (1997)
  Rafik Schami

- *Sabriya: Damascus Bitter Sweet* (1997)
  Ulfat Idilbi

- *Menstruation* (2001)
  Ammar Abdulhamid

Lebanon

- *Sitt Marie Rose: A Novel* (1982)
  Etel Adnan

- *The Stone of Laughter* (1998)
  Hoda Barakat

- *The Rock of Tanios* (1994)
  Amin Maalouf

- *Memory for Forgetfulness: August, Beirut 1982* (1982)
  Mahmoud Darwish

- *Death in Beirut* (1976)
  Tawfiq Yusuf Awwad

Janet Wallach's *Desert Queen* (2001) is a highly entertaining account of the often sensuous adventures of feisty Victorian traveller (and friend to TE Lawrence), Gertrude Bell. You can read Bell's own gossipy account of her carousing with Bedouin tribesmen in *The Desert and the Sown*, first published in 1907. If you find the colonial travellers from this period intriguing, you'll enjoy Lawrence's controversial classic *Seven Pillars of Wisdom*.

In *Travels with a Tangerine* (2001), Tim Mackintosh Smith engagingly documents his travels to Damascus, the Crusader and Assassin castles (for more information on the latter, see the boxed text The Assassins, p170), Hama and Aleppo as he retraces the journeys of the famous 14th-century Arab traveller, Ibn Battuta. William Dalrymple follows in the footsteps of another earlier traveller – a 6th-century monk – in *From the Holy Mountain* (1998). Dalrymple's visits to Aleppo, Damascus, Beirut and Bcharré offer some keen observations.

For vivid local perspectives on the Syrian and Lebanese capitals, read Siham Tergeman's *Daughter of Damascus* (1994) and Jean Said Makdisi's *Beirut Fragments* (1990). *Daughter of Damascus* is a personal account of growing up in the atmospheric Souq Saroujah in the first half of the 20th century, while *Beirut Fragments* focuses on the difficult and dangerous day-to-day life during the civil war, as told by Edward W Said's sister.

INTERNET RESOURCES

Al-Mashriq (http://almashriq.hiof.no/) Enormous array of info and images on the Levant.

Lebanon.com (www.lebanon.com) Travel info, maps, hotels, restaurants, online shopping.

Lebanon's Ministry of Tourism (www.lebanon-tourism.gov.lb) Lebanon's official tourism site – one day it might even finish the English version!

Lebanon Panorama (www.lebanonpanorama.com) Panoramic 360-degree views of Lebanon.

Lonely Planet (www.lonelyplanet.com.au) Succinct summaries on travelling to Syria and Lebanon, Thorn Tree bulletin board, and the subwwway section with links to the most useful travel resources elsewhere on the Web.

Syria's Ministry of Tourism (www.syriatourism.org) Quite good official travel site.

Syria-Net (www.syria-net.com) Wide range of links on Syria, including news and culture.

Itineraries
CLASSIC ROUTES

SYRIAN SOJOURN
Two weeks / Syria

Spend three full days in **Damascus** (p75), visiting its **Old City** (p83) to see the Umayyad Mosque, its souqs, and historic houses. Visit the **National Museum** (p94) – in preparation for Syria's archaeological sites. Do day trips to the village **Maalula** (p118), the convent at **Seidnayya** (p118) and the monastery at **Mar Musa** (p121). **Bosra** (p122) is a must, with its Roman theatre.

From Damascus, fly to **Aleppo** (p172). Allow two days to explore Aleppo's citadel, its Al-Jeida quarter and get lost in the alleyways of its souqs. From Aleppo, take day trips to the ruined basilica of **Qala'at Samaan** (p196), and the **Dead Cities** (p200) of Jerada, Ruweiha, Serjilla and Al-Bara. Move on to **Hama** (p160) to see its norias (wooden waterwheels), take a couple of days to visit **Apamea** (p167), **Qasr ibn Wardan** (p170) and the **beehive villages** (p171) of Sarouj and Twalid Dabaghein. Head to the coast to **Tartus** (p136) and **Arwad island** (p138), and visit **Lattakia** (p143). Return via Tartus to see the immense **Krak des Chevaliers** (p132) and stay in **Homs** (p155). Allow a day or two in **Palmyra** (p204) for the ruins (they're at their best at first light; see the boxed text Visiting Palmyra, p205), before returning to Damascus.

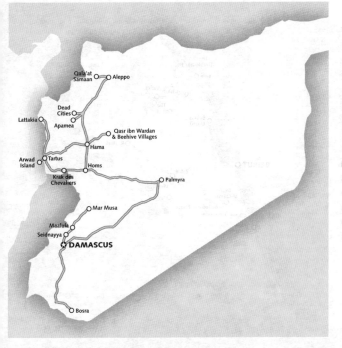

Your Syrian Sojourn is a busy but satisfying two-week trip that covers the best Syria has to offer. Starting off in Damascus the trip moves on through captivating sights and ends with two of the best in the Middle East, Krak des Chevaliers and Palmyra.

LOOPING LEBANON

Two weeks / Lebanon

Begin by spending a few days in buzzy **Beirut** (p233), before cruising up the coast to pretty **Byblos** (p280) for its picturesque old port, timing your explorations so that you are strolling around the ruins at sunset – a sublime experience. Head to **Tripoli** (p300) next, taking a few days to explore its ancient khans (inns), mosques, hammams, souqs and the crusader castle in nearby Enfe.

Enjoy the dramatic vistas and charming villages of the **Qadisha Valley** (p310) on your way to **Bcharré** (p312) and **The Cedars** (p314). Outside of winter you can take the mountain road to the Bekaa Valley and **Baalbek** (p327) to enjoy the best-preserved Roman temples in the world. Drop in to Zahlé for lunch and to one of the **Bekaa's vineyards** (p324) for some wine-tasting.

Next, visit the exquisite Umayyad ruins of **Aanjar** (p325) before heading to the Chouf Mountains and the charming village of **Deir al-Qamar** (p292). Nearby is the lavish **Beiteddine Palace** (p294) and its delightful gardens with Byzantine mosaics. Make your way to **Sidon** (p337) to see its stylish **Musée Du Savon** (p341), **labyrinthine souq** (p341) and **Sea Castle** (p340).

Head south to **Tyre** (p345) for its pretty bay and ruins, which include the world's largest **Roman hippodrome** (p348). Tyre is a good base for exploring the formerly occupied south (see the itinerary for Southern Souqs, p17). Head back along the coast to Beirut for one last taste of the city's vibrant nightlife.

Looping Lebanon takes you to all of Lebanon's best sights starting and finishing in the capital, Beirut. The route can be covered in 10 days, but doing it over two weeks is a more relaxing trip. Note that during winter you cannot cross from Bcharré to Baalbek.

ROADS LESS TRAVELLED

THE EUPHRATES & THE EMPTINESS   Five days / The Euphrates River

Alongside the Nile and Tigris, the Euphrates is one of the great Middle East rivers. Flowing through the northeastern region of Syria bordering Turkey and Iraq, this area is known as the Jezira, or 'island'. Its fertile grounds yield wheat, cotton and oil. To explore this region, from **Aleppo** (p172), head east to **Raqqa** (p217). This dusty little town will be your base to visit **Qala'at Najm** (p217), built by Nurredin, and **Qala'at Ja'abar** (p217), a Mesopotamian citadel overlooking Lake al-Assad; you can also swim and picnic with the locals at the **Ath-Thaura** (p217) dam. A visit to **Rasafa** (p219) is a must – an immense walled city with ruins of three basilicas, it rises dramatically out of the empty desert.

From Raqqa travel southeast to the bustling market town of **Deir ez-Zur** (p220). Basing yourself here for a few days, you can do a couple of day trips or take one very long day to see the various archaeological sites along the Euphrates River towards the Iraqi border. **Dura Europos** (p224), an extensive Hellenistic/Roman fortress city, has breathtaking views of the desert. The mud-brick ruins of **Mari** (p225) might not offer beautiful vistas, but this is one of the most important ancient Mesopotamian sites. Take time in Deir ez-Zur to enjoy the riverside setting, Bedouin-influenced culture and colourful souq, before heading for the stunning Roman ruins of **Palmyra** (p208) before travelling south to vibrant Damascus.

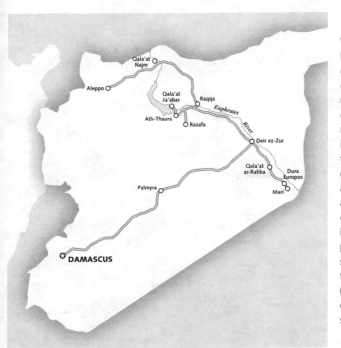

While this area is best seen with your own transport, you can still do this trip utilising the variety of public transport methods available in Syria. Some travellers have done this journey as a bicycle trip – an unforgettable experience, providing you are well prepared for the searing seasonal temperatures (for more advice on when to go, see p9).

SOUTHERN HIATUS

Five days / South Lebanon

Military checkpoints, land mines, giant posters of martyrs and streets lined with Hezbollah flags might have you thinking you're in a war zone, but southern Lebanon is the most hospitable part of the country. Say *'salaam 'aalaykum'* to someone in the South and you'll not only get a warm Arabic greeting in response but an enormous twinkle-eyed smile. And while the South has been slower to recover than the rest of Lebanon, there's still plenty to see.

From **Beirut** (p233) travel down the coast, through banana plantations and citrus orchards, to **Sidon** (p337). Spend a couple of days exploring its labyrinthine **souq** (p341), the beautifully restored **Khan al-Franj** (p340), **Sea Castle** (p340), stunning **Musée Du Savon** (p341) and dining at an **Ottoman palace khan restaurant** (p342) at the seafront. You can also explore the Phoenician **Temple of Echmoun ruins** (p343), near Sidon.

Head further south to **Tyre** (p345), a World Heritage Site, to see ancient ruins and the world's largest, best-preserved **Roman hippodrome** (p348). Visit Tyre's picturesque fishing harbour, the atmospheric old souq and lovely beaches. From Tyre do a day trip into Hezbollah territory. Fought over for the past 1000 years, **Beaufort Castle** (p352) was occupied by the Israelis for over 20 years, and has commanding views of Israel and Syria. A visit to the notorious **Al-Khiam Detention Camp** (p353), now a Hezbollah-run museum, is a sobering experience, but an absolute must. Then head to the border town of Kfar Kila to **Fatima Gate** (p353), the well-known wartime border crossing. Then it's back to Beirut.

The south is great for getting away from the tourist trail. After a run down the coast, from Tyre you can take a (long) day trip to areas that were, until recently, under Israeli occupation. There's better accommodation in Tyre than in Sidon, so you can shorten the trip by doing Sidon in one full day.

TAILORED TRIPS

ARCHAEOLOGICAL ADVENTURE

If exploring archaeological sites is your thing, Syria and Lebanon have a long list of ancient ruins as impressive as Pompeii or Persepolis. Start your adventure in the old town of **Damascus** (p75). **Apamea** (p167), with its 2km-long main street and grey granite colonnades is impressive, **Krak des Chevaliers** (p132) is a must for fans of Crusader castles, and the city of **Palmyra** (p208) must be one of the world's greatest sites.

In Lebanon, **Tyre** (p345) boasts Roman and Byzantine ruins and the world's largest **Roman hippodrome** (p348). **Sidon's** (p337) **Sea Castle** (p340) dates back to Phoenician times although the present structure was built by the Crusaders. The **Temple of Echmoun** (p343) is the best preserved of the Phoenician ruins.

In **Beirut's downtown** (p247) you will find excavations from the Bronze Age and Roman remains. **Byblos** (p280) has 7000 years of history to explore in its Phoenician, Greek, Roman and Crusader ruins. Although **Tripoli** (p300) was settled around 1400 BC its Crusader castle and medieval structures are most intact. **Baalbek** (p327), with its monumental temples, is the most impressive ancient site in Lebanon, followed by the Umayyad ruins of **Aanjar** (p325). **Bosra** (p122), in the south of Syria, was once the capital of the Roman province of Arabia.

SOUQS & SHOPPING

The souqs of Lebanon and Syria are a shopper's paradise. You can find nargileh at the **Ottoman-era souqs** (p348) in Tyre, luxurious Oriental soaps and unique hammam products at the **Musée Du Savon** (p341) in Sidon. Back in **Beirut** (p233), you can buy handicrafts and home décor at the **Artisans du Liban et d'Orient** (p264) by the Ain al-Mreisse seashore. The **Princesse and Sultan Artisanat** (p264) has arabesque drink coasters influenced by the floor-tile designs of Lebanese houses! Nearby, **CD-Thèque** (p264) has the best selection of CDs and DVDs, and books on Middle East photography and visual arts. Scour the restored **Byblos souq** (p284) for retro souvenir guidebooks to the town and ruins, and buy ancient fish fossils at **Mémoire Du Temps** (p284). **Tripoli** (p300) and **Aleppo** (p172) offer more traditional souq shopping: olive soap, textiles, spices and sweets. The souqs in **Damascus** (p111) provide the ultimate Oriental shopping experience: frankincense, perfumes, hand-crafted wooden inlaid furniture, backgammon boards-cum-chess sets and boxes, copper and brass coffeepots and trays, carpets, Damascene tablecloths, brocades and silks, unusual antiques, gold and silver jewellery, and Aladdin slippers. Don't leave without a kitsch box of the Syrian version of Turkish delight from **Al Ghraoui Confiseur Chocolatier** (p100), 'purveyors to Queen Victoria'.

THE GOOD LIFE

Good food, good wines, good hotels. Let's start by checking in to Beirut's **Hotel Monroe** (p255). Breakfast is fine here, but lunch on superb Italian at **La Posta** (p258) and dine on modern-fusion cuisine at **Food Yard** (p258). Stop at Jounieh's **Chez Sami** (p279) for succulent seafood before an overnight stay (in a room with sea views) at **Byblos Sur Mer** (p285) in Byblos. Reserve a table for dinner at **Bab El Mina** (p286). Over lunch at Pepe's **Byblos Fishing Club** (p286) pay homage to the '60s jetset whose pics adorn the walls. If you like winters in Megève, you'll love the lodge style of **L'Auberge des Cèdres** (p316) at The Cedars. Outside winter, take the mountain road to the Bekaa and the **Ksara Winery** (p324), picking up some wines before heading to Damascus.

In Damascus, a room with mountain views is a must at the **Cham Palace** (p103) where it can reserve **Old Town** (p105) for lunch and **Elissar** (p105) for dinner. Fly to Aleppo for an Oriental palace experience in the **Diwan Rasmy hotel's** (p189) Governor's Suite. Lunch at **Cordoba** (p190) for tasty Armenian food, and for dinner try **Beit Wakil's** (p191) delicious cherry kebabs or **Beit as-Sissi's** (p191) antique bazaar interior. True foodies should line up with the locals on early winter mornings for hot steaming bowls of the best **foul** (p191) in Aleppo.

ARCHITECTURAL GEMS TOUR

If you love snooping into other people's homes, then Syria and Lebanon are your dream destinations. Damascus' **Old City** (p83) has hundreds of historic houses and palaces. Some are now museums, cafés and restaurants, while many are currently undergoing restoration and being opened to the public. **Maktab Anbar** (p92), **Azem Palace** (p163) and **Beit Nizam** (p92) are all very special. Also, marvel at the **Umayyad Mosque** (p86), one of the most notable buildings of Islam and an architectural and decorative wonder.

Aleppo's elegant **merchant mansions** (p182) and **Ottoman palaces** (p182) are increasingly being converted into magical boutique hotels and restaurants. Beit Wakil, Dar Zamaria Martini and Diwan Rasmy give you the opportunity to admire a gilded ceiling from your bed or listen to a trickling fountain from your dinner table.

Lebanon's magnificent **Beiteddine Palace** (p294), a combination of Arab and Italian architecture, is considered to be the greatest achievement of 19th-century Lebanese architecture. Nearby, the **Mir Amin Palace** (p296) is now a luxury hotel. A short distance away, the village of **Deir al-Qamar** (p292) has some of the best-preserved examples of 17th- and 18th-century provincial architecture in Lebanon. On the waterfront at Sidon, a beautifully restored Ottoman khan is now a restaurant, appropriately named the **Rest House** (p342).

The Authors

TERRY CARTER   Coordinating Author

Terry has lived in the Middle East since 1998, when his wife, Lara, accepted an offer he didn't understand. Having found the United Arab Emirates (UAE) on a map and being bored with looking at publishing schedules in Sydney, he quit his job and started packing.

His first overseas foray from the UAE was to Lebanon, a place he'd heard so much about from Australian-Lebanese friends. He claims he'd fly there for dinner if the flights were cheaper. Over the past few years he and Lara have visited almost every country in the Middle East (war permitting) and are halfway through their second passports.

Happily freelancing from Dubai, Terry has recently completed his Masters dissertation on representations of nationalism in the UAE media.

LARA DUNSTON   Coordinating Author

For the five years that her family toured Australia in a caravan, young Lara marked the journey in her *Jacaranda Junior World Atlas*. For her undergraduate film degree she learnt about cinema by country: Russian avant-garde, Italian neorealism, French New Wave. Her Master's research in South America was planned around film festivals: Rio Cine, Mar del Plata, Havana. For her PhD, Lara explored what for her is an inextricable link between mobility and the moving image. Now running the Dubai Women's College Communication Technology programme, Lara is fully committed to student learning outcomes, particularly the one on global awareness. She uses the CNN City Weather List to plan her and Terry's travels, and has visited most destinations in the last six years in the UAE.

OUR FAVOURITE TRIP

Our long weekend in Lebanon and Syria is all about good food, good wine, good times. Arrive Beirut (p233). La Posta (p258) for lunch, Bay Rock Café (p259) for sundown nargileh, dinner at Food Yard (p258) and a Rue Monot club of the minute. Early start for Tripoli (p300). Stick foot in Mediterranean before heading to Bcharré (p312) so we can say we skied and swam on same day. At L'Auberge des Cèdres (p315) we sip Ksara red by fireplace. Aleppo (p172) next, checking into palatial Diwan Rasmy (p189) before hitting the souq (p192). Beit Wakil (p189) for dinner; Beit as-Sissi bar (p191) post-supper. Last stop Damascus (p75) and Omayad Hotel (p104). Revisit Old Town atmospheric streets for umpteenth time. Forget material world in tranquil courtyard of Umayyad Mosque (p86). Elissar (p105) for dinner. Walk home through dark silent streets of this ancient city.

ANDREW HUMPHREYS   Preliminary Research for Syria

Andrew has lived, travelled and worked in the Middle East on and off since 1988. Originally trained in London as an architect, he slid into writing through a growing fascination with Islamic buildings. He has since earned his living as a writer, travelling desert and valley on assignment. Andrew has also authored Lonely Planet's *Cairo*. He now lives in London.

CONTRIBUTING AUTHORS

Greg Malouf Born into a Lebanese-Australian family, Greg is an acknowledged champion of modern Middle Eastern cuisine, and is one of Australia's most admired chefs and food writers. Regular trips to the Middle East inspire Greg in his culinary pursuits. Greg is the author of *Arabesque* and *Moorish* and he runs the acclaimed restaurant Mo Mo (Melbourne, Australia).

Geoff Malouf Also an accomplished restaurateur, Greg's brother Geoff runs Cafe Zum Zum, a busy establishment in inner-city Melbourne. Together, Geoff and Greg host culinary tours to Syria and Lebanon.

Dr Caroline Evans Having studied medicine at the University of London, Caroline completed general practice training in Cambridge. She is the medical adviser to Nomad Travel Clinic, a private travel-health clinic in London, and is also a general practitioner specialising in travel medicine. Caroline has acted as expedition doctor for Raleigh International and Coral Cay expeditions. Caroline wrote the Health chapter in this book.

History

The modern states of Syria and Lebanon came into being little more than 50 years ago, but before this the region had a shared history going back many thousands of years. Any history of this region naturally also deals with modern-day Jordan, and Israel & the Palestinian Territories (I&PT).

EARLY EMPIRES & ALPHABETS

The area of modern-day Syria and Lebanon can lay claim to having one of the oldest civilisations in the world. The shores of Lebanon were settled from around 10,000 BC. Archaeological finds at Ugarit (c 6600 BC), on the Mediterranean coast, and at Mari (c 4500 BC), on the Euphrates River, bear evidence of advanced settlements that would later become sophisticated city-states. This is in evidence at Byblos (p280), where the layers of development can be seen most clearly in the excavations.

By around 2500 BC the coast was colonised into city-states by the people who came to be known as the Phoenicians. For over 1500 years they would watch the ebb and flow of great civilisations before the tide ebbed for them too.

The emerging city-states were very much independent entities. They were first brought together under the rule of the Akkadians, who marched out of Mesopotamia (modern-day Iraq) in search of conquest and natural resources. Under the rule of Sargon of Akkad (r 2334–2279 BC) the eastern Mediterranean area flourished, particularly ports such as Byblos, which grew wealthy on trade with the Egyptians, who needed plentiful supplies of timber (from Mt Lebanon), a resource lacking in their own country.

The name Syria is believed to have first been applied by the Greeks, and by Roman times it referred to the part of the empire that lay between Egypt in the south and Anatolia in the north.

By about 1550 BC Egypt had removed itself from under the occupation of Asiatic Hyksos invaders, who had fought for control of the country for just over a century. To be sure that the threat did not return, the pharaohs pursued their former tormentors north, which led to a period of expansion of the Egyptian empire.

In 1480 BC, a revolt organised by more than 300 local rulers was easily crushed and Egypt was by this time firmly established in what is now

RECOMMENDED READING LIST

Pity the Nation (by Robert Fisk) A comprehensive and unflinching account by a long-term resident of Lebanon. Acknowledged as the quintessential read for anyone interested in Lebanon's recent trials.

The Crusades through Arab Eyes (by Amin Maalouf) Offers an antidote to the 'traditional' Western histories of the Crusades. Essential reading for students of Middle Eastern history.

The Book of Saladin (by Tariq Ali) A fictionalised account of the life of the great Muslim leader. Detailed and thought-provoking it recounts day-to-day life and grand events.

Holy War: The Crusades and Their Impact on Today's World (by Karen Armstrong) Draws parallels and makes connections between historical and current events in the Middle East. A scholarly and even-handed tome.

A Peace to End All Peace: The Fall of the Ottoman Empire and the Creation of the Modern Middle East (by David Fromkin) Details the events of WWI in the Middle East, and the continuing fallout.

TIMELINE **6600 BC** | **2500 BC**

First evidence of advanced human settlement at Ugarit. | The Lebanese coast is colonised by the Phoenicians.

The Phoenicians by Donald Harden is a comprehensive and authoritative study of the famed ancients.

Palestine and southern Syria. In the north, however, the various principalities coalesced to form the Mitanni empire. They held off all Egyptian attempts at control, helped in part by their invention of the horse-drawn chariot.

The Mitanni empire was subsumed by the encroachments of the Hittites (1365 BC) from a region that corresponds today with central Turkey. By 1330 BC all of Syria was firmly in the hands of the Hittites.

The region became a battleground for the Egyptian and Hittite ancient superpowers. They clashed at the bloody Battle of Kadesh on the Orontes River in Syria around 1300 BC. The battle saw the Egyptians retreat south.

Finally, the two opposing forces signed a treaty of friendship in 1284 BC. It left the Egyptians with the south and the Hittites with what corresponds to modern-day Syria and Lebanon.

Living in tandem with the Egyptians and Hittites were the Phoenicians, a Semitic people. The Phoenicians occupied a series of towns along the Mediterranean coast and successfully traded with Egypt to the south, Mesopotamia to the east and Anatolia to the north. By being great traders and having no military ambitions, they were not seen as a threat to the great powers of the region. However, despite their innovations and skills as artisans and traders, the Phoenicians never became unified politically, and instead remained independent city-states along the Lebanese shore. Gebal (Byblos, later Jbail) and Tyre (also known as Sour) were the most important of these cities, followed by Sidon (Saida) and Berytus (Beirut).

A SPOIL OF WAR

Much of the success of the sea peoples in warfare was owed to their use of iron for weapons and armour, a material that neither the Egyptians nor the Hittites possessed.

By the 13th century BC the Egyptian empire was in decline and was under threat on several fronts. In the eastern Mediterranean this threat came from the 'Peoples from the Sea', of whom little is known, except that one of these peoples were the Philistines, who settled on the coastal plain in an area that came to be known as the Plain of Philistia. From this is derived the name Palestine, or 'Filasteen' in Arabic. These sea peoples – possibly from the Aegean – overthrew the Hittites, destroying Ugarit in the process.

Adding to the melange was a further influx of new people, the Aramaeans, a seminomadic race from the deserts to the south. The Aramaeans settled mainly in the north including Halab (Aleppo) and Hamath (Hama). Although the Aramaeans managed to stand their ground against the expansionist ambitions of the kingdoms of Judea and Israel to the south, they were unable to repel the attentions of the powerful Assyrian empire

2334–2279 BC	1550–1300 BC
The region flourishes under the rule of Sargon of Akkad.	Egyptians control much of Lebanon and southern Syria.

(1000–612 BC) to the east and by 732 BC all of Syria was under the command of Sargon II.

For the next 400 years Syria was little more than a spoil of war, being ceded to the Babylonians after their king Nebuchadnezzar defeated the Assyrians, then to the Achaemenid Persians who captured Babylon in 539 BC.

Of all of these occupying empires – the Assyrians, Babylonians and Persians – little trace remains today in Syria, except for some spindly columns on the Mediterranean coast at Amrit, which bear distinct Persian ancestry.

THE GREEKS & ROMANS

Alexander the Great defeated the forces of King Darius III at Issus (333 BC) in what's now southeast Turkey, opening the way for his armies to storm through Syria and Palestine on his way to Egypt. On his death, his newly formed empire was divided among his generals. Ptolemy I gained Egypt and southern Syria, while Seleucus I Nicator established a kingdom in Babylonia that spread to include the north Syrian centres of Antioch, Apamea, Lattakia and Cyrrhus.

The Seleucids disputed the Ptolemys' claim to Palestine, finally succeeding in ousting them in 198 BC under the leadership of Antiochus III. A further aggressive campaign of expansion by the Seleucids brought them up against the new power of Rome. In the resulting clash, the Seleucids were defeated and in 188 BC Antiochus was forced to cede all his territories in Asia Minor. However, it wasn't until 64 BC that the Roman legate Pompey finally abolished the Seleucid kingdom, making it a province of Rome with its capital at Antioch.

Antioch became the third-most important imperial city after Rome and Alexandria, and Syria grew rich on trade and agriculture. New trade routes were developed and towns such as Palmyra, Apamea, Bosra, Damascus and Lattakia were replanned and expanded.

In the 3rd century AD the Sassanian Persians (or Sassanids) invaded northern Syria but were repelled by the Syrian prince Odainat of Palmyra. He was granted the title dux orientalis (commander of the east) by his Roman overlords for his efforts, but died shortly afterwards. Suspected of complicity in his death, his widow, the beautiful and ambitious Zenobia, assumed the title Augusta and, with her sights set on Rome, invaded western Syria, Palestine and Egypt. In 272, Aurelian destroyed Palmyra and carted Zenobia off to Rome as a prisoner (for more details see p205).

The year after emperor Constantine converted to Christianity (313), the new religion dominated the empire as it was now legitimised. This rosy state of affairs was abruptly shattered in the 7th century when the Persians once again descended from the north, taking Damascus and Jerusalem in 614 and eventually Egypt in 616, although Byzantine fortunes were revived when the emperor Heraclius invaded Persia and forced the Persians into a peace agreement. In the south, however, the borders of the empire were being attacked by Arab raiders – no new thing – but these Arabs were different. They were ambitious followers of the teachings of a prophet named Mohammed and they called themselves Muslims.

> The name Phoenicia was given to the collection of city-states on the Lebanese coast by the Greeks.

1365–1284 BC	**1000 BC**
Hittites spread their rule to include modern-day Syria and Lebanon; the Phoenicians begin their Golden Age.	Writing in linear script emerges at Ugarit and Byblos.

THE UMAYYADS

The Umayyads, descendants from the tribe of the Prophet Mohammed, ruled the entire Islamic world, creating an empire larger than Rome's, stretching from the Indus River to the Pyrenees mountains. Theirs was a period of great achievement that saw the building of such monuments as the Umayyad Mosque in Damascus and the Mosque of Omar and the Dome of the Rock in Jerusalem. Nevertheless, it was also a time of almost unremitting internal struggle, and Damascus found itself constrained to put down numerous revolts in Iraq and Arabia.

THE ADVENT OF ISLAM

With the Byzantine empire severely weakened by the Persian invasion, the Muslims met with little resistance and in some cases were even welcomed.

In 636 the Muslim armies won a famous victory at Yarmouk, near the modern border between Jordan and Syria. The Byzantine forces could do little but fall back towards Anatolia. Jerusalem fell in 638 and soon all of Syria was in Muslim hands.

Within 15 years of the Battle of Yarmouk the Sassanian empire had disappeared and the Arab Muslims had reached the Oxus River on the northern frontier of modern Afghanistan.

Because of its position on the pilgrims' route to Mecca, Syria became the hub of the new Muslim empire which, by the early 8th century, stretched from Spain across northern Africa and the Middle East to Persia (modern Iran) and India. Mu'awiyah, the governor of Damascus, had himself declared the fifth caliph, or successor to Mohammed, in 658 and founded a line, the Umayyads, which would last for nearly a hundred years (see the boxed text The Umayyads, above).

Umayyad rule was overthrown in 750, when the Abbasids seized power. This new and more solemn religious dynasty moved the capital of the Arab world to Baghdad, thus beginning a succession of subjugations to non-Syrian rulers that would last 1200 years, only ending when the French pulled out of Syria in April 1946.

The Abbasids, too, had their share of problems, and by 980 all of Palestine and part of Syria (including Damascus) had fallen under Fatimid Cairo's rule.

THE CRUSADES

It was into this vacuum of power that the Crusaders arrived. A plea from Pope Urban II in November 1095 for the recapture of the Church of the Holy Sepulchre in Jerusalem resulted in the embarkation of hundreds of thousands of people on the road to the Holy Land. All along the Crusaders' route, cities such as Antioch, Aleppo, Apamea, Damascus, Tripoli, Beirut and Jerusalem, weakened by their own rivalries and divisions, were exposed to the invaders' untempered violence.

The Crusaders comprised a range of people – from peasants to knights, even entire families.

The atrocities inflicted on the population of Ma'arat an-Nu'aman (see p199) in December 1098 were perhaps the nadir of Crusading behaviour, but the taking of Jerusalem on 15 July 1099 was also marked by the same excesses of savagery, and only a handful of Jewish and Muslim inhabitants escaped alive.

Following the capture of the Holy City the Crusaders built or took over a string of castles, including the well-preserved Krak des Chevaliers (p132). Nureddin (Nur ad-Din), son of a Turkish tribal ruler, was able to unite all of Syria not held by the Franks and defeat the Crusaders in Egypt. His

732 BC	**333 BC**
The powerful Assyrian empire takes over the whole of Syria.	Alexander the Great defeats Darius III and storms through Syria.

SALADIN (1138–93)

In contrast to the reputed barbarous antics and dishonourable reputation spaded out to the Crusaders, Saladin (Salah ad-Din) tends to be portrayed as a true knight in the romanticised European tradition of chivalry. He was born in Tikrit (in modern Iraq) to Kurdish parents. At the age of 14 he joined other members of his family in the service of Nureddin of the ruling Zangi dynasty. Rising to the rank of general, by the time Nureddin died in 1174, Saladin had already taken over de facto control of Egypt. He quickly took control of Syria and in the next 10 years extended his control into parts of Mesopotamia, careful not to infringe too closely on the territory of the by-now largely powerless Abbasid caliphate in Baghdad.

In 1187 Saladin crushed the Crusaders in the Battle of Hittin and stormed Jerusalem. By the end of 1189, he had swept the Franks out of Lattakia and Jabla to the north and castles such as Kerak and Shobak (both in Jordan) inland. This provoked Western Europe into action, precipitating the Third Crusade and matching Saladin against Richard I 'the Lionheart' of England. After countless clashes and sieges, the two rival warriors signed a peace treaty in November 1192, giving the Crusaders the coast and the interior to the Muslims. Saladin died three months later in Damascus.

campaign was continued by Saladin (Salah ad-Din; see the boxed text, above), who recaptured Palestine and most of the inland Crusader strongholds. Saladin's compromise with the Assassins (for more information see the boxed text The Assassins, p170) led to the Crusaders remaining on the coast.

Prosperity returned to Syria with the rule of Saladin's dynasty known as the Ayyubids, who parcelled up the empire on his death. They were succeeded by the Mamluks, the freed slave class of Turkish origin that had taken power in Cairo in 1250, just in time to repel the onslaught from the invading Mongol tribes from Central Asia in 1260. Led by the fourth of their sultans, Beybars – one of the great warrior heroes of Islam – the Mamluks finally managed to rid the Levant of the Crusaders by capturing their last strongholds: Acre in 1291 and the fortified island of Ruad (Arwad, see p138) in 1302. Not quite as chivalrous as Saladin, Beybars torched Antioch, a devastation from which the city never recovered. Beybars also winkled the Crusaders out of their mountain castles and put them to flight.

However, more death and destruction was not far off and in 1401 the Mongol invader Tamerlane sacked Aleppo and Damascus, killing thousands and carting off many artisans to Central Asia. His new empire lasted for only a few years but the rout sent Mamluk Syria into decline for the next century.

Arab Historians of the Crusades, edited by Francesco Gabrieli, gives the Arabs' perspective of the Crusades.

THE OTTOMAN TURKS

By 1516 Palestine and Syria had been occupied by the Ottoman Turks and would stay that way for the next four centuries. Most of the desert areas of modern Syria, however, remained the preserve of Bedouin tribes.

Up until the early 19th century, Syria prospered under Turkish rule. Damascus and Aleppo were important market towns for the surrounding desert as well as being stages on the various desert trade routes and stops on the pilgrimage route to Mecca. Aleppo also became an important trading centre with Europe (see p175).

By the 19th century, though, groups of Arab intellectuals in Syria and Palestine (many of them influenced by their years of study in Europe)

64 BC	272 AD
The region becomes a province of the Roman empire.	Zenobia is defeated by Aurelian and sent to Rome as a prisoner.

had set an Arab reawakening in train. The harsh policies of the Young Turk movement of 1909 further encouraged opposition and the growth of Arab nationalism.

WWI & THE FRENCH MANDATE

During WWI, the region was the scene of fierce fighting between the Turks, who had German backing, and the British based in Suez. The enigmatic British colonel TE Lawrence, better known as Lawrence of Arabia (see p189), and other British officers involved with the Arab Revolt encouraged Arab forces to take control of Damascus and Emir Faisal, the leader of the revolt, to set up a government in 1918.

When Arab nationalists proclaimed Faisal king of Greater Syria (an area that included Palestine and Lebanon) and his Hashemite brother, Abdullah, king of Iraq in March 1920, the French, who the following month were formally awarded the mandate over Syria and Lebanon by the League of Nations, moved swiftly to force Faisal into exile.

In 1932 Lebanon's first-and-only census was carried out, confirming a slight Christian majority.

Employing what amounted to a divide-and-rule policy, under pressure from the Lebanese Christian Maronites the French split their mandate up into Lebanon (including Tyre, Beirut and Tripoli); a Syrian Republic, whose Muslim majority resented their presence; and the two districts, Lattakia and Jebel Druze. The French attempt to create a Lebanese nation fell foul of growing Arab nationalist sentiment, which held that Arabs should live in a greater Arab homeland, rather than arbitrarily drawn nation states. For the Maronites, who looked towards Europe, Arab nationalism was a threat. Hostility to the French led to uprisings in 1925 and 1926 and France twice bombarded Damascus.

Scant attention was paid to the opposition and in 1926 the French and their Maronite allies drew up and passed a new constitution for Lebanon, sowing the seeds of the country's troubled future. The document formalised a largely symbolic power-sharing formula, but Maronites still managed to secure a virtual monopoly on positions of power and Sunni Muslims boycotted the constitution, which was suspended in 1932. In 1936, the Franco-Lebanese treaty was signed, promising eventual independence for Lebanon; the following year a new constitution was drawn up but not ratified by the French.

Syrian maps still show the area known as Alexandretta, now the Hatay district of southern Turkey, as belonging to Syria.

In Syria, a Constituent Assembly set up in 1928 to hammer out a constitution for partial independence was dissolved because it proposed a single state, including Lebanon, as the successor to the Ottoman province. This was unacceptable to the French.

In 1932 the first parliamentary elections took place in Syria. Although the majority of moderates elected had been hand-picked by Paris, they rejected all French terms for a constitution. Finally, in 1936, a treaty was signed but never ratified; under the deal, a state of Syria would control Lattakia and Jebel Druze as well as the sanjak (subprovince) of Alexandretta, the present-day Turkish province of Hatay. After riots by Turks in the sanjak protesting against becoming part of Syria, the French encouraged Turkey to send in troops to help supervise elections. The outcome favoured the Turks and the sanjak became part of Turkey in 1939. Syria has never recognised the outcome, which further sharpened feeling against France.

The Umayyads begin a dynasty that would soon cover the entire Muslim world.

The Abbasids seize power, beginning 1200 years of foreign control.

WWII & INDEPENDENCE

When France fell to the Germans in 1940, Syria and Lebanon came under the control of the puppet Vichy government until July 1941, when British and Free French forces took over. The Free French promised independence, but this did not come for another five years, after violent clashes in Syria in 1945 had compelled Britain to intervene. Syria took control of its own affairs when the last of the British troops pulled out in April 1946.

In Lebanon, the various religious and political factions came together in 1943 to draw up the Lebanese National Covenant, an unwritten agreement dividing power along sectarian lines on the basis of the 1932 census. The president was to be Maronite, the prime minister a Sunni, and the speaker of the house a Shiite. Parliamentary seats were divvied-up between Christians and Muslims on a ratio of six to five. The Maronites were also given control of the army, with a Druze chief of staff.

A History of the Arab Peoples by Albert Hourani is tough reading but possibly the best book on the development of the modern-day Arab world.

When, in November 1943, the fledgling Lebanese government of President Bishara al-Khouri went a step further and passed legislation removing all references to French Authority in the constitution, the French retaliated by arresting the president, and members of his cabinet, and suspending the constitution. Britain, the US and the Arab states supported the Lebanese cause for independence, and in 1944 the French began the transfer of all public services to Lebanese control, followed by the withdrawal of French troops. Independence was declared in 1946.

POST-INDEPENDENCE SYRIA
A Land of Confusion

Civilian rule in Syria was short-lived, and was terminated in 1949 by a series of military coups that brought to power officers with nationalist and socialist leanings. By 1954, the Ba'athists in the army, who had won support among the Alawite and Druze minorities (see p44), had no real rival.

Founded in 1940 by a Christian teacher, Michel Aflaq, the Arab Ba'ath Socialist Party was committed to the creation of a greater Arab state. In a merger with Egypt under President Nasser in 1958, Syria became the Northern Province of the United Arab Republic. Although this was at first a popular move with many Syrians, the Egyptians treated them as subordinates, and after yet another military coup in September 1961, Damascus resumed full sovereignty. Although outwardly civilian, the new regime was under military control and it made few concessions to Ba'ath and pro-Nasser Pan-Arabists, resulting in yet another change of government in March 1963.

In 1960 a National Assembly of the United Arab Republic came together, with 400 Egyptian and 200 Syrian deputies.

A month before the Ba'ath takeover in 1963, which first propelled an air force lieutenant-general, Hafez al-Assad, into a government headed by General Amin al-Hafez, the Iraqi branch of the party seized power in Baghdad. Attempts were made to unite Iraq, Egypt and Syria but the parties failed to agree on the tripartite federation. The Ba'ath Party in Iraq was overthrown in November 1963.

Syria was now on its own. The Ba'ath Party's economic policy of nationalisation was meeting with much dissatisfaction, expressed in a disastrous and bloodily repressed revolt in the city of Hama in 1964. Worse, the Ba'athists' Pan-Arabism implicitly gave non-Syrians a significant say in Syrian affairs, an issue that led to a party split. In February 1966, the

The First Crusade sets out for the Holy Land.	Saladin storms Jerusalem, then Beybars drives off the Crusaders for good.

ASSAD'S SUCCESS

After seizing power in November 1970, Hafez al-Assad was sworn in as president of Syria for seven years on 14 March 1971. He was never to relinquish control. Assad managed to hold power longer than any other post-Independence Syrian government with a mixture of ruthless suppression and guile. His success can be attributed to a number of factors: giving disadvantaged and minority groups a better deal; stacking the bureaucracy and internal security organisations with members of his own Alawite faith (which led to widespread repression and silencing of opposition both at home and abroad); and an overall desire, no doubt shared by many Syrians, for political stability.

In the 1980s economic difficulties helped fuel growing discontent with Assad's regime. The main opposition came from the militant Muslim Brotherhood, who objected to Alawite-dominated rule, given that the Alawites accounted for only 11.5% of the population (see p41). The Brotherhood's opposition has sometimes taken a violent course. In 1979, 32 Alawite cadets were killed in a raid in Aleppo. Anti-Ba'ath demonstrations were held in that city in 1980. In February 1982 as many as 25,000 people were killed in the town of Hama when the army brutally quashed a revolt led by Sunnis who ambushed Syrian security forces and staged a general insurrection. Since then, little has been heard of the opposition.

ninth coup saw Amin al-Hafez ousted and the self-proclaimed socialist radical wing of the party took control of the government. Hafez al-Assad, the rising strongman, was instrumental in bringing about the fall of the party old guard.

War But No Peace

The Arab World: Forty Years of Change by Elizabeth Fernea and Robert Warnock covers the recent history of the Middle East and makes a good primer to the region.

The socialist government was severely weakened by defeat in two conflicts. The first disaster came at the hands of the Israelis in the June 1967 war. Later known as the Six Day War, it was launched by Israel partly in retaliation for raids by Syrian guerrillas on Israeli settlements and also because the Egyptians were massing troops near the Israeli border. The end result was a severe political and psychological reversal for the Arab states and saw vast areas of land fall into Israeli hands. Syria lost the Golan Heights and Damascus itself was threatened.

Next came the Black September hostilities in Jordan in 1970. In this clash, the Jordanian army smashed Syrian-supported Palestinian guerrilla groups who were vying for power in Jordan. At this point Hafez al-Assad, who had opposed backing the Palestinians against the Jordanian army, seized power in November 1970. He was sworn in as president in 1971. For details see the boxed text Assad's Success, p28.

On 6 October 1973, Syria, in a surprise offensive coordinated with Egypt, sent 850 tanks across the 1967 cease-fire line to regain the lost Golan Heights. It was also an attempt to regain karama (dignity) after previous ignominious defeats. Three days after hostilities started, Israeli planes bombed Damascus. The Arab offensive failed; an Israeli counterattack was halted only 35km from Damascus. Although Assad grudgingly accepted a UN cease-fire on 22 October (as Egypt had done), his troops kept up low-level harrying actions in the Golan area. Egypt signed an armistice in January 1974 but it was not until the end of May that Syria did the same.

1260–1516	1401
The Mamluks have their turn ruling the region.	The Mongol invader Tamerlane sacks Aleppo and Damascus, killing thousands.

Syria Today

After 30 years of iron-fisted and often bloody presidential rule, Hafez al-Assad died on 10 June 2000, aged 69, sending the country into a 40-day official mourning period. His replacement was his son, 34-year-old Bashir al-Assad. Bashir, whose budding career as an ophthalmologist in London apparently gave him the perfect credentials for a job at the top of Syrian politics, was sworn in for a seven-year term in July 2000.

In fact, the possibility of genuine reform seems almost far-fetched considering that Bashir was hand-picked by his father, and that the country's constitution was literally changed overnight to validate this undemocratic choice by reducing the minimum age for president from 40 years to 34, so Bashir would qualify.

Internationally, Syria's hardline stance vis-à-vis Israel over the return of the Golan Heights and alleged support for extremist organisations such as Hezbollah (Party of God) continues to stand in the way of improved relations with the West. As recently as 2002, the US president George W Bush was tarring Syria with the accusation of being an associate of a perceived 'axis of evil'. European leaders, however, are reading from a different, less hysterical, script and Britain's Tony Blair has been just one of a number of key Western statesmen to drop in on Damascus in recent times to encourage the young new president in a direction that might one day see Syria entering a new era of openness.

Assad's oldest son Basil was groomed for the top slot until his death in a high-speed car accident in January 1994 – curiously earning him the epithet 'Basil the Martyr'.

POST-INDEPENDENCE LEBANON
The Seeds of Discontent

Bringing the nascent state's diverse and mutually suspicious sectarian groups together was no easy task, but in the early days after independence, the government of President al-Khouri struggled to make the National Covenant work. However, although the agreement was an effective short-term compromise, as a long-term solution to the country's diverse mixture of religious and economic interests it was too inflexible.

Soon after it came into being, the country was hit with major political and economic challenges. In 1948 the devaluation of the French franc (to which the Lebanese currency was tied) damaged the country's economy. The same year saw the last act of colonialism in the area, when the British oversaw the partition of its British Mandate for Palestine and promptly

---

THE PALESTINIAN DISPOSSESSED

After their arrival in Lebanon after fleeing Jewish forces in 1948, the Palestinians had initially had a sympathetic reception. Urban middle-class Palestinians were able to participate in the laissez faire economy and some Christians were even granted Lebanese citizenship. The rest were given basic housing in UN-run camps. But as time wore on, the Palestinian presence became a threat to Lebanon's increasingly shaky National Covenant. To the pro-Western Maronites, the presence of the Palestinians, who were sympathetic to the anticolonial doctrines of Nasserism and Arab nationalism, strengthened Lebanon's Arab nationalist challenge to their power. Gradually, restrictions were imposed on the ability of Palestinians to work or move around. Under President Chehab, army intelligence posts were established inside the camps to try and control Palestinian political activity.

1516	1914 to 1918
The Ottoman Turks occupy the Syrian region.	The Arab Revolt culminates in the formation of a government by Emir Faisal.

withdrew. In the Arab-Israeli War (1948–49) that followed, Jewish forces flooded into Palestinian areas and evicted thousands before establishing the State of Israel. Between 250,000 and 500,000 Muslim and Christian Palestinian refugees flooded into Lebanon, welcomed at first (when it was thought their stay would be temporary), but nonetheless upsetting the sectarian balancing act. In 1950, economic ties with Syria were cut, placing further strain on the economy.

Increasing support for the burgeoning Arab nationalist movement, which was sweeping the region, also had a destabilising effect. In 1951, the Sunni prime minister, Riad al-Solh, was assassinated by Syrian nationalists and, the following year, growing unrest led to the resignation of the government. The new president, Camille Chamoun, an avowedly pro-Western Maronite, added fuel to the fire. He assumed power in 1952, the same year as Egypt's revolution. When Egypt's president Nasser, widely seen as a leftist revolutionary by the West, nationalised the Suez Canal in 1956, Chamoun supported the attempted Israeli-British-French invasion of Egypt. The rest of the Arab world, still smarting from colonial domination, supported Nasser.

Chamoun's disregard for the principles of the National Covenant and insensitivity to the feelings of non-Christian Lebanese precipitated the country's biggest crisis yet in 1958. The previous year he had enthusiastically signed the Eisenhower Doctrine. This Cold War document allowed the USA to 'use armed forces to assist any nation...in the Middle East requesting assistance against armed aggressors from any country controlled by international communism'. When Egypt and Syria united as the United Arab Republic in 1958, Chamoun immediately announced that Lebanon would not join, inflaming Arab nationalist sentiment still more.

When Chamoun then won parliamentary elections, amid widespread allegations of fraud and probably with the help of the CIA, he tried to change the constitution and allow himself a second term as president. Violence that had been simmering in the background broke out throughout the country, pitting pro-Western Maronites against their largely (but not entirely) Muslim pro-Arab nationalist opponents. A panicked Chamoun requested American help and in July 1958, some 15,000 American marines landed on the shores in Beirut, creating an uproar in the Cold War world.

Chamoun's mismanagement was his downfall, and the moderate chief of staff, Fouad Chehab, replaced him. He presided over the withdrawal of the American troops and appointed Rashid Karami, leader of the Muslim insurrectionists in the north, to the post of prime minister, ushering in a brief period of calm in which Lebanon's economy appeared to flourish. Chehab made some attempts to even out the distribution of wealth, however the prosperity was largely concentrated in Beirut and along the coast. The hinterland was neglected, with virtually no industry, a burgeoning population growth and extreme poverty.

Chehab's successor, Charles Hélou, who came to power in 1964, attempted, less successfully, to continue the reforms. But this was the freewheeling 1960s, for which Lebanon is still famous. The fact that the government did little to redistribute the spoils or pay attention to the dispossessed did not bother the rich Lebanese, who partied with the international jet set at the Casino du Liban.

'Chamoun tried to change the constitution and allow himself a second term as president'

1920	1932
The French take over Syria and Lebanon and Faisal is forced into exile.	The first parliamentary elections take place in Syria.

The Six Day War & the Palestinians

Lebanon may not have sent troops to fight in the 1967 war but, along with the rest of the Middle East, was profoundly affected by the conflict. The humiliating loss of what remained of Palestine in 1967 radicalised the Palestinians, thousands of whom had been languishing in the hope of returning to their homes for almost 20 years. This, and the fresh influx of refugees into Lebanon, Jordan and Syria, turned Palestinian camps throughout the Middle East into de facto centres of guerrilla resistance to the Israeli occupation. Well armed and increasingly radical, the guerrillas had the sympathy of many ordinary Arabs, who identified with the humiliation of their position. Arab governments, while helpful on the surface, saw in the Palestinians a potential threat to their own less-than-open regimes and cracked down on the guerrilla activities. The Lebanese government was too weak to impose such restrictions. As a result, an increasing number of guerrilla attacks on I&PT were launched from Lebanon.

Israeli forces retaliated with attacks across the border in May 1968. Events escalated in December the same year when an Israeli airliner was machine-gunned at Athens airport. Two days later the Israelis launched an attack on Beirut airport and destroyed 13 Lebanese passenger aircraft – a clear warning not to allow any further attacks from Lebanese soil.

In 1968 and 1969 Lebanese forces clashed violently with Palestinians, who demanded to run their own camp security and be free to launch attacks into I&PT. But Lebanon's weak army was no match for the guerrillas and under pressure from Lebanese Muslims, the government signed the Cairo Agreement with the Palestine Liberation Organisation (PLO), in which most of the Palestinians' demands were met and the camps were moved away from civilian towns to protect civilians from injury during reprisal raids.

Maronite opposition to the Cairo Agreement was immediate. The right-wing Christian Phalange party began to arm and train its young men in Maronite mountain strongholds around the Qadisha Valley. In March 1970, fighting broke out in the streets of Beirut between Palestinian guerrillas and Phalangists. Tensions rose still further in September, when, after heavy fighting, the Jordanian army drove Palestinian guerrillas out of their country. Following their defeat in what became known as Black September, the guerrillas flocked into Lebanon where they continued their attacks into Israel with scant regard for the effect on the local (mainly Shiite) population, who were displaced by Israeli retaliatory attacks and subsequently migrated to the rapidly growing slums around Beirut.

The country became more factionalised and the government became more and more powerless to stop it. Groups armed themselves and formed private militias along religious/political (and clan/tribal) lines. The fiercely militant Maronite president, Suleiman Franjieh, who came to power in 1970, did little to prevent the dangerous build-up.

Underlying all this were the old political tensions between the pro-Western Maronites and the pro-Arab nationalist Muslims. A loose grouping of left-wing Arab nationalists and Muslims, led by Kamal Jumblatt, formed the National Movement and allied with the Palestinians to push for constitutional reforms that would break the existing guarantees of Maronite power. The Phalange, complaining that the Palestinian resistance had now become a magnet for radicals who threatened the National

Israel & the Palestinian Territories (I&PT) invaded Lebanon (or parts of Lebanon) in 1968, 1973, 1978, 1982, 1983, 1991 and 1992.

The Christian Phalange party was formed in the 1930s by a member of the Gemayel clan.

| Syria and Lebanon is under the control of the puppet Vichy government. | Syria and Lebanon are granted independence. |

Covenant, developed close ties with the Israelis to try and rid the country of the Palestinians. The Israelis armed the Phalange and waves of violent confrontation began to escalate, pitting the Lebanese army and Phalange militia against the Palestinians and the militias of the National Movement. Although Lebanon avoided direct involvement in the October War in 1973, Israel's reprisals against Palestinian attacks following the conflict only exacerbated the intensity of the clashes.

The Civil War

Although violence was already becoming commonplace in Lebanon, it is generally agreed that the civil war began on 13 April 1975, when Phalangist gunmen attacked a bus in the Beirut suburb of Ain al-Rummaneh and massacred 27 of its Palestinian passengers. Tit-for-tat killings and the spiral into anarchy intensified. When four Christians were found shot dead in a car in December 1975, Phalangists stopped all cars around Beirut and checked identity cards, before slitting the throats of any Muslims found. Muslim militias soon followed suit with Christians. By the end of the day, known as Black Saturday, some 300 people were dead. A month later, the Phalange led other militias in the siege and massacre of Palestinian refugees in the camps of Qarantina and Tell al-Zaatar. The Palestinians responded by attacking the town of Damour, just south of Beirut, and massacring most of its Christian inhabitants.

Set up as an 'interim' force, the United Nations Interim Force in Lebanon (Unifil) remained in Lebanon for over 20 years.

Fighting continued and Beirut was soon partitioned between the Christian East and Muslim West along what became known as the (infamous) Green Line and the rest of the country was likewise controlled, area by area, along lines marked out by the various religious sects. This state of affairs would last throughout the 17-year civil war, although loyalties would change and sides would re-form many times.

SYRIAN INTERVENTION

In 1976, the Syrians, alarmed at the prospect of partition of Lebanon and possible Israeli occupation, tried to end the fighting. By May there were an estimated 40,000 Syrian troops in the country. Initially sympathetic to the National Movement and the Palestinian cause, disagreements with the National Movement's leader, Kamal Jumblatt, caused them to switch sides and they moved through the country trying to crush the Palestinian guerrilla groups, hoping to install a pro-Syrian government. As a staunch Arab nationalist power, the Syrian alliance with the Maronites was condemned by other Arab countries and later that year the Arab League brokered a ceasefire. An Arab peace-keeping force, the Arab Deterrent Force (ADF), was established, but most of its troops were Syrian and it was largely ineffective. In March 1977 Kamal Jumblatt was assassinated, leading to a series of massacres of Christian villagers by Druze locals in the Chouf Mountains.

ISRAELI INVASIONS

Continued Palestinian attacks on Israel in March 1978 gave the Israelis the pretext to launch an attack on southern Lebanon in an effort to destroy the PLO and its bases in Lebanon. Following demands for withdrawal by the Security Council, the UN formed the United Nations Interim Force in Lebanon (Unifil) to oversee the withdrawal and 'restore international

1948	1960s
The State of Israel is created and Palestinian refugees flood into Lebanon.	The Lebanese economy booms, international jet-setters arrive for holidays, but the lives of the poor stay unchanged.

peace'. The Israeli forces withdrew, but instead of handing over to Unifil, they created their own militia, the South Lebanon Army (SLA), installed a pro-Israeli Christian, Saad Haddad as its head, and proclaimed the area south of the Litani River 'Free Lebanon'.

Meanwhile, fighting between the Syrian ADF soldiers and Christian militiamen flared up in Beirut. By 1981 the Syrians had switched allegiance again and joined with the Palestinians to lay siege to the Phalange-controlled town of Zahlé in the Bekaa Valley. Worried by Phalange links to the Israelis, their presence in the Bekaa was too close for Syrian comfort. The two countries appeared to be on the brink of all-out war, however the Phalange withdrew and an American-brokered cease-fire came into force.

The cease-fire proved to be short-lived. Although the Palestinians by and large adhered to it, Israel's right-wing government was determined to crush the PLO once and for all. In the view of Israel's generals, its very existence was fanning the flames of Palestinian nationalism in the occupied territories of the West Bank and Gaza. So, on 6 June 1982, after an exchange of small attacks with the Palestinians, the Israeli army marched into Lebanon, one contingent pushing the Syrians out of the Bekaa Valley, the rest sweeping northward until they reached Beirut. The invasion was accompanied by a devastating bombing campaign that laid waste large parts of Tyre, Sidon, Damour and Nabatiye.

There were more than 150 cease-fires during the first eight years of Lebanon's civil war.

About a week after the invasion began, the Israelis began their siege of West Beirut, where the PLO leadership was based. In the coming two months, the city was subject to an almost continuous bombardment with deadly suction bombs, cluster bombs and phosphorus shells. The city was devastated and the overwhelming majority of the 18,000 dead and 30,000 injured were civilians. On 21 August, following a US-brokered agreement, the PLO left Beirut under multinational supervision. Two days after their evacuation, which many took to be a sign that the Maronites had won the war, Phalange-leader Bashir Gemayel was, with Israeli help, elected president. Three weeks later a huge bomb was placed outside Phalange headquarters, killing Bashir and 60 of his supporters. Responsibility for the attack was never claimed.

SABRA & SHATILA

The day after the killing of Bashir Gemayel (see above for details), Israeli forces moved into West Beirut, in violation of the US-sponsored agreement. Three days later, Israel's Phalange allies, bent on revenge for Bashir's assassination, entered the Palestinian refugee camps of Sabra and Shatila, on the outskirts of Beirut, to root out 'terrorists'. In a brutal two-day rampage of rape and murder, the militia (which may also have had help from Saad Haddad's SLA) killed as many as 2000 Palestinians, mostly women and children.

An Israeli inquiry later found that, despite the denials of the defence minister, Ariel Sharon, Israeli troops were fully aware of what their Phalange allies were doing. Not only were they stationed around the camp, they offered logistical help, lending bulldozers for the digging of mass graves and even dropping flares through the night so the Phalange could better find their targets.

News of the massacres shocked the world and international condemnation was swift. Multinational peace-keeping forces, comprised of French, British, American and Italian troops returned to Beirut and tried, unsuccessfully, to keep the peace.

1964	1967
In Lebanon, Charles Hélou comes to power.	The Six Day War with Israel ends with Syria's loss of the Golan Heights.

MULTINATIONAL FORCES

Following the arrival of the peacekeepers after the Sabra and Shatila massacre (for details see p33), Bashir Gemayel's brother, Amin, was elected president, although at first he controlled little more than Beirut and part of Mt Lebanon. The Israelis had pulled back to a position a few kilometres south of Beirut, and occupied the south, while the north of the country was dominated by the Syrians. In both these areas the fighting continued.

In Tripoli, PLO leader Yasser Arafat, who had returned to Lebanon with a much smaller group of fighters, was engaged in fierce fighting with other Syrian-supported Lebanese and breakaway Palestinians. Palestinian refugee camps were once again pawns in the game for political supremacy. Both they and the city of Tripoli were ravaged in the fighting. In December 1983, under multinational-force protection, Arafat left Lebanon again, this time for Tunis.

Fighting also raged in the Chouf Mountains. Inhabited by Druze and Christians, the area had been relatively peaceful throughout the war. It was now occupied by the Israelis, who brought in Phalangist militiamen in 1982. Phalangist harassment of Druze civilians led to reprisals that escalated into widespread sectarian violence. The fighting threatened to engulf Beirut when Druze leader, Walid Jumblatt, shelled Beirut airport and attacked Lebanese army positions in the city. At this moment, the Israelis pulled out of the mountains. The Lebanese army joined with the Phalangists against the Druze (who were helped by the Shiite militia, Amal). The Druze had the upper hand until the US, in its Cold War fervour, claimed that they were in fact acting for the Syrians, under the orders of Moscow. American warships then bombarded Druze positions. Shortly after, yet another cease-fire was negotiated.

The US was becoming increasingly bogged down in the war. When the multinational forces arrived, Beirut, for a time, appeared to be safe, even as the areas around it were paralysed by fighting. However, the US was increasingly seen to favour the Israelis and the severely compromised government of Amin Gemayel, and opposition to them and the other peacekeepers grew. Any lingering illusions that the multinational force would bring an end to the war were brutally shattered when in April 1983, the US embassy in Beirut was destroyed by a powerful blast that left 63 dead and 100 wounded. Although the Americans stayed on, the simultaneous attacks by suicide bombers on the US and French military headquarters in Beirut the following October, which left 265 US marines and 56 French soldiers dead, shook their resolve and paved the way for their retreat, which followed in February 1984.

'The Shiites had always been Lebanon's poor'

THE SHIITE RENAISSANCE

Responsibility for the attacks on the Americans and French was claimed by a little-known organisation called Islamic Jihad, the armed wing of a radical, Iranian-backed Shiite group known as Hezbollah, a new – but soon to be well-known – character in the ever-growing cast of the civil war. The Shiites had always been Lebanon's poor. They were largely excluded from the Sunni-Maronite power struggles and ignored by the government. Concentrated in the south, they had borne the brunt of Israeli retaliatory

1970	1973
Hafez al-Assad seizes power in Syria and begins 30 years of iron-fisted rule.	Syria, in a surprise offensive, sends 850 tanks across the 1967 cease-fire to regain the Golan Hights.

attacks for Palestinian raids, had suffered brutal repression at the hands of Israeli occupiers and their Lebanese proxies, and been turned into destitute refugees stuck in shantytowns around Beirut. With Syrian approval, Iranian Revolutionary Guards stationed themselves in the Bekaa Valley and began to train and preach to the disaffected. They provided fertile ground for Hezbollah's message of overthrowing Western imperialism and the anti-Muslim Phalange. The organisation's effectiveness, and willingness to sacrifice its own in suicide bombings, turned it into a feared fighting force.

In 1984 Hezbollah began to use one of Lebanon's most chilling militia tactics, kidnapping. Although Lebanese were often targeted by one militia or another and either held for ransom or killed, several high-profile abductions of Westerners, such as CIA bureau chief William Buckley (who was tortured and killed) and Associated Press bureau chief Terry Anderson (later released), resulted in widespread press coverage and the exodus of most Westerners from Beirut.

BATTLE OF THE CAMPS

Brutal in its treatment of Shiites and Palestinians in the south and relentlessly targeted by guerrilla fighters and suicide bombers, I&PT was gradually removing its troops and handing control to Haddad's SLA. It was also arming other Christian militias to do its bidding. In early 1985 the last Israeli troops withdrew, preserving for themselves a self-proclaimed security zone along the border controlled by the SLA.

Once the Israelis withdrew, the militias that it had encouraged clashed with Druze and Shiite militias around Sidon in the south, while in West Beirut, fighting continued between Sunni, Shiite and Druze militias. Amid the confusion, the PLO began to filter back into Lebanon, leading to more fighting around the Palestinian camps. The attacks were led by the Shiite Amal militia, worried that the return of the Palestinian fighters would lead to Israeli intervention and yet more suffering for the people in the south. Vicious fighting continued through 1985 and 1986, laying waste to already-battered camps and inflicting thousands of casualties.

In the summer of 1986, the Syrians returned to West Beirut and their numbers increased over the coming months. Damascus was able to institute an uneasy cease-fire, but although the Syrians were able to lift the siege of the camps in Beirut over the following winter (and then prevent the re-establishment of the PLO), the camps in South Lebanon remained under Amal control until the beginning of 1988.

GENERAL AOUN & THE TAIF ACCORD

Although real power now lay in the hands of the militias, the government still technically existed. By September 1988 Amin Gemayel's term of office was due to expire, but, due to militia violence, deputies trying to vote for a new president were unable to reach the parliament. With only hours to go until his term was up, Gemayel appointed his chief of staff, General Aoun, to head an interim military government. Aoun's staunchly anti-Syrian stance was dimly viewed in Damascus and Syria opposed his appointment, as did the USA. Gemayel also

'the government still technically existed'

1975	1978
Years of fighting between Palestinians and Phalangists lead to civil war in Lebanon.	Israeli forces launch an attack on Lebanon in an effort to destroy Palestinian bases.

THE TAIF ACCORD

A serious attempt to negotiate a peace settlement finally came in the autumn of 1989. Diplomatic efforts by a committee consisting of Morocco's King Hassan II, King Fahd of Saudi Arabia and President Chadli of Algeria proposed a comprehensive cease-fire and a meeting of the parliament to discuss a Charter of National Reconciliation, which, while retaining the confessional-based distribution of power in the government (the confessional system refers to government representation based on stated religion), attempted to even out the balance. On 23 September the cease-fire was implemented and the National Assembly met in Taif, Saudi Arabia. The charter, known as the Taif Accord, was formally ratified on 5 November 1989 despite General Aoun's opposition. René Mouawad was elected president, but only 17 days later was assassinated by opponents of the agreement. Parliament, fearing this would trigger yet another round of war, immediately appointed Elias Hrawi to take his place.

appointed three Christian and three Muslim officers to serve under Aoun, but the Muslims refused to take up their posts. Instead, Selim al-Hoss, Gemayel's Muslim former prime minister, formed his own rival government in West Beirut. By the end of 1988, it appeared that the partition of the country into Muslim and Christian ministates had finally come to pass.

Perhaps inevitably, violence between Christian and Muslim militias once again raged across the Green Line. Aoun was determined to drive the Syrians from Lebanon and the fighting continued for most of the coming year. Aoun angered the Syrians still more by receiving arms from Iraq, Syria's implacable enemy.

The first signs of hope of peace came in the form of the Taif Accord of 1989 (for details see the boxed text The Taif Accord, p35). Aoun continued to oppose the agreement and fighting once more broke out, this time between Aoun and rival Christian militias who disagreed with his stance. Fighting also broke out between Hezbollah and Amal militias, first in Beirut, then in the south.

Nevertheless, in August 1990 the National Assembly voted to amend the constitution to adopt the reforms of the Taif Accord. When Syria supported the US-led military campaign in the Gulf War, the US allowed Syrian troops to join with the Lebanese army in getting rid of General Aoun. With the exception of the still-occupied south, Aoun's removal led to the first period of lasting peace in Lebanon for 15 years.

Later in the same year, Syria formalised its dominance over Lebanese affairs with the signing of the Treaty of Brotherhood, Co-operation and Co-ordination, followed in 1992 by a defence pact. Although they had a mixed reception, both agreements held. According to the Taif Accord, Syrian forces were to withdraw from Lebanon, but while they began to pull out in March 1992, the withdrawal was only partial and the Syrian army is still present today.

The Post-War Period

Even with peace shakily restored, the many militias remained armed and in March 1991 the delicate process of disarming and extending government authority over the country began. The Syrian and Lebanese armies

1982	1983
Israel invades Lebanon; the Palestinian refugee camps of Sabra and Shatila become the scene of a massacre.	The radical Shiite group of Hezbollah emerges in Lebanon to become a major player in the region.

jointly gained control of most of Lebanon's territory. The south, occupied by Israel through the SLA militia, was an exception. Palestinian bases remained around Sidon, and Hezbollah fighters were allowed to keep their arms in order to fight the occupation.

Violence continued to flare along the southern border of Lebanon, with tit-for-tat mortar attacks punctuated by Israeli offensives in June 1991 and 1992. The latter was yet another attempt to destroy Palestinian and Hezbollah bases, and displaced as many as 300,000 Lebanese.

By mid-June 1992, all Western hostages who were still alive in Lebanon had been released and the following October the country's first parliamentary elections in 20 years took place. Despite a boycott by much of the Christian community, Rafiq Hariri, a Lebanese-born Saudi entrepreneur, became the new prime minister of Lebanon. He also assumed the post of finance minister and set about rebuilding the shattered country.

Hariri tried to redress the imbalance brought about by the Christian boycott of the elections and in 1994 attempted to bring more Christians into the government. He was blocked by both the Syrians and by President Hrawi, and offered his resignation. He was reappointed after Syrian mediation, but the same events were repeated in 1995.

While Beirut and the north of the country were rebuilt, the south suffered from Hezbollah battles and Israeli attacks. In March 1995 a senior Hezbollah official was assassinated by a rocket attack on his car near Tyre. In response to counterattacks from Hezbollah, Israel launched another campaign, Operation Grapes of Wrath, in April 1996. This was a combined land-sea-air offensive, ostensibly aimed at Hezbollah positions, but it extended far beyond the south and involved attacks on Lebanon's painstakingly rebuilt infrastructure, destroying Beirut's power station and blockading ports. The attack was clearly intended to pressure the Lebanese government to act against Hezbollah. It was during this attack that the Qana massacre took place; for details see the boxed text Bitter Wine from Grapes of Wrath (p352).

'on 24 May 2000, the Israeli army finally withdrew from the south'

Although both sides initially respected the agreement, Israel once again launched attacks, bombing Beirut's power stations in 1999, while Hezbollah continued its hit-and-run guerrilla attacks on the SLA and on Israel's northern border. Sustained losses led to increased calls within Israel for a withdrawal, and on 24 May 2000, the Israeli army finally withdrew from the south.

The withdrawal was celebrated within Lebanon. Members of Hezbollah, which had already transformed itself from a fanatic, suicide-bombing group into an efficient political party, with popular and well-managed social welfare programmes, became heroes overnight. However, many Lebanese questioned how the power vacuum would be filled. The death of Syrian president Hafez al-Assad only a few days after the withdrawal further increased the uncertainty. Even with the international border between Lebanon and Israel demarcated, the fate of relations between the two countries remains dependent on peace talks between Syria and Israel. Moreover, at least 350,000 Palestinians remain in Lebanon, unwelcome by most Lebanese and subject to severe hardship. Their presence will continue to be a destabilising factor, one

1989	1992
The Taif Accord sees a cease-fire declared between the warring factions in Lebanon.	Lebanon's first parliamentary elections in 20 years are held.

that is unlikely to be removed until Israel and the Palestinian Authority agree on their fate.

President Hrawi was replaced by Emile Lahoud following presidential elections in October 1998. Prime Minister Hariri was replaced in 1998 by Selim al-Hoss, and returned to power in elections held in September 2000. Presidential elections are planned for later in 2004. See also Snapshot Lebanon (p232) for an up-to-date look at events in Lebanon.

The Culture

THE NATIONAL PSYCHE
Syria

The first thing you'll notice in Syria is the hospitality. Those travelling from Western countries with preconceived ideas about 'terrorist training grounds' and 'rogue states', will find little to support these notions on the streets of Syria. The friendliness and offers of tea and a chat are constant and only occasionally linked to the sale of a carpet! However, underneath this hospitality, the Syrians can be a little reserved – perhaps tied to the fact that most people still believe someone's always listening. During Hafez al-Assad's reign there were nearly as many secret service officers as there were posters of the leader. This has taught Syrians to politely change the subject when conversation turns to politics.

Don't be surprised, however, at how many questions *you* are asked – about your family, where you live, your life and how much you earn! While many visitors consider the constant questions about family as being too personal, remember that family is of paramount importance throughout the Middle East. Having a large, healthy family is seen as a gift from God and in traditional Arab greetings it's the first thing you ask about after saying hello.

So after visiting Syria, next time you hear about 'evil regimes', you'll know to separate the people from those that govern them – just as the Syrians politely do when meeting you.

The Institute of the Arab World, Paris, has a wonderful website, rich with information, at www.imarabe.org.

Lebanon

Those visitors flying in to Beirut and trying to negotiate a cab might not initially agree, but Lebanon is one of the friendliest places in the world to visit. The city has an energy that emanates from its people. Lebanese who only speak Arabic will still know 'welcome' and deliver it with a smile. Given the substantial Lebanese diaspora, everyone you meet probably has a brother or a cousin living in your country – a link that will win you instant friends.

Ask about one of the reasons for the diaspora – the civil war – and you'll generally be greeted with a shrug of the shoulders, as if the war happened around the time the first boat sailed into Byblos harbour. Most Lebanese want to move on – and changing the subject to politics will certainly do that! Unlike their more reserved neighbour, Syria, talking

---

RESPONSIBLE TOURISM

- Do ask before taking close-up photographs of people.
- Don't worry if you don't speak the language – a smile and gesture will be understood and appreciated.
- Do have respect for local etiquette. Men should shake hands when formally meeting other men, but not women unless the woman extends her hand.
- Don't wear revealing clothing. Guys, if you're wearing shorts the locals will think it's funny that you've gone outside without your pants and your dignity.
- Don't display affection in public.
- Do be patient, friendly and sensitive.

politics in Lebanon is a national sport, and virtually no aspect of the government and what it's doing right or wrong is out of bounds.

While unemployment and corruption are hot topics, the Lebanese certainly don't get dejected about it. Lebanese like to enjoy life and good times with family and friends are the most important thing. Spend a little time getting to know the Lebanese and they'll probably consider you both.

LIFESTYLE
Syria

Regardless of religious sect or ethnic background, family is the core unit of Syrian life. Unlike most Western countries, several generations of the one family will often live together. The elderly are greatly respected and are not placed in nursing homes, as there are usually enough family members willing to take care of the them. When a person dies there are three days of mourning when friends and relatives pay their respects. Family and individual pride is very strong and this is one reason that, despite being a relatively poor country, you'll rarely see begging on the streets.

A gateway into a wealth of information about the Arab world is at www.al-bab.com.

Marriage is a major social event in Syria. There is pressure on women to get married young and more than a little advice on prospective marriage partners is forthcoming from the family – especially from the older women! These days young people have a greater say in whom they marry, but both sets of parent must agree, and many living in rural areas still have partners chosen for them. Young couples who are engaged usually meet under supervision, generally a male member of the girl's family, and in the Muslim population they never live together before marriage. It's common for a couple to save money to buy their own place and often delay marriage until they are financially stable, while others will marry and stay at home for a few years.

The conduct of young women is constantly scrutinised and they are expected to uphold the standing of their family. Bringing shame on the family can occur through something as simple as being alone with a man not from her immediate family – when girls marry they are expected to be virgins.

Education is becoming increasingly important as a key to a wealthier life. Having a family member attend university is a source of great pride for most Syrians, who simply cannot afford to have a potential income earner spending time at university. During the 1990s it was a goal of many upwardly mobile Syrians to get a Green Card or study in the USA. Today that destination has lost its appeal somewhat, as it has for many Middle Eastern nations, and Europe is now a preferred destination for career and study.

For most of the desert-dwelling Bedouin of Syria, the seminomadic life has been replaced by a more settled life in a town or city. There are still a few who keep to the old lifestyle and many who work a 'normal' job, getting out to the desert as often as possible to enjoy its peace and solitude.

Lebanon

Family is central to life in Lebanon as well. Extended families are the still the norm and children tend to live at home until married. For many Lebanese this is either to save money for their own place or simply because they can't afford to rent, given their salaries. While family life among Muslims is somewhat similar to that in Syria, Christians in Lebanon, especially the young, take great pleasure in their social freedoms.

While these freedoms superficially appear similar to the West, there is a limit to what is deemed acceptable behaviour. Drinking heavily, sleeping around or taking drugs is frowned upon in Lebanese society, but of course, this far exceeds what is acceptable in other countries in the Middle East.

Marriage is of utmost importance in Lebanon and expected of everyone. For women to remain unmarried into their 30s is rare and raises eyebrows, as well as questions of moral behaviour. For a man still single at 30, like anywhere in the Middle East, it simply means he's waiting for the right girl, although there will come a point where his sexuality will be called into question. There's generally an expectation that people will marry within their religion.

While men are the undisputed heads of the household in Muslim families, increasingly in Christian families women have careers and contribute to decision-making in the household. To achieve the career–home balance, wealthier families often have a full-time maid, who looks after the children and takes care of household duties such as cleaning.

A university education is highly valued in Lebanon and for those who are not from a wealthy family it usually involves juggling a part-time job of at least 20 hours a week alongside attending classes. Many study with a view to getting a Green Card for the USA or entry to another country where they can earn higher salaries. Many young students feel that qualifications alone aren't enough to secure a good job in Lebanon and that having family connections is just as important.

The brain drain from Lebanon is a constant topic of conversation among Lebanese families, as nearly every family has a member living in another country, and seemingly always having a better life than those back home. The reality is slightly different. For many who left during the war, their new country has become a permanent home, the memories of war often a stumbling block to ever returning permanently. For others it's a temporary financial move, a way to pay for a house back in Lebanon that they could never afford on salaries at home.

POPULATION
Syria

More than half of Syria's total population of around 17 million live in a city, concentrated between Damascus (1.6 million) and Aleppo (3.7 million), as well as between Lattakia and Tartus on the coast. Syria's Muslims make up around 90% of the population and this statistic includes the Ismailis, Alawites and Druze as well as Sunni and Shiite. The Alawites have traditionally occupied the mountainous ranges along the coast, which to this day are known as the Jebel Ansariyya, or Jebel an-Nusariyya, after the founder of the Alawite sect.

The Christian population makes up the other 10% and mainly consists of Armenian and Greek Orthodox. Syria also has a Palestinian population of around 300,000, many of whom live on the outskirts of Damascus.

Syria has a youthful population, with over 40% under 14 years of age and population growth at around 2.5%, down from previous decades but still one of the highest in the region. Life expectancy is 67 years of age for men and 71 for women and has been steadily increasing over the last few years.

Lebanon

Lebanon's population of just over four million people is boosted by anywhere between 250,000 and 500,000 Palestinian refugees, half of whom are living in camps. Given the high unemployment rate in Lebanon, there is also a large contingent of guest workers, mainly from Syria, Egypt, Sri Lanka and the Philippines.

Home Works by Christine Tohme and Mona Abu Rayyan (eds) is a thought-provoking compilation of lectures, photos, performances, exhibits and films from a forum on cultural practices in Lebanon, Syria, Palestine, Egypt, Iran and Iraq.

For a Beirut-based photographic archive from the Arab world go to www.fai.org.lb.

An online store featuring Arab books available in English is www.arabworldbooks.com/bookstore.

The population is urban-based, with around 90% of people living in cities. These cities are mainly situated along the coastline, with Beirut being the most populated city (over 1.5 million), followed by Tripoli, Sidon and Tyre. Inland, only Zahlé is notable in terms of population, with around the same number of inhabitants as Sidon.

The population growth rate is low for the region at 1.4% and the number of children per household is two, also low for the Middle East. Lebanon has a youthful population, and more than 30% are under 15 years of age.

Lebanon hosts more than a dozen 'official' religious groups, including Judaism, five Muslim groups and 11 Christian denominations; Muslims are estimated at nearly 70% of the population. Before the civil war, the statistics were, according to most sources, closer to 50:50 between Muslims and Christians. Migration of Christians during and after the civil war, and higher birth rates among Muslims, are considered to be the key reasons.

The Shiite population is the largest of the Muslim sects, and is concentrated in the South, the Bekaa Valley and suburbs south of Beirut. The Sunni population is found in Beirut, Tripoli and Sidon. The Chouf Mountains are the traditional home of the Druze, and the Maronite Christians are historically from the Mt Lebanon region.

RELIGION
Islam

Islam was founded in the early 7th century AD by the Prophet Mohammed, who was born around 570 in Mecca. The basis of Islam is a series of divine revelations in which the voice of the archangel Gabriel revealed the word of God to Mohammed. These revelations started when he was 40 and continued throughout the rest of his life. They were originally committed to memory and later transcribed. This text forms the Quran, literally meaning 'recitation' and great care is taken not to change one single dot of the holy Quran.

Mohammed started preaching in 613, three years after the first revelation, but could only attract a few dozen followers. Having attacked the ways of Meccan life – especially the worship of idols – he also made many enemies. In 622 he and his followers retreated to Medina, an oasis town some 360km from Mecca. It is this Hejira, or migration, which marks the beginning of the Muslim calendar.

In Medina, Mohammed quickly became a successful religious, political and military leader. After several short clashes with the Meccans, he finally gathered 10,000 troops and conquered his home town, demolishing the idols worshipped by the population and establishing the worship of the one God.

Mohammed died in 632, but the new religion continued its rapid spread, through the remarkable wave of conquests achieved by Mohammed's successors, the four caliphs (or Companions of Mohammed). By the end of the 7th century Islam had reached across North Africa to the Atlantic, and having consolidated its power, invaded Spain in 710.

THE CALL FOR PRAYER

Muslims pray five times a day:

Fajr Between dawn and sunrise
Zuhr Just after the height of the midday sun
Asr In the afternoon
Maghrib Just after the sun sets
Isha During the evening

ISLAM & THE WEST

Islam has been much maligned and misunderstood in the West in recent years. Any mention of it usually brings to mind one of two images: the 'barbarity' of some aspects of Islamic law such as flogging, stoning or the amputation of hands; or the so-called fanatics out to terrorise the West (an image that has been greatly strengthened since 11 September 2001).

For many Muslims, however, and particularly for those in the Middle East, Islam is stability in a very unstable world. Many of them are keenly aware that Muslims are seen as a threat by the West and are divided in their own perceptions of Western countries. Not without justification, they regard the West's policies, especially towards the Arab world, as aggressive and they often compare its attitudes to them with those of the medieval Crusaders. Despite this view that Western culture is dangerous to Muslim values and the growing influence of anti-Western religious groups, many Muslims still admire the West. It is common to hear people say they like it, but that they are perplexed by its treatment of them.

If the West is offended by the anti-Western rhetoric of the radical minority, the majority of Muslims see the West, especially with its support of Israel, as a direct challenge to their independence.

Although the violence and terrorism associated with the Middle East is often held up by the Western media as evidence of blind, religiously inspired bloodthirstiness, the efficient oppression of the Palestinian Arabs by Israeli security forces has, until fairly recently, barely rated a mention. The sectarian madness of Northern Ireland is rarely portrayed as a symbol of Christian 'barbarism' in the way political violence in the Middle East is summed up as simple Muslim fanaticism. It is worth remembering that while the 'Christian' West tends to view Islam with disdain, if not contempt, Muslims generally accord Christians great respect as believers in the same God.

Just as the West receives a distorted view of Muslim society, so too are Western values misread in Islamic societies. The glamour of the West has lured those able to compete (usually the young, rich and well educated), but for others, it represents the bastion of moral decline.

These misunderstandings have long contributed to a general feeling of unease and distrust between nations of the West and the Muslim world, and often between individuals of those countries. As long as this situation persists, Islam will continue to be seen in the West as a backward and radical force bent on violent change, rather than as simply a code of religious and political behaviour that people choose to apply to their daily lives, and which makes an often difficult life tolerable.

THE FAITH

Conversion to Islam is simply achieved by a profession of faith (the shahada) in front of two witnesses. This is the first of the five pillars of Islam, the five tenets which guide Muslims in their daily life – see the boxed text The Five Pillars of Islam (p44) for more details.

To Muslims, Allah is the same God that Christians and Jews worship. Adam, Abraham, Noah, Moses and Jesus are all recognised as prophets, although Jesus is not recognised as the son of God. According to Islam, all these prophets partly received the word of God, but only Mohammed received the complete revelations.

SUNNIS & SHIITES

Not long after the death of Mohammed, Islam suffered a major schism that divided the faith into two main sects: the Sunnis and the Shiites. The split arose over disputes about who should succeed Mohammed, who died without an heir. The main contenders were Abu Bakr, who was father of Mohammed's second wife Ayesha and the Prophet's closest companion, and Ali, who was Mohammed's cousin and husband to his daughter Fatima. They both had their supporters, but Abu Bakr was declared the first caliph, an Arabic word meaning 'successor'.

THE FIVE PILLARS OF ISLAM

Shahada (The Profession of Faith) 'There is no God but Allah and Mohammed is his prophet.' *La il-laha illa Allah Mohammed rasul Allah.'* This is the fundamental tenet of Islam and is often quoted at events such as births and deaths. The first part is used as an exclamation good for any time of life or situation.

Salat (The Call to Prayer) This is the obligation to pray in the direction of Mecca five times a day, when the muezzins call the faithful to prayer from the minarets. Prayers can be performed anywhere if a mosque is not available and Muslims often travel with a prayer mat and pray wherever they can. The midday prayers on Friday are the most important of the week.

Zakat (The Giving of Alms to the Poor) This was a fundamental part of the social teaching of Islam. It has become formalised in some states into a tax, which is used to help the poor. In other countries it is a personal obligation to give and is a spiritual duty rather than the Christian idea of charity.

Sawm (Fasting) Ramadan, the ninth month of the Islamic calendar, commemorates the month when the Quran was revealed to Mohammed. In a demonstration of Muslims' renewal of faith, they are asked to abstain from sex and from letting *anything* pass their lips from dawn to dusk for an entire month.

Haj (Pilgrimage) The pilgrimage to Mecca is the ultimate profession of faith for the devout Muslim. Ideally, the pilgrim should go to Mecca during the last month of the year, Zuul-Hijja, to join with Muslims from all over the world in the pilgrimage and subsequent feast. See also the boxed text The Haj (p366) for more details.

Ali finally became the fourth caliph following the murder of Mohammed's third successor, Uthman. He in turn was assassinated in 661 after failing to bend to the military governor of Syria, Mu'awiyah. A relative of Uthman, Mu'awiyah had revolted against Ali over the latter's alleged involvement in Uthman's killing and set himself up as caliph.

Ali's supporters continued to hold fast to their belief in the legitimacy of his line and became known as the Shiites (Partisans of Ali). They believe in 12 imams (spiritual leaders), the last of whom will one day appear to create an empire of the true faith.

The Sunnis are followers of the succession of the caliphs.

ISLAMIC MINORITIES

In Syria, the Shiites and other Muslim minorities, such as the Alawites and Druze, account for about 16% of the population. Many of the Druze in Syria were originally from Lebanon.

Alawites

The Alawites are an offshoot of the mainstream Shiite branch of Islam. Their origins are uncertain but it's believed the sect was founded on the Arabian Peninsula in the 9th century by a preacher named Mohammed ibn Nusayr. Their basic belief is that there is one God with a hierarchy of divine beings, the highest of whom is Ali (see Sunnis & Shiites, p43), hence the name Alawites, or 'followers of Ali'.

Like the Ismailis, a similar sect who also lived in the coastal mountains (see the boxed text The Assassins, p170), the Alawites have always suffered persecution at the hands of ruling Sunni dynasties. Saladin (Salah ad-Din) and his Ayyubid dynasty, the Mamluks and the Ottoman Turks massacred Alawite communities, forced them to convert or imposed crippling taxes. Alawites traditionally worked the poorest lands or held down the least skilled jobs.

That situation radically changed early in the 20th century when the French courted the Alawites as allies and granted them a self-ruled enclave in the mountains around Lattakia. From there the Alawites managed to entrench themselves into national politics to the extent that, since Hafez al-Assad, an Alawite, took power in 1970, this minority sect of one million now holds complete power over the 16 million majority Sunni population.

HEJIRA CALENDAR

The principal Islamic holidays are tied to the lunar Hejira calendar. The word Hejira refers to the flight of the Prophet Mohammed from Mecca to Medina in AD 622, which marks the first year of the calendar (year 1 AH). The calendar is about 11 days shorter than the Gregorian (Western) calendar, meaning that Islamic holidays fall 11 days earlier each year. See also the boxed text Islamic Holidays (p45).

Ras as-Sana New Year's Day. Celebrated on the first day of the Hejira calendar year, 1 Moharram.

Ashura Day of public mourning observed by the Shiites, 10 Moharram.

Moulid an-Nabi A lesser feast celebrating the birth of the prophet Mohammed on 12 Rabi' al-Awal.

Ramadan & Eid al-Fitr When the faithful are called upon as a community to renew their relationship with God. The month in which the Quran was first revealed.

Druze

The Druze religion is an offshoot of Shiite Islam and was spread in the 11th century by Hamzah ibn Ali and other missionaries from Egypt who followed the Fatimid caliph Al-Hakim. The group derives its name from one of Hamzah's subordinates, Mohammed Darazi. Darazi had declared Al-Hakim to be the last imam and God in one. When Al-Hakim died in mysterious circumstances, Darazi and his companions were forced to flee Egypt.

Most members of the Druze community now live in the mountains of Lebanon, although there are some small Druze towns in the Hauran, the area around the Syria–Jordan border. Their distinctive faith has survived intact mainly because of the secrecy that surrounds it. Not only is conversion to or from the faith prohibited, but only an elite, known as 'uqqal (knowers), have full access to the religious doctrine, the hikmeh.

The hikmeh is contained in seven holy books that exist only in handwritten copies. One of the codes it preaches is taqiyya (caution), under which a believer living among Christians, for example, can outwardly conform to Christian belief while still being a Druze at heart. They believe that God is too sacred to be called by name, is amorphous and will reappear in other incarnations. Although the New Testament and the Quran are revered, they read their own scriptures at khalwas (meeting houses) on Thursdays.

Christianity

There are many different churches and rites representing the three main branches of Christianity – Eastern Orthodox, Catholic and Protestant – but the main Christian sect in Lebanon is Maronite, a Roman Catholic church of eastern origin.

MARONITE CHURCH

The Maronite church traces its origins back to the 4th century AD and to the monk, St Maro (also called St Maron), who chose a monastic life on the banks of Nahr al-Aasi (Orontes River) in Syria. It is said that 800 monks joined his community and began to preach the gospel in the surrounding countryside. After his death, his followers built a church over his tomb, which became an important sanctuary. Later, a monastery grew around the church. This became a centre from which early missionaries set out to convert people.

The Byzantine emperor Heraclius visited the monastery in 628 to discuss his ideas for mending the rifts in Christianity. His new doctrine was that of monothelitism, according to which the will of Jesus Christ, both divine and human, was defined as one and indivisible. The Western orthodoxy later condemned this idea as heretical. But the Syrians of Lebanon remained attached to monothelitism, which grew to be identified with their national and religious aspirations. This led to their isolation from both the Orthodox and Jacobite (Syrian Orthodox) sections of the Lebanese community.

Two major events charted the course of the Maronites. Firstly, the Arab conquest put an end to Christian persecutions of heretical groups. Secondly, serious differences led to the expulsion of the Patriarch of Antioch, and at the end of the 8th century, the Maronites elected their own national patriarch, who took the title Patriarch of Antioch and the East – a title still held today.

During the Crusades, the Maronites were brought back into contact with the Christian world and the Church of Rome. A gradual process of Romanisation took place, but the church still worshipped in Syriac (a dialect of Aramaic spoken in Syria) and maintained its own identity. Today the Maronite sect is considered a branch of Roman Catholicism.

EASTERN ORTHODOX CHURCH

This branch of Christianity is well represented in Lebanon. There are many Greek and Armenian Orthodox Churches, as well as a small Jacobite (Syrian Orthodox) community.

Greek Orthodox has its liturgy in Arabic and is the mother church of the Jacobites (Syrian Orthodox), who broke away in the 6th century. Jacobites use only Syriac, which is closely related to Aramaic, and was the language of Christ. Armenian Orthodox (also known as the Armenian Apostolic Church) has its liturgy in classical Armenian and is seen by many to be the guardian of the national Armenian identity.

CATHOLIC CHURCHES

The largest Catholic group in Lebanon is the Maronites, but other Catholic rites represented include Greek Catholics (also know as Melchites), who come under the patriarch of Damascus; Syrian Catholics, who still worship in Syriac; and Armenian Catholics, whose patriarch lives in Beirut. There is also a small community of Catholics who worship in either the Chaldean rite or the Latin rite. The Middle East–based patriarchs are often responsible for the worldwide members of their churches.

SPORT
Lebanon

By far the most popular sport in Lebanon (and Syria) is football (soccer) and it still remains a male-dominated pastime for participants and armchair fans alike. Basketball is increasing in popularity and Lebanon has hosted several regional championships.

While for most, football and basketball are spectator sports, extreme sports are becoming more popular in Lebanon. Jet skis and skidoos feature heavily, while the average Lebanese skier can make a green run at Faraya look like an extreme activity!

Wind- and kite-surfing are increasing in popularity and Lebanon offers reasonable conditions for both sports. Board sports such as surfing and snowboarding gain in popularity every year.

Lebanon's attempts to get a Formula 1 Grand Prix have been thwarted by Bahrain now running a round of the World Championship. How people would tell the difference between Grand Prix competitors and the average Lebanese driver on their way to Beit Mery, we don't know…

MULTICULTURALISM
Syria

To the casual observer, Syria appears to be a homogeneous, Arab-Muslim country. However, around 10% of the population is Christian, and a proportion of the Muslim community is Alawite and Druze. In terms of ethnic background the largest minority group in Syria is the Kurds, who make up around 10% of the population and remain a people without a homeland, with the rest of the Kurdish population based in Turkey, Iraq and Iran. They continue to maintain a strong cultural identity, as well as hopes for an independent state.

A large range of Arab culture links can be found at www.arabianfest.com.

The Armenian community, mainly based in Aleppo, keeps their traditions and culture alive, as they do also in the Beirut suburb of Borj Hammoud. The Armenian language is widely spoken and mass is celebrated in the classical Armenian dialect. Syria also has a Palestinian population of around 300,000, many of whom live on the outskirts of Damascus.

Lebanon

Lebanon's population consists of people from a wide variety of ethnic backgrounds, but today religion is the dominating factor in Lebanon's multicultural mix. One needs only look at the law in relation to divorce, separation and child custody – each handled by the respective authority of each religion – to see how important a role religion plays. Even the two highest positions in the country are split along religious lines, with the president always a Christian and the prime minister Muslim.

Both Right and Left Handed: Arab Women Talk About Their Lives by Syrian author Bouthaina Shaaban dispels some myths about Arab women in spirited interviews with freedom fighters, scholars, poets and mothers of martyrs.

One of the interesting aspects of Lebanon's religious and cultural mosaic, is that it's a country consisting of minorities, many of them in Lebanon to escape persecution in other countries. One of the key reasons proffered by many attempting to untangle the causes of the civil war point to these groups trying to assert their position.

One group still attempting to be accepted with any position at all is the Palestinian refugees. Estimated anywhere between 250,000 and 500,000, the Palestinians have no real rights in Lebanon – only a tiny proportion have been granted citizenship, and unless you take a trip out to a refugee camp their presence as a cultural force in Lebanon is almost nonexistent.

In many ways, the divisions between minorities in Lebanon are still strong. Lebanon's attempts to 'balance' the country by dividing positions proportionally, according to religion, only highlight differences rather than create harmony.

Despite this, it's too simplistic to judge a person's religion based on behaviour alone in Lebanon. While some claim that the religious differences are directly aligned with tastes and attitudes towards art, culture and food, spending only a short amount of time in Lebanon will serve to break these stereotypes.

WOMEN IN SYRIA & LEBANON

The place of women in Syria and Lebanon today defies traditional classification, although these women must tackle many of the same problems facing women globally. Key issues of concern to women include, but are not limited to, human rights, access to education, gender discrimination, equal opportunity, fairer laws relating to household expenses, violence against women, annulment, divorce, alimony, and custody laws.

Middle Eastern Muslim Women Speak by Basima Qattan Bezirgan and Elizabeth Warnock Fernea (eds) is a hefty anthology of lively autobiographical writings by and about Middle Eastern women. Topics cover tradition, transition, colonialism, nationalism and future directions.

Following the release of survey findings in October 2003 which revealed that in 80% of divorce or separation cases Lebanese law gave custody of children to the man, the Lebanese Council to Resist Violence Against Women strengthened its lobbying to change legislation. The focus of its attention is the outdated 'Lebanese Personal Status Law', which gives men overwhelming power, virtually considering women the private property of men.

Perhaps due to their socialist leanings and connections to the former Soviet Union, women in Syria have long had equal opportunities and excelled in fields such as education, health, engineering and architecture, and have attained good positions in the legal and political fields. Twenty-four of the 250 members of parliament are women, and two are ministers. The General Women's Union, established in 1967, has branches across the country, and has worked hard to encourage women to take a more active social and political role in society.

However, what seems to be of greater concern to women in the media, business, public life and academia, and is increasingly gaining attention, is the visibility and image of women in Syria and Lebanon. Many regional organisations have been active, often with Unesco's support, in the area of improvements relating to the representation of women in the media, and rectifying the distorted images of Arab Muslim women in the West is an important challenge facing these women today.

MEDIA

See p82 (Syria) p240 (Lebanon) for general information on newspapers and magazines available.

Syria

Prospects of media liberalisation were high when Bashir al-Assad came to power, but regional tensions and government interference have seen plans fall far short of expectations. While Internet service providers were finally able to start selling subscriptions in 2000, much of the population still can't afford access, let alone a computer.

For most Syrians, news still comes via traditional means. The dailies – three in Arabic and one in English – are mouthpieces for the government and its Ba'ath Party. It's possible for private citizens to start a newspaper but it's easy for the government to shut it down via 2001's press laws.

Television is state-run and the only time you'll find anything approaching a critique of life under the Al-Assad regime is during Ramadan (see p365) programming. Comedies and soap operas attempt to cast a critical eye over life in Syria, but are edited before screening.

Radio doesn't fare much better. While there are no privately owned Syrian radio stations, private Lebanese companies can broadcast in Syria. Dance music doesn't trouble the censors, however, and no one has ever been arrested for playing too much Fairouz (p52).

Lebanon

The much discussed 'liberal' media of Lebanon doesn't really hold up to close scrutiny – it just looks better than the rest of the Middle Eastern media and journalists tend to practise self-censorship in order to keep their jobs. Lebanon allows elected politicians to have active ownership of media outlets. This has now reached a point where a political party is not in the game unless it has a mouthpiece television station, newspaper, or both.

While there is plenty of media – several television stations, a dozen daily newspapers and countless magazines – many are losing money because of Lebanon's small population base. Among these, thankfully, are a couple of publications that appear to express their views very freely. An Nahar, an Arabic daily, is openly critical of Syria's involvement in Lebanon and the Daily Star sometimes publishes articles that have you wondering whether the next day's edition will make it to the newsstand.

DID YOU KNOW?

In 2003, a music concert in Sidon featuring singing stars of a hit TV show started with a bang – dynamite exploded outside the stadium, the blast attributed to religious groups who found the concert a little too 'non-Islamic'.

A Beirut-based contemporary Arab music radio station is at www.sawtelghad.com.

Television ownership falls along political, religious and party lines, and the two most popular are the Lebanese Broadcasting Corporation (LBC), appealing to Maronite Christians, and Future Television, targeting Sunni Muslims. Both are very popular regionally.

ARTS

Syria and Lebanon have vibrant arts scenes, both traditional and contemporary. In the summer many villages have a festival in which traditional dance and music play a part. There are also the large festival events, such as Baalbek, attracting the biggest music stars and international acts (see p327). At smaller contemporary arts festivals, such as Al Shams in Beirut, you can see cutting-edge film, theatre, visual arts and music. The Damascus International Film Festival (p102), one of the oldest in the region, has recently been revitalised, and the Beirut Mid East Film Festival (p253) has taken on the responsibility for rejuvenating cinema regionally. Lebanon's visual arts scene is visible at its many galleries and exhibition spaces, such as the terrific Arab Image Foundation and Espace SD (p242). While Syrian artists and cultural practitioners are producing provocative work, you are more likely to read about it than see it on the streets. Contemporary Middle Eastern culture has been the flavour of the month in Europe for the past six years, so you are more likely to stumble across an interesting Middle Eastern exhibit or film in Paris or Madrid than you are in Damascus or Beirut.

Greetings from Beirut Shift! (www.shift.de) is a funky and funny Lebanese-German co-produced postmodern text on the infinite representations of Beirut. Playful use of photos, graphics, stories, stats and words. One very cool souvenir!

Literature

The first great literature in Arabic came from the Arabian Peninsula. The Holy Quran is considered to be the finest example of classical Arabic writing. Al-Mu'allaqaat, a collection of the earliest Arabic poetry, predated the Quran, and was a celebrated text.

Al-Mu'allaqaat means 'the suspended', and refers to the tradition of hanging poems for public view. That explains those pages you see decoratively hanging across the street during *eid* (see p365).

Seen & Heard: A Century of Arab Women in Literature and Culture by Mona N Mikhail is a collection of serious essays on the representation of Arab women in literature, film and popular culture.

SYRIA

Syria became the focal point of classical Arabic poetry by the 10th century. However, as the Arab world became dominated by the Ottoman Turks, its literature faded, continuing to stagnate until the 19th century. Lebanon's most famous poet, Khalil Gibran, should be given due credit for its rejuvenation. A writer, painter and philosopher, Gibran became a mystical hero after the release of *The Prophet* in 1923. For more on Gibran, see p312. The most popular poet was a Damascene, Nizar Qabbani, who transformed formal Arabic poetry with everyday language, and was adored in the

---

THE GREATEST ARAB POETS

Abu Nuwas (d 815) – companion to 8th-century Baghdad Abbasid caliph Haroun ar-Rashid, who spent his summers at Raqqa on the Euphrates River, wrote humorous accounts of court life and countless odes to the wonders of wine.

Al-Mutanabbi (d 965) – the Syrian 'Shakespeare of the Arabs'. Born in Al-Kufah, he spent his youth bragging to local Bedouin that he was a prophet.

Abu Firas al-Hamdan (932–68) – an Aleppan who wrote most of his poetry while a prisoner in Byzantium.

Abu Ala Al-Ma'ari (973–1057) – born in Ma'arat an-Nu'aman, the blind 'philosopher of poets and poet of philosophers' was a recluse, his writings marked by a heavy scepticism about the decadent, fragmented society surrounding him.

TOP MODERN POETRY TITLES

Modern Arabic Poetry (edited by Salma Khadra Jayyusi) Ninety poets from 15 Middle East countries: Gibran, Adunis and Darwish to contemporary poets published here in English for the first time.

On Entering the Sea: The Erotic and Other Poetry of Nizar Qabbani An English translation of the work of Nizar Qabbani.

The Poetry of Arab Women (edited by Nathalie Handal) Powerful contemporary poetry by more than 80 female poets from the Arab world, including Syria and Lebanon, which destroys many stereotypes about Arab women.

Unfortunately, It Was Paradise (by Mahmoud Darwish) An uplifting collection spanning four decades from a Palestinian-Lebanese poet, awarded France's Chevalier de l'Ordre des Arts et des Lettres de la République Française (Knight of Arts and Belles Lettres) medal, who has penned some 20 collections.

1950s for his love poems. After the wars with Israel, his poetry expressed the Arabs' collective feelings of humiliation and outrage. His writing was banned and Qabbani forced into exile, where he died in 1998 at the age of 75. President Assad organised his burial place in Damascus, where a street was named in his honour.

The novel as an artform emerged with the awakening of Arab national consciousness after WWII. Since then Egyptians such as Nobel Prize–winning Naguib Mahfouz, Lebanese, Palestinians and Syrians have dominated the Middle Eastern literary scene, although in Syria repression has kept most writing banal or forced authors into exile. Zakariya Tamir, Syria's master of the children's story, deals with everyday city life marked by a frustration and despair born of social oppression, which may explain why he ended up in London. Initially his work was realist in manner, but increasingly he turned to fantasy. *Snow at the End of Night* deals in a hallucinatory manner with the theme of family dishonour. In *Tigers on the Tenth Day and Other Stories,* his fables are instruments of social criticism. Ghada al-Samman, who wrote *Beirut Nightmares,* takes her readers on angst-ridden rides through social alienation and constraint, dealing with the plight of women torn between love and traditional values. Of the writers who remain in Syria, the most celebrated and outspoken is Ulfat Idilbi, who writes about the late Ottoman empire and French Mandate and the drive for liberation and independence. *Sabriya: Damascus Bitter Sweet* is critical of the mistreatment of women by their families. Much of its anger stemmed from Idilbi's own experience of being married off at 16 to a man twice her age.

LEBANON

Lebanon has had a flourishing publishing industry since the 19th century, producing a number of literary figures and some great novels, such as a slim book about the civil war by Etel Adnan. *Sitt Marie Rose: A Novel* is an experimental narrative about a Christian schoolteacher murdered in front of her deaf-mute pupils after falling in love with a Palestinian refugee, with its story told from the killers' perspectives. Many Lebanese writers who live abroad include London-based Tony Hanania, whose *Unreal City* is the story of a young scion from a feudal family who leaves for England, returns to war-torn Lebanon and falls in with Hezbollah fighters as he searches for meaning amid anarchy. Feminist Hanan al-Shaykh's *Story of Zahra* is a harrowing account of the civil war, while *Beirut Blues* is a series of long, rambling letters that contrast Beirut's cosmopolitan past with the book's war-torn present. Paris-based Amin Maalouf has been widely published. His most enchanting book, *The Rock of Tanios,* set in a Lebanese village where the

---

THE THOUSAND & ONE NIGHTS

Long before the novel, a deeply rooted tradition of Arabic literature existed in the form of oral storytelling. Before print, tales, epics, fables and histories were circulated by professional storytellers. A standard entertainment was to entrance audiences with tales attributed to Sheherezade from *The Thousand and One Nights*, or *Arabian Nights*, a mixed bag of colourful and fantastic tales that were periodically committed to manuscript from the 12th century onwards. Collectively they comprise thousands of stories, sharing a core of 271 common tales that employ the same framing device – the nightly telling of the stories by Sheherezade to save her neck from the misogynistic King Shahriyar. In the earliest written versions available, the adventures, enchantments and goings-on take place in the semifabled Baghdad of Haroun ar-Rashid (r AD 786–809), and in the Damascus and Cairo of the Mamluks (1250–1517). The *Nights* provides a wealth of rich period detail, from shopping lists and slave prices, through to vivid descriptions of the types and practices of assorted conjurers, harlots, thieves and mystics.

Sheikh's son disappears after rebelling against the system, is considered by many to be his masterpiece.

Cinema & Television

Middle Eastern movies have often been treated as products of a single, unified 'Arab world', yet the unifying factors – Pan-Arab identity, Arab nationalism and Islam – also represent the range of identities characteristic of the region. The most successful industries are those in Egypt, Iran and Turkey, however countries less developed in terms of film production, such as Syria and Lebanon, have produced carefully crafted movies that reflect upon issues specific to their cultures and countries. Despite Hollywood's dominance of their cinema screens, Syrian and Lebanese filmmakers have created films of great beauty that have given voice to people often denied expression.

An online store with the best selection of Arab films on video and DVD is at www.arabfilm.com.

SYRIA

Syria was one of the first Arab countries to develop a cinema industry, yet its production has always been intermittent. It got off to a dazzling start in 1928 with Ismail Anzur's stunning silent film, *Under the Sky of Damascus*. After a flurry of film-making activity following independence in the 1940s nothing much was made until the 1960s when a state organisation was created to promote film production and distribution. Ever since, the state has supported screen education, sending many of its filmmakers to Moscow for training, and financing first feature films. Omar Amiralay, a still active director/curator/critic, made a groundbreaking documentary, *Daily Life in a Syrian Village* (1974), and Mohamed Malas directed *Dreams of the City* (1984), an evocative fictional study of Damascus. Abdulatif Abdulhamid's brilliant first feature was *The Nights of the Jackal* (1989).

The brightest spot on the drama scene in Syria in recent years has been television rather than film. Since the 1980s, when the government allowed independent companies to produce television content there has been a boom in quality series and soap operas, many of which are successfully sold abroad. Most of the talent graduating from the National High Institute for Drama head straight for lucrative TV work. A highlight of Syrian television drama was the enormously successful *The Silk Market*, by Nihad Sirees, an Aleppan novelist and screenwriter. The drama presented the city of Aleppo, its culture and dialect, on television for the first time.

Arab Cinema: History and Cultural Identity by Viola Shafik is an excellent narrative history and analysis of cinema in the Middle East from its birth through to the present with good coverage on Syrian and Lebanese cinema.

In December 2003 Syria held the 13th edition of its biannual international film festival with the theme 'Embrace the World', 450 films on show, an all-women jury and the release of 20 publications. The festival celebrated the 40th anniversary of the National Film Organisation and Syrian cinema's diamond jubilee.

LEBANON

Transit Visa by Akram Zaatari and Mahmoud Hojeij (eds) is a cool collection of cultural reflections of young artists from Lebanon, Syria, Egypt, Jordan and Iran on ideas to do with 'city' and 'place' in video/documentary work.

When the Egyptian industry was at its peak, churning out some 350 films a year in the late 1950s, Lebanon was producing a paltry dozen films a year. Lebanese filmmaking remained artisanal in nature, reflected in movies such as those of the great Georges Nasser, who made the tragic *Towards the Unknown* in 1957. In the 1960s, when state intervention in the Egyptian industry drove many Egyptians into exile, levels of production rose rapidly in Lebanon to about 200 films from 1965 to 1975. The downside was that Lebanese cinema became an industry driven by expatriates, and it wasn't until the 1970s that a number of talented Lebanese directors emerged, including Andre Gedeon, Maroun Baghdadi and Bohrane Alaouie. The civil war brought the industry to a virtual halt, with most filmmakers forced to work outside the country, seldom having their films shown within. Baghdadi continued to work (winning an award at Cannes), as did Roger Assaf, Samir Nasri and Mohammed Sweid. Lebanon produced some notable films following the war. Paris-based Jocelyn Saab has made documentaries in Lebanon with European money. *Once Upon a Time in Beirut* incorporates footage from 300 different films dating from 1914 to 1975. In 1998, *West Beirut* won international critical acclaim. Directed by Ziad Duweyri (a former cameraman for US director Quentin Tarantino), the tender and funny film tells the semi-autobiographical story of a teenager living in West Beirut during the first year of the civil war. That same year, Mai Masri made a highly acclaimed award-winning documentary, *Children of Shatila*, which looks at the history of the notorious refugee camp through children's eyes. War was also the theme of Ghassan Shalhab's film *Beyrouth Fantome*, which tells the story of a former militiaman who returns to the city in the late 1980s after a 10-year absence.

For an Arabic music website, try www.musicoflebanon.com

Although Lebanon has four film schools, six television stations, three decent film festivals (the Mid East Film Festival Beirut, Docu-Days and Al Shams), and the recently established Beirut Middle East Film Foundation, the film industry is yet to fully recover. Nevertheless, Beirut has become a hub for advertising and music video productions.

Music

Music is everywhere in Syria and Lebanon. Fairouz wafts all the way down from bullet-riddled Hamra apartment blocks, Amr Diab blasts from the stereos of passing cars, Haifa hails from boom-boxes on the beach, while the REG Project emanates from cool Rue Monot bars.

Arabic music links are at www.maqamworld.com.

Arab music today reflects a successful synthesis of indigenous harmony, taste and instruments, combined with some Western instruments and influences. In the Syrian desert the Bedouin have long had simple, but mesmerising, musical traditions. The chanting of men drifting across the desert from a distant wedding on a still night is truly haunting. Up close, the musical side of the evening's festivities is clearly rooted in ancient traditions. A row of men, arm in arm, gently sway backwards and forwards engaged in a trance-like chant, singing to a lone, veiled woman, who dances before them with restrained sensuality.

In recent years the Bedouin sound has been updated to produce a unique semi-electric, semitraditional and thoroughly hypnotic style of music. The music you hear on the Arab street has little to do with timeless desert traditions but has its roots in Egypt which, for much of the past hundred years, has been the undisputed cultural capital of the Arab world. If the artists weren't always Egyptian-born, they were Egyptian-bred, groomed and broadcast. Syria's most famous singer, Farid al-Atrache, spent most of his life in Cairo. See the boxed text Farid al-Atrache (below).

The most popular style of music focuses on a star performer backed by anything from a small quartet to a full-blown orchestra. The all-time great remains Umm Kolthum, an Egyptian diva renowned in the Arab world as the 'Nightingale of the East' (Kawkab ash-Sharq), who died in 1975. The only singer who has come close to supplanting her in the affections of the Arabs is Fairouz, a Lebanese torch singer who has enjoyed star status since first recording in Damascus in the 1950s. She later became an icon for Lebanon during the civil war (which she sat out in Paris) and her concert in downtown Beirut after the end of the fighting attracted 40,000 people and provided a potent symbol of reunification. In her late 60s, she still occasionally performs, most recently in Dubai with her son Ziad, a renowned experimental jazz performer.

Although the kind of orchestra that backs such a singer is a curious cross-fertilisation of East and West – instruments such as violins, piano, wind and percussion instruments predominate, next to such local species as the oud (lute) – the sounds that emanate from them are anything but Western. There is the seduction of the East in the backing melodies and the melancholic, languid tones you'd expect from a sun-drenched and heat-exhausted region.

Held in such esteem as they still are, singers like Farid al-Atrache, Umm Kolthum and Fairouz have little appeal to younger generations of Syrians and Lebanese who have grown up on a diet of Arabic pop. Characterised by a clattering, hand-clapping rhythm overlaid with synthesised twirlings and a catchy repetitive vocal, the first Arab pop stars came out of Cairo. While the Arab world's biggest selling song ever, Amr Diab's 'Nour al-Ain' (1998), was an Egyptian product, these days the Egyptians are being beaten at their own game by Lebanese, Syrian, Iraqi, and other Gulf-based artists. Amr Diab, for example, is the Ricky Martin of the Middle East, and attracts a huge following.

A popular musician marrying classical Arabic music with contemporary sounds is Marcel Khalife, hailing from Amchit, near Byblos. An oud player with a cult following, many of his songs have a controversial political side, such as a composition for the dead of Sabra and Shatila (see p33).

Contemporary Arabic fusion remixes of oriental trip-hop, lounge, drum and base, acid jazz and traditional music, for both the dance floors and chilling out, have taken the Middle East and Europe by storm over the last few years. DJs such as Elie Attieh are the new stars, along with Beirut-based REG

DID YOU KNOW?

Syrian megastar singers include George Wassouf and Mayada El Hennaway and Iraq-born Kazem al-Saher.

A comprehensive site on the Lebanese singing legend, Fairouz, can be found at www.fairouz.com

DID YOU KNOW?

There's an ongoing debate in the Arabic pop world about talent versus looks. Newer artists like Nancy and Haifa, as well as the 4 Cats, are being accused of caring more about their looks than their singing, as well as being criticised for their raunchy videos.

FARID AL-ATRACHE

Although he lived most of his life in Cairo and was made a star in Egypt, Farid al-Atrache was born in Suweida in the Hauran region of Syria. A crooner or singer of populist sentimental songs, he appeared in more than 30 films during the 1940s and '50s. More than just an 'Arab Sinatra', he was a highly accomplished oud (lute) player and composer, who succeeded in updating Arabic music by blending it with Western scales and rhythms and the orchestration of the tango and waltz. He died in Beirut in 1974, was buried in his adopted home of Egypt, but lives on in the Arab world through continued sales of cheap cassettes that are played in shops, restaurants and bars throughout both countries (and indeed the whole Middle East).

Project – Ralph Khoury, Elie Barbar and Guy Manoukian – who specialise in Arab deep house and lounge. You'll hear these sounds at the Rue Monot clubs and bars, and Damascus cafés such as Moulaya and Galerie Abdel.

If you don't know locals or read Arabic, it's difficult to see live music in the Middle East, as the megastar concerts are generally only advertised in the Arabic language press. You will find some live oud music in restaurants in Damascus and Aleppo, however in Beirut there are few live-music venues. Other than at festivals, such as Baalbek or Beiteddine (see p364), your best chance of catching a performance is at a wedding or party, which is where nearly all Arab singers and musicians get their start!

Architecture

The earliest architectural efforts undertaken by Muslims were mosques, which inherited much from Christian and Graeco-Roman models. The Umayyad Mosque in Damascus (p86) was built on the site of a Christian basilica, which itself had been the successor of a Roman temple, and is one of the earliest and grandest of Islam's places of worship.

With the spread of Islam, various styles soon developed and the vocabulary of Islamic architecture quickly became very sophisticated and expressive, reaching its apotheosis under the Mamluks (1250–1517). The Mamluks extended the types of buildings to include the madrassa (theological school), *khanqah* (Sufi monastery) and mausoleum complex. These were typically characterised by the banding of different coloured stone (a technique known as *ablaq*) and by the *muqarnas,* the elaborate stalactite carvings and patterning around windows and in recessed portals. The Mamluks were also responsible for the transformation of the minaret from the Umayyad Mosque's square tower into a slender cylindrical shape. The Ottoman Turks defeated the Mamluks, and during the Ottoman era Damascus and Aleppo flourished, growing rich on trade monopolies. Much of the architecture from this time reflects that wealth. The most prevalent Ottoman building type is the khan (travellers' inn).

There are still examples of traditional architecture in Lebanon, however many of the old buildings have suffered the same redevelopment fate as the rest of the Mediterranean. Beirut's old houses are usually large and airy with a courtyard garden, a terrace overgrown with vines and large arched windows, often inset with coloured glass. The style is a mix of Arabic layout and Italian influence. Examples can still be seen on the Ain al-Mreisse Corniche and in the backstreets of Achrafiye and near the American University of Beirut (AUB). Most buildings constructed since the 1960s are concrete blocks, although there are some modernist gems, particularly in Achrafiye. In the Beirut Central District, many of the buildings were too damaged by the war to be saved, and reconstruction is being done in the 'spirit' of the original.

In regional Lebanon, styles vary. In the north, Tripoli has a wealth of medieval and Islamic architecture, and a fine collection of 18th-century merchants' houses can be seen in the small town of Amchit, north of Byblos. Deir al-Qamar, in the Chouf Mountains, is a well-preserved village, with some beautiful 18th- and 19th-century villas and palaces. Beiteddine Palace (Beit ad-Din, see p294), also in the Chouf Mountains, is a melange of Italian and traditional Arab architecture, although it is more remarkable for its lavish interiors than any architectural innovation.

Interior designers are doing wonderful work in Lebanon today. For the most part, thoughtful, playful and stylish, it's often a shame that many places are either private residences or clubs that don't last long enough for people to pay a visit. One notable exception is the B 018 nightclub (p263).

www.b018.com – sure, it's a website of a nightclub, but the concept and execution of the architecture and interior design make it worth a look.

Contemporary Arab Representations: Beirut/Lebanon by Catherine David (ed) is a brilliant publication, part of a project by visual artists, photographers, architects, writers and poets aimed at encouraging cultural exchange between Arabs and the rest of the world.

Unlike Rue Monot clubs, situated on the former Green Line, architect Bernard Khoury created an homage to the past at a site that was formerly a quarantine zone, a refugee camp and the site of an appalling massacre during the war.

While contemporary Lebanese architecture and interior design is notable, the scene in Syria is notable only for its absence.

Painting, Visual Arts & Photography

If you think of painting in the Western sense, you may think there is little artistic tradition in the Arab world. Islam's taboo on the depiction of living beings means that the Arabs have traditionally limited their artistic endeavours to calligraphy and patterning, hence the term 'arabesque'. In the late 19th century a smattering of educated Levantines travelled abroad and returned to form schools of fine art, although their styles were all imported. A regional identity did, however, begin to emerge in the latter half of the 20th century.

In Lebanon, the first art school, the Academie Libanais des Beaux-Arts, was established in 1937 and 20 years later AUB established its Department of Fine Arts. The two institutions nurtured a growing artistic community. In the 1950s and '60s a number of galleries opened to showcase its art, and the private Sursock Museum, in Achrafiye, also began to show new artists. In the 1960s a group of artists and scholars, headed by Jenine Rubeiz, formed Dar al-Fan (literally Place of Art) to provide a forum for artists to gather and discuss their work. The art scene re-established itself with vigour after the war and there is a thriving artistic community in Beirut. Apart from Khalil Gibran, famous 20th-century artists include the painters Hassan Jouni, Moustafa Farroukh and Mohammed Rawas. Better-known contemporary painters include Marwan Rechmawi, Bassam Kahwaji, Amin al-Basha, Helen Khal and Etel Adnan (who, like Gibran, is also a writer).

Many galleries exhibit sculpture as well as painting. One of the current Lebanese stars is Salwa Raodash Shkheir, while a permanent sculpture display can be seen at the workshop and galleries at the home of the Basbous brothers in Rachana village, to the north of Beirut. Their larger works line the streets nearby and attract many visitors, especially on weekends. See p287 for details.

The photography and visual arts scene is the most vibrant and cutting-edge of all the arts in the region, and can be experienced at local galleries such as Espace SD. At the 2003 International Biennale of Contemporary Art, Lebanese artist Salwa Zeidan won a prize for her abstract paintings, which combine strength and vigour with a gentle transparency. Zeidan has exhibited her work in more than 32 international exhibitions and had more than 17 solo exhibitions.

Theatre & Dance

With a limited number of theatre venues and little funding in Syria and Lebanon, young writers and performers find it difficult to get a start. Most theatres are based in Beirut, and prominent Lebanese playwrights such as Roger Assaf, Jalal Khoury and Issam Mahfouz are trying to encourage younger artists, and a revitalised Lebanese theatre scene is gradually emerging.

The Théâtre de Beyrouth in Ain al-Mreisse (Minet al-Hosn) puts on high-quality performances (often experimental works) by young actors and playwrights. It also hosts foreign productions and is a likely place to find quality English- or French-language theatre. Al-Medina Theatre (p264) is a performance venue based in West Beirut, which shows plays, primarily in

Berlin's House of World Cultures holds innovative exhibitions/events, such as DisORIENTation, Contemporary ArabArt from the Middle East at www.hkw.de.

Beirut's Espace SD gallery website features info on the exhibitions and artists at www.espacesd.com.

Visit the artist's Brummana atelier at www.salwazeidan.com.

BELLY DANCING

This ancient form of dance, known in the east as *raks sharki* and to the world as belly dancing, sums up the eastern nightclub experience. The dance is characterised by its sensual hip movements and graceful arm movements – and also by the skimpy costumes worn by the practitioners. When Westerners first saw this dance, they were struck by its erotic quality and this image has stayed with the dance ever since. Not surprisingly, Europe in the 18th century had no equivalent dance and the degree of skin shown in oriental dancing was shocking to Christian Europeans of that time.

Professional belly dancers can earn a fortune for a single performance. Others make do with large denomination notes tucked into their costume as a tribute from their appreciative audience. The top dancers are usually Egyptian, although some Russian dancers have become stars in their own right across the Middle East, which has resulted in Egypt refusing to issue licences to foreign dancers.

The origins of the dance are unclear. Some scholars think they come from the professional dancers of medieval Spain. Others think belly dancing has a connection with pagan fertility dances performed in temples. These days the dance is performed as entertainment in clubs and restaurants and still plays an important role at traditional weddings. The belly dancer who performs at weddings represents the transition from virgin bride to sensual woman.

If you find yourself confronted by a gyrating torso at a club, etiquette requires that you place a rolled or folded banknote into the bra or waistband of the dancer without too much physical contact. The belly dancer will then move on to another table and repeat the performance. Those who don't enjoy public humiliation should note that in some clubs the dancer will embarrass members of the audience by getting them up to dance.

Arabic. In Achrafiye, Theatre Monot tends to show French-language productions. The AUB campus has a theatre, which sometimes performs plays in English, although the quality of the productions varies wildly.

The traditional Levantine dance, the *dabke*, is an energetic folk dance performed at weddings and celebrations throughout the region. People join hands and are led by a 'master' dancer. The dance can also be seen in tourist-oriented restaurants where dancers wear the traditional costume of the mountains and portray aspects of village life. Far more fun is when a spontaneous *dabke* erupts at a wedding or social occasion, and people form circles and start to move. You may also catch a glimpse of some *raks sharki* (belly dancing) at a wedding or a 'women only' social occasion. Belly dancers, with their gyrating hips and spangled bikinis, are one of the Middle East's most famous sights, and belly dancing is still very popular in the region, although these days many dancers are not even Arab.

Caracalla is the closest thing Lebanon has to a national dance troupe. Founded by Ahmed Caracalla, the choreographer of the Baalbek Festival in the 1960s, the group's performances are inspired by oriental dance, but combine opera, dance and theatre. With colourful costumes and musicals based on diverse sources, from Shakespeare to modern Lebanese literature, they can be seen at some of Lebanon's summer festivals, and at the Theatre Monot in Achrafiye.

DID YOU KNOW?

Egyptian belly dancer, Tahiyya Karioka, was the undisputed 'Queen of Oriental Dancing', starring in hundreds of films. In-between films she liked to relax by getting married, something she did 17 times before her death in 1999.

Environment

THE LAND
Syria

There are four broad geographical regions of Syria: a coastal strip, backed by mountains, which then flatten out into cultivated plains, quickly giving way to desert.

The coastline is not particularly extensive, stretching for just 180km between Turkey and Lebanon. In the north, the coast is almost fronted by the Jebel Ansariyya range of peaks (also known as the Jebel an-Nusariyya) with an average height of 1000m that forms a formidable and impenetrable north–south barrier dominating the whole coast. The mountains angle inland somewhat to give space to the Sahl Akkar (Akkar Plain) in the south. Deep ravines mark the western side of the range, while to the east the mountains fall almost sheer to the fertile valley, Al-Ghab, of the Orontes River (Nahr al-Aasi), that flows north into Turkey.

The Anti-Lebanon Range (Jebel Libnan ash-Sharqiyya) marks the border between Syria and Lebanon and averages 2000m in height. Syria's highest mountain, Jebel ash-Sheikh (the Bible's Mt Hermon), rises to 2814m. The main river flowing from this range is the Barada, which has enabled Damascus to survive in an otherwise arid region for over 2000 years.

Other smaller ranges include the Jebel Druze, which rises in the south near the Jordanian border, and the Jebel Abu Rujmayn in the centre of the country, north of Palmyra.

The Fertile Crescent is, as the name suggests, Syria's main agricultural region and forms an arc in which are cradled the major centres of Damascus, Homs, Hama, Aleppo and Qamishle. The Euphrates and Orontes Rivers provide water for intensive farming, while away from the water sources, dry-land wheat and cereal crops are grown.

The Syrian desert, a land of endless and largely stony plains, occupies the whole southeast of the country. The oasis of Palmyra is on the northern edge of this arid zone and, along with other oases, used to be an important centre for the trade caravans plying the routes between the Mediterranean and Mesopotamia.

Lebanon

Lebanon is one of the world's smallest countries, but within its borders are several completely diverse geographical regions. There is a very narrow, broken, coastal strip on which the major cities are situated. Inland, the Mt Lebanon Range rises steeply with a dramatic set of peaks and ridges; the highest, Qornet as-Sawda, reaches over 3000m southeast of Tripoli. South of Beirut are the Chouf Mountains, which get progressively lower in altitude as you head south. The unusual feature of this mountain range is its nonporous layer of rock, which forces water to the surface in big enough quantities to produce large springs at up to 1500m. This means that in addition to an abundance of picturesque waterfalls, Lebanon has cultivation at unusually high altitudes.

The Mt Lebanon Range gives way steeply to the Bekaa Valley, 150km from end to end, which, although low in comparison to the mountain peaks, is still 1000m above sea level. Flanked on both sides by mountains, the Bekaa Valley lies in a rain shadow and is considerably more arid than the rest of the country; nevertheless, it is the major agricultural area, producing wine, vegetables and, until recently, cannabis.

'Lebanon is one of the world's smallest countries'

The Anti-Lebanon Range to the east of the Bekaa Valley forms a natural border with Syria and rises in a sheer arid massif from the plain.

WILDLIFE
Syria
ANIMALS

Officially, wolves, hyenas, badgers, wild boar, jackals, deer, bears and even polecats still roam some corners of Syria, but don't expect to see these on your travels.

The number of bird species found in Syria and their population densities are both low. While Syria has only a small number of major wetlands, they are significant for globally threatened species of birds.

Syria's big claim to faunal fame is as the original home of the golden (or Syrian) hamster *(mesocricetus auratus)*. Mention of the animal first appeared in a 1797 publication entitled *The Natural History of Aleppo*. The majority of the millions of golden hamsters that have been kept worldwide as pets are descended from one single pregnant female that was trapped near Aleppo in 1930. The pups were bred in a laboratory and then released into the British pet market in the 1940s. Since then, only 10 more hamsters have ever been caught in Syria, so chances of spotting one in the wild are slim.

PLANTS

Heavy clearing has all but destroyed the once plentiful forests of the mountain belt along the coast of Syria, although some small areas are still protected. Yew, lime and fir trees predominate in areas where vegetation has not been reduced to scrub. Elsewhere, agriculture dominates, and there's little or no plant life in the unforgiving stretches of the Syrian desert.

Lebanon
ANIMALS

Lebanon has a huge variety of bird life, in part due to its location as a resting place for many species as they migrate between Africa and Europe or Asia. Some 135 species of bird have been observed off the Lebanese coast, while further out at the Palm Islands Reserve over 300 have been seen. A variety of nesting birds make their homes on the islands, including the mistle thrush, tern, broad-billed sandpiper, osprey and various types of finch.

The Bekaa Valley is another extremely important migratory stop for millions of birds, including storks (which pass through every April), hoopoes, red-rumped swallows, buzzards, golden eagles and kestrels.

Lebanon's love affair with the car is echoed by its obsession with guns. On almost any mountain track in the country you will find spent bullet shells – not from the war, but from hunters. Hunting, combined with pollution, has had a massive negative effect on Lebanon's wildlife, but thanks to conservation efforts over the past decade, some species are returning. Wolves, wild boar, ibexes and gazelles remain endangered species in Lebanon, but they have been sighted in the Chouf Cedar Reserve, along with wild cats, porcupines and badgers.

Marine life has also been given a boost by the establishment of the Palm Islands Reserve. Mediterranean turtles, which had disappeared from the Lebanese coast, have begun nesting there in recent years.

PLANTS

The most famous flora in Lebanon – the cedar tree – is now found on only a few mountaintop sites, notably at Bcharré and near Barouk in the Chouf

Mountains. These lonely groves are all that remain of the once-great cedar forests, however there are some sites where new trees are being planted. It will take centuries before new forests look anything like their predecessors. For information on The Cedars, see p314.

In spite of widespread deforestation before, during and after the war, Lebanon is still the most densely wooded of all the Middle Eastern countries. Many varieties of pine, including Aleppo pine, flourish on the mountains, in addition to juniper, oak, beech and cypress. In spring there is an abundance of wild flowers on the hills and mountains, including the indigenous Lebanon violet.

Much of the coastal land is cultivated with fruit trees, such as oranges, lemons, medlars, bananas and olives. In the Bekaa Valley most of the arable land is given over to agriculture, including grape growing.

In Beirut many of the magnificent, mature palm trees that once lined the Corniche were blown up during the civil war. Replanting schemes are taking place, but it will be 20 years or more before tall palms sway in the Beirut breeze again.

'Lebanon is still the most densely wooded of all the Middle Eastern countries'

NATIONAL PARKS & RESERVES
Syria

Syria has one of the lowest ratios of protected areas to total land area of any country in the Mediterranean region. However, Syria has a significant protected wetland, the Sabkhat al-Jabbul Nature Reserve. This large, permanent saline lake is located in Halap province, 30km east-southeast of Aleppo. The area is important for a large number of water birds, including the greater flamingo.

There are a number of protected rangelands and many more slated to become protected, but their individual sizes are quite small.

Lebanon

Although there are over 30 areas in Lebanon that are protected by ministerial decrees, it's mainly in the country's three nature reserves that conservation is actually being practised. They are the main hope for the future of the country's threatened flora and fauna. The reserves are overseen by the Protected Areas Directorate at the Ministry of the Environment and receive funding from a variety of NGOs and international organisations, as well as the government.

CHOUF CEDAR RESERVE

This is Lebanon's largest nature reserve, and it covers over 50,000 hectares – some 5% of the country's entire area. Established in 1996, it is the best managed and easiest to visit of the three reserves. It boasts six cedar forests, including three that contain old-growth cedars. A huge variety of flora and fauna, including a number of endangered species, is found here and, like the other reserves, it contains areas used as resting places for migratory birds. For more information, see p297.

HORSH EHDEN FOREST NATURE RESERVE

This reserve is situated 35km from Tripoli and 100km from Beirut in the northern stretch of the Mt Lebanon Range, just 3km from the summer resort of Ehden. The reserve is a unique natural habitat supporting rare indigenous trees and plants, including the Cicilian fir, Lebanon violet, Ehden milk vetch and dozens of others. It also provides a habitat for rare birds and butterflies and is the last natural archetype of Lebanon's ancient indigenous forests. For more information, see p312.

PALM ISLANDS RESERVE

Incorporating Palm Island, Sanani Island and Ramkine Island, the reserve lies 5km off the coastal city of Tripoli. Its area covers 5 sq km of land and sea and it's an important nesting place for marine birds as well as turtles and Mediterranean monk seals. For more information, see p307.

AAMIQ MARSH

Aamiq Marsh lies halfway between Chtaura and Lake Qaraoun, at the foot of the eastern slopes of Jebel Barouk, and is Lebanon's last major wetland formed by Nahr al-Riachi (Riachi River) and its underground source. The area is a haven for migrating and aquatic birds but the wetland was in a perilous state until recently. A Christian nature conservation organisation has been working with local landowners to improve the area. See p327 for more information.

ENVIRONMENTAL ISSUES
Syria

One of the key issues for Syria is water conservation. Syria is located in a very arid area of the Middle East. Water scarcity is compounded by a rapidly growing population, development and pollution of natural water supplies. A huge amount of Syria's water supply goes towards agriculture, however the amount of money that Syria earns from agriculture is small. On top of this, the Turkish Greater Anatolia Project involves dams and power plants being built on the Tigris-Euphrates basin. Some estimates have stated that the amount of water flowing through the Euphrates in Syria will be reduced by 40%. Problems for the Syrian Euphrates translate to even greater problems for Iraq's waterways.

There is a Syrian National Environmental Action Plan (NEAP), which will attempt to prevent misuse of land and water resources. It will look at issues such as desertification (reducing fertile land to desert through misuse); deforestation (of what's left of Syria's forests); desalination of water resources; the reuse of treated wastewater; and the prevention of chemical and microbiological contamination of water resources. As with Lebanon, these types of projects need full government backing and long-term commitment, something that doesn't appear to be high on the agenda of either country.

Lebanon

Ravaged by 15 years of anarchy, decades of unfettered building and weak state control, Lebanon's environment suffered greatly through the 20th century and remains extremely fragile.

During the war land mines were embedded in much of the country. Paradoxically, this actually protected some areas, such as the Chouf, by keeping humans away.

The absence of basic services during the war meant that solid waste was dumped throughout the country. Although the worst of these excesses has been cleaned up with the creation of massive landfill sites, the continuing lack of environmental awareness and inadequate waste disposal mean that most water sources are polluted.

By the mid-1990s Lebanon did not have a single functioning wastewater treatment plant, and raw sewage was pouring out to sea. A number of treatment plants have been rehabilitated and new ones are being built, but offshore water quality remains a concern. The dumping of medical waste, particularly along the country's coast, also continues to be a serious problem.

AL MASHRIQ

A directory site with useful links to Lebanese green groups.

almashriq.hiof.no/base/environment.html

GREENLINE

A volunteer organisation promoting environmental awareness and conservation.

www.greenline.org.lb

In the south, the land is littered with mines and unexploded ordnance (for more information see the boxed text Warning, p339). However, in the eyes of many environmentalists, the occupation has saved the area. Beaches to the south of Tyre remain unspoilt and there has been little interest in 'developing' an area that was so unstable. As in the Chouf, the mines have prevented encroachment on the countryside.

Although Beirut is on the coast and has strong sea breezes, air pollution is a major problem. There are some 1.5 million cars in Lebanon and a huge proportion of them are in Beirut.

Against this litany of woes there are positive signs, however. The fact that a Ministry of the Environment even exists is a step in the right direction, even though it is weak and rarely consulted by other ministries. More encouraging is the establishment of a number of environmental organisations and there are now more than 30 NGOs working in this field in Lebanon. Greenpeace has an office in Beirut, and a growing number of local green groups are actively fostering grass-roots opposition to the worst environmental problems.

Ecotourism is also having a positive effect. Trekking and other adventure-travel organisations are rapidly growing in Lebanon and promoting environmental concerns to thousands of locals, and some foreign visitors, each year. See Trekking, p357, for some ecofriendly operators.

There are also campaigns under way to promote awareness of the dangers of pesticide use. Some restaurants in Beirut are now trying to use organic produce and farmers are being taught alternatives to chemical pesticides and fertilisers. Nevertheless, this is all NGO-driven and without government support. While green organisations are discussing conservation plans for the country, the environment minister is signing off new quarries.

DID YOU KNOW?

Beirut's long-suffering taxi drivers have been ordered to switch back to petrol engines for environmental reasons, after most switched to diesel engines for economic reasons.

Food & Drink
Greg Malouf & Geoff Malouf

There is no better way to gain an understanding of the Syrian and Lebanese psyches than by observing the role that food, and in particular entertaining, plays in everyday life. It would be an understatement to say that, for the people of the Levant, life revolves around food. From the cradle to the grave, a dish or a feast marks every milestone in life. If you're travelling with children, they will fall in love with this gregarious, family-oriented culture, and they'll always be welcome in restaurants.

Lebanese food has often been described as the 'pearl of the Arab kitchen'. The country is the gateway to the Mediterranean, linking the cultures of East and West, and it has stylised its cuisine to appeal to Western palates. Lebanon inherited the art of trading and the ability to please from the Phoenicians, and from the Arabs, the art of hospitality.

A host's generosity is measured by the amount of food on the table, and it's often the subject of gossip. An old rule of entertaining advises people to serve up twice the amount of food that they expect their guests to eat! A word of advice, then, to a guest in the home of a Syrian or Lebanese – take everything offered, because to decline will greatly offend your host.

While Syrians and Lebanese generally love their meat, if you're vegetarian you can still eat very well in the region (much mezze is vegetarian), and you won't have to survive solely on felafels. The abundance of fresh local produce means that there's almost always a meat-free option.

> Greg Malouf is one of Australia's most admired chefs and food writers. Born into a Lebanese-Australian family, he is an acknowledged champion of modern Middle Eastern cuisine. He is the author of *Arabesque* and *Moorish* and he runs the acclaimed restaurant Mo Mo (Melbourne, Australia). Geoff Malouf, Greg's brother, is also an accomplished restaurateur, running Café Zum Zum, a busy establishment in inner-city Melbourne. Together, Greg and Geoff host culinary tours to Syria and Lebanon.

STAPLES & SPECIALITIES
Mezze

The very core of Syrian and Lebanese hospitality is typified by mezze. This huge array of small starters precedes the main course. Dishes range from pickled vegetables to offal and savoury pastries *(samboosik)*. In a normal *azeemieh* (invitation) or *hafli* (party), the preferred way of entertaining is in a banquet style.

The dips – hummus (chickpea and tahini) and *baba ghanoug* (smoky eggplant) – are served on long oval platters and garnished with chopped parsley, paprika and olive oil. In Damascus, *baba ghanoug* (which means 'father's favourite') takes the form of an eggplant salad with diced tomato, onion, parsley, garlic and lemon.

The ever-popular *tabbouleh* (a salad of bulgur wheat, parsley and tomato, with a sprinkling of sesame seeds, lemon and garlic) is accompanied with bowls made of lettuce cups, enabling diners to dispense with cutlery and scoop up the tangy olive oil and lemon. Vine leaves are also popular – they're rolled with spiced lamb and rice and served with platters of fresh greens.

For the daring gastronome, there's finely chopped, fresh lamb's fry served raw with a piece of fat *(liyye)* found only in the tail of a regional breed of sheep. Or try chicken livers and frogs legs sautéed in lemon, garlic and coriander.

Bastoorma, an Arabic pastrami thickly coated with fenugreek, garlic and chilli, is made by Turkish and Armenian butchers. It's a breakfast favourite, usually fried in paper-thin slices with eggs. On a breakfast table you may also find *labneh*, a wonderfully thick and creamy yogurt cheese, sprinkled with fruity olive oil.

Traditionally all meals are eaten with *khoobz Arabi*, the ancient flat bread of the Arabic world, often used as a scoop.

These are just some of the many mezze dishes. The best advice for the *ajnabi* (foreigner) is to not go in hard at this stage of the meal – the best is yet to come!

Mains

Just when you are rising to wish your host warm thanks and goodnight, the main course arrives on the table. In a private home this might be a whole oven-roasted lamb, stuffed with spiced mince, rice, almonds and pine nuts. This is served on the birth of a male in the family, or on the arrival of an honoured guest.

Arabesque: Modern Middle Eastern Food by Greg and Lucy Malouf lists the 42 most essential ingredients from the region and offers insights into how the chef should use them to create authentic dishes.

In a restaurant the mains usually consist of a variety of skewered meats. Chicken and lamb kebabs, barbecued on charcoal, arrive on the table covered with *khoobz Arabi*. Another main course dish, *kafta,* is made of minced lamb, onion and spices, topped with a tossed salad of parsley, onions, olive oil and sumac (a tangy, lemony spice).

The celebrated chicken and rice dish, *roz a djaj,* always completes the banquet. Rice is cooked in chicken stock with aromatic spices such as cinnamon and allspice, and roasted chicken pieces are placed on top with toasted almonds and pine nuts.

In Damascus, don't miss *makhlooba* (literally 'upside-down') rice. It's cooked in stock and spices with chickpeas, onions and off-the-bone lamb shanks, then pressed in a deep bowl and turned upside down to reveal a delicious work of art. The vegetarian version incorporates eggplants with almonds and pine nuts.

Moolookhiye is a triumph of textures and flavours, combining fragrant rice with chicken, lamb and slimy but sexy spinach-like leaves called mallow. Don't let the slime fool you, this is comfort food at its Bedouin best, and an aphrodisiac to boot! Generally, *moolookhiye* is garnished with toasted *khoobz Arabi,* cumin and onions soused in vinegar. It can be hard to find in restaurants, but sometimes appears as a lunch special on Sunday. The dish originated in Egypt, and was adapted in Syria and Lebanon to suit local tastes.

DID YOU KNOW?

In Syria, *labneh* is spread on thick *khoobz Arabi* and rolled up – it's then called *arus* (the bride).

Another dish starting with the letter M is *moghrabiye* (which means 'Moroccan'). It's made of steamed, spiced semolina pellets, like a giant couscous, and is served with chicken, lamb shanks and little pickled onions. It's a popular dish especially in Lebanon's Tripoli and Syria's Damascus.

TRAVEL YOUR TASTEBUDS

The cuisine of Syria and Lebanon is world-renowned and has influenced chefs well beyond the region. Try some of these delights:

k'nefi bi djeben – breakfast Beirut-style, sweet cheese wrapped in a sesame roll and drizzled with orange blossom syrup

limonada – a simple lemon-and-sugar cordial is made magic with a dash of orange blossom essence

makhlooba – a topsy-turvy speciality of Damascus made with flavoured rice, lamb shanks (or eggplant) and chickpeas moulded in an upturned bowl

roz a djaj – a famous dish of roast chicken with almonds and pine nuts served on rice flavoured with cinnamon and allspice

WE DARE YOU

liyye – a piece of fat from the tail of a special breed of sheep, served as a mezze dish with raw lamb's fry

moolookhiye - a slimy meat-and-rice dish to get you in the mood – it's flavoured with mushy mallow leaves, which have a reputation as an aphrodisiac

Kibbeh

A cook's skills are judged by their success in preparing Lebanon's national dish – *kibbeh*. These croquettes of ground lamb, cracked wheat, onion and spices are served in many regional variations. In Damascus they're shaped into mini footballs and stuffed with spiced lamb, pine nuts and walnuts, then shallow-fried until golden brown. In Beirut they're served raw like a steak tartare, accompanied with fresh mint leaves, olive oil and spring onions.

Raw *kibbeh* (*kibbeh nayye*) in itself has many variations. In northern Lebanon you often find mint and fresh chillies mixed through the meat. In Aleppo, a chilli paste is layered on top of the *kibbeh* with walnuts and onions.

Kibbeh saniye is essentially *kibbeh* flattened out on a tray with a layer of spiced lamb and pine nuts in between. This is served with natural yogurt on the side.

Before the arrival of food processors, the matron of the household or village pulverised lamb for the *kibbeh* in a mortar and pestle. To produce an even texture requires great skill and strength in the arms. Driving through the mountains of Lebanon on a Sunday morning you can hear the chimes of these stone 'food processors' like church bells calling the faithful to eat.

DID YOU KNOW?

British soldiers in the Middle East during WWII used to call *kibbeh* 'Syrian torpedoes', which describes their shape rather well.

Fish

The warmer waters of the Mediterranean Sea are home to an abundance of fish species. Most popular are the red mullet *(Sultan Ibrahim)*, sea bass *(lookoz)* and sole *(samak moossa)*. Although very simple to prepare, whole fish dishes are probably the most loved.

There are two standout favourites. *Samak sa'ayadiye* is a seafood paella made of rice cooked in fish stock, brown onions and spices. Onions are caramelised and scattered on top of the rice with toasted pine nuts. *Sammki harra* is usually a whole fish (sea bass), oven-baked with a mixture of coriander, fresh chillies, walnuts and onions stuffed inside. When it's almost cooked, tahini sauce is poured on top and it's returned briefly to the oven. This is a firm favourite along Lebanon's coast, especially in Tripoli where the dish originated.

Samak bi loz is a dish that reflects the influence of French cuisine. It's a whole trout baked with almonds and it's served in restaurants near trout farms, such as in Aanjar (p326) and at Nahr al-Aasi (p333) in the Bekaa Valley.

DID YOU KNOW?

Sole is known as *samak moossa*, or Moses fish – because of its thinness it is said to have been cut in half when Moses divided the Red Sea.

Desserts

Diners in Syria and Lebanon usually opt for fresh fruit after a meal. When in season, fruit is in plentiful supply from the fertile agricultural regions. Lebanon's abundant snowfalls guarantee a flavoursome crop season after season.

Regional fruits to look out for include: oranges and tangerines from Lebanon's southern coastal strip; apples and pears from the elevated hinterland of northern Lebanon and the banks of Syria's Nahr al-Aasi; grapes and melons from the Bekaa Valley; and sweet cherries and figs of different varieties from Mt Lebanon. In Syria, don't miss the white mulberry as well as the conventional purple variety *(toot shami)*. The fruit of the prickly pear is always plentiful in the hot, dry conditions.

If dessert is offered it will be *mahalabiye* which is a milk custard similar to blancmange, laced with orange blossom essence, almonds and pistachios. *Halawat bi djeben* is a stringy, sweet cheese with dollops of *ashta* (clotted cream skimmed from the top of boiling milk) and sugar syrup. *Asmaleyye* (literally 'gold sovereign') is a sandwich of *kataifi* pastry filled with *ashta* and sprinkled with pistachios.

The traditional baklava usually makes an appearance. These sweet filo pastry morsels of crushed pistachios, almonds, cashews or peanuts come in all shapes – try lady fingers *(asabeeh),* the nest of the nightingale *(aash el-bulbul)* or eat and give thanks *(kol wa shkor)*.

Syria is renowned for *barazi* which is a large biscuit of sesame seeds and pistachios. Also popular in Syria is *bor'ma*, a mosaic of pistachios wrapped in angel hair noodles and sliced into discs.

DRINKS
Spirits & Beer

Arak (lion's milk) is always drunk with mezze, a process that usually takes a couple of hours. This aniseed-based cousin to ouzo is the preferred drink of the region, and complements mezze perfectly. It's combined with water and ice into a potent mixture served in small glasses. See Arak on p326 for more information.

Next on the list of favourites, especially in Beirut, is scotch – always an upmarket brand and always served straight with ice.

There are breweries producing beer for the locals in both Syria and Lebanon. In Syria the most popular labels are Barada in Damascus and Al Chark in Aleppo. In Lebanon the favourite is Almaza, a light brew made under licence from the popular Dutch brewer Amstel.

Wine

Recently wine has become an acceptable part of a meal in the region. Lebanon has produced some excellent wines, based on the 'old-world' style, which have gained some popularity among connoisseurs.

Winemaker Gaston Hochar took over an 18th-century castle, Château Musar (see p325 for details), in Ghazir just 24km north of Beirut in 1930. Together with his sons, Hochar created a wine that, despite the civil war, was able to win important awards in France, including the prestigious Winemaker's Award for Excellence. Ninety percent of the produce from this family winery is exported.

The main wine-growing areas are Kefraya and Ksara in the Bekaa Valley. The success of these wines can be attributed to the climate and soil composition of the region. In 1857 Jesuit fathers introduced quality viticulture at the Ksara Winery (p324), using European growing techniques. A natural wine cellar that was discovered and used by the Romans was enlarged, creating a series of tunnels with the ideal temperature for storing wine.

See the boxed text Lebanese Wine (p324) for more information on Lebanon's thriving wine industry.

Coffee & Tea

As in many societies, coffee *(ahwa)* is an important social lubricant. The black, syrupy Arabic coffee is served in small Chinese teacups. It's usually laced with cardamom and sweetened according to taste: *moorra* (no sugar), *wasat* (a little sugar) or *helwi* (sweet). See also the boxed text Coffee Craze, p262. In Syria, unlike Lebanon, tea is popular. A distinct Arabic blend is served sweet and black in small glasses. At night *zhurat* (chamomile tea with dried wild flowers and rosehip) is prepared. In Beirut one might ask for *ahwa bayda* (a few drops of rose-water added to boiling water).

DID YOU KNOW?

Traditionally yogurt is not put on the same table with fish – an old wives' tale claims eating the two together will poison the diner.

DID YOU KNOW?

There is only one correct way to pour a glass of arak: first pour about two fingers of arak, then add the water and finish off with one ice cube. Any other order will provoke frowns from onlookers.

Juice & Other Drinks

There are many street stalls in both Syria and Lebanon selling freshly squeezed juice, just the thing in summer. As Lebanon is an important citrus-growing area, orange juice is very popular. *Limonada* is a simple drink of lemon juice and sugar, which sounds basic enough until the orange blossom essence is added. This gives the drink a refreshing, perfumed quality.

For a revitilising, delicately flavoured drink, try *jallab* (a date drink with floating pine nuts and pistachios), or *ma'wared* (distilled rose petals served with ice).

CELEBRATIONS
Holy Days

Food plays an important part in the religious calendar of the region. Holy days usually involve hours of preparation in the kitchen.

Claudia Roden's The New Book of Middle Eastern Cooking is filled with mouth-watering recipes from across the Middle East.

The Muslim fasting period of Ramadan offers a good insight into the diversity of festive food. Once the sun sets, a feast is spread on the table with an emphasis on sweet energy foods, to get the believers through the next day of fasting. At this time of year the pastry shops of Tripoli and Damascus are full of special Ramadan sweets. The traditional colour for Ramadan food is white, and desserts are filled with *ashta*. Beverages like *kharroob* (carob) and tamar hindi (a tamarind drink) accompany great feasts of grilled lamb and chicken with almond rice. Platters of dates on the table remind diners of the Prophet Mohammed's only source of food while fasting in the desert.

Easter is the most important time in the calendar for eastern Christians. Good Friday's abstinence from meat brings out dishes such as *m'jaddara*, a dish of spiced lentils and rice. Another Easter dish is *shoraba zingool* (sour soup with small balls of cracked wheat, flour and split peas). The sourness reminds Christians of the vinegar on the sponge offered by the Roman centurion to Christ on the cross. *Selak*, rolls of silver beet (Swiss chard) stuffed with rice, tomato, chickpeas and spices, are also served. The fast is broken on Easter Sunday with round semolina cakes called *maamoul*, stuffed with either walnuts or dates.

The Armenian Christmas, the Epiphany (6 January), has the women busy making *owamaut* (small, deep-fried honey balls).

On Eid el-Barbara, a Christian feast day similar to the American Halloween, a bowl of boiled barley, pomegranate seeds and sugar is offered to masquerading children.

Special Occasions

An important aspect of food in the region is its association with different milestones in an individual's life.

Food from Biblical Lands by Helen Corey is an easy-to-use guide to Syrian and Lebanese cooking. A video is also available.

When a baby is born a pudding of rice flour and cinnamon called *mighlay* is served to family and friends. Sugar-coated almonds and chickpeas are the celebratory treats when the baby's first tooth pushes through.

At death a loved one is remembered with a banquet. This takes place after the burial in Christian communities, and one week later in Muslim communities. The only beverage offered is water and unsweetened *ahwa*.

It is believed that the spirit of the departed stays among the living for 40 days before it travels on to the afterlife. At this point the family offers another banquet to relatives and friends.

WHERE TO EAT & DRINK

Syrian and Lebanese restaurants offer a unique eating experience. Restaurants in both countries serve the traditional mezze-and-main-course banquet, and a variety of other cuisines are available in Lebanon. The mezze part of the meal is much the same wherever you eat, however some restaurants specialise in particular main courses, for example grilled meats or seafood.

At *kebabji ahwa* (restaurants that specialise in kebabs), you will find long metal troughs, the width of a skewer, filled with lighted charcoal. Skewers of lamb, chicken and beef *kafta* are evenly cooked to customers' tastes (Arabs like their meat well done).

In Beirut the restaurant scene is all about keeping up appearances – wearing the right clothes and being seen in the right establishment. Usually the décor is state of the art and restaurant locations take full advantage of the magnificent views. A restaurant can be precariously perched on the edge of a mountain or offer sunset views over the Mediterranean, or both. But the prices reflect these upmarket tastes – in Lebanon you can expect to pay between LL80,000 and LL140,000 a head, and don't forget the service charge of 15%.

In Syria you can get the same meal you would get in Lebanon for a quarter of the price. It won't have as much finesse, but the quality will be just as good and in some cases, even better. In Damascus you can say to the waiter *'ah zowaak'* ('I'll leave it up to you') and still pay only S£1065 a head no matter how many dishes are placed on the table. In Lebanon this isn't the case and you need to be specific when ordering. Many of the good restaurants in Damascus are set up in old Arabic mansions with traditional outside courtyards complete with a fountain. Restaurants in Syria tend to focus on regional specialities.

Sonia Uvezian's Recipes and Remembrances from an Eastern Mediterranean Kitchen includes anecdotes, proverbs and recipes from Syria, Lebanon and Jordan.

Quick Eats

You don't need to blow your budget eating out in expensive restaurants with the vast array of takeaway food on offer.

For breakfast nothing beats a big, hot bowl of fava beans drizzled with olive oil, lemon and cumin, especially on a cold Damascus morning. This is the traditional *foul m'damas* served throughout the Middle East, but it takes on a distinctly Syrian flavour with the addition of chickpeas and tomatoes. In Beirut, breakfast is *k'nefi bi djeben* (sweet cheese and semolina in a doughy sesame roll with a sugar syrup and orange blossom).

In the mountains of Lebanon, a porridge-like dish called *kishik* is served with fried lamb pieces and onions. It's designed to warm you from the inside during the snowed-out winters.

Shwarma is the Lebanese and Syrian equivalent of the Turkish doner kebab. Strips of lamb or chicken are sliced from a vertical turning spit and served with tahini and greens in *khoobz Arabi*. To enhance the flavour and moistness of the meat, fat from the tail of the sheep is skewered to the top of the pyramid and allowed to dribble down slowly and evenly while the spit is turning.

Felafel balls are one of the world's most widely recognised snack foods. These golden spheres of ground chickpeas, coriander, onions, garlic and heaps of cumin are usually stuffed in a sandwich of *khoobz Arabi* with tahini, lettuce, pickled turnip and tomato.

Fabulous *farooj mishwee* is hard to beat. A whole chicken is split, placed in a wire rack, barbecued on charcoal and served with copious amounts of garlic that has been whipped to a mayonnaise consistency. Down it with Almaza beer, *khoobz Arabi* and a few greens while watching the sun set over the Mediterranean Sea – it doesn't get any better than this.

Other delicious fast-food options are savoury pastries eaten straight out of the oven. *Manaeesh* is the name given to the variety of pizza-like

The Lebanese Kitchen by Abla Ahmed is a cornucopia of centuries-old Lebanese recipes for modern chefs.

PRESERVING THE HARVEST

Due to the rugged terrain in the Levant, especially in Lebanon, communities often thrived in isolation for centuries, giving rise to wonderful regional cuisines. The climate and availability of produce also influenced the menu. High altitudes and snowed-out winters led to the development of ingenious food preservation methods that could take a family through the harsh winter months.

All this changed with the arrival of refrigeration and modern food-storage technologies. Nevertheless, traditional food preservation techniques are kept alive in rural areas and are relished by urban dwellers who look suspiciously on food they know is not in season.

When something is in season, Syrians and Lebanese always take full advantage of the situation. Fruits and vegetables from the summer harvest are blanched and pickled to be stored in the *moonay* (food cellar or pantry).

Bayt injen makdoos are baby eggplants blanched, then split open and stuffed with garlic, chilli and walnuts. They're put into jars of olive oil and allowed to pickle for a month. No table is complete without olives, which are pickled in brine. Long thin cucumbers and beetroot-coloured turnips are also pickled.

Huge pots of cubed and fried lamb with onions and spices are kept in rendered fat to be brought out and cooked with eggs in the depths of winter, or added to a stew of winter vegetables, pulses and rice.

Labneh (a type of yogurt cheese) is rolled into individual balls and stored in jars filled with olive oil. In summer cracked wheat mixed with yogurt is laid out to dry and then stored for the winter. It makes a hearty bowl of *kishik*, which is served like porridge in the mornings.

snacks eaten for breakfast or at any other time of the day. The most popular *manaeesh* is *manaeesh bi-zaatar*, a mixture of dried wild thyme and sesame seeds mixed with olive oil which is spread on dough and baked. *Fatayer bi jibne* is like a pasty stuffed with *haloumi* cheese. The speciality from the town of Baalbek is lamb *sfeeha* (spiced lamb with onion, tomato and chilli baked on a thin pastry crust and side-served with yogurt).

HABITS & CUSTOMS

The age-old Arabic custom of respect and hospitality to guests puts certain obligations on both host and guest. A lot of these obligations are really just good manners, however there are certain subtle patterns of behaviour that you should follow if you are invited to eat in a private home.

A Taste of Syria by Virginia Jerro Gerbino and Philip Kayal consists of recipes from Aleppo, as handed down by the authors' grandparents.

In most homes, whether Christian or Muslim, the men usually gather separately from the women. This is not a strict religious or social requirement (though this may not be the case in rural Muslim areas), just a social practice that has evolved over time.

Men and women come together at the table where the host will welcome you with a toast. You should follow this with a reciprocal toast, wishing the host and the family good health. If appropriate, you could also congratulate the family on a birth, or offer commiserations on the sudden death of a loved one.

When the meal begins, it is important to accept as much food as possible when it is offered to you. If you say 'no thanks' continually, it can offend the host.

EAT YOUR WORDS

Wrap your tongue around the language of food before you sample the regional cuisine.

Useful Phrases

Bring a variety of dishes for the mezze please.
jeebelna tishkeeli mezza a'amil ma'aroof.

Bottoms up!
kassak!

After you.
tfaddal (m) tfaddali (f).

The bill, please.
al hessab, a'amil ma'aroof.

Side serve of chilli.
shwayt harr.

Open.
maftooh.

Closed.
m'sakar.

Is that dish very spicy?
hal akle-harra?

I don't eat meat.
anna ma baqel laham.

With no garlic.
bedun toom.

How much is the fish by the kilo?
addesh el kilo samak?

What's the special of the day?
shoo al sah'an al yomi?

Do you have a table?
undak tawle?

Menu Decoder

Note that because of the imprecise nature of transliterating Arabic into English, spellings will vary; for example, what we give as kibbeh may appear variously as 'kibba', 'kibbe', 'kibby' or even 'gibeh'.

bamiye – okra stewed with tomatoes, onions and spices served with fragrant rice

fattoosh – a Lebanese bread salad with purslane, tomatoes, cucumbers and sumac dressing

fattoosh al-batinjan – Damascus version of fattoosh using fried eggplant tossed with pomegranate syrup

harak isbao – a Damascus favourite of green lentils with tamarind and pomegranates

kibbeh – minced lamb, bulgur wheat and pine nuts shaped into a patty and deep fried

kibbeh nayye – ground lamb and cracked wheat served raw like steak tartare

labneh – thick yogurt cheese with olive oil

loobiye bi zhet – green beans cooked in garlic, onions and crushed tomatoes

mahashi – stuffed vine leaves, eggplant or silver beet rolls

mashawi – grilled meats on charcoal

m'jaddarah – lentil and rice with caramelised onions, served with a cabbage salad

moosa'a' – eggplant, chickpea and onion with crushed tomatoes

selek – silver beet stuffed with chickpeas and rice

Food Glossary

BASICS

foorn – bakery
helwanji – pastry shop
ma'alaka – spoon

mataam – restaurant
showki – fork
sikeen – knife

COOKING TERMS

halal – Islamic meat; meaning that the animal has been slaughtered using the halal method
labaniyye – cooked in yogurt
maa le – salty
mi'klay – fried
mishwee al-faham – charcoal grilled

mooghli – boiled
muhammar – roasted
nayye – raw
sayniye – baked
yabis –s dried (herbs)

STAPLES

adas – lentils
khoobz – bread

khoobz Arabi – Arabic flatbread
roz – rice

MEAT

lahame – meat

samak – fish

OTHER DISHES & CONDIMENTS

ashta – clotted cream
baharat – spices
ejja – omelette
filfil – pepper
jibna – cheese
ma'al-ward – rose-water
mele – salt

naana – mint
shoraba – soup
tahini – sesame paste
toom – garlic
za'atar – spice mix
zaytoon – olives, olive oil

DRINKS

ahwa – Arabic coffee
arak – aniseed-based spirit, similar to ouzo

chai – tea

Syria

CHRIS BARTON

SYRIA

Syria سورية

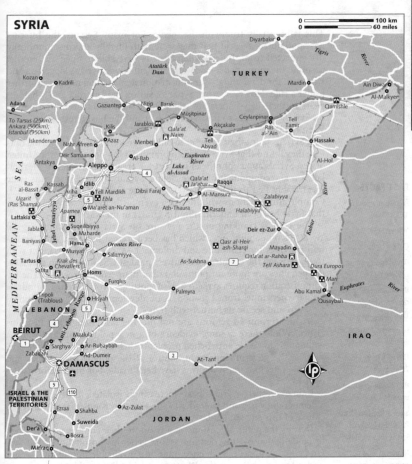

SYRIA

Snapshot Syria

In 2000, when Bashir al-Assad succeeded his father, Hafez al-Assad, Syria held its collective breath in anticipation of what the new president would deliver to his people.

While Bashir came to power promising widespread political, economic and administrative reforms, the likelihood of genuine change seemed remote given his undemocratic appointment by his father and the challenges of treading a fine line between the demands of powerful Islamic forces, relations with the West – particularly the USA – and pressures for less-restrictive practices at home.

Nevertheless, as with any country facing threats from the USA and Israel & the Palestinian Territories (I&PT), the people are generally behind the young leader, although privately many Syrians will express their dismay that he hasn't opened up the country more to outside influences.

This is especially true with the media. For many Syrians, the Internet has spotlighted a world that they were both literally and metaphorically disconnected from. Indeed when Syrians were able to open an Internet account, the more media-savvy and affluent young Syrians logged on and stayed on for days, hungry for information denied them under the former leader's rule. However, what Syrians read on the Internet and what appears in their newspapers are still a world apart. For more information on Syrian's attitudes to the West see p39 and the boxed text Islam & the West (p43).

If Syrians point their browser to online versions of Western media outlets, they'll find that Syria has been branded a 'rogue state' by the United States. Syria's apparent official support for organisations such as Hezbollah is a key component of these claims. Syrians, however, see this issue inextricably tied to that of the return of the Golan Heights from I&PT. Complicating relations with the West even further is Washington's claim that Syria has been undermining US efforts in the war in Iraq.

The USA is cranking up the pressure on Syria with its controversial 'Syria Accountability Act', which has been passed into law. This legislation provides for economic and diplomatic sanctions on Syria, but with trade between the countries a relatively modest US$300 million annually, the penalties are more for political, rather than economic, effect. The US administration requires Syria to stop supporting terrorist groups, withdraw military personnel from Lebanon, cease development of unconventional weapons and secure its border with Iraq.

Bashir's promised reforms are not moving fast enough to satisfy his critics. While there is some evidence of a new political openness and a willingness to tackle entrenched problems such as corruption in the civil service, the government's tight control of the populace continues and few concrete, long-term reforms have been made. For more information see p74.

In many respects Syria appears increasingly isolated, its people without a democratic voice and its leader facing some decisions that will alter the course of this ancient land.

Despite the political tensions, as a visitor to their country you are likely to be delighted by the friendliness and generous hospitality of the Syrian people you meet. Such encounters are invaluable in building greater understanding between the Western and Muslim worlds. For more on Syrian culture, see p39.

FAST FACTS

Population: around 17.2 million

Inflation: 1.5%

GDP per capita: US$993

Official unemployment rate: around 7%

Unofficial unemployment rate: much higher!

Main exports: Oil and oil products, food and livestock

Literacy rate: 93% men, 78% women

Over 40% of Syrians are under 14

Borders: Iraq, Israel & the Palestinian Territories, Jordan, Lebanon, Turkey

Number of times flag has changed since Independence: several

Damascus دمشق

DAMASCUS

CONTENTS

On a journey from Mecca, legend has it, the Prophet Mohammed looked down from the mountainside on Damascus but refused to visit the city because he wanted to enter paradise only once, and that was when he died. The allure of the city that made the Prophet turn away is the same that has attracted travellers through the ages – Damascus is the first natural landing place for the traveller from the east, where the desert stretches thousands of miles all the way to the Indian Ocean.

The town grew here because it's the spot where the Barada River, flowing down from the mountains to the west, leaves an oasis of greenery in its path. Murray's *Guide to Syria & Palestine* of 1868 paints a picture of enchantment: 'Tapering minarets and swelling domes, tipped with golden crescents, rise up in every direction from the confused mass of white terraced roofs; while in some places their glittering tops appear above the deep green foliage, like diamonds in the midst of emeralds…'

Tragically, today Syria's capital is a paradise lost. The life-giving river is largely a dry khaki-coloured mud bed and the fabled fields and orchards have been replaced by concrete urban sprawl – home to some six million people.

More happily, beyond often disappointing first impressions, there is still magic in Damascus. The Old City is still the Damascus of the Orient, filled with bazaars and blind alleys, minarets, mosques and fountain courtyards, street-cart vendors and coffeehouses. What's more, far from being a relic, it's an area currently undergoing a revitalisation, spawning exciting new restaurants and bars in age-old premises.

HIGHLIGHTS

- Wander around the **Old City** (p83) – sure there are major sights to see but taking your eyes off the map for a while is just as much fun
- Marvel at the magnificence of the **Umayyad Mosque** (p86), one of the most notable buildings of Islam and an architectural and decorative wonder
- Shop in the exotic **Souq al-Hamidiyya** (p86), a cross between a Parisian passage and a department store
- Check out the decorative **Damascene houses** (p91) – more like *objets d'art* than residences
- Dine at one of the **Old City restaurants** (p104), marrying superb food with exceptional settings and attentive service
- While away an evening at a coffeehouse such as **Ash-Shams** or **An-Nafura** (p107) – a favourite Damascene pastime

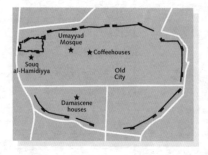

- TELEPHONE CODE: 011

HISTORY

'...no recorded event has occurred in the world but Damascus was in existence to receive news of it. Go back as far as you will into the vague past, there was always a Damascus... She has looked upon the dry bones of a thousand empires and will see the tombs of a thousand more before she dies.'

Mark Twain, The Innocents Abroad, 1869

Damascus lays a strong claim to being the oldest continuously inhabited city in the world. Hieroglyphic tablets found in Egypt make reference to 'Dimashqa' as one of the cities conquered by the Egyptians in the 15th century BC, but excavations from the courtyard of the Umayyad Mosque have yielded finds dating back to the 3rd millennium BC. The name Dimashqa appears in the Ebla archives and also on tablets found at Mari (2500 BC).

In the earliest times, it was a prize city, constantly fought over. Early conquerors include the fabled King David of Israel, the Assyrians in 732 BC, Nebuchadnezzar (circa 600 BC) and the Persians in 530 BC. In 333 BC it fell to Alexander the Great. Greek influence declined when the Nabataeans occupied Damascus in 85 BC. Just 21 years later, Rome's legions sent the Nabataeans packing and Syria became a Roman province.

Under the Romans Damascus became a military base for the armies of legionnaires fighting the Persians. Hadrian declared the city a metropolis in the 2nd century AD and during the reign of Alexander Severus it became a Roman colony.

With the coming of Islam, Damascus became an important centre as the seat of the Umayyad caliphate from 661 to 750. When the Abbasids took over and moved the caliphate to Baghdad, Damascus was plundered once again.

After the occupation of Damascus by the Seljuk Turks in 1076, the Crusaders tried unsuccessfully to take the city. They made a second attempt in 1154; this time a general of Kurdish origin, Nureddin (Nur ad-Din) came to the rescue, occupying Damascus himself and ushering in a brief golden era. During his time business prospered, triggering a corresponding building boom. Notable monuments from the era include the Maristan Nureddin, Madrassa an-Nuri and the Hammam Nureddin, the oldest public bath in Syria.

A brief occupation by the Mongols separates the successors of Nureddin as rulers from the Mamluks of Egypt, who rose to power in 1260. During the Mamluk period, Damascene goods became famous worldwide and attracted merchants from Europe. This led to the second Mongol invasion under Tamerlane, when the city was flattened and the artisans and scholars were deported to the Mongol capital of Samarkand. The Mamluks returned soon after and proceeded to rebuild the city.

From the time of the Ottoman Turk occupation in 1516, the fortunes of Damascus started to decline and it was reduced to the status of a small provincial capital in a large empire.

The Turkish and German forces used Damascus as their base during WWI. When they were defeated by the Arab Legion and the Allies, a first, short-lived Syrian government was set up in 1919.

The French, having received a mandate from the League of Nations, occupied the city from 1920 to 1945. They met with massive resistance and at one stage in 1925 bombarded the city to suppress rioting. French shells again rained on the city in the unrest of 1945, which led to full independence a year later when French and British forces were pulled out and Damascus became the capital of an independent Syria.

ORIENTATION

There are two distinct parts to Damascus: the Old City and everything else. The Old City is tightly defined by its encircling walls, while modern Damascus sprawls around it stretching off in all directions: climbing the slopes of Jebel Qassioun (Mt Qassioun) to the north and petering out on the plains to the south. However, all the parts that are likely to be of most interest to a visitor are contained in roughly 2 sq km and easily accessed on foot. Be warned, though, the official street signs do not always correlate with the commonly known names of various streets and squares – we give both where appropriate.

The Old City lies on the lowest ground around the banks of the Barada River. It's still partially walled and oval in form. The main access from the new city is via the covered Souq al-Hamidiyya. This leads directly

DAMASCUS

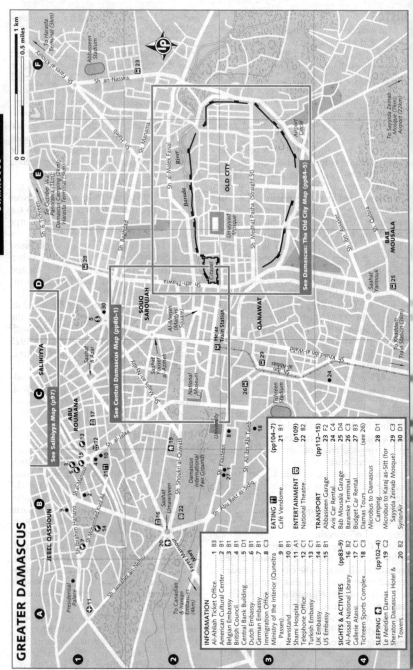

GREATER DAMASCUS

0 ————— 1 km
0 ————— 0.5 miles

To Harasta Terminal (3km)

Abbaseen Stadium

Sh an-Nassira

Sh Maysaloun

Sh al-Malek Fasal

Barada River

OLD CITY

See Damascus: The Old City Map (pp84–5)

Airport Circle

To Sayyida Zeinab Mosque (7km); Airport (22km)

BAB MOUSALA

Saahat Yarmouk

Sh Ibn al-Assad

Sh Qbiha

Sh Medhat Pasha (Straight St)

Umayyad Mosque

Citadel

Sh ath-Thawra

To October War Panorama (1km); Damascus Camping (2km); Harasta Terminal (3km)

Sh 6 Tishreen

SOUQ SAROUJAH

Al-Merjeh (Martyrs) Square

Hejaz Train Station

QANAWAT

Sh Khalid ibn al-Walid

To Khaddam Train Station (3km)

Sh Ibn al-Abbas

Tichreen Stadium

National Museum

Saahat Youseff al-Azmeh

Sh Maysaloun an-Nasr

Saahat 8 Azar

SALHIYA

See Salhiyya Map (p97)

ABU ROUMANA

Sh al-Jalaa

University

Damascus International Fair Grounds

Sh Filasteen

Sh Ali bin Abi Taleb

Sh Abu Bakr as-Sidiq

Saahat Umawiyeen

JEBEL QASSIOUN

Sh Ibrahim Hanano

Sh Shoukri al-Quwatli

Sh al-Marmar

Sh Mohammed Kurd Ali

To Canadian & French Embassies (4km)

Presidential Palace

Sh Jawahra an-Nehru

DAMASCUS IN...

Two Days

Head straight for the **Old City** (p83), taking in **Souq al-Hamidiyya** (p86) on your way to the splendid **Umayyad Mosque** (p86). Walk through the gold and spice souqs to **Azem Palace** (p90) and continue through the spice souqs taking Straight St to **Old Town restaurant** (p105) for lunch. Once rejuvenated, spend the afternoon fossicking through the fascinating and better-value antique and souvenir stores in **Straight St** (p91) and the **Christian Quarter** (p92). Rest up for your late-dinner booking at **Elissar** (p105).

Start off day two with a couple of educational hours at the **National Museum** (p94). Stroll through **Handicrafts Lane** (p111) to compare prices with the souqs, dropping in to see the magnificent interior of the **Hejaz train station** (p93) on your way back to the Old City for lunch at **Narcissus** (p107). Spend the afternoon admiring the historic **Damascene houses** (p91), then drop in for coffee at **An-Nafura** (p107). Head to one of the restaurants with a floor show of **whirling dervishes** (p104).

Four Days

On days one and two follow the two-day itinerary and then on days three and four take day trips to the beautiful village of **Maalula** (p118), the convent at **Seidnayya** (p118), and the monastery at **Mar Musa** (p121). **Bosra** (p122), with its magnificent Roman theatre, is a must.

to the centrepiece Umayyad Mosque. South of the mosque is Sharia Medhat Pasha, the ancient Straight St, which bisects the Old City on an east–west axis.

The heart of the modern city is Al-Merjeh (al-*mer*-dzey, where 'dz' sounds like the second 'g' in garage), which is the popular name for Saahat ash-Shohada (Martyrs' Square), a landscaped traffic island about 500m west of the Old City walls. Most of the cheap hotels and restaurants are around here.

The rest of what could be considered 'downtown' Damascus lies north and west of Al-Merjeh. The main street is two blocks west and begins at the old Hejaz train station as Sharia Said al-Jabri; it then cuts a kilometre-long swathe north to the grand entrance of the Central Bank building, changing its name twice en route. Here you'll find the post office, main tourist office, some airline offices and many mid-range restaurants and hotels. About halfway along this main street is Saahat Yousef al-Azmeh (Yousef al-Azmah Square), a focal point for the modern city centre, into which all roads seem to run. The road that runs off to the west, Sharia Maysaloun, has more airline offices, the swish Cham Palace and a scattering of restaurants that get more expensive the further west you go.

At its extreme western end, Maysaloun intersects with Sharia al-Jala'a, which is the main thoroughfare through the wealthy diplomatic district, known as Abu Roumana. Here you are already on the lower slopes of Jebel Qassioun; there's plenty of greenery and the air seems distinctly fresher and more breathable than down below.

Maps

The best street map is one produced by Freytag & Berndt – distinguished by a red-and-green cover. It shows the country at a scale of 1:800,000 and also carries very good city plans of Damascus and Aleppo. It's widely available in Syria, where it's published under licence by the Librairie Avicenne (see Bookshops, below) and costs S£250. There's also another sheet map put out by GEO Projects, at a scale of 1:1,000,000, and also with city plans.

The tourist offices throughout Syria have free handout city and regional maps but these are generally way out of date and of very little use.

INFORMATION
Bookshops

Family Bookshop (Map pp80-1; ☎ 222 7006; Saahat al-Najmeh; ☺ 9am-1.30pm & 4.30-8pm Mon-Thu & Sat, 10am-1pm Fri) South of Sharia Maysaloun, it's also worth checking out for its small stock of old eclectic fiction.

Librairie Avicenne (Map pp80-1; ☎ 224 4477; 4 Sharia Attuhami; ☺ 9am-2pm & 4.30-8.30pm Sat-Thu) One block south of Cham Palace, this is possibly the best bookshop in the country for foreign-language publications.

DAMASCUS

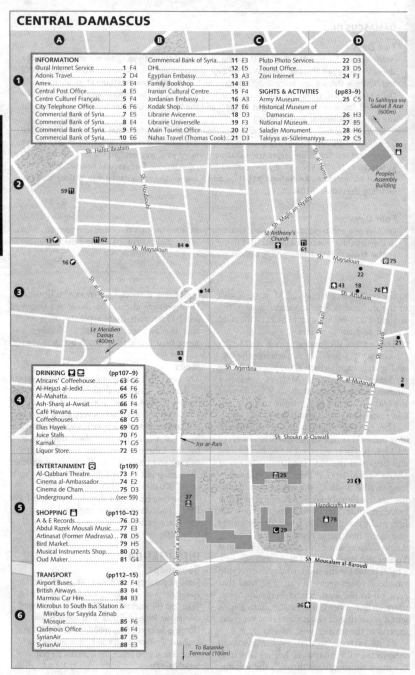

CENTRAL DAMASCUS

INFORMATION
@ural Internet Service	1 F4
Adonis Travel	2 D4
Amex	3 E4
Central Post Office	4 E5
Centre Culturel Français	5 F4
City Telephone Office	6 F6
Commercial Bank of Syria	7 E5
Commercial Bank of Syria	8 E4
Commercial Bank of Syria	9 F5
Commercial Bank of Syria	10 E6
Commerical Bank of Syria	11 E3
DHL	12 E5
Egyptian Embassy	13 A3
Family Bookshop	14 B3
Iranian Cultural Centre	15 F4
Jordanian Embassy	16 A3
Kodak Shop	17 E6
Librairie Avicenne	18 D3
Librairie Universelle	19 F3
Main Tourist Office	20 E2
Nahas Travel (Thomas Cook)	21 D3
Pluto Photo Services	22 D3
Tourist Office	23 D5
Zoni Internet	24 F3

SIGHTS & ACTIVITIES (pp83–9)
Army Museum	25 C5
Historical Museum of Damascus	26 H3
National Museum	27 B5
Saladin Monument	28 H6
Takiyya as-Süleimaniyya	29 C5

DRINKING (pp107–9)
Africans' Coffeehouse	63 G6
Al-Hejazi al-Jedid	64 F6
Al-Mahatta	65 E6
Ash-Sharq al-Awsat	66 F4
Café Havana	67 E4
Coffeehouses	68 G5
Elias Hayek	69 G5
Juice Stalls	70 F5
Karnak	71 G5
Liquor Store	72 E5

ENTERTAINMENT (p109)
Al-Qabbani Theatre	73 F1
Cinema al-Ambassador	74 E2
Cinema de Cham	75 D3
Underground	(see 59)

SHOPPING (pp110–12)
A & E Records	76 D3
Abdul Razek Mousali Music	77 E3
Artinasat (Former Madrassa)	78 D5
Bird Market	79 H5
Musical Instruments Shop	80 D2
Oud Maker	81 G4

TRANSPORT (pp112–15)
Airport Buses	82 F4
British Airways	83 B4
Marmou Car Hire	84 B3
Microbus to South Bus Station & Minibus for Sayyida Zeinab Mosque	85 F6
Qadmous Office	86 F4
SyrianAir	87 E5
SyrianAir	88 E3

To Salihiyya via Saahat 8 Azar (600m)

Peoples' Assembly Building

Sh. Hafez Ibrahim

Sh. Houboubi

Sh. al-Hama

Sh. Majlis an-Nyaby

St Anthony's Church

Sh. Maysaloun

Sh. Maysaloun

Sh. Brazil

Sh. Affuham

Sh. al-Jala'a

Le Meridien Damas (400m)

Sh. Arjentina

Sh. al-Mutanabi

Sh. Muradi

Sh. Shoukri al-Quwatli

Jisr ar-Rais

Handicrafts Lane

Sh. al-Jama'a as-Siriyya

Sh. Mousalam al-Baroudi

To Baramke Terminal (100m)

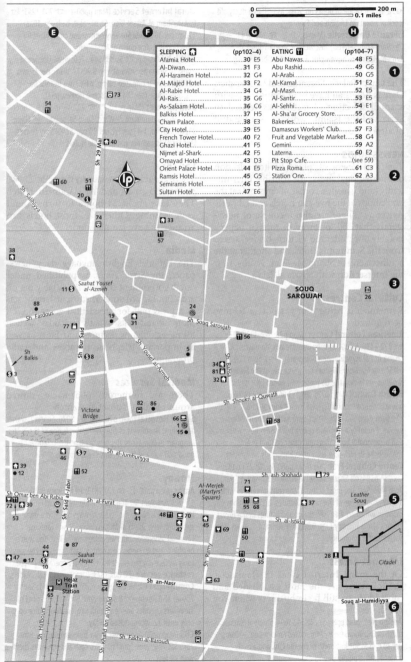

SLEEPING	(pp102–4)
Afamia Hotel	30 E5
Al-Diwan	31 F3
Al-Haramein Hotel	32 G4
Al-Majed Hotel	33 F2
Al-Rabie Hotel	34 G4
Al-Rais	35 G6
As-Salaam Hotel	36 C6
Balkiss Hotel	37 H5
Cham Palace	38 E3
City Hotel	39 E5
French Tower Hotel	40 F2
Ghazi Hotel	41 F5
Nijmet al-Shark	42 F5
Omayad Hotel	43 D3
Orient Palace Hotel	44 E5
Ramsis Hotel	45 G5
Semiramis Hotel	46 E5
Sultan Hotel	47 E6

EATING	(pp104–7)
Abu Nawas	48 F5
Abu Rashid	49 G6
Al-Arabi	50 G5
Al-Kamal	51 E2
Al-Masri	52 E5
Al-Santir	53 E5
Al-Sehhi	54 E1
Al-Sha'ar Grocery Store	55 G5
Bakeries	56 G3
Damascus Workers' Club	57 F3
Fruit and Vegetable Market	58 G4
Gemini	59 A2
Laterna	60 E2
Pit Stop Cafe	(see 59)
Pizza Roma	61 C3
Station One	62 A3

Has a decent range of books on Syria, as well as a dusty old stock of novels in English and French.

Librairie Universelle (Map pp80-1; ☎ 230 0744; ☾ 9am-8pm Sat-Thu) Just west of Sharia Yousef al-Azmeh. Has more novels plus a shelf of art books.

The Cham Palace, Sheraton and Le Meridien Damas hotels all have bookshops, each with a small selection of gift books related to Syria and the Islamic world plus a handful of airport novels.

NEWSSTANDS

Time and *Newsweek*, plus a limited selection of international press, are available intermittently (and usually a couple of days' old) at the bookshops in the five-star hotels and Librairie Avicenne. There are also a couple of newsstands that sell an array of foreign papers: notably one under the Victoria Bridge, across from the Semiramis Hotel, and another at the southern end of Sharia Majlis an-Nyaby, near the intersection with Sharia al-Jala'a.

Cultural Centres

Remember to bring your passport as ID may be required.

American Cultural Center (Map p78; ☎ 333 8413; fax 332 1456; http://usembassy.state.gov/damascus; 87 Sharia Ata al-Ayyoubi, Abu Roumana; ☾ 1-5pm Sun-Thu) Off Sharia Mansour. Visitors can make use of the library facilities, including the US press, and watch CNN news.

British Council (Map p78; ☎ 333 0631; fax 332 1467; www.britishcouncil.org/syria; Sharia Karim al-Khalil; ☾ 9am-8pm Sun-Thu, 10am-5pm Sat) Off Sharia Maysaloun. Primarily a teaching centre but it does have a library and occasionally hosts films and other cultural events – visit the website or pick up a copy of its bimonthly newsletter.

Centre Culturel Français (Map pp80-1; ☎ 231 6181; fax 231 6194; off Sharia Yousef al-Azmeh, Bahsa; ☾ 9am-9pm Mon-Sat) The most active of the cultural centres with a busy programme of live music, lectures, art exhibitions etc, many of which are free (see the posted listings in the foyer). There's also a **library** (☾ 9.30am-1.30pm, 4-7.30pm Mon-Sat, closed Fri morning).

Internet Access

Of the many Internet cafés in Damascus, the following are the most established and most likely to still be in business when you get there.

Amigo Net (Map pp84-5; ☎ 542 1694; Sharia al-Kassaa, north of Bab Touma; ☾ 24hr, closed for cleaning 8-10am; per 30 min S£50) Just north of the Old City, and a really smart-looking place.

@ural Internet Service (Map pp80-1; ☎ 231 1253; 1st fl, Ash-Sharq al-Awsat Bldg, Sharia al-Itehad; ☾ 10am-11pm; per 30 min S£50) Very central and convenient for most hotels, 100m north of Al-Merjeh.

Beit Jabri (Map pp84-5; ☎ 544 3200; www.jabrihouse .com; 14 Sharia as-Sawwaf; ☾ 9.30-12.30am; per 15 min S£50) A popular café (see Eating, p106) in a historic Damascene house (see Old Damascene Houses, p92).

Zoni Internet (Map pp80-1; ☎ 232 4670; 3rd fl, Abdeen Bldg, Sharia Hammam al-Ward, Souq Saroujah; ☾ 10am-11pm Sat-Thu, 1-11pm Fri; per 30 min S£40) Very convenient for Al-Haramein and Ar-Rabie Hotels.

Laundry

There are at least two **laundry shops** (Sharia Bahsa; per item S£25-35) around Al-Haramein Hotel. They take about 24 hours to turn around your washing. Otherwise, most hotels can arrange to have laundry done.

Media

The national English-language daily newspaper, the *Syria Times*, is published under direct government control. Predictably big on anti-Zionist, pro-Arab rhetoric it largely acts as a press puff for presidential goings-on. Of more interest is its 'What's on Today' section listing exhibitions, lectures and films as well as important telephone numbers and radio programmes.

Medical Services

There are numerous pharmacies dotted around Saahat Yousef al-Azmeh.

Shami Hospital (Map p78; ☎ 371 8970; Sharia Jawaher an-Nehru) Northwest of the centre, this is one of the better hospitals in Damascus. Reports say that the treatment is good and some of the doctors speak English.

Money

Amex (Map pp80-1; ☎ 221 7813; 1st fl, Sharia Balkis; ☾ 8.30am-8pm Sat-Thu, 9am-1.30pm & 5-8pm Fri) This local agency is above the Sudan Airways office on a small street between Sharia al-Mutanabi and Sharia Fardous. Financial services on offer are extremely limited. You won't be able to get advances on a card, or cash travellers cheques (only replace any stolen). It does however operate a **poste restante service** (PO Box 1373, Damascus) for cardholders.

Commercial Bank of Syria (CBS; Map pp80-1; Saahat Yousef al-Azmeh; ☾ 8.30am-8pm Sat-Thu, to 2pm Fri) Travellers cheques are dealt with in a 1st-floor office open only until 12.30pm, closed Friday.

CBS (Map pp80-1; opposite Hejaz train station; ☾ 9am-7pm Sat-Thu, 9am-2pm Fri) Takes cash and travellers cheques with no fuss.

CBS (Map pp80-1; Sharia Bur Said) Exchanges cash only.

CBS (Map pp80-1; cnr Sharia Said al-Jabri & Sharia Jumhuriyya)

CBS (Map pp80-1; west side of Al-Merjeh; �־ 9am-6pm Sat-Thu, 10am-2pm Fri) Happy to change cash and travellers cheques.

CBS (Map pp84-5; just inside Bab ash-Sharqi; �־ 9am-7pm Sat-Thu, to 2pm Fri)

CBS (Map p78; Sheraton hotel, Saahat Umawiyeen; �־ 9am-9pm) Changes cash and travellers cheques.

CBS (Map p78; Le Meridien Damas hotel; Sharia Shoukri al-Quwatli; �־ 9am-9pm) Changes cash and travellers cheques; insists on seeing the receipts for your travellers cheques.

CBS (Map pp80-1; Cham Palace; Sharia Maysaloun; �־ 24hr) Reception changes cash and travellers cheques.

Nahas Travel (Map pp80-1; ☎ 223 2000; Sharia Fardous) The Thomas Cook agent. You can't cash travellers cheques here, only arrange for replacements for any stolen (this can take up to 10 days). Also the agent in Syria for Visa and MasterCard, but can't give advances against your plastic. If you ask you might be directed to places that can oblige.

You can obtain cash advances on a Visa card at a couple of places around Al-Merjeh, although at unfavourable rates – look for shops with a Visa sign in the window.

ATMS
There is an ATM at the airport where you can withdraw cash from savings accounts – although depending on your bank there could be a hefty fee. There's also one in the gold souq, a couple near Saahat Yousef al-Azmeh and one at the Cham Palace hotel.

Photography
Sharia al-Jumhuriyya is the film and photography street, with a bunch of photo labs and camera-repair shops.

Kodak Express (Map pp80-1; Sharia Mousalam al-Baroudi; �־ 9am-7pm Sat-Thu) About 100m west of Hejaz train station. Stocks a wide range of quality film; credit cards accepted. Developing in one hour costs S£25 for processing plus S£10 per print. Slides, so we were told, could be done in one day for S£200 plus S£7 per transparency.

Pluto Photo Services (Map pp80-1; Sharia Maysaloun) Just west of Cham Palace; good for emergency camera repairs or spares.

Post
Central post office (Map pp80-1; Sharia Said al-Jabri; �־ 8am-7pm Sat-Thu, 9am-noon Fri & national holidays) In an ugly, monolithic building, just down from Hejaz train station. The parcel post office is outside and around the corner.

DHL (Map pp80-1; ☎ 222 7692; Sharia Omar ben Abi Rabia; �־ 8am-8pm Sat-Thu, 9am-2pm Fri) Not far from the post office, and east toward Sharia Shoukri al-Quwatli.

Express Mail Service (EMS; �־ 8am-5pm, except Fri) In the parking lot behind the central post office.

Poste restante (Map pp80-1; Sharia Said al-Jabri; �־ 8am-5pm, closed Fri) In the central post office at the counter to the left on entering and fairly efficient. You'll need your passport as proof of identity. There's a S£10 charge per letter.

Telephone & Fax
There are card phones at every major junction in Damascus. For more details on card phones and phonecards see p373.

City telephone office (Map pp80-1; Sharia an-Nasr; �־ 24hr) A block east of the Hejaz train station. Telegram and faxes can be sent from this office during vaguely set daytime hours; for the latter a passport is required.

Tourist Information
The staff at both the following tourist offices are friendly, speak English and do their best, but beyond some free maps, they have little to offer and are poorly informed on the sorts of things that most visitors might want to know.

Main tourist office (Map pp80-1; ☎ 232 3953; Sharia 29 Mai; �־ 9.30am-7pm Sat-Thu) Just north of Saahat Yousef al-Azmeh.

Tourist office (Map pp80-1; Ministry of Tourism bldg; �־ 9am-2pm Sat-Thu) Near the National Museum and Takiyya as-Süleimaniyya.

Visa Extensions
Immigration office (Map p78; Sharia Filasteen; �־ 8am-2pm except Fri) One block west of the Baramke terminal. Go to the 2nd floor to fill out the forms (questions in Arabic and French only), to be completed on the spot and handed over along with S£25 and three photos – **Kodak Express** (Map pp80-1; Sharia Mousalam al-Baroudi; �־ 9am-7pm Sat-Thu), just west of Hejaz train station, can do them in 10 minutes (eight for S£200). Visa extensions of one month are given. Return to pick up your passport at 1pm the next day.

SIGHTS
Old City   المدينة القديمة
Although settlement on this site dates back to as early as the 15th century BC, and strong evidence of a Roman-era street plan occasionally shows through, the character of the Old City is essentially medieval Islamic. It remains unchanged from that time to an astonishing degree.

DAMASCUS: OLD CITY

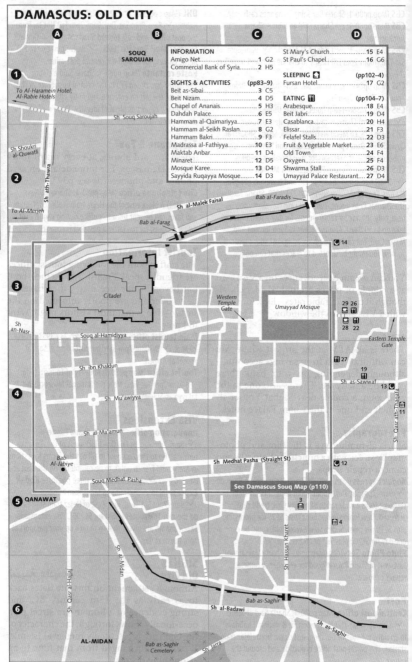

INFORMATION	
Amigo Net	1 G2
Commercial Bank of Syria	2 H5

SIGHTS & ACTIVITIES	(pp83–9)
Beit as-Sibai	3 C5
Beit Nizam	4 D5
Chapel of Ananais	5 H3
Dahdah Palace	6 E5
Hammam al-Qaimariyya	7 E3
Hammam al-Seikh Raslan	8 G2
Hammam Bakri	9 F3
Madrassa al-Fathiyya	10 E3
Maktab Anbar	11 D4
Minaret	12 D5
Mosque Karee	13 D4
Sayyida Ruqayya Mosque	14 D3

St Mary's Church	15 E4
St Paul's Chapel	16 G6

SLEEPING	(pp102–4)
Fursan Hotel	17 G2

EATING	(pp104–7)
Arabesque	18 E4
Beit Jabri	19 D4
Casablanca	20 H4
Elissar	21 F3
Felafel Stalls	22 D3
Fruit & Vegetable Market	23 E6
Old Town	24 F4
Oxygen	25 F4
Shwarma Stall	26 D3
Umayyad Palace Restaurant	27 D4

SOUQ SAROUJAH

To Al-Haramein Hotel;
Al-Rabie Hotels

Sh Souq Saroujah

Sh Shoukri al-Quwatli

Sh ath-Thawra

To Al-Merjeh

Sh al-Malek Faisal

Bab al-Faradis

Bab al-Farag

Citadel

Western Temple Gate

Umayyad Mosque

Eastern Temple Gate

Sh an-Nasr

Souq al-Hamidiyya

Sh Ibn Khaldun

Sh Mu'awiyya

Sh as-Sawwaf

Sh al-Ma'amun

Bab Al-Jabiye

Souq Medhat Pasha

Sh Medhat Pasha (Straight St)

Sh Qasr ath-Thaqafi

See Damascus Souq Map (p110)

QANAWAT

Sh al-Midan

Sh Hassan Kharet

Sh Qasr al-Hijaz

Bab as-Saghir

Sh al-Badawi

AL-MIDAN

Bab as-Saghir Cemetery

Sh Jarra

Sh as-Saghir

DAMASCUS

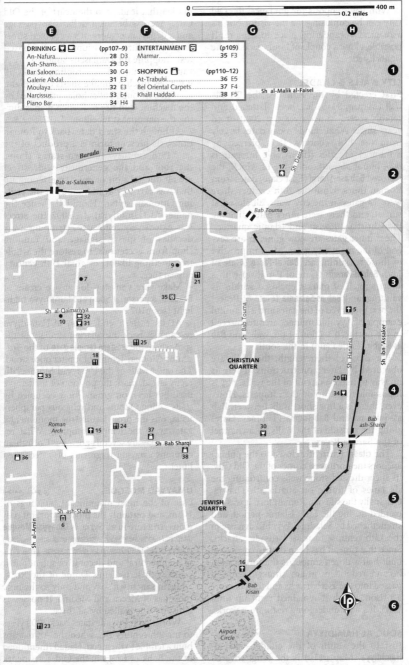

0 ——— 400 m
0 ——— 0.2 miles

DAMASCUS

Barada River

Bab as-Salaama

Sh al-Malik al-Faisel

Bab Touma

Sh Diasa

CHRISTIAN QUARTER

Sh al-Qaimariyya

Sh Bab Touma

Sh Hanania

Sh Ibn 'Assaker

Roman Arch

Sh Bab Sharqi

Bab ash-Sharqi

JEWISH QUARTER

Sh ash-Shalla

Sh al-Amin

Bab Kisan

Airport Circle

With few signposts for guidance, the Old City can be confusing for the visitor but it's a magical, meandering place to explore. If possible, allow a couple of hours each for the sights listed.

CITY WALLS & CITADEL

First erected by the Romans, the **Old City wall** (Map pp84–5) has been flattened and rebuilt several times over the 2000 or so years since. What stands today dates largely from the 13th century. It is pierced by a number of gates (the Arabic for gate is *bab*, plural *abwab*), only one of which, the restored **Bab ash-Sharqi** (East Gate) dates from Roman times. Until the 20th century there were 13 gates in the city walls, all closed at sunset, and there were inner gates dividing the Christian, Jewish and Islamic quarters. These inner gates are now gone, as are several of the main city gates. Most impressive of those remaining are **Bab al-Faraq** (Gate of Joy); **Bab al-Faradis** (Gate of Paradise) with a short stretch of market enclosed within its vaulting; and **Bab as-Salaama** (Gate of Peace) the best preserved of the gates and a beautiful example of Ayyubid military architecture; all in the northern section of the wall, and **Bab as-Saghir** (Little Gate) in the south.

For most of their length, the walls are obscured by later constructions. There is no way to make a circuit of the walls, nor is it possible to get up on the ramparts. However, there is a fine short walk between Bab as-Salaama and **Bab Touma** (Thomas' Gate) along the outside of the walls by a channel of the Barada River.

The **citadel** (currently closed to the public) anchors the northwest corner of the Old City, its sheer dressed-stone walls confronting the six lanes of traffic on Sharia ath-Thawra. Originally the site of a Roman fort, it was expanded during the early Islamic period, and strengthened by Saladin's Ayyubid dynasty in the 13th century, to resist Crusader attacks. Since that time, it has been destroyed and rebuilt half-a-dozen times. As the fortification became redundant in any strategic sense, it passed into use as a barracks and then became a prison, which it remained right up until 1985. It's now undergoing restoration work.

SOUQ AL-HAMIDIYYA   سوق الحميدية

Just to the south of the citadel, **Souq al-Hamidiyya** (Map p110) is the long, covered market that leads into the heart of the Old City. A cross between a Parisian passage and a department store, it's a cobbled street lined with glitzy emporiums (see the boxed text Shopping the Damascus Souq, p111). A vault of corrugated-iron roofing blocks all but a few torch-beamlike shafts of sunlight, admitted through bullet holes punctured by the machine-gun fire of French planes during the nationalist rebellion of 1925.

Although the street dates back to Roman times, its present form is a product of the late 19th century; the two-storey shops, the roof and the generously wide street are all due to a bit of civic smartening up that was carried out in honour of the visiting Ottoman sultan, Hamid II (hence the name, Al-Hamidiyya). In 2002 the street was extensively renovated, stripping away decades of messy signage and random shop-front accretions, to restore the whole to something like its original 19th-century appearance.

Make sure you stop for an ice cream at **Bekdach**, a personal Souq al-Hamidiyya highlight (see p107).

At its eastern end, Souq al-Hamidiyya re-emerges back into glaring sunlight at the spot where the **western temple gate** of the 3rd-century Roman Temple of Jupiter once stood. The outer walls of the Umayyad Mosque, directly ahead, mark the position of the temple itself but here, on ground now occupied by stalls selling Qurans and religious paraphernalia, was the propylaeum (the monumental gateway to the temple complex). What remains today are several enormous Corinthian columns carrying fragments of a decorated lintel.

UMAYYAD MOSQUE   الجامع الاموي

One of the most magnificent buildings of Islam, and certainly the most important religious structure in all Syria, is **Umayyad Mosque** (Map p87; admission S£50; ☾ dawn until after sundown prayers, closed 12.30-2pm Fri for noon prayers). In terms of architectural and decorative splendour it ranks with Jerusalem's Dome of the Rock, while in sanctity it's second only to the holy mosques of Mecca and Medina. It possesses a history unequalled by all three.

Worship on this site dates back 3000 years to the 9th century BC, when the Aramaeans built a temple to their god, Hadad (mentioned in the Book of Kings in the Old Testament).

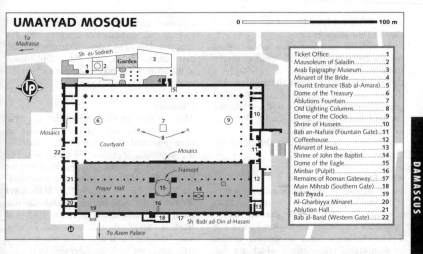

UMAYYAD MOSQUE

0 ————— 100 m

Ticket Office...............................1
Mausoleum of Saladin................2
Arab Epigraphy Museum.............3
Minaret of the Bride...................4
Tourist Entrance (Bab al-Amara)...5
Dome of the Treasury.................6
Ablutions Fountain......................7
Old Lighting Columns................. 8
Dome of the Clocks....................9
Shrine of Hussein.....................10
Bab an-Nafura (Fountain Gate)...11
Coffeehouse.............................12
Minaret of Jesus.......................13
Shrine of John the Baptist..........14
Dome of the Eagle.....................15
Minbar (Pulpit).........................16
Remains of Roman Gateway.......17
Main Mihrab (Southern Gate)....18
Bab Ziyada 19
Al-Gharbiyya Minaret..................20
Ablution Hall............................21
Bab al-Barid (Western Gate).......22

DAMASCUS

With the coming of the Romans the temple became associated with the god Jupiter and was massively expanded.

A cousin to the great temples to Bel/Baal at Palmyra (p209) and Baalbek (p329), the walls of the mosque as seen today were just the inner court of the temple. Around this was a large courtyard with four access points – traces of two of these grand gateways still exist and are described in the Souq al-Hamidiyya (p86) and Sayyida Ruqayya Mosque (p89) sections. After Constantine embraced Christianity as the official religion of the Roman Empire, Jupiter was ousted from his temple in favour of Christ. The former pagan shrine was replaced by a basilica dedicated to John the Baptist, whose head was said to be contained in a casket here.

When the Muslims entered Damascus in AD 636 they converted the eastern part of the basilica into a mosque but allowed the Christians to continue their worship in the western part. This arrangement continued for about 70 years. But, during this time, under Umayyad rule Damascus had become capital of the Islamic world and the caliph, Khaled ibn al-Walid, considered it necessary to empower the image of his city with 'a mosque the equal of which was never designed by anyone before me or anyone after me'.

Consequently, the Christians were elbowed out of the basilica while all the old Roman and Byzantine constructions were flattened, and for the next 10 years over 1000 stonemasons and artisans were employed in building a grand new mosque. According to historical accounts, practically every wall was covered with rich mosaics, precious stones were set into the prayer niches, and the wooden ceiling was inlaid with gold and hung with 600 lamps, also of gold. It cost seven years of taxes from the whole of Syria to build. While the mosque has been ravaged by invading Mongols, rocked by earthquakes and gutted by fire, what remains is impressive.

Visiting the Mosque

The tourist entrance is through the northern Bab al-Amara, and the ticket office is close by in the little archaeological garden. Women are provided with a black robe, which must be worn in the mosque. Men in shorts or sleeveless shirts will also be asked to don one. As in all mosques, shoes must be removed at the threshold. Photography is permitted.

Mausoleum of Saladin (Salah ad-Din)

قبر صلاح الدين

In the small archaeological garden that lies along the north wall of Umayyad Mosque are a few columns dating back to the original Roman Temple of Jupiter and a small white building topped by a rust-red dome, which is the **Mausoleum of Saladin** (Map above; ⊙ 10am-5pm). The famed, chivalrous adversary of the Western Crusaders died in Damascus in 1193, and the original mausoleum was erected on this site that same year. It was restored with funds made available by

Kaiser Wilhelm II of Germany, during his visit to Damascus in 1898.

As with the man himself, who was famed for his austerity, the mausoleum is a very modest affair. Inside are two cenotaphs – the walnut-wood one on the right, richly decorated with motifs of the Ayyubid period, contains Saladin's body, while the modern tomb in marble on the left was donated by Kaiser Wilhelm.

Admission is included in the ticket for Umayyad Mosque.

Arab Epigraphy Museum
For most visitors this will be a case of a museum building being more engaging than its contents. The **Arab Epigraphy Museum** (Map p87; adult/student S£150/10; ☉ 9am-2pm Wed, Thu & Sat-Mon, 9-11.30am Fri) has a small calligraphic exhibit of illuminated manuscripts, which are dull unless you have a particular passion for such things; however, the 15th-century Madrassa al-Jaqmaqiyya in which the collection is exhibited is a fine example of characteristic Mamluk-era architecture.

Courtyard
The northern part of the mosque is an expansive, open courtyard with a white limestone floor, flanked on three sides by a two-storey arched arcade. The fourth side is the façade of the prayer hall, dominated by a central section covered with a gilding of golden **mosaics**. Much of this work is the result of 1960s renovations; you can imagine how spectacular the courtyard area must have appeared when all the walls shimmered.

A larger expanse of mosaic also remains on the western arcade wall. Stretching some 37m in length, and executed in shades of green and lime on a background of gold, the mosaic depicts fairytale-like clusters of towers and domes, alternating with heavily foliated trees. Scholars have yet to decide on what it all represents but Damascenes claim it's the Barada Valley, and the paradise Mohammed saw in Damascus.

In the centre of the courtyard is an odd square-shaped **ablutions fountain** topped by a wooden-canopied pulpit, which is a fairly recent addition, while flanking it are two old **columns** that used to hold lamps. The small octagonal structure on the western side, decorated with intricate 14th-century mosaics and standing on eight recycled Roman columns, is the **Dome of the Treasury**, once used to keep public funds safe from thieves. It's counterbalanced by a domed structure on the east side, built in the 18th century and known as the **Dome of the Clocks** because it's where the mosque's clocks used to be kept.

Minarets
There are three minarets, which date from the original construction. However each one has been renovated and restored at later dates by the Ayyubids, Mamluks and Ottomans. The one on the northern side, the **Minaret of the Bride**, is the oldest; the one in the southwestern corner, the Mamluk-styled **Al-Gharbiyya minaret**, is the most beautiful; while the one on the southeastern corner, the **Minaret of Jesus**, is the tallest, and so-named because local tradition has it that this is where Christ will appear on earth on Judgment Day.

Prayer Halls
On the southern side of the courtyard is the rectangular prayer hall, its three aisles divided by a transept. The hall as seen today is the Ottoman reconstruction that took place after the devastating fire of 1893. At the centre of the hall above the transept, resting on four great pillars, is the **Dome of the Eagle**, so-called because it represents the eagle's head, while the transept represents the body and the aisles are the wings.

Looking somewhat out of place in the sanctuary is the green-domed marble-clad **shrine of John the Baptist** (Prophet Yehia to Muslims). The story goes that during the building of the mosque, back in the early 8th century, a casket was discovered buried under the old basilica floor. It contained the biblical character's head, still with skin and hair intact, and that's what's in the shrine. However, this is only one of several claimed final resting places for the gory relic and unless the saint was endowed with multiple heads, the authenticity of any such claims has to be seriously doubted.

The eastern side of the mosque contains the **shrine of Hussein**, son of Ali and grandson of the Prophet. He was killed by the Umayyads at Kerbala in Iraq. The shrine attracts large numbers of Shiite Muslims (Ali is regarded as the founder of Shiism) and black-clad Iranians are a common sight, making straight across the courtyard for this part of the mosque.

Shrine of John the Baptist in the prayer hall of
Umayyad Mosque (p88), Damascus, Syria

PAUL DOYLE

Brightly coloured clothing on display
in the Souq al-Hamidiyya (p86),
Damascus, Syria

Brass serving tray inside the 18th-century Azem Palace (p90), Damascus, Syria

CHRISTINA DAMEYER

Beehive houses (p171), near Hama, Syria

Ancient Roman ruins of Apamea (p167), Syria

Ancient norias (p162), Hama, Syria

NORTH OF THE MOSQUE

Less than 100m northwest of the Umayyad Mosque are two fine old **madrassas**, facing each other across a narrow alley. Both of these schools were erected in the 13th century during the ascendancy of the Ayyubids. On the left (west), **Madrassa al-Adeliyya** (Map p110) was begun under Nureddin and continued under a brother of Saladin, Al-Adel Seif ad-Din, whose grave it contains. Its façade is considered a classic example of Ayyubid architecture. At the time of writing, the interior was in turmoil as a new construction project was underway.

Mausoleum of Beybars   قبر بيبرس

Madrassa az-Zahariyya (Map pp84–5), on the eastern side of the alley, was originally a private house belonging to the father of Saladin. Following the death in 1277 of the great Mamluk sultan and nemesis of the Crusaders, Beybars, the building was converted into his **mausoleum** (9am-5pm, closed 12.30-2.30pm Fri). Someone will usually be on hand to open up the tomb chamber. It's badly in need of attention, but there's a band of splendid mosaic decoration done in a style similar to that in the nearby Umayyad Mosque. The tomb itself is a surprisingly minimalist 20cm-high flat slab, topped by what look like two giant marble Toblerones, marking the resting places of the sultan and his son.

From the madrassas a good route is to head north, past the doorway of **Hammam az-Zahariyya** (see Hammams, p99), and then bear to the right; following this narrow alley leads you to a small square right in front of the main entrance of Sayyida Ruqayya Mosque.

Sayyida Ruqayya Mosque
جامع السيدة الرُقيّة

If they built mosques in Las Vegas, this is what they'd look like. For centuries the mausoleum of Ruqayya bint al-Hussein ash-Shaheed bi-Kerbala (Ruqayya, the Daughter of the Martyr Hussein of Kerbala) was hidden among the clutter of tumbledown Damascene housing, just to the north of Umayyad Mosque. In 1985, the Iranians (Ruqayya being a Shiite saint) began construction of a mosque around the mausoleum, designed very much in the modern Persian style. While the portico, courtyard and main 'onion' dome are relatively restrained and quite beautiful, the interior of the prayer hall is a riot of mirrors decorated with mosaics. The whole complex strikes a very discordant note with the predominant khaki and dun of the rest of the Old City. Non-Muslim visitors are welcome (except during Friday noon prayers).

North of Sayyida Ruqayya Mosque is **Bab al-Faradis** (see City Walls & Citadel, p86). Following the lane that runs due east, then turning right (south) at the T-junction leads to a crossroad marked by the scant, half-buried remains of the **eastern temple gate** (Map pp84–5), which served as the eastern entrance to the compound of the Roman Temple of Jupiter (the site now occupied by Umayyad Mosque).

Back toward the mosque is one of the loveliest stretches of alleyway (vines strung overhead and the walls hung with the vividly coloured wares of carpet sellers) before the way widens slightly to accommodate a burbling fountain and An-Nafura and Ash-Shams, two lazily atmospheric **coffeehouses** (p107). The former has been around over 200 years.

Beside the coffeehouses, a broad flight of stairs carries the alley up to the eastern wall of Umayyad Mosque, shaped by elements of what was originally part of the main Roman-era monumental entrance to the inner courts of the temple – now the mosque's **Bab an-Nafura** (Fountain Gate). The street loops around the southern wall of the mosque (see below) and reconnects with Souq al-Hamidiyya.

SOUTH OF THE MOSQUE

South of Umayyad Mosque is the heart of the **Damascus souq** (Map p110), with stretches of stalls devoted to spices, gold, sweets, perfume and fabrics. If you can drag yourself away from the colourful and fragrant displays, there are also wonderful bits of architecture, including numerous khans and a small beautiful palace complex.

One of the liveliest thoroughfares, with its glittering gold and silver sellers is **Souq as-Silah**, running due south from Bab Ziyada (set into the southern wall of Umayyad Mosque), out of which crowds of men emerge after prayers. After no more than 100m you can turn right (west), which leads you to Azem Ecole, Madrassa an-Nuri and

Maristan Nureddin; left and then straight ahead is the splendid Azem Palace (see below). Continuing due south takes you to **Souq al-Bzouriyya** (Seed Bazaar), heavily scented with cumin, coffee and perfumes. A little way along, on the left, is **Hammam Nureddin** (see Hammams, p99), the most elegant of Damascus' old bathhouses, and, just beyond, the grand entrance to **Khan As'ad Pasha** (Map p110; ☪ 8am-2pm Sat-Thu), arguably the finest and most ambitious piece of architecture in the Old City – a cathedral among khans. Built in 1752 under the patronage of As'ad Pasha al-Azem, it encompasses a vast space achieved through a beautiful arrangement of eight small domes around a larger circular aperture, allowing light to stream in above a circular pool. The domes are supported on four colossal grey-and-white piers that splay into elegant arches.

Beyond the khan, the souq intersects with Straight St (see opposite).

Azem Ecole   مدرسة العظم

Built in 1770 by a member of the Azem family (successive generations of whom governed Damascus from 1725 to 1809), **Azem Ecole** (Map p110) is a former madrassa and a little gem of urban Ottoman architecture. It has a beautiful tight little courtyard, hemmed in by a delicate three-storey gallery, the upper floor of which is wood. Currently it houses an expensive souvenir store (see Shopping, p111).

Madrassa an-Nuri   المدرسة النورية

Just 50m beyond Azem Ecole, at the start of a street devoted to gold and jewellery, **Madrassa an-Nuri** (Map p110) is easy to pick out because of its crimson, pimpled domes. The structure is fairly modern and not particularly noteworthy but inside is a surviving part of a madrassa dating from 1172, which houses the mausoleum of Nureddin, the uncle of Saladin, who united Syria and paved the way for his nephew's successes against the Crusaders. It's not necessary to enter the building to see the tomb chamber, instead walk down the narrow market alley beside the madrassa and peer in through a big iron-grille opening in the wall.

Maristan Nureddin   بيمارستان نور الدين

Located 150m west of Madrassa an-Nuri, **Maristan Nureddin** (Map p110) was built in 1154, under the patronage of Nureddin, as a hospital and was the most advanced medical institution of the time (Arab medicine was far in advance of anything practised in the West, until Europe caught up during the Renaissance). Remarkably, it stayed in use as a centre of healing right up until the 19th century. Today it serves as a **Science & Medical Museum** (adult/student S£300/15; ☪ 8am-2pm Sat-Thu), filled with old medical and surgical odds and ends from Roman to Ottoman times, many of which look more like implements of torture. Notably bizarre exhibits include an electric-shock machine, a birthing chair and a great number of stuffed and pickled creatures, the bodily parts of which were ground, diced, snorted or otherwise ingested as cures.

Azem Palace   قصر العظم

If you are only going to visit one old building in Damascus (in addition, of course, to Umayyad Mosque) then it should be this, a stunning tour de force of all that's best about Damascene architecture.

Azem Palace (Map p110; adult/student S£300/15; ☪ 9am-5.30pm Wed-Mon Apr-Sep, 9am-3.30pm Wed-Mon Oct-Mar, closed 12.30-2.30pm Fri) comprises a complex of buildings, courtyards and gardens that were built between 1749 and 1752 as a private residence for the governor of Damascus, As'ad Pasha al-Azem. It remained the Azem residence until the beginning of the 20th century, when the family moved outside the Old City and the house was sold to the French to become their Institute of Archaeology and Islamic Art. The palace was badly damaged by fire during uprisings against the French in 1925 but has been beautifully restored.

On entering turn left then right, which leads through into the main courtyard with a central pool and fountain. The courtyard is fringed by low buildings, which are all a mixture of black basalt, limestone and sandstone, giving a beautiful and subtle banding effect. This technique, known as *ablaq*, is a characteristic theme throughout Levantine and Egyptian architecture; it was particularly popular under the Mamluks, but also later adopted by Ottoman masons.

This area served as the *haramlek* (family quarter). Each of the rooms off the courtyard is sumptuously decorated with wooden panelling, lustrous blue tiling, painted ceilings and coloured paste work – a technique in which a pattern is incised into stone and then filled in with pastes made from different coloured stones to give the effect of an immensely complicated stone inlay.

The rooms all contain mannequin displays, each with a different theme (a musical party, the pilgrimage, a wedding), which is why the palace is also known as the Museum of the Arts & Popular Traditions of Syria. However these displays distract from the sublime architecture and interiors.

STRAIGHT STREET (WESTERN END)

Although it's now more commonly known as Sharia Medhat Pasha (the western part) or Sharia Bab Sharqi (the eastern), the main east–west street that bisects the Old City was historically known as **Straight St** (Map pp84–5), from the Latin, Via Recta. It isn't straight at all but bends slightly in a couple of places, hence, as Mark Twain wrote in *The Innocents Abroad,* St Luke in the Bible is 'careful not to commit himself; he does not say it is the street which is straight, but "the street which is called Straight". It is a fine piece of irony; it is the only facetious remark in the Bible, I believe.'

Straight or not, this was the main street of Damascus during Greek and Roman times, when it would have appeared something like the main avenues still seen at Apamea

(p167) or Palmyra (p204). It was four times its present width and planted with a seemingly endless row of columns that supported a canvas street covering.

The street is busiest at the western end, where it's largely devoted to shops selling textiles and clothes. There are several old khans in this area, their gates still locked at night: on the north side are the pretty little **Khan az-Zeit** (Map p110) and the **Khan Jakmak** (Map p110); while on the south is **Khan Süleiman Pasha**, built in 1732, with a central courtyard that was formerly roofed by two domes. The domes collapsed at some point, leaving the courtyard now open to two great circular discs of sky.

Aside from the old houses (described in the boxed text History with Potential, below) there are few notable monuments or sites south of the western stretch of Straight St, but the twisting narrow alleyways are picturesque, tranquil and well worth exploring.

OLD DAMASCENE HOUSES

Damascus has a hidden treasure: unseen behind the walls of the Old City are hundreds of houses built around courtyards and featuring their own distinctive decoration (see the boxed text History with Potential). Unfortunately, much of this treasure is in a state of disrepair, but a loop off Straight St

---

HISTORY WITH POTENTIAL

During the 18th century, while members of the powerful Al-Azem family were governors of the city, domestic architecture flowered and the houses of this period were almost secret works of art. Hidden behind featureless façades, inside European visitors were stunned to find there were decorated ceilings and walls, richly painted and covered with gilded wood, coloured glass hanging lamps, mosaic and marble floors with mother-of-pearl inlay in stone, indoor fountains and lush interior gardens blooming with bouganvillea and citrus trees.

Divans or cushions covered with embroidered silk were placed around the walls of the raised seating areas. Persian rugs overlapped on the floors. All bedding was stored in giant, built-in wall cupboards concealed behind painted doors, and the only free-standing piece of furniture was a huge mother-of-pearl inlaid chest, in which a bride kept her trousseau.

By the beginning of the 20th century, new European-style suburbs were growing up outside the Old City. Fuelled by the appeal of glazing and central heating, electricity and plumbing, many families left these homes and poorer folk moved in; unable to afford the upkeep, many of the residences fell into a state of disrepair. Just one hundred years earlier, every notable family lived in a traditional house in the Old City, but now only a couple of families have remained.

Over the last decade or so numerous restaurants have opened in the Old City, all in converted old residences. Those passionate about preserving the Old City have bought houses and are restoring them. Perhaps all this activity is helping to persuade the authorities to take a more dynamic attitude towards the Old City, which may in turn help to promote and preserve the historical richness of these grand traditional houses.

takes in several examples, all of which have benefited from extensive renovation.

Just a few steps away from Khan Süleiman Pasha, **Beit Aqqad** (Map p110; ☎ 223 8038; www.videnskabsministeriet.dk in Danish; 8-10 Souq as-Souf; ☽ 9am-3pm Sat-Wed, 9am-1pm Thu) was formerly the home of a rich family of textile merchants. It now houses the Danish Institute in Damascus. Visitors are allowed into the courtyard, which is graced by a massive expanse of the most gorgeous inlaid-stone decoration – it looks just like one of those inlaid boxes sold in the souq.

Head south down Sharia Hassan Kharet and take the first left for **Beit as-Sibai** (Map pp84-5; Sharia al-Qabbani; ☽ 8am-2pm Sun-Thu), built between 1769 and 1774, and beautifully restored in recent years. Petite, delicate and very homely, it's the sort of place you could actually imagine yourself living in. In fact, for a time during the 1990s it served as the residence of the German ambassador. Now it stands empty and, as with many of these grand old places, the authorities don't quite know what to do with it. At present it serves occasionally as a set for historical TV dramas and as an atmospheric venue for ministerial functions.

Walking on past the Sibai house, and turning right at the T-junction, leads to **Beit Nizam** (Map pp84-5; Sharia nasif Pasha; ☽ 8am-2pm Sun-Thu), another breathtakingly beautiful 18th-century house, although in this case, executed on a far grander scale. It has been organised around two large courtyards, the one to the rear coloured by orange trees and rose bushes. In the mid-19th century it served as the French consulate.

A two-minute walk east through the back alleys brings you to the **Dahdah Palace** (Map pp84-5; 9 Sharia ash-Shalla; ☽ 9am-1pm & 4-6pm), an 18th-century residence owned by the elderly Mr Dahdah. If you ring the bell his amiable wife, who speaks good English, may be free to show you around the many beautiful rooms, one of which operates as a dusty antique shop (see Shopping, p111).

From the Dahdah Palace, backtrack to Sharia al-Amin and bear left along Straight St, then right for the **Maktab Anbar** (Map pp84-5; Sharia Qasr ath-Thaqafa; ☽ 8am-2pm Sun-Thu). This is a relatively late house, built only in 1867 but on an extravagant scale. Its owner was a Jew who, so the story goes, travelled to India as a servant and came back with a hat full

of diamonds. He built lavishly in what was at the time derided as 'modern style'. His profligacy was his ruin and when in 1890 he couldn't pay his taxes, the house was seized and pressed into service as a school. These days it houses the architects responsible for the preservation and renovation of the Old City.

From Maktab Anbar continue north and take the first left after the mosque; 50m along on the right is **Beit Jabri** (Map pp84-5; ☎ 544 3200, www.jabrihouse.com; 14 Sharia as-Sawwaf; ☽ 9.30-12.30am). Its courtyard has recently been partially restored and opened up as a hugely popular café (see Eating, p106). One room is an Internet café. Take a look at the heavily restored *qaa* (reception room) up the steps at the far end of the courtyard.

GALLERIES

In the Old City, **Gallerie Albal** (Map pp84-5; ☎ 544 5794; Sharia Shaweesh; ☽ 9.30-12.30am) is a café with an exhibition space above that hosts regularly changing shows (see also Drinking, p107). There are several other art galleries in Abu Roumana, northwest of the city (see p99).

CHRISTIAN QUARTER

No longer gated, the **Christian Quarter** (Map pp84–5) begins approximately where a small **Roman arch** stands on a mean patch of grass beside Straight St. It's all that remains of what was probably a grand triple arch, which once marked an important intersection. Occupying the northeastern part of the Old City, the quarter is home to numerous churches representing various denominations: Syrian Orthodox; Greek Orthodox; Armenian; Greek Catholic; Syrian Catholic; and Maronite; among others. The wealth and education of the city's Christians is reflected in a thriving commercial atmosphere, and a rapidly expanding dining and drinking scene centred on Sharia Bab Touma and its surrounding streets.

Chapel of Ananias كنيسة حنانيا

In the far northeastern corner of the quarter is the **Chapel of Ananias** (Map pp84-5; Sharia Hanania; ☽ 9am-1pm & 3-6pm Wed-Mon), the old cellar of which is reputedly the house of Ananias, an early Christian disciple – see the boxed text Biblical Damascus, opposite.

BIBLICAL DAMASCUS

Christianity has been on the scene in Damascus since early in the 1st century. Saul of Tarsus, who had been the scourge of Christians in Jerusalem, was riding to Damascus on the instructions of the Jewish high priests in order to harass the Christians there. En route he was blinded by a vision of God near the village of Darayya outside Damascus. He was led into the city to the home of a Christian named Judas. There he was cured of his blindness by Ananias, who had also received a vision: 'Arise, and go into the street which is called Straight...' (Acts 9:11). Converted, Saul of Tarsus became Paul the Apostle, and was baptised in the Barada River; later he spread the word of God throughout the Roman Empire.

His conversion so outraged the Damascene Jews, who considered him a renegade, that he was forced to flee the city: 'And through a window in a basket was I let down by the wall, and escaped' (2 Corinthians 11:33).

The houses of Ananias and Judas, and the 'window' of St Paul are all commemorated in Damascus and held in reverence by the city's Christian communities. But it's as well to remember, as highlighted in Cook's *Guide to Palestine & Syria* (1934), that 'the holy places of Damascus undergo a change every few years'. In this guide the current traditions are presented.

To find the chapel, take the last street on the left (Sharia Hanania) before Bab ash-Sharqi; it's at the far north end, in a crypt below the house, where you (sometimes) pay to enter.

Sharia Hanania is predictably busy with souvenir and antique shops, along with restaurants and bars.

St Paul's Chapel   كنيسة مار بولس

The Old City gate, **Bab Kisan** (Map pp84–5), purportedly marks the spot where the disciples lowered St Paul out of a window in a basket one night, so that he could flee from the Jews, having angered them after preaching in the synagogues – see the boxed text Biblical Damascus. Beside the gate, which has been sealed since at least the 18th century, is **St Paul's Chapel**, dedicated to the saint. Follow the driveway up to the new convent on the left and push open the heavy wooden doors into the back of Bab Kisan, which now contains the small chapel.

Central Damascus   Map pp80–1

The modern city is short on sights and largely bereft of beauty. The main thing to do is to visit the National Museum and its neighbour, Takiyya as-Süleimaniyya. The backstreets of the Souq Saroujah district are also worth a wander and, if you haven't already had enough of the splendours of the Damascene take on vernacular architecture, then the Historical Museum of Damascus is a beautiful place. The old neighbourhood of Salihiyya, on the lower slopes of Jebel Qassioun, is worth some exploration.

AL-MERJEH   المرجه

Writing in 1875, Isabel Burton, wife of the British consul, describes the 'green' Merjeh as looking like a 'village common'. By the end of the 19th century it was the hub of Damascus: a small park; where the city's best hotels were; and a terminus for trams. Damascus was the first city in the Ottoman empire to possess electric trams, with six lines converging here, and the power supplied by a waterfall on the Barada River. Another century on and the trams are gone. Al-Merjeh is now a traffic island with a tiny fume-wreathed patch of grass at the centre. The whole area is dominated by the huge construction site on its northern side (destined to be a grand mosque and offices of the Ministry of Religion).

The square is now officially known as Saahat ash-Shohada (Martyrs' Square). The martyrs referred to were victims of the French bombardments in 1925. The strange column at the centre, topped by what looks like a bronze birdhouse, has nothing to do with martyrs; instead, it commemorates the opening of the first telegraph link in the Middle East – the line from Damascus to Medina.

As the focus of the city has shifted north and west, Al-Merjeh has been left behind, and the area has slid downmarket. Although the surrounding streets remain busy, the trade is in cheap eateries, pastry shops and low-budget hotels.

HEJAZ TRAIN STATION   محطة الحجاز

A little south and west of Al-Merjeh, Saahat Hejaz (Hejaz Square) is another of the city's former grand spaces, created to show off the **Hejaz train station** on its southern side. Completed in 1917, the station was the northern terminus of the new Hejaz Railway, which was meant to ferry pilgrims down to Medina (see the boxed text The Hejaz Railway, p385). Compared with the grand transport palaces of Europe, the station is a provincial affair but the interior, though badly neglected and not improved any by the luridly painted presidential hagiography, still has a nicely decorated ceiling.

The actual platforms of the station are closed for renovation and all trains now leave from the Khaddam station. Behind the station two carriages have been converted into a bar-café, Al-Mahatta (see p109), while out front is a steam locomotive dating from 1908, which finds some use as a poster hoarding, and a public water fountain erected at the same time as the station was built and still serving its intended purpose.

SOUQ SAROUJAH سوق ساروجه

A compact historical area of wonky streets lined with small shops and punctuated by medieval tombs, mosques and antiquated street furniture, Souq Saroujah (Saddlers' Bazaar) is the most-friendly part of Central Damascus for strolling.

It was common practice in medieval times for the areas immediately outside the city walls to develop as burial places for the dead; you can still see this today with large areas of cemeteries lying to the south of the old cities of both Damascus and Aleppo. Occasionally, however, the needs of the living would overwhelm those of the dead. Such was the case with the area now known as Souq Saroujah. During the Ayyubid era the fields just north of the Barada River became a favoured location for the tombs and mausoleums of nobles, and for several hundred years this site served as an exclusive burial ground. As the city expanded under the Ottomans, and space within the city walls was at a premium, the cemeteries became built over with the houses of well-off Turkish civil servants and military officers.

Unfortunately, the needs of the living are pressing once again, and many of the fine old houses have been demolished in the cause of redevelopment. Of the handful that remain, **Beit al-Haramein** and **Beit Ar-Rabie** now serve as backpackers' hotels (see Al-Haramein

Hotel, p102, and Ar-Rabie Hotel, p102). The similarly venerable **Beit Shami** is open as the Historical Museum of Damascus.

Historical Museum of Damascus

متحف تاريخ دمشق

Like a down-market version of the Old City's Azem Palace, the **Historical Museum** (Sharia ath-Thawra, Souq Saroujah; adult/student S£150/10; ☺ 8am-2pm Sat-Thu) is in an attractive old house with eight richly decorated rooms off a central courtyard. A couple of rooms hold half-hearted displays of photos and diagrams relating to the Old City, and there is a superb large-scale model of the same, but it's the rooms themselves, decorated in typical Damascene fashion with inlaid marble, carved wood and painted ceilings, that are of greatest interest,.

The museum is not signposted and it's a little difficult to find. It's off Sharia ath-Thawra, just where the flyover comes down north of Sharia Souq Saroujah, beside two tall modern buildings. It's on Ministry of the Interior property and visitors have to pass through a guarded gate to reach the arched entrance.

NATIONAL MUSEUM المتحف الوطني

The most important of Syria's museums is the **National Museum** (Map p95 ; Sharia Shoukri al-Quwatli; adult/student S£300/15; ☺ 9am-6pm Wed-Mon Apr-Sep, 9am-4pm Wed-Mon Oct-Mar) and it could well be argued that you would profit from a visit before and after seeing the main sites around the country.

Enter through a shady **garden** that acts as an overflow for pieces that the museum, overburdened by riches, cannot house inside. Tickets are purchased at the gate and occasionally bags and cameras have to be left in the office at the entrance.

The entrance to the museum is striking – it's the main gate of the Qasr al-Heir al-Gharbi, a desert palace/military camp west of Palmyra dating from AD 688, the time of the Umayyad caliph, Hisham. It was transported to Damascus stone by stone and reconstructed as part of the museum façade.

Within the museum, the exhibits are presented thematically and grouped into pre-classical, classical and Islamic sections. Most of the exhibits are labelled only in French or Arabic and some have no explanation at all. *The Concise Guide: National Museum of*

Damascus is available at the gift shop but it's anything but, and consequently very off putting. Devoid of any context, the endless procession of small, largely nondescript objects can become a bit numbing, but you should definitely see the synagogue and the Hypogeum of Yarhai, both in the east wing.

The **lobby** is devoted to Qasr al-Heir al-Gharbi, with large black-and-white photos of the palace with its façade still in situ. Upstairs is an airy new gallery displaying a series of fine carved-stone screens removed from the Qasr. There are also two large wall paintings kept hidden behind royal-blue drapes, which the custodian takes great pleasure in whisking aside with a dramatic flourish.

En route to the west wing and preclassical galleries is an attractive **fountain courtyard**, constructed to resemble the type of inner sanctuary common to many of the more opulent Damascus dwellings built during the Mamluk and early Ottoman eras.

Preclassical Galleries

The first room (No 1 on the museum map), the **Ugarit Room** is devoted to finds from Ugarit (p148) and contains stone tablets inscribed with what is believed to be the world's earliest alphabet. The **Long Gallery** (No 2) contains finds from ancient Syria, including more from Ugarit, and from other sites. It leads into the **Ebla Room** (No 3), and then on to the two **Mari Rooms**, devoted to artefacts from the Mesopotamian city of Mari (p225) in the extreme southeast of the country, near what is now the border with Iraq. The distinctive statuettes in here with their fur skirts and lively black eyes, date back to around the second millennium BC, making them roughly the same age as the Great Pyramids of Giza.

Islamic Galleries

The first room of the Islamic galleries (No 6) contains **Raqqa artefacts** – pottery and stucco panels recovered from the old Abbasid city of Raqqa (p217) destroyed by Mongols in 1260. A staircase leads up to the **Modern Art Galleries**, while the long corridor running north (No 7) begins with carved wooden fragments of a ceiling found at Qasr al-Heir al-Gharbi, goes on to **Islamic coins** and then leads to **jewellery and weaponry** (No 8), where some heavy jewellery pieces and wonderfully or-

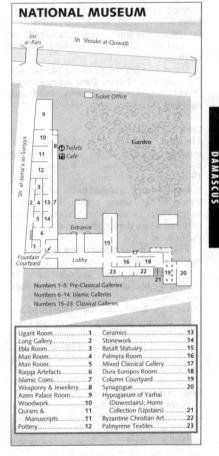

NATIONAL MUSEUM

Jisr ar-Rais — Sh Shoukri al-Quwatli

Ticket Office

Sh al-Jama'a as-Suriyya

9
10
8 Toilets
11 Café
12
3
2 4 13 7
5 14
6
1

Garden

Entrance

Fountain Courtyard Lobby 15
17
16 18
23 22 19 20
21

Numbers 1–5: Pre-Classical Galleries
Numbers 6–14: Islamic Galleries
Numbers 15–23: Classical Galleries

Ugarit Room	1	Ceramics	13
Long Gallery	2	Stonework	14
Ebla Room	3	Basalt Statuary	15
Mari Room	4	Palmyra Room	16
Mari Room	5	Mixed Classical Gallery	17
Raqqa Artefacts	6	Dura Europos Room	18
Islamic Coins	7	Column Courtyard	19
Weaponry & Jewellery	8	Synagogue	20
Azem Palace Room	9	Hypogaeum of Yarhai	
Woodwork	10	(Downstairs); Homs	
Qurans &	11	Collection (Upstairs)	21
Manuscripts	11	Byzantine Christian Art	22
Pottery	12	Palmyrene Textiles	23

nate weaponry are displayed. They embody the two traits for which the Mamluk dynasty was renowned: artistry and violence.

Off the far end is **woodwork** (No 10), where a large room is devoted to the intricate style of woodwork that developed throughout the Islamic era as a result of the religious ban on figurative representations. This room is dominated by two great cenotaphs: the one nearest the entrance, decorated with a beautiful star motif, dates from 1250; while the second dates to 1265 and comes from the Khaled ibn al-Walid Mosque in Homs. For more information on the mosque, see p258. Other objects here are pieces of domestic furniture from some of the old houses of Damascus.

DAMASCUS

North of the woodwork room is the **Azem Palace Room** (No 9), which is a reconstruction of a room from Azem Palace (p90) in the Old City. Only parts of the room are original.

The remaining rooms of the Islamic galleries are devoted to the **Quran and manuscripts** (No 11), **pottery** (No 12), **ceramics** (No 13) and **stonework** (No 14).

Classical Galleries

The classical galleries are probably the most interesting part of the museum and make up the whole east wing. The first room (No 15 on the map) contains a large collection of **basalt statuary**, executed in the black stone typical of the Hauran region. There's also an excellent mosaic here, recovered from Lattakia, which depicts the Orontes River in the form of a god.

The busts in the **Palmyra Room** (No 16) are representations of the dead from Palmyra; they would have fitted like seals into the pigeonhole-like chambers in which bodies were stored. To see how this worked, pass through the **Dura Europos Room** (No 18; p224), which contains jewellery and ceramics from this Roman site on the Euphrates, and down the stairs to the **Hypogeum of Yarhai** (No 21), which is an amazing reconstruction of an underground burial chamber from the Valley of the Tombs at Palmyra. Seeing this helps to make sense of the funerary towers at Palmyra, and some of the exhibits at the museum there (which is where this reconstruction truly belongs). For more information on the Valley of the Tombs, funerary towers and the Palmyra museum, see p207.

Beside the staircase down to the hypogeum is a staircase that goes up to the **Homs Collection** (No 21 upstairs), so-named because much of it was found in and around that city. Alongside some exquisite gold jewellery, there are coins depicting Venetian Doges, the Roman emperor, Philip the Arab, and Alexander the Great.

The other attraction worth seeing is the **synagogue** (No 20), which is across the colonnaded courtyard. This dates from the 2nd century and was discovered at Dura Europos, from where it was removed and reconstructed here. Other than its age, what is particularly interesting are the frescoes that cover the walls, from floor to ceiling, of the interior. Executed in a colourful naive style, they depict scenes from Old Testament events, from the crowning of King Solomon, through to the reign of David, the story of Moses and the flight from Egypt. This is a real oddity in that depictions of the human form go against Talmudic traditions. While the frescoes are very faded (hence the low level of light in the room), it's remarkable that they've survived at all – something that occurred only because the synagogue lay buried under sand for centuries until its discovery in the 1930s.

TAKIYYA AS-SÜLEIMANIYYA التكية السليمانية
Lying immediately east of the National Museum, **Takiyya as-Süleimaniyya** was built over six years, beginning in 1554, to the design of the Ottoman empire's most brilliant architect, Sinan. A favourite of the emperor, Süleiman the Magnificent, Sinan would later go on to create the gorgeous Süleymaniye Mosque that dominates the skyline of İstanbul.

The Takiyya (an Ottoman term for a Sufi hostel) is a much more modest affair than the İstanbul mosque and one that blends local Syrian styles (the alternating layers of black and white stone and honeycomb-style stonework over the main entrance) with typically Turkish features (the high central dome and tell-tale pencil-shaped minarets). It has two parts: the mosque to the south; and an arcaded courtyard with additional rooms on the north side that would have housed pilgrims. This former hostel area is now the Army Museum (see below).

Under the patronage of Süleiman's successor, Selim II, the Takiyya compound was extended with the addition of a small madrassa (theological school). Built around a central courtyard and fountain, the madrassa now serves as the **Artisanat**, an appealing handicraft market, where the former students' cells are now workshops and ateliers (see also Shopping, p110).

ARMY MUSEUM المتحف الحربي
An ill-considered and inappropriate use of the Takiyya, this **Army Museum** (Sharia Shoukri al-Quwatli; adult/student S£15/5; ☉ 8am-2pm Wed-Mon) has a mixed collection of military hardware from the Bronze Age to the near present. Exhibits range from flint arrowheads to a pile of the twisted remains of planes shot down in the 1973 war with Israel & the

Palestinian Territories (I&PT). An interesting anachronism is a display on the theme of Soviet-Syrian space cooperation.

Salihiyya الصالحيه

Strung out along the lower slopes of Jebel Qassioun, north of the modern city centre, Salihiyya is a ramshackle old quarter of small shops, markets and Islamic architecture. The district was first developed in the 12th century, when Nureddin settled Arab refugees here who had fled the Crusader massacres in Jerusalem (1099). What grew up in the subsequent four centuries was a lively if straggly zone of mosques, mausoleums and other religious institutions. Though few of these places can be viewed from the inside, most of them are strung out along one particular street, Sharia Madares Asaad ad-Din, and passing by the domes and decorated portals makes for a pleasant one- or two-hour walk.

The reason that few buildings here can be visited is that while ancient enough to warrant having preservation orders slapped on them, the needs of the locals are so pressing that the monuments are almost all still in private service – albeit rarely for the purposes intended. So it is that the small 14th-century **Tomb of Emir Kajkar** serves now as a Christian Union care centre, while the neighbouring **Tomb of Amat al-Latif** (1243), harbours a human-rights organisation. The **Madrassa Morsidiyya**, complete with the only surviving example of a square 13th-century minaret in Damascus, is a kindergarten, while over the

street a 14th-century tomb, with elaborate carved-stone decoration around the doorway, is presumably now somebody's home, judging by the satellite dish on the dome.

There are one or two hidden gems that are worth gaining access to, if at all possible. Tucked down a side street called Sharia ibn al-Muqaddam, the 14th-century **Jamaa al-Jedid** (New Mosque) was in the process of being rebuilt when we last visited, probably in honour of the tomb it contains within, which belongs to Ismat ad-Din Khatun, wife of first Nureddin and then his successor Saladin. The burial chamber is richly decorated and certainly worth a look.

Back on the main street, and just a little distance east facing a small square, is the modest **Mosque of Mohi ad-Din**. Architecturally undistinguished (although it does possess a beautiful late-Mamluk minaret), this is very much a community mosque, with washing hanging from lines strung between the columns and men dozing in the shade of the prayer hall. It's also a popular centre of pilgrimage – buried here is the body of Sheikh Mohi ad-Din al-Arabi (who died in 1240) a great Sufi mystic, whose writings are supposed to have greatly influenced Dante in his descriptions of hell. The tomb is down a flight of steps off to the left-hand side of the entrance courtyard; the claustrophobic chamber is filled by a cenotaph enclosed in a glitzy silver casing and illuminated by fluorescent green light. It's not unusual to find large family groups picnicking happily down here.

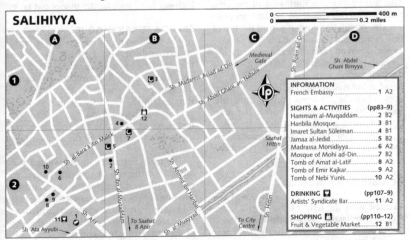

SALIHIYYA

| | | 0 | 400 m |
| | | 0 | 0.2 miles |

INFORMATION	
French Embassy.................... 1	A2

SIGHTS & ACTIVITIES	(pp83–9)
Hammam al-Muqaddam............2	B2
Hanbila Mosque......................3	B1
Imaret Sultan Süleiman............4	B1
Jamaa al-Jedid.......................5	B2
Madrassa Morsidiyya...............6	A2
Mosque of Mohi ad-Din...........7	B2
Tomb of Amat al-Latif.............8	A2
Tomb of Emir Kajkar...............9	A2
Tomb of Nebi Yunis................10	A2

DRINKING 🍸	(pp107–9)
Artists' Syndicate Bar.............11	A2

SHOPPING 🛍	(pp110–12)
Fruit & Vegetable Market........12	B1

RICHARD BURTON

Adventurer, explorer, scholar and translator of *The Thousand and One Nights* and *Karma Sutra*, Sir Richard Burton (1821–90) held the post of British consul in Syria from 1869 to 1871. Although the consulate building was in the city, the fact that the great gates were sealed at night made Burton and his wife Isabel feel claustrophobic. Instead, they chose to live in Salihiyya, which at that time was a Kurdish village of 15,000 inhabitants, on the mountainside overlooking Damascus and separated from the city by fields of orchards. Their house, as described in Isabel's letters, was flanked on one side by a mosque and on the other by a hammam, and had a rooftop terrace where the Burtons would entertain guests. They also had a house in Bludan in the Barada Gorge and Burton would ride into Damascus once a week to attend to consular duties. However, being the colourful unconventional character that he was, Burton lost no time in making enemies. After only two years into his post, the foreign office in London felt compelled to remove him following numerous petitions of complaint, so ending what he would later refer to as the two happiest years of his life.

As you leave the mosque, **Imaret Sultan Süleiman**, just slightly back along and across the main street, is another building designed by Sinan (see Takiyya as-Süleimaniyya, p96, for more details).

Historian Ross Burns, in his *Monuments of Syria: A Historical Guide,* also suggests that **Hanbila Mosque** is worth a visit for the Crusader columns in the courtyard; however it's often locked.

To reach Salihiyya, walk north from Saahat 8 Azar (also known as Saahat Arnous) in Central Damascus, up Sharia Jamal Abdel Nasser, cross a main road and continue up Sharia Afif, past the French embassy on your left.

Greater Damascus

JEBEL QASSIOUN   جبل قاسيون

That bare rocky rise northwest of the city, **Jebel Qassioun** (Mt Qassioun; 1200m), provides a useful orientation tool. It's from the top of this mount that Mohammed is said to have looked down on Damascus and made the observation that opened this chapter (p76). The distinctly urban view today is hardly one of paradise but it is worth the effort, especially at dusk, when the city lights up. Unfortunately, there is no public transport up to the most popular viewing points and the only option is to hire a taxi. You'll have to negotiate for the driver to wait and return with you; a fare of S£200 would seem reasonable.

OCTOBER WAR PANORAMA   بانوراما حرب تشرين

Created with the help of the North Koreans, this **memorial** (Sharia 6 Tishreen; adult/student S£300/15; ☺ 9am-9pm Wed-Mon) to the 1973 war

with I&PT is an extraordinary effort. A lower floor is filled with portraits of former president Hafez al-Assad in the company of various heads of state, but the main focus is the battle over the Golan Heights, and particularly the fighting around the town of Quneitra. A mini-cinema screens a film of the conflict, while on an upper floor there's a combined 3-D mural and diorama depicting the Israeli devastation of the town. Unfortunately, everything is in Arabic only, but it's still worth seeing if you're planning a visit to Quneitra (p129).

The panorama is located about 2km northeast of the centre, on the road to the Harasta bus terminal; take a Harasta microbus (see p112) and ask to be let out when you spot the parking lot on the opposite side of the highway filled with fighter planes and tanks.

SAYYIDA ZEINAB MOSQUE   جامع السيدة زينب

About 10km south of the city centre stands an extraordinary Iranian-built mosque on the site of the burial place of Sayyida Zeinab, granddaughter of Mohammed. Stylistically, the mosque is similar to that of Sayyida Ruqqaya in the Old City (with a glistening gold onion-shaped **dome** and brilliant blue **tiles** covering its façade and twin, freestanding **minarets**), only it's all on a much larger scale.

The main entrances to the sanctuary are on the northern and southern sides, and non-Muslims may enter the courtyard that surrounds the central **mausoleum**. The faithful kiss and stroke the silver grate surrounding Zeinab's tomb, seemingly in the hope of thus attracting to themselves some of the holiness of this much-venerated descendant of the Prophet.

To get here, take a microbus for Karajat as-Sitt (S£5) from Sharia Fahkri al-Baroudi in the city centre. At Karajat as-Sitt change vehicles for another that will take you on to the mosque (S£5). A taxi from the city centre to the mosque and back should cost between S£200 and S£300, but as a foreigner you'll be lucky to get a driver to agree to that.

GALLERIES

We recommend visiting **Gallerie Atassi** (Map p78; ☎ 332 1720; 35 Sharia ar-Rawdah, off Sharia al-Jalaa, Abu Roumana; ❂ 10am-2pm, 6-9pm Sat-Thu), which is Damascus's premier independent art space. It has a busy programme of regularly changing exhibitions, including exchanges of work with institutions abroad. Lavish catalogues accompany every show, and the Atassi also publishes fine art books.

ACTIVITIES
Hammams

If you only visit one hammam in Damascus, then it probably should be the **Hammam Nureddin** (Map pp84-5; ☎ 222 9513; Souq al-Bzouriyya, Old City; ❂ 9am-midnight), in the covered street that runs between the Umayyad Mosque and Straight St. Founded in the mid-12th century (though much remodelled since then), it is one of the grandest as well as the oldest functioning hammams in the country. It has an excellent, superheated steam room, and the full deal of massage, bath and sauna with towel, soap and tea costs S£240 (bath only is S£125); but it is strictly men only.

Second favourite is the less touristy **Hammam Bakri** (Map pp84-5; ☎ 542 6606; Sharia Qanayet al-Hattab; ❂ 9am-midnight), which is in the Christian Quarter and charges about S£190 for the full scrub and massage. Groups of women are accepted but by special reservation only.

More or less opposite the Minaret of the Bride at the rear of the Umayyad Mosque is the comparatively bland **Hammam as-Silsila** (Map p110; ☎ 222 0279; ❂ 9am-11pm). It has cottoned on to tourists and charges S£350 for the full package. Women generally can't get in, but mixed groups can arrange to take the place over for a hefty consideration in dollars.

Hammam az-Zahariyya (Map p110; ❂ 8am-midnight), next to the madrassa of the same name, just north of Umayyad Mosque, has also been in use since the 12th century but alterations over the centuries have completely deprived it of any charm. Nevertheless, the place is clean and well looked after and it does the job. A scrub, sauna, massage and tea costs S£240, but be aware that it's hard to relax when someone's whispering 'Good? Baksheesh!' in your ear every thirty seconds. At the time of research, Monday was reserved between 9am and 5pm for women only.

Just north of Sharia al-Qaimariyya, another hammam with regular sessions for women is **Hammam al-Qaimariyya** (Map pp84-5; Zuqqaq Hammam; ❂ men 7am-noon, 5pm-midnight, women noon-5pm), 300m east of Umayyad Mosque; this place is a local establishment.

Swimming

There is an Olympic pool at the **Tichreen Sports Complex** (Map p78; Sharia Ali ibn Abi Taleb; single entry S£50, monthly pass S£500; ❂ 6am-8pm, women only 7-9am) southwest of the Baramke terminal.

Otherwise, most of the big hotels open their pools in summer. They don't come cheap – the Cham Palace is the cheapest and it charges nonguests S£400 a day; the Sheraton and Le Meridien both charge around S£500 for nonguest day usage.

WALKING TOUR

Wandering the historic Old City streets is the most wonderful thing to do in Damascus. The walk is around 4km and should take anywhere from a couple of hours to half a day. For something different (most people enter by Souq al-Hamidiyya), begin your tour at the Bab Al-Jabiye end of Sharia Medhat Pasha. This will take you directly into the hustle and bustle of this ancient road and centre of commerce known as **Straight St** (**1**; p91). As you make your way along this exotic street you'll pass scores of tiny stores selling textiles, *jalabiyya* (robes), *keffiyeh* (chequered scarves worn by Arabs), coffee, olive oil, and spices. Notice the tattooed faces of the Bedouin ladies shopping, and the dignified faces in the framed portraits hanging at the back of most stores – a sign of respect to past family members, who ran these small businesses decades before. If you look up you will see bullet holes caused by planes at the end of the French Mandate.

When you reach the end of the covered part of the souq, take a slight detour into

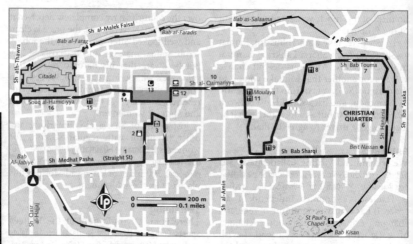

the spice souq on your left, and **Al Ghraoui Confiseur Chocolatier** (2), 'purveyors to Queen Victoria', for a retro box of chocolates. If you're in the mood for some peace and tranquillity before you push on, slip into the beautiful **Azem Palace** (3; p90) to enjoy the glorious garden. Don't get too distracted, however, as there is a lot to see! Return to Straight St and continue in the direction you were heading, passing the small shops selling wooden spoons and plastics, pots and pans, and sweets and nuts. You are likely to be offered a taste of pistachios or cashews – don't hesitate to try before you buy!

You'll start to notice antique shops and second-hand stores selling tarnished brass and copperware, wooden furniture, boxes and backgammon streets, carpets and kilims, coloured Oriental lamps and other old Damascene delights. More interesting and original souvenirs can be found here and further along Straight St in the direction of Bab ash-Sharqi, than can be found in Souq al-Hamidiyya. Drag yourself away from the great shopping to note the **Roman arch** (4; p92), evidence that this was the main street in Roman and Greek times.

Once you arrive at **Bab ash-Sharqi** (5; p86), turn left into Sharia Hanania and the **Christian Quarter** (6; p92). Yes, there are even more shops, but there are also some historic sites that are worth a look, including the courtyard of the fine old Beit Nassan. Turn left here, admiring this characterful residential street until you arrive at busy **Sharia Bab Touma** (7).

Cross the street, continuing until you get to the fork in the road. Take a left – noting **Elissar** (8; p105), the restaurant you'll want to return to for dinner, but continue along the winding street until you get to the restaurant **Old Town** (9; p105). You'll deserve your delicious mezze lunch and the best *mouhamarra* (red-pepper-and-walnut dip) in Syria in this splendid renovated old house.

After lunch return briefly to Straight St, then take a sharp right, and follow this street until you arrive at **Sharia al-Qaimariyya (10)**. This is one of the most lively intersections in the Old City, with a shwarma shop on one corner and a sweet shop on another, and numerous locals lining up for both! Backtrack for a coffee to perk you up, while watching young Damascenes mellowing out on nargileh, at the almost bohemian **Galerie Abdal** (11; p107) or **Moulaya** next door. Otherwise, save your caffeine fix for later and continue along one of the most charming lanes, lined with quaint stores and vines hanging over the street, in the whole of Damascus. At the end of Sharia al-Qaimariyya you'll find two of the most atmospheric old **coffeehouses** (12; p107). Stop at An-Nafura to get your caffeine fix, while being entertained by the dying art of the *kahawai* (storyteller) – see the boxed text Keeping the Story Going (p108). Take a left and follow the walls of **Umayyad Mosque** (13; p86), but save your visit to this exquisite building for another day when you aren't too tired to appreciate it (unless you're looking for some well-earned peace and tranquillity).

Otherwise, pass under the **old temple gateway (14)** stopping for the best ice cream in town at **Bekdach** (**15**; p107), and perhaps one last spot of shopping in the magnificent **Souq al-Hamidiyya** (**16**; p86).

COURSES
Language
Courses in Arabic are offered at the following centres.

British Council (Map p78; ☎ 333 0631; fax 332 1467; www.britishcouncil.org/syria; Sharia Karim al-Khalil, off Sharia Maysaloun; ☒ 9am-8pm Sun-Thu, 10am-5pm Sat) Offers regular and intensive courses in both Modern Standard Arabic (MSA) and Syrian Colloquial Arabic (SCA) at three different levels.

Damascus University (☎ 212 9864; Arabic Language Department, Faculty of Letters) Offers six Arabic courses in one academic year with each course lasting two months. Each class is five days a week, 3½ hours a day.

DAMASCUS FOR CHILDREN
While the family is of prime importance for all Middle Eastern destinations, children-specific activities are thin on the ground in Damascus. Unlike Beirut, the better restaurants in Damascus are not as accommodating for kids as one might expect, but the **Old Town** restaurant (p105), fares better than most. A must (for kids of all ages) is an ice-cream from **Bekdach** (p107) in Souq al-Hamidiyya. In the souqs, urban-dwelling youngsters should enjoy the shopping experience – especially seeing sweets sold off a cart.

Hotels with facilities suitable for children (including babysitting) are **Le Meridien Damas,** **Semiramis Hotel** and **Sheraton Damascus Hotel & Towers.** (See p103 for more details.)

Children will enjoy the garden area of the **National Museum** (p94), although the exhibits inside are not geared towards children. Boys and girls with a bent for the aeronautical will enjoy looking at the old propeller and jet-powered aircraft at the **Army Museum** (p96).

The rest of the time though, you'll find yourself explaining the significance of the sights, certainly enough to keep any adult busy!

TOURS
Really, the best way to see Damascus is on foot – perhaps with a taxi back to your lodgings after a long day's walk! The city is small enough to manage, if you follow the suggestions in the boxed text Damascus in… (p79), and the Walking Tour (p99).

If time is important, several travel agents in the area around the Cham Palace offer half-day and one-day excursions as far as Palmyra and Bosra. They operate mainly in spring and summer, and you're looking at around US$35 per person for the transport – if there is sufficient demand to fill a microbus. For day trips outside Damascus, see the Around Damascus chapter (p116) for information.

FESTIVALS & EVENTS
International Flower Show Held in Damascus every May.
Silk Road Festival Held in late September, it celebrates Syria's long cultural history with events held in Aleppo, Damascus and Palmyra.

GAY & LESBIAN DAMASCUS
Homosexuality is illegal in Syria and very much frowned upon in the general population. In fact, the public position is that homosexuality doesn't exist in Syria. Of course it's no less or more prevalent than anywhere else in the world. but Damascus is not the place to flaunt it.

That said, cruising amongst gay men does occur, notably in the souqs and in the area around Cham Palace, but as always in Middle Eastern countries, discretion is advised. There have been arrests for behaviour seen as being 'homosexual'. Overall though, the secret police are far more interested in people who are politically subversive, rather than those wishing to make a dent in Syria's 100% heterosexual statistics.

As a gay visitor to Damascus, your best option is to make some contacts before you arrive. The following websites are good places to start:

- www.globalgayz.com.com
- www.gaymiddleeast.com

For lesbian-specific information, a good website is www.bintelnas.org.

Damascus International Film Festival Held in November and December every odd-numbered year; it shows an eclectic range of films, including many pan-Arab productions. There's also a theatre festival.

SLEEPING

The good news is there's plenty of accommodation across all price brackets in Damascus. The not-so-good news is that there are no real sparkling gems in any of the price ranges. There are a number of relatively good hostels and hotels, but these places tend to fill up fast, especially in summer, and it's recommended that you book in advance.

Note that at the time of writing, lamentably there are no hotels in the Old City; most are concentrated in Central Damascus.

Where room rates are specified in US dollars, the hotel expects payment in same. Credit cards are not accepted unless otherwise stated.

Budget

HOTELS

With a couple of notable exceptions, the bulk of the cheap accommodation is to be found grouped around Al-Merjeh. This is a good place to be as it's central to the sights and there are plenty of cheap eating places around. But beware, some of the hotels double as brothels – at the time of writing, this is not the case with any of the places reviewed here.

In any case, the true travellers' ghetto lies in the Souq Saroujah district, centred on pretty Sharia Bahsa, a little lane north off Sharia Shoukri al-Quwatli. Here you'll find Al-Haramein and Ar-Rabie, Damascus' two popular backpacker institutions.

Hotels in this category generally do not have air-con, although there are exceptions (look for the air-con icon 🔀 in the following reviews). At other hotels, if you're lucky, you may be provided with a fan.

Balkiss Hotel (Map pp80-1; ☎ 222 2506; Al-Merjeh; s/d S£350/500; 🔀) Two blocks east of Al-Merjeh this hotel has reasonably clean rooms with private bathrooms, some with air-con. Those on the top floor are bright and well lit (but hot in summer). The clientele is predominantly Arab and Iranian.

Al-Haramein Hotel (Map pp80-1; ☎ 231 9489; fax 231 4299; Sharia Bahsa, Souq Saroujah; roof mattress S£100, dm/s/d/tr S£185/235/395/450) An old house off a picturesque alley, the rooms are basic

with no private bathrooms and there are only two toilets. There are however hot showers in the basement, and the covered central courtyard is a big plus. This place is *the* budget travellers' favourite in Damascus, so book in advance to secure a room.

Ar-Rabie Hotel (Map pp80-1; ☎ 231 8374; fax 231 1875; Sharia Bahsa, Souq Saroujah; roof mattress S£150, dm/s/d/tr with shared showers S£175/250/395/550, d/tr with shower S£600/675) Another big backpackers' fave – this one's an old house with a particularly attractive vine-trailed fountain courtyard in which to kick back after a day's sightseeing. There's an excellent atmosphere – a good place to meet fellow travellers – and if the rooms are a little basic they are at least clean.

Al-Rais (Map pp80-1; ☎ 221 4252; Sharia as-Sandjakdar; d with private bathroom S£500) One block east and south of Al-Merjeh, this one's very popular with visiting Arabs and little or no English is spoken. The basic rooms have recently benefited from a fresh paint job and some have also gained sparkling new private bathrooms.

Nijmet al-Shark (Map pp80-1; ☎ 222 9139; Al-Merjeh; s/d S£300/500) The best budget bet if the two Sharia Bahsa favourites are full, it has basic but clean rooms and most have immaculate private bathrooms. The location, right on the Al-Merjeh, is also excellent. Some rooms can be noisy (so check a couple out first) and there is not much English spoken.

CAMPING

Damascus Camping (Harasta Camping; ☎ 445 5870; per person S£300) for those really want to pitch a tent in an approved ground, facilities (a toilet, a shower and cooking equipment) are basic but clean. About 4km north of town on the road to Homs, but the distance from the city centre is a drag. To get here catch a Harasta microbus on the south side of Sharia Shoukri al-Quwatli, ie heading east.

Mid-Range

From budget to mid-range is a hefty leap in price, but some of the mid-range options do offer good value for money. Given the state of much of Damascus' bottom-end accommodation, this is one town where it may be worth spending more.

Afamia Hotel (Map pp80-1; ☎ 222 8963; fax 221 4683; Sharia Omar ben Abi Rabia; s/d US$21/28; 🔀) Behind the post office, it's a bit gloomy and impersonal, and the beds are on the narrow side, but rooms all have good new private bathrooms. It takes the overspill from the superior Sultan.

City Hotel (Map pp80-1; ☎ 221 9375; Sharia Omar ben Abi Rabia; s/d US$21/28; ✿) Also known as the Hotel al-Medina, it was in the process of a massive overhaul at the time of writing. However the completed 4th floor had excellent rooms kitted out with new carpets, bedding, satellite TV, and even hairdryers in the new private bathrooms. Manager Mohammed Bkirati spent 17 years in Boston and has the drawl to prove it. The hotel is just south of Shoukri al-Quwatli, 400m west of Al-Merjeh.

Al-Diwan (Map pp80-1; ☎ 231 8567; Sharia Souq Saroujah; s/d with breakfast US$24/28; ✿) Recently refitted, the rooms are immaculate – almost Scandinavian in their pristine white pine. All come with a gleaming private bathroom. There's also a pretty little breakfast room. Exceptional value. It's up on the 5th floor with a badly signed entrance beside the access to a large car park; not to be confused with the nearby Iwan.

French Tower Hotel (Map pp80-1; ☎ 231 4000; fax 231 4002; Sharia 29 Mai; s/d US$24/30; ✿) Just north of the tourist office, this one occupies the top floors of a modern apartment block. Rooms are clean, bright and frilly with modern private bathrooms. There's also a very nice breakfast terrace with views of northern Damascus and Jebel Qassioun. Excellent value.

Fursan Hotel (Map pp84-5; ☎ 542 1949; Sharia Bab Touma; s/d US$15/21; ✿) About as close as you can get to staying in the Old City – it's right across from Bab Touma, the northern gate into the Christian Quarter. While this makes it inconvenient for downtown Damascus, given the liveliness of the Bab Touma area it might not prove a problem. The place is aged but has some fine Art Deco detailing, period furniture and huge rooms with good private bathrooms. Another good-value hotel.

Al-Majed Hotel (Map pp80-1; ☎ 232 3300; www.al majed-group.com; s/d US$30/40; ✿) Just off Sharia 29 Mai, behind Cinema al-Ambassador, this modern multistorey block has comfortable spacious rooms all kitted out with fridge, satellite TV and spotlessly clean bathrooms. It's perhaps a touch utilitarian, but for the quality the price is hard to beat.

Orient Palace Hotel (Map pp80-1; ☎ 223 1351; fax 221 1512; Saahat Hejaz; s/d US$32/38; ✿) In a busy area across from the Hejaz train station, the Orient has been around since the 1920s, and depending on your level of enthusiasm it either retains plenty of period charm or resembles a gloomy 19th-century medical institution. Rooms are big, and although a bit fusty, they're clean and most have balconies.

Ramsis Hotel (Map pp80-1; ☎ 221 6702; Al-Merjeh; s/d US$17/23) Despite its winning location overlooking the main square, age has not lent charm to the rooms of this hotel, which are spartan and well worn, although they're kept clean.

As-Salaam Hotel (Map pp80-1; ☎ 221 6674; fax 221 5031; Sharia ibn Sina; s/d US$22/29; ✿) In a quiet location, south of Takiyya as-Süleimaniyya and the National Museum, it's extremely clean and all rooms come with private bathroom and fridge. Recommended.

Sultan Hotel (Map pp80-1; ☎ 222 5768; fax 224 0372; Sharia Mousalam al-Baroudi; s/d US$21/28; ✿) Just west of the Hejaz train station, this is the most popular mid-range hotel with Western travellers. Some of the rooms are shabby (although most have air-con and private bathrooms) but if you're the kind of traveller who spends a lot of time at the front desk asking questions, the multilingual staff generally have the answers. There's a small library of books to borrow, a guests' notice board and a reception/breakfast (US$3) area with satellite TV.

Top End

At the time of writing, Damascus had nothing as charming as the boutique hotels of Aleppo, but there are persistent rumours that something similar is in the pipeline for the Old City. A grand new Four Seasons hotel is also under construction in the city centre. Prices below do not include taxes, which add another 10%.

Cham Palace (Map pp80-1; ☎ 223 2300; www.cham hotels.com; Sharia Maysaloun; s US$150-210, d US$160- 240; ✿ ▣ ▨) One of the better hotels in the national chain and the most conveniently located of the large five-star places: just one block west of Saahat Yousef al-Azmeh, right in the middle of the new city centre. It has a wonderful lobby – worth a look even if you're not staying – but many of the 400 rooms are small and it's worth checking a couple out before setting your bags down. Major credit cards accepted and it also has an ATM.

THE AUTHOR'S CHOICE

Omayad Hotel (Map pp80-1; ☎ 221 7700; www.omayadhotel.net; 1 Sharia Brazil; s US$86-91, d US$100-105; ❄) One of the city's elder hotels that comes complete with a lovely Art Deco lobby, a characterful bar, several restaurants, and wine and cheese nights. The rooftop restaurant-bar has stunning views of the city and mountains – splendid on a starry night! You may be lucky enough to be there while there's a wedding on and have the opportunity to join in on the celebrations. The hotel's 80 large rooms have been refurbished and modernised to four-star standard and are very comfortable. The location is also excellent (right around the corner from Cham Palace). Major credit cards accepted.

Le Meridien Damas (Map p78; ☎ 373 8730; www .lemeridien.com; Sharia Shoukri al-Quwatli; s US$205-220, d US$240-260; ❄ 🖥 🍸) About 10 to 15 minutes' walk west of the city centre, this is a standard 350-room five-star place. But it at least has a reasonable locale with plenty of surrounding greenery, plus all the usual amenities, including a shopping mall, business centre, pools, health club and tennis courts. Major credit cards accepted.

Omayad Hotel (Map pp80-1; ☎ 221 7700; www .omayadhotel.net; 1 Sharia Brazil; s US$86-91, d US$100-105; ❄) This is one of our favourites. Read the boxed text The Author's Choice (above) to find out why.

Semiramis Hotel (Map pp80-1; ☎ 223 3555; www .semiramis-hotel.com; Sharia Shoukri al-Quwatli, Victoria Bridge; s US$110-150, d US$130-170; ❄ 🍸) A modestly sized five-star hotel with a decent central location (but with no views to speak of). It has indoor and outdoor pools and a gym, plus an extremely good Chinese restaurant and a lively nightclub that regularly features Arab singers. Major credit cards accepted.

Sheraton Damascus Hotel & Towers (Map p78; ☎ 373 4630; www.starwood.com; Saahat Umawiyeen; s US$175-260 d US$205-310; ❄ 🖥 🍸) A 300-room complex at the western end of Sharia Shoukri al-Quwatli, 2km from the centre. Near to nowhere, and sandwiched between major highways, it's a terrible location unless you have your own transport. Numerous restaurants, bars, the full array of amenities

and great service go some way to making up for this inconvenience.

EATING

Generally speaking, the cheapest restaurants are all around Al-Merjeh. A variety of slightly more expensive options are scattered throughout the city centre, mostly within a few minutes walk of Saahat Yousef al-Azmeh, with almost all of the top-end places in the Old City.

Restaurants

Most Damascus restaurants, unless otherwise stated, open around 11am for lunch and serve through until well after midnight – usually until the last diners are ready to leave, which can be 2am or even 3am. Remember, locals dine late and most places don't get busy until 10pm or later. Reservations are rarely necessary, except where noted.

OLD CITY

It's only as recently as the 1990s that the first restaurants opened in the Old City. Now there are at least a dozen fine-dining options, most of them in the Christian Quarter, with more opening all the time.

Abu al-Azz (Map p110; ☎ 221 8174; just north of Souq al-Hamidiyya; buffet dinner per person S£400; ⊙ 9am-late) Although it's a tourist trap, this place is fun all the same. A narrow staircase off a busy covered lane leads up to two floors of an Oriental-themed restaurant, complete with pantomime trappings. Food is the standard mezze and kebabs, served buffet style in the evening, or à la carte during the day. From about 9pm there's entertainment in the form of whirling dervishes and musicians. Watch out for overcharging. No alcohol is served.

Arabesque (Map pp84-5; ☎ 543 3999; Sharia al-Kineesa, Christian Quarter; mains S£250-400; ⊙ noon-midnight) A stylish take on the Old Damascene dining experience, Arabesque is semiformal and the food is continental European (excellent steaks in sauces). Quality is superb and there's a decent selection of local wine. No credit cards accepted.

Casablanca (Map pp84-5; ☎ 541 7598; Sharia Hanania, Christian Quarter; mains from S£350; ⊙ noon-late) Near Bab Sharqi, this place is up at the top end of the market, specialising in French cuisine, with a menu inclined heavily towards steak in sauces, and seafood. The food is excellent and there's live music in the evenings; alcohol is served and major credit cards are accepted.

Elissar (Map pp84–5; ☎ 542 4300; Sharia ad-Dawamneh, Bab Touma, Christian Quarter; dinner for 2 people S£800; ☾ 12.30pm-late) Another one of our favourite restaurants. Read the boxed text to find out why.

Al-Khawali (Map p110; Sharia Bab Touma; mains from S£300; ☾ noon-2am) Off Straight St, this beautiful refurbishment of an old Damascene house serves typical Arabic cuisine with some Syrian specialities. The food is good and the different dining rooms are quite beautiful.

Old Town (Map pp84–5; ☎ 542 8088; off Sharia Bab Sharqi, Christian Quarter; pasta around S£125, local beer S£65; ☾ 1pm-late) This was one of the pioneer Old City courtyard restaurants and it set the formula. It's more relaxed than most, with an Arabic, French and Italian menu. No credit cards.

Oxygen (Map pp84–5; ☎ 544 4396; Sharia Bab Touma, Christian Quarter; dishes S£200-300; ☾ noon-2am) Aimed at the hip and youthful, it features a prominent bar area, big-screen MTV and over-the-top décor, including a stage-set statue of the Damascene god Hadad. There was no menu when we visited, but the dishes coming out of the kitchen were Continental European eg meat fillets and pasta.

Umayyad Palace Restaurant (Map pp84–5; ☎ 222 0826; fax 224 8901; 22 Sharia al-Masbagha al-Khader; buffet lunch/dinner per person S£350/600; ☾ noon-2am) Halfway down a tight squeeze of an alley, south of Umayyad Mosque, is this cavernous basement restaurant kitted out like Ali Baba's cave with baubles and trinkets, kilim-covered benches, dazzling mother-of-pearl inlaid furniture and hanging greenery. Evening dining is recommended for the entertainment, which includes whirling dervishes (at 9pm), acrobats and musicians. Huge fun, but no alcohol.

CENTRAL DAMASCUS Map pp80–1
The cheaper restaurants are in the Al-Merjeh area, but quality improves as you move north.

Al-Arabi (Al-Merjeh; meals around S£250) Situated on a pedestrianised street off the southwestern corner of Al-Merjeh, Al-Arabi is the name of two adjacent cheap restaurants, both run by the same management and sharing the same extensive menu with an unusually wide range of meat and vegetable

dishes. The food is hit and miss and there are no prices given. Staff act a little offhand but if you can get a table out on the pavement it's worth it.

Damascus Workers' Club (An-Nadi al-Umal; meals S£150-200; ☾ 5pm-midnight Sat-Thu) Hidden behind a modest door in a wall opposite the Majed Hotel, off Sharia 29 Mai and behind Cinema al-Ambassador, is an unexpected delight amid the concrete drabness of the city centre. This garden restaurant in the sprawling courtyard of an old house, complete with fountain and plenty of greenery. The food is standard fare, such as mezze and kebabs, but it's reasonably well prepared and cheap. Beer is served.

Al-Kamal (☎ 222 1494; Sharia 29 Mai; meals S£100-150; ☾ 11am-midnight) Located next to the main tourist office, it resembles a Parisian bistro with its air of busy efficiency, regular clientele (including a smattering of elderly madams) and good-value *plats du jour*. The menu features many home-style dishes, such as mixed-vegetable stews, but the best are on the changing daily menu – try the *kabsa* (spiced rice with chicken or lamb). No alcohol served.

Laterna (☎ 232 3185; Najet Kassab Hassan, off Sharia 29 Mai; dishes S£200-400; ☾ 9-1am) Somebody has spent a fortune on this place and it shows in its sinuous playful décor inspired by Dali, with furniture made to match, and a glass floor with goldfish swimming beneath. Food is less exciting – pasta, steak and chicken dishes. Alcohol is served; major credit cards are accepted.

Al-Sehhi (☎ 221 1555; Sharia al-Abed, off Sharia 29 Mai; dishes around S£70; ⏱ noon-midnight) A modest family restaurant that confines itself to the basics – mezze, grilled meats, and very good *fatta* (an oven-baked dish of chickpeas, minced meat or chicken, and bread soaked in tahini; S£70). It's clean and efficient with a separate 'family area' for women diners and a menu in English and Arabic. No alcohol.

ABU ROUMANA   Map p78

The most moneyed part of the city has some of the most-Westernised places to eat. A bunch of cafés, pizza parlours and boutique restaurants is grouped around what's known as 'Restaurant Square', which is just 200m west of the top end of Sharia al-Jalaa. Of these, we list just one: find it and you've found the rest. As a visitor you're likely to find the eateries lacking in atmosphere and a little pretentious. Still, if you want to see how the other half of Damascus lives, here's where.

Café Vendome (☎ 333 3137; Sharia Abdul Malek; ⏱ 8.30-1am) This glass-fronted café faces the square, with a bar and a restaurant deeper inside. It's loud and lively, with music TV and a menu that kicks off with club sandwich and salad lunches and soars up to steak and seafood. A steak sandwich and juice is approx S£200; Amex, MasterCard and Visa are accepted.

Quick Eats
OLD CITY

The best bet is the small alley east of Umayyad Mosque; east of the two coffeehouses are a couple of very good **shwarma stalls** (Map pp84–5) and a **felafel stall** (Map pp84–5) that does a truly fat felafel with salad for S£25 – probably the best value in town. There's another collection of hole-in-the-wall **shwarma and felafel places** (Map p110) in the covered market lane that runs north off Souq al-Hamidiyya, just before you reach the mosque. At the end of this lane turn left and you'll come to two extremely popular local places, **Shwarma Majed** (Map p110) and **Castello Fast Food**, (Map p110) for Western-style hamburgers and hot dogs.

Beit Jabri (☎ 544 3200; www.jabrihouse.com; 14 Sharia as-Sawwaf; meals per person less than S£150; ⏱ 9.30-12.30am) This an historic Damascene house (see Old Damascene Houses, p92) with a large courtyard that serves as a café. There's an extensive snack menu beginning with breakfast and progressing through mezze to mains, such as *fatta*, kebab, *shish tawouq* (marinated chicken grilled on skewers). There are also fresh juices and nargileh. The place is hugely popular with locals, and very female friendly. It accepts Amex, Diners, MasterCard and Visa.

CENTRAL DAMASCUS   Map pp80–1

The side streets off Al-Merjeh are crowded with cheap eateries, mostly offering the staples of shwarma and felafel, while some pastry shops also do some good savouries (see Self-Catering, opposite). There are also a couple of good cheap juice places right on the square. Fresh juices cost between S£35 and S£50.

If you are staying in the vicinity of the post office, then **Al-Santir** is a good little toasted-sandwich and juice bar that's handy for breakfast when you're sick of boiled eggs, bread and jam.

Al-Masri (Sharia Said al-Jabri; dishes from S£65; ⏱ 7.30am-5pm) An excellent, cheap lunch place heavily patronised by local office workers. The name means 'the Egyptian' and much of the menu (which is in English, with prices) is the kind of home-cooked fare you'd find in the backstreet eateries of Cairo, including no-frill dishes, such as *shakshouka* (fried egg and mince meat), *foul* (mashed fava beans, garlic and lemon) and a variety of *fatta*.

Gemini (☎ 333 7095; Sharia al-Amar Izzedin al-Jazzari; meals per person S£300-500; ⏱ noon-2am) Off Sharia Maysaloun, this is about the hippest eatery in town. It's very popular with moneyed Damascenes, who reserve the tables by the windows. The menu is Continental European (chicken, steak and seafood), plus some lighter lunch fare. Extremely popular for weekend lunches and late dinners, so make a booking. Alcohol is served; MasterCard and Visa are accepted.

Pit Stop Café (☎ 333 7095; Sharia al-Amar Izzedin al-Jazzari, off Sharia Maysaloun; crepes S£120; ⏱ 8-2am; ✪) A bright, lively and modern snack joint below the Gemini restaurant, serving sandwiches, crepes and other quick eats, as well as milk shakes and ice creams. The Pit

Stop is a good place in which to cool off on a hot afternoon.

Pizza Roma (3 Sharia Odai bin ar-Roqaa; pizza around S£100; ☺ 11am-late) Off Sharia Maysaloun, west of Cham Palace, and run by a guy who used to work for Pizza Hut in Abu Dhabi. He has adapted the idea and this takeaway or eat-in joint does an acceptable American-style deep-pan pizza. There are also spaghetti dishes, lasagne and burgers.

Station One (☎ 333 4575; Sharia Maysaloun; ☺ 1pm-1am) An informal snacking place that resembles a Syrian take on the American diner. It's a popular hang-out with Westernised youth. Expect the likes of good salads, shwarma and chicken. Prices are reasonable and there's no alcohol.

Self-Catering

For the do-it-yourself crowd, there is a good **fruit and vegetable market** (Map pp80–1) wedged between Al-Merjeh and Sharia Shoukri al-Quwatli. There is also another one on Sharia al-Amin in the Old City (Map pp84–5). For things like milk and cheese, there's a decent grocery store, **Ash-Sha'ar** (Map pp80–1), next to the coffeehouses, just off the eastern side of Al-Merjeh. For hot freshly baked bread, go to the hole-in-the-wall bakeries at the northern end of Sharia Bahsa, just north of Al-Haramein and Ar-Rabie Hotels in the Souq Saroujah area.

Of the many pastry shops on the southern side of Al-Merjeh, one of the best is **Abu Rashid** (Map pp80–1), down the alley at the southeastern corner of the square and up at the top of the steps. It also does savouries like *kibbeh* (meat-filled cracked wheat croquettes), cheese or meat borek (filled pastries) and something called *ouzi sarrar*, which is a bit like a big, round samosa – rice, meat, peas and spices in a pastry ball.

Bekdach (Map p110; Souq al-Hamidiyya) is the purveyor of extraordinary ice creams made with sahlab (like semolina powder), and makes a great dessert stop. The ice creams are gooey and elastic; a takeaway cone with a topping of crushed pistachio nuts is S£25.

DRINKING
Coffeehouses & Cafés

OLD CITY   Map pp84–5

Galerie Abdal (☎ 544 5794; Sharia Shaweesh; ☺ 9.30-12.30am) A Western-style café, albeit set in the thoroughly 'Eastern' surrounds of an old Damascus house, with a bustling arty, student air. It's loud and gossipy, and very female-friendly. **Moulaya**, next door, is another funky place that's popular with locals.

Narcissus (☎ 543 1205; Sharia al-Amin; ☺ 10am-late) Full of hip young groups smoking nargileh and eating Arabic food (the menu is the on the wall). Narcissus is another beautiful old house with a wooden sign outside that reads 'coffeehouse'.

Beit Jabri (☎ 544 3200; www.jabrihouse.com; 14 Sharia as-Sawwaf; ☺ 9.30-12.30am) Also doubles as a café (p106), with plenty of locals dropping by for tea, coffee, juice and nargileh.

The most atmospheric place to relax in Damascus is at either of the two coffeehouses nestled in the shadow of the Umayyad Mosque's eastern wall. **Ash-Shams**, on the north side of the street, occupies a former hammam, which makes for an excellent setting for a coffee and nargileh – although it's much more entertaining to sit outside and watch the activity in the street. Unfortunately, there have been complaints of over charging. No such complaints at **An-Nafura** (The Fountain; Map pp84–5), on the southern side of the street, and by far the older of the two. At 7pm each evening the local *hakawati* (professional storyteller) takes up the chair inside. His performance is all in Arabic but it's still worth catching for the accompanying dramatic flourishes and the novelty of witnessing one of the last few practitioners of an art form that was once such a vital part of popular Middle Eastern culture – see the boxed text Keeping the Story Going (p108).

CENTRAL DAMASCUS   Map pp80–1

In Central Damascus, there are a couple of coffeehouses on one of the side streets leading east off Al-Merjeh, although they are not particularly friendly places. Better is **Al-Hejazi al-Jedid** (Sharia an-Nasr), a big, open-air coffeehouse near the Hejaz train station. Just north of the Cham Palace, **Ar-Rawda** (Sharia Majlis an-Nyabi) is a large, modern coffeehouse that is noisy with the staccato clacking of slammed dominoes and backgammon counters. Chess is also played here. Nargileh is a little more expensive than normal at S£80, but tea and coffee are the standard S£25.

One place particularly popular with travellers is the rooftop coffeehouse **Ash-Sharq al-Awsat**, just north of Al-Merjeh and next to

KEEPING THE STORY GOING

In one of the tales in The Thousand and One Nights, a king commissions a merchant to seek out the most marvellous story ever. The merchant sends out his slaves on the quest and at last success is achieved – a slave hears a suitably wondrous story told in Damascus by an old man who tells stories every day, seated on his storyteller's throne.

Jump forward several hundred years or so from the time in which the tales were set, and here in Damascus today there is still an old man who tells stories every day, seated on his version of a storyteller's throne. His name is Abu Shady and he's the last of the Syrian hakawati (professional storytellers).

Enjoying a fairly low status (on a par with quack doctors, astrologers and charm sellers), hakawati were a common feature of Middle Eastern city street life as far back as the 12th century. With the spread of coffee-drinking during Ottoman times, the storytellers moved off the street and into the coffeehouse.

He recites walking to and fro in the middle of the coffee room, stopping only now and then, when the expression requires some emphatical attitude… Not unfrequently in the midst of some interesting adventure…he breaks off abruptly and makes his escape…the auditors suspending their curiosity are induced to return at the same time next day to hear the sequel.

Alexander Russell, The Natural History of Aleppo, 1794

As with so many Arab traditions, the art of public storytelling has largely failed to survive the 20th century, supplanted in the coffeehouses first by radio, then by television. According to Abu Shady, the last professional storyteller in Syria went into retirement in the 1970s. Abu Shady, who as a boy was a frequent member of the audience in coffeehouses, decided to revive the profession in 1990. Since then he's been appearing nightly, at one of the fine old coffeehouses in the lee of Umayyad Mosque. Costumed in baggy trousers and waistcoat, with a moustache like that of Groucho Marx and a fez on his head, he recounts nightly from his volumes of handwritten tales. These include the legendary exploits of Sultan Beybars or Antar ibn Shadad, both Islamic heroes and – as Abu Shady tells it – regular doers of fantastic feats, sorcery and cunning roguery.

The assembled listeners know the historical facts (they were learnt at school), but it's the way Abu Shady tells it, interjecting jokes and comments, working the audience, punctuating the words with waves of his sword, smashing it down on a copper-top table for startling emphasis. The audience responds with oohs and aahs, cheering and interjecting comments of their own. Sadly, the numbers present are small. Abu Shady says that nobody has the time any more to listen to stories. He believes that there's no future for a hakawati and that when he stops telling his stories, it will finally bring to a close the era of the storyteller.

the blue-tiled Iranian cultural centre on the corner by the Shoukri al-Quwatli flyover. **Café Havana** (Sharia Bur Said) has something of a history as a haunt for coup planners and other plotters in the days before former president Hafez al-Assad got a firm grip on the country.

Bars

While there's no shortage of restaurants serving alcohol, there are few dedicated bars. This is a situation however that's changing rapidly, especially in the Old City's Bab Touma area, which is currently nightlife central for Damascus. In the hippest of nightspots (a short list that includes Marmar and Underground), things don't really kick

off until around midnight. Thursday and Saturday are the big nights.

OLD CITY   Map pp84–1

No alcohol is served in the Muslim neighbourhoods of the Old City, so all the action focuses on the Christian Quarter.

Bar Saloon (148 Sharia Bab Sharqi; ☾ noon-10pm Mon-Sat) This is a liquor store-cum-bar graced by a topless pin-up and frequented by a regular bunch of elderly reprobates, usually half cut on arak and engaged in heated, slightly slurred debate. Visitors will initially feel they've encroached on some private old bohos' club but it's less exclusive than first appearances suggest and the beer's cheap.

The rest of the quarter's bars are a very different proposition, catering primarily to the city's well-off youth.

Piano Bar (Sharia Hanania, Bab Sharqi; local beer S£140; ☾ noon-midnight) A mainstay of the Damascus scene, it's a little uptight and pricey but it's worth dropping in for the spectacle of a Syrian karaoke night.

Oxygen (☎ 544 4396; Sharia Bab Touma; ☾ noon-2am) Another popular and fashionable drinking venue (see p105).

CENTRAL DAMASCUS   **Map pp80–1**
Karnak (Al-Merjeh; ☾ 11am-late) Conveniently near most of the budget accommodation off the main square, above Hotel Siyaha. It's a real booze hole populated by regulars knocking back beer or arak until two in the morning. You wouldn't bring your mother here.

Damascus Workers' Club (An-Nadi al-Umal; beer S£60; ☾ 5pm-midnight Sat-Thu) Although it serves food (see Eating, p105), it is equally okay with patrons who choose only to drink.

Al-Mahatta (The Station; behind Hejaz train station; beer S£100) Two ancient carriages with gorgeous period interiors have been pressed into service as this strange little bar-café. The café part is accommodated under awnings stretched beside the carriages, while the hard stuff is served inside in dimly lit, polished and lacquered surrounds. Notions of glamour are dispelled by fellow drinkers, who tend toward heavily made-up tarts and dodgy-looking blokes. Delightfully seedy but not altogether comfortable.

GREATER DAMASCUS
There are several bars located north of the city centre.

Artists' Syndicate Bar (Map p97; Sallat ar-Rawak al-Arabi; Sharia at-Tantawi; ☾ 5pm-midnight) Up toward the Salihiyye district, this is another open-air garden bar-restaurant in residential surrounds; out of the way, perhaps, but worth knowing about if you're in the area.

Some of the restaurants in the Abu Roumana neighbourhood, such as **Café Vendome** (p106) and **Gemini** (p106) include bars, but for serious late-night action locals head for **Underground** (right).

Liquor Stores
CENTRAL DAMASCUS Map pp80–1
Takeaway beer and arak are available from **Elias Hayek** (Sharia Ramy; ☾ 10am-8pm Sat-Thu)

a liquor store on one of the side streets running south off Al-Merjeh. There is another liquor store on Sharia Omar ben Abi Rabia.

ENTERTAINMENT
Cinemas
Cinema de Cham (Map pp80–1; Cham Palace hotel; Sharia Maysaloun; tickets S£150) The only cinema to screen English-language films. The programming is restricted to carefully selected Hollywood blockbusters, usually well out of date. To find out what's showing, drop by the cinema.

Nightclubs
Marmar (Map pp84-5; ☎ 544 6425; Sharia Dawamneh, Bab Touma; ☾ noon-late) The happening Old City night spot. Tucked down a tiny passageway signed by a neon squiggle, it's basically an old house kitted out with a pub-like serving area, a few tables, a DJ booth and room to dance. Come the weekend, it's pounding with a heaving, sweaty, foxy young crowd.

Underground (Map p78; Sharia al-Amar Izzedin al-Jazzari, off Sharia Maysaloun; ☾ late until very late) A new purpose-built club venue beneath the Pit Stop Café/Gemini restaurant. Seriously fashionable, frighteningly pricey.

Theatre & Music
The **National Theatre** (Map p78; Saahat Umawiyeen) is at the western end of Sharia Shoukri al-Quwatli, and north of the tourist office is the large **Al-Qabbani theatre** (Map pp80–1; Sharia 29 Mai). Not a lot goes on at either but you can ask at the tourist office for details of what's on. Otherwise, some of the cultural centres, particularly the French, have fairly active programmes of events and performances – for contact details see Cultural Centres p82. The **Centre Culturel Français** (see p82) sponsors performances by local musicians – check its notice board for details.

Traditional Dance
Abu al-Azz (Map p110) and **Umayyad Palace Restaurant** (p105) in the Old City include a floorshow as part of the package. The Umayyad Palace Restaurant features whirling dervishes and musicians, plus a troupe of singers, sword fighters, and human-pyramid builders (with the restaurant dwarf as the top of the pyramid).

SHOPPING

The best and most obvious place to shop in Damascus is at its extensive souq (see below), which spreads through much of the northwestern quarter of the Old City. The stores and emporiums then continue east along **Straight St**, which is lined with small family-run businesses that tend to specialise in one particular type of product, such as copperware, handmade furniture, carpets, even sword-making – although sadly the long tradition of Damascene steel is now reduced to one or two practitioners making ceremonial pieces. The selection of goods tends to be better in these places than at the emporiums in the souq, and prices are certainly keener. There's more of the same in the Christian Quarter, particularly around **Sharia Hanania**, which is the well-trodden tourist route up to the Chapel of Ananias.

For gift grazing in Central Damascus, visit what the tourist office calls **Handicrafts Lane**, a small stone alleyway that's part of the Takiyya as-Süleimaniyya complex, just south of Sharia Shoukri al-Quwatli. Off the lane is a Turkish madrassa, **Artisanat**, where the former student cells are now occupied by craftspeople engaged in weaving, marquetry and painting. The whole complex, small though it is and limited in choice, is lovely and it is certainly worth a look.

For nontourist-oriented shopping, the main commercial area is just north of Cham Palace, and centred on **Sharia al-Hamra** and

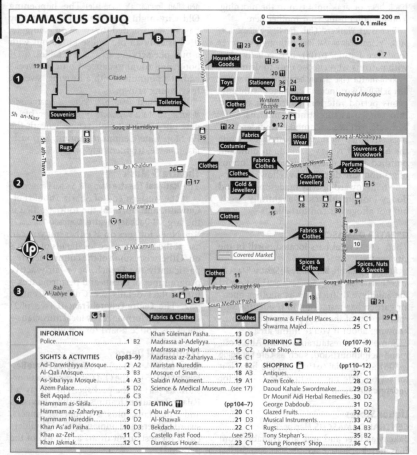

DAMASCUS SOUQ

0 — 200 m
0 — 0.1 miles

INFORMATION		
Police	1	B2

SIGHTS & ACTIVITIES	(pp83–9)	
Ad-Darwishiyya Mosque	2	A2
Al-Qali Mosque	3	B3
As-Siba'iyya Mosque	4	A3
Azem Palace	5	D2
Beit Aqqad	6	C3
Hammam as-Silsila	7	D1
Hammam az-Zahariyya	8	C1
Hammam Nureddin	9	D2
Khan As'ad Pasha	10	D3
Khan az-Zeit	11	C3
Khan Jakmak	12	C1

Khan Süleiman Pasha	13	D3
Madrassa al-Adeliyya	14	C1
Madrassa an-Nuri	15	C2
Madrassa az-Zahariyya	16	C1
Maristan Nureddin	17	B2
Mosque of Sinan	18	A3
Saladin Monument	19	A1
Science & Medical Museum	(see 17)	

EATING	(pp104–7)	
Abu al-Azz	20	C1
Al-Khawali	21	D3
Bekdach	22	C1
Castello Fast Food	(see 25)	
Damascus House	23	C1

Shwarma & Felafel Places	24	C1
Shwarma Majed	25	C1

DRINKING	(pp107–9)	
Juice Shop	26	B2

SHOPPING	(pp110–12)	
Antiques	27	C1
Azem Ecole	28	C2
Daoud Kahale Swordmaker	29	D3
Dr Mounif Aidi Herbal Remedies	30	D2
George Dabdoub	31	D2
Glazed Fruits	32	D2
Musical Instruments	33	A2
Rugs	34	B3
Tony Stephan's	35	B2
Young Pioneers' Shop	36	C1

Map labels: Souq al-Asrouniyya, Household Goods, Toys, Stationery, Qurans, Umayyad Mosque, Clothes, Western Temple Gate, Toiletries, Souvenirs, Citadel, Sh an-Nasr, Souq al-Hamidiyya, Fabrics, Costumier, Bridal Wear, Souq al-Abbabiyya, Rugs, Sh ath-Thawra, Sh ibn Khaldun, Clothes, Fabrics & Clothes, Souvenirs & Woodwork, Perfume & Gold, Clothes, Gold & Jewellery, Souq an-Niswan, Costume Jewellery, Sh Mu'awiyya, Clothes, Souq al-Bzouriyya, Sh al-Ma'amun, Covered Market, Fabrics & Clothes, Bab Al-Jabiye, Clothes, Clothes, Spices & Coffee, Spices, Nuts & Sweets, Sh Medhat Pasha (Straight St), Souq al-Attarine, Souq Medhat Pasha, Fabrics & Clothes, Clothes the pedestrianised **Sharia Salihiyya**. These two virtually parallel streets are full of mostly clothes shops, with everything from veil specialists to the likes of Benetton.

For information on shopping around in Syrian souqs, see the boxed text The Art of Bargaining, p372.

Antiques

Dahdah Palace (Map pp84-5; 9 Sharia ash-Shalla; ☽ 9am-1pm & 4-6pm) Has a room full of 'finds' including coins, figurines and tiles recovered from demolished Damascene houses, although beware, it pays to do some groundwork before buying that bargain of a lifetime. For more on the Dahdah Palace, see Old Damascene Houses, p91.

Carpets & Rugs

At the western end of Souq al-Hamidiyya there's a grouping of rug and carpet traders but give them a miss and instead concentrate on the eastern end of Straight St, just beyond the Roman arch. There are several shops in the area with good selections, including **Bel Oriental Carpets** (Map pp84-5) and **George Dabdoub** (Map p110).

Cloth, Textiles & Garments

For all this kind of thing, focus any searches on Sharia Medhat Pasha (the western end of Straight St), Souq al-Khayyatin, and the Bab Sharqi area (the very eastern end of Straight St). **Azem Ecole** (see below) has what it claims is the last working silk loom in Damascus, the products of which are sold in-house (tragically, largely in the form of that most traditional of Damascene apparel, the tie). Several stores on the same street sell black-and-white *keffiyeh* (chequered scarves).

Handicrafts Lane in Central Damascus is a good source of embroidered clothing made by Palestinians living in refugee camps in Syria.

Crafts & Handicrafts

In Souq al-Hamidiyya (Map p110) initial prices in the souvenir-craft shops can be ridiculous, but it is a good place to at least check out what's on offer. One exception is **Tony Stephan's** at No 156. It stocks a variety of merchandise from textiles through inlaid woodwork and jewellery, to copper and brassware, and while the prices are certainly not bargain basement, the quality is unsurpassed. **Azem Ecole** (☎ 221 3208) is a gorgeous sales space in a former madrassa, with some beautiful items including Bedouin jewellery and silk products that are hand-woven on site. Prices, however, are high and the selection limited.

George Dabdoub, on the small square in front of the entrance to Azem Palace, sells

---

SHOPPING THE DAMASCUS SOUQ

The Damascus souq (Map p110) is not as strictly ordered as its Aleppo counterpart, with few areas devoted strictly to a single type of goods. The main covered market, **Souq al-Hamidiyya**, starts with glitzy souvenir shops and ends with prayer beads and Qurans. In between, the majority of stores sell clothing of some description, typically poor quality, if not outright trash. But trashy can be fun – there are dress shops to make a drag queen swoon, while some of the lingerie has to be seen to be believed.

Alleyways to the north are more routinely domestic – toiletries, household items, toys, school books and stationery. South is more colourful, particularly narrow, sloping **Souq Khayyatin** (Tailors' Souq), filled with cubbyhole traders dealing in bolts of fine cloth and richly coloured garments, from the practical (scarves and pants) to the peacock (belly-dancing outfits and wedding dresses).

The most aromatic and enchanting passage is **Souq al-Bzouriyya** (Seed Bazaar), which is the covered area running south from Umayyad Mosque. This mixes jewellery with perfumes, spices, nuts and sweets, all illuminated in the evening by glowing chandeliers. It's an alluring place in which to linger and examine little curiosities, such as the glazed-fruit shop and, just around the corner, Dr Mounif Aidi's herbal remedies. Al-Bzouriyya gives way to **Souq al-Attarine**, actually a stretch of Sharia Medhat Pasha (Straight St), which is devoted to spices and coffee.

Shops in the souq start to close at around 6pm, and by 7pm nearly all the shutters are down. Most of the souq stays closed all day Friday, although the shops and businesses in the Christian Quarter close on Sunday instead.

jewellery, brass, icons, brocade and carpets. The courteous manner of its staff and the fair prices make it a good place to shop.

For brass work, about the best selection we encountered was at **At-Trabulsi** (Map pp84-5; 175 Straight St).

For those attractive inlaid boxes, chests and backgammon boards, pay a visit to **Khalil Haddad** (Map pp84-5; 115 Sharia Bab Sharqi; 10am-8pm Mon-Sat), who fronts the actual workshop in which this exquisite work is produced. There are also many other workshops along Sharia Bab Sharqi and the surrounding streets with similar quality handicrafts.

Music

CDS & CASSETTES

Abdel Razek Mousali (Map pp80-1; Sharia Bur Said) Just south of Saahat Yousef al-Azmeh in the city centre, and specialises in the giants of the Arab world: artists such as Umm Kolthum, Fairouz, Farid al-Atrache and Abdel Halim Hafez. The selection is extensive and if what you're looking for is not on the shelves you will probably find it in the back catalogue stored away in drawers. Prices are cheap at S£300 for most CDs, or S£60 for cassettes.

A & E Records (Map pp80-1; Sharia Muradi), just off Maysaloun opposite Cham Palace, has recordings of contemporary Arab world music and a limited selection of tapes of Western artists.

MUSICAL INSTRUMENTS

If you are at all interested in Arabic music, or a musician yourself, you might be keen to visit the small workshop of an **oud maker**, the oud (flute) being the most popular instrument in the Middle East. In a small, open-fronted space on Sharia Bahsa in Souq Saroujah, he finishes and strings the shells, which are produced in another small, nearby workshop. Less well-made models sell for around S£1500, while finer examples go for between S£4000 and S£5000. Ouds are also sold at the **musical instruments shop** (Map pp80-1; opposite People's Assembly Bldg) in the city centre, and at a few overpriced places along Souq al-Hamidiyya. The oud is a difficult instrument to master and Western-trained musicians may find the different styles of tuning and playing it a little bewildering at first.

GETTING THERE & AWAY

See Getting There & Away in the Transport chapter (p380) for information on transport options between Damascus and the rest of the country.

Air

There are several **SyrianAir** (central sales & reservations 223 2154, 223 2159, 222 9000) offices scattered about the city centre including on Sharia Fardous (Map pp80-1) on Sharia Said al-Jabri across from the Hejaz train station (Map pp80-1), and up on Saahat Maghrebiyya (Map p78).

From Damascus, SyrianAir flies several times daily to and from Aleppo (S£900, one hour), three times weekly to Deir ez-Zur (S£742, one hour), three times weekly to Qamishle (S£1200, 80 minutes), and twice a week to Lattakia (S£532, 45 minutes). Return fares are exactly double the single fare.

For a list of the main carriers that fly in and out of Damascus see Airports & Airlines, p380. The telephone numbers for Damascus international airport are 543 0201/9.

AIRLINE OFFICES

You'll find almost all of the airline offices in the Mohandiseen Building, opposite Cham Palace on Sharia Maysaloun, or on Sharia Fardous, one block to the south. Working hours are typically 9am to 5pm Sunday to Thursday, closed Friday.

Bus

There are two main bus stations in Damascus. **Harasta terminal** (Karajat Harasta)

ARRIVING IN DAMASCUS BY AIR

The **Damascus international airport** (543 0201/9) is 26km southeast of the city centre, and a taxi to the city costs S£500, (S£300 if you walk to the main road). The airport bus brings new arrivals into Baramke terminal, the bus station 1.5km southwest of Al-Merjeh. This is also where you will be deposited if you're arriving by bus from Amman or by bus/service taxi from Beirut. If you're approaching Damascus from the north (from Aleppo or Turkey), you'll be dropped off at Harasta terminal, the northern bus station; from here take a microbus to Al-Merjeh or a taxi.

is about 6km northwest of the city centre and has departures for all destinations north. To get up to Harasta, you can take a microbus from Al-Merjeh or the eastern end of Shoukri al-Quwatli for S£5. A taxi will cost S£50 maximum.

The other main station is **Baramke terminal** (Karajat Baramki; Map p780), which is about a 15- to 20-minute walk southwest of Al-Merjeh. The station occupies a square block, which is divided into three separate sections: viewed from the north, in front to the left are local microbus services and behind are the buses to the south (Bosra, Der'a and Suweida); the front right quarter is for service taxis to Beirut and Amman; behind is the Karnak lot with international services to Jordan, Lebanon, Egypt and the Gulf.

In addition there are several other microbus and minibus stations serving regional destinations (for details see Microbus & Minibus, p114).

For a description of the various kinds of buses, see p389 in the Transport chapter.

NORTH OF DAMASCUS

All the big private bus companies have departures from Harasta terminal. Prices are similar and typical one-way fares include Aleppo (S£150, five hours), Deir ez-Zur (S£175, seven hours), Hama (S£85 to S£90, 2½ hours), Homs (S£70, two hours), Lattakia (S£120 to S£150, 4½ hours), Palmyra (S£100, four hours) and Tartus (S£100 to S£110, 3½ hours). Cheaper Karnak buses also depart from here to most of these destinations.

Be warned, the touts are particularly ferocious here and as soon as you've cleared the security checks at the entrance to the station, guys will be tugging at your sleeve to lead you toward whichever office happens to be paying the highest commission. Shrug them off and make a beeline for one of the more reputable companies, such as Qadmous (straight ahead) or Al-Ahliah (over to the right).

Booking in advance is rarely necessary but several companies that do have offices in Central Damascus include **Al-Ahliah** (Map p78) on Sharia Filasteen, west of the immigration office) and **Qadmous** (Map pp80–1), in the same arcade as the Kairowan Hotel by Victoria Bridge and also on Sharia al-Hamra, just north of Cham Palace.

SOUTH OF DAMASCUS

Damas Tours (Map p78) runs good buses (with air-con) out of Baramke terminal to Bosra (S£50, two hours, every two hours from 8am until 10pm), and to Suweida (S£40, one hour 40 minutes, approximately every hour from 8am until 8.35pm). Al-Muhib also runs (from Baramke) good Bosra buses at exactly the same times as Damas Tours and for the same price, and regular services to Suweida. Der'a (S£50, one hour 20 minutes) is serviced by As-Soukor and Al-Wassim (companies that leave from Baramke terminal) – the latter has the better buses.

LEBANON, JORDAN, EGYPT & THE GULF

From its Baramke terminal, Karnak has eight buses a day to Beirut (S£175, 4½ hours) departing roughly every hour between 7.30am and 6.30pm, plus two buses at 7am and 3pm daily to Amman (S£300 or JD5, six or seven hours depending on border formalities).

You can also go to Amman by train and Amman or Beirut by service taxi – for details see Service Taxi, p115.

The Aman bus company has a daily service to Riyadh (S£1500) at 11am, one to Jeddah (S£1000) on Tuesday, Thursday and Saturday, and buses to Kuwait (S£2500) on Saturday, Wednesday and Thursday. These buses also go from the Baramke terminal (eastern half) and tickets should be bought in advance.

For Egypt there is just one Karnak bus a week and that's at 8pm Sunday from Baramke terminal. It costs US$43, including the ferry fare from Aqaba to Nuweiba. The trip takes about 30 hours.

TURKEY

Buses to İstanbul (S£1500, 30 hours) and other Turkish destinations, such as Antakya (S£350) and Ankara (S£1200) all depart from the Harasta terminal. However, the various companies that run the buses all have offices downtown, on a side street just west of Victoria Bridge, so it's probably a good idea to book a day or so in advance, when you can also check departure times.

Note, if you are on a tight budget then it's cheaper to get local transport to Aleppo and on to the border, and then get Turkish buses once you're across.

Car & Motorcycle

If you are travelling independently by car or motorcycle, see Car & Motorcycle, p390, for more information. Another, and probably more relaxing, option is to hire a car and a driver for a day (see Cars & Drivers, p391, for details). For car-rental options try the following:

Avis (Map p78; ☎ 223 9664)

Budget (☎ 212 2220)

Europcar (Map pp80-1; ☎ 222 9300; Sheraton Damascus Hotel & Towers, Saahat Umawiyeen)

Europcar (Map pp80-1; ☎ 222 9200; Le Meridien Damas, Sharia Shoukri al-Quwatli)

Hertz operates through **Chamcar** (☎ 223 2300)

Marmou (Map pp80-1; ☎ 333 5787)

Microbus & Minibus

It's generally easier to use buses, but there are a few destinations where a microbus or minibus is the only option, including for journeys to Quneitra and Zabadani and all stops along the Barada Gorge, plus Ad-Dumeir, Seidnayya, Maalula and An-Nabk and all destinations to the immediate north of Damascus.

The main microbus stations are at **Baramke terminal** (see Bus p112) and **Bab Mousala garage** (Karajat Bab Mousala, also known as Karajat Der'a; Map p78), which is in the district of Bab Mousala about 2km south of the Old City. From here there are services for the Hauran region including Suweida, Shahba and Der'a (for Bosra and the Jordanian border). Although there are microbuses to Bab Mousala from a stop on Sharia Fakhri al-Baroudi (one block south and east of the Hejaz train station) the easiest way to get to the depot is by taxi, which should cost about S£25 from the vicinity of Al-Merjeh.

There are further minibus/microbus stations in the northeast of the city: **Abbasseen garage** (Karajat Abbasseen; Map p78), which is about 200m south of the Abbasseen stadium and just east of Saahat Abbasseen, and the **Maalula garage** (Karajat Maalula), just to the south of Saahat Abbasseen. These are where you come to catch transport to destinations to the immediate north of Damascus. Again, the easiest way of getting here from the city centre is by taxi (S£25).

Train

Although one of the landmarks of Central Damascus is **Hejaz train station**, it's currently closed for an extensive renovation. All services now go from **Khaddam train station** (☎ 888 8678), about 5km southwest of the centre. You'll have to take a taxi to get there; it will cost between S£30 and S£50 from Al-Merjeh. There's one train service a day to Aleppo (1st/2nd class S£85/57, six hours) departing 4pm and travelling via Homs and Hama, and a weekly train to Lattakia (S£90/60, six hours) departing 3pm Thursday and travelling via Tartus and Banias. Tickets for these trains can also be bought at the Hejaz station – providing you can find some one on duty. There's also a weekly train to İstanbul departing 5.30am Tuesday; the sleeper fare is US$66 (a 1st-class seat is half that). The journey takes two full days, arriving in İstanbul around midnight Wednesday. Tickets for this train, which must be booked at least 24 hours in advance, can only be bought from Khaddam.

A twice-weekly train connects Damascus and Amman. It leaves Damascus for Amman on Monday and Thursday at 8am (S£160, eight to ten hours) and at the same times departs Amman for the trip in the opposite direction. Be warned, there are no comforts on board, such as a buffet or working toilets and carriages are battered and dust-filled as half of the windows are jammed open (see Train, p385, for more information about this service).

GETTING AROUND
To/From the Airport

There's a Karnak airport service (S£20, 30 minutes, half-hourly between 6am and midnight) that runs between the airport forecourt (directly outside the arrivals/departures hall) and the southwestern corner of the Baramke terminal. You might be charged a further S£10 per item of large luggage.

A taxi into the city centre, organised at one of the taxi counters in the arrivals hall, costs US$10. One of Syria's few ATMs can be found to the left of the taxi counters, and it's worth taking the opportunity to withdraw some pounds before you leave the airport. If you're taking a taxi from the centre out to the airport, expect to pay anything from S£200 to S£500 (US$4 to US$10), depending on your luck and/or bargaining skills.

For more information, see the boxed text Arriving in Damascus by Air on p112.

Bicycle

There's a group of about four or five bicycle repairs and spares shops lined up along Sharia Khaled ibn Walid, about 500m due south of the main post office. Don't expect to find any esoteric parts for your mono-shocked mountain bike though.

Bus

Bigger town buses still operate but the microbuses are handier. Tickets cost S£5 or a book of five is S£20 from the ticket booths.

Microbus

Damascus' battered old city buses are ceding ground quickly to a mass onslaught by very nimble little microbuses, which have now become a firm fixture in Lebanon as well.

The city is compact and you should not really have a great need to use either, except in rare cases. The microbuses run set routes, and generally pick up and set down at marked stops, although the drivers are pretty flexible about this. The fare ranges from S£3 (if anyone has coins) to S£5.

The main central terminal is at Jisr ar-Rais, the flyover west of the National Museum. From here you can get microbuses to Bab Touma, Muhajireen, Mezzeh, Abbasid Square (or Abbasseen garage for Seidnayya and Maalula) and Harasta terminal, the northeastern bus station. The latter two can

also be picked up along Sharia Shoukri al-Quwatli.

Microbuses for Bab Mousala garage (Map p78) leave from another station on Sharia Fakhri al-Baroudi, as do others that take you to the minibus for Sayyida Zeinab Mosque.

Route names are posted in Arabic on the front of the bus.

Service Taxi

The main service-taxi station is at the **Baramke garage** (Map p78), just south of the city centre. Taxis leave just as soon as they fill up throughout the day and night for Amman (S£400, five hours) and Irbid (S£250, 3½ hours) in Jordan, and Baalbek (S£300, 2½ hours) and Beirut (S£300, four hours) in Lebanon.

Taxi

While there appears to be thousands of yellow Damascus taxis motoring down every street, finding one with a working meter is an increasingly rare sight. The standard fare for a cross-town ride should be about S£25. State your destination (many drivers appear to only know one landmark – Cham Palace) and ask your price before getting in.

Note, it's extremely difficult to find an empty taxi between 2pm and 4pm (rush hour) on working days. If you have to catch a bus from Harasta at this time, allow a good hour for getting to the terminal.

Around Damascus & the Hauran
ضواحي دمشق وحوران

AROUND DAMASCUS
& THE HAURAN

Heading south from Damascus towards the Jordanian border, about 100km away, fertile agricultural land gives way to harsh, scrubby grassland. This area, known as the Hauran, is a basalt plain straddling the Syria-Jordan border. The black rock gives the villages and towns of the area a strange, brooding quality that is best explored at Bosra. With its impressive Roman remains it's one of Syria's highlights and a must-do day trip from Damascus. Other places worth visiting include Suweida, with its excellent museum, and the ruins at Shahba and Qanawat which are both close enough to Suweida to be visited on the same trip.

The other popular trip to the south is one for followers of the ever-changing Middle East political scene. The ghost town of Quneitra, captured by the Israelis during the Arab-Israeli War of 1967, was deliberately destroyed on their withdrawal and remains a ghost town today. Lying within the UN-monitored Golan Heights, it requires special permission from the Ministry of the Interior for the visit.

There are several places of interest to the northwest, off the Damascus–Aleppo Hwy (Hwy 5). This region is a bastion of Christianity and is dotted with several predominantly Christian towns and villages and a handful of remote monasteries.

The other picturesque region near Damascus is the Barada Gorge, incised into the Jebel Libnan ash-Sharqiyya (Anti-Lebanon Range) to the west. Half the fun of this region is getting to it via the snail-paced, narrow-gauge steam train. The other half is in watching the locals at leisure, especially on a Friday, enjoying the Syrian weekend.

AROUND DAMASCUS & THE HAURAN

HIGHLIGHTS

- Relive the time when **Bosra** was the capital of the Roman province of Arabia with a visit to its **theatre and citadel** (p123)

- Discover why picturesque **Maalula** (p118) is perhaps Syria's prettiest village

- Get monastic for a night or two at **Mar Musa** (p121) while enjoying spectacular views

- Check out beautiful 4th-century mosaics from Shahba at the **Suweida museum** (p127)

- Join the summer picnic throng on the slow-and-steady steam train to scenic **Barada Gorge** (p121)

- Visit the ghost town of **Quneitra** (p129) in the UN-patrolled demilitarised zone of the Golan Heights

AD-DUMEIR
الضمير

☎ 011

The so-called **Roman temple** at Ad-Dumeir (or Ad-Dmeir), a dusty, nondescript little village some 40km northeast of Damascus on the Palmyra road, is something of a conundrum. Conventional wisdom has the temple dating from the 3rd century and dedicated to Zeus, but some maintain that it started life as a public fountain.

Whatever the case, the temple (off the main street about 100m east of the microbus stop) has been restored to an impressive state and is well worth a look. The squat, rectangular structure sits deep in a pit that resulted from intense excavations and reconstruction work. A local caretaker has the keys and will admit visitors for a small tip of about S£50. If he's not around when you arrive, someone will fetch him. You can see Greek inscriptions on the wall as you enter, and again in several spots inside where there are carved reliefs.

Getting There & Away
There are regular microbuses to Ad-Dumeir (S£15, 45 minutes) from the Abbasseen garage in northeast Damascus; see p114 for details on how to get to the garage.

SEIDNAYYA
صيدنايا

☎ 011

At first glance you could just about mistake the modern Greek Orthodox **Convent of Our Lady**, for another Crusader castle. In fact, the convent stands on the site of one of the most important places of Christian pilgrimage in the Middle East, a status derived from its possession of a portrait of the Virgin Mary, purportedly painted by St Luke. All manner of miracles have been attributed to this icon, to the extent that at the time of the Crusades, the Christians considered Seidnayya to be second in importance only to Jerusalem. Veneration of the icon is still strong, but what is particularly fascinating is the fact that it attracts Muslim pilgrims as well as Christians.

Legend has it that the Byzantine emperor Justinian founded the convent in the 6th century, probably on the site of an earlier Greek or Roman shrine, but it has been rebuilt so many times there's little of antiquity remaining in the present structure. It's possible to identify bits of medieval masonry in the lower courses of some of the walls, but most of the structure dates from the 19th century. After ascending a flight of steps, enter through a small doorway and proceed across a courtyard to the main chapel – off to the left – which is crammed with modern icons and other testimonies of faith from the convent's visitors. The pilgrimage shrine containing the famed relic is to the right of the chapel, in a small dark room.

After visiting the chapels it's worth wandering through the courtyards and up the various steps to the roof, from which there are great views over the town and the plains beyond.

The **Feast of Our Lady of Seidnayya** is held on 8 September each year, and if you're in the region it constitutes a spectacle worth attending. The main celebrations begin on the night of the 7th and both Christian and Muslim pilgrims attend from all over the Middle East.

The town itself, dating back to the 6th century BC, is set in a spectacular position in the heart of the Jebel Libnan ash-Sharqiyya, but is modern and nondescript, with little of interest beyond the convent, and warranting no more than a half-day excursion. It's possible to combine Seidnayya with a visit to Maalula – although public transport between the two is infrequent and you might have to ask someone for a ride.

Sleeping
Seidnayya Tourist Hotel (☎ 595 3739; s/d US$17/21; 🖭) At the southwestern end of the main street, about 15 minutes' walk from the convent, this place has decent rooms with private bathroom. The views from the hotel are pleasant.

It's also possible to obtain a room at the **Convent of Our Lady** for a modest donation.

Getting There & Away
There are regular microbuses to Seidnayya (S£15, 40 minutes) from the Maalula garage in northeast Damascus; see p114 for details on how to get to the garage.

MAALULA
معلول

☎ 011

Set in a narrow valley in the foothills of the Jebel Libnan ash-Sharqiyya, Maalula is a beautiful little village in which the houses – many painted a sandy yellow or a silvery

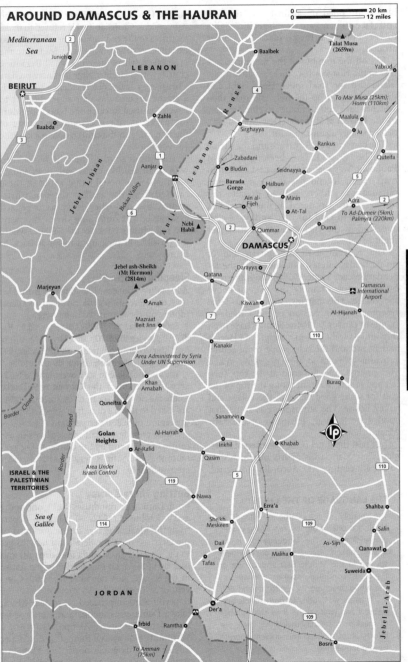

AROUND DAMASCUS & THE HAURAN

0 — 20 km
0 — 12 miles

Mediterranean Sea

Junieh

BEIRUT

LEBANON

Baabda

Zahlé

Baalbek

Talat Musa (2659m)

Yabrud

To Mar Musa (25km); Homs (110km)

Maalula

Ju

Sirghayya

Rankus

Quteifa

Aanjar

Zabadani

Bludan

Seidnayya

Barada Gorge

Halbun

Minin

Adra

Ain al-Fijeh

At-Tal

To Ad-Dumeir (5km); Palmyra (220km)

Bekaa Valley

Nebi Habil

Qummar

DAMASCUS

Duma

Jebel Libnan

Anti-Lebanon Range

Lebanon Range

Jebel ash-Sheikh (Mt Hermon) (2814m)

Qatana

Darayya

Marjeyun

Amah

Kiswah

Damascus International Airport

Mazraat Beit Jinn

Al-Hijanah

Kanakir

Area Administered by Syria Under UN Supervision

Khan Arnabah

Buraq

Quneitra

Sanamein

Golan Heights

Al-Harrah

Khabab

Ar-Rafid

Inkhil

ISRAEL & THE PALESTINIAN TERRITORIES

Area Under Israeli Control

Qasim

Border Closed

Sea of Galilee

Nawa

Shahba

Ezra'a

Salin

Sheikh Meskeen

As-Sijn

Qanawat

Dail

Maliha

Tafas

Suweida

JORDAN

Der'a

Irbid

Ramtha

To Amman (75km)

Bosra

Jebel al-Arab

blue – are piled up against a vertiginous cliff face. There are few specific sights to see, but it's a lovely place to wander around.

Get off the minibus at the main intersection in the village, where there's a little traffic island and the road splits. Head right and then right again up the hill. The road then switches back and continues to climb steeply to the **Convent of St Thecla** (Deir Mar Takla), tucked snugly against the cliff.

The convent developed around the shrine of St Thecla, said to have been a pupil of St Paul, who was one of the earliest Christian martyrs. As legend has it, she was being pursued by soldiers sent to execute her for her faith. Cornered against the cliffs she prayed to God for help and, lo, a cleft appeared in the rock face, facilitating her flight to safety.

The convent itself is modern and of no particular interest but ahead lies the legendary escape route. Cut through the rock by the waters draining the plateau above the village. This narrow, steep-sided defile resembles a miniversion of the famed siq (gorge or canyon) at Petra. Shrines have been dug into its walls and in a couple of places it widens out and the sides slope more gently, providing popular local picnic spots. When you emerge onto the road at the top, turn left and follow the route along the top of the cliff for some good views of the village and valley below. The atmosphere is somewhat spoiled by the ugly intrusion of the Safir Maalula hotel.

Just past the hotel is the **Monastery of St Sergius** (Deir Mar Sarkis), parts of which date to the 4th century AD. According to legend,

Sergius (Sarkis) was a Roman legionary who converted to Christianity. He refused to make sacrifices to the god Jupiter, for which he was executed. A very low doorway leads into the monastery, where there is a small Byzantine church with a circular altar that may predate Christianity – possible evidence for this is a groove around the altar edge, thought to have been used to catch the blood spilt during pagan sacrificial ceremonies. Some of the fine icons in the church date back to the 13th century.

The hillside south of the church is riddled with small cell-like caves with neat, square openings. It's thought that some of these caves date to the earliest years of Christianity, but now they serve as oversized garbage bins. Continuing down this way, the road loops back to the village, where it's possible to pick up a minibus back to Damascus.

Sleeping & Eating

As Maalula is an easy half-day trip from Damascus, there should be no need to spend money on the expensive hotel here.

Safir Maalula (☎ 777 0250; safir@net.sy; s/d Oct-May US$79/95, Jun-Sep US$95/112; ☑) The Safir offers four-star accommodation with full amenities, including a restaurant, coffee shop and bar.

It's also possible to stay overnight in basic accommodation at the **Convent of St Thecla**. There are no fixed room rates; instead guests are asked to make a donation – something in the region of S£250 per person.

There are a few small snack places in the centre of town and by the convent. The restaurant at the Safir is very good and prices are reasonable.

Getting There & Away

From Damascus, minibuses (S£12, one hour) and microbuses (S£22, 50 minutes) depart from the Maalula garage in the northeast of the city (see p114 for details on how to get to the garage). In Maalula they drop off and pick up at the main intersection at the centre of the village, just downhill from the Convent of St Thecla.

If you want to proceed on to Mar Musa, take a Damascus minibus and ask to be let off on the Damascus–Aleppo Hwy (just a 10-minute ride away); there, flag down any bus or minibus going north (for Homs or Aleppo) and ask to be let off at An-Nabk.

THE LANGUAGE OF THE CHRIST

The mainly Greek Catholic village of Maalula is one of the last remaining places where Aramaic, the language of Jesus, is still spoken. Aramaic was once widely spoken in the Middle East and is one of the oldest continually spoken languages in the world, reaching its zenith around 500 BC. It bears similarities to both Arabic and Hebrew and while these days the number of speakers is steadily dwindling, there are efforts afoot to keep this ancient tongue from disappearing.

Silk tablecloths for sale, Aleppo (p192), Syria

ANDREW BURKE

JOHN ELK III

Interior passage of the Citadel (p181), Aleppo, Syria

Spice stall in the souq (p193), Aleppo, Syria

JOHN ELK III

Ruins in one of the Dead Cities, Serjilla (p200), Syria

The ruined basilica built around the pillar of St Simeon, Qala'at Samaan (p196), Syria

MAR MUSA   مار موسى

At Mar Musa (also known as Deir Mar Musa, the Monastery of Mar Musa) it's very much like the last 1500 years never happened. The monastery is a throwback to the 6th-century heyday of Byzantine Christianity, when the deserts and rocky landscapes of the eastern Mediterranean hinterland provided shelter for thousands of tiny, isolated, self-sustaining and pious communities. Mar Musa is one of the very few of these desert monasteries to survive. It's way off the beaten track, 14km from the nearest town, and the last stretch, along a steep-sided rocky gorge, must be travelled on foot. Entered through the tiniest of doorways, it's not until you are standing on the monastery's terrace that you realise the complex is perched high on the edge of a cliff, facing east over a vast, barren plain.

According to the monks the monastery was founded in the 6th century AD by an Ethiopian royal named Moses (or Musa), who favoured monastic life to the throne. He fled his outraged family, finding refuge first in Egypt and then Palestine, before founding several monasteries in present-day Syria, including this one based on the site of an old Roman watchtower. By the 11th century, the monastery was the seat of a local bishopric and it flourished into the 15th century, gradually declining until it was finally abandoned in the 1830s. An Italian former Jesuit rediscovered it in the 1980s and with the help of the local Syrian Catholic community, undertook to renovate the place and have it reconsecrated.

Since 1991 the monastery has been home to a small group of monks, nuns and novices (who numbered just six at the time of writing). As well as being mixed sex, Mar Musa is doubly unconventional, in that it is also ecumenical, with both Syrian Catholics and Syrian Orthodox Christians represented within the community.

The pride of the monastery is its ancient church, which contains some beautiful frescoes, some dating to the 11th century.

Visitors are made very welcome and it's possible to stay here. Basic accommodation (including bedding) and simple meals are free, but guests must take an active part in the community's life and help with cooking and other work.

Getting There & Away

To get to Mar Musa take a microbus to An-Nabk (النبك; S£35, 50 minutes), 80km northeast of Damascus on the road to Homs and Aleppo. Microbuses depart from the Abbasseen garage (see p114). Coming from Maalula on a Homs or Aleppo bus, you'll be dropped off on the highway at the An-Nabk turn-off, from where it's a 2km walk to the town centre. Wait around and somebody is bound to pick you up and give you a ride in.

Once in An-Nabk, you have to sort out transport to Mar Musa, which is 14km northeast across some extremely stony terrain. You could attempt to bargain with the microbus drivers – best price S£600 – or instead, walk 100m down the main street to the taxi office, where you should be able to cut a deal for S£300, including the ride there and back (about 40 minutes each way), and a two-hour wait.

Vehicles can't go all the way to the monastery; you must walk the last 1.5km along a winding path halfway up a steep-sided gully, which degenerates in places into a scramble over rocky outcrops.

BARADA GORGE   وادي بردى

The Barada River flows into Damascus from the west, winding down from the Jebel Libnan ash-Sharqiyya and through low foothills to reach the city. The valley through which it flows is extremely picturesque, and Damascenes escape the city by flocking here on Fridays and throughout summer for picnics by the river. For the traveller, however, the main attraction is possibly the narrow-gauge train trip up the valley.

The antiquated wooden carriages are loaded with a great variety of people – from elderly veiled women with children and grandchildren in tow, to teenage boys sporting the latest Western clothes and ghetto blasters – all being hauled by a groaning, wheezing Swiss-built steam train.

The train crawls as far as Sirghayya, a small village just short of the Lebanese border, where it's turned around on a revolving platform for the return journey. Most passengers alight before this, at **Zabadani** (الزبداني) – only 50km from Damascus, but a painful three- to four-hour journey. Zabadani's 1200m altitude means that it is considerably cooler than the capital, and the hills around the town are clustered with holiday homes, while the main street is lined with chic restaurants and cafés. Downhill from the station is the older part of the village, with an old mosque and Catholic church.

Bludan (بلودان) is 7km east of Zabadani at an altitude of 1400m. It's a smaller, more exclusive getaway spot. Although pleasant enough, it really doesn't have much to offer the traveller, and is accessible only by microbus.

The return train to Damascus departs about three hours after arriving in Zabadani. However, you can catch a microbus down to **Ain al-Fijeh** (عين الفيجه) to have a look around before picking up the train (or microbus), or simply ride all the way back to Damascus. On the way to Ain al-Fijeh you pass through Barada Gorge and it's just to the west of here, on the mountain of Nebi Habil that, according to local legend, Cain buried Abel after killing him.

Getting There & Away

The Zabadani Flyer, as it's known to expat wits, runs only from June to October, leaving from the Khaddam train station at 8am Tuesday, Thursday, Friday and Sunday. The fare is S£30. On other days the train only goes as far as Ain al-Fijeh (S£20).

Microbuses for Zabadani (S£20, 45 minutes) leave from the eastern part of Baramke garage in Damascus year-round.

EZRA'A   ازرع
☎ 015

Although not the most significant of destinations, if time allows it is definitely worth trying to squeeze Ezra'a into a trip to the Hauran region. If you're heading for Bosra, it's quite easy to go via Ezra'a and then to Der'a.

Ezra'a has two of Syria's oldest functioning churches. The Greek Orthodox **Basilica of St George** (Kineeset Mar Jirjis) has been a working church since the 6th century and remains in a remarkably unchanged state. An inscription above the west entrance (to the left of the current entrance), reads:

> What once was a lodging place for
> demons has become a house of God;
> where idols once were sacrificed, there
> are now choirs of angels;
> where God was provoked to wrath,
> now He is propitiated.

It's dated AD 515, indicating that the church stands on the site of an earlier pagan temple. There are no fixed opening times; if the church is locked, ask around for the caretaker. For background on St George and Syria, see the St George's Monastery section (p135).

Virtually next door is the Greek Catholic **Church of St Elias**. It also dates from the 6th century but it has been much altered over the years and as a result isn't as impressive as its Orthodox neighbour.

Getting There & Away

Minibuses to Ezra'a depart from the Bab Mousala garage in Damascus (p114) or from the main bus station at Der'a, although you may have to change at Sheikh Meskeen (often just called Sheikh), 15km west of Ezra'a. The minibus drops you off in central Ezra'a and the churches are 3km to the north – you'll need a taxi.

BOSRA   بصرى
☎ 015

Bosra (or more properly Bosra ash-Sham) is a fascinating place. Apart from having one of the best-preserved Roman theatres in existence – certainly the best theatre encompassed by an Arab fortress – the rest of the town is constructed almost entirely of black basalt blocks around and over old sections of Roman buildings. Altogether it's a strange mixture of architectural styles, and as the Cook's Travellers' Handbook of 1934 says, 'a zealous antiquary might find weeks of profitable enjoyment among the ruins'. That remains true to this day, though for most people a day trip from Damascus leaves ample time to see everything at a leisurely pace.

Note that the eating options in Bosra are less than stellar, so pack a lunch.

History

Bosra is mentioned in Egyptian records as early as 1300 BC (as Busrana) and during the 1st century AD it became the short-lived capital of the Nabataean kingdom, eclipsing Petra in the south. However, it's historical importance was secured when, following Rome's annexation of the region, the renamed Nova Trajana Bostra became capital of the Province of Arabia and garrison for a Roman legion. A new road linked Bosra with both Damascus to the north and

CROSSING INTO JORDAN

If you are looking for the best way to get between Damascus and Amman, then just stick with the regular twice-daily direct bus (which goes by the alternative border crossing at Nasib/Jabir, southeast of Der'a). True, you could maybe knock a dollar or two off the fare doing it yourself by a combination of minibuses and service taxis, but the inconvenience renders the exercise uneconomical. However, if you are down in the Hauran already and don't want to double back to Damascus, crossing the border independently is straightforward enough, although it can involve a bit of hiking. Service taxis shuttle directly between the bus stations in Der'a and Ramtha (on the Jordanian side), and cost S£150 or JD2 per person.

Otherwise, you will need to hitch or walk. Try to get a local bus from the bus station into the centre, to save yourself the first 3km of walking. From there, head south out on the Jordan road (signposted) and hitch or walk the 4km to the Syrian checkpoint. Once through formalities here, it's another 3km or 4km to the Jordanian checkpoint. The soldiers here may not allow you to walk the last kilometre or so to the immigration post, but are friendly and will flag down a car or bus for you. From Ramtha, minibuses go on to Mafraq, Irbid and Zarqa, from where you can proceed to Amman.

There is no departure tax and a Jordanian visa can be picked up on the spot at the border post for JD10 (approximately US$15).

Amman to the south and the town grew as an important trading centre. The surrounding countryside was also something of a bread basket, providing a sound economic foundation for the Bosrans' wellbeing. When local-boy Philip became emperor of Rome (AD 244–49), he raised the town to the status of metropolis, and coins bearing his likeness were minted there.

During the Byzantine era, Bosra was the seat of a primate overseeing 33 priests, and during the 6th century the largest cathedral in the region was built here. Prior to the town's fall to the Muslims in 634, tradition has it that the young Mohammed, passing through the town with his merchant uncle's caravans, encountered a wise Nestorian monk named Boheira. It's told that the boy and the monk engaged in theological discussions and the monk, recognising greatness in Mohammed, revealed his future vocation as the Prophet.

In response to two attacks by the Crusaders in the 12th century, both of which were repelled, the Ayyubids fortified the old Roman theatre, transforming it into a citadel. Throughout the Middle Ages, Bosra's position on the pilgrimage route to Mecca assured its continued prosperity, and because of the legend of Mohammed and the monk, pilgrims often stopped here for up to a week. However, during Ottoman times declining security in the region led to pilgrims using a route further to the west, through Der'a, and Bosra lapsed into obscurity.

Today the friendly inhabitants of Bosra live among the ruins of the old town, seemingly oblivious to the history contained within.

Orientation & Information

The ruins and modern town lie just to the north of the main east-west road between Der'a and Suweida. Al-Muhib buses drop off outside their office 100m short of the citadel; Damas Tours buses and microbuses from Der'a pass the citadel and drop off 400m further along the road, passing along the way the new **tourist information office** (🕑 9am-2.30pm Sat-Thu). There's a **Commercial Bank of Syria exchange booth** (CBS; 🕑 9.30am-2pm & 4-7pm) near the entrance to the theatre/citadel; it takes cash and travellers cheques. Money can also be changed at the Bosra Cham Palace hotel.

Sights
CITADEL & THEATRE

The **citadel** (adult/student S£300/25; 🕑 9am-6pm Mar-Nov, to 4pm Dec-Feb) is a unique construction in that it began life as a massive Roman theatre and later had its fortifications grafted on. It's a wonderful experience to be lost in the dark, oppressive fortress halls and then to pass through a sunlit opening to find yourself suddenly looking down on a vast terraced hillside of stone seating.

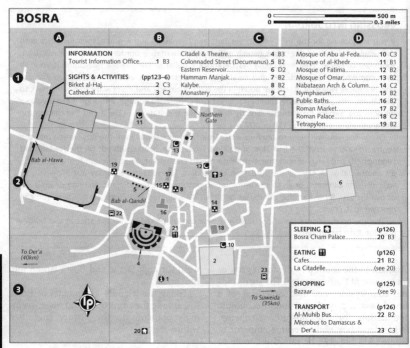

BOSRA

0	500 m
0	0.3 miles

INFORMATION
Tourist Information Office.........**1** B3

SIGHTS & ACTIVITIES (pp123–6)
Birket al-Haj.............................**2** C3
Cathedral..................................**3** C2
Citadel & Theatre.....................**4** B3
Colonnaded Street (Decumanus).**5** B2
Eastern Reservoir......................**6** D2
Hammam Manjak......................**7** B2
Kalybe.......................................**8** B2
Monastery..................................**9** C2
Mosque of Abu al-Feda...........**10** C3
Mosque of al-Khedr.................**11** B1
Mosque of Fatima....................**12** B2
Mosque of Omar......................**13** B2
Nabataean Arch & Column.....**14** C2
Nymphaeum............................**15** B2
Public Baths..............................**16** B2
Roman Market..........................**17** B2
Roman Palace...........................**18** C2
Tetrapylon................................**19** B2

Northern Gate

Bab al-Hawa

Bab al-Qandil

To Der'a (40km)

To Suweida (35km)

SLEEPING (p126)
Bosra Cham Palace...................**20** B3

EATING (p126)
Cafes...**21** B2
La Citadelle............................(see 20)

SHOPPING (p125)
Bazaar.....................................(see 9)

TRANSPORT (p126)
Al-Muhib Bus..........................**22** B2
Microbus to Damascus & Der'a..................................**23** C3

The theatre was built early in the 2nd century AD, when Bosra was the capital of the Roman province of Arabia. It's estimated that it would have seated 15,000 people and is a rarity among theatres of the time in that it is completely freestanding, rather than built into the side of a hill. Buried under an accumulation of sand and long obscured by the addition of later buildings, the theatre's full glory was only laid bare in the 20th century. The stage is backed by rows of Corinthian columns and the whole facade was originally in white marble. The stage would have had a wooden roof and the rest of the theatre would have been covered by silk awnings. As if this wasn't atmospheric enough, it was customary during performances to spray perfumed water into the air, allowing a fragrant mist to descend soothingly upon the spectators.

The citadel was built around the theatre in stages. The first walls were built during the Umayyad and Abbasid periods, with further additions being made in the 11th century by the Fatimids. Following Crusader attacks in 1140 and 1183, the Ayyubids strengthened the fortifications by constructing more towers between 1202 and 1251. The result is a ring of eight towers connected by thick walls, which encircle the theatre like a protective jacket.

The southwest tower contains one of those ubiquitous museums of popular culture and tradition; with scenes of Arab life depicted using mannequins and various exhibits of clothing and utensils. It's often closed, and if you want to see inside, backtrack and ask at the ticket desk for the key. Another tower contains a cafeteria on the first floor.

The theatre blossoms into life once every other year for the biennial **Bosra Festival** (odd years), when it becomes a venue for drama and concerts – see p363.

OLD TOWN

The remains of the old Roman town lie to the north of the theatre, covering an area of about 1 sq km. Until recently much of the site lay buried under the contemporary town but there has been an ongoing project to relocate the modern buildings and recover the Roman-era structures. Unfortunately, this also involves some clumsy reconstruction –

he resulting erratic colonnades of mis-sized,
runken columns are not exactly what the
Roman engineers envisaged.

The best way to approach the old town is
o walk around the north side of the citadel
and then bear right for the Bab al-Qandil.
here is no admission fee for the old town
and as the site is unbounded, there are no
ixed opening hours.

The **Bab al-Qandil** (Gate of the Lantern)
s a triumphal arch, with one great central
rch flanked by two smaller arches. It dates
rom the early 3rd century and an inscrip-
ion on one pillar states that it was erected
n memory of the Third Legion, which was
arrisoned here. Through the arch you will
ee a modern Bosran home, built with stone
cavenged from the ruins – which has at
east ensured that the building sits harmo-
iously amidst its ancient surrounds.

The gate marks an intersection with the
ld town's main east-west street, the **decu-
nanus**, which has been excavated to reveal its
obbled surface and parallel rows of column
ases. At the western end of the decumanus
ises the **Bab al-Hawa** (Gate of the Wind), a
lain, single-arched structure that's flanked
y the remains of the Roman-era city walls.

Returning east, the large dilapidated struc-
ure off to the right (south) is what remains
f the **public baths**. Though the building is in
bad state, it is possible to get some sense
f how it functioned. You enter off the de-
umanus into a large octagonal room (with a
ollapsed ceiling) that would have served as
he changing hall; from here you pass into
he frigidarium (cold room), which leads to a
epidarium (warm room) with a calidarium
hot room) to either side.

Almost opposite the baths are four enor-
nous Corinthian columns set at an angle
o the decumanus – this is what's left of the
ymphaeum, or public water fountain. On
he side of the street heading north you can
ee another column and lintel incorporated
nto a modern house. It is believed that
his is what remains of a pagan sanctuary,
r **kalybe**, built by a Bosran king to protect
is daughter from death. A dismal failure it
eems, as the daughter was brought a bunch
f grapes in which a scorpion was hiding. It
romptly stung and killed her.

This street leads north, past the remains
f a long rectangular **Roman market** with
aved plaza, to the **Mosque of Omar**, claimed

by some to have been built by (and named
for) Caliph Omar, under whose leadership
Syria was conquered in 636. If it is true, this
would make it one of the earliest mosques in
the world. However, historians identify the
mosque in its present form as being wholly
Ayyubid, which dates it to the 12th or 13th
centuries. It's still in use as Bosra's main
mosque and madrassa.

Nearly opposite the mosque, the **Hammam
Manjak** was only fully revealed in the early
1990s. Built in 1372 under the Mamluks,
it's a bathhouse that served the passing
pilgrim trade.

After walking around the hammam, head
back south but bear left to the small **Mosque
of Fatima**, which is notable for a square
minaret that stands separate from the main
building. The mosque was built by the Fatimids in the 11th century and named after
the Prophet's daughter. North of the mosque
is the oldest **monastery** in Bosra, thought to
have been built in the 4th century. Popular
tradition has it that this is where Mohammed met the monk Boheira. The facade has
been totally rebuilt but the side walls and
apse are original. The square in front of the
monastery is a makeshift **bazaar** where a couple of stalls sell a dusty collection of antiques
and bric-a-brac.

South of the monastery lies the **cathedral**
(c 512), in a sorry state of decay. It represents one of the earliest, and not entirely
successful, attempts to surmount a square
base with a circular dome and was rebuilt
a number of times before its final demise.
The Byzantine emperor Justinian used the
church as the model for cathedrals he built
in Constantinople and Ravenna, both of
which still stand. There's considerably less
to look at here, with only the nave and two
antechambers still standing, but many of the
stones lying about the site are carved with
religious symbols.

Continuing south, this small street intersects with the eastern end of the decumanus,
marked by a **Nabataean arch and column**. As
well as marking the edge of the Roman
city, the gate was probably the main entrance to a Nabataean palace complex that
archaeologists suspect lies immediately east
of here, yet to be uncovered. Excavations
have, however, been conducted on a Roman
palace just to the south, beyond which is a
massive Roman reservoir, 120m x 150m,

which goes by the name of **Birket al-Haj** (Pool of the Pilgrimage) – a clear reference to the era when Bosra was a popular rest stop for pilgrims on their way to Mecca.

Sleeping & Eating

Bosra Cham Palace (☎ 790 881/2/3; www.chamhotels .com; s/d US$100/120; ❄ ▢ ⧉) Bosra's only accommodation is an expensive yet unappealing place a few hundred metres south of the theatre. Reservations are essential during the biennial (odd years) festival in September.

When it comes to eating you're really at the mercy of the cafés and restaurants around the plaza beside the citadel/theatre, which regularly overcharge for their awful food. Alternatives include some cheap felafel and grilled chicken places on Sharia Ghasasena down toward where the Der'a microbuses depart from, or there's the **La Citadelle**, the expensive house restaurant at the Bosra Cham Palace, where at least the prices are given up front.

Getting There & Away

Damas Tours and Al-Muhib buses both run direct services between Bosra and the Baramke garage in Damascus (S£50, two hours). For departure times from Damascus see p113. Return buses from Bosra are every two hours, with the first bus at 6am and the last at 6pm. It's wise to double check departure times at the bus company office when you arrive in Bosra, and buy your return ticket in advance. Allow at least two hours for a quick visit.

The alternative way is to take a microbus to Der'a (S£15, 30 minutes) and change there for Damascus (S£50, 1½ hours). Microbuses for Der'a depart from Sharia Ghasasena, 400m east of the tourist office.

There are no buses of any sort from Bosra to Suweida and your only options are to take a taxi (possibly S£500) or to hitch.

SHAHBA   شهبا

☎ 016

About 90km south of Damascus, Shahba was founded as Philipopolis by the Hauran's most famous son, Emperor Philip of Rome. Construction of the town began in AD 244, the year of his accession, and it was laid out in a Roman grid pattern oriented to the cardinal points of the compass, with four great gates in the surrounding walls. Unfortunately, the building was halted abruptly when Philip was murdered only five years

into his reign. Despite this, the town continued to thrive for another hundred years or so (as the magnificent 4th-century mosaic now held in the museum of nearby Suweida testify) but it was later abandoned. It came to life again only in the 19th century, when it was settled by the Druze, who still account for almost the entire population.

The road from Damascus climbs from the plain below up towards Shahba, entering via the partially reconstructed Roman north gate, proceeding down the main street of modern Shahba, which follows the line laid down by the ancient town's *cardo* (main north-south street). A roundabout at the town centre (where passengers alight) denotes the old intersection with the Roman-era east-west decumanus. Ruins are visible all around, and all the sights of interest are no more than a few minutes' walk away.

If you head right along the partly intact cobbled decumanus, past four stubby **columns** on the right (the remains of a temple portico), you'll see a number of buildings of interest on the left ranged around a large open space that was once the **forum** of the Roman Philipopolis. The best preserved of these buildings, on the south side of the square, appears to have been a family **shrine**, dedicated probably to Philip's father, Julius Marinus. A set of stairs in the southeast corner gives access to the roof for a view over the site. The impressive structure on the western side of the forum, consisting of a series of niches arranged in a semicircle, is the remains of a palace facade. Just behind the shrine lies a modest **theatre**, with fish sculpted on the walls of the vaulted passages that lead to the seats.

Following the street that runs in front of the theatre 400m west, you reach the meagre remains of the town's **Roman baths** and, on the opposite side of the street just a little further along, a small **museum** (adult/student S£150/10; ⏱ 9am-6pm Wed-Mon Mar-Nov, 9am-4pm Wed-Mon Dec-Feb). The principal exhibits here are some fine 4th-century mosaics dug up in town.

Getting There & Away

Suweida buses (see opposite) all pass through Shahba, which is just 20km to the north of the regional capital. Perhaps the ideal way of visiting is to take one of these buses, hop off in Shahba, then later continue south to Suweida by catching one of the frequent microbuses

(S£5, 15 minutes) on the main street. Otherwise, minibuses from Damascus (S£18, 1¼ hours) run direct to Shahba from the Bab Mousala garage.

SUWEIDA السويدا

☎ 016

Capital of the Hauran, Suweida has a place in the hearts of many Syrians for two reasons: it's the centre of the viticulture industry (some of the country's best wines and arak come from around here) and it's also the birthplace of Farid al-Atrache, a giant of the golden age of Arab music (see the boxed text Farid al-Atrache on p53). However, for the casual visitor anything that might once have been of interest in this largely Druze settlement has long been swept away by modern expansion. The town centre is unremarkable, with perhaps the only points of interest being the old Ottoman-era **Governor's Residence** and an **arch with columns**, all that remain of an old city gate just southwest of the market area, and now stranded on a roundabout on the Der'a road.

Orientation & Information

The main bus station is on the northern edge of town, a little over a kilometre from the centre, and just west of a large roundabout with a bronze relief of Basel al-Assad on horseback as its centrepiece. The **tourist information office** (🕑 9am-2.30pm Sat-Thu) is just north of the roundabout. For the museum, head due east from the roundabout, following the road uphill; after a kilometre or so there's a major road junction and the museum is the outsized, grey institutional building just over the road, up to the left. To get to the town centre from either the bus station or the museum, walk due south and the roads will lead to central Saahat Assad (Assad Square), which resembles a large parking lot and is distinguished only by a prominent statue of the ex-president. Surrounding it are a small produce market and several modest shopping streets. There's a branch of the **CBS** (🕑 9am-2.30pm Sat-Thu) that will change cash one block east of Saahat Assad.

Sights
MUSEUM

The French helped to build and organise Suweida's **museum** (adult/student S£300/25; 🕑 9am-6pm Apr-Sep, to 4pm Oct-Mar, closed Tue), which opened in

November 1991. It holds an impressive collection, covering periods in the history of the Hauran from the Stone Age to the Roman era. Prehistoric pottery, an extensive array of mostly basalt statuary, and, upstairs, a popular-tradition section (wax dummies in traditional garb and various items) comes complete with descriptions in Arabic and French only. The main attractions are six 4th-century mosaics from Shahba, displayed in the domed central hall.

The neighbourhood just west of the museum, through which you pass when walking from the bus station, is graced by villas of remarkable opulence, all built with foreign remittances from Venezuela – a country that's a second home to a significant percentage of Suweida's population in much the same way that Philadelphia is to Amar.

Sleeping & Eating

Rawdat al-Jabal Hotel (☎ 221 347; Sharia ash-Shohada; beds S£150) This hotel benefits from a central location but otherwise is a grubby dive with four-bed dorms only, and grim communal toilets and cold showers.

There are a few local eateries around the town centre; the **Al-Amir** (Sharia 29 Mai), just to the south of the centre, is clean, serves standard Syrian fare and has good service. To get there, walk east from Saahat Assad, take the second right and it's about 200m down. Otherwise, **Asrar** (Sharia Hafez al-Assad), just west of the centre on the main north-south road through town, is slightly more formal and does shwarma (Syrian doner kebab), grilled chicken and kebabs.

Getting There & Away

Damas Tours, Al-Muhib buses and Al-Wassim all run luxury buses between Damascus (Baramke garage) and Suweida (S£40, one hour 40 minutes). Departures in both directions are roughly half-hourly between 6am and 10pm. A minibus from Damascus (from the Bab Mousala garage) takes 1¾ hours and costs S£22, or you can take a faster microbus for S£40.

QANAWAT قناوات

☎ 016

The village of Qanawat was a member of the Roman-inspired Decapolis, a politico-economic alliance of cities in Syria/Jordan that included such major centres as Jerash,

Philadelphia (Amman) and Gadara (Umm Qais) in Jordan. It flourished during the time of Trajan (AD 98–117) but began to decline with the arrival of Islam. It was all but abandoned before being resettled by Druze in the 19th century.

Today it's a small agricultural hamlet of low black-stone buildings, many of them constructed with recycled bits from more ancient structures. It's a short minibus ride northeast of Suweida, hop out at the *al-muderiyya* (town hall). This small, single-storey building has an entrance gate surmounted by the colours of the Syrian flag; notice that the building to the right has a block at its bottom left corner that was once carved with three busts.

Beside the town hall, a road is signposted 'To the ruins'. It runs up beside the picturesque gorge of the Wadi al-Ghar, and from the road, visible down below on the far side of a stream, are the ruins of a **theatre** and a **nymphaeum**.

At the top of the hill is an open square with Qanawat's most interesting monument; known as the **Saray** (Palace; adult/student S£150/10; ⊙ 8am-sunset). Historians believe this small, badly deteriorated complex was a combination of temples. The most intact building is Roman and dates from the second half of the 2nd century AD. It was later converted into a basilica under the Byzantines and the whole area was given over to Christian worship. On entering, the recessed niches you see to the right were once a small shrine, and each of the three probably held a small statue; they are still used as a focus of worship today. The second area, with two rows of still-standing columns, is dominated by a monumental gateway on the north side. Carved grapes form part of its decoration – evidence of the centuries-old connection between Suweida and viticulture.

As you leave the Saray, take the first left for a fine underground **cistern**, now minus its roof covering so the buried rows of stone arches and the water-logged pit they stand in are all exposed to the sky. Beyond are the poor remains of yet another **temple**, this one possibly dedicated to Zeus.

Return to the town hall for the minibus back to Suweida, but first take a quick stroll 200m south, where off to the right (west) are seven columns standing atop an almost square platform, all that remains of the **Helios**

temple. Today it's hemmed in by sparse and scrubby farmers' gardens, out of which local doggedly coax whatever fruit and vegetable they can.

Getting There & Away

From Suweida old, battered but colourful minibuses depart from a side street just shy of a traffic-light junction 200m north of Saahat Assad. Departures are frequent in the morning, less so in the afternoon (S£2, 10 minutes).

GOLAN HEIGHTS
مرتفعات الجولان

The Golan Heights in the southwest of the country mark the only border between Syria and Israel. Originally Syrian territory, the Golan was lost to the Israelis in the Six Day War of 1967. After the Yom Kippur War of 1973, a delicate truce was negotiated between Syria and Israel by then–US secretary of state Henry Kissinger, which saw Syria regain some 450 sq km of lost territory. A complicated demilitarised buffer zone, supervised by UN forces, was also established, varying in width from a few hundred metres to a couple of kilometres.

In 1981 the Israeli government upped the stakes by formally annexing part of the Golan and moving in settlers. In Israeli eyes the heights are an indispensable shield against potential Syrian attack. The Syrians, of course, see things differently.

Since the Middle East peace process was kicked into gear with the 1991 Madrid conference, Israel and Syria have so far danced a reluctant tango with no tangible results. With peace signed between Israel and Egypt, and Israel and Jordan, Syria remains in a sense the odd one out. But its position is straightforward enough – Israel must execute a complete withdrawal from the whole of the Golan Heights before Syria will contemplate peace. The Syrian hardline approach has been met by an equally intransigent response from Israel. With the current troubles raging in Israel and the Palestinian Territories and all the associated security fears, it's hard to see the Golan Heights stalemate being broken any time soon.

While general travel in this most politically sensitive of regions is not allowed, you can visit the town of Quneitra.

QUNEITRA   القنيطرة

It's been 30 years since a shot has been fired in Quneitra, but the ruins serve as a bitter reminder of conflict. Once the area's administrative capital, before the Israelis withdrew from the town after the 1973 cease-fire, they evacuated the 37,000 Arabs here and systematically destroyed Quneitra, removing anything that could be unscrewed, unbolted or wrenched from its position. Everything from windows to light fittings were sold to Israeli contractors, and the stripped buildings were pulled apart with tractors and bulldozers.

Quneitra today is a ghost town. The rubble of demolished houses lies next to the empty shells of mosques and churches rising among strangely peaceful scenes of devastation. The main street's banks and shops that once prospered are lifeless, and the pockmarked local clinic has become the centrepiece for what has become something of a propaganda exhibit demonstrating the hard-nosed approach of the Israelis.

For some years, Quneitra has been under Syrian control within the UN-patrolled demilitarised zone. There is a UN checkpoint right in the town, and barbed wire on its outskirts marks the border between Syrian territory and Israeli-occupied land. From the town you can easily make out Israeli communications and observation posts on the heights to the west. Much of this area also has land mines.

Before visiting Quneitra, it's worth paying a visit to the Panorama in Damascus (see p98).

Entry Permits

To visit Quneitra you must obtain a permit from the **Ministry of the Interior** (⏰ 8am-2pm Sun-Thu), just off Saahat Adnan al-Malki in Abu Roumana, the embassy district of Damascus. To reach it from the square, head west uphill with the steep grassy park on your right. Almost immediately you will see a flight of stairs going up – the office is just to the left at the top, signposted by T-shirted, machine gun-wielding guards. You must bring your passport, and you should be issued the permit within about 15 minutes. You have the option of having the pass for that particular day or for the following day – if it's already past about 10am ask for it to be for the following day, or you'll be really tight on time.

Getting There & Away

From the Baramke garage in Damascus, catch a microbus to Khan Arnabah (أرنبة خان; S£20, one hour). This is a small end-of-the-earth, UN-frequented town about 10km short of Quneitra. From here the odd minibus or microbus (S£5) makes the final run past the Syrian and UN checkpoints into Quneitra itself, or you can hitch. At the last checkpoint you'll be asked for your permit and presented with a 'tour guide' – a Syrian intelligence officer who probably won't speak English but will make sure you don't wander off into any minefields.

The Coast & Mountains

الساحل السوري والجبال

CONTENTS

THE COAST & MOUNTAINS

Syria's 183km-long coastline is dominated by the rugged 250km-long Jebel Ansariyya mountain range that runs along its entire length. Squeezed between the highland and the sea is a narrow coastal strip that widens towards the south, where the country is extremely fertile and heavily cultivated. The port city of Lattakia (Al-Lathqiyya), with its beach resorts and the ruined ancient city of Ugarit (Ras Shamra), lie in the north. From here roads lead north to Turkey, east across the mountains to Aleppo, and south to Tartus, a secondary port that preserves remnants of its medieval Crusader past.

The mountains behind Lattakia contain Syria's only forests and these are easy on the eyes after the often-featureless interior. Excessive clearing of the forests for timber has led to large areas being reduced to scrub, although the government has laid aside some sections for preservation. Perhaps more interesting for the traveller is that much of this area was in Crusader hands for centuries. They left behind a chain of hilltop eyries and precipitously located castles, the undisputed king of which is the stalwart Krak des Chevaliers.

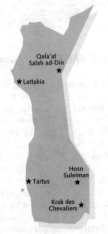

HIGHLIGHTS

- Marvel at **Krak des Chevaliers** (p132), possibly the finest Crusader castle in the world
- Sample the atypical port town of **Lattakia** (p143) with its tree-lined boulevards and sidewalk cafés
- Speculate on how the temple of **Hosn Suleiman** (p142) was constructed so high up in the picturesque mountains
- Witness why TE Lawrence thought **Qala'at Salah ad-Din** (p150) was the most sensational thing in castle building
- Kick back at **Tartus** (p136), a quiet port town and a pleasant place to unwind for a couple of days

THE COAST & MOUNTAINS

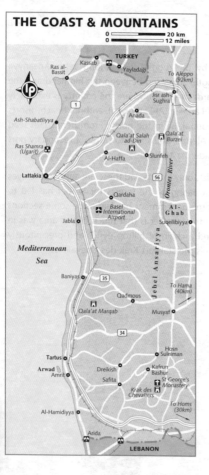

THE COAST & MOUNTAINS

0 ———— 20 km
0 ———— 12 miles

exploring it. A torch is handy for some of the darker passages and rooms.

The castle is easily visited by public transport as a day trip from Tartus or Hama – see Getting There & Away (p135) for practical details. However, visiting by car (rental or hired with driver from your hotel) allows for exploring the surrounding countryside and hilltop resort towns, which is highly recommended. Anybody passing through en route to Homs, Tartus or elsewhere, can leave bags and packs at the ticket office.

History

The castle addresses the only significant break in the Jebel Ansariyya. Anyone who held this breach, known as the Homs Gap, between the southern end of the range and the northern outreaches of the Anti-Lebanon Range (Jebel Libnan ash-Sharqiyya), was virtually assured authority over inland Syria by controlling the flow of goods and people from the ports through to the interior. Even today, this gap carries the major road link from Homs to Tartus, as well as the oil pipeline from the fields in the far east of the country to the terminal at Tartus.

The first fortress that is known to have existed on this site was built by the Emir of Homs in 1031. He was briefly displaced in 1099 by the hordes of the First Crusade passing through on its way to Jerusalem, and was then given the complete push some 11 years later when the Christian knights, now established in the Holy City, began to extend their gains throughout the region. Around the middle of the 12th century the elite Knights Hospitaller replaced the First Crusaders and built and expanded the Krak into its present form.

The knights built well and despite repeated attacks and sieges, the fortress was never truly breached. Instead, the Crusaders simply gave it up. When the Mamluk sultan Beybars marched on the castle in 1271, the knights at the Krak were a last outpost. Jerusalem had been lost and the Christians were retreating. Numbers in the castle, which was built to hold a garrison of 2000, were depleted to around 200. Surrounded by the armies of Islam and with no hope of reprieve, the fortress must have seemed more like a prison than a stronghold. Even though they had supplies to last for five years, after a month under siege the

KRAK DES CHEVALIERS   قلعة الحصن

☎ 031

Author Paul Theroux described Krak des Chevaliers as the epitome of the dream castle of childhood fantasies of jousts and armour and pennants. TE Lawrence simply called it 'the finest castle in the world'. Take their word for it, the remarkably well-preserved **Krak des Chevaliers** (Qala'at al-Hosn; adult/student S£300/30; ⏱ 9am-6pm Apr-Oct, to 4pm Nov-Mar) is one of Syria's prime attractions and should not be missed. Impervious to the onslaught of time, it cannot have looked a great deal different 800 years ago, and such is its size and state of completeness that you could easily spend several hours absorbed in

Crusaders agreed to depart the castle under terms of safe conduct.

Beybars garrisoned the castle with his own Mamluk troops and further strengthened the defences. Today, it is possible to distinguish the Frankish aspects of the castle, with their Gothic and Romanesque building styles, and those of the Arabs – there are some beautiful, typically Islamic geometric designs carved into some of the structures on the upper levels of the main complex.

Sights
THE OUTSIDE WALL
The castle comprises two distinct parts: the outside wall with its 13 towers and main entrance; and the inner fortress. The whole is built on a foundation of solid rock, with a moat hacked out of the rock separating the outer and inner sections.

The **main entrance** (1) leads to a sloping ramp with steps wide enough to allow the garrison's horses to be ridden two abreast. The **first tower** (2) on the left was a guard room and, next to it, the **long hall** (3) served as stables – it's now a dark storeroom filled

with building equipment. The ramp eventually emerges in a more open area where the passage doubles back on itself to lead up into the inner fortress, as well as continuing on ahead to exit via another **tower** (5), which gives access out into the moat area. As you emerge look back at the outer face of the doorway to see, carved into the stone, representations of two lions facing each other, possibly symbols of the English Crusader king, Richard I 'the Lion-Heart'.

The **moat** (10) here is usually full of stagnant water. When the castle was occupied, this water was used to fill the **baths** (6), which you can get down to by a couple of dogleg staircases over in the corner to your left. These stairs lead into a tight complex of rooms and those familiar with hammams will recognise the layout: there's a central chamber with a stone fountain and off it, private washrooms, a couple of which still contain stone basins. This was a Mamluk or later addition.

The cavernous room on the southern edge of the moat measures 60m by 9m and the roof is formed of one single vault – quite an

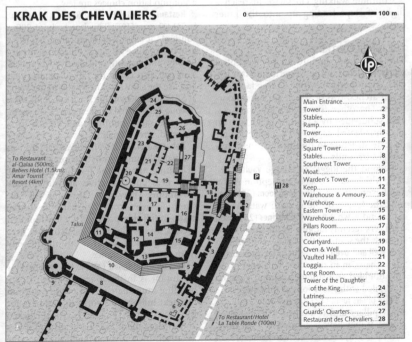

KRAK DES CHEVALIERS

0 — 100 m

To Restaurant
al-Qalaa (500m);
Bebers Hotel (1.5km);
Amar Tourist
Resort (4km)

Talus

To Restaurant/Hotel
La Table Ronde (100m)

Main Entrance.....................1
Tower...................................2
Stables................................3
Ramp...................................4
Tower...................................5
Baths...................................6
Square Tower......................7
Stables................................8
Southwest Tower.................9
Moat..................................10
Warden's Tower.................11
Keep..................................12
Warehouse & Armoury.......13
Warehouse.........................14
Eastern Tower....................15
Warehouse.........................16
Pillars Room......................17
Tower.................................18
Courtyard...........................19
Oven & Well.......................20
Vaulted Hall.......................21
Loggia................................22
Long Room.........................23
Tower of the Daughter
   of the King.......................24
Latrines..............................25
Chapel................................26
Guards' Quarters................27
Restaurant des Chevaliers...28

impressive feat in stone. It was most likely used as **stables** (8). On exiting the western end of the hall two sets of stairs (these are quite decrepit, so be careful of your footing) give access to the battlements above. From up here it is possible to gain access to each of the three towers that punctuate the southern wall. The **square tower** (7) bore the brunt of the 1271 attack and was later rebuilt by Beybars. The **southwest tower** (9) was also rebuilt; its central pillar, which supports the upper levels of the construction, bears an inscription in Arabic recording Beybars' full title, which translates as 'the Manifest King, Pillar of the World and the Faith, Father of the Victory'.

Walking around between the two walls from the southwest tower, you reach the **Tower of the Daughter of the King** (24) in the northwestern corner, unusual in that it is wider than it is deep. On the façade are three rows of triple-pointed arches. A large projecting gallery, where rocks were hurled at assailants, is concealed in the face. The eastern face of this tower has a rear gate opening onto the moat.

Continue walking clockwise to reach a flight of steps leading up into the inner fortress.

THE INNER FORTRESS

The steps lead up into an open, central **courtyard** (19). On the western side is a **loggia** (22), or portico, with a Gothic façade of seven arches, two of which are open doorways. The other five arches are windows, each subdivided by a delicate pillar with an acanthus-leafed capital. It's a surprisingly delicate structure to find in such massively brutal surrounds.

Beyond the loggia is a large **vaulted hall** (21), which was probably a reception room, and beyond this, a 120m **long room** (23) running the length of the western wall. At the north end is what were the **latrines** (25), used until very recently judging by the smell, while towards the south of the hall are the remains of a **well and oven** (22), the latter measuring more than 5m in diameter. This area probably doubled as a storage area and granary, stockpiled with provisions against sieges.

The **pillars room** (17) has five rows of heavy squat pillars and is vaulted with fist-sized stones. It may have been used as a refectory. Several nearby rooms were **warehouses** (13, 14

and 16). In one are the remains of massive pottery oil jars and in another there's an oil mill, more oil jars and a well.

Back in the courtyard, the **chapel** (26) has a nave of three bays of vaults. It was converted to a mosque after the Muslim conquest and the minbar still remains. The staircase that obstructs the main door is a later addition and leads to the upper floors of the fortress.

The upper floor of the Tower of the Daughter of the King is a **café** with expensive tea, coffee and cold drinks, and terrible food. There are also toilets up here. You can make your way over to the round tower in the southwest corner known as the **Warden's Tower** (11); this was where the Grand Master of the Hospitallers had his quarters. From the tower's roof are some magnificent views; haze permitting, to the west you should be able to make out the solitary pale figure of Safita's keep.

Sleeping & Eating

Given that Krak des Chevaliers is only just over an hour from Tartus, Homs or even Hama, most people visit on a day trip – hence, accommodation choices are few.

Restaurant/Hotel La Table Ronde (☎ 740 280; fax 741 400; rooms S£500) This hotel, about 200m south of the castle's main entrance, has a few grubby rooms with squat toilets; rooms are wholly unappealing and vastly overpriced. You can also camp (S£150 to pitch a tent and use the shower). The food is better value at S£175 per person for shish kebab or *shish tawouq* (marinated chicken grilled on skewers) plus salad, hummus and French fries, but mediocre in quality.

Bebers Hotel (☎ 741 201; s/d US$20/25) This was still partially under construction at the time of writing, though the few finished rooms were neat and attractive, all with private bathrooms. Many of the 31 rooms will have stunning views from their balconies of the castle in full side-profile just a few hundred metres away. The hotel is two hills over from the castle, about a 20-minute walk from the main entrance.

Restaurant al-Qalaa (☎ 740 493, 740 003) This restaurant is in the lone white two-storey building immediately west of the castle, on the next hilltop. It's worth dining here for the views alone. The food is grilled chicken and mezze (about S£250 a head) and if you ask nicely owner Anran might show you the guest book signed by Sean Connery (a visitor here in June 2001).

Getting There & Away

Krak des Chevaliers lies some 10km north of the Homs–Tartus highway. It is roughly halfway between the two towns and can be visited on a day trip from either, or en route from one to the other. Coming from Damascus or Hama, it's necessary to change bus in Homs – see the Going to Krak des Chevaliers boxed text (p159) for transport details. The Cairo and Riad hotels in Hama (see p164) run organised tours to the castle.

Doing it yourself from Tartus, you need to catch a Homs microbus and ask to be let out at 'Qala'at al-Hosn' (the local term for the castle). You'll be dropped off on the main highway at the turning for the castle, where there's usually a microbus waiting to shuttle passengers up the hill; expect to have to haggle over the fare – it should be S£10 but the best we could bring it down to was S£50.

To return, hitch a lift with a microbus (another S£50) from the castle back down to the junction on the Homs–Tartus highway. Here you can flag down a passing microbus back/onward to Homs or Tartus.

AROUND KRAK DES CHEVALIERS

☎ 031

The landscape surrounding Krak des Chevaliers is beautiful – low, rolling, emerald-green hills, shaded with foliage. The high altitude cools the temperature and the small villages and towns such as **Amar**, **Dreikish**, **Mashtu Helu** and **Safita** which dot the hilltops are popular summer resorts, not just with native Syrians but with many thousands who now live overseas and return annually for vacations. Other than the keep at Safita (see p141), the area's main sight is St George's Monastery, which lies in a valley a few kilometres northwest of the Krak. Unfortunately, there's no way of getting around by public transport, so the only way to see this highly attractive part of the country is to hire a car or sign up for an organised tour in Hama or Tartus.

St George's Monastery   دير مار جرجس

St George is one of the most popular Christian saints in the Middle East, where in Arabic he's known as Mar Jirjis. Traditionally he's held to have been a Palestinian conscript in the Roman army who was executed in the 3rd century AD for tearing up a copy of the Emperor Diocletian's decree forbidding the practise of Christianity. Legends about him grew from the 6th century onwards and these stories were likely carried back to Europe by returning Crusaders; in 1348 England's Edward III made George patron of the Knights of the Garter. Long before then, there were churches dedicated to him throughout the Middle East, and the first church on this particular site was built possibly as early as the 6th century AD.

The **monastery** (Deir Mar Jirjis; ⏱ 6am-8pm) of today is fully functioning, and takes the form of a modern, large walled compound at the bottom of a valley, with the guardian Krak des Chevaliers clearly visible high on a hilltop just a few kilometres away. A guide greets visitors and shows them to the 'New Church', dating from 1857, adorned with a fine carved-wood iconostasis depicting various scenes from the life of Christ, and topped by a row of wooden birds about to take flight. The 13th-century 'Old Church' accessed across a lower, sunken courtyard has a smaller, even more intricate iconostasis, which is over 300 years old and depicts scenes from the life of St George.

To get here, take the road from the highway towards Nasira and 4km after the turnoff for Hosn and the Krak take a fork to the left. If you don't have transport you could arrange to go by taxi from the Krak; there and back, plus an hour or so waiting time, should cost no more than S£200.

Sleeping

Although there's plenty of accommodation around, it's highly seasonal; from mid-June to mid-September you need to book well in advance.

Amar Tourist Resort (☎ 730 512; Wadi Nassarah, Amar; low-season d US$25; ▨ ▣) The resort is a sizable set-up with a large pool and restaurants, but all facilities are closed up through winter. Rooms are huge but shabby; prices vary with the season.

Al-Fahd Hotel (☎ 730 822, 730 559; Al-Mishtaia; d with breakfast US$20; ▣) The hotel is around 2km from the monastery, right on the main road. It's a modest place with simple clean rooms – all doubles – complete with private bathrooms and balconies with views of the Krak. There is a dining room and the owner speaks good English.

Francis Hotel (☎ 730 946/7/8; www.francishotel.net; Wadi Nassarah, Amar; ste US$75-95; ✖ ▢ ▩) Several kilometres from the Krak, this hotel is a recently completed apartment hotel on a hillside overlooking Amar. Suites are large and splendid – prices vary according to the season. Plus there's a big pool, restaurant and bar. Reception staff speak excellent English.

Al-Wadi Hotel (☎ 730 456; fax 730 399; Al-Mishtaia; s/d US$60/72; ✖ ▩) Next door to Al-Fahd, this hotel is a big modern place, recently made even bigger by the addition of a new annexe. Prices are high, but it's a very good four-star hotel with full amenities.

TARTUS طرطوس
☎ 043

Tartus, Syria's second port, is a small, quiet town that is unlikely to set many pulses racing, but which makes for a pleasant place to relax for a couple of days. The town's principal attraction is the compact remnants of the Old City (known to the Crusaders as Tortosa), which is a fascinating little warren. There's also the once-fortified island of Arwad, which lies 3km offshore and is reached by water taxi. Syrians love Tartus for its beaches but anyone game to pick through the junk on the sand and go for a dip should note the occasional dribble of sewage into the sea.

See Around Tartus (p140) for details on the Phoenician site of Amrit, the keep at Safita, and Hosn Suleiman. Tartus is also a good base for visiting Krak des Chevaliers (p132), or the fortress of Qala'at Marqab (p142).

History
Tartus seems to have been first established by the Phoenicians as a service town for the island of Arados (Arwad) and given the name Antarados (meaning 'Anti-Arados' or 'Opposite Arados'). It wasn't until the time of the Byzantines that Antarados became important – it's said that the emperor Constantine preferred the Christian community on the mainland to the pagans on the island, and the town became known as Constantina. With the collapse of the Byzantine empire, the town passed into the hands of the Arabs, from whom it was wrested in 1099 by the Crusaders.

Under the new name of Tortosa, the town was strategically important for the Crusaders as it kept their sea links open with Europe. They turned the place into a fortified stronghold and built a cathedral in honour of the Virgin Mary, who had long been associated with this site. In 1152, after Muslim forces had briefly taken Tortosa, control of the town was given to the elite Knights Templar.

In 1188, Saladin (Salah ad-Din) led another Muslim assault and forced the Crusader knights to fall back to the main fortified keep, the town's last defence. This they held, and eventually the Muslims withdrew. The Knights Templar set about refortifying the town and also defending the approaches with a series of castles. These precautions enabled them to hold Tortosa against a further two major attacks by the Mamluks but eventually, as the last of the Crusader strongholds elsewhere in the Holy Lands fell, the knights realised their days were numbered and retreated to Arwad. There they maintained a garrison for 12 years before finally departing for Cyprus.

The town languished – hence its modest size – and only really began to flourish once Syria gained independence. With the subsequent partitioning off of Lebanon and the handing over of the Antakya region to Turkey, Syria found itself with only one functioning port (Lattakia), making it necessary to revive Tartus.

Orientation
The heart of town is the area around Sharia al-Wahda, which stretches between the roundabout with the clock tower at its eastern end and the fishing harbour at its western end. Just to the north is the Old City, south are the town's few shopping streets. The Qadmous bus station is around 500m north of the clock-tower roundabout; minibuses and trains halt out on the main highway, Sharia 6 Tichreen, which marks the eastern edge of town – from here it's a 15- to 20-minute walk to the centre. The commercial port is north of the town.

Information
Commercial Bank of Syria (CBS; cnr Sharia Khaled ibn al-Walid & Sharia al-Orouba; ✆ 8am-noon Sat-Thu) On the northeast side of the Old City. It changes cash and travellers cheques (S£40 commission).

Immigration Office (✆ 8am-2pm Sat-Thu) Just south of Sharia Jamal Abdel Nasser, one block east of the park (it's well signposted). Visa extensions (less than one hour

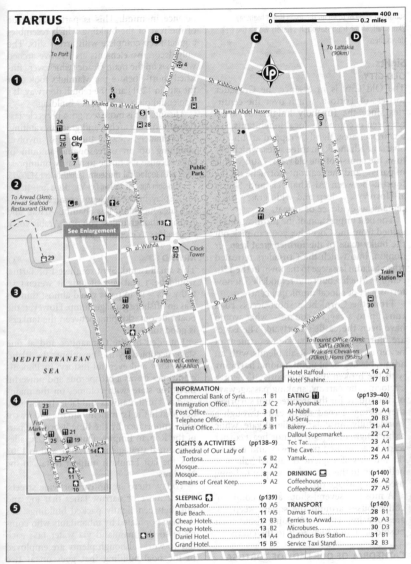

TARTUS

See Enlargement

MEDITERRANEAN
SEA

INFORMATION
Commercial Bank of Syria............1 B1
Immigration Office.......................2 C2
Post Office..................................3 D1
Telephone Office.........................4 B1
Tourist Office..............................5 B1

SIGHTS & ACTIVITIES   (pp138–9)
Cathedral of Our Lady of
    Tortosa...................................6 B2
Mosque......................................7 A2
Mosque......................................8 A2
Remains of Great Keep................9 A2

SLEEPING   (p139)
Ambassador................................10 A5
Blue Beach.................................11 A5
Cheap Hotels..............................12 B3
Cheap Hotels..............................13 B2
Daniel Hotel...............................14 A4
Grand Hotel...............................15 B5

Hotel Raffoul..............................16 A2
Hotel Shahine............................17 B3

EATING   (pp139–40)
Al-Ayounak................................18 B4
Al-Nabil.....................................19 A4
Al-Seraj....................................20 B3
Bakery......................................21 A4
Dalloul Supermarket...................22 C2
Tec Tac.....................................23 A4
The Cave...................................24 A1
Yamak......................................25 A4

DRINKING   (p140)
Coffeehouse..............................26 A2
Coffeehouse..............................27 A5

TRANSPORT   (p140)
Damas Tours..............................28 B1
Ferries to Arwad.........................29 A3
Microbuses................................30 D3
Qadmous Bus Station..................31 B1
Service Taxi Stand......................32 B3

to process) require two photos, two completed forms, along with S£30 for an excise stamp.

Internet Centre (☎ 315 906; Sharia ath-Thawra; per 30 min S£50; ☒ 10am-10pm) As you walk down Ath-Thawra, it's on the left-hand side about 1.5km south of the clock-tower roundabout; look for a blue Ericsson sign. If you reach Hotel Cliopatra, it's across the street about 100m back.

Post Office (cnr Sharia Jamal Abdel Nasser & Sharia

6 Tichreen; ☒ 8am-8pm Sat-Thu, to 2pm Fri) About a 15-minute walk from the centre of town.

Telephone Office (Sharia Adnan al-Maleki; ☒ 24hr Sat-Thu, to 8pm Fri) Just north of the Khaled ibn al-Walid and Ath-Thawra junction. There are also a couple of card phones at the post office.

Tourist Office (☎ 223 448; Sharia 6 Tichreen; ☒ 8am-2pm Sat-Thu) Inconveniently located on the southeast edge of town on the main Homs highway, 2km south of the train station. It's hardly worth the trek down there.

Sights
OLD CITY

The Old City is in essence the Crusader fortress of Tortosa, which over the centuries since the (un)holy knights departed has been occupied by local inhabitants. It's a compact area, tightly wrapped around by Sharia al-Khandek on three sides, which follows the course of the **old walls** – still visible in parts – and the seafront Corniche on the fourth. Between Al-Khandek and Sharia al-Horreyya, a deep and wide grassy ditch remains as evidence of a **moat**.

The best impression of the fortifications is gained from the Corniche: you can pick out the bulky mass of the former **great keep**, or donjon, into which the Crusaders retreated when Saladin lay siege to the town in the 12th century. Much rebuilt and remodelled, it now forms part of a local municipal centre.

From the Corniche a short access road runs up to a ragged square – what would have been the castle's **courtyard**. The edges are blurred by a ramshackle assortment of newer structures, but it all blends with an admirable degree of unintentional harmony with the broken old stonework. It's worth exploring the narrow, snaking passageways off the square for the architectural surprises they spring; a road north exits through a wonderfully muscular medieval gate, while a short flight of steps in the northeast corner leads to an arched passageway and then to the remains of a splendid vaulted hall, now half-open to the sky and very open to being used as a garbage tip.

A mosque, several shops and a couple of coffeehouses around the square keep the area buzzing with locals going about their business, all of which adds to the charm.

CATHEDRAL OF OUR LADY OF TORTOSA
كاتدرائية طرطوس

Part cathedral, part fortress, Our Lady of Tortosa was constructed by the Crusaders in the 12th century, although a chapel dedicated to the Virgin Mary possibly existed on this site as early as the 4th century AD. Rebuilding on the existing consecrated site means that the Crusader cathedral stood outside the walled enclave and hence was designed with its own defence in mind. This is particularly true of the rear of the building which resembles a great keep complete with arrow slits. The only decorative elements are the five arched windows on the main façade (which were finished shortly before the Mamluks took over the city in 1291) and the rebuilt doorway. It's a splendid piece of Crusader building.

The interior is more recognisably ecclesiastic with soaring arches and graceful vaulting. Unfortunately, viewing the interior involves coughing up an unreasonable amount of cash because it's home to a fairly unimpressive **archaeological museum** (adult/student S£300/15; ☣ 9am-6pm Apr-Sep, to 4pm Oct-Mar, closed Tue). Items on display in the museum come from various sites including Ras Shamra, Arwad and Amrit, although unless you read Arabic you'll be at a loss to identify them.

ARWAD
أرواد

This small island, 3km southwest of Tartus, would be a real gem if only it weren't so filthy. As it is, in parts you'd almost think it was an offshore garbage dump. However, the boat ride out, skipping between the tankers, is good fun.

Founded by the Canaanites and at one stage occupied by the Egyptians, the island has a long and eventful history. In Phoenician times it was a prosperous and powerful maritime state, with colonies on the mainland at Amrit, Baniyas and Jabla. It gradually declined in the 1st millennium BC and was of little importance by the time it became part of the Roman Empire. During the Crusades it assumed strategic importance and in 1302 was the last Frankish outpost to fall to the Muslims.

Today, there are no cars or wide streets, only a maze of narrow lanes that jog and jink between tightly packed buildings. It's densely populated by inhabitants who commute to the mainland via water taxi each day to work, although plenty are employed in the boat-building that goes on at two sites on the island, on the north and south tips. At any given time there will be several timber skeletons of boats in various stages of construction. Otherwise, there's little else specific to see. Not much is left of the island's defensive walls (just a stretch on the western side of the island), but two forts remain; the one that you see off to the right as you come into the harbour is closed to the public, but there's another on the island's highest point that houses a small **museum** (adult/student S£150/10; ☺ 9am-6pm Apr-Sep, to 4pm Oct-Mar, closed Tue). Nothing is labelled but the attendants are eager to show off their English and guide you around. To find the museum just head directly inland from the harbour and you'll come across it eventually – the whole island only measures 800m by 500m.

Sleeping

Decent accommodation is thin on the ground in Tartus. There are several cheapies (about S£150 a bed) clustered around the junction of Ath-Thawra and Al-Wahda but these are dire – bedding down on one of the mattresses in these places could be the start of a meaningful relationship with a dermatologist. There are a couple of places near the seafront too, notably the **Ambassador** and **Blue Beach** on Sharia Tarek ibn Ziad, which were formerly quite grand but are now little better than dosshouses. The owners still have the nerve to ask for S£800 a double, presumably because of the sea views.

Daniel Hotel (☎ 312 757; fax 316 555; Sharia al-Wahda; s/d S£300/600) The pick of the town's accommodation, the Daniel's location is as central as it gets, while rooms are spacious with large beds (with crisp, white sheets) and new private bathrooms. Management are helpful and speak English. During summer the hotel runs half-day trips to Krak des Chevaliers and to an island beyond Arwad for swimming.

Hotel Raffoul (☎ 220 616, 220 097; Saahat Manchieh; beds per person S£200) Across from the cathedral, this hotel has only 10 rooms, but it's good value. Two of the rooms have private bathrooms, the rest share facilities. It's quiet and very well looked after. If the hotel is locked up you need to go to the grocer's store on the nearby corner, owned by the same guy who runs the hotel.

Hotel Shahine (☎ 315 001; fax 221 703; Sharia Ahmed al-Azawi; s/d US$24/30; ✹) Modern but badly aged, this eight-storey place is one block back from the sea. Rooms on the 3rd floor and above have oblique sea views. All have air-con, private bathroom and fridge.

Grand Hotel (☎ 317 797; fax 315 683; Corniche al-Bahr; s/d US$30/40; ✹) An old-style four-star, the Grand has character, is well looked after and most rooms have sea views, making the rates something of a bargain. The downside is that it's about 1km from the centre and

surrounded by the concrete shells of half-finished buildings. The hotel accepts credit cards.

Shahine Tower Hotel (☎ 329 100; fax 315 290; Sharia Tarek ibn Ziad; s/d US$80/100; ✹) Tartus' only luxury accommodation, the Shahine has 14 floors and 156 rooms. Money has been spent on lots of marble and brass, and rooms are suitably plush, but the overall feel is cold and impersonal, like a vast mausoleum. Credit cards are accepted.

Eating
RESTAURANTS

The local speciality, unsurprisingly, is fish, but it comes with a hefty price tag. It's sold by weight and starts at S£400 per kilogram and can shoot up to four times as much, depending on the type of fish (although the best is sent south to Lebanon, where it fetches far more money). About the cheapest place to eat fish is probably the no-frills **Al-Nabil** (see Cafés & Quick Eats, below), but most locals head over to Arwad for one of the open-air fish restaurants around the harbour. At somewhere like **Arwad Seafood Restaurant** you're taken to the fridge to select your fish and it's then either baked or grilled for you and served with complimentary bread, hummus and salad. You'll be lucky to get away with a bill of S£600 for two.

Cave (☎ 220 408; Corniche al-Bahr; ☺ noon-late) Occupying a vaulted hall burrowed into the sea wall of the old city, the Cave has atmosphere in spades and the food is excellent too. The house speciality is seafood (pricey) but there are also beautifully cooked grilled meat dishes. Expect to spend S£300 to S£500 per head. Alcohol is served and Diners Club, MasterCard, and Visa are all accepted.

Yamak (☎ 328 755; Sharia al-Amara; ☺ noon-2am) Up on the 4th floor of the nondescript Chamber of Commerce & Industry building opposite the fishing harbour, this restaurant is a fairly souless space, only partly redeemed by the views out to sea. Choose between an iced display of the day's catch, or kebabs. Kebabs and a couple of beers will come to around S£500 for two.

CAFÉS & QUICK EATS

The usual cheap restaurants and snack places (for felafel, shwarma, grilled chicken) are clustered around the clock tower and Sharia al-Wahda, and south down Ath-Thawra.

There's also a cluster of cheap-eats places along Sharia Ahmed al-Azawi (500m south of Sharia al-Wahda), which is where the local kids hang out.

Al-Ayounak (☎ 326 086; 7 Sharia Ahmed al-Azawi; ◷ noon-midnight) This small snack bar at the seafront end of the street is run by a very friendly guy who lived in Sydney for 17 years. The pizzas are excellent and it serves beer (S£50).

Al-Nabil (Sharia al-Amara) One block back from the fishing harbour (just round the corner from the Daniel Hotel), Al-Nabil specialises in heavily spiced and salted baked fish but also does more regular dishes like chicken and kebabs for around S£100. Local beer (S£50) is available too.

Al-Seraj (off Sharia Tarek ibn Ziad; ◷ 11am-late Sat-Thu) Signposted in Arabic only (السراج), this place is worth searching out for its friendly service, clean surrounds and very decent, cheaply priced local fare, as well as pizzas. Beer is also served.

Tec Tac (Corniche al-Bahr; ◷ 10-2am) One of a string of coffeehouses along the seafront between the fishing harbour and the Old City, Tec Tac is notable for serving food (cheap local fare) and beer. It's also very female friendly, attracting plenty of local girls sharing nargileh (water pipes).

SELF-CATERING

The very good, modern and small **Dalloul supermarket** (Sharia al-Quds) just east of the public park has groceries and Western toothpaste, shampoo and sanitary napkins. For freshly baked bread, rolls and croissants, there's a small **bakery** next to Al-Nabil restaurant. A **liquor store** a couple of doors from the Daniel Hotel sells beer.

Drinking

The best bet for an evening in Tartus would be to settle into a **coffeehouse** – there are several along the seafront just north of the fishing harbour, but the preferred choice is **Tec Tac** (see above), which is clean and bright, and serves beer as well as nargileh. There's also a bar in the lobby of the **Shahine Tower Hotel**, but it's a fairly gloomy affair.

Getting There & Away

BUS

Qadmous has a station just off the big roundabout north of the park. Buses depart hourly for Damascus (S£110, four hours), as well as frequent services to Aleppo (S£115, four hours), Hama (S£65, 1½ hours) and Homs (S£40, one hour). Small buses to Lattakia (S£35, one hour) and Baniyas (S£12, 30 minutes) go every 15 to 20 minutes.

Damas Tours has an office just off Sharia ath-Thawra, near the Old City, from where there are six departures a day for Damascus and five to Lattakia (prices as for Qadmous).

Al-Ahliah (Sharia ath-Thawra) is south of the centre; destinations and fares are as for Qadmous, although departures are less frequent.

MICROBUS

Microbuses depart from the main highway, Sharia 6 Tichreen, in front of the little-used train station. Departures include Lattakia (S£35, one hour), Baniyas (S£15, 30 minutes), Homs (S£30, one hour), Safita (S£10, 30 minutes) and Al-Hamidiyya (for Amrit; S£5, 15 minutes).

SERVICE TAXI

Service taxis congregate around the clock tower. Demand is not very high so you may have to wait quite a while for one to fill up. They charge much more than bus prices. Destinations include Damascus, Homs and Lattakia, as well as Beirut and Tripoli.

TRAIN

The only train for Damascus passes through at 12.45am Friday and costs S£67/45 (1st/2nd class) and you have to change at Homs. The sole weekly service to Lattakia is at 7.30pm Thursday.

Getting Around

Although you're not likely to use them very often, the local buses can make life a little easier. A ticket booth is located about 200m north of the clock tower. A pink ticket valid for four rides (punch a corner at a time) will cost S£10.

AROUND TARTUS

Tartus is a good base from which to explore the mountainous hinterland and several interesting sites. Closest to town is Amrit, although as with many of Syria's pre-Classical sites, this is really one for the keen amateur archaeologist. Alternatively, head inland and up into the hills. The local transport hub up here is Safita, an attractive hilltop town with an impressive Crusader keep. From Safita you can push on to Hosn Suleiman – there isn't that much there but the scenery along the way is beautiful.

Tartus is also a convenient base for day trips to the castles of Qala'at Marqab to the north, on the way to Lattakia, and to Krak des Chevaliers, on the road to Homs. It takes about an hour to get to either of these places.

Amrit   عمريت

Two quite odd-looking monuments, erected as long ago as the 6th century BC, dominate the mysterious ancient site of Amrit, 8km south of Tartus. Known later to the Greeks as Marathos and conquered by Alexander the Great in 333 BC, Amrit had fallen by the wayside by the time it was incorporated into the Roman Empire.

The so-called *meghazils* (spindles) stand in what was once a necropolis and, although no-one is entirely sure how to explain the origins of this settlement, it appears that Phoenicians from Arwad made the area a kind of satellite or religious zone. The taller of the monuments has four lions carved in a Persian style around the base. Both towers stand above underground funeral chambers (you'll need a torch to poke around them) and betray a curious mix of Hellenistic, Persian and even Egyptian influences in their decoration.

About 1km to the north you will find the remains of a **temple** built to serve a cult centred on the springs here. The main feature is a deep basin cut out of the rock, which would once have formed an artificial lake. The water that filled the basin came from the nearby spring and was considered to have curative powers. Just 50m to the north you can make out the shape of a small stadium.

GETTING THERE & AWAY

Take Al-Hamidiyya microbus (الحميدية; S£5) from Sharia 6 Tichreen near the train station in Tartus and ask to be let off at the track leading to Amrit – mention you want 'al-athaar'. The track leads off towards the sea from the main road. After about 1.5km you will pass an army post (there are firing ranges around here). Some 200m further on, immediately after passing some communication towers, you can see the temple remains in the distance on the left – these are reached by turning onto the dirt track by the

sign reading 'Rest Camp'. Continue along the paved road and take the dirt track beside the sign announcing 'Amrit Touristic Project'. This will bring you to the *meghazils*.

To get back to Tartus, return to the main road and flag down a microbus.

Safita   صافيتا

☎ 043

This restful mountain town is dominated by a striking Crusader-era **keep** (☯ 8am-1pm & 3-6pm), all that remains of the once-powerful 'Castel Blanc'. Originally built in the early 12th century as part of the outlying defences of Tartus, the castle was rebuilt and strengthened after damage sustained in an attack by the Ayyubid ruler Nureddin (Nur ad-Din). It was garrisoned by the Knights Templar until 1271 when they were driven out by Beybars, who shortly after went on to take Krak des Chevaliers.

From the very chaotic central town intersection where most microbuses drop off their passengers, take the road leading uphill to the west. After about 500m the keep is visible ahead. Continue until you see a cobbled lane off to the right and follow it under the arched gate of what remains of the castle's defensive perimeter.

At 27m high, the keep is the largest of all surviving Crusader towers. It consists of just one single lower floor and one great upper floor (plus a sub-floor passage that leads to a cistern for water storage). The lower level was a grand church with an elegant barrel-vaulted ceiling and an apse in the east wall. Only the arrow slits in the walls betray the room's military function. The church still operates, serving the local Syrian Orthodox community.

Stairs in the southwest corner lead to the upper level, which consists of a large hall divided by massive trunk-like stone pillars (note the absence of corresponding pillars in the church below – no wonder the walls are so thick). This upper room probably served as a dormitory for the knights, who lived in monastic conditions.

Another flight of steps leads you up to the roof and expansive views; to the southeast it's sometimes possible to make out Krak des Chevaliers (the two were thus linked in the Crusaders' chain of communications) and, to the south, the snowcapped peaks of northern Lebanon.

Opening hours are not strictly adhered to. Although entrance is free a tip of S£50 or S£100 is in order.

GETTING THERE & AWAY

The microbus from Tartus costs S£10; it departs from just south of the traffic circle in front of the train station. The journey takes about 30 minutes.

From Safita, microbuses for Hosn Suleiman (S£20) depart from Sharia Maysaloun, 100m south of the town's main intersection. There are also microbuses to Homs (S£35) from a side street off Maysaloun. If you want to go to Krak des Chevaliers from here, take a Homs microbus (you'll have to pay full fare) and ask to be let off at the junction for Qala'at al-Hosn.

Hosn Suleiman   حصن سليمان

A worthwhile excursion north of Safita involves journeying 25km along some of the highest mountain ridges of the Jebel Ansariyya to arrive at a remarkable testament to thousands of years of religious fervour. Outside the village of Hosn Suleiman are partial temple walls constructed of huge stone blocks, some of them as large as 5m by 3m. What makes them all the more striking is that they were here, high in the mountains, days distant from anywhere, at a time when travel was by foot or on horse.

Although evidence suggests the site has been home to temples of one religious persuasion or another since the Persian occupation of the Levant, what you can see today was erected mainly under Roman domination in the 2nd century AD.

Four gates permit entry to a large rectangular enclosure. A partially collapsed cella, which is the focal point of worship and offerings in the temple, rises from the centre of the site. The gates preserve the most intact decoration, with columns, niches and inscriptions (the clearest of these can be observed above the east gate). The east and west gates both display the same sculptural adornments: the figure of a bearded man stands above the lintel, while the same area on the inside is dominated by figures depicting two youths and a lion's head. As you pass through each gate, look up to see the outspread wings of an eagle.

Across the road are the less extensive ruins of what appears to be another temple compound, but little is known about its history or function.

GETTING THERE & AWAY

Microbuses (S£20) run at irregular intervals from Safita, taking about 40 minutes. Most go right past the site so just holler to be let out when you can see the ruins. To get back to Safita, stand on the road and flag down any passing public transport.

QALA'AT MARQAB   قلعة مرقب

After Krak des Chevaliers and Qala'at Salah ad-Din, probably the third most impressive of Syria's Crusader castles is the brooding **Qala'at Marqab** (adult/student S£300/15; 9am-6pm Apr-Sep, 9am-4pm Wed-Mon Oct-Mar), built from black basalt rock. It's not as complete as the Krak or as strikingly located as Salah ad-Din, but set out on a spur it does command almost limitless views across the Mediterranean to the west and over the valleys dropping away to the east and south.

The original castle was a Muslim stronghold, founded possibly as late as 1062. During the early 12th century it passed into Crusader hands and was part of the principality of Antioch before being sold in 1168 to the Knights Hospitaller. It was the Hospitallers who gave the castle its present shape, concentrating their fortifications on the southern flank where the gentler slopes made the site most vulnerable. Their work was well done (according to TE Lawrence, Marqab combined 'all the best of the Latin fortifications of the Middle Ages in the East') and the castle stood up to two major assaults in the 13th century. Saladin (Salah ad-Din), who in 1188 successfully captured the nearby castle that now bears his name, did not even bother with Marqab but just marched right by, preferring to concentrate on easier targets.

Historians suspect that the main reason for its eventual fall in 1285 to the Mamluk sultan Qalaun (successor to Beybars) was, as with the breaching of Qala'at Salah ad-Din, a lack of manpower for the extensive defences. Qalaun brought down Marqab by 'mining'; his soldiers dug under the foundations of the castle walls and towers, propping up the tunnels with wooden beams. By lighting a fire and burning the beams, the tunnels collapsed and brought down the defences above them. Following the surrender of the Crusaders, the Mamluks repaired the castle – you can identify their handiwork in the telltale white bands of the south tower – and continued to use it until they lost power to the Ottomans, who had little use for castles and kept it as a prison.

Touring the Castle

The exterior walls and towers are the most impressive elements of the castle, while the interior areas are gradually being overrun by vegetation. The entrance is now through the square **gate tower** (2) in the west wall. After entering, turn right and walk down between the inner and outer walls and then up the short flight of stairs on the left to what was the inner **courtyard** (3) and the focus of activity in the castle. Across from where you enter the courtyard is a Gothic-style **chapel** (6) with two fine doorways and fragments of an original fresco depicting the Last Supper.

Keep heading south past the chapel to the three-storey semicylindrical **main keep** (7). An internal staircase leads up to the roof from where you can clearly make out the castle's concentric plan (echoing Krak des Chevaliers) and enjoy some superb views of the coast. To the north and east are the barely distinguishable remnants of **storerooms** (4) and possibly dining and living quarters.

Although it is possible to access the large wilderness that is the northern part of the castle, where there are the remains of a cemetery and an old Arab village, the area is snake infested.

Getting There & Away

Take a microbus (S£5) from Baniyas for Zaoube – it goes right past. You may have to wait a while as services are infrequent. Hitching is your best bet on the way back down. Baniyas is reached by microbus from Tartus (S£15, 20 to 30 minutes) or Lattakia (S£20, 40 minutes).

LATTAKIA   اللاذقية

☎ 041

Lattakia is not a typical Syrian town. A busy port since Roman times, it is less inward-looking than the rest of the country. The odd sign in Greek, and many more in Russian, point to the town's openness to the sea and its traffic with outsiders, while the results of this foreign exchange can be seen in wide, tree-lined boulevards and a smattering of sidewalk cafés – as opposed to the more

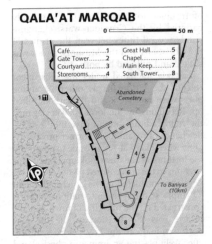

QALA'AT MARQAB

Café....................1	Great Hall...........5
Gate Tower.........2	Chapel.................6
Courtyard...........3	Main Keep...........7
Storerooms.........4	South Tower.........8

Abandoned Cemetery

To Baniyas (10km)

traditional Arabic coffeehouse. Lattakia is one of the least conservative cities in the country. Helped by the influx of money that came its way when local-boy Hafez al-Assad ruled the roost (see History, p21, for more on Syria's first president), until quite recently Lattakia had almost as many chic bar-restaurants as the capital, while its inhabitants have always been snappy dressers, especially the girls – here, the headscarf gives way to tight jeans and shoulderless tops, and you may even see a miniskirt or two.

Its comparative liberalism aside, Lattakia has no real attractions, but it does make a comfortable base for visits to the ruins of Ugarit and Qala'at Salah ad-Din (see Around Lattakia, p148).

History

Lattakia's history dates back to at least 1000 BC, when it was a small Phoenician fishing village. Alexander the Great passed through the town in 333 BC shortly after his renowned victory over the Persians at Issus, but it didn't become a settlement of any importance until the arrival of the Seleucids, the dynasty founded by one of Alexander's generals in the 4th century BC. They gave the town its name, 'Laodicea', in honour of the mother of Seleucus I. During Roman times, Marc Antony granted the town its autonomy and in the 2nd century AD it briefly served as the capital of the Roman province of Syria.

A string of serious earthquakes during the 5th and 6th centuries were precursors of troubles to come. Lattakia was badly battered by the Crusader wars, changing hands several times between the armies of the Christians and the Muslims, and it was sacked and pillaged by both.

Lattakia stagnated under the subsequent rule of the Ottomans as other Levantine ports were preferred, and its harbour silted up. Rebellions by the local Alawites against the ruling administration gave the town little chance of regaining its former prosperity. Only when Hafez al-Assad came to power did the fortunes of the town look up; family connections to the area ensured plenty of local redevelopment, including the largely redundant 'Olympic' stadium and international airports constructed on the outskirts of town. Equally bizarre was the decision to site the new port terminal on the city centre seafront, effectively placing an immense physical and visual concrete barrier between the town and the Mediterranean Sea, to which Lattakia has traditionally owed its character.

Orientation

The main north-south street is Sharia Baghdad, home to the main bank, shops and a smattering of cafés and coffeehouses. The other main street is the downmarket Sharia 14 Ramadan, which comes off the northern end of Sharia Baghdad and then runs northeast for 1.5km to the tourist information centre. Partway along, 14 Ramadan widens out to accommodate a central strip of ornamental fountains and a statue of Al-Assad, a traffic-snarled area hazardous to pedestrians known as Saahat al-Sheikh Daher (Sheikh Daher Sq). Many of the cheap hotels and eateries are clustered around here.

The train and bus stations are almost 2km east of the centre. From either of these transport terminals it takes about 20 to 25 minutes to walk to Saahat al-Sheikh Daher; a taxi will cost S£25.

Information

CBS (Sharia Baghdad; 8.30am-1.30pm & 5-8pm Sat-Thu) Changes cash and travellers cheques, no commission charged. Otherwise, you can change money 24 hours a day at the Côte d'Azur de Cham hotel at Shaati al-Azraq (Blue Beach).
Center Net (465 310) Sharia al-Mutanabi; 11am-11pm; S£50 per half-hr) Extremely well located among the cafés and restaurants of the 'American Quarter'.
Immigration Office (Saahat Jumhuriyya; 8am-2pm Sat-Thu) Some distance from the centre, beyond the tourist

information centre, on the far side of a large traffic roundabout. You need an absurd six passport photos, although after much shuffling between desks you will get your extension issued within an hour or so.
Internet Cafe Clic (466 113; 1st fl, 12 Sharia 14 Ramadan; noon-midnight; S£40 per half hr) A superchic set-up with beverage bar and excellent hardware.
Main Post Office (8am-6pm Sat-Thu) Some distance from the centre, just north of the train station in a little alley off Sharia Suria. If you can hang onto your postcards it would be more convenient to post them elsewhere.
Telephone Office (Sharia Seif al-Dawla; 8am-10.30pm) Just west of Sharia Baghdad. There are no operator calls except for emergencies; you must buy a phonecard and wait for a free phone. Phonecards bought in Damascus or Aleppo will not work here.
Tourist Information Centre (416 926; Sharia 14 Ramadan; 8am-8pm Sat-Thu) Located in the foyer of a municipal building at the eastern end of town. The friendly staff speak English.

Sights & Activities

Lattakia has precious little to show for its 3000 or so years of history. More or less the only existing monument is a right-angled **tetraporticus**, a grouping of four columns, which is all that's left of a Roman gateway that once marked the eastern end of the 2nd-century-AD main street. It's on Sharia Bur Said, a short walk southwest of the train station.

Neither is there much remaining to represent the city's medieval Islamic heritage. The oldest parts are off and around Sharia al-Quds; plenty of historic fragments can be found down the various side alleys. Just east of the Ugarit cinema keep an eye out for a stone-vaulted passageway down which are a couple of doorways and windows with some splendid carved stonework. The area just beyond here, around the old fruit and vegetable market, is worth exploring but the squeamish might want to avoid the passageways used by the butchers.

A **museum** (Sharia Jamal Abdel Nasser; adult/student S£300/15; 8am-6pm Apr-Sep, to 4pm Oct-Mar, closed Tue) near the waterfront, housed in what was once an old khan (travellers inn), contains some pottery and written tablets from Ugarit, chain-mail suits and a section devoted to contemporary art. Most descriptions are in Arabic only and the experience of Lattakia would hardly be diminished by giving it a miss.

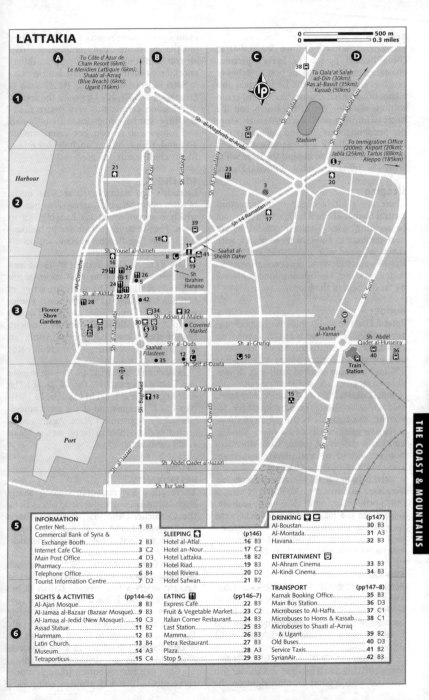

LATTAKIA

0 — 500 m
0 — 0.3 miles

To Côte d'Azur de
Cham Resort (6km);
Le Meridien Lattique (6km);
Shaati al-Azraq
(Blue Beach) (6km);
Ugarit (16km)

To Qala'at Salah
ad-Din (30km);
Ras al-Bassit (35km);
Kassab (50km)

To Immigration Office
(200m); Airport (20km);
Jabla (25km); Tartus (88km);
Aleppo (185km)

Harbour

Stadium

Sh al-Maghreb al-Arabi

Sh 8 Azar

Sh Antakya

Sh Al-Hamadany

Sh al-Bahka

Sh Omar bin Abdel Aziz

Sh 14 Ramadan

Saahat al-
Sheikh Daher

Sh Yousef al-Azmeh

Sh Ibrahim
Hanano

Al-Corniche

Sh al-Akhtal

Flower
Show
Gardens

Sh al-Mutanabi

Sh Adnan al-Maleki

Covered
Market

Sh al-Quds

Sh al-Ghafiqi

Sh Suria

Saahat
al-Yaman

Sh Abdel
Qader al-Husseiny

Saahat
Filasteen

Sh Seif al-Dawla

Train
Station

Sh al-Yarmouk

Sh Baghdad

Sh al-Quwatli

Sh al-Uruba

Port

Sh al-Jazaar

Sh Abdel Qader al-Jazairi

Sh Bur Said

THE COAST & MOUNTAINS

INFORMATION

Center Net	1	B3
Commercial Bank of Syria & Exchange Booth	2	B3
Internet Cafe Clic	3	C2
Main Post Office	4	D3
Pharmacy	5	B3
Telephone Office	6	B4
Tourist Information Centre	7	D2

SIGHTS & ACTIVITIES (pp144–6)

Al-Ajan Mosque	8	B3
Al-Jamaa al-Bazaar (Bazaar Mosque)	9	B3
Al-Jamaa al-Jedid (New Mosque)	10	C3
Assad Statue	11	B2
Hammam	12	B3
Latin Church	13	B4
Museum	14	A3
Tetraporticus	15	C4

SLEEPING (p146)

Hotel al-Atlal	16	B3
Hotel an-Nour	17	C2
Hotel Lattakia	18	B2
Hotel Riad	19	B3
Hotel Riviera	20	D2
Hotel Safwan	21	B2

EATING (pp146–7)

Express Café	22	B3
Fruit & Vegetable Market	23	C2
Italian Corner Restaurant	24	B3
Last Station	25	B3
Mamma	26	B3
Petra Restaurant	27	B3
Plaza	28	A3
Stop 5	29	B3

DRINKING (p147)

Al-Boustan	30	B3
Al-Montada	31	A3
Havana	32	B3

ENTERTAINMENT

| Al-Ahram Cinema | 33 | B3 |
| Al-Kindi Cinema | 34 | B3 |

TRANSPORT (pp147–8)

Karnak Booking Office	35	B3
Main Bus Station	36	D3
Microbuses to Al-Haffa	37	C1
Microbuses to Homs & Kassab	38	C1
Microbuses to Shaati al-Azraq & Ugarit	39	B2
Old Buses	40	D3
Service Taxis	41	B2
SyrianAir	42	B3

BEACHES

Six kilometres north of town, **Shaati al-Azraq** (Blue Beach) passes for Syria's premier coastal resort. Access to the best stretches of beach is controlled by the Le Meridien and Cham hotels; each charges S£250 per person to nonguests for use of the beach and the hotel swimming pool. Both hotels also hire out pedal boats, jet skis and sailboards.

To get to Shaati al-Azraq take a waiting microbus (S£5) from behind the large white school building on Saahat al-Sheikh Daher.

Sleeping

There are a lot of cheap options around central Saahat al-Sheikh Daher but few can be recommended. Sanitary conditions are near perilous in some of these places, with sheets yellowed with stale sweat, and shared showers and toilets pungent enough to make your eyes water. The options listed below are by far the best of the bunch.

BUDGET

Hotel al-Atlal (☎ 476 121; Sharia Yousef al-Azmeh; beds per person S£250) This hotel is a quiet, family-run establishment with freshly laundered sheets and a pleasant common area with satellite TV and a fridge stocked with soft drinks. Shower facilities are shared but clean.

Hotel Lattakia (☎ 479 527; Sharia Yousef al-Azmeh; dm/d S£125/200) The current backpackers' favourite, the Lattakia is tucked away down a narrow alley north of Al-Ajam Mosque and has a variety of rooms from dorms to doubles with or without private bathroom, and even a complete apartment.

Hotel Safwan (☎ 478 602; mziadeh22@excite.com; Sharia Mousa bin Nosier; s/d/tr S£300/500/700; ✻) Just a little north of the centre close to the seafront, the Safwan is a bit run-down (especially the reception area) but some of the rooms are fine – look at a few before choosing. Most have private bathrooms, and a few have balconies.

MID-RANGE

Hotel an-Nour (☎ 423 980; fax 468 340; Sharia 14 Ramadan; s/d US$13/19; ✻) This is similar in standard to the nearby Riad but it's the better choice because of its comfortable lounge area and breakfast room. Breakfast is included in the price.

Hotel Riad (☎ 479 778; fax 476 315; Sharia 14 Ramadan; s/d US$13/19; ✻) The Riad is a modernish two-star with a good location right on the main square. Some rooms are a little shabby but the sheets are clean; some rooms have air-con, some only a fan (with no price difference). Front-facing rooms have balconies.

Hotel Riviera (☎ 421 803; fax 418 287; Sharia 14 Ramadan; s/d US$52/76; ✻) Opposite the tourist information centre, this very smart, modern three-star has professional, friendly staff and rooms with air-con, hot water, satellite TV and fridge. Prices include breakfast. Major credit cards accepted.

TOP END

Lattakia's two luxury hotels are 6km north of town out at Shaati al-Azraq (Blue Beach), which is inconvenient for hanging out in town. They're largely patronised by holidaying Syrians. See Beaches (above) for details on getting to these hotels.

Côte d'Azur de Cham Resort (☎ 428 700; www .chamhotels.com; Shaati al-Azraq; d with garden/sea view US$67/100; ✻ ▢ ▣) The more attractive of Lattakia's two five-stars, this resort comes with a surprisingly sexy swathe of beach complete with palms. Facilities are excellent. Out of season rates (October to April) can be significantly cheaper. Major credit cards accepted.

Le Meridien Lattiquie (☎ 428 736; www.lemeridien .com; Shaati al-Azraq; s/d US$99/126; ✻ ▢ ▣) The only international hotel in Lattakia, Le Meridien has 274 rooms and all the usual amenities but it's a charmless place. Again, rooms are heftily discounted in the off season. Major credit cards accepted.

Eating

RESTAURANTS

There are a few restaurants along Sharia Baghdad and a couple of seafood places along the Corniche. Otherwise, head for Sharia al-Mutanabi, home to so many Western-style eateries that it has acquired the nickname the 'American Quarter'.

Italian Corner Restaurant (☎ 477 207; cnr Sharia al-Mutanabi & Sharia al-Akhtal; ☽ noon-late) This restaurant offers a few average Italian dishes and better pizza. It has a very pleasant covered terrace, which is a good place to sip local or imported beer, or even cocktails. Expect to pay S£200 to S£250 per head.

Last Station (☎ 468 871; 20 Sharia al-Mutanabi; ☽ noon-late) This is a definite restaurant, as opposed to a bar/restaurant (though it does serve alcohol), it has a menu comprising international and Middle Eastern standard dishes. Expect to pay around S£200 to S£250 a head. Recommended.

Petra Restaurant (☎ 477 027; Sharia al-Akhtal; ☾ noon-late) With its Middle Eastern name, Greek motif interior and a predominantly Italian/international menu, this restaurant is suffering a bit of an identity crisis. It's probably all supposed to add up to 'classy', but is let down by the food which is merely average. Expect spaghetti, pizza, steak and seafood at S£200 to S£300 per head. Alcohol is served.

Plaza (☎ 461 013; Sharia Jamal Abdel Nasser; ☾ noon-late) This large banqueting hall of a restaurant sticks to the standard Syrian fare and does it passably well. Best seats (if the weather is good) are on the large balcony area. Alcohol is served.

CAFÉS & QUICK EATS

The cheapest source of dining is around the Saahat al-Sheikh Daher area. A quick hunt turns up the old faithfuls – felafel, kebabs and shwarma – as well as a basic but good spit-rotisserie **chicken restaurant** (S£100 for a whole chicken plus salad, hummus and bread) next door to the Hotel Riad.

Olabi Coffee (3 Sharia Yousef Shahour, off Sharia Baghdad) This place does decent filter coffee plus croissants and muffins, making it a good change from the standard Syrian hotel breakfast of bread, cheese, apricot jam and a boiled egg. Opens early.

Cesar (☎ 475 403; Sharia 8 Azar; ☾ 11am-late) This is one of two restaurants (the other is signed in Arabic only) in the narrow alley that runs along the south side of Al-Ajan Mosque connecting with Sharia 8 Azar. Both places do grilled meats and mezze, along with a few Continental dishes such as escalopes and pastas. The food is fine and moderately priced (expect to pay S£150 to S£200 each), the atmosphere is good, and beer is served. The friendly manager at Cesar speaks good English.

Express Café (☎ 456 200; 22 Sharia al-Mutanabi; ☾ 9.30am-midnight) This gleaming new US-style diner offers burgers, steaks, pizza and hot and cold sandwiches. The menu is in English with prices; most dishes are in the S£80 to S£150 range. It also does good milk-shakes and there's a bar downstairs.

Mamma (☎ 416 929; Sharia 8 Azar; ☾ 11am-late) This is a tiny, but very popular takeaway-style place that does reasonable pizzas (S£80

to S£120), as well as spaghetti bolognaise (S£65), burgers (S£80) and escalope (S£150), among others. Beer is served.

Stop 5 (☎ 477919; 27 Sharia al-Mutanabi; ☾ noon-late) Resembling a bar rather than a restaurant – with shelves of spirits, posters advertising happy hours, and a TV locked into MTV – the food (burgers, escalopes, pizza, pasta) is good and very affordable with most dishes in the S£75 to S£125 range.

SELF-CATERING

There's a small **fruit and vegetable market** just north of the big white high school on Sharia 14 Ramadan, although the **main market** (Sharia al-Ghafiqi) is just east of the Ugarit cinema. For bread and other groceries, there are a few little places down Sharia Ibrahim Hanano.

Drinking

Al-Boustan (Sharia Baghdad) This is an excellent Continental-style café with pavement seating for people-watching. It's great for a kick-start morning coffee and not a bad place to while away the evening.

Al-Montada (Sharia Adnan al-Maleki) Near the museum, Al-Montada offers a modern take on the coffeehouse – a restaurant-like façade fronts a large, fan-cooled hall that becomes packed every night with locals sipping tea and coffee, watching TV, puffing on nargileh and playing chess and cards. Foreigners are made welcome.

Havana (Sharia Ibrahim Hanano) The grittiest and most fun place for a beer, it has an open-air terrace up on the 1st floor overlooking a small square in the souq (market) area. It serves local Al-Chark (S£50), as well as imported Almaza (S£100) from Lebanon. Otherwise, you can drink without dining at **Stop 5** (above) and possibly at **Italian Corner Restaurant** (opposite).

Getting There & Away

AIR

Lattakia's Basel International Airport lies about 25km south of town, close to Jabla. There is a grand total of three flights a week: two for Damascus (S£532, 45 minutes) and the other for Cairo (hence the designation 'international'), which costs US$175 one way. A taxi to the airport from Lattakia will cost about S£300.

There is a town centre office of **SyrianAir** (☎ 476 863; 8 Sharia Baghdad).

BUS

The **main bus station** (Sharia Abdel Kader al-Husseiny) is about 200m east of the train station. At least a dozen companies have their offices here, including Al-Ahliah and Qadmous, and between them they offer frequent services to Damascus (S£150, four hours), Aleppo (S£100, 3½ hours) and Tartus (S£35, one hour). Buses also go to Antakya, Iskendrun, Ankara and İstanbul in Turkey, and to Amman, Beirut and Cairo.

The cheaper Karnak buses also depart from this station but the **Karnak booking office** (☎ 233 541; Sharia Seif al-Dawla; ☼ 7.30am-8.30pm) is at the southern end of the town centre, just off Sharia Baghdad. Karnak services include two a day to Damascus (S£125) stopping in Tartus and Homs, one a day to Aleppo (S£65), and one service a day each to Beirut (S£175, with a stop in Tripoli), Antakya (S£200) and İstanbul (S£1500).

There's a second bus station between the main station and the train station from where old, clapped-out vehicles totter forth for Damascus (S£55) and Aleppo (S£40); cheap, yes – recommended, no.

MICROBUS

Lattakia's enormous **microbus station** is either side of Sharia al-Jalaa, about 1km north of the centre beside a sports stadium. From here a confusion of services depart frequently for Baniyas (S£10, 45 minutes), Tartus (S£35, one hour), Homs (S£60, two hours), Al-Haffa (for Qala'at Salah ad-Din; S£20, 45 minutes) and Kassab (S£20, 1½ hours) for the Turkish border.

Microbuses for Ugarit (Ras Shamra) and Blue Beach (Shaati al-Azraq) depart from

---

TO TURKEY ON THE CHEAP

The cheapest way to get to Turkey starts at the microbus station in Lattakia. Take a service for Kassab (S£20). You actually want to be dropped off 2km before the mountain village, where the road passes within 50m of the border – ask the driver for 'Turkiyya'. Once across the border you'll have to haggle with any taxi driver you find (pay no more than US$1) or try to hitch. You want to be taken on to Yayladaği from where you can pick up a *dolmuš* (minibus) for Antakya and onward connections.

---

a back alley down the side of the big white school on Saahat al-Sheikh Daher.

TRAIN

There are four trains a day between Lattakia and Aleppo (1st/2nd class S£67/40), and this is the rare occasion when we recommend taking the train over the bus. The scenery on this line is beautiful as the track winds its way through the mountains, rattling through tunnels and high over bridges across valleys below. The trip takes 3½ hours on the 6.40am and 3.20pm trains, and 2½ hours on the 1.30pm and 5pm express services. The station is 1.5km east of the town centre on Saahat al-Yaman.

SERVICE TAXI

Service taxis to Beirut and Tripoli in Lebanon leave from a rank on Sharia 14 Ramadan outside the Hotel Kaoukab as-Sharq. They depart when full (and they fill up faster in the mornings) and the one-way fare to Beirut is US$10 per person.

AROUND LATTAKIA

Few travellers visit Lattakia for its own sake; most step over to make the easy half-day trip to Ugarit or Qala'at Salah ad-Din, or both. If you are pushed for time, we'd recommend the latter, as much for its beautiful location as for the fortifications.

The scenery around this region is lovely – it's extremely fertile country, full of orchards surrounded by high cypress hedges, and in season you'll encounter fruit stalls along the road selling apples and oranges.

Ugarit (Ras Shamra)   رأس شمره

Although there's little to see today, **Ugarit** (adult/student S£300/15; ☼ 9am-6pm Apr-Sep, to 4pm Oct-Mar) was once the most important city on the Mediterranean coast. Academics consider it to be the world's first international port, and evidence suggests that a settlement on this site was trading with Cyprus and Mesopotamia as far back as the 3rd millennium BC. Ugarit was at its peak around 2000 to 1800 BC, when it enjoyed a healthy trade providing the Egyptian pharaohs with timber and exporting the city's trademark bronzework to the Minoans of Crete. With the immense wealth accrued from trade, the city's royal palace was developed into one of the most imposing and

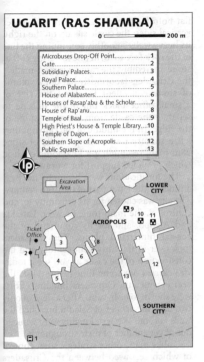

UGARIT (RAS SHAMRA)

0 ——————— 200 m

Excavation Area

LOWER CITY

ACROPOLIS

Ticket Office

SOUTHERN CITY

---

famous edifices in western Asia. Ugarit's wealth was matched by its learning and innovation. For instance, the palace had a piped water system and drainage, as did the houses of the well-to-do.

The most significant achievement of all, however, was the development of the Ugaritic alphabet. Tablets discovered at this site are inscribed with what is thought to be one of the world's earliest alphabets. Prior to the one developed at Ugarit the two known systems of writing were hieroglyphics (developed by the Egyptians) and cuneiform (from Mesopotamia), both of which involved hundreds of pictograms that represented complete words or syllables. Ugaritic is a greatly simplified system of 30 symbols, each of which represents one sound. Some of the tablets discovered list these 30 letters in alphabetical order, providing a key for archaeologists to decipher the texts that were unearthed at the site. These include stock accounts, commercial records, diplomatic correspondence and descriptions of gods and religion. Taken together the texts are a fantastically important source of informa-

tion on early life in Syria and the eastern Mediterranean region.

It's also thought the Ugaritic alphabet may have been adopted and adapted by the Greeks and Romans, thus making it the ancestor of modern European alphabets.

Ugarit's fall was swift and occurred around 1200 BC at the hands of the Philistines. The city never recovered; the invasions heralded the beginning of the Iron Age, and Ugarit was left behind by the changing technology.

SIGHTS

Ugarit was built in stone and, although the buildings are long gone, the foundations and the lower courses of some walls are visible. There's not that much to take in and it doesn't help that the site is poorly maintained, to the point where some parts are completely overgrown. While there's no information or signposting, it's of little consequence as the significant artefacts turned up by the digs (since the 1920s) have been removed to museums in Lattakia, Aleppo and Damascus, as well as to the Louvre in Paris. It's one of those situations where you may find yourself wondering what on earth you are paying the admission for and, more to the point, where the money is going – it certainly isn't on site maintenance.

On the right of the track up to the ruins is the original **city entrance**, although now it looks more like a large drainage outlet. Once inside, you can gain an impression of the layout of the place from the low hill in the northeastern quarter of the site that once served as Ugarit's **acropolis**. What you see stretched out below is a massive jumble of blocks with poorly defined streets and buildings. Among the ruins are vaulted tombs, wells and water channels.

Two temples dominated the acropolis; one was dedicated to the storm god, Baal, the supreme deity for the Canaanites, Phoenicians and Aramaeans, the other to Dagon, the father of Baal and the god associated with crop fertility. What little remains of the **Temple of Baal** (8) is found to the northwest of the acropolis, while the **Temple of Dagon** (10), of which only some of the foundations can be made out, is about 50m to the east.

Ugarit's **royal palace** (3) and related buildings were in the west of the city, a short way south of the tourist entrance. Presenting itself now as something of a labyrinth, the main entrance in the northwestern corner of the palace is marked by the bases of two pillars. Inside, the palace rooms are loosely organised around a series of courtyards. It was in storerooms of the palace that a good many of the precious Ugaritic archives were unearthed. The area between the palace and the acropolis was given over largely to private housing.

The Mediterranean Sea is just visible through the trees to the west. It has receded 100m or so since Ugarit's heyday. Don't try to walk directly through to the water as this is a military area. If you follow the road back a bit, you'll find some quiet stretches of water and beach.

GETTING THERE & AWAY

Local microbuses make the 16km trip to Ugarit (ask for Ras Shamra) every hour or so from a back alley behind Saahat al-Sheikh Daher. Ask the driver where to get off for 'al-athaar' (the ruins). Coming back, flag down any passing microbus, or it's easy enough to hitch.

Qala'at Salah ad-Din (Saône)
قلعة صلاح الدين

Although it is much less celebrated than Krak des Chevaliers, TE Lawrence was moved to write of Qala'at Salah ad-Din, 'It was I think the most sensational thing in castle building I have seen'.

To Lawrence, the castle was Saône (in Arabic, Sayhun), which is the name that the Crusaders knew it by, after Robert of Saône, one of the original Crusader builders. The name Qala'at Salah ad-Din was only officially adopted in 1957.

Qala'at Salah ad-Din (adult/student S£300/15; ☉ 9am-6pm Apr-Oct, to 4pm Nov-Mar, closed Tue) is a sensational place largely because of its setting – the castle is perched on top of a heavily wooded ridge with near-precipitous sides dropping away to surrounding ravines.

Approaching from the nearby village of Al-Haffa, the first sighting is from the top of the ridge to the north, and the distance across to the castle is almost less than the depth of the valley between. The road then slithers down in a tight coil of switchbacks, crossing a stream at the bottom before winding its way back upwards. Nearing the top, the road turns sharply to enter a flat-bottomed, narrow canyon with sheer vertical sides; the castle sits up on the right, its heavy walls smoothly continuing the line of the rock face to form one towering cliff of stone. Incredibly, the canyon is man-made – the Crusaders laboriously hacked a volume of stone equivalent to about the size of a small office block out of the hillside to separate the castle from the main spine of the ridge. In the middle of the canyon, they left a solitary freestanding needle of stone 28m high, resembling a Pharaonic obelisk, which provided support for a drawbridge.

The fortifications were begun by the Byzantines in the latter part of the 10th century. The site was chosen for its proximity to, and control of, the main route between Lattakia and Aleppo, and for its command of the coastal hinterland plains. The Crusaders took over in the early 12th century and the construction of the castle as you see it today was carried out some time before 1188, the year in which the Crusaders' building efforts were shown to be in vain. After a siege of only two days the armies of Saladin breached the walls and the Western knights were winkled out of yet another of their strongholds.

Unlike many other strategic sites, control of which seesawed between the Crusaders and the Muslims, this one stayed in the hands of the Islamic armies. As its importance declined, the castle was abandoned. A small village occupied the lower courts at some point but its remoteness eventually caused it to be deserted too.

SIGHTS & ACTIVITIES
Touring the Castle

The castle is approached up a flight of concrete steps on the south side, which climb toward a **gate tower** (7), where entry tickets are purchased. Passing through the tower into the castle's interior, a right turn leads to the inner courtyard area of the upper castle. The two **towers** (8 and 9) in the southern wall are both relatively intact and it's possible to climb the internal staircase in each up to the 1st floor and roof for fine views of the surrounding countryside.

To the left of the furthest of the towers, a doorway leads to a flight of steps descending into the square sunken space of a former **water cistern** (10); a doorway from the cistern links to an adjacent large, low pillared hall that served as **stables** (11). Incredibly, the

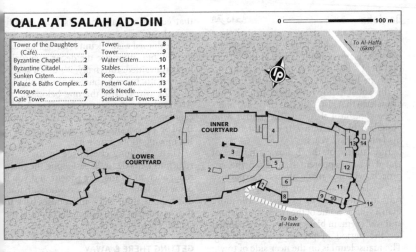

QALA'AT SALAH AD-DIN

Tower of the Daughters (Café).....................1	Tower...........................8
Byzantine Chapel............2	Tower...........................9
Byzantine Citadel............3	Water Cistern............10
Sunken Cistern...............4	Stables.......................11
Palace & Baths Complex...5	Keep...........................12
Mosque..........................6	Postern Gate.............13
Gate Tower.....................7	Rock Needle..............14
	Semicircular Towers...15

0 [============] 100 m

To Al-Haffa (6km)

INNER COURTYARD

LOWER COURTYARD

To Bab al-Hawa

damp space still smells of horses. From the stables it's possible to access two of the three small **semicircular towers** (15) of the eastern wall; these were originally built by the Byzantines and later strengthened by the Crusaders.

North of the stables is the largest and most heavily fortified of the castle's towers, the **keep** (12), or donjon, with 5m-thick walls. It was always assumed that any attack would come from along the ridge to the east. In fact, when the attack came, Saladin split his forces: half occupied the defenders here as expected, but a second force bombarded the northern walls with catapults from the hilltop across the valley. The missiles breached the walls of the lower courtyard and the Crusaders, who were of insufficient number to defend such a huge fortress, were unable to stop the Muslims streaming in. An intact staircase gives access to the roof of the keep, and views down into the defile that are vertigo-inducing.

The ruins to the north of the keep include the **postern gate** (13), from where the drawbridge was lowered onto the rock needle. A metal gantry protrudes from the unsealed gateway so the nerveless can step out and peer directly down into the defile.

The most prominent structure in this part of the castle is the **palace and baths complex** (5), easily identifiable by its high, typically Islamic entrance, decorated with stone stalactites and carved geometric patterning. This dates back to the Ayyubid period (1169–1260). Inside is a reception hall with *iwans* (vaulted halls), and beyond that the main room of the baths with a star-patterned floor around a central fountain.

From the palace a path leads north to a modest doorway that, if you step through, gives way to the dizzying spectacle of a cathedral-sized **sunken cistern** (4), which is still partially filled with water. Follow the same path west, passing the remains of the original **Byzantine citadel** (3) up to the right, to the **Tower of the Daughters** (1), which today serves as a small café. From here you can look down on the lower (western) castle, which is completely ruined and overgrown, and inaccessible. Complete the circuit by returning to the gate tower.

GETTING THERE & AWAY

Take a microbus to the village of Al-Haffa (الحفة; S£20, 45 minutes); they depart from the far end, right-hand side (as you come from town) of Lattakia's vast microbus lot. From Al-Haffa the castle is a gruelling 6km walk uphill and downhill – keep on heading east out of the village then follow the signs. The best bet is to haggle with a taxi driver at Al-Haffa; there are usually several cabs waiting around where the microbuses stop. The local price is S£20 per person but getting a ride for this will test your negotiating skills. The microbus drivers at the station in Lattakia will drive you to the castle and back for S£200, which isn't a bad deal for a group of four.

Qardaha القرداحة

Known to all Syrians as the birthplace of Hafez al-Assad, Syria's first president, Qardaha is now equally famed as the former president's last place of rest. Following his death in June 2000, his body was interred in this small hilltop town in a purpose-built **mausoleum** that also contains the grave of his eldest son, Basil al-Assad, 'the martyr' who ploughed his car into a tree, predeceasing his father by six years.

Indications of the hallowed nature of Qar-daha are apparent right from the approach, which is made along an expansive and well-maintained four-lane highway that runs from the coast up to what is little more than a village. Some of the trees, street lamps and walls remain black as they were painted for the period of presidential mourning. The mausoleum is on the near side of town; look off to the left for a red-tiled pagoda-like roof on a large villa and ask the driver to stop at the crossroads ahead. Take the road

that curves up past the villa to a spindly arched gate.

The domed mausoleum is an Islamic star in plan, but otherwise the décor is surprisingly restrained. Internally, it's a vast space, heavy with incense, but empty of all else save the two graves: the one belonging to Al-Assad is in the centre, a low bench-like cenotaph lying in a sunken section of floor. Basil occupies a similar grave off to one side. It's moving in its simplicity.

There's nothing else to see in town. To return to Lattakia, walk east along the main road; after 400m the way widens and you'll come to a large statue of guess who with four dopey lions at his feet – microbuses back to the coast depart from diagonally opposite the statue. There will probably be one waiting.

GETTING THERE & AWAY

Services for Qardaha (S£10, 35 to 40 minutes) depart from Lattakia's vast microbus lot (near end, on the right).

Orontes Valley

وادي العاصي

The Orontes Valley, bordered by the coastal strip to the west and the scorched desert to the east, provides a distinctively different experience than Aleppo to the north and Damascus to the south. While Syrians try to break land speed records between the aforementioned cities, there are enough attractions in the region to make this more than just a blur outside the window of a bus.

Hama, Syria's fourth largest city is an attractive stop on the journey. Famed for its large *norias* (water wheels) and riverside parks, it's most active in summer when the wheels groan with the flow of the Orontes River, known as Nahr al-Aasi, or the 'Rebel River'. The name in Arabic is attributed to the fact that the river flows from south to north – the opposite of most rivers in the region.

The striking roman ruins of Apamea are well worth visiting for the colonnaded grace of its cardo maximus, both longer and wider than Palmyra's. Careful restoration over the last few decades has turned this once shapeless site into an evocative one. Far less complex in structure are the intriguing beehive houses found at Sarouj and Twalid Dabaghein, which are still used as dwellings. These conical mud-brick structures are an arresting sight.

While the castle of Musyaf is suitably imposing, the castle's connection with one of Islam's most fascinating sects, the Assassins, is the highlight. This radical, mystical group was known for their ability to infiltrate their enemy and kill its leader, lending their name to the Western term 'assassin'.

HIGHLIGHTS

- Kick back in **Hama** (p160) – enjoy the top-end hotels for just a few dollars a night, and mingle with the locals at its first-class outdoor eateries
- Explore **Apamea** (p167), perhaps Syria's second most impressive archaeological site after Palmyra and definitely one for fans of colonnades
- Scale the heights of Jebel Ansariyya for the **view over Al-Ghab** (p166), the best view in Syria
- Visit the intriguing **beehive houses** (p171) in Sarouj, which are still used as dwellings
- Take advantage of the photo op in front of Hama's groaning **norias** (p162) which are up to 20m in diameter

ORONTES VALLEY

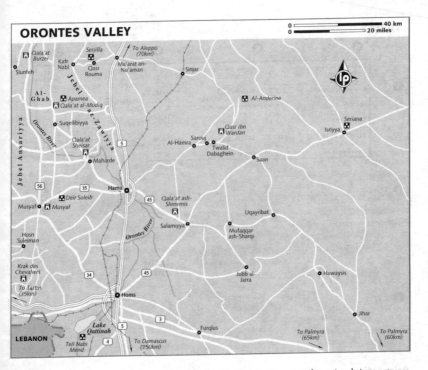

ORONTES VALLEY

HOMS   حمص

☎ 031

Homs, Syria's third-largest city, has a history stretching back to the 1st millennium BC and at one time gave birth to a dynasty of Roman emperors. These days, the major boast of Homs is its huge oil-refining industry. With little else to offer, this is often the butt of Syrian humour – it's said that the only thing refined about Homs is its oil. Still, the city remains an important crossroads, where routes east to Palmyra and west to Tartus and the coast intersect with the main north-south Aleppo–Damascus highway. Most travellers have to pass through at some stage. The shortage of things to see is compounded by a lack of decent budget accommodation, so few choose to stay, instead treating the city as little more than a bus interchange. If you find yourself here with time to kill, then the little-visited souq is well worth exploring.

History

Digs at the tell (artificial hill) – to the south of the centre of the modern city – indicate there were settlements in pre-Classical times.

However, Homs only gained importance during the Roman era. Formerly known as Emesa, the town benefited from close ties with Palmyra, 125km to the east.

Its regional importance was further enhanced around AD 187 when Julia Domna, daughter of an Emesan high priest, married a Roman garrison commander, Septimius Severus, who six years later would become emperor of Rome. They founded a Syro-Roman dynasty that spanned four emperors (reigning from AD 211 to 235).

Unfortunately it was a dynasty most noted for its rapid decline into depravity. Most notorious of all was Elagabalus, whose four-year reign of chaos was abruptly terminated, when he was assassinated by his own Praetorian guards, seeking to restore some order to the empire.

Under the Byzantines, Homs became an important centre of Christianity, and it still has a very large Christian population. After falling to a Muslim army in AD 636 led by the general Khaled ibn al-Walid (revered as the warrior that brought Islam to Syria), Homs became an equally fervent centre of Islam.

ORONTES VALLEY

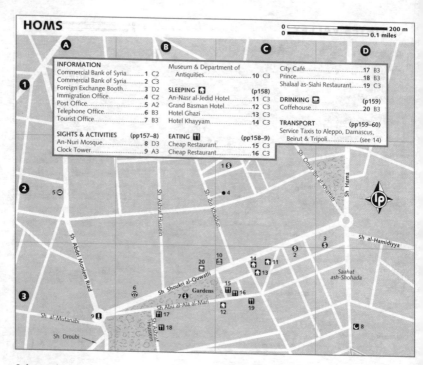

HOMS

INFORMATION	Museum & Department of	City Café..............................**17** B3
Commercial Bank of Syria..........**1** C2	Antiquities.........................**10** C3	Prince....................................**18** B3
Commercial Bank of Syria..........**2** C3		Shalaal as-Siahi Restaurant........**19** C3
Foreign Exchange Booth............**3** D2	**SLEEPING** (p158)	
Immigration Office....................**4** C2	An-Nasr al-Jedid Hotel............**11** C3	**DRINKING** (p159)
Post Office................................**5** A2	Grand Basman Hotel...............**12** C3	Coffeehouse..........................**20** B3
Telephone Office......................**6** B3	Hotel Ghazi............................**13** C3	
Tourist Office...........................**7** B3	Hotel Khayyam.......................**14** C3	**TRANSPORT** (pp159–60)
		Service Taxis to Aleppo, Damascus,
SIGHTS & ACTIVITIES (pp157–8)	**EATING** (pp158–9)	Beirut & Tripoli.................(see 14)
An-Nuri Mosque......................**8** D3	Cheap Restaurant...................**15** C3	
Clock Tower.............................**9** A3	Cheap Restaurant...................**16** C3	

Orientation

Central Homs lies either side of the main east-west axis of Sharia Shoukri al-Quwatli, a short but wide strip of a road punctuated at either end by a large roundabout; the one at the western end is distinguished by a clock tower. Cheap accommodation and eats are found in the side streets south of Quwatli. The old city and souq lie southeast. The bus stations are around 2km northeast of town.

Information

INTERNET ACCESS

At the time of writing there was just one Internet café, **Compuserv** (☎ 499 990; Sharia Hafez Ibrahim; ⏰ 10am-11pm; per 30 min S£50), a super-chic place with moulded curved booths, smoked plate glass windows and potted palms. It feels more like an upmarket women's hairdresser. It's just off the map: follow Sharia Droubi 200m south to an intersection with a main road (Sharia Bab Houd), along which you continue west. Sharia Hafez Ibrahim is the first right, and the Internet café is just another couple of hundred metres along on the left-hand side.

MONEY

Commercial Bank of Syria (CBS; Map p156; ⏰ 8am-12.30pm Sat-Thu) Changes cash or travellers cheques.
Foreign-exchange booth (Map p156; ⏰ 8am-7pm) Also cashes travellers cheques; it shuts for a few hours in the early afternoon for lunch.

POST

Post office (Map p156; Sharia Abdel Moniem Riad; ⏰ 6am-5.30pm Sat-Thu) About 150m north of the clock-tower roundabout.
Telephone office (Map p156; Sharia Shoukri al-Quwatli; ⏰ 8am-8pm Sat-Thu, to 1pm Fri) Just east of the same roundabout; there are several card phones inside and cards are available from the counter.

TOURIST INFORMATION

Information booth (Map p156; ☎ 473 898; ⏰ 8am-2pm & 5-8pm Sat-Thu) In the park on the south side of Sharia Shoukri al-Quwatli. There's no printed information here and the people running it, who seem to know very little, are prone to locking up shop and disappearing for large parts of the day.

VISA EXTENSIONS

For visa renewals, the **immigration office** (Map p156; Sharia ibn Khaldun; ⏰ 8.30am-2pm Sat-Thu) is on he 3rd floor of an administration building, ust north of Sharia Shoukri al-Quwatli. On he ground floor there are photo studios that do passport photos.

Sights

OLD CITY & SOUQ   المدينة القديمة والسوق

Little remains of the old city of Homs. Its walls and gates were largely demolished in the Ottoman era, although there is a short section of **fortified wall** with a circular corner tower just south of Sharia Shoukri al-Quwatli. Half a kilometre to the south a large earthen mound marks the site where a **citadel** once stood.

A little way south of the roundabout at the eastern end of Al-Quwatli is the imposing yet undistinguished 20th-century façade of the **An-Nuri Mosque** (Jamaa an-Nuri, also known as Jamaa al-Kebir; Map p156), which is actually much older than first appearances might suggest. Just north of the prayer hall, the mosque courtyard contains a curious long, low platform and an ancient capital is embedded in the western end of the platform.

The mosque also marks the beginning of the **souq**, which is large and busy and although it lacks the charm of those in Aleppo or Damascus, its narrow lanes are thankfully free of souvenir stalls.

CHRISTIAN QUARTER

Another route of exploration is to head east from the mosque along Sharia Abi al-Hawl, which leads into the old Christian Quarter. Along the street numerous expanses of black-and-white stonework mark out buildings of considerable age, all still in use as shops and dwellings. Encouragingly, there are plenty of signs of renovation and reconstruction.

Continue due east, straight over a cross-road and past Pappay Pizza (see p157) until you see a small gateway topped by a cross that leads through to the **Church of the Girdle of Our Lady** (Kineesat al-Zunnar; Map p157; Sharia Qasr ash-Sheikh). In 1953, the patriarch of Antioch, Ignatius Aphraim, declared a delicate strip of woven wool and silk, found in the church six months earlier, to be a girdle worn by the Virgin Mary. The story is that it had

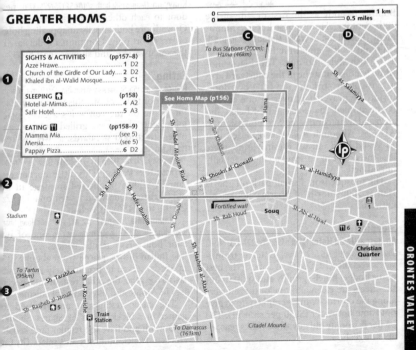

GREATER HOMS

SIGHTS & ACTIVITIES	(pp157–8)
Azze Hrawe	1 D2
Church of the Girdle of Our Lady	2 D2
Khaled ibn al-Walid Mosque	3 C1

SLEEPING	(p158)
Hotel al-Mimas	4 A2
Safir Hotel	5 A3

EATING	(pp158–9)
Mamma Mia	(see 5)
Mersia	(see 5)
Pappay Pizza	6 D2

To Bus Stations (200m); Hama (46km)

See Homs Map (p156)

To Tartus (95km)

Stadium

Fortified wall   Sh Bab Houd   Souq

Christian Quarter

Train Station

To Damascus (161km)   Citadel Mound

Sh al-Korniche   Sh Hafez Ibrahim   Sh Droubi   Sh Abdel Moniem Riad   Sh Ibn Khaldun   Sh Hama   Sh as-Salamiyya   Sh Shoukri al-Quwatli   Sh al-Hamidiyya   Sh Abi al-Hawl   Sh Hashem al-Atasi   Sh Tarablus   Sh al-Korniche   Sh Ragheb al-Jamali

0   1 km
0   0.5 miles

ORONTES VALLEY

survived intact since the Ascension of Mary into Heaven, preserved in one container or another in a church on this spot. The church is an attractive little grey-stone building with a red pantile roof, and is still an active centre for Syrian Orthodox worship.

From the church follow the road that heads off to the north, taking the first right for the **Azze Hrawe** (Map p157; Sharia Omar al-Mokhtar; 8am-2pm Sat-Thu), a recently restored Mamluk-era residence of impressive size that is now supposedly open to the public as a National Folklore Museum, but doesn't stick to its advertised opening hours and is often closed.

MUSEUM

Accommodated in the gloomy Department of Antiquities building on the main street, the **museum** (Map p156; Sharia Shoukri al-Quwatli; adult/student S£300/15; 8am-4pm Apr-Oct, to 3p-m Nov-Mar) contains a rather lacklustre collection comprised of artefacts, from prehistoric to early Islamic, unearthed in the Homs region. Labelling is in Arabic only.

KHALED IBN AL-WALID MOSQUE

جامع خالد إبن الوليد

Built as recently as the first decade of the 20th century, Homs' best-known monument, **Khaled ibn al-Walid Mosque** (Map p157), isn't old – it's an attractive example of a Turkish-style mosque. The black-and-white banding of stone in the courtyard area is particularly striking, if a little overdone. Inside the prayer hall, over in one corner, is the domed mausoleum of Khaled ibn al-Walid, who conquered Syria for Islam in AD 636. Although it is well recorded that Al-Walid lived out his life in Homs, there is some doubt as to whether he is actually buried here.

The mosque is in a small park off Sharia Hama, 500m north of Sharia Shoukri al-Quwatli.

Sleeping

An-Nasr al-Jedid Hotel (Map p156; 227 423; Sharia Shoukri al-Quwatli; s/d S£200/300) Entered from a side street off Al-Quwatli, it's about the best of the budget hotels: grubby and spartan but the sheets are clean and one of the showers along the corridor can be cranked up to give out some hot water (S£50 per shower). The owner is a polite old guy who speaks reasonable English.

Hotel al-Mimas (Map p157; 220 224; mh@mail.s Sharia Malab al-Baladi; s/d US$24/30;) A modern ish five-storey place with rooms featurin big plump beds, fridge, balcony, priva bathroom and air-con. It's very clean an the best value in town. The drawback that it's about 2km (west) out of the centr Attached is a small travel agency that ca arrange tours of Homs and the region.

Safir Hotel (Map p157; 412 400; www.safirhote .com; Sharia Ragheb al-Jamali; s/d US$110/125;) One of Syria's best five-stars hotels. In ad dition to thoroughly luxurious rooms, has a pleasant bar area, a couple of decen restaurants and a bookshop with a sma selection of titles on Syria and the Midd East. Credit cards are accepted. It is 2kr southwest of the centre (a brief S£25 tax ride), just south of Sharia Trablous, whic is the western continuation of Sharia Ba Houd.

The cheap hotels are on or just south o Sharia Shoukri al-Quwatli between the tour ist office and the souq. They're a grim bunch it's better to upgrade to Al-Mimas or get ou of town before nightfall. **Hotel Ghazi** and **Hote Khayyam** (Map p156; both s/d/tr S£175/275/375), nex door to each other on a side street off Al Quwatli, are both equally unappealing hotel of last resort only. Communal toilets are o the squat variety, and showers cost S£35.

Eating

Prince (Map p156; Sharia Ashraf Hussein; 9am-midnigh Next door to City Cafe, this is an okay plac for eating on the run – it's a basic snac joint with shwarma, grilled chicken an other street-food standards, as well as fres fruit juices.

Pappay Pizza (Map p157; Sharia Qasr ash-Sheik noon-11pm Mon-Sat) This little corner res taurant with a bright red frontage in th old Christian Quarter does reasonable pizz (S£100 to S£150), as well as sandwiches.

Mamma Mia (Map p157; 412 400; Safir Hotel, Shar Ragheb al-Jamali; noon-midnight) is one of tw Safir house restaurants; it does very cred ible Italian dishes, priced from about S£25 upwards, served in bright, lively surrounds **Mersia** (24 hr), the other restaurant, special ises in Arabic and international cuisine.

The cheap restaurants are grouped to gether one block south of Sharia Shoukr al-Quwatli and have the regular fare: kebab: chicken, felafel, hummus and salad. **City Caf**

(Map p156; ☎ 239 755; Sharia Abu al-Ala al-Mari; ☯ 24 hr) is perhaps the best of the lot. It's a modern coffeehouse-type place that does similar food to everywhere else, but it has an attractive interior with kilim-covered benches and a pleasant shaded terrace facing the clock tower.

Drinking

Majmu ar-Rawda as-Siyahi (Sharia Shoukri al-Quwatli) is a big shady garden coffeehouse (whose name means something along the lines of 'Tourist Garden Association') on the north side of the main street, close to the clock tower. It is now rivalled in popularity however by the far smarter **City Cafe** (Map p156; ☎ 239 755; Sharia Abu al-Ala al-Mari; ☯ 24 hr), as a place for a drink and a nargileh (water pipe).

Otherwise, the hub of Homs social life – for those with cash – is the **Safir Hotel** (Map p157; ☎ 412 400; Sharia Ragheb al-Jamali), particularly its poolside café, which operates through the summer months. At other times, the hotel's **Abu Nawas bar**, where a local beer costs S£135, is fairly lively Thursday through Sunday nights.

Getting There & Away

BUS

There are two bus stations: the Karnak minibus station, which is about 1.5km north of the city centre up the Hama road; and the main 'luxury' bus station ('karajat Pullman'), which is about 1km further out. To get to the main station from the Karnak station, turn right out of the main entrance and walk 500m to a large roundabout; bear right there and the luxury bus station is 400m straight ahead. To get between either of these stations and the city centre by taxi should cost no more than S£25 – for information on microbuses see p114.

At the main station are all the usual private companies, including Al-Ahliah and Qadmous. From here there are frequent departures to Damascus (S£70, two hours), Aleppo (S£75 to S£85, 2½ hours) and Tartus (S£40, one hour). There are buses to Hama from here but it's more convenient to catch a microbus – see p114 for details.

Buses operate from Karnak station to Damascus (S£60, six daily), Aleppo (S£75, twice daily), Palmyra (S£65), Tartus (S£40, once daily), Lattakia (S£65, two hours, twice daily) and Beirut (S£250, twice daily).

GOING TO KRAK DES CHEVALIERS

Unless you're coming from the coast, getting to Krak des Chevaliers (p132) by public transport involves a change of bus (or minibus or microbus) at Homs. There are two options. One is to take a microbus to the village of Al-Hosn, which is just below the castle – you can walk up from the drop off point. These depart from the chaotic microbus lot, which is part of the Karnak garage. They leave regularly throughout the day until around 4pm; the fare is S£25.

Alternatively, if you arrive at the main bus station, you can easily switch to a Tartus minibus (£30), which depart from the north end of the bus station. Tell the driver you want 'Qala'at al-Hosn' and, fingers crossed, you'll be dropped off on the main highway at the turning for the castle, where there's usually a microbus waiting to shuttle passengers up the hill.

MINIBUS & MICROBUS

Bright, new microbuses flit in and out of the main bus station, most of them going to Hama (S£20, 40 minutes); they depart as soon as they're full and you can generally turn up at any time, climb straight in, and expect to be away in less than 10 minutes.

From Karnak station, battered old minibuses go everywhere including Hama (S£10), Tartus (S£20) and Palmyra (S£25). Fares are considerably cheaper than the bigger buses, but these things are cramped and uncomfortable with nowhere to put baggage. From the Karnak there are buses to Baalbek/Beirut/Tripoli for S£150/200/200.

TRAIN

The station is a good half-hour walk from the centre. Take the street heading southwest of the clock tower, until it merges with the main road, Sharia Tarablus. At the second set of lights turn left down Sharia al-Mahatta, and head to the rather grandiose station at the end. There are two departures a day: south to Damascus (1st/2nd class S£47/34, 3.30am) and north to Aleppo (S£45/32, 7pm).

Getting Around

To get into town from either bus station cross the main road and flag down any passing microbus (S£3). These all skirt west of the centre, along Sharia al-Corniche. Look out for a major junction with traffic lights; hop out here, cross over and head south down Sharia Abdel Moniem Riad, which after 400m will bring you to the clock-tower roundabout.

HAMA
حماه
☎ 033

With the Orontes River flowing through the city centre, its banks lined with trees and gardens and the ancient, groaning *norias* (water wheels), Hama is one of Syria's more attractive towns. While there isn't an awful lot to see, the peaceful atmosphere, good restaurants and excellent hotels combine to make it a very pleasant place to spend a few relaxing days. Use the comforts of Hama as a base for excursions to some of the very worthwhile sites further north up the Orontes Valley (see p153), or to places further afield such as Krak des Chevaliers (see p132) or the Dead Cities (see p200).

History

Excavations on the city's central tell have revealed that the locale was settled as long ago as the Neolithic Age. There are historical references to an Aramaean kingdom of Hamah (or Hamath), which traded with Israel during the reigns of biblical David and Solomon (1000 to 922 BC). Occupied later by the Assyrians, Hama joined Damascus in a revolt against their foreign conquerors in 853 BC, defeating the troops of Shalmenaser. Under Sargon II, however, the Assyrians wreaked their revenge, and in 720 BC the city was razed and its citizens deported. By the time of the Seleucids, the Greek dynasty established by one of Alexander's generals, the town had been renewed and rechristened Epiphania after the ruler Antiochus IV Epiphanes (r 175–164 BC). It remained an important Roman and Byzantine centre until its capture by the Arabs in AD 637.

The town prospered under the Ayyubids, the dynasty founded by Saladin, but was often fought over by rival dynasties in Damascus and Aleppo, which it lay between.

The most recent chapter in Hama's history has been one of the country's saddest. It was here in 1982 that the repressive nature of Hafez al-Assad's regime was most brutally demonstrated. The details of what happened that bloody February are hazy at best but

it appears that about 8000 government troops were moved in to quash a rebellion by armed members of the then-outlawed Muslim Brotherhood. Fighting lasted three weeks and the level of destruction was immense. Only those who knew the city before this calamity can fully measure the damage, although as recently as 1955 travel writer Robin Fedden could write in his book, *Syria: An Historical Appreciation,* that Hama was 'extraordinarily unspoilt with houses that overhung the water and an extensive old town in which modern buildings barely intrude'; this is no longer the case. The heart of the old town was completely razed.

Orientation

Central Hama sticks to the switchbacks of the southern bank of the Orontes River. Its main drags, Sharia Shoukri al-Quwatli, run east-west, and Sharia Said al-A'as/Jamal Abdel Nasser run north-south. Immediately west of the centre is the 'old town' and the citadel mound, and west of this is the traditionally Christian neighbourhood of Al-Medina with its two main shopping streets, Sharia al-Mutanabi and Ibn Rushd. It's all very compact and easy to get around on foot.

Arriving by bus, you are most likely to be dropped off on Sharia al-Buhturi, the riverside street, one block north of the main cluster of hotels on Al-Quwatli.

Information
INTERNET ACCESS

The Cairo and Riad hotels both offer online computer access to their guests, otherwise try one of the following:

City M@il (☎ 214 466; 8 Sharia Abdel Alwani; ⏱ 10.30am-midnight; per 30 min S£50) Behind the post office.

Al-Mustaqbal (☎ 210 135; Sharia al-Buhturi; ⏱ 8am-midnight; per 30 min S£30) In back of the Afamia Restaurant near the Qadmous bus office – look for the sign saying 'Future'.

Rendevo (☎ 211 686; Sharia al-Qalaa; ⏱ 11am-2am; per 30 min S£30) Beside the Citadel.

MONEY

The local main branch of the **CBS** (Sharia Shoukri al-Quwatli; ⏱ 8.30am-12.30pm Sat-Thu) is just east of the clock tower and next door to the post office. It accepts cash and travellers cheques (no commission) at the exchange counter on the 1st floor. For a small transaction fee,

HAMA

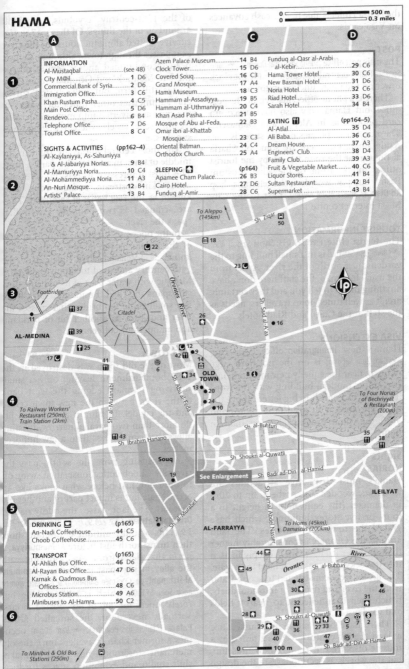

To Aleppo (145km)

Sh. Ziqat

To Railway Workers' Restaurant (250m); Train Station (2km)

Orontes River

Citadel

AL-MEDINA

OLD TOWN

Sh. al-Mutanabi

Sh. Abu al-Feda

Sh. Said al-A'ass

To Four Norias of Bechriyyat & Restaurant (200m)

Sh. Ibrahim Hanano

Souq

Sh. al-Buhturi

See Enlargement

Sh. Shoukri al-Quwatli

Sh. Badr ad-Din al-Hamid

ILEILYAT

To Homs (45km); Damascus (200km)

Sh. al-Murabet

AL-FARRAYYA

Sh. Jamal Abdel Nasser

To Minibus & Old Bus Stations (250m)

River

Orontes

Sh. al-Buhturi

Sh. Shoukri al-Quwatli

Sh. Badr ad-Din al-Hamid

the Noria Hotel is able to give cash advances on Visa cards.

POST

The **main post office** (Sharia Shoukri al-Quwatli; ⓧ 8am-5pm Sat-Thu) is centrally located, beside the clock tower on the main junction in town.

There is a phone office, just behind the post office, but Hama now also has Easycomm card phones, as in Aleppo and Damascus. The number of phones on the street is currently small, but there are some on Sharia al-Buhturi at the roundabout, by the tourist office, and in front of the Khan Rustum Pasha. Buy phonecards at the telecoms shop **Ad-Diah** (3 Sharia Abdel Alwani), next to the City M@il Internet centre.

TOURIST INFORMATION

The **tourist office** (☎ 511 033; Sharia Said al-A'as; ⓧ 8am-2pm Sat-Thu) is in a small building in the gardens, just north of the river. Apart from the usual free map, the staff here don't have anything much to tell you and they certainly aren't as well tuned-in to travellers' needs as the staff at the Cairo and Riad hotels.

VISA EXTENSIONS

Hama's new **immigration office** (Sharia Ziqar; ⓧ 8am-2pm Sat-Thu) is on the northern edge of town, near the equally new museum, in a two-storey modern building with the word 'Passport' in English in big letters above the main entrance. You need four photos and S£50; the whole process takes less than an hour.

Sights

NORIAS النواعير

Hama's most distinctive attractions are its *norias*, wooden water wheels up to 20m in diameter (the equivalent in height to a four- or five-storey building), which have graced the town for centuries. The land around the Orontes is considerably higher than the river itself, which is deeply incised into its rocky bed, making it hard to irrigate. The *norias* were constructed to scoop water from the river and deposit it into aqueducts, which then channelled it to nearby fields and gardens.

There have been *norias* in Hama since at least the 5th century AD, as attested by a mosaic displayed in Hama's new museum, but the wheels as seen today are the design

of the 13th-centruy Ayyubids, who built around 30 of the things. Of these, 17 *norias* survive, dotted along the course of the river as it passes through town, although all have been reconditioned and/or rebuilt during the late Mamluk and Ottoman times. The *norias* still turn, but only during spring and summer; at other times the waters of the river are diverted into more modern irrigation schemes elsewhere, reducing water supplies.

The most central *norias* are right in the middle of town in an attractive park setting. The most impressive wheels, however, are about 1km upstream, and are collectively known as the **Four Norias of Bechriyyat**. They are arranged as two pairs on a weir that spans the river.

In the opposite direction, about 1km west of the centre, is the largest of the *norias*, known as **Al-Mohammediyya**. It dates from the 14th century and used to supply the Grand Mosque with water. Part of its old aqueduct still spans the road. Beside the *noria* there is a small stone footbridge that crosses the river and leads to another bit of parkland and an open-air coffeehouse.

OLD TOWN المدينة القديمة

Most of the old town was destroyed in the 1982 bombardment, leaving only a small surviving remnant edging the west bank of the river, between the new town centre and the citadel. In sum, it amounts to little more than two parallel narrow, twisting alleys that run for less than a few hundred metres.

Approaching from the south, pass the riverside Choob coffeehouse, then swing off to the right, just before what looks like an arched gate but is in fact part of another old **aqueduct**. The lane passes the oddly named **Oriental Batman** (☎ 224 957; ⓧ 9am-9pm Sat-Thu 3-9pm Fri), a junky antique-cum-craft shop, then turns north just before **Al-Mamuriyya**, a *noria* that dates from 1453. Sticking with the alley, it jogs past the historic **Hammam al-Uthmaniyya** (ⓧ men 8am-noon & 7-11pm, women noon-5pm; S£150), which is still working but rarely open for all of its posted hours. Virtually next door, the so-called **Artists' Palace** (Ateliers des Peintures; ⓧ 9am-10pm) occupies a former khan (travellers inn); the old merchant storerooms now used as makeshift studio and exhibition spaces for local rtists, some of whose work is for sale. The chan doesn't really compare with those seen n Damascus and Aleppo, but a little further s a much more noteworthy monument, the Azem Palace.

Ross Burns, historian and author of the sage *Monuments of Syria*, regards the **Azem Palace** (Beit al-Azem; adult/student S£150/10; 🕙 9.30am-.30pm Wed-Mon) as 'one of the loveliest Ottoman residential buildings in Syria'. It's the former residence of the governor Asaad Pasha al-Azem, who ruled the town from 1742. The palace has strong echoes of the more grandiose building of the same name n Damascus, which is hardly surprising as the latter was also built by Al-Azem after he was transferred to the capital. Burns singles out the *haramlek* (women's quarters), the area to the right of the entrance, as being particularly noteworthy.

A short distance north of Azem Palace, a modest but attractive little riverside **mosque** was built by the Muslim commander Nureddin, uncle of Saladin, in the late 12th century. If you cross the bridge beside the mosque, you have a very picturesque view of the river and three *norias*, which are, from east to west, **Al-Kaylaniyya**, **As-Sahuniyya** and **Al-Jabariyya**.

CITADEL & GRAND MOSQUE القلعة والجامع الكبير

The term 'citadel' is a bit of a misnomer, because it refers to what used to be rather than what is. What the locals call Al-Qalaa, or 'the castle', is actually no more than a great earthen mound, or tell. Danish archaeologists who carried out extensive work on the tell found evidence of continuous settlement since Neolithic times, particularly during the Iron Age. Sadly, apart from a few unrecognisable fragments, nothing remains as all the stone was long ago carted off for use in other buildings. The area has been landscaped and developed into a picnic and recreation area, with a small café; it's popular with locals, particularly on Fridays and public holidays.

Looking north from the tell, just over the river, is the small **Mosque of Abu al-Feda**, resting place of the noted 14th-century soldier-turned-poet of that name, who was also a noted historian, astronomer and botanist. His treatise on geography was a major source for European cartographers from the Renaissance onwards. He was elevated to become emir of Hama in 1320. During his rule, Abu al-Feda commissioned his own mosque and tomb beside the Orontes in what he wrote was 'one of the most delectable of spots'.

About 400m southwest of the citadel is the **Grand Mosque** (Sharia al-Hassanein; 🕙 sunset-sunrise), which, after being almost completely destroyed in the fighting of 1982, has since been faithfully restored. It was originally built by the Umayyads in the 8th century, along the lines of their great mosque in Damascus. It had a similar history, having been converted from a church that itself had stood on the site of a pagan temple.

HAMA MUSEUM متحف حماة الأثري

Located about 1.5km north of the centre, Hama's new regional **museum** (Sharia Ziqar; adult/student S£300/15; 🕙 9am-4pm Nov-Mar, to 6pm Apr-Oct) is housed on the ground floor of what appears to be a municipal office. It's a charmless place that attracts few visitors and there are just a half-dozen rooms, each devoted to a particular era, including: Neolithic and Palaeolithic; the Iron Age; Roman; and Islamic. There's some interesting material on finds at the citadel mound, including a fine 2.5m-high basalt lion that once guarded the entrance to an Iron Age palace. Other stand-out items are an exquisitely rendered 3rd-century mosaic, depicting a group of young women playing music and dancing, and a fragment of a 5th-century Byzantine mosaic, recovered from Apamea, that depicts a *noria*.

To get to the museum walk, north uphill along Sharia Said al-A'as and take the first left after the large new **Omar ibn al-Khattab Mosque**, which was completed in 2001.

SOUQ السوق

Hama was never a great trading centre and today its main **souq** (off Sharia al-Murabet) is modest with hardly any of the great commercial khans that fill the old cities of Aleppo or Damascus. The two noteworthy khans that Hama does possess have long since been pressed into other uses: **Khan Rustum Pasha** (1556), just south of the town centre on Sharia al-Murabet, is an orphanage (although it's occasionally open to the public as an exhibition space); while **Khan Asad Pasha** (1751), also on Sharia al-Murabet but further south, is now a local Ba'ath Party branch.

Tours

The Cairo and Riad hotels in Hama run excursions with flexible itineraries determined by the wishes of the group. Popular options are full-day trips involving two or three scattered locations (eg Apamea and Musyaf or the Dead Cities combined with Qala'at Saladin) that would be hard to get to in one go using public transport. Prices are typically S£500 per person (not including admissions), based on four people sharing the transport. It's not cheap but if you're pushed for time this may be a good way of doing things.

It's also possible to hire a car and driver and put together your own itinerary; expect to pay between US$40 and US$50 for the day. Ask at your hotel if you'd like to arrange a car-driver package.

Sleeping
BUDGET

There are really only two budget options worth considering in Hama, but both are superb.

Cairo Hotel (☎ 222 280; cairo_hotel@ayna.com; Sharia Shoukri al-Quwatli; dm/s/d/tr S£157/300/450/550; 🗶 🖳) Near the clock tower, this hotel offers possibly the best budget accommodation in Syria. Rooms are spotlessly clean with fridge, satellite TV, and gleaming private bathrooms, or you can sleep on a mattress on the roof for S£100. There's also a good little breakfast area, free tea on arrival, and a small library of books to borrow. Staff are extremely friendly and speak English. The hotel also runs a range of trips around the region – see the Tours (above). Fantastic.

Riad Hotel (☎ 239 512; riadhotel@scs-net.org; Sharia Shoukri al-Quwatli; dm/s S£150/300 d S£350-550; 🗶 🖳) In direct and not necessarily friendly competition with its neighbour, the Cairo, to which it is identical in almost all respects, the Riad is also fantastic.

In the unlikely event of both these hotels being booked out, your budget options are down to two flophouses, where S£125 gets you a filthy bed (free bugs). Look for **Funduq al-Amir** (Hadat Abi Taleb), in a lane off Sharia Shoukri al-Quwatli, or **Funduq al-Qasr al-Arabi al-Kebir** ('Hotel' in English) near the vegetable market, just south of Sharia Shoukri al-Quwatli.

MID-RANGE

Hama Tower Hotel (☎ 226 864; fax 521 523; d US$31; 🗶) In the centre of town, one block north of Sharia Shoukri al-Quwatli, this hotel occupies the top floors of a tower block overlooking the river. The views are great but the hotel is badly maintained – rooms are grubby and battered. Rates seem to be negotiable.

New Basman Hotel (☎ 521 802; fax 517 776; Sharia Shoukri al-Quwatli; s/d US$13/19; 🗶) Once a fairly ordinary place, this place has been taken in hand by the management of the nearby Riad. Since then it's undergone a much-needed overhaul. Some of the rooms still need attention but overall it's not bad; there are a couple of massive suites that sleep five (US$29) and are excellent value for groups. Rooms have fan, bath and TV; and some have air-con.

Noria Hotel (☎ 512 414; bader@mail.sy; Sharia Shoukri al-Quwatli; s/d US$18/28; 🗶 🖳) Run by Badr Tonbor, who also owns the Cairo, this large, modern, three-star has a smart reception area fronted by extremely competent and friendly staff, and good spacious rooms with air-con, fridge and satellite TV. Triples and suites are available. Guests can also take advantage of the tours organised out of the Cairo Hotel.

Sarah Hotel (☎ 515 941; Sharia Abu al-Feda; s/d US$21/28; 🗶 🖳) This hotel is in a good location in the old quarter of Hama, and has a good range of facilities including a laundry service, direct-dial phones and a café-restaurant; the hotel itself, however, is very impersonal. It's one of the newer hotels in town, yet the place is already looking decidedly shabby.

TOP END

Apamee Cham Palace (☎ 525 335; www.chamhotels.com; Sharia abi Nawas; s/d US$100/120 plus tax; 🗶 🖳 🖭) While this place has all the five-star features you expect from the Cham hotel chain, it's located across the river from the citadel and well away from the buzz of the town centre. It's a disquietingly gloomy place with all the life of a mausoleum and is generally empty unless there's a tour group in town.

Eating

Although you can find it elsewhere in Syria, a Hama speciality worth trying is *halawat al-jibn* – a soft cheese-based, doughy delicacy, drenched in honey or syrup and often topped with ice cream. A lot of places around Sharia Shoukri al-Quwatli sell it – a few sell nothing else.

RESTAURANTS

Dining in Hama is pleasurable – just as well given that there's little else to do here at night. At places such as Al-Atlal, the Family Club or the Four Norias the drill is to turn up late (not before 9pm), and pass a few hours over a succession of mezze accompanied by *arak* (ouzo-like drink), finished off with a nargileh. Most places stay busy until well into the early hours.

Al-Atlal (☎ 222 234; Sharia al-Buhturi; ☽ noon-late) A relatively new place in town, serving what is possibly the best food in Hama. Choose between the indoor section and the outdoor area, with its tree-shaded terrace beside the river. There's no menu, but expect all the usual mezze and meaty grills. The restaurant sign is in Arabic only, but it's the first place on the left as you walk along Sharia al-Buhturi, east from the centre. No alcohol is served; credit cards aren't accepted.

Dream House (☎ 411 687; Sharia al-Khandak; ☽ 10-1am) Also a fairly newish place in Al-Medina quarter, just two blocks north of the orthodox church, Dream House is a bit soulless, but very clean and smart, and the food is good. The menu – in English with prices – runs from pizza and filling burgers with fries and salad (S£100 to S£130), up to steaks, fillets and Middle Eastern grills (S£120 to S£175). Alcohol is served, and payment by AmEx, MasterCard or Visa is possible on bills of US$10 or over.

Family Club (Nadi al-Aili; Sharia Kawakili, Al-Medina; ☽ 6pm-late) This is an open-air terrace on the 1st floor, at the rear of a building a block north of the orthodox church (the club is run by the church). It's used as a social and drinking club by the wealthier citizens of Hama and is a frequent venue for weddings and parties. Anybody is welcome to show up though, and it's definitely worth a visit because the food is excellent. There's no menu – just order any mezze you can think of, and chances are they'll have it. Prices are reasonable and alcohol is served.

Four Norias (Sharia al-Buhturi; per person S£250-300; ☽ noon-late) This place is just over 500m east of the centre, on the banks of the river beside – what else – four *norias*. It's a large open-air place popular with groups and families and gets pretty lively on summer evenings. Food is the standard mezze and kebabs. Alcohol is served.

Sultan Restaurant (☎ 235 104; per person S£100-150; ☽ noon-11pm) Benefiting from a wonderful setting in part of a waterside Mamluk-era complex in the old town, the main dining room here is bare stone with wooden ceilings and a central fountain. Best of all, right outside is one of the great old *norias*, which provides a groaning aural backdrop to your meal. The menu is limited to mezze and kebab, but the menu is in English and items are priced. No alcohol is served. To get here, pass through the low, vaulted tunnel beside the An-Nuri Mosque.

QUICK EATS

In the couple of blocks along Sharia Shoukri al-Quwatli, west of the Cairo Hotel and in the side streets running north to the river, there are all the usual cheap felafel, shwarma, kebab and chicken restaurants. Go for the one doing the most business with the locals.

SELF-CATERING

For fruit there is a good little **market** just off the western end of Sharia Shoukri al-Quwatli, while for groceries there's a Western-style **supermarket** (cnr Sharia Ibrahim Hanano & Sharia Al-Mutanabi) which, though small, is decent and well stocked. You can get takeaway beer at a couple of **liquor stores** at the north end of Sharia al-Mutanabi, near the citadel.

Drinking

Engineers Club (Nadi al-Mohandiseen; Sharia al-Buhturi; ☽ noon-late) This club, just a short walk east of the city centre, is an open-air garden restaurant, which many use primarily as a bar.

Railway Workers' Restaurant (Al-Mahatta al-Omali; ☎ 511 498; Sharia al-Wahda al-Arabiyya; ☽ 4-8pm) Housed in the old railway-station building in the western part of town, this faintly seedy club features tuneless female singers. It makes for a fun one-off experience, but note the limited opening hours. To get there, follow Sharia Ibrahim Hanano west until reaching a major junction; the club is on the south side of this junction, in a distinctive French Mandate–era building.

The open-air **Choob coffeehouse** is set in a garden of shady eucalyptus trees and has views of the river and *norias*. There is also another open-air coffeehouse, **An-Nadi**, next to the big city centre *noria* and facing the Choob across the river; and another by Al-Mohammediyya *noria*, west of the Citadel.

Getting There & Away
BUS

Hama has no central station for luxury buses. Instead, the main bus companies (including Al-Ahliah, Qadmous and Al-Rayan) have their offices in the town centre – and all services pull up out front.

Al-Ahliah (Sharia al-Buhturi) has the greatest number of departures and the times are posted inside the office in English; it has services to Damascus (S£85 to S£90, 2½ hours, every half hour 5am to 9am then hourly until 11.30pm), Aleppo (S£65, 2½ hours, hourly from 6.30am to 11.15pm), Homs (S£20, 45 minutes), Tartus (S£70, two hours), Lattakia (S£100, three hours), Idlib (S£50, one hour) and Raqqa (S£145, five hours). Note, if you're travelling to Homs, departures by microbus (see below for details) are far more frequent.

Qadmous (Sharia al-Buhturi), facing the river west of the main bridge, has only two buses a day to Damascus (7.15am and 3.15pm) but frequent departures to Aleppo, Lattakia and Tartus, as well as three buses a day to Qamishle via Hassake, and the only direct services to Palmyra (S£85, three hours; 8am, 7.30pm and 11.15pm), all of which continue on to Deir ez-Zur. Qadmous also has twice-daily services to Beirut/Tripoli (S£250, 9.30am and 11am).

There are no direct services to Krak des Chevaliers from Hama; you have to change at Homs, see Going to Krak des Chevaliers (p132).

MICROBUS & MINIBUS

The main microbus station is a 10-minute walk from the centre of town at the southwestern end of Sharia al-Murabet in a triangular lot at the junction with the main Damascus road. From here there are regular departures to Homs (S£20, 30 minutes) and also to Musyaf (S£20, 45 minutes), Salamiyya (S£15, 40 minutes) and Suqeilibiyya (for Apamea, S£20, 40 minutes).

For microbuses to Al-Hamra (for Qasr ibn Wardan; S£15) there's a separate minibus station north of the river on Sharia al-Arkam – head up Sharia Said al-A'as, past the tourist office and take the fourth street on your right; it's about a 10-minute walk from the centre.

The minibus station is a further 200m left and along the Damascus road. Services depart from here for Homs (S£10), Salamiyya (S£15), Suqeilibiyya (S£10), Musyaf (S£10), Maharde and other surrounding towns. Battered old buses go from here to Aleppo (S£25), Damascus (S£32) and Lattakia.

TRAIN

The train station is 1.5km from central Hama. Trains to Damascus (1st/2nd class S£57/40, four hours) stop in Hama at 2.30am, while services in the opposite direction, for Aleppo (S£34/23, 2½ hours), stop at 8pm.

Getting Around

Local buses may come in handy for getting to and from the bus and train stations, both of which are uncomfortably far from the town centre. Buses leave from Sharia al-Buhturi beside the bridge. You pay the S£2 fare on the bus. Alternatively, a yellow taxi will cost S£25 to either the old bus and minibus station or the train station.

There's a **bicycle repairs and spares place** (26 Sharia Said al-A'as) on the main road heading north out of the centre in the direction of Aleppo; go past the tourist office and up the hill, and it's on your left before you get to the big new mosque.

AROUND HAMA

There are three main excursions to make from Hama around the Orontes Valley. You can travel north to the Roman-era ruins of **Apamea**, west into the hills to the Assassins' castle of **Musyaf**, or east out to the Byzantine ruins of **Qasr ibn Wardan**. Each of these trips takes about half a day but could be extended by adding in extras, such as stopping off at **Qala'at Sheisar** on the way to Apamea, or swinging past **Qala'at ash-Shmemis** (قلعة الشميص) on the way back from Qasr ibn Wardan.

Hama also makes a good base for visiting **Krak des Chevaliers** (see p132), via a change of bus at Homs, while the **Dead Cities** are only 60km to the north and easily reached by microbus – see above for more details.

All these trips can be done fairly easily through a combination of public transport and hitching, or alternatively you could take advantage of the organised tours offered by some of Hama's hotels (p164).

Al-Ghab الغاب

From Hama the Orontes River flows northwest for 50km and then into Al-Ghab plain, a vast green valley stretching between Jebel

Ansariyya to the west and Jebel az-Zawiyya to the east. It's said that in ancient times the pharaoh, Thutmose III, came here to hunt elephants, and a thousand years later Hannibal was here teaching the Syrians how to use elephants in war.

Under the Seleucids, the plain must have been both rich and fertile as it supported large cities such as Apamea, but as the population dwindled the untended land degenerated into a swamp. In recent times however, with World Bank help, this low-lying area of some 40 sq km has been drained and crisscrossed with irrigation ditches, returning it to its former status as one of the most fertile areas in Syria.

Qala'at Burzei · برزاي قلعة

One for completists only, at Qala'at Burzei you will find the minimal remains of a once sizable Crusader castle. The castle was built in the 12th century but fell to Saladin not long after, in 1188. The most intact part of the ruins is the watchtower that guarded the eastern approach, and you can also pick out the keep on the far western side. It's a bit of a scramble to get up to the ruins, so wear decent footwear.

The site is about 4km north of the turn-off for Slunfeh on the Jisr ash-Shughur road (No 56) and is accessed by a side road off to the west.

Apamea · أفاميا

If it weren't for the unsurpassable magnificence of Palmyra, Apamea (a-*fam*-ia, in Arabic) would be considered a wonder and one of the unmissable highlights of Syria. As it is, the ruinous site is like a condensed version of Zenobia's pink sandstone desert city, but built in grey granite and transposed to a high, wild grassy moor overlooking Al-Ghab plain.

The site has no set opening hours as it's unfenced and there's nothing to stop anyone wandering across it at any time. However, an admission fee (adult/student S£300/15) is payable at one of two ticket offices; ticket officials patrol the site.

The site lies about 1km north of the main road; the turn-off is marked by a long, low, old grey-stone building, which houses a museum devoted to mosaics. It's well worth a visit. A combined ticket for both mosaic museum and site can be purchased for S£350.

HISTORY

Founded early in the 3rd century BC by Seleucus I, a former general in the army of Alexander the Great, Apamea became an important trading post and one of the four key settlements of the empire to which he gave his name. It was connected by road to another key Seleucid town, Lattakia (Laodicea), which served it as a port. Seleucus had great skills as a diplomat; while Laodicea was named after his mother, he also took due care to keep things sweet with his Persian wife, Afamia, by naming this settlement after her.

As a result of the rich pasture of Al-Ghab, Apamea was renowned for its horses. According to Greek historian Strabo, the city had some 30,000 mares and 3000 stallions, as well as 500 war elephants.

Apamea was seized by the general, Pompey, for the Romans in 64 BC, and only entered into its true golden era in the 2nd century AD, when much of the city was rebuilt after an earthquake in AD 115. The results of this reconstruction are what you see at the site today.

In its heyday, Apamea boasted a population of about 500,000 and was notable enough to be visited by Mark Antony, accompanied by Cleopatra, on his return from staging a campaign against the Armenians on the Euphrates River. Prosperity continued into the Byzantine period but then the city was sacked by the Persians in AD 540 and again in 612. Barely a quarter of a century later, Syria was seized by the Muslims and Apamea fell into decline. It assumed importance during the Crusades when the Norman commander, Tancred, took possession of the city in 1106. The occupation however was short-lived and Nureddin won the city back 43 years later. Eight years on the city was all but flattened in a devastating earthquake.

The site wasn't abandoned completely: a nearby hilltop that had served as an acropolis under the Seleucids and Romans became a citadel under the Mamluks. It sheltered a small village, which later became a popular stopover for pilgrims on their way south to Mecca. The village, which takes its name Qala'at al-Mudiq from the citadel, has long since outgrown its fortified walls and now tumbles down the hillside to the main road.

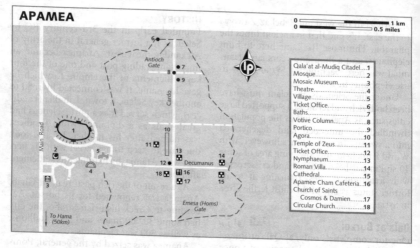

APAMEA

Qala'at al-Mudiq Citadel....**1**	
Mosque....................**2**	
Mosaic Museum............**3**	
Theatre...................**4**	
Village...................**5**	
Ticket Office..............**6**	
Baths....................**7**	
Votive Column.............**8**	
Portico...................**9**	
Agora...................**10**	
Temple of Zeus...........**11**	
Ticket Office..............**12**	
Nymphaeum..............**13**	
Roman Villa..............**14**	
Cathedral................**15**	
Apamee Cham Cafeteria..**16**	
Church of Saints	
Cosmos & Damien.......**17**	
Circular Church...........**18**	

SIGHTS

Mosaic Museum

Just off the main road, at the foot of the hill that leads up to Apamea, is a restored Ottoman khan that dates from the 18th century and was used as a trading post on the route to Mecca from Constantinople. It is now the fabulous setting for a distressing **mosaic museum** (adult/student S£150/10; ☼ 9am-2.30pm Wed-Mon). The mosaics include some very, very fine pieces and are housed in the former stables around the central courtyard, along with an odd assortment of architectural bits and pieces. The distressing part is the level of neglect, with leaks in the building's roof causing unchecked water damage.

On exiting the museum, turn right and follow the road left, then right, up the hill for the site. Ignore the guys on motorbikes who offer to show you the way or give you a lift, saying that it's too far to walk – it's not. From where the hustlers are generally encountered, at the top of the hill, it's only about 400m further to the ticket office and main entrance to the ruins.

Theatre

Part way between the museum and the site proper, and off to the right, is a hollow filled with the barest vestiges of what was a 2nd-century-AD theatre. After serving as a convenient quarry for the neighbouring village for centuries, the remains are less than impressive, yet archaeologists believe that this may once have been the largest theatre

in the eastern Roman Empire, bigger even than the one at Bosra.

Cardo

The main feature of the ruins of Apamea is the north-south **cardo** (main street), marked out along much of its length by parallel colonnades. Several lesser decumani (cross-streets or east-west streets) intersected the cardo, and the main surviving **decumanus** now serves as the modern access road to the site – you'll walk or ride up it from the main highway. The junction of the cardo and decumanus is the main entry point for the site; here are the ticket office and the pricey Apamee Cham Cafeteria.

At 2km Apamea's cardo is longer than the one at Palmyra. Many of its columns, originally erected in the 2nd century AD, bear unusual carved designs and some have twisted fluting, a feature that is unique to Apamea. Visitors to this site as recently as 50 years ago would have seen nothing of this; in what's termed 'reconstructive archaeology', the columns have been recovered from where they once lay, scattered and overgrown with weeds, and have been re-erected by a Belgian team that has been working here since the 1930s.

North of the main junction, parts of the cardo still retain its original paving, visibly rutted by the wear of chariot wheels. To the right are the remains of a **nymphaeum** (public water fountain), while a little further on and off to the left, two rows of column bases lead to a pile of stone blocks that were once part of the entrance to the **agora** (forum). Considerably further to the north is an impressive and beautiful **portico**, set forward of the main colonnade and composed of taller columns crowned by a triangular pediment. Just beyond the portico is the base of a large **votive column** in the middle of the street: this would have marked an important intersection.

Beyond the column is the best-restored section of the cardo, with raised paved areas either side of the street, and behind them the lower portions of facades that would most likely have been shops – it's possible to gain a clear impression here of how the cardo must have looked in its heyday. The northernmost end of the cardo is marked by the recently restored **Antioch Gate**, beyond which once stretched the ancient city's necropolis.

Decumanus   دوكومانوس
About 400m east from the main junction and café area, there are the remains of a **Roman villa** with an impressive entrance and colonnaded courtyard. Across the way is a **cathedral** from about the 5th century.

Citadel   القلعة
The citadel of Qala'at al-Mudiq, which sits atop a spur just west of the ruins of Apamea, is, typically, more impressive from the outside. It dates from the 13th century and occupies what had been the acropolis of the ancient city. Inside is a tumbledown village; it's an unkempt, grimy little place – especially after rain – but, given time to spare, it is worth visiting for the views out over Al-Ghab, and of the theatre and ruins.

GETTING THERE & AWAY
Microbuses (S£20, 40 minutes) regularly run the 45km from Hama to the village of Suqeilibiyya, where it's necessary to change to a microbus for Qala'at al-Mudiq (S£10, 10 minutes). The whole trip takes about an hour, except on Friday, when you can wait ages for a connection. You need to tell the driver to let you off at the museum – 'al-mathaf. See p164 for more information about organised tours from Hama.

Musyaf   مصياف
The solid castle of **Musyaf** (adult/student S£150/10; 8am-6pm Apr-Oct, to 4pm Nov-Mar, closed Tue) sits in the foothills of Jebel Ansariyya, about 40km

west of Hama. While it's far from being the most impressive of Syria's many fortresses, the outer walls are intact and suitably imposing, especially viewed against the mountain backdrop. And there are the colourful historical associations.

It's not known when the first fortifications were erected on this site, but there was definitely a castle of some sort here in 1103 because it was seized by the Crusaders. They didn't have enough manpower to garrison it and by 1140 it had passed into the hands of the mysterious Ismaili sect, more dramatically known as the Assassins (see the boxed text, p170).

As Shiites, the Ismailis were at odds with Syria's ruling Sunni Ayyubid dynasty and so they waged guerrilla warfare. They successfully assassinated several important Sunni figures, and in 1175 and 1176 made two attempts on the life of the sultan, Saladin, himself. The warlord's immediate response was to meet the Ismaili threat head on and in the same year as the second attempt on his life, he laid siege to their stronghold of Musyaf. What happened next is unknown and is the source of an intriguing legend, for almost as soon as it was begun, Saladin called off the attack. The story has it that in the midst of his camp, surrounded by his personal guards, Saladin woke suddenly one evening to see a shadowy figure slip out of his tent and found at the foot of his bed a dagger and a note of warning from the leader of the Assassins.

Some sort of agreement must have been reached between the two parties because Saladin did not attack the Ismailis again and their attempts on his life ceased. It wasn't until 100 years later, and the campaigns of the Mamluk warrior sultan, Beybars, that the Assassins were finally driven out and Sunni orthodoxy was secured in Syria.

The entrance to the castle is via a flight of stairs at the south, which leads up into the main keep. Opening hours are a bit hit-and-miss: if the caretaker is not around when you arrive, go to the tea stall on the east side of the castle (the opposite side to the town) and the guy there will be able to find him for you.

GETTING THERE & AWAY
Minibuses to/from Hama and Homs cost S£10 and S£15, respectively; microbuses cost S£20 and S£25. Avoid making the journey on Friday when services are greatly reduced.

Musyaf is also conveniently visited en route to Krak des Chevaliers (see p132), for example as part of an organised tour with one of the Hama hotels (p164).

Qasr ibn Wardan قصر إبن وردان

About 60km northeast of Hama, **Qasr ibn Wardan** (adult/student S£150/10) lies on a road that goes to nowhere. There's little out here but hard-baked earth and dust, but it's a fascinating journey all the same – in the space of little more than an hour you pass from the comforting surrounds of cosily urban Hama to a landscape that in parts resembles Mars.

Erected by the Byzantine emperor, Justinian, in the mid-6th century as part of a defensive line that included Rasafa and Halabiyya on the Euphrates, Qasr ibn Wardan was a combined military base, palace and church. Its appearance, however, would seem to belie any defensive function; rather than a frontier outpost it looks more like a modestly grand public building that would be more at home on some city square.

One theory for this is that Qasr ibn Wardan was a base from which to consolidate control over the local Bedouin population, and as such it was meant to impress upon the nomads the strength and status of their would-be overlords.

The palace, assumed to have been home to the local governor, is the building closer to the road and the caretaker will usually open this up first. There are no set opening hours. The best-preserved part is the south façade, constructed of broad bands of black basalt and yellow brick, through which you enter into a hall with rooms off to either side. Many of the stones lying around are carved with symbols and you can pick out variously a jar, some scales, a sheep and a fish. In the courtyard two large stones are carved with a sundial and a calendar. On the north side of the courtyard are the former stables while on the east side, to the right as you enter, is a small bath complex.

The church is architecturally similar in style to the palace but smaller. Its basic form is a square, and it was once capped by a large dome (long since disappeared) and ringed by galleries on three sides. The fourth side is rounded off by a semicircular and half-domed apse that's common to many early Byzantine churches. Stairs in the northwestern corner lead to an upper gallery, which originally would have been reserved for women.

Admission is payable to the caretaker who lives in the house at the side of the road. If you walk into the courtyard someone will see you and run to get him – meanwhile you'll probably be sat down and offered strong syrupy coffee or tea.

Around Qasr ibn Wardan

Between Qasr ibn Wardan and the village of Al-Hamra, lie the hamlets of **Sarouj** (سروج)

THE ASSASSINS

The Ismailis were an extreme Muslim sect that leaned towards the mystical. They were little loved by orthodox Sunnis, who regularly persecuted them. Not surprisingly perhaps, since the doctrine of these followers of Ismail (the 8th century son of the sixth imam) included murder as a means of removing obstacles to the propagation of their faith. Under their charismatic 12th-century leader Sinan, known to the Europeans as the 'Old Man of the Mountain', the surrounding Muslims and Crusaders came to fear and respect the Ismailis.

The Ismaili 'Assassins', so called – according to one account – because they smoked hashish (an Arabic word from which 'assassin' is said to be derived) before embarking on their murderous exploits, attempted on a couple of occasions to kill both Nurredin and Saladin, two of Islam's principal champions against the Crusaders. Among the Christian rulers to end up on the wrong end of their poison-tipped swords was Raymond II of Tripoli, who bit the dust around 1150, and Conrad de Montferrat, king of Jerusalem, about 40 years later.

By the late 13th century, however, Sultan Beybars had not only all but finished off the Crusader presence in the Levant, but had also taken the Ismaili fortresses and stripped the group of any political importance.

Anyone interested in knowing more should get hold of a copy of The Assassins by Bernard Lewis.

and **Twalid Dabaghein** (دباقين توالد) with their curious – see the boxed text above.

Hitchers could ask to be dropped off to look around and pick up another lift later. The Cairo and Riad hotels in Hama (p164) both include a visit to the beehive houses as part of their organised trips out to Qasr ibn Wardan.

AL-ANDERINE   العندرين

Beyond Qasr ibn Wardan, a further 25km of rough road leads northeast to **Al-Anderine**, which is another Byzantine settlement of which precious little remains today. The defensive settlement was dominated by a cathedral, but only a few pillars still stand.

GETTING THERE & AWAY

Although public transport doesn't go all the way out to Qasr ibn Wardan, it is still relatively easy to get there under your own steam. Take a minibus from Hama (see p166) to Al-Hamra (S£15, 45 minutes). From Al-Hamra you have to hitch the remaining 20km and although there's not much traffic going this way, whatever there is will most likely stop and take you on. You shouldn't have to wait much longer than 10 minutes or so for a ride out and about the

same for the ride back. Sarouj is 53km from Hama and Twalid Dabaghein is 50km from Hama, most hire a taxi for the trip.

Isriyya   أثريا

Only the main temple remains of the ancient desert settlement of **Seriana**. Apart from a missing roof, the temple is largely in one piece. Dating from the 3rd century AD, the stone employed is the same as that used in much of the construction in Palmyra. Seriana was in fact an important way station in the imperial Roman road network, with highways to Palmyra, Chalcis, Rasafa and Homs (ancient Emesa) all meeting here.

GETTING THERE & AWAY

Getting to Isriyya can be a bit trying. Buses and microbuses regularly ply their trade between Hama and Salamiyya (السلمية), but this part of the trip is best done with a driver or hire car. You could hire a service taxi for about S£600 one way. Otherwise, you could take a microbus the first 45km northeast to Saan (S£10). From there you have another 45km of road to travel, and may still be obliged to deal with a service taxi for the remainder of the trip.

Aleppo حلب

While Damascus was always the precious 'holy' city, the seat of rulers and wary of foreigners, Aleppo, Syria's second city, has been one of commerce since Roman times. Aleppo (or Halab) today retains that air of people going about business, as they have done for centuries. The streets speak a rhythm of sounds – from horse-drawn carts over cobblestones to the more frenetic pace of donkey-riding couriers, still the fastest way through the atmospheric, labyrinthine souqs (markets) fragrant with soap, spices and shwarma.

With a population nudging three million, early in the 20th century Aleppo saw its Christian population (between 20% and 30% of the total) swollen by thousands of Armenians and other Christian minorities driven out of Anatolia by the Turks. In certain quarters of the city there are almost as many signs in the condensed-looking script of Armenian as in Arabic.

Alongside this distinctive script, travellers will note some signs in Russian along the city centre shopping streets – Aleppo being a beneficiary of the dissolution of the USSR. During the 1990s, a steady stream of traders from the former Soviet republics bustled through on large-scale shopping sprees. Most recently Aleppo has witnessed a new breed of local investors and entrepreneurs. This has included spending on Aleppo's wonderful World Heritage–listed buildings, immaculately restored and housing a new wave of boutique hotels and restaurants, promising to restore some of its former panache to the city.

HIGHLIGHTS

- Get lost in **Aleppo's souq** (p176), arguably the most vibrant and untouristy in the whole Middle East

- Steam-clean yourself at the **Hammam Yalbougha an-Nasry** (p186), one of the most attractively restored hammams in all Syria (it's open to women, too)

- Spend a night at one of Aleppo's wonderful **boutique hotels** (p189) and try to stop yourself extending your booking

- Visit **Qala'at Samaan** (p196), the hilltop remains of a sumptuous Byzantine cathedral dedicated to an ascetic who lived his life on top of a pillar

- Tiptoe around the **Dead Cities** (p200), the eerie shells of abandoned ancient towns and villages scattered across the landscape

Qala'at Samaan ★
★ Aleppo
Dead Cities ★

■ TELEPHONE CODE: 021

HISTORY

Aleppo vies with Damascus for the title of the world's oldest continually inhabited city. In fact, a handful of other Middle Eastern towns make this claim too, but texts from the ancient kingdom of Mari on the Euphrates River indicate that Aleppo was already the centre of a powerful state as long ago as the 18th century BC, and the site may have been continuously inhabited for the past 8000 years. Its pre-eminent role in Syria came to an end with the Hittite invasions of the 17th and 16th centuries BC, and the city appears to have fallen into obscurity thereafter.

During the reign of the Seleucids, who arrived in the wake of Alexander the Great's campaign, it was given the name Beroia, and with the fall of Palmyra to the Romans, it became the major commercial link between the Mediterranean and Asia. The town was destroyed by the Persians in AD 611 and fell to the Muslims during their invasion in 637. The Byzantines overwhelmed the town in 961 and again in 968 but they could not take the Citadel.

Three disastrous earthquakes also shook the town in the 10th century and Nureddin (Nur ad-Din) subsequently rebuilt the town and fortress. In 1124 the Crusaders under Baldwin laid siege to the town.

After raids by the Mongols in 1260 and 1401, in which Aleppo was all but emptied of its population, the city finally came into the

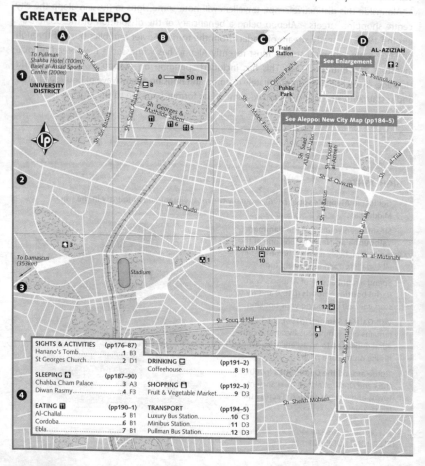

GREATER ALEPPO

SIGHTS & ACTIVITIES	(pp176–87)		
Hanano's Tomb	1 B3		
St Georges Church	2 D1	**DRINKING**	(pp191–2)
		Coffeehouse	8 B1
SLEEPING	(pp187–90)		
Chahba Cham Palace	3 A3	**SHOPPING**	(pp192–3)
Diwan Rasmy	4 F3	Fruit & Vegetable Market	9 D3
EATING	(pp190–1)	**TRANSPORT**	(pp194–5)
Al-Challal	5 B1	Luxury Bus Station	10 C3
Cordoba	6 B1	Minibus Station	11 D3
Ebla	7 B1	Pullman Bus Station	12 D3

Ottoman Turkish orbit in 1517. It prospered greatly until an earthquake in 1822 killed over 60% of the inhabitants and wrecked many buildings, including the Citadel.

As long as four centuries ago European merchants – particularly French, English and those of the various city states of Italy – had established themselves here. However, the flood of cheap goods from Europe in the wake of the Industrial Revolution, and the increasing use of alternative trading routes, slowly killed off a lot of Aleppo's trade and manufacturing. Today the major local industries are silk-weaving and cotton-printing. Products from the surrounding area include wool, hides, dried fruits and, particularly, pistachios for which Aleppo is justly famous.

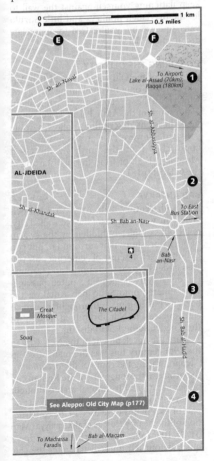

See Aleppo: Old City Map (p177)

ORIENTATION

There are two distinct parts to central Aleppo: the New City with the bulk of the places to stay and eat, and the Old City with all the sightseeing. The New City centre lies south of the large public park, focused on the vast but characterless public plaza of Saahat Saad Allah al-Jabri. West of this square is the modern commercial centre – seen by very few visitors – while east, is the main travellers area, bounded by Sharia al-Baron, Sharia al-Quwatli, Sharia Bab al-Faraj and Sharia al-Maari. In this tightly hemmed quadrilateral are most of the cheap hotels and budget eateries. Sharia al-Baron is also home to most travel agents, airline offices, banks and cinemas.

The Old City lies southeast of the New City, a 10-minute walk away. The two are separated by a couple of drab, wide avenues (Sharia al-Mutanabi and Sharia Bab Antakya) that feel more Murmansk than Middle East. The heart of the Old City is the compress of streets that make up the city's famed souq. Its main thoroughfares run east–west, slipping by the south face of the Great Mosque and terminating at the massive earthen mound of the Citadel. To the north of the Old City is the Christian-Armenian quarter of Al-Jdeida, an area with its own distinct character, and a buffer between old and new Aleppo.

INFORMATION
Bookshops

The best bookshop in Aleppo is at the Chahba Cham Palace (p189), just out west on Sharia al-Qudsi. It has a reasonable selection of books about Syria and the Arab world in general, plenty of locally produced guidebooks, as well as a handful of novels in both English and French. There's also a limited range of international newspapers available. It is a S£35 to S£40 taxi ride out there.

Internet Access

Aleppo has few Internet cafés but you can expect to find many more by the time you visit.

Concord Internet Café (Map pp184-5; Sharia al-Quwatli; per 30 min S£50; ☼ 9am-11pm) It's above a pastry café.

Internet Ramsis (Map pp184-5; ☎ 211 1102; Sharia al-Baron; per 30 min S£50; ☼ 11am-midnight) In the Ramsis Hotel.

Libraries

Librairie Said (Map pp184-5; cnr Sharia Qostaki al-Homsi & Sharia Litani) Has a small selection of dusty old novels as well as the odd Syria coffee-table book.

Medical Services

There are several pharmacies on Sharia al-Quwatli around the junction with Sharia Bab al-Faraj.

Dr Farid Megarbaneh (☎ 221 1218) This recommended doctor speaks excellent English and French.

Money

For travellers cheques, you could go to one of the two branches of the Commercial Bank of Syria (CBS) located on Sharia Yousef al-Azmeh north of Al-Quwatli. You are required to show the receipts for your cheques. At both branches there is a commission of S£25. You could also try the reception at your hotel.

CBS Branch No 2 (Map pp184-5; ⌚ 8.30am-1pm & 2-6pm) 100m further north of No 6, next to the cinemas.

CBS Branch No 6 (Map pp184-5; ⌚ 8.30am-1.30pm Sat-Thu) It's marked by a big sign in English but the entrance is hidden at the back of an arcade and the office is on the 1st floor.

Exchange Office (Map pp184-5; cnr Sharia al-Quwatli & Sharia Bab al-Faraj; ⌚ 9am-7.30pm) Convenient but doesn't accept travellers cheques.

Post

Aleppo is dotted with Easycomm cardphones; they're not too hard to find, especially around the Sharia al-Baron area.

DHL (Map pp184-5; off Sharia al-Quwatli; ⌚ 9.30am-11pm)

Main Post & Telephone Offices (Map pp184-5; Saahat Saad Allah al-Jabri; ⌚ 8am-5pm, until 10pm for telephones) The monolithic Soviet-style building is on the southwest side of the main square. The parcels office is around the corner to the left of the main entrance.

Tourist Information

Tourist Office (Map pp184-5; ☎ 222 1200; Sharia al-Baron; ⌚ 9am-2pm Sat-Thu) In the gardens opposite the National Museum. Usually the best you'll get is a free map.

Immigration Office

Visa extensions (Map pp184-5; Sharia al-Qala'a; ⌚ 8am-1.30pm Sat-Thu) On the 1st floor of a building just north of the Citadel. Bring four passport photos and then fill out forms in quadruplicate. The processing takes one to 1½ hours and there's a fee of S£25; extensions of up to two months are possible. The office is up the stairs and through the right-hand

door in the facing wall. Passport photos can be taken at the shacks lining the road across from the immigration office.

SIGHTS
The Old City   المدينة القديمة

At one time walled and entered only by one of eight gates, the Old City has long since burst its seams and now has few definable edges. Exploring its seemingly infinite number of alleys and cul-de-sacs could occupy the better part of a week, depending on how inquisitive you are. We recommend visiting at least twice: once on a busy weekday to experience the all-out five-senses assault of the souq, and a second time on a Friday when, with all the shops closed, the lanes are silent and empty. Relieved of the need to keep flattening yourself against the wall to let the overladen donkeys and little Suzuki vans squeeze by, you're free to appreciate architectural details.

EXPLORING THE OLD CITY

Coverage of the Old City begins at Bab Antakya, one of only two remaining city gates, which is on the street of the same name about 500m south of the Amir Palace Hotel. From here the sight descriptions follow a route eastward. However, the area is just as easily approached from the north via the Great Mosque (p178), or from the east starting at the Citadel (p181).

BAB ANTAKYA   باب أنطاكية

The 13th-century Bab Antakya (Antioch Gate), the western gate of the old walled city, is all but completely hidden by the swarm of busy workshops that surround it, but you definitely get a sense of 'entering', as you pass under its great stone portal and through the defensively doglegged vaulted passageway. Emerge onto Souq Bab Antakya, the bazaar's bustling main thoroughfare, which runs due east to halt abruptly at the foot of the Citadel, some 1.5km distant.

Until the development of the New City in the 19th century this was the main street in Aleppo, tracing the route of the *decumanus*, the principal thoroughfare of the Roman city of Beroia. A great triumphal arch is thought to have stood on the site of Bab Antakya and part of its remains were used in the construction of the nearby **Mosque of al-Kamiliyya** (Map p177), 100m ahead on your left. Before this, a quick detour left immediately after the gate

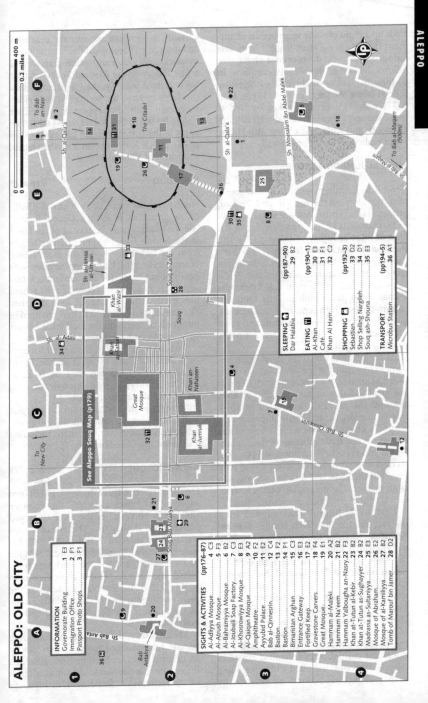

ALEPPO

ALEPPO: OLD CITY

0   0
0.2 miles
400 m

Sh al-Qala'a
To Bab an-Nasr
The Citadel
Sh al-Qala'a
Sh Moualam ibn Abdel Malek
To Bab al-Maqam (500m)
Sh Bab al-Maqam

Sh al-Jamaa al-Jumuwi
Souq al-Zarb
Khan al-Wazir
Souq
Khan as-Sabun
Sh al-Adasi
Khan an-Nahaseen
Great Mosque
Khan al-Jumruk
See Aleppo Souq Map (p179)

To New City

Sh Bab Qinnesrin
Souq Bab Antakya
Sh Bab Anta
Bab Antakya

leads up a flight of stone steps beside a ham-mam (bathhouse) – often flagged by towels airing outside – and up onto a street that follows the line of the old city ramparts. In addition to good views, there's the interesting little **Al-Qaiqan Mosque** (Crows' Mosque; Map p177) with its doorway flanked by Byzan-tine columns, a façade studded with column segments, and a block inscribed with Hittite script embedded in the south wall.

KHAN AL-JUMRUK & OTHERS

خان الجمرك و غيره

Beyond Al-Kamiliyya mosque, a corrugated-iron roof blots out the sunlight and the souq proper starts. To the left are entranceways to two adjacent khans (travellers' inns), the **Khan at-Tutun as-Sughayyer** (Map p177) and the **Khan at-Tutun al-Kebir** (Map p177) – that's the little and big khans of Tutun, although in fact they're both fairly modest in scale. A few steps along and on the right is **Al-Bahramiyya Mosque** (Map p177) built in early Ottoman style in the late-16th century. From here on, virtually every building is a khan and there are a few in particular that are definitely worth investigating.

At the point at which the street again be-comes spanned by stone vaulting, slip off to the right, then take an immediate left to reach the great gateway of the magnificent **Khan al-Jumruk** (Map p179). Completed in 1574, this is the largest and most impressive of Aleppo's khans. At one time it housed the consulates and trade missions of the English, Dutch and French, in addition to 344 shops. Its days as a European enclave are now long gone but the khan is still in use, serving as a cloth market. The decoration on the interior façade of the gateway is particularly fine.

Next to Al-Jumruk (but entered from the east side) is the much smaller **Khan an-Nahaseen** (Khan of the Coppersmiths; Map p179), which dates from the first half of the 16th century. Until the 19th century, rooms on the 1st floor housed the Venetian consul, and during the 20th century they were the residence of the Belgian consul. Madam Jenny Poche, descended from the last of the Venetian consuls (and mother of the present Belgian consul), maintains the property, which may well qualify as the oldest continuously inhabited house in Aleppo. Its rooms are filled with a beguiling variety of historic collections gathered by

various family members over the centuries and include archaeological finds, antiquities, mosaics, precious early photography and a fine library where Madam Poche's father once waltzed with Agatha Christie. Visitors (no large groups) are welcomed on Friday mornings only by appointment; either phone **Madam Poche** (☎ 221 5712, 094 443 327) or apply at the current Belgian consulate (Map p179), which is close by in Khan al-Qattin, just south of Khan al-Wazir.

THE SOUQ   Map p179

السوق

Not as extensive as Cairo's Khan al-Khalili or as grand as İstanbul's Grand Bazaar, Aleppo's **souq** is nonetheless one of the finest in the Middle East. Its appeal derives largely from the fact that it is still the main centre of local commerce. If an Aleppine housewife needs some braid for her curtains, a taxi driver needs a new seat cover, or the school kids need satchels, it's to the souq that they all come. Little here seems to have changed in hundreds of years and the local trade has yet to be displaced by sightseers and tourists.

Parts of the souq date from the 13th cen-tury, but the bulk of what stands today belongs to the Ottoman era (largely 16th-to 19th-century). A walk through the souq could take all day, particularly if you accept some of the many invitations by the polyglot stall owners to stop and drink tea. For infor-mation on what to buy and where, including a detailed map, see Shopping (p192).

GREAT MOSQUE   Map p179

الجامع الكبير

On the northern edge of the souqs is the Great Mosque (Al-Jamaa al-Kebir), the younger sibling (by 10 years) of the great Umayyad Mosque in Damascus. The mosque was started by Caliph Al-Walid (r AD 705–15) who had earlier founded the Great Mosque in Damascus (p86) and the work was com-pleted by his successor Caliph Suleiman (r AD 715–17). However, aside from the plan, nothing survives of the original mosque as the building has been destroyed and re-built countless times.

Miraculously, the mosque's freestanding **minaret** has managed to survive in exactly its original form, as built in 1090, although it does have a pronounced lean as a result of an earthquake. Standing 47m high, it's

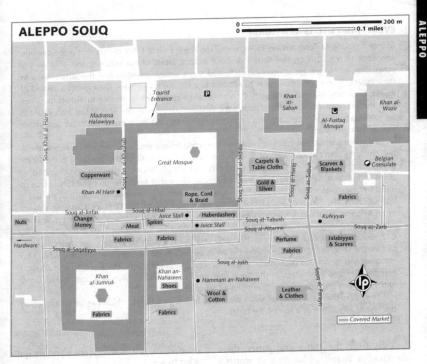

ALEPPO SOUQ

a beautiful thing, rising up through five distinct levels adorned with blind arches to a wooden canopy over a muezzin's gallery (ie of the mosque official who calls the faithful to prayer).

While it's not possible to climb the minaret, visitors are allowed inside the mosque. There's no admission fee but footwear must be removed, which will then be watched over by a custodian who customarily receives S£25.

Entrance is directly into the courtyard, the floor of which is decorated by a checkerboard of black and white marble geometric patterns. Under a strong sun, the reflected light is so harsh it hurts the eyes, while the heated marble is painful under shoeless feet.

Inside the prayer hall is a fine 15th-century carved *minbar* (pulpit). Behind the grille to the left of this is supposed to be the head of Zacharias, the father of John the Baptist. Notice the many padlocks fastened to the grille, placed here temporarily by locals who believe that a few days soaking up the *baraka* (blessings) from the tomb will lend them additional strength.

Madrassa Halawiyya   المدرسة الحلوية

Opposite the western entrance of the mosque, this rather dilapidated former theological college (built 1245) stands on the site of what was once the 6th-century Cathedral of St Helen. The prayer hall opposite the entrance incorporates all that remains of the cathedral, which is a semicircular row of six columns with intricately decorated acanthus leaved capitals. For several hundred years the cathedral and the Great Mosque (built in the cathedral's gardens) stood side by side, serving their respective faiths, who would appear to have worshipped in harmony. The cathedral was only seized by the Muslims in 1124 in response to atrocities committed by the Crusaders. The prayer hall is often kept locked but ask around and someone will search out the custodian.

AROUND THE GREAT MOSQUE   Map p179

The souq is at its most labyrinthine immediately south and east of the Great Mosque. This is where you'll find gold and silver, carpets and kilims (see Shopping, p192).

EVERYTHING OLD IS NEW AGAIN

Author Anthony M Tung writing in *Preserving the World's Great Cities* claims that more damage was done in the 20th century to the precious historic fabric of our urban spaces than at any other time in history. He blames concrete and steel, industrialisation and the automobile. In this respect, Aleppo and Damascus have been lucky. Enjoying perhaps their greatest period of wealth under the Mamluks and early Ottomans, when cash from commerce furnished the cities with the grandest of architecture, both were well into decline by the end of the 19th century, languishing in the 20th century, and subsequently missing out on many of the most destructive aspects of modernism.

As a consequence, few cities anywhere in the world have a medieval heritage as rich as these two. But they aren't wholly without scars. In the case of Aleppo, misguided planning in the 1950s ploughed major new roads through the Old City, causing considerable damage, compounded by the new building construction that went alongside. Since that time Aleppo's Old City has been listed by Unesco as a World Heritage Site – keeping company with monuments such as the Great Wall of China, the Pyramids and Machu Picchu. More significantly, the Old City is also the subject of an ongoing rehabilitation project being carried out by the local municipality in conjunction with the German government (via the offices of the German Agency for Technical Cooperation; GTZ; www.gtz-aleppo.org). Begun in 1993 and very much a work still in progress, objectives are to halt the deterioration of the residential areas by improving housing and services, while also restoring and renovating monuments, ensuring their continued usage. The aim is to nurture local communities and businesses in the hope that the Old City will survive as a historic but living entity, and not become just another open-air museum piece.

For visitors there's a series of walks described in free brochures, which can be picked up at the tourist office and at a few of the hotels.

Away from the glitter and patter, there are another couple of khans well worth a look. In the block east of the Great Mosque is the early-16th-century **Khan as-Sabun** (Soap Khan), largely obscured by a clutter of shops but with a very distinctive, richly decorated Mamluk façade. Internally it's one of the prettiest of khans, with vine-hung trellising and the brightly hued wares of carpet sellers draped over the upper balconies.

The 17th-century **Khan al-Wazir** (Minister's Khan), a block further east, also has a beautifully decorated gateway. It's one of the grandest such structures in Aleppo and largely unaltered by modern development.

BAB QINNESRIN   Map p177

باب قنسرين

Sharia Bab Qinnesrin is the southern continuation of Souq an-Nahaseen, the Coppersmiths' Souq – which no longer has any coppersmiths at all – and it runs down to Bab al-Qinnesrin, which is the surviving southern Old City gate. It's been a prime beneficiary of the attentions of the GTZ and the Old City rehabilitation project (see the boxed text Everything Old Is New Again, above). It only stretches for a little

over 500m, but in that stretch there's quite a lot to see.

Towards the bottom of Souq an-Nahaseen, just before Sharia Bab Qinnesrin, a short passageway leads to **Al-Adliyya Mosque**, built around 1550 and one of the city's major Ottoman-era mosques. It's worth a quick look inside for the fine tiling. To the south, the street doglegs round the jutting corner of a small khan, now used by shoe wholesalers, beyond which noses are set twitching by the fragrant smells emanating from **Al-Joubaili Soap Factory**, ages-old and still producing soaps the traditional way using bay plants and olive oils.

Directly across the street, stepped back slightly behind railings, is the wonderful **Bimaristan Arghan**, one of the most enchanting buildings in the whole of Aleppo. It dates from the 14th century and was constructed as a hospital. The main entrance gives access to a beautifully kept courtyard with a central pool overhung by greenery. Diagonally across, a doorway leads through to a series of tight, claustrophobia-inducing passages, one of which terminates in a small octagonal, domed courtyard. Off this are 11 small cells; these are where the dangerously insane were confined when the bimaristan served as an asylum – a role it performed until as recently as the 20th century.

Continuing south, you reach the huge, solid and tunnel-like **Bab al-Qinnesrin** gate. It's in a superb state of preservation and, like Bab Antakya, incorporates a defensive dogleg.

CITADEL
Map p177

القلعة

Rising up on a high mound at the eastern end of the souq, the **Citadel** (☎ 362 4010; adult/student S£300/15; ☷ 9am-6pm Wed-Mon) is Aleppo's most obvious landmark. It dominates the city and was long the heart of its defences.

The mound the Citadel stands upon is not, as it seems at first sight, artificial: it's a natural feature and one that originally served as a place of worship, as evidenced by two basalt lions unearthed here and identified as belonging to a 10th-century BC temple.

It's thought that the first fortifications were erected up here at the time of the Seleucids (364–333 BC), but everything today dates from much later. The Citadel served as a power base for the Muslims during the time of the Crusades and it's at this time, during the 12th century, that the moat, 20m deep and 30m wide, was dug and the lower two-thirds of the mound were encased in a stone glacis. Much rebuilding and strengthening occurred during the period of Mamluk rule (AD 1250–1517) and it's largely their work that survives. There are plans to turn the street circling the Citadel into a pedestrian area with cafés and shops.

Touring the Citadel
To enter, you cross the moat by a stepped bridge on the south side, carried by eight arches. Any attacking forces would have been incredibly exposed on the bridge as they confronted the massive **fortified keep**, from which defenders could rain down arrows and pour boiling oil through the row of machicolations. The **bastion**, off to the right, was added in the 14th century to allow for flanking fire on the bridge.

Once through the first great gate, set to the right rather than dead in front to prevent charges with a battering ram, is a succession of five further right-angle turns with three sets of steel-plated doors forming a formidable barrier to any would-be

aggressors. Some of the doors still remain and one of the lintels of the doorways has carvings of entwined dragons; another has a pair of lions, echoing the millennia-old use of lions as guardians against evil, as seen in the National Museum (p183).

The rubble left in the wake of pillage and earthquakes, overgrown by weeds, covers most of the area on the summit of the mound. A path leads north. On the right is a series of doorways, one of which has steps leading down to two sunken chambers that once served as a cistern and prison. Beyond the doorways a set of stairs doubles back to lead up to the remains of an **Ayyubid Palace** dating from the early 13th century. The most striking remains are of a soaring entrance portal with stalactite stone decoration. To the rear of the palace is a recently renovated Mamluk-era hammam.

A path from the hammam leads back towards the fortified keep and its heavily restored throne room with a magnificent intricately decorated wooden ceiling.

Back on the main path, off to the left is the small 12th-century **Mosque of Abraham**, attributed to Nureddin and one of several legendary burial places for the head of John the Baptist.

At the northern end of the path, opposite what is now a café, is the 13th-century **great mosque**, a rather grandiose title for a building of such humble dimensions. The café is housed in an Ottoman-era barracks, and it's from here that you get the best views over the collage of roofs, domes and minarets. The replica Roman **amphitheatre** over to the east is new and clumsily built in concrete to accommodate infrequent opera and concert performances; find out if anything is happening by asking at the ticket office.

SOUTH OF THE CITADEL
Map p177

Virtually opposite the entrance to the Citadel is the Ayyubid **Madrassa as-Sultaniyya**. The prayer hall has a striking mihrab (niche indicating the direction of Mecca) with eye-catching ornamentation achieved through multicoloured marble inlays, but unfortunately this part of the building is often locked. Also here is the **mausoleum of Al-Malek az-Zaher Ghazi**, a son of Saladin (Salah ad-Din), and one-time occupant of the Citadel.

Across the road to the west is a low, multidomed mosque set in gardens. Known as **Al-Khosrowiyya Mosque**, it's notable for being one of the earliest (1537) works of the famed Turkish architect Sinan. It still serves as the main place of worship for the neighbourhood and each Friday streams of men and young boys make a beeline to assume their place for noon prayers.

To the east of Madrassa as-Sultaniyya is **Hammam Yalbougha an-Nasry**, source of naked indolence and steamy pleasure, and an Aleppine must – see Activities (p186).

Al-Jdeida

Map pp184–5

الجديدة

Al-Jdeida quarter is the most charming part of Aleppo. It's a well-maintained warren of narrow, stone-flagged lanes with walls like canyons. The façades that line the alleys are blank because the buildings all look inwards into central courtyards. But every so often one of the studded black doors with their clenched fists for knockers is open and passers-by get a glimpse of the private realms inside.

Much of the architecture here dates from the Ottoman era, which makes this quarter less old than the Old City, hence its name Al-Jdeida, 'the new'. It developed as an area for prosperous traders, who were largely Maronite and Armenian Christians, getting rich on the city's trade.

The quarter is currently undergoing something of a rebirth. With the backing of an enlightened city mayor, private investors have been encouraged to purchase and renovate properties in the quarter and convert them to commercial usage. At the moment there are two fantastic boutique hotels occupying former merchants' mansions and an ever-growing number of restaurants and bars sprouting in striped-stone courtyards and cellars.

AROUND SAAHAT AL-HATAB

ساحة الحطب وحواليها

If there's a heart to Al-Quarter, then it's Saahat al-Hatab (Hatab Square), lined with shops selling oriental jewellery. To the north is **Sharaf Mosque**, one of the neighbourhood's earliest monuments, built in the reign of the Mamluk sultan Qaitbey (r 1468–96). At the western corner, just the other side of **Orient House Antiques** (p193), a stylised sculpture of two robed women marks the turn for Sharia as-Sissi. Along here on the right **Beit as-Sissi**

(Sissi House) is a 17th-century residence that was one of the first of the area's many historic houses to be restored and recycled it's now a top-class restaurant (p191). About 50m further on the left, **Beit Wakil** is two 18th-century houses lovingly transformed into a stunning boutique hotel and adjacent courtyard restaurant (p191).

Backtrack across Saahat al-Hatab and make a beeline south along Sharia al-Kayyal and on the right is a door with a plaque announcing **Beit Ghazzali**. This is the largest house in the quarter. It was built some time in the late 16th/early 17th century, served as an Armenian school for much of the 20th century, and is the subject of ongoing restoration. Some of the walls have fine painted decoration and there's a splendid private hammam. Except for the caretaker and his family the house is currently unoccupied while the authorities decide what to do with it. Knock on the door to be let in for a look around. A little baksheesh is in order.

MUSEUM OF POPULAR TRADITION

تحف التقاليد الشعبية

A little further down from Beit Ghazzali is yet another house, Beit Ajiqbash (built 1757) now pressed into service as the **Museum of Popular Tradition** (☎ 333 6111; Haret al-Yasmin; adult/student S£150/10; ☉ 8.30am-2pm Wed-Mon) with scenes and artefacts relating to local life in bygone times. The architecture of the house and the décor are very fine and worth paying to see.

CHURCHES & CATHEDRALS

The quarter is home to five major churches each aligned to a different denomination. Immediately west of the museum is the Syrian Catholic **Mar Assia al-Hakim Church** built in 1625 and happy to admit visitors who come knocking. Next stop is the 19th-century **Greek Orthodox Church** and further beyond that, still on Haret al-Yasmin, is the entrance to the 17th-century **Armenian Cathedral of the 40 Martyrs**. If possible, it's worth visiting on a Sunday to observe the Armenian mass which, as performed here is still pervaded with an almost sensuous aura of ritual and mystery. It starts at 10am and lasts two hours.

North of these three are also the **Maronite Cathedral** (Saahat Farhat) and a smaller **Greek Catholic Church**, both of which date only to the 19th century.

The New City
Map pp184–5

Most visitors' experience of modern Aleppo is limited to the Bab al-Faraj area, a low-rise neighbourhood of cubbyhole shops, small businesses and *mekaniki* (car repair workshops). A huge area east of the baroque **clock tower**, which appears like a bomb site, is under redevelopment and is shortly to be graced by a large Sheraton hotel.

In the meantime, the most pleasant part of the New City is the large **public park** that lies northwest of the hotel district. It's nicely laid out with pathways meandering through well-tended greenery, and with an impressive fountain entrance off Sharia Saad Allah al-Jabri. If you're through with walking for the day this is as good a place as any to bring a book and find a bench for a bit of relaxation.

Up around the north end of the park is the district of **Al-Aziziah**, an upmarket neighbourhood developed during the 19th century and home to Aleppo's moneyed families, most of whom are Christian.

NATIONAL MUSEUM
المتحف الوطني

Aleppo's **National Museum** (☎ 221 2400; adult/student S£300/15; ♥ 9am-1pm & 4-6pm Wed-Mon), right in the middle of town, could be mistaken for a sports hall were it not for the extraordinary colonnade of giant granite figures that fronts the entrance. Standing on the backs of cartoonishly stylised creatures, the wide-eyed characters are replicas of pillars that once supported the ceiling of

an 8th- or 9th-century BC temple-palace complex at Tell Halaf near the border with Turkey in the northeast of the country.

The ticket office is just inside the building on the left. There's a decent guidebook to the museum for S£200, although most of the exhibits have some sort of labelling in English.

From the entrance hall the exhibits are displayed chronologically in an anticlockwise direction.

Tell Brak
تل براك

Tell Brak is 45km north of Hassake in far northeastern Syria. It and other neighbouring sites were excavated by Sir Max Mallowan, husband of Agatha Christie. Most of the exhibits in this room are finds from his digs, although many of the best pieces went to the British Museum in London.

Mari
ماري (تل الحريري)

This room contains some of the museum's best pieces, unearthed at Tell Hariri, the site of the 3rd-millennium BC city of Mari, on the Euphrates River near the present-day Iraqi border (p225). Look for the tableaux of delicate carved-shell figurines of a general and his fettered prisoners and chariots, which attests to the high level of artistry existent at this early time; it's on the wall opposite Case 4. Just past the tableaux is a wonderful greened bronze lion. It's less refined than the shell figurines but has a winningly doleful expression. Along with a twin, now in the Louvre in Paris, it was discovered flanking a temple doorway.

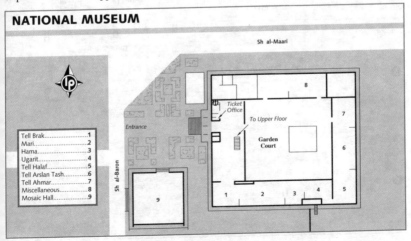

NATIONAL MUSEUM

Sh al-Maari

Ticket Office

To Upper Floor

Entrance

Garden Court

Sh al-Baron

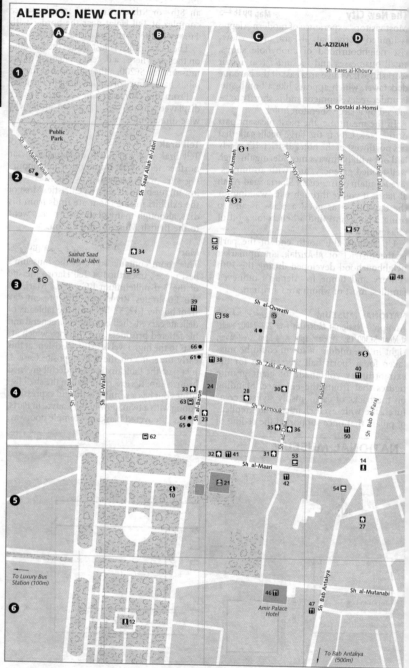

ALEPPO: NEW CITY

AL-AZIZIAH

Sh Fares al-Khoury

Sh Qostaki al-Homsi

Public
Park

Sh al-Malek Faisal

67 ●

Sh Saad Allah al-Jabri

Sh Yousef al-Azmeh

● 1

Sh al-Ayyubi

Sh ash-Shohada

Sh Jbrail Dalal

● 2

57

Saahat Saad
Allah al-Jabri

34

55

7

8

48

39

Sh al-Quwatli
@ 3

56

58

4 ●

66 ●

61 ●

38

5

40

Sh Zaki al-Arsuzi

Sh al-Walid

Sh al-Jalaa

33

24

28

30

Sh Rashid

63

23

Sh Yarmouk

64 ●

65 ●

35

36

50

Sh Bab al-Faraj

62

Sh ad-Dala

32

41

31

53

14

21

42

54

10

27

To Luxury Bus
Station (100m)

46

Sh al-Maari

Sh Bab Antakya

Sh al-Mutanabi

47

12

Amir Palace
Hotel

To Bab Antakya
(500m)

0			200 m
0			0.1 miles

INFORMATION

Commercial Bank of Syria No 2....**1**	C2
Commercial Bank of Syria No 6....**2**	C2
Concord Internet Café.............**3**	C3
DHL................................**4**	C3
Exchange Office...................**5**	D4
Internet Ramsis..............(see 33)	
Librairie Said....................**6**	E1
Main Post & Telephone Office....**7**	A3
Parcels Office....................**8**	A3
Police.............................**9**	E3
Tourist Office....................**10**	B5

SIGHTS & ACTIVITIES (pp176–87)

Armenian Cathedral of the	
40 Martyrs....................**11**	F3
Assad Statue.....................**12**	B6
Beit Ghazzali....................**13**	F3
Clock Tower......................**14**	D5
Greek Catholic Church...........**15**	F3
Greek Orthodox Church..........**16**	F3
Latin Cathedral..................**17**	E1
Mar Assia al-Hakim Church......**18**	F3
Maronite Cathedral..............**19**	F3
Museum of Popular Tradition..**20**	F3
National Museum.................**21**	C5
Sharaf Mosque...................**22**	G2

SLEEPING (pp187–90)

Ambassador Hotel................**23**	B4
Baron Hotel......................**24**	C4
Beit Wakil.......................**25**	F2
Dar Zamaria Martini.............**26**	G2
Hanadi Hotel.....................**27**	D5
Hotel al-Faisal..................**28**	C4
Hotel al-Jawaher................**29**	E5
Hotel Somar......................**30**	C4
Hotel Syria......................**31**	C5
Hotel Yarmouk...................**32**	C5
Ramsis Hotel.....................**33**	B4
Tourism Hotel....................**34**	B3
Tourist Hotel....................**35**	C4
Zahrat ar-Rabie (Spring	
Flower Hostel)................**36**	C4

EATING (pp190–1)

Al Mir Restaurant................**37**	G2
Al-Andalib.......................**38**	C4
Al-Fehaa.........................**39**	B3
Al-Kindi Restaurant.............**40**	D4
Aleppo Dairy Qattib.............**41**	C5
Amman Supermarket.............**42**	C5
Bazar Al Charq...................**43**	E6
Beit as-Sissi....................**44**	F2
Cantara..........................**45**	F3
Fountain Café....................**46**	C6

Fruit & Vegetable Market.......**47**	D6
Fruit Stall.......................**48**	D3
Haj Abdo Al Fawwal.............**49**	G2
Juice Bars & Liquor Stores......**50**	D4
Mashrabia........................**51**	F3
Yasmeen House...................**52**	F3

DRINKING (pp191–2)

Al-Mathaf........................**53**	C5
As-Sahel.........................**54**	D5
Ash-Shams.......................**55**	B3
Kazar Café.......................**56**	C3
Open-Air Bar.....................**57**	D2

ENTERTAINMENT (p192)

Cinemas..........................**58**	C3

SHOPPING (pp192–3)

Orient House Antiques...........**59**	F2
Sh al-Adasi......................**60**	G6

TRANSPORT (pp194–5)

Air France.......................**61**	B4
Karnak & Turkish Bus Station...**62**	B4
Karnak Bus Office................**63**	B4
KLM..............................**64**	B4
Lufthansa........................**65**	B4
SyrianAir........................**66**	B4
SyrianAir........................**67**	A2

Sh Litani

Sh as-Sissi

Saahat Farhat

Saahat al-Hattab

AL-JDEIDA

Souq

Sh al-Tilal

Sh al-Kayyali

Sh al-Khandak

Sh Hammam an-Nar

Souq

Sh al-Adasi

To Old City;
Great Mosque (250m)

Behind the lion are two fine, almost life-sized statues, one in diorite representing the prince Ishtup-Ilum, and the other in limestone of the Lady of the Well Spring (pictured on the S£50 note). The Lady has a hollow interior through which a pipe was run that spewed water out of the vase in her hands.

Hama حماه
These exhibits are of finds made from excavations at the citadel in Hama, which date back to around 1000 BC. Note the two lions which, like those at Mari, were set as guardians to ward off evil.

Ugarit اوغاريت (رأس شمره)
Many of the objects in this room display evidence of the links between this one-time busy port (p148) and Egypt. In Case 1 there are some bronze figures which are wholly Egyptian and may have been gifts from a pharaoh to the king of Ugarit (Ras Shamra). In Case 4, one of the alabaster vessels bears the name of Ramses II in hieroglyphs, while beside Case 5 is a limestone Egyptian obelisk.

Tell Halaf تل حلف
This hall is dominated by more of the giant figures similar to those at the entrance to the museum; however, while those outside are replicas, some of these are millennia-old. The figures are believed to represent gods and a goddess; the central one is thought to be Haddad, the weather god, symbolically linked to the bull (on which he stands). The colossi were originally flanked by two, similarly wide-eyed and comical sphinxes, and a replica of one stands over to the left. The large panels are plaster casts of originals that once adorned Tell Halaf's palace walls – the originals were destroyed during WWII in a bombing raid on a German museum.

Tell Arslan Tash تل ارسلان طاش
The best display here is the astonishing collection of ivory carving. The pieces were discovered in the remains of a palace at Tell Arslan Tash, an Aramaean city (ancient name Hadatu) in the northeast of the country, excavated by the French early last century. They are not Syrian in origin and have been identified as coming from Phoenicia and dated to the 9th century BC. For such a cold, hard medium, some

of the pieces display a surprisingly touching warmth and fluidity, such as the cow licking her calf and the grazing gazelles. Others, like the Ugarit pieces earlier, bear a strong Egyptian influence: there's a series depicting the birth of the god Horus from a lotus flower, which is very similar to an alabaster carving of Tutankhamen emerging from a lotus on display in the Egyptian Museum in Cairo.

Tell Ahmar تل احمر
Tell Ahmar is the site of another ancient Aramaean city, and is on what is now the Syrian–Turkish border, 20km south of the crossing point of Jarablos. The wall paintings displayed in this room were removed from the remains of a palace excavated by the French in the 1920s. They date from around the 8th century BC.

Miscellaneous
These halls contain exhibits from digs in progress.

Upper Floor
Up here is a modern art gallery that suffers from a lack of labelling and serves only to show that 20th-century Syrian art has been heavily influenced by various European movements. Of more interest is the Islamic arts hall which contains brasswork, coins, a Mamluk tomb and a superb 3m square model of the Old City of Aleppo.

Mosaic Hall
There is a separate mosaic hall entered from the museum garden but at the time of writing it was closed to the public.

ACTIVITIES
Hammams
The **Hammam Yalbougha an-Nasry** (Map p177; ☎ 362 3154; near the Citadel; entry S£200, massage S£100, rubdown S£50; ☉ 10-2am, women only 10am-5pm Mon, Thu & Sat) is one of Syria's finest working bathhouses and something of a state showpiece. It was originally constructed in 1491 but it had been destroyed and rebuilt several times before the latest restoration, completed in 1985. Note the sun clock inside the dome above the reception area. The hammam is just southwest of the Citadel's entrance.

The Yalbougha an-Nasry is something of a popular tourist stop. If that somehow detracts from the experience, there are other possibilities. **Hammam an-Nahaseen** (Map p179; men only; entry S£150), in the heart of the souq just south of the Great Mosque, has also been recently renovated, though not with the tourist in mind so most of the old architectural features have been obscured.

Hammam Na'eem (Map p177), also known as Hammam al-Jedida, is a quiet and clean place just north of the main souq street. To find it, coming from Bab Antakya along the main souq street, take the first left after the start of the corrugated iron roofing and it's just ahead on the right.

Organised Tours

Ahmed Modallal (☎ 267 1719; fax 225 1606) is a genial guy with excellent English who guides Syria's expat and diplomatic community around the City. We met him at the Great Mosque, where he claims his father was the muezzin for years. He certainly seemed to know his stuff and his prices were reasonable at US$5 per person for a two-hour tour. You can set your own itinerary or he'll whisk you along on one of his own devising.

Halabia Travel & Tourism (☎ 224 8497; www .halabia-tours.com) is run by the very friendly and extremely knowledgeable Abdel Hay Kaddar. It will organise visas and meet you at the Turkish border. A variety of tours are on offer.

Swimming

People wanting to cool off with a simple and relaxing swim can try the **Basel al-Assad sports centre** (☎ 266 6497; ☼ only 10am-2pm Wed, 3-6pm Wed & Fri, women only 10am-2pm Mon & Thu, 3-6pm Mon), out west next to the Pullman Shahba Hotel. The other days are for families.

Nonguests can also use the pool at the **Chahba Cham Palace** (Map pp174-5; admission S£400; ☼ summer only).

SLEEPING

The accommodation scene in Aleppo is steadily improving, with the arrival in recent times of two superb boutique hotels in Al-Jdeida, now joined by a third in the vicinity of the Citadel. The first hotel in the Old City has also opened, and that's bound to trigger a slew of copycats. Otherwise, beware when looking for budget accommodation – good, clean lodgings are hard to find, and the handful of recommended places fill up fast. Book in advance if possible.

Budget

Most budget hotels are in the block bounded by Sharia al-Maari, Sharia al-Baron, Sharia al-Quwatli and Sharia Bab al-Faraj. Sharia ad-Dala, where many of the hotels are, is Aleppo's auto tyre shop street – not exactly the kind of ambience to write home about. Hot water in these hotels generally comes only in the evening and/or early morning.

Hanadi Hotel (Map pp184-5; ☎ 223 8113; Bab al-Faraj; s/d/tr S£450/900/1350; ☒) Once you can get past its Barbie-esque colour scheme (pink, pink and more pink), it's a well looked-after, spotlessly clean hotel. All rooms have private bathrooms (albeit with squat toilets) and some have air-con. There's also a washing machine, ironing facilities and a breakfast courtyard, and management organises trips around the region. It's well located 100m south of the clock tower.

Hotel al-Jawaher (Map pp184-5; ☎ /fax 223 9554; Bab al-Faraj; s/d/tr S£350/750/1050) In a handy location just off Bab al-Faraj, this hotel has basic but clean rooms, most with decent new private bathrooms. There are a couple of attractive common areas hung with rugs and kilims, and satellite TV in the reception. It's often fully booked so reservations are recommended.

Hotel Somar (Map pp184-5; ☎ 221 2198; Sharia ad-Dala; s/d US$15/21; ☒) Pleasant rooms come with their own showers and toilets and there's a nice little courtyard. It's a fine budget place, but charges unwarranted mid-range room rates.

Hotel Syria (Map pp184-5; ☎ 221 9760; Sharia ad-Dala; s/d S£200/350, with private bathroom S£250/400; ☒) A block south of the famed Tourist Hotel, this place has tolerable loddings. Sheets are changed regularly, the rooms have functioning ceiling fans and the bathrooms have hot water.

Tourist Hotel (Map pp184-5; ☎ 221 6583; Sharia ad-Dala; r per person S£350, with breakfast) Run by the formidable Madam Olga, this remains Aleppo's best budget option – as long as you don't need air-con. It's homely, immaculately clean and there's always hot water. Some rooms have shared bathrooms, others have private bathrooms. Booking in advance is essential.

Hotel Yarmouk (Map pp184-5; ☎ 221 7510; Sharia al-Maari; s/d S£250/500; ☒) Just east of the junction with Sharia al-Baron, the Yarmouk doesn't get too many tourists (mostly Russian traders) but it has benefited from a recent overhaul;

Maari; s/d S£250/500; ⚇) Just east of the junction with Sharia al-Baron, the Yarmouk doesn't get too many tourists (mostly Russian traders) but it has benefited from a recent overhaul; rooms are clean with good private bathrooms and fan. It's a decent fall-back if the others are full.

Zahrat ar-Rabie (Spring Flower Hostel; Map pp184-5; ☎ 221 2790; 373hotur@mail.sy; Sharia ad-Dala; dm/s S£175/250, d S£300-500) This was once one of the most popular backpacker joints in Aleppo, but rooms are tiny, dark, grubby and overpriced for what they offer. Lonely Planet has received a number of reports from female travellers of staff members using peepholes to watch guests in the shower.

Mid-Range

Most of Aleppo's mid-range hotels are run-down and the choices are a little limited. Dar Halabia is a welcome addition, but given that the Old City pulls the shutters down about 7pm, there's only a couple of eating options nearby. The renovated rooms of the Baron are a good choice if you can bargain them down to a good price. If neither of these two appeal, consider pushing your budget up to the splendours of the Beit Wakil, Dar Zamaria Martini or Diwan Rasmy.

Ambassador Hotel (Map pp184-5; ☎ /fax 222 3362; 6 Sharia al-Baron; s/d US$21/25; ⚇) This is a dated 1940s place with the odd redeeming feature (eg the tiered foyer). Rooms are spartan but clean, some with new private bathrooms, all with fridge and satellite TV. Attracts a mainly Arab clientele.

Baron Hotel (Map p177; ☎ 221 0880/1; hotelbaron@mail.sy; 8 Sharia al-Baron; s US$30-35, d US$40-45) The Baron is one of those old, slightly eccentric Middle Eastern character pieces – see the boxed text (below). Be prepared for a bit of a trade-off: for its air of Gothic romance, let go any attachments to more physical luxuries. That said, it is being renovated (but not with the level of detail it should be receiving), and several rooms have now been totally refurbished to include new bathrooms. See also its entry under Bars, p192.

Dar Halabia (Map p177; ☎ 332 3344; halabiatour@net.sy; Sharia Lisan ad-Din al-Khatib; s/d US$30/40; ⚇) The only hotel in the Old City opened its doors in 2001. It's a conversion of a couple of old houses, and has 16 rooms on two levels around a central courtyard. It's lovely and good value, although quiet at night when the whole quarter is deathly silent.

Hotel al-Faisal (Map pp184-5; ☎ 221 7768; fax 221 3719; Sharia Yarmouk; s/d US$24/30; ⚇) Around the corner from the Baron, this modern three-star is popular with tour groups. The rooms are extremely clean with central air-con and good private bathrooms.

Ramsis Hotel (Map pp184-5; ☎ 211 1102; www.ramsishotel.com; Sharia al-Baron; s/d US$59/75; ⚇ ▣) Recently renovated, this Art Deco hotel has modern and extremely comfortable rooms. The hotel also has a coffee shop (with Lavazza coffee), bookshop and Internet café.

Tourism Hotel (Map pp184-5; ☎ 225 1602/3/4/5; fax 225 1606; Saahat Saad Allah al-Jabri; d US$50) This modern place on the New City's square has clean rooms, fridge, TV and private bathrooms.

THE BARON HOTEL

Built at a time when travel invariably involved three-week sea voyages, a set of garden shed–sized trunks to be carried by porters and a letter of introduction to the local consul, the **Baron Hotel** (Map p177; ☎ 221 0880/1; hotelbaron@mail.sy; 8 Sharia al-Baron; s US$30-35, d US$40-45) belongs to a very different era. When it went up (1909–11), the hotel was on the outskirts of town 'in gardens considered dangerous to venture into after dark' and from the terrace guests could shoot ducks on the neighbouring swamp.

The Baron quickly became known as one of the premier hotels of the Middle East, helped by the fact that Aleppo was still a busy trading centre and staging post for travellers. The Near Eastern extension of the *Orient Express* used to terminate in Aleppo and the rich and famous travelling on it generally ended up staying in the Baron. The old leather-bound visitors book turns up names such as aviators Charles Lindbergh, Amy Johnson and Charles Kingsford-Smith, as well as TE Lawrence (also see the boxed text Lawrence of Arabia, opposite), Theodore Roosevelt and Agatha Christie, who wrote the first part of *Murder on the Orient Express* while staying here. Kept securely stashed in the safe, the visitors book sadly isn't available for viewing but you can see a copy of Lawrence's bar bill displayed in the lounge.

LAWRENCE OF ARABIA

Born in 1888 into a wealthy English family, Thomas Edward Lawrence studied archaeology, which led him in 1909 and 1910 to undertake excavations in Syria and Palestine.

With the outbreak of WWI, Lawrence became an intelligence agent in Cairo. Highly regarded in this capacity, he adopted an attitude that was both unobtrusive and nonconformist. In 1915, as a specialist on Middle Eastern military and political issues, he recorded his ideas on the Arab question and these were taken into consideration by British intelligence. Supporting the cause of the Arab revolt and manifesting his own hostility towards French politics in Syria, Colonel Lawrence favoured the creation of a Sunni and Arab state. He also became the main architect of the English victory against the Turks. It was during this time that Lawrence claims that he was flogged for rebuffing the sexual advances made by a Turkish commandant. This was meant to have occurred at Der'a – which most travellers pass through on the way to the ruins at Bosra. However, it's the conclusion of several of Lawrence's biographers that the whole sadistic encounter never took place and was a complete fabrication on the part of Lawrence.

But it was the desert revolt of October 1918 that etched Lawrence's name into legend. At the side of Emir Faisal, whom he made the hero of the Arab revolt, and of the English General Allenby, Lawrence conquered Aqaba. He then entered Damascus in triumph, marking the final defeat of the Ottoman forces. Syria then became a joint Arab-English state.

Returning to England, Lawrence defended his ideas at the peace conference and served as the special interpreter of the Hashemites. In 1921, following the conference in Cairo at which both Lawrence and Churchill participated, he was sent to Transjordan to help the Emir Abdullah – the great-grandfather of the current King Abdullah II of Jordan – to formulate the foundations of the new state. Nevertheless, he later left this position and enrolled in 1922 with the Royal Air Force (RAF), under the assumed name of Ross, first as a pilot, then as a mechanic. He left the RAF in February 1935 and was killed in May that year in a motorcycle accident.

Top End

In Beit Wakil, Dar Zamaria Martini and Diwan Rasmy, Aleppo has three of the most seductive hotels in Syria. Therefore there's no reason to consider staying at the charmless Chahba Cham Palace or Pullman Shahba. You could also check if the new luxury Sheraton in the Bab al-Faraj area has opened (www.starwood.com/sheraton).

Beit Wakil (Map pp184-5; ☎ 221 7169; fax 224 7083; Sharia as-Sissi; s/d US$80/100; ✱) Situated in Al-Jdeida quarter and opened in 1998, this is an 18th-century house lovingly restored and converted into a small boutique hotel with rooms arranged around a beautiful yellow-and-black striped courtyard. Aside from two suites, the rooms are plain and boxy but have stone bathrooms complete with fonts taken from old hammams. A second courtyard acts as a restaurant and bar (p192). Reservations necessary. Credit cards are accepted.

Dar Zamaria Martini (Map pp184-5; ☎ 363 6100; zazahtl@net.sy; s/d US$85/115; ✱) Also in Al-Jdeida quarter, this hotel integrates three old courtyard houses dating from the 17th and 18th centuries. It has 22 rooms and a fine restaurant. While the renovation of the building itself is wonderful, the hotel lacks the simple elegance of Beit Wakil, although the rooms are significantly more comfortable. Credit cards are reluctantly accepted.

Diwan Rasmy (Map pp174-5; ☎ 331 2222; s/d/ste US$50/65/85; ✱) Aleppo's newest hotel is an elegant conversion of two connected historic houses, with 32 rooms and four suites off two large covered courtyards. Several of the rooms incorporate stone vaulting, while the suites have stunning panoramic views of the Citadel just 400m to the south. There's an inhouse restaurant and coffeehouse. Room rates are an absolute bargain; the only drawback is the fairly isolated location, about 10 minutes' walk from Al-Jdeida quarter. Credit cards are accepted.

Pullman Shahba Hotel (☎ 266 7200; fax 266 7213; Sharia al-Jamaa; s/d US$80/100; ✱) Out in the west of town, opposite the University Hospital, this is a four star–style place, not too big but still a bit Siberian and gloomy. Given the hotel's distance from the centre, it has little to recommend it. Credit cards are accepted.

Chahba Cham Palace (Map pp174-5; ☎ 266 1600; www.chamhotels.com; Sharia al-Qudsi; s/d US$160/190; ✱ ✱) Also well out in the west of the city (but with great views), this is Aleppo's show-piece. It has all the usual facilities including tennis courts, heath club, a pool and two cinemas. Credit cards are accepted.

EATING

Known for its use of hot peppers and chillies, Allepine cuisine is quite distinctive within Syria. Dining here can be a real pleasure. However, although street-food joints are ubiquitous, the good restaurants are concentrated in only two areas: Al-Jdeida and Al-Aziziah.

Most Aleppo restaurants, unless otherwise stated, open around 11am for lunch and serve through until well after midnight – usually until the last diners are ready to leave, which can be 2am or even 3am. Remember, locals dine late and most places don't get busy until 10pm or later. Reservations are rarely necessary, except where noted.

Old City
RESTAURANTS

Although at the time of research there were no restaurants in this most touristed of areas, the Diwan Rasmy hotel (p189) has two dining areas.

CAFÉS & QUICK EATS

It's surprisingly difficult to find food in the Old City. Other than the couple of cafés listed below, there are the occasional felafel sellers in the souq, particularly in the area immediately south of the Great Mosque, which is also the location for a couple of fresh juice stalls.

Al-Khan (Sharia al-Qala'a; ☽ 8.30am-10pm) One of the row of cafés facing the Citadel (second in when approaching from the souq, distinguishable by its white sun umbrellas), Al-Khan has a menu in English, with prices. The place is clean and, unlike most of the others, it doesn't routinely overcharge.

Khan Al Harir (☎ 331 7756; Sharia al-Qala'a, Souq ibn al-Khashab; ☽ 8.30am-10pm) Arabic food is served in this sleek, new, postmodern restaurant complete with fish tanks in the walls.

New City
RESTAURANTS

Al-Andalib (Map pp184-5; Sharia al-Baron; ☽ noon-late) A rooftop restaurant one block north of the Baron Hotel, this place has a boisterous atmosphere. The set menu platter (S£200)

includes kebabs, huge amounts of salads, hummus, *baba ghanoug* (purée of grilled aubergines with tahini and olive oil) and fries. The food is basic but fresh and it's good value for what you get but there's an insidious service charge of S£50. Beer is served.

Bazar Al Charq (Map pp184-5; ☎ 224 9120; btw Sharia al-Mutanabi & Sharia Hammam al-Tal; ☽ noon-late) Delicious food served in a cavernous atmospheric restaurant decorated to resemble a bazaar. Great (and very popular) lentil soup for S£80 and tasty *toshka* (Armenian toasted meat and cheese sandwiches). Alcohol is served and there's live music on Thursday and Saturday.

A better dining scene is north in the elegant district of Al-Aziziah. Crammed together on or near Sharia Georges & Mathilde Salem are about half a dozen restaurants, most with pavement tables occupied by young males sipping imported beer and toying with their mobile phones, while inside groups of jewellery-bedecked women chatter and pick at mezze.

Ebla and **Al-Challal** (Map pp174-5; ☎ 224 3344) Both of these places on Sharia Georges & Mathilde Salem have indoor and outdoor sections – in the case of the Ebla there's a lovely, old-world, canopied terrace with potted trees. Al-Challal is more chic and modern. Its menu combines mezze and Middle Eastern grills (around S£120) with international dishes, such as escalopes and steaks (S£160 to S£220). The menu at Ebla is similar but prices are more modest. Beer is served at both restaurants.

Cordoba (Map pp174-5; ☎ 224 0868; Sharia George & Mathilde Salem; ☽ 9am-late) While it's not one of the best looking restaurants on the strip the food (Armenian and Aleppine specials) makes up for it. Try the *maajouka* (meat cheese pistachios and peppers shaped into a pattie). Also worth trying is the *bastrame* (spicy potatoes). If you're not sure what to order, just ask. Alcohol is served.

CAFÉS & QUICK EATS

In the block bounded by Sharia al-Maari, Sharia Bab al-Faraj, Sharia al-Quwatli and Sharia al-Baron are plenty of cheapies offering the usual fare – prices are more variable than the food so check before you sit down. One place well worth book-marking is Al Fehaa, just off Sharia al-Baron across from the cinemas, which is a clean and hugely popular felafel place, open all hours for takeaway only. There's a row of excellent late-opening juice bars at the Bab al-Faraj end of Sharia Yarmouk.

Fountain Café (Map pp184-5; Amir Palace Hotel; Sharia al-Mutanabi; ☽ 8.30am-midnight) This café offers a welcome air-con retreat from the heat and dust outside. Sandwiches (club, steak, chicken, mortadella, ham) are S£95 to S£160 and quite substantial. The iced milkshakes (S£70) are excellent.

Al-Kindi Restaurant (Map pp184-5; Sharia Zaki al-Arsuzi) Just off Bab al-Faraj, this is one of a cluster of similar kebab restaurants, all of which offer reasonable food at budget prices. It has an extensive menu in English made up of kebabs (S£80 to S£100), grilled meats, and mezze in the S£20 to S£30 range.

Al-Jdeida
Map pp184–5

RESTAURANTS
Beit as-Sissi (☎ 221 9411; Sharia as-Sissi; ☽ noon-late) This place is a restored 17th-century house with dining in a stunning courtyard setting (and wood-panelled rooms for the colder months). It specialises in Aleppine cuisine – Syrian standards with a twist. There is a fabulous mix of mezze on offer, although the grills are disappointingly familiar. Expect to pay S£250 to S£350 per head – well worth every piastre. Alcohol is served; credit cards are accepted.

Beit Wakil (☎ 221 7169; Sharia as-Sissi; ☽ noon-late) Similar in many respects to Beit as-Sissi, which is just across the alley, it also delights with some equally interesting dishes. The cherry kebabs are a must as well as stuffed deep-fried intestines (much better than they sound), and mutton patties filled with feta cheese. Excellent. Prices are similar to Beit as-Sissi. Alcohol is served; credit cards are accepted. See also the review under Sleeping, p189.

Cantara (☎ 225 3355; Sharia al-Kayyali 1; ☽ noon-midnight Wed-Mon; dishes up to S£200) This is another courtyard restaurant that's quite pretty but not in the same league as Beit Wakil or Beit as-Sissi. It's very informal and offers an Italian-style menu with plenty of pasta and meat, and pizzas baked in view. Prices are reasonable. Credit cards are accepted; there's no alcohol.

Mashrabia (☎ 224 0249; Sharia Aidah; ☽ 9-1am; meals around S£250 per head) This self-described restaurant-pub has a diverse menu and live music. The food is reasonably priced and the bar has an extensive cocktail list.

Al Mir Restaurant (☎ 211 6880; Saahat al-Hatab; ☽ noon-late) A beautifully restored building houses this new restaurant serving pastas, salads and French food. It serves alcohol and is reasonably priced. A good choice if Beit as-Sissi and Beit Wakil are booked up.

Yasmeen House (☎ 222 4462; Sharia al-Kayyali 1; ☽ from 8pm; kebabs S£160, mixed mezze S£120) Yasmeen accommodates groups with its bench-like tables in a large courtyard but it's attractive nevertheless. The menu (in English with prices) offers about half-a-dozen nicely presented kebabs accompanied by a house selection of mixed mezze – specify which mezze you'd like. Beer is served.

QUICK EATS
Opening early every morning on Saahat al-Hatab is Haj Abdo Al Fawwal, *the* best place to get Aleppan-style *foul* (fava bean paste), here delicately spiced with cumin, red pepper, garlic and lemon. Crowds gather around the tiny shop from 7am, bearing containers of every size and description, pushing and shoving their way to the front for their share of this aromatic dish.

Self-Catering
For basics such as bread, cheese, jam and biscuits, the **Amman supermarket** (Map pp184-5; Sharia al-Maari) is a good place. It also sells toiletries including toothpaste, soap and shampoo. For fresh fruit, there is a **fruit and vegetable market** (Map pp184-5; Sharia Bab Antakya), or there's an excellent **fruit stall** (Map pp184-5; Sharia Jbrail Dalal), 200m north of the Bab al-Faraj money exchange office.

Across the road from the National Museum, **Aleppo Dairy Qattib** (Map pp184–5) stocks a range of delicious cheeses, olives and pickles; look for the red and white mirrored 'happy cow' sign.

If you take an empty mineral water bottle to the juice stalls on Sharia Yarmouk (opposite), they'll fill it up for you to take away. Among the juice stalls there are also two **liquor stores** (Map p177) where you can get Al-Chark beer for S£35.

DRINKING
Aleppo is not a late-night city and there's not much going on beyond midnight. The better places to be are promenading around

Al-Aziziah area or ducking between the bar-restaurants in Al-Jdeida.

Cafés & Coffeehouses

Al-Mathaf (Map pp184-5; Sharia al-Maari) In the city centre, while definitely not picturesque or possessed of good views, is this decent-enough, basic coffeehouse where the clientele are used to stray foreigners from the nearby hotels. It opens early and is a good option for a morning cup of tea.

As-Sahel (Map pp184-5; Sharia al-Maari) This upstairs coffeehouse is close to Bab al-Faraj and the clock tower. The place is grungy (in an old Aleppine sort of way) and the entrance is in the side street, through the reception of the As-Sahel Hotel.

Ash-Shams (Map pp184-5; Saahat Saad Allah al-Jabri) On the corner of the big, main New City square, this is a good people-watching place and a busy venue for Aleppo's chess players.

Kazar Café (Map pp184-5; Sharia Yousef al-Azmeh) A smart café, popular with locals, and with one of the few real espresso machines in Aleppo!

If you are dining up in Al-Aziziah there's also a good, big post-prandial **coffeehouse** (Map pp174-5; Sharia Georges & Mathilde Salem), across from the park.

Bars

Aleppo is Al-Chark territory, which is the less appealing of Syria's two local brews and there's not exactly a wealth of venues in which to drink it. History lovers will probably head to the bar at the **Baron Hotel** (Map p177; ☎ 221 0880/1; 8 Sharia al-Baron), where they can discuss just how many of former guest TE Lawrence's tales were true. The bar is a small room off to the left as you enter the hotel, with a few armchairs and six stools at a high dark-wood bar facing an arch of shelves half-filled with half-empty bottles of spirits. It feels like a chapel and makes for a fitting place to commune with ghosts of guests past. Alternatively, during the summer months the staff put some chairs and tables out on the terrace. Local beer is S£100, or you can pay S£150 for a can of whatever they have of the imported variety.

For fewer ghosts and more life, there's a huge **open-air bar** (Map pp184-5; Sharia ash-Shohada), just 200m north of Bab al-Faraj. With seating for a couple of hundred, it's a large garden with vines strung overhead

and splashing fountains, all walled around to protect innocent eyes from the sight of alcohol being consumed. The place is also a restaurant but there's no obligation to eat. A beer is S£55.

There are also a couple of underground bars at Beit as-Sissi (p191) and Beit Wakil (p189) in Al-Jdeida quarter. The one at Beit as-Sissi is buried deep in former cellars – it's a cave-like grotto with goblin faces leering out of the rock walls, while the one at Beit Wakil has colourful postmodern décor. The nearby Mashrabia (p191) is a popular drinking spot. In summer, cocktail-sipping patrons spill out into the alley, and from 10pm Wednesday, Saturday and Sunday there's live music.

ENTERTAINMENT

Cinemas

There is no shortage of cinemas (Map pp184–5) along Sharia al-Baron and its northern extension Sharia Yousef al-Azmeh. Most of what they screen is martial arts, trashy B-movies and any Hollywood movie that has Cameron Diaz in it. Perhaps the most entertaining aspect is the airbrushed posters outside advertising the movies. These slightly risqué (for Syria, at least) posters, used to entice the almost exclusively male customers, generally depict the very scenes that have been removed by the censor. Still, it's fun trying to figure just what movie the poster is for.

Music & Dance

One of Syria's two remaining troupes of whirling dervishes infrequently performs at the Bimaristan Arghan in the Old City (p180). For details of performance dates and times check with the tourist office.

SHOPPING

The main place to shop in Aleppo is the souq, which is the best place to shop for textiles. For nargilehs (water pipes) and inlaid backgammon boards visit Sharia al-Adasi (Map pp184–5), which is north of the main souq area; walk east from the front of the Great Mosque and then cut north (left) up the third lane.

If you want to browse in relative peace and quiet, try the Souq ash-Shouna (Map p177), which is a regulated handicrafts market just behind the coffeehouses on the southwestern side of the Citadel. Here you can take your time to inspect goods and quality with minimum fuss and everything has a fixed price. With these price tags in mind you can then, if you choose, see if you can bargain a lower price elsewhere.

On the fringes of the souq **Sebastian** (Map p177; ☎ 332 3672; Sharia al-Qala'a; ⏱ 8am-8pm Sat-Thu) sells a good range of quality scarves, tablecloths, rugs etc. The brothers running this souvenir/handicrafts shop are fluent variously in German, Italian, French, English and quotations from Wilde.

Sharia Bab Antalya (Map p177) is the place to go for basic olive soap, while you'll find more upmarket soaps and hammam products in Souq as-Sabun (Map p179).

Over in Al-Jdeida the Beit as-Sissi store (p191) and **Orient House Antiques** (Map pp184-5; 1st fl, Saahat al-Hatab) are great for antiques and historical bric-a-brac. In the New City, there are also several antique stores on Sharia al-Kayyadi at the Sharia al-Khandak end near the chocolate shops, while Saahat al-Hatab is the place to go for jewellery.

Shopping the Aleppo Souq Map p179

Generally speaking, Aleppo's souq is much less touristy than that in Damascus and, away from the central area just behind the Great Mosque, pressure to buy is low-key. In fact, because Aleppo's souq is geared to local trade it's very likely that you won't find a lot to buy. Exceptions might be textiles, gold, silver, carpets and olive soaps.

Aleppo's bazaar is broken down into the usual demarcations – gold in one alley, spices in another, carpets in one corner, scarves across the way. The exception to this is the main Souq al-Attarine, which is a mix of everything: hardware to the west, select items of clothing to the east, spices and perfumes in the middle counteracting the stench from butchers stalls.

South of Souq al-Attarine the laneways are given over almost exclusively to fabrics, clothing and shoes. Textiles have always been an important component of Aleppo's trade and places such as Souq al-Jukh still operate as major wholesale cloth markets.

North of Al-Attarine the souq is at its most dense. Squeezed around the Great Mosque are veins of parallel narrow alleys that in places are barely wide enough for a single person. Some of the specialisations

here are fascinating: the Souq al-Hibal is devoted to shops selling cord, braid and rope, while one lane south the Souq at-Tabush is filled with stalls selling nothing but buttons, ribbons and all manner of things necessary for a woman who runs up her family's clothes.

The Souq az-Zarb area is a good place to look for plain or gaudy *jalabiyyas*, the thin cotton gowns worn by women and men alike and which make excellent night dresses; or, as a souvenir, a *keffiyeh*, the distinctive black-and-white or red-and-white headdress that is worn by traditional Muslim and Bedu Arabs, particularly in Occupied Palestine, Jordan, Syria and the Gulf States.

Shops in the souq close around 6pm. The souq is closed on Friday when the whole area is eerily deserted and many of the small passageways and khans are inaccessible, locked up behind great old wooden gates. In addition, some shops, such as many of those in the gold souq, are also closed on Sunday.

GETTING THERE & AWAY

Air

Aleppo has an international airport with some connections to Turkey, Europe and other cities in the Middle East, although it is not easy to find a travel agent who will organise international flights to Aleppo. SyrianAir has flights to İstanbul every Friday for S£8030 and to Cairo every Tuesday and Wednesday for S£8811.

Internally there are two or three flights most days to Damascus (S£900, one hour).

SyrianAir (Map pp184-5; ☎ 224 1232; www.syrian-airlines.com) has an office on Sharia al-Baron but if you are booking international flights you may be directed to its **head office** (Map pp184-5; ☎ 222 0501; Saahat Saad Allah al-Jabri).

Other airline offices include:
Air France (☎ 223 2238; Sharia al-Baron)
Alitalia (☎ 222 2721; Sharia Saad Allah al-Jabri)
British Airways (☎ 227 4586; Sharia Qostaki al-Homsi)
KLM (☎ 221 1074; Sharia al-Baron)
Lufthansa (☎ 222 3005; Sharia al-Baron)

Bus

The **luxury bus station** (Map pp174-5; Sharia Ibrahim Hanano) for long-distance buses is about 500m west of the National Museum. More than 30 private companies, including Qadmous and Al-Ahlia, have their own sales shacks around the edge of the bus bays. It's easy to shop around but there's not that much difference in prices. Destinations include Damascus (£150, five hours), Deir ez-Zur (S£135, five hours), Hama (S£65, 2½ hours), Homs (S£75 to S£85, three hours), Lattakia (S£100, 3½ hours), Qamishle (S£175, eight hours), Raqqa (S£85 to S£90, three hours) and Tartus (S£120, four hours). Departures are frequent so there's no need to book ahead.

There are also seven daily buses from here to Beirut (S£300, six hours).

CITY BUS STATION   Map pp174-5

South of Amir Palace Hotel is a vast area of dusty, rubbish-strewn bus bays stretching over 500m. This area incorporates four adjacent stations serving, from north to south, local city buses, old battered regular intercity buses, intercity 'Pullmans', and minibuses that cover the region around Aleppo. For information on the distinguishing characteristics of these bus types, see p389.

Hard-core budget travellers might want to check out the 'Pullman' station, from where

---

ARRIVING IN ALEPPO

Most buses pull into the **luxury bus station** (Map pp174-5; Sharia Ibrahim Hanano); from here it's a brief five-minute walk east to Sharia al-Baron and the bulk of the budget and mid-range hotels. However, anyone staying at the Beit Wakil, Dar Zamaria Martini or Diwan Rasmy hotels would be better to get a taxi; pay no more than S£35.

For arrivals by train, the **train station** (Map pp174-5) is about 1.5km north of the centre. To walk from here down to the vicinity of the budget hotel district takes about 20 to 25 minutes; head due south from the station keeping the park on your right until reaching a large open plaza (Saahat Saad Allah al-Jabri), at which point take a left down Sharia al-Quwatli.

Those flying in should take a taxi from outside the airport terminal hall. It takes around 20 minutes and will cost about S£500. Taking a taxi from the street back to the airport will only cost around S£300.

---

there are coach services to destinations all over the country. These buses are older and less comfortable than services departing from the main bus station, but fares are generally about two-thirds the cost. Different bays are allotted to various competing companies and you buy tickets in the large booking hall before boarding.

EAST BUS STATION

Old battered buses head out of here for all destinations east including Raqqa and Deir ez-Zur. Fares are cheaper than those charged on the services out of the main bus station, but then comfort levels are also significantly less and given the length of these journeys that's probably an important factor. About the only occasion on which you might wind up at this station is to pick up an Ain al-Arab microbus for a visit to Qala'at Najm (p217). The station is way out east of the Old City and the only way there is by taxi (S£35).

INTERNATIONAL/KARNAK STATION

Actually little more than a parking lot, this station (Map pp184-5) is shared between state-owned Karnak buses and several private companies running services to Turkey and a handful of other international destinations.

It's immediately north of the tourist office and behind the Sharia al-Baron **Karnak bus office** (Map pp184-5; ☎ 210 2482; ⏱ 7am-8pm). At the time of research Karnak had three buses daily to Damascus (S£130), six to Hama (S£60) and Homs (S£75), two to Lattakia (S£65), and one to Deir ez-Zur (S£125) via Raqqa (S£75), plus a nightly service to Amman (S£450) departing at 10pm, and three buses daily to Beirut (S£250) via Tripoli (S£175). However, Karnak is cutting back its operations so check with the office for a current timetable.

At the same station are sales offices for four companies who between them run at least five buses a day to İstanbul (about S£950, 22 hours) and plenty more to Antakya (S£200 to S£250). Note that the İstanbul service involves a change of bus at Antakya. From the same station you can also get buses to Amman (S£450, nine hours), departing nightly at 11pm, plus less frequently to Cairo (S£1000) and Riyadh (S£1200).

Car Rental
Europcar has a desk at the Chahba Cham Palace and Pullman Shahba Hotel. For details of average rental rates, see p391.

Service Taxi
Next to the Pullman bus station is a service taxi stand. This is the expensive but quick way to travel. Sample fares include (for the whole taxi) Hama S£150, Damascus S£400 and Beirut S£700.

Train
Trains to Lattakia (1st/2nd class S£67/40) depart at 6am, 7am, 3.30pm and 4.45pm. The scenic trip takes either 2½ or 3½ hours depending on the service. There are two overnight services to Damascus (seven hours) departing at 10.30pm and 12.30am; tickets cost S£85/57 in 1st-/2nd-class seating, or S£325 for a sleeper. There are two daily services at 3pm and 10.15pm for Qamishle (8½ hours) in the northeast, via Deir ez-Zur. Fares to Qamishle are S£132/87, and S£350 for a sleeper. Fares to Homs are S£34/23 (2½ hours).

A limited form of rail travel between Turkey and Syria has persisted, and there is one weekly service that continues to run between İstanbul and Aleppo/Damascus. It departs Haydarpaşa station at 8.55am Thursday morning, arriving 2.34pm in Aleppo (£19) the following day, terminating at Damascus

at 8.06pm (£24). The sleeper supplement is £17/17 (Aleppo/Damascus) for a single or £11/11 per person in a double.

A weekly train for İstanbul departs each Tuesday at 11.05am taking about 36 hours; sleeper berths cost S£1950 (US$36), 1st-class seats are S£1050 (US$19). There's also now apparently a weekly service for Tehrān departing 11.30am Monday.

GETTING AROUND
Everything in the city is reachable on foot, which is good because the city bus system is unfathomable. The City Bus Station (see opposite) is behind the Amir Palace Hotel, off Sharia Bab Antakya, but there doesn't seem to be any information about routes. Tickets (S£10) are bought from the driver.

Taxi
Car buffs may like to ride in a regular taxi just for the hell of it. They are mostly enormous, lumbering old American limousines from the 1940s and '50s painted bright yellow and with plenty of polished chrome. An average across-town ride should cost no more than about S£25.

AROUND ALEPPO
There are enough worthwhile sites around Aleppo to warrant at least two or three days' exploring. One day spent around Qala'at Samaan and another among the Dead Cities to the south could turn out to be highlights of your trip. The fact that these sites are out of the way, probably necessitating some hitching, is half the fun. However, good weather is a prerequisite as you're out in open, exposed countryside, which will quickly turn to mud underfoot in rain.

Although all of the sites around Aleppo are accessible by public transport, if you're short on time try hiring a car and driver. Just go to the tourist office in Aleppo and before you get within 100m you'll be intercepted by a 'guide' offering his services. In practice, many of these guys don't know that much about the sites and some of them speak virtually no English but that's not really an issue because you only want them for their wheels. The going rate is about US$50 for a full day, from early morning until early evening, although some travellers have reported being able to bargain drivers down to US$20. Be warned, if a driver agrees to such a

AROUND ALEPPO

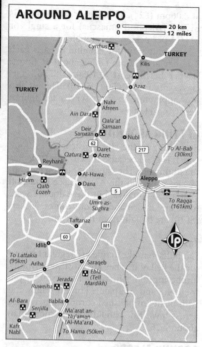

0 ———— 20 km
0 ———— 12 miles

them all into one trip without your own car. Qala'at Samaan, the jewel of the collection, is fairly accessible by public transport and from there it's possible to push on to Ain Dara and get back to Aleppo by minibus in one long day. Alternatively, you could combine Qala'at Samaan with Qalb Lozeh, if you do a little backtracking. Cyrrhus is more problematic and requires cash and time, and if you are planning on visiting the Dead Cities to the south then it's probably not worth the expense to duplicate the experience here.

QALA'AT SAMAAN قلعة سمعان

The ruined basilica of **Qala'at Samaan** (adult/ student S£300/15; 9am-6pm Wed-Mon Apr-Sep, 9am-4pm Oct-Mar) is probably the must-see site of the many archaeological remnants that dot the countryside north of Aleppo. Enough remains of the basilica to impress, with a glorious situation high on a rocky outcrop. The views are excellent. From Aleppo, it's an easy half-day trip; if you set off by 9am you'll be back by early afternoon.

The structure takes its name from a peculiar individual named Simeon. Born in AD 392, Simeon was the son of a shepherd who opted at a young age for life in a monastery. However, finding monastic life insufficiently ascetic, he retreated to a cave in the barren hills where he lived under a regime of self-imposed severity.

Word got around of this extremely pious individual and people began to visit to seek his blessing. Simeon apparently greatly resented this invasion of his solitude and was driven to erect a 3m-high pillar on which he took up residence so that people couldn't touch him. The legend goes that as his tolerance of people decreased he erected ever higher pillars. In all he's said to have spent close to 40 years on top of his pillars, the last of which was 18m in height. There was a railing around the top, and an iron collar around his neck was chained to the stone to stop him toppling off in the middle of the night.

Simeon's increasingly eccentric behaviour eventually drew pilgrims from as far as Britain and France, where he was known as Simon Stylites, a name derived from the Greek word for pillar, *stylos*. The notion of stylism caught on and Simeon inspired a fashion for pious pillar-top dwelling that spread all the way to Central Europe, where it eventually faltered in the face of a colder climate.

low price it will be with great reluctance and you can expect plenty of wheedling later for more cash – it's better to pay a fair price and save yourself hassle.

With such an arrangement you dictate your own itinerary. For example, with a car you will be able to cover in a full day all the sites described in the North & West of Aleppo section (below), or all those described in South of Aleppo (p199).

One driver/guide who has been recommended for his fairness and reasonable rates is **Basheer Kadour** (574 4043). Alternatively, you could sign up for one of the tours run by the guys at the Zahrat ar-Rabie hostel (p188); you don't need to be a guest. They offer several itineraries, of which the most popular is a four-hour jaunt up to Qala'at Samaan taking in Qatura and Mushabbak, which costs S£400 per person for a party of four, S£600 for two, exclusive of site admissions.

North & West of Aleppo

The half-dozen major sites north and west of Aleppo are scattered across Jebel Samaan in such a way that it is impossible to combine

St Simeon would preach daily from his perch, and shout answers to his audiences' questions. However, he refused to talk to women and even his mother was not allowed near the column.

When he died in 459, Simeon was possibly the most famous person in the 5th-century world and his body was taken to be buried in the great Christian centre of Antioch (present-day Antakya). In addition, an enormous church was built around the famous pillar. It had a unique design with four basilicas arranged in the shape of a cross, each opening onto a central octagonal yard covered by a dome. Beneath the dome stood the pillar. One basilica was used for worship, the other three housed the many pilgrims. Completed in 490 after 14 years of building, at the time it was the largest church in the world.

With the arrival of Islam in Syria, the Byzantine Christians were put on the defensive and the church complex was fortified, hence the name Qala'at (fortress). It eventually fell to the Islamic Fatimid dynasty in 1017 and was apparently never again used as a place of worship.

The church today is remarkably well preserved. The main Romanesque façade still stands, while behind it the arches of the octagonal yard are reasonably complete. There's plenty of ornamental carved stonework to admire, although Simeon's pillar is in a sad state. It is nothing more than a boulder, reduced centuries ago by pilgrims chipping away at it for holy souvenirs.

The views of the barren hills to the west are stunning and the ruins of Deir Samaan can be seen down to the southwest at the foot of the hill.

DEIR SAMAAN دير سمعان

Deir Samaan originally began life as the small Greek agricultural village of Telanissos. But like some ancient Corfu, during the first part of the 5th century it found itself being rapidly transformed by a steady influx of outsiders, in this case not tourists but their forerunners, pilgrims. As the antics of Simeon drew ever larger crowds, so the village expanded to provide hostelries, churches and three monasteries to accommodate the pilgrims (hence the new name of Deir Samaan, 'Monastery of Simeon').

With the building of the basilica on top of the hill the two were connected by a procession way (Via Sacra). A monumental arch remains partway up the slope marking the old route. In the village there are skeletons of two of the monasteries, a church and the bazaar, plus 150m south of the arch there are two very impressive hostelries and a tomb chapel hewn out of rock and reached by a stone bridge.

Local people have taken up residence around the ruins and built their own dwellings – often with stone recycled from ancient Deir Samaan – but they don't mind if you wander around.

The ruins cover an extensive area at the foot of the hill of Qala'at Samaan and you can scramble down after viewing the basilica on top. Alternatively, at the point where the road forks at the foot of the hill, instead of bearing right up to Qala'at Samaan, swing left and the ruins are on either side of the road 200m further on.

Getting There & Away

Take a minibus from the minibus station in Aleppo (part of the City Bus Station complex, p194) to the village of Daret Azze (S£10, 50 minutes), departing every half-hour or so. During the trip keep a lookout for the 5th-century Mushabbak basilica standing alone in fields off to the left about two-thirds of the way along the route. From Daret Azze it's about 6km to Qala'at Samaan. The minibus driver may offer to take you the extra distance or you can negotiate with a local taxi, but they'll ask at least S£100. The cheapest option is to hitch. While there isn't much traffic on the road, any vehicle that comes by will invariably stop. The last minibus from Daret Azze to Aleppo leaves at about 8pm.

QATURA قطوره

About 2km west of Daret Azze on the road to Qala'at Samaan is the turn-off to Qatura. Follow this road off to the west and you come to more ruins, which include some Roman-era tombs cut into the rock. The last tomb on the road is carved with a reclining figure in much the same style as at Palmyra. You can also quite clearly make out Latin and Greek inscriptions.

When you pick up a lift out of Daret Azze you can ask to be let off at the Qatura junction and the ruins and tombs are not much of a walk from there. You shouldn't have any trouble picking up a lift onwards to Qala'at Samaan or back to Daret Azze.

AIN DARA عين دارة

A thousand years before Christ, a Hittite temple dedicated to the goddess Ishtar stood on an acropolis off the present-day road that now leads north from Qala'at Samaan to the mainly Kurdish town of Nahr Afreen. The temple was destroyed in the 8th century BC, rebuilt and then gradually gave way to other constructions.

Excavations on the mound where the temple formerly stood have revealed its layout and, most interestingly, some extraordinary basalt statues and reliefs, which litter the **site** (adult/student S£150/10; ☼ daylight hrs). The single most impressive statue is a huge lion tipped over on its side. However, that said – and despite recent restoration efforts by a Japanese team – the site overall yields little and doesn't really repay the trouble taken to reach it. A local caretaker, who will probably greet you and do his best to show you around, collects the admission fee.

Getting There & Away

Ain Dara is around 18km north of Qala'at Samaan. You can continue hitching from Deir Samaan toward Nahr Afreen (you want the road that goes through Deir Samaan, not the one that leads up to Qala'at Samaan) and get dropped off at the turn-off to Tell Ain Dara. Alternatively, from Aleppo catch a minibus direct to Nahr Afreen (S£13) and from there take one of the irregular pick-ups to Ain Dara (S£10) which is 7km to the south. It will drop you at the turn-off just before the village; you can see the acropolis in the distance. Follow the road around (about 2km), or cut across the path and onion fields directly to the site.

CYRRHUS (NEBI HURI) النبي هوري

In the remotest of spots, overlooking the Turkish border and deep in Kurdish territory, is the 3rd-century provincial town of Cyrrhus (Nabi Houri to the locals). No-one has lived here for ages and very little is left of the town today but it once held quite a strategic position for troops of the Roman Empire and boasted a citadel, a theatre and a cathedral.

From the dusty town of Azaz the road takes you through cheerful countryside, dotted with wheat fields and olive groves, across two 3rd-century humpback Roman bridges on the Sabun River and past a Roman-era **mausoleum**. This pyramid-capped monument has survived well, partly because it

was preserved by local Muslims as a holy site (the ground floor has been recycled as the tomb of a local Muslim prophet named Houri). Here you branch right off the road to the site, which is just 200m further on.

The easiest structure to distinguish, of what is a fairly decrepit bunch of ruins, is the theatre. Of the town walls, colonnaded street and basilica in the north of the town, not much remains, but scramble up through the ruins past the theatre to the Arab citadel at the top for sweeping views across to the Turkish mountains. You can be virtually guaranteed of having this particular place to yourself.

Getting There & Away

Minibuses run from Aleppo to Azaz (S£10), from where you have no real choice but to bargain with one of the taxis for the remaining 28km to the site. Do not be surprised to be hit for as much as S£800 for the ride there and back. You can try to hitch but there is precious little traffic on this road. The same taxis also run people to the Turkish border for S£100 (for the car, not per person). You could try to rent a minibus or microbus at the Aleppo City Bus Station (p194) for the day to do Cyrrhus and Qala'at Samaan. This would probably cost about S£1000, which isn't so bad if you have a big enough group.

QALB LOZEH قلب لوزه

One of the very best preserved examples of Syrian-Byzantine ecclesiastical architecture, the church of **Qalb Lozeh** (adult/student S£150/10; ☼ daylight hrs) predates St Simeon by perhaps only a few decades. It was built as a stop-off point for pilgrims en route to see Simeon on his pillar. The entrance to the church, flanked by two three-storey towers, and its walls, not to mention the semicircular apse, are almost completely intact. Even some stone slabs of the roof have been retained, but the once impressive arch between the towers has been lost forever. The simple elegance of the structure, clean lines of the columns around the apse and classical decoration make this church an obvious precursor to the Romanesque style that would later dominate the breadth of European church-building.

Getting There & Away

Qalb Lozeh lies a short way south of the main road from Aleppo to the Turkish border and Antakya. To get there take a minibus from Aleppo to Harim, which is a small, attractive provincial town crowned by an Ayyubid castle. From Harim you'll need to negotiate a taxi.

South of Aleppo

Ebla, Ma'arat an-Nu'aman, Jerada and Ruweiha are all just off the main Aleppo–Hama highway and are easily reached by public transport (plus a bit of hitching). They could all be visited in a single day. However, the most interesting sites are possibly Al-Bara and Serjilla and these deserve a half-day in themselves. If you have a car at your disposal you could see the whole lot in one day. All of these sites can just as easily be visited from Hama.

EBLA (TELL MARDIKH)   تل مرديخ

Lying about 60km south of Aleppo, the ancient city of **Ebla** (Tell Mardikh; adult/student S£300/15; 8am-7pm Wed-Mon Apr-Sep, 8am-5pm Wed-Mon Oct-Mar) is of enormous fascination to archaeologists and historians but considerably less so to most visitors.

The Italian teams that have been excavating the site since 1964 have discovered that it was one of the most powerful city-states in Syria in the late 3rd millennium BC (known as the Early High Syrian period), but was sacked before the close of the millennium, probably by Sargon of Akkad. In its heyday, Ebla probably controlled most of northwestern Syria and it again rose for a relatively brief period from about 1900 to 1750 BC, before being destroyed in 1600 BC by Hittite invaders. Troops of the First Crusade passed by thousands of years later, when it was known as Mardic Hamlet.

In recent times, digs at Ebla have unearthed more than 15,000 clay tablets in a Sumerian dialect, providing a wealth of information on everything from economics to local administration and dictionaries of other tongues. However, only a small portion of the cuneiform secrets has been unlocked.

The site lies over a rise about 1km beyond the village of Tell Mardikh. You buy your ticket outside the small museum dedicated to the story of the excavations, and then continue along the road and over the rise. The shallow remains of the city lie before you, dominated by the limestone tell that once formed the core of the city's fortress. Note it's

strictly forbidden to go clambering over the site. Stick to the ill-defined trails around the edge of the ongoing excavations. The most interesting ruins are probably those labelled 'Palace G', just west of the acropolis, which display remains of a royal staircase, walls and columned halls. Beyond that, and lots of trenches and holes in the ground, there's very little here to see at all and anybody who has paid S£300 for a ticket may find themselves wondering why.

Getting There & Away

Take any Hama-bound minibus or microbus, or to be sure of not paying the full fare for Hama, one of the less frequent ones to Ma'arat an-Nu'aman (ask for Al-Ma'ara), and ask to be let off at the Tell Mardikh turn-off. From there it is a 20-minute walk through the village of Tell Mardikh to the site. It's quite likely that you may be offered a lift by one of the tractors buzzing between the archaeological digs and the village.

MA'ARAT AN-NU'AMAN (AL-MA'ARA)   معرّة النعمان

This lively little market town is nothing special in itself, although it was witness to a gruesome bit of history when the Crusaders disgraced themselves even more than usual. On 12 December 1098, under the command of Count Raymond of Toulouse, the Crusaders attacked the fortified Muslim town of Ma'arat an-Nu'aman, slaughtering thousands. But the horror was less in the carnage of killing than what followed: 'In Ma'ara our troops boiled pagan adults in cooking pots; they impaled children on spits and devoured them grilled', confessed one of the Crusader chroniclers. The food provisions the Crusaders had hoped to find in the town hadn't been there and, literally dying of starvation, they had resorted to eating the bodies of the dead.

The main point of interest here is the **Mosaic Museum** (adult/student S£300/15; 9am-6pm Wed-Mon Apr-Sep, 9am-4pm Wed-Mon Oct-Mar) housed in the 16th-century Khan Murad Pasha. Most of the mosaics covered the floors of the more important or luxurious buildings and private houses of the clusters of 5th- and 6th-century Byzantine towns, which are now collectively referred to as the Dead Cities. Not quite as old is the lovingly executed mosaic of Assad, which takes pride of place facing the entrance. The museum is about 50m to the north of the bus station, on the right side of a large square.

Further north and off to the right is the **Great Mosque**, whose 12th-century minaret was rebuilt after an earthquake in 1170. From the mosque, head to the right of the square and north for a few hundred metres – where the street opens out you'll see the sad remains of a medieval **Citadel**, which now serve as cheap accommodation for a few families.

Getting There & Away

There are frequent minibuses to Ma'arat an-Nu'aman (S£20, one hour) from Aleppo's minibus station (part of the City Bus Station, p194). Sleeker and faster microbuses (S£25) go from the microbus station a little further south on Sharia al-Baron. You'll find that bigger, older and lumbering buses also do this run (S£15), departing from the Pullman station (also part of the City Bus Station).

Dead Cities

The main attraction of the region around Aleppo is the so-called Dead Cities, a series of ancient ghost towns among the limestone hills that lie between the Aleppo–Hama highway in the east and the Orontes River in the west. They date from the time when this area was part of the hinterland of the great Byzantine Christian city of Antioch. There are reckoned to be some 600 separate sites, ranging from single monuments to nearly whole villages complete with houses, churches, baths and even wine presses. Taken together they represent a great archive in stone from which historians can put together a picture of life in antiquity.

The great mystery is why the towns were abandoned. Some of the sites, especially Serjilla, have an eerie quality, as though their occupants had just vanished. The most current theory is that these towns and villages were emptied by demographic shifts; trade routes changed and the people moved with them. However, not all the areas are completely abandoned – some of the Dead Cities form part of present-day villages with people inhabiting the ancient ruins or incorporating oddments of antiquity into the structure of their homes.

The number of sites is simply overwhelming – we can describe only a handful of the most interesting and most easily accessible.

If you have the inclination, you could spend weeks pottering around, stumbling across Byzantine ghosts that have yet to be described in any guidebook. Keep in mind that wild dogs inhabit some of these areas and it's wise to keep a watchful eye when exploring.

JERADA & RUWEIHA   جاراده ورويحة

Jerada is the closest of these twin Dead Cities to the Aleppo–Hama highway, which it over-looks from a position up on low rocky hills. The site is partially occupied, with some of the big old houses serving as barns for villagers who have built their own dwellings on the northern fringes of the ruins. These ruins include the extensive remains of noble houses, a 5th-century Byzantine cathedral and a six-storey watchtower. Some of the simple geometric designs on column capitals and lintels is vaguely reminiscent of Visigothic work done in Spain around the same time.

Hit the road again and follow it for another 2.5km or so across a barren lunarlike land-scape to reach the striking, scattered remains of Ruweiha. The most imposing building here is the 6th-century **Church of Bissos**, now home to a local family. Its transverse arches are thought to be among the oldest of their kind. Just outside, the domed mausoleum hous-ing the body of Bissos (possibly a bishop) has since found its echo in similar designs throughout the Arab world. Few people live among the ruins now, although the occasional family gets up here for a Friday picnic.

SERJILLA   سرجلا

Serjilla and Al-Bara (opposite) are two of a cluster of five or more Dead Cities strung out on either side of a country lane that runs north from the green-domed mosque just outside Kafr Nabl. About 2km after the mosque you'll see a sign for **Shinshira** point-ing off to your right, then after a further 2km just off to the left are the grey stone remnants of **Mahardiyya** buried within some straggly olive groves. Both of these Dead Cities are worth exploring, but if you're pushed for time, skip them and look out instead for the signposted turn-off to Serjilla, to the right. If you are hitching, be warned, it's about a 4km walk from this junction down to Serjilla and next to no traffic comes along this way.

Serjilla (adult/student S£150/10) is undoubtedly the most eerie and evocative of the Dead Cities. Serjilla has the greatest number of semi-complete buildings, all of which sit in a natural basin in windswept and hilly moorland. Although having been deserted for about 15 centuries, the stone façades are clean and sharp-edged and the surrounding ground is covered with short grass. There are no wild bushes or uncontrolled undergrowth; the place has quite a spooky air of almost human-maintained orderliness about it.

At its centre is a small plaza flanked by a two-storey tavern and a large bathhouse. Now stripped of the mosaics that once decorated it, the latter building is quite austere but the mere existence of Christian-era baths is itself a source of curiosity. Next door lies an *andron* (men's meeting place), and further east a small church. Spreading away are substantial leftovers of private houses and villas. You pass down narrow grassy lanes between high stone walls punctuated by carefully carved windows and doors, and half expect a householder to step out on a quick errand to fetch something from the market.

The admission fee is payable to a guard who hovers around the car park at the edge of the site.

AL-BARA   باره

Al-Bara is the most extensive of the Dead Cities. It's also the furthest north from Kafr Nabl; you continue on beyond the turning for Serjilla and past another small Dead City called **Bauda**.

Occupying a good position on the north–south trade route between Antioch and Apamea and being surrounded by rich arable land, from humble beginnings in the 4th century AD Al-Bara rapidly became one of the most important centres of wine and olive oil production in the region. Even when the trade routes shifted in the 7th century (resulting in the abandonment of many neighbouring towns), Al-Bara prospered and grew. It boasted large villas, three monasteries and numerous churches – at least five can still be picked out among ruins that cover 6 sq km.

The town weathered the coming of Islam and remained predominantly eastern Christian – and the seat of a bishopric subordinate to Antioch – until its occupation by the Latin Crusaders in the very last years of the 12th century.

It was from Al-Bara that the Crusaders set out to perpetrate their horrible cannibalistic episode at Ma'arat an-Nu'aman in 1098.

Twenty-five years later they were driven out and Al-Bara reverted to Muslim control. It's thought that the town became depopulated in the latter part of the 12th century following a severe earthquake.

As it stands today, there's no obvious route around the site. Unlike at Serjilla, the land here is densely covered by trees and bushes and you have to squeeze through the undergrowth to discover the old buildings and ruins. Be careful where you tramp, though, as small plots are still intensively worked in among the ancient stones – the land remains good and olives, grapes and apricots still thrive here as in Byzantine times.

The most striking structures to look out for are a couple of **pyramid tombs**, 200m apart. Decorated with Corinthian pilasters and carved acanthus leaves, the tombs are a very visible testament to the one-time wealth of the settlement. The larger of the two still holds five sealed, decorated sarcophagi.

From the pyramids you can wander south past an underground tomb with three arches to a large, well-preserved monastery, or head north to find the ruins of the five churches.

Take plenty of water and food as there's not much to be had in the town, although you will stand out so much that an invitation to tea is more than likely.

GETTING THERE & AWAY
You need to take a microbus or minibus for Ma'arat an-Nu'aman (commonly referred to as Al-Ma'ara) – see p199. For Jerada and Ruweiha ask to be let off at Babila, 7km before Al-Ma'ara. From where you are dropped off you can see the ruins over to the west, 3km away. If you start walking you're bound to be offered a lift before you get too far.

To get to Al-Bara, Serjilla and the other neighbouring Dead Cities, you stay on the minibus all the way into Al-Ma'ara where you then pick up a microbus for Kafr Nabl (S£5), some 10km away. From Kafr Nabl it's a further 6km to Al-Bara. The microbus drivers will offer to take you for an outrageous price but your best bet is to start walking out of the village, following the main street, then after about 1.5km bear right at the large new mosque with the green dome; it won't be long before a passing car offers you a lift.

Palmyra to the Euphrates

تدمر إلى نهر لفرات

PALMYRA TO THE EUPHRATES

CONTENTS

Palmyra, Syria's prime historical attraction, is an oasis is in the middle of a vast emptiness, with the Orontes River to the west and the Euphrates to the east. But this apparent emptiness is deceptive. The desert of this northeastern region of Syria is dotted with ancient sites of both archaeological significance and beauty – little could surpass the spectacle of the Palmyra ruins with a backdrop of the rising or setting sun.

The vast desert is not only home to the splendours of past civilisations. For many Bedouin and other seminomadic people, life continues here as it has done for centuries, and while their method of transport may have changed – from camel to pick-up truck – the hospitality of these nomads living in an inhospitable environment has not. The chance to share a cup of tea with the Bedouin may well be a highlight of your visit to Syria.

The harsh, extreme northeast of the country is also home to about one million Kurds, a stateless people still struggling towards some day attaining their own homeland. It is here also that the cool green ribbon of the Euphrates, which provides welcome relief for the traveller, continues its journey before emptying into the Gulf after having travelled more than 2400km from its beginnings high in the mountains of eastern Anatolia in Turkey.

HIGHLIGHTS

- Rising at dawn for first light at the **Palmyra** (p205) ruins for a couple of hours of photography-perfect light before the coaches arrive

- Stepping back 5000 years and imagining the ancient civilisation of the Mesopotamians at **Mari** (p225), with its peculiar ziggurat

- Accepting an offer of coffee with the Bedouin near **Qamishle** (p227), for the unique experience of sharing a brew with desert nomads

- Arriving at the intriguing and striking ruins of **Rasafa** (p219), rising up out of the featureless desert

- Enjoying the wonderful setting of the ancient site of **Dura Europos** (p224) overlooking the Euphrates River

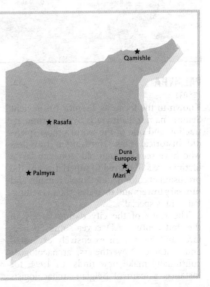

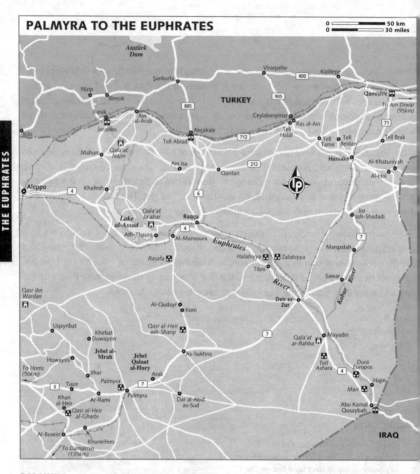

PALMYRA تدمر

☎ 031

Known to the locals as Tadmor (its ancient Semitic name), Palmyra is Syria's prime attraction and one of the world's most splendid historical sites. Hard-bitten travellers who have seen enough old stones to last a lifetime are still moved to superlatives by the profusion of colonnades, temple remains and funerary towers and their desert oasis setting. Palmyra is special.

The ruins of the city dating largely to the 2nd century AD cover some 50 hectares and have been extensively excavated and restored. Nevertheless, archaeologists continually make new finds. In 1994, for instance, a team of Belgian archaeologists stumbled across some Roman tombs southeast of the Temple of Bel. The new town is rapidly growing around the ruins, spreading especially towards the west, and now has more than 40,000 inhabitants. They exist on a mix of agriculture, trade and tourism. Nearby is an air-force base, and jet fighters occasionally scream over the ancient ruins on training runs.

History

Tadmor (Palmyra) receives mention in texts discovered at Mari that date back as early as the 2nd millennium BC. Early rulers included the Assyrians and Persians, before the settlement was incorporated into the realm of the Seleucids, the empire founded by a former general of Alexander the Great. From an early time Tadmor was an indispensable staging post for caravans travelling between the Mediterranean and the lands of Mesopotamia and Arabia. It was also an important link on the old Silk Road from China and India to Europe and the city prospered greatly by levying heavy tolls on the caravans.

As the Romans expanded their frontiers during the 1st and early 2nd centuries AD to occupy the eastern Mediterranean littoral, the Seleucid dynasty failed. Tadmor became stranded between the Latin realms to the west and those of the Parthians to the east. This was a situation the oasis turned to its benefit, keeping the east-west trade routes open and taking the role of middleman between the two clashing superpowers. The influence of Rome grew, and the city they dubbed Palmyra (City of Palms) became a tributary of the empire and a buffer against rivals to the east. The Palmyrenes were permitted to retain considerable independence, profiting also from rerouted trade following the defeat of the Petra-based Nabataeans by Rome.

The emperor Hadrian visited in AD 130 and declared Palmyra a 'free city', allowing it to set and collect its own taxes. In 212, under the emperor Caracalla (himself born of a Syrian mother), Palmyra became a Roman colony. In this way, its citizens obtained equal rights with those of Rome and exemption from paying imperial taxes. Further wealth followed and Palmyra spent lavishly, enlarging its great colonnaded avenue and building more and larger temples.

As internal power struggles weakened Rome, the Palmyrenes strengthened their independence. A local noble, Odainat, defeated the army of one of Rome's long-standing rivals, the Sassanians, and proclaimed himself 'king'. In 256 the emperor Valerian bestowed upon Odainat the title of 'Corrector of the East' and put all Roman forces in the region under his command.

The most glorious episode in Palmyra's history – which also led to the city's subsequent rapid downfall – began when Odainat was assassinated in 267. His second wife, Zenobia, took over in the name of their young son, Vabalathus. Rome refused to recognise this arrangement, particularly as Zenobia was suspected of involvement in her husband's death. The emperor dispatched an army to deal with the rebel queen. Zenobia met the Roman force in battle and defeated it. She then led her army against the garrison at Bosra, then the capital of the Province of Arabia, and successfully invaded Egypt.

With all of Syria and Palestine and part of Egypt under her control, Zenobia declared her independence from Rome and had coins minted in Alexandria bearing her image and that of her son, who assumed the title of Augustus, or emperor.

Claiming to be descended from Cleopatra, Zenobia was, it seems, a woman of exceptional ability and ambition. Though she was headstrong and wilful, the 18th-century historian Edward Gibbon also said of her in his *Decline and Fall of the Roman Empire*:

> She equalled in beauty her ancestor Cleopatra and far surpassed that princess in chastity and valour. Zenobia was

---

VISITING PALMYRA

Although visitors can no longer expect to enjoy the ruins in solitude, the flow of tourists is still often little more than a trickle. Added to which, the site is so vast that it is easy to lose yourself and imagine that you're a 19th-century adventurer stumbling across the fallen, half-buried city for the very first time. This is especially true at first light. For this reason, if no other, avoid visiting Palmyra as a day trip from Damascus or Hama because no matter how early you set off, you'll arrive too late to see the ruins at their best.

The unhurried traveller could easily spend several days wandering around the main site, which spreads over a very large area, bounded by what have come to be known as Zenobia's walls. Then there are the funerary towers and underground tombs, as well as Qala'at ibn Maan, the Arab castle on the hill. A visit of less than two days sells the experience short for most travellers. It's also highly recommended that you see the site both at sunrise, when the early morning light infuses the stone with a rich pink hue, and again at sunset, ideally watching the sun drain from the ruins from the vantage point of the castle or the rocky outcrops to the south.

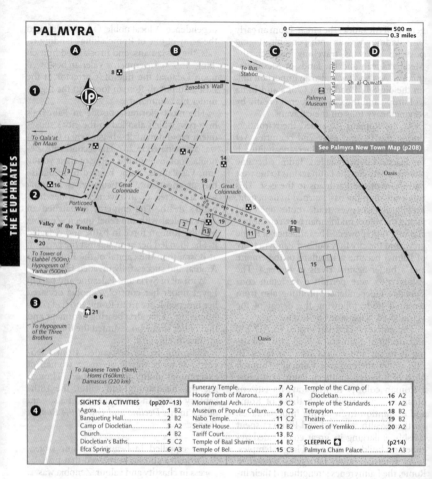

PALMYRA

0 _____ 500 m
0 _____ 0.3 miles

To Bus Station
To Qala'at ibn Maan
Zenobia's Wall
Sh. As'ad al-Amir
Sh. al-Quwatli
Palmyra Museum
See Palmyra New Town Map (p208)
Oasis
Great Colonnade
Great Colonnade
Porticoed Way
Valley of the Tombs
To Tower of Elahbel (500m); Hypogeum of Yarhai (500m)
To Hypogeum of the Three Brothers
Oasis
To Japanese Tomb (5km); Homs (160km); Damascus (220 km)

SIGHTS & ACTIVITIES (pp207–13)		Funerary Temple	7 A2	Temple of the Camp of	
Agora	1 B2	House Tomb of Marona	8 A1	Diocletian	16 A2
Banqueting Hall	2 B2	Monumental Arch	9 C2	Temple of the Standards	17 A2
Camp of Diocletian	3 A2	Museum of Popular Culture	10 C2	Tetrapylon	18 B2
Church	4 B2	Nabo Temple	11 C2	Theatre	19 B2
Diocletian's Baths	5 C2	Senate House	12 B2	Towers of Yemliko	20 A2
Efca Spring	6 A3	Tariff Court	13 B2		
		Temple of Baal Shamin	14 B2	SLEEPING	(p214)
		Temple of Bel	15 C3	Palmyra Cham Palace	21 A3

esteemed the most lovely as well as the most heroic of her sex. She was of dark complexion. Her teeth were of a pearly whiteness and her large black eyes sparkled with an uncommon fire, tempered by the most attractive sweetness. Her voice was strong and harmonious. Her manly understanding was strengthened and adorned by study.

The Roman emperor Aurelian, who had been prepared to negotiate, could not stomach such a show of open defiance. After defeating Zenobia's forces at Antioch and Emesa (Homs) in 271, he besieged Palmyra itself. Zenobia was defiant to the last and instead of accepting the generous surrender terms

offered by Aurelian, made a dash on a camel through the encircling Roman forces. She headed for Persia to appeal for military aid, only to be captured by Roman cavalry at the Euphrates.

Zenobia was carted off to Rome in 272 as Aurelian's trophy and reputedly paraded in the streets, bound in gold chains. She spent the rest of her days in Rome, possibly in a villa provided by the emperor, although other sources claim she chose to starve to death rather than remain captive.

Whatever happened to the vanquished queen, her defeat marked the end of Palmyra's prosperity. A further rebellion in 273 in which the Palmyrenes massacred a garrison of 600 Roman archers, elicited a brutal response and Aurelian's legionaries slaughtered large numbers and put the city to the torch. Palmyra never recovered. The emperor Diocletian (r 254–305) later fortified the broken city as one in a line of fortresses marking the eastern boundary of the Roman Empire, and Justinian further rebuilt the city's defences in the 6th century. The city survived primarily as a military outpost and the caravan traffic all but dropped away.

In 634 the city fell to a Muslim army led by Khaled ibn al-Walid, and from this time Palmyra all but fades from history. Architectural and archaeological evidence tells that the Arabs fortified the Temple of Bel, which became host to a small village, and a castle was built on a nearby hilltop, but the great city itself was largely abandoned. Its structures were devastated by earthquake and largely covered over by wind-blown sand and earth.

It wasn't until 1678 that Palmyra was 'rediscovered' by two English merchants resident in Aleppo. Few followed in their footsteps; the buried desert city was five days' journey from civilisation in an area made dangerous by bandits and hostile tribes. It took a 1751 expedition, which resulted in drawings and the first tentative excavations, to truly pique travellers' interest. Throughout the rest of the 18th and 19th centuries a steady flow of intrepid visitors made the expedition out from Aleppo or Damascus, although it wasn't until the early 20th century that the first scientific study began. The earliest surveys were carried out in the 1920s by the Germans. In 1929 the French took over. Work intensified following WWII, and continues to this day.

Orientation

Modern Palmyra is laid out on a grid pattern. The main street is Sharia al-Quwatli, which runs east from the main square, Saahat ar-Rais, on the western edge of town. On the south side of this square is the museum. The ancient site is just over 500m southwest of here along a road that crosses a reconstructed section of Zenobia's walls, which runs just behind the museum. The town is tiny and can be walked from end to end in 10 minutes.

Arriving buses drop off in one of three places: the Karnak office in the centre of town; the Sahara Cafe on the northern outskirts of town, from where a taxi will cost

S£25; and near the new Palmyra bypass in the west of town, from where it's a 10-minute walk, straight on ahead, to the town centre. (See Getting There & Away, p215, for more details on buses.)

Information

At the time of writing there we no internet cafés in Palmyra, though at least one of the hotels may be online by the time you read this. Ask around when you arrive.

CBS Exchange Booth (Commercial Bank of Syria; Map p208; Saahat ar-Rais; ☽ 8am-8pm Sat-Thu) In front of the museum; it takes cash and travellers cheques. The Palmyra Cham Palace (p214) also changes cash and travellers cheques 24 hours a day.

Post Office (Map p208; Saahat ar-Rais; ☽ 8am-2pm) Also has a couple of cardphones in front of the main entrance, accessible 24 hours. There's another cardphone just inside the Temple of Bel compound.

Tourist Office (Map p208; ☎ 910 574; Saahat ar-Rais; ☽ 8am-2pm) Across from the museum. Staff can organise guides.

Sights

PALMYRA MUSEUM   متحف تدمر

It's debatable whether anyone but keen amateur archaeologists benefit greatly from a visit to Palmyra's modest **museum** (Map p208; adult/student S£300/15; ☽ 8am-1pm & 4-6pm Apr-Sep, 8am-1pm & 2-4pm Oct-Mar, closed Tue). With no labelling to speak of and poor presentation, it provides no context for understanding the site and adds little to the experience of Palmyra. There are a few highlights, however.

In the second room is a fine large-scale model of the Temple of Bel that gives an excellent impression of how the complex would have looked in its original state. In the next room are some fascinating friezes depicting camel trains and cargo ships, attesting to the importance trade played in the wealth of Palmyra.

Continuing anticlockwise, the western gallery has a couple of very dynamic mosaics that were found in what are presumed to have been nobles' houses, located just east of the Temple of Bel. One mosaic represents a scene from the Iliad in which Ulysses discovers Achilles disguised in women's clothes and concealed among the daughters of the king of Scyros (this scene is also portrayed in a fresco in the Hypogeum of the Three Brothers – see p212); the other depicts centaurs hunting deer. Also in this hall is a large photo of Qasr al-Heir ash-Sharqi, the early Islamic desert fortress that's a popular day trip from Palmyra (p215).

The far end of the museum, the eastern gallery, contains the most outstanding piece in the collection, a 3m-high statue of the goddess Allat, associated with the Greek Athena, and found in 1975 by Polish archaeologists. Also in this room is a collection of coins, including some depicting Zenobia and her son, which were discovered in 1991.

The last few rooms hold countless busts and carved portraits that formed part of the panels used to seal the loculi in Palmyra's many funerary towers and hypogea. To see exactly how this arrangement worked, pay a visit to the Japanese Tomb (p213). Many of these sculpted portraits possess an uncanny animation – it's quite unnerving to think that you're gazing on the faces of people who died close to 2000 years ago.

THE RUINS   Map p206

Follow the road that runs south from directly opposite the tourist office to reach the Temple of Bel and the monumental arch, the latter being perhaps the best place to start exploring. Depending on the heat and your energy levels, you may need to organise transport to visit Qala'at ibn Maan (the

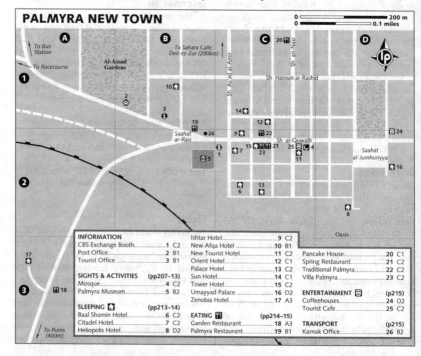

PALMYRA NEW TOWN

0 — 200 m
0 — 0.1 miles

To Bus Station
To Racecourse
Al-Assad Gardens
To Sahara Cafe; Deir ez-Zur (200km)
Sh As'ad al-Amir
Sh an-Nasr
Sh Haroun ar-Rashid
Saahat ar-Rais
Sh al-Quwatli
Saahat al-Jumhuriyya
Oasis
To Ruins (400m)

AN EXPENSIVE PRECEDENT

Admission fees at Palmyra have doubled in recent times, making the high cost of visiting Syrian sites a popular conversation topic among travellers. There's nothing new in this. In fact, visitors have been grumbling about the cost of visiting Palmyra for over 200 years.

The Middle East has always attracted intrepid female explorers and adventurers – Gertrude Bell, Lady Jane Digby and Freya Stark to name just three – but Lady Hester Stanhope was one of the more extreme examples. She was the niece of a British prime minister and, as such, a one-time resident of 10 Downing St. On the death of her beloved uncle and her removal from the centre of British politics, Lady Hester decided to travel abroad and find herself a new court. Along with her retinue she travelled in the Middle East, interfering in local affairs but winning the admiration of the Arabs, who regarded her as a queen.

One of her greatest moments of glory was, in 1813, riding into Palmyra on an Arab stallion at the head of her travelling procession. On this occasion she was hosting a fete for the local Bedouin, during which she ordered that a silver dollar be given to all present. To the grand sheikh of the Bedouin she presented a piece of paper, handwritten, on which she directed him to charge every traveller who visited the ruins a thousand piastres. 'This enormous tax,' wrote traveller John Carne in *Letters from the East* (1826), 'which it is impossible to escape causes several travellers to leave Syria without seeing the finest ruin in the world'. One visitor who did attempt to evade the tax, reports Carne, had his hut set on fire by the Arabs.

At least the impecunious traveller of today is able to visit a great deal of the site for free and finds cash admissions barring the way only to a few selected sections, such as the Temple of Bel and the Museum of Popular Culture. And if the traveller decides to give these sights a miss and hold back on the cash, the chances of having the hotel burned from under them are these days very slim.

Arab castle), the Valley of the Tombs and the underground hypogea; most hotels are keen to oblige, charging on average S£200 for a combined trip to the tombs and castle.

When heading out to the ruins, an early start is advisable to beat the heat – from May through to September the sun can be merciless. Take plenty of water and wear a hat.

Although there is no admission fee to the site, the museums, Temple of Bel, Qala'at ibn Maan and some of the tombs charge admission, and the total can quickly top S£1000 (US$20), not including possible transport costs. The site itself has no fixed opening times but paying attractions keep set hours.

Temple of Bel معبد بل

The most complete structure and single most impressive part of the ruins is this **temple** (adult/student S£300/15; 8am-1pm & 4-6pm Apr-Sep, 8am-1pm & 2-4pm Oct-Mar), also known as the Sanctuary of Bel. Bel is assumed to be the most important of the gods in the Palmyrene pantheon, although very little is known about Palmyra's deities. He was most likely an imported masculine version of the Babylonian goddess Belili, the mother goddess, and identified with the Romans' Jupiter.

Raised on a slight tell (mound) indicating the existence of a pre-Classical settlement on this site, you enter the temple through the ticket office, just north of the main monumental entrance. The keep-like form of this entrance was created by the Arabs when they converted the temple into a fortress; an inscription in a recessed arch dates the work to 1123–24.

The complex consists of two parts: a huge walled courtyard, or **temenos**, and, at its centre, the temple proper or cella. Originally the courtyard was surrounded by a 15m-high wall but only the northern side is original, dating from the 2nd or 3rd century AD. The rest is of Arab construction. A double colonnade used to run around three sides of the interior while the fourth (western) side had a single row of columns much taller than the others. Some of these can be seen to the right and left of the entrance.

Just to the left of the entrance inside the courtyard is a **sunken passage** that enters the temple from outside the wall and gradually slopes up to the level of the courtyard. This was probably used to bring sacrificial animals into the precincts. The podium of the **sacrificial altar** is on the left, and beside it are the foundations of a **banqueting hall**. The remains of another platform are to the right and this was possibly used for religious purification ceremonies.

The **cella** was completed in AD 32, a date given in a dedication inscribed on a pedestal found inside, and now exhibited in the Palmyra Museum. It's unusual in that the entrance is in one of the sides rather than at an end, and is offset from the centre. Inside is a single chamber with *adytons* (large niches) at either end. The *adyton* ceilings, carved from single slabs of stone, are magnificent: the northern ceiling has a cupola featuring seven busts of divinities and the 12 signs of the zodiac, while the southern ceiling has a circular pattern of acanthus leaves surrounded by a ring of geometric patterning all inset within a square frame, itself surrounded by an elaborate pattern of hexagonal coffers. The stepped ramp leading to the southern portico suggests that it may have contained a portable idol used in processions.

Around the back of the shrine is a pile of old railway tracks that were used to remove trolleys of rubble during the original excavations.

Museum of Popular Culture
متحف التقاليد الشعبية

The whitewashed building just by the Temple of Bel was originally the residence of the Ottoman governor of Palmyra. It later became a prison, and now houses a **museum** (adult/student S£150/20; ☽ 8.30am-2.30pm) dedicated to portraying scenes from traditional life recreated using mannequins. It's better than most of its kind and there's lots of interesting information about the Bedouin tribal system written in French.

Great Colonnade
الشارع الطويل

The spine of ancient Palmyra was a stately colonnaded avenue stretching between the city's main funerary temple in the west and the Temple of Bel in the east, and covering a distance of almost 1km. Unlike in the typical Roman model, Palmyra's main avenue was far from straight, pivoting decisively at two points – a result of piecemeal growth and improvisation. Where the modern asphalted road slices across the ancient way is an imposing **monumental arch**. Dating from the reign of Septimius Severus, when Palmyra was at its peak, the construction is

actually two arches, joined like a hinge to swing the street through a 30 degree turn, aiming it at the Temple of Bel.

The section of street between the Bel temple and the arch has largely vanished, with just a few sparse columns to indicate the route the colonnades once took, but the section west of the arch is magnificent. This section lies at the heart of the ancient civic centre; it has been heavily restored and gives a very clear idea of how the city must have appeared in all its original pomp and grandeur.

The street itself was never paved, probably to save damage from camel caravans, but flanking porticoes on either side were. Each of the massive columns that supported the porticoes has a small jutting platform about two-thirds of the way up, designed to hold the statue of some rich or famous Palmyrene who had helped pay for the construction of the street.

Nabo Temple
معبد نبو

The ruined area to the left immediately after passing through the arch is a small trapezoidal temple built in the 1st century AD and dedicated to Nabo, the Palmyrene god of destinies. All that's left are the temple podium, lower courses of the outer walls and some re-erected columns.

Diocletian's Baths
حمامات ديوكلسيان

On the north side of the great colonnaded way, four columns standing forward of the line of the portico announce the location of what was once a public bathhouse founded by Diocletian. These columns once carried a pediment over the entrance, but this has been lost. The baths survive only as trenches and as outlines scored in the baked earth.

Theatre

Palmyra's theatre lies on the south side of the street accessed between two arches in the colonnade. Until the 1950s it was buried beneath sand but since then has been extensively restored.

Beneath the platforms on many of the columns are inscriptions with names for the statues that once stood there: representations of prominent people including emperors, princes of Palmyra, magistrates, officials, high-ranking priests and caravan chiefs.

The freestanding stage façade of the theatre itself is designed along the lines of a

PALMYRA FESTIVAL

Since 1993, Palmyra has been the scene of a popular annual **folk festival**. Horse and camel races take place on the hippodrome below Qala'at ibn Maan, and in the evenings there are music and dance performances, some of which take place in the old theatre in the ancient civic centre. Aimed largely at tourists, the festival runs for three or four days, usually towards the end of April or beginning of May.

palace entrance, complete with a royal door and smaller doors on either side. From the rear of the theatre, a pillared way once led south to a gate in the city walls dating from the era of Justinian. North of this pillared way are the substantial remains of the Tariff Court and agora (below).

Tetrapylon   التترابيل

This is probably the single most photographed monument at Palmyra, marking the second pivot in the route of the colonnaded street. It consists of a square platform bearing at each corner a tight grouping of four columns. Each of the four groups of pillars supports 150,000kg of solid cornice. A pedestal at the centre of each quartet originally carried a statue. Only one of the 16 pillars is of the original pink granite (probably brought from Aswan in Egypt); the rest are coloured concrete and look it – a result of some rather hasty reconstruction carried out in the 1960s.

From here the main colonnaded street continues northwest, while smaller pillared transverse streets lead southwest to the agora and northeast to the Temple of Baal Shamin.

Agora   السوق العامة

The agora was the hub of Palmyrene life, the city's most important meeting space, used for public discussion and as a market where caravans unloaded their wares and engaged in the trade that brought the desert oasis its wealth. What remains today is a clearly defined courtyard measuring 84m by 71m. Numerous pillars survive to indicate that the central area was once enclosed by porticoes on all four sides and that the pillars carried statues. The dedications reveal that the portico on the north held statues of Palmyrene and Roman officials, the eastern one had senators, the western portico was for military officers, while on the south side, merchants and caravan leaders were honoured. Sadly, today no statues remain and most of the pillars are small stumps.

Adjoining the agora in the northwest corner are the remains of a small **banqueting hall** used by the rulers of Palmyra. South of the agora is another large, walled rectangular space, known as the **Tariff Court**, because this is where the great tariff stella (now residing in the St Petersburg Hermitage) was found. The enormous stone tablet dates from AD 137 and bears the inscription 'Tariff of Palmyra', setting out the taxes payable on each commodity that passed through the city.

The small structure at the north end of the court, closest to the theatre, has a semicircular arrangement of tiered seating leading archaeologists to believe that it may have been the city's **Senate**, or council building.

Temple of Baal Shamin   معبد بعلشمين

Dating from AD 17 and dedicated to the Phoenician god of storms and fertilising rains, this small shrine is all that remains of a much larger compound. It stands alone 200m north of the main colonnaded street, near the Zenobia Hotel, in what was a residential area of the ancient city. Baal Shamin was an import, like Bel, who only really gained popularity in Palmyra when Roman influence was at its height.

Although the temple gate is permanently padlocked closed, it is possible to peer inside. Fronting the temple, the six columns of the vestibule have platforms for statues, and carry inscriptions. The column on the far left, dated AD 131, has an inscription in Greek and Palmyrene that praises the secretary of the city for his generosity during the imperial visit of 'the divine Hadrian' and for footing the bill for the temple's construction.

Funerary Temple

Beyond the tetrapylon the main street continues for another 500m. This stretch has seen much less excavation and reconstruction than elsewhere and is still littered with tumbled columns and assorted blocks of masonry. The road ends at the impressive portico of a funerary temple, dating from the 3rd century AD. The portico with its six columns stands as it was found but the walls are a relatively recent reconstruction. This was the main residential section of town and streets can be seen leading off to both sides. There is scattered masonry everywhere, in places literally heaped into small hillocks of statuary fragments and decorated friezes and panels.

Camp of Diocletian   مخيم ديوكلسيان

Southwest of the funerary temple, reached via a porticoed way, is an extensive complex known as Diocletian's camp. Dating from the late 3rd or early 4th century AD, it comprises the remains of a monumental gateway, a tetrapylon and two temples, one of which, the **Temple of the Standards**, dominates from an elevated position at the head of a flight of worn steps. The 'camp' was erected after the destruction of the city by Aurelian. The extent of the complex and the fact that it was built on top of, and incorporates, earlier structures of evident grandeur has led some historians to speculate that it occupies what had been the palace of Zenobia.

Behind the complex a section of fortified wall climbs a steep hill – from where there are excellent views of the site – then descends, edging around the southern edge of the city.

VALLEY OF THE TOMBS   Map p206
وادي القبور

To the south of the city wall at the foot of low hills is a series of variously sized, freestanding, square-based towers. Known as the **Towers of Yemliko**, they were constructed as multistorey burial chambers, stacked high with coffins posted in pigeonhole-like niches. The niches, or loculi, were then sealed with a stone panel carved with a head and shoulders portrait of the deceased; you can see dozens of these stone portraits in the Palmyra Museum, and also in the National Museum at Damascus (p94).

The tallest of the towers – at four storeys high – is the most interesting. It dates from AD 83 and although it is kept locked you can peer in through the barred entrance. There is also an interesting carved lintel above the doorway and an inscription further up identifying the family interred within. A rough path winds up behind the towers to the top of a rocky saddle for a wonderful view of the Palmyrene landscape.

Further west, deeper into the hills, are plenty more of these funerary towers, some totally dilapidated, others relatively complete. By far the best preserved is the **Tower of Elahbel** (adult/student S£150/10), which is situated about 500m west of the Yemliko group. Built in AD 103, it has four storeys and could purportedly accommodate up to 300 sarcophagi. It's possible to ascend an internal staircase to visit the upper storey tomb chambers and to get out onto the roof. Also here is the chamber that formerly housed the **Hypogeum of Yarhai**, dismantled and reconstructed in the National Museum.

To visit Elahbel it's necessary to buy a ticket at the Palmyra Museum and join an organised foray led by a caretaker; these depart at 8.30am, 10am, 11.30am and 4.30pm Wednesday to Monday (no 11.30am visit Friday) and 9am and 11am Tuesday. From October to March the last visit is 2.30pm. At all other times the tomb is locked. The visit also includes the Hypogeum of the Three Brothers, which makes it worthwhile.

HYPOGEUM OF THE THREE BROTHERS
مدفن الاخوان الثلاثة

In addition to the funerary towers, Palmyra boasts a second, later type of tomb, the hypogeum, which was an underground burial chamber. As with the towers, this chamber was filled with loculi fitted with stone carved seals. The best of the 50 or more hypogea that have been discovered and excavated, apart from the Hypogeum of Yarhai (left), is the Hypogeum of the Three Brothers, which lies just southwest of the Palmyra Cham Palace hotel.

The tomb dates from AD 160–91. It is very modest in size but contains some beautiful frescoes, including portraits of the three brothers in oval frames. There are also three large sarcophagi topped by figures reclining on couches. You'll notice that these figures, like many in the Palmyra Museum, are headless; the official Palmyra guide suggests that this is because early tomb robbers found they could quite easily sell the stone heads.

The hypogeum can only be visited as part of an organised group – see the Valley of the Tombs, left.

THE JAPANESE TOMB

Discovered in 1994 and opened to the public in 2000, this underground tomb takes its name from the nationality of the archaeological team responsible for its immaculate restoration. The tomb dates from AD 128 and is occupied by two brothers with the unlikely names of Bwlh and Bwrp. The entrance is richly decorated and gives way to a main gallery lined with a pigeonhole arrangement of loculi sealed with carved busts and decorated with an ornate frieze and painting of a family banqueting scene. Two side chambers contain sarcophagi topped by family sculptures. The ensemble is superb and helps make sense of all the miscellaneous bits of sculpture exhibited in the Palmyra Museum.

The tomb is in the Southeast Necropolis, which is several kilometres beyond the Palmyra Cham Palace. It's not attractive scenery to hike through, but if you do want to walk continue on the road south of the hotel for 2km taking an immediate left after the petrol station, and the necropolis is a further 3km. The best way to get here is in a car, either by taxi or as part of an organised trip. Either way, check with the museum first that the tomb is open.

QALA'AT IBN MAAN   قلعة إبن معن

To the west of the ruins perched high on a hilltop, **Qala'at ibn Maan** (adult/student S£300/15; ◉ approximately 9am-dusk) is most notable as the prime viewing spot for overlooking the ruins of Palmyra. The castle is said to have been built in the 17th century by Fakhreddine (Fakhr ad-Din al-Maan II), the Lebanese warlord who challenged the Ottomans for control of the Syrian desert. However, it's also possible that some sort of fortifications existed up here well before then.

The castle is surrounded by a moat, and a footbridge allows access to the rooms and various levels within. However, it's not necessary to enter the castle to enjoy the views. The best time to go up is in the late afternoon, with the sun to the west, casting long shadows among the ruins below. To reach the castle on foot is quite a hike with a scramble up a steep zigzagging path to reach the summit. Approaching by car is easier and most of the hotels in town organise sunset trips up to the castle for around S£100, which is about the same as you would pay in a taxi.

Activities
SWIMMING
The Garden Restaurant (p214) has a small spring-filled and slightly sulphurous pool surrounded by date palms. The Zenobia Hotel (p214) charges S£100 per person, and nonguests can use the pool at the Palmyra Cham Palace (p214) for S£300.

Sleeping
Palmyra is very much affected by the seasonal tourism trade. In the peak season, from around April to September, beds can be scarce and prices inflated. Out of season, there are far more beds than visitors, and competition becomes fierce. At such times do not accept the first rate quoted. It should be pointed out, though, that the places willing to make these drastic discounts may later try to make money by reneging on the agreement or adding supplementary charges for hot water or extortionate charges for breakfasts.

BUDGET
All of Palmyra's budget accommodation is located on or just off the main street in the new town, Sharia al-Quwatli.

Baal Shamin Hotel (Map p208; ☎ 910 453; roof mattress S£75, dm/s/d/tr S£125/150/300/450) This place is run by mountain-of-mirth Mohammed Ahmed, who camps in the lobby and entertains guests with tea, coffee and, occasionally, booze. Many travellers who aren't even staying here end up hanging with Mohammed for the fun of it. Rooms are basic but serviceable with clean ensuites.

Citadel Hotel (Map p208; ☎ 910 537; Sharia As'ad al-Amir; dm/d S£200/500; ◉) Facing the side of the museum, this is a prime site which the owners exploit to the max (confirm the price and check your bill). There's a wide range of rooms, including some good new ones on the upper floor with air-con, new bathrooms and views of the ruins. Check a few out before choosing. Visa cards accepted.

New Afqa Hotel (Map p208; ☎ 791 0386; roof mattress S£100, s/d S£250/500) This could be a decent option: rooms are comfortable if a little spartan, and there's a spacious reception with satellite TV and beer in the fridge.

New Tourist Hotel (Map p208; ☎ 910 333; Sharia al-Quwatli; beds in share r S£150, s/d S£175/275, with private bathroom S£200/325) At one time this was about the only hotel in town. It's failed to keep up with the times and is looking a bit grotty and battered, although the communal lounge with kilim-covered benches is cosy.

Sun Hotel (Map p208; ☎ 911 133; dm/s/d S£150/250/500) This relatively new budget place is run by an amiable guy named Mohammed. Some of the rooms are a little gloomy, but all come with clean ensuites. Ask for a fan.

Umayyad Palace (☎ /fax 910 755; Saahat al-Jumhuriyya; d S£400) This one has potential with an attractive arrangement of rooms, most with private bathrooms, around a pleasant central courtyard area.

Campers can pitch tents out back of the Zenobia Hotel (this page) for S£250, including use of hot showers, or over the road among the date palms at the Garden Restaurant for S£100 per person.

MID-RANGE

Out-of-season mid-range hotel rates can very quickly drop down into the budget range, so if Palmyra is looking quiet it might be worth seeing what deals can be had.

Heliopolis Hotel (Map p208; ☎ 913 921; heliopolis-palmyra@usa.net; Saahat al-Jumhuriyya; s/d US$40/50; ✯) Opened in 1998, this is a five-storey, three-star place and probably marks the start of a trend to overdevelop the small town. However, it has beautiful, large rooms with all modern facilities; many rooms have unsurpassable views over the oasis to the ruins – make sure you ask. MasterCard and Visa are accepted.

Ishtar Hotel (Map p208; ☎ 913 073; fax 913 260; Sharia al-Quwatli; s/d US$20/30; ✯) This is about the first place you come to on the left as you enter the town. Rooms – all with ensuites but varying greatly in size – have benefited from a recent refit (new carpets, mattresses and furniture). There's a basement bar and plans for a rooftop café-restaurant.

Orient Hotel (Map p208; ☎ 910 131; fax 910 700; s/d US$20/25; ✯) This one is favoured by many of the adventure tour companies and rightly so, the rooms are spotlessly clean with gleaming ensuites complete with towels and toiletries. The large bright reception area is also particularly pleasant. Great value for the money.

Palace Hotel (Map p208; ☎ /fax 911 707; s/d with private bathroom US$17/24; ✯) This hotel is quiet, set back off the main street, and well looked after. Rooms vary in quality but all have air-con and clean ensuites; some have good views of the ruins. The place is used a lot by French groups but manager Khaled also speaks English.

Tower Hotel (Map p208; ☎ 910 273; fax 910 116; Sharia al-Quwatli; s/d US$15/21) A modern three-star with smallish but attractive rooms – frilly bed spreads, gleaming ensuites, all with air-con and some with excellent views of the ruins. Very good value.

TOP END

Palmyra Cham Palace (Map p206; ☎ 912 230-9; www.chamhotels.com; s/d US$160/190; ✯ ✯) Near the old Efca Spring some 2km south of the new town, the hotel has recently undergone an extensive renovation. Now, at least as far as the foyer is concerned, it resembles something you might expect to find in Las Vegas, not the Syrian desert. It has a couple of indifferent restaurants, a bar, shops and a pool but is too expensive for what it offers. Major credit cards accepted.

Zenobia Hotel (Map p208; ☎ 910 107; zenobia-hotel@net.sy; s/d US$60/78; ✯) Although built around 1900, The Zenobia is short on any kind of charm, period or otherwise, but owes its popularity to a location right on the very edge of the ruins. Reservations are a must but specify that you want one of rooms 101 to 106, which are the only rooms (out of 24) with views (which are wonderful), otherwise it's just not worth the money. Amex, MasterCard and Visa are all accepted.

Eating

Palmyra is certainly not celebrated for its dining opportunities. Most travellers seem to end up at one of two restaurants on Sharia al-Quwatli: **Traditional Palmyra** or **Spring Restaurant** across the street. There's little to choose between them. The food is unremarkable, although the Bedouin-style *mansaf* (rice dish) at the Traditional Palmyra is reasonably good (S£250 for two). Both places have a pleasantly laid-back atmosphere.

Garden Restaurant (Map p208; ☎ 911 421; Old Damascus Road; ☾ noon-midnight) This is exactly what it says on the sign: a restaurant in a garden, it's set on the edge of the oasis surrounded by date palms, close to the Zenobia Hotel. The food (mezze and grilled meats) doesn't quite live up to the setting but it's tolerable. Expect to pay S£200 to S£250.

Pancake House (Map p208; ☎ 913 733; Sharia an-Nasr; ☾ 8am-3pm & 6-11pm) A relatively new venture, this is one of the best places in town. The menu is limited to a handful of savoury and sweet options (S£150 each) plus the ubiquitous *mansaf* (S£200), but all ingredients are fresh, and the food is good. Excellent milkshakes (S£50) and juices too. Seating is in a small courtyard under a date palm or in a Bedouin carpet-covered room.

Palmyra Restaurant (Map p208; Saahat ar-Rais; 11am-late) On the main square, opposite the museum, the Palmyra does fairly average food (mezze and kebabs; expect to spend S£200 to S£250) but does a roaring trade in coach parties. The garden setting with fountains and plenty of leafy shade is a big plus. Alcohol is served.

Villa Palmyra (Map p208; ☎ 913 600; Sharia al-Quwatli; 6pm-midnight) While the hotel is overpriced, the 4th-floor restaurant is about as close as it gets to fine dining in Palmyra. Staff can be a little disinterested in nongroup diners, but the food is well prepared and well cooked. Expect to spend S£200 to S£300. Alcohol is served.

Entertainment

Once the sun goes down and you can't look at the old stones any more, there's very little to do in Palmyra. But before the light completely fades, it's worth taking a seat at the outdoor terrace at the **Zenobia Hotel** (p214) to cool off with a chilled Barada beer (S£100) while watching the ruins turn a flaming pink. Back in the town, the Ishtar Hotel (p214) and Villa Palmyra restaurant (above) both have almost identical cave-themed basement bars, but the best place for a couple of ales is the open-air section of the **Palmyra Restaurant** (above), where there's no obligation to eat and a bottle of local beer goes for S£75.

Plenty of travellers choose to hang out at the restaurants on Sharia al-Quwatli or at the **Tourist Cafe**, a traditional coffeehouse next to the mosque further along the same street. Alternatively, the **Baal Shamin Hotel** (p213) has a rooftop Bedouin tent with beer (S£50).

Getting There & Away
BUS

Palmyra doesn't have a bus station. The government-run Karnak bus company has its office and bus stop conveniently on the main square opposite the museum but its services are infrequent; they include just three buses a day to Damascus (S£100, three

hours), six a day to Deir ez-Zur (S£75, two hours), of which the 1.30pm service continues to Hassake and Qamishle, and one a day to Homs (S£65, two hours) at 3pm. Check the office for other times.

The other option is to go with Qadmous. Its buses stop at the Sahara Cafe on the edge of town, some 2km north of the museum; a taxi should cost S£25. Services for Damascus (S£115, three hours) depart at 9.30am, 11.30am and on the half-hour thereafter until 7.30pm. There are buses to Deir ez-Zur (S£85, two hours) on the hour every hour between 10am and 10pm. These buses originate in Damascus and cannot be booked in advance; turn up at the ticket office out front of the Sahara 15 minutes in advance and hope that there are available seats. The Qadmous office in the town centre is freight only and doesn't sell passenger tickets.

MINIBUS

Minibuses (S£40) and microbuses (S£60) for Homs (two hours) depart frequently throughout the day from the eastern end of the main street at Saahat al-Jumhuriyya.

QASR AL-HEIR ASH-SHARQI
قصر الحير الشرقي

If you have some time and cash to spare, an excellent excursion from Palmyra is to head 120km northeast of the oasis into the desert to see one of the most isolated and startling monuments to Umayyad Muslim rule in the 8th century AD, Qasr al-Heir ash-Sharqi (the so-called East Wall Palace). The palace here held a strategic position, commanding desert routes into Mesopotamia. As support from the nomadic Arab tribes (of which they themselves were a part) was one of the main Umayyad strengths, it is no coincidence that they made their presence felt in the desert steppes.

The palace complex and rich gardens, once supplied by an underground spring about 30km away, covered a rough square with 16km sides. Built by the Umayyad caliph Hisham abd al-Malek (r AD 724–43), the palace long outlived its founders. Haroun ar-Rashid, perhaps the best known ruler of the Abbasid dynasty that succeeded the Umayyad, made it one of his residences, and evidence suggests that it was only finally abandoned as late as the 14th century.

THE BEDOUIN

Mounted on a camel, swathed in robes and carrying a rifle for security and a coffee pot for hospitality, the archetypal Arab, as portrayed by Omar Sharif in *Lawrence of Arabia*, is no more. Certainly not in Syria, anyway. Although still known as bedu, these days few of Syria's 100,000 Bedouin population could be regarded as desert wanderers. They used to make their living guiding caravans across the deserts and supplying camels and protection against bandits but the overland trade routes died with the coming of the aeroplane. Most Bedouin are now settled in towns and villages and the furthest they roam is to find new pastures for their goats and sheep. For the most part, the camels are long gone and, instead, most Bedouin drive battered pick-ups.

Many of the Bedouin continue to wear traditional dress though, and this can include, for men, a *kanjar* (dagger) – a symbol of dignity, but these days used for precious little else. Women tend to dress in colourful garb, or sometimes black robes, and occasionally sport facial tattooing and kohl around the eyes.

Another aspect of Bedouin tradition still very much in evidence is their famed hospitality. Born of the co-dependency the nomads developed in order to survive in the desert, modern-day hospitality manifests itself in unmitigated generosity extended to strangers. Should you be fortunate enough to encounter the Bedouin (and in Palmyra this is quite possible as an increasing number of the hotels are arranging trips out to Bedouin camps) you can expect to be invited into their black goat-hair tents (*beit ash-sha'ar*; literally 'house of hair'), and offered bitter coffee, then sweet tea and possibly even something to eat. Money is not expected in return so you should try to be a gracious guest and not take advantage of their hospitality.

Sights

The partly restored walls of one of the main enclosures, with their mighty anddefensive towers, are the most impressive remaining sign of what was once a sumptuous anomaly in the harsh desert. The ruins to the west belong to what may have been a **khan** (travellers' inn). In the southeastern corner are remnants of a **mosque**; the column with stairs inside between the two areas was a minaret. The remains of **baths** are to the north of the main walls. Traces of the old perimeter wall can just be made out to the south, and border the best track leading here from the highway.

This castle has a counterpart southwest of Palmyra, **Qasr al-Heir al-Gharbi** (West Wall Palace), but little of interest remains at the site; its impressive façade was dismantled and reconstructed at the National Museum in Damascus (p94).

Getting There & Away

The only way to get to Qasr al-Heir ash-Sharqi is by private transport. Most of the hotels in Palmyra are more than happy to oblige with a car and driver. The castle has become a standard excursion, with most hotels charging around S£1200 to S£1500 for a half-day trip. The cost is per car, so for a group of four it's not that expensive.

Some of the hotels also offer the worthwhile combination of Qasr al-Heir ash-Sharqi and Rasafa (p219), another desert development associated with Hisham lying 80km to the north along a desert trail.

LAKE AL-ASSAD بحيرة الاسد

By the time the Euphrates enters Syria at Jarablos (once the capital of the Neo-Hittite empire) it is already a mighty river. To harness that power for irrigation and hydroelectricity production, one of the Assad regime's most ambitious plans, to dam the Euphrates, went into effect in the 1960s.

Work began at Tabaqah in 1963 and the reservoir started to fill in 1973. Now that it's full, it stretches for some 60km. The dam is Syria's pride and joy and the electricity produced was supposed to make the country self-sufficient.

The flow of the Euphrates, however, has been reduced by the construction of the Atatürk Dam in Turkey, and Syria and Iraq are concerned that the Turks may at any time decide to regulate the flow for political reasons. The decision by İstanbul in late 1995 to proceed with construction of a further dam, the Birecik, has only served to heighten the two Arab countries' worst fears. The Turks deny all claims of having used their position to reduce the flow of the river, attributing any slowing down to natural causes.

While the lack of water in the river has been a disappointment, the regular power

WAYNE WALTON

The monumental arch of the ruins at Palmyra (p208), Syria

Traditional Bedouin dress
(p216), Palmyra, Syria

JOHN ELK III

CHRISTINA DAMEYER

A camel with traditional saddle in the ancient
theatre (p210), Palmyra, Syria

Traditional Arabic sweets for sale, Damascus (p75), Syria

CHRIS BARTON

Village girls, Syria

Strong coffee in a small porcelain cup, Lebanon

cuts that were once a daily reality across the country have been all but eliminated.

The dormitory town of Ath-Thaura (the Revolution; الثورة) was built at Tabaqah to accommodate the dam workers and peasants who had to be relocated because of the rising water levels. Not only villages but also some sites of both historical and archaeological importance were inundated. With aid from Unesco and other foreign missions, these were investigated, documented and, whenever possible, moved to higher ground. The 27m-high minaret of the Maskana Mosque and the 18m-high minaret from Abu Harayra were both segmented and then transported, the latter to the centre of Ath-Thaura.

Qala'at Ja'abar   قلعة جعبر

Impressive from a distance, Qala'at Ja'abar, a citadel built entirely of bricks in classic Mesopotamian style, is a disappointment once inside. It is situated on a spit of land connected to the bank of Lake al-Assad, about 15km north of Ath-Thaura. Before the lake was built, the original castle had rested on a rocky perch since before the arrival of Islam, and had then been rebuilt by Nureddin (Nur ad-Din) and altered by the Mamluks.

The castle makes a great backdrop for a day by the lake, and on Friday this is an extremely popular spot with locals. It's a great place for a picnic. It is also an ideal place for a swim, unless you happen to be a woman, in which case it could be decidedly uncomfortable.

You will have to pass through Ath-Thaura to get to the citadel, and it may be worth a quick look at the dam. The town itself, however, has little to recommend it.

GETTING THERE & AWAY

Without your own car, Qala'at Ja'abar can be difficult to get to. It's necessary to go via Ath-Thaura, either coming from Raqqa (S£25 by microbus) or Aleppo (S£50 by bus). Raqqa is the much closer base; from Aleppo it can be a long and hassle-filled day. From the centre of Ath-Thaura, you have to head out towards the north of town and try to hitch across the dam (*as-sidd*). The turn-off for the citadel is a few kilometres further on to the left, and from here it's about another 10km.

Friday is a good day to hitch across the dam, as the place is truly crowded with day-trippers. On other, quieter days, be prepared for long waits, or negotiate with a local driver: expect to pay about S£200 from Ath-Thaura.

Note that there are few, if any, buses or microbuses from Ath-Thaura to anywhere after about 4pm.

QALA'AT NAJM   قلعة نجم

Qala'at Najm, the northernmost castle of its kind along the Euphrates in Syria, has been partly restored. Originally built under Nureddin in the 12th century, it was later reconstructed under Saladin (Salah ad-Din). It commands a natural defence position over the Euphrates plain, and the views out across what was once a strategic crossing point are alone worth some effort.

To get here, take a bus for Ain al-Arab (عين العرب) from the East Bus Station in Aleppo (p194; S£30, two hours) and get off at the village of Haya Kebir. You may be able to get an Ain al-Arab bus from Aleppo's City Bus Station, too (see p194). From Haya Kebir it's 15km to the castle, and hitching is the only way.

An early start is essential, as there is not a lot of traffic on this dead-end trail. The road passes through rolling wheat fields that form a cool green carpet in spring. It appears there are no buses at all to Ain al-Arab on Friday.

RAQQA   الرقة
☎ 022

Raqqa is a small dusty town with little to detain a traveller, but in the 8th and 9th centuries AD, as the city known as Rafika, it was reputedly a glorious place that served as a summer residence of the legendary Abbasid caliph Haroun ar-Rashid (r AD 786–809), of *The Thousand and One Nights* fame (see the boxed text on p5). The area around the city had been the site of numerous cities that had come and gone in the preceding millennia, including Nikephorion, founded by the Seleucids (sometimes attributed by legend to Alexander the Great). After the Mongol invasion in 1260, Rafika virtually ceased to exist.

Orientation & Information

The heart of town is a busy traffic-filled square, Saahat Saa'a (Clock Square), with a clock tower as its centrepiece. The site of the

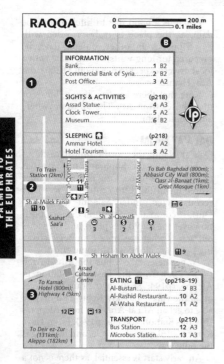

RAQQA

0	200 m
0	0.1 miles

INFORMATION
Bank...1 B2
Commercial Bank of Syria...........2 B2
Post Office...................................3 A2

SIGHTS & ACTIVITIES (p218)
Assad Statue................................4 A3
Clock Tower................................5 A2
Museum......................................6 B2

SLEEPING (p218)
Ammar Hotel...............................7 A2
Hotel Tourism.............................8 A2

To Train Station (2km)

To Bab Baghdad (800m); Abbasid City Wall (800m); Qasr al-Banaat (1km); Great Mosque (1km)

To Mansour

Sh al-Malek Faisal

Saahat Saa'a

Sh al-Quwatli

Sh Hisham Ibn Abdel Malek

Assad Cultural Centre

To Karnak Hotel (800m); Highway 4 (5km)

To Deir ez-Zur (131km); Aleppo (182km)

EATING (pp218–19)
Al-Bustan....................................9 B3
Al-Rashid Restaurant.................10 A2
Al-Waha Restaurant...................11 A2

TRANSPORT (p219)
Bus Station................................12 A3
Microbus Station.......................13 A3

old city lies to the east, reached by following Sharia al-Quwatli. The central bus station is on Sharia Saa'a, 300m due south of the clock tower. There's a **post and telephone office** on the east side of Saahat Saa'a, and a local branch of the **CBS** (Sharia al-Quwatli) with no sign in English that can change cash only.

Sights & Activities

Only a few scant, badly worn remnants that barely hint of the city's old glory remain. The partly restored, mid-12th-century **Bab Baghdad** (Baghdad Gate) lies about a 15-minute walk to the east of the clock tower. Built of mud-brick, it's relatively modest in scale, and stands marginalised, off to the side of the modern road. Running north from the gate is a heavily restored section of the old **Abbasid city wall**, punctuated at regular intervals by the bases of what were once more than 100 towers. Unfortunately, the trench in which the walls lie now serves as a makeshift garbage dump. After about 500m, there's a break in the walls for Sharia Tahseh (also known as Sharia Shbat); take the first left inside the walls and 200m down is the

9th-century **Qasr al-Banaat** (Maidens' Palace), with four high-arched *iwans* (vaulted halls) around a central courtyard.

Continue west along Sharia Tahseh and north of the first major intersection (with Sharia Seif ad-Dowla) are the remains of the **Great Mosque**, built during the reign of the Abbasid caliph Al-Mansur in the 8th century and reconstructed in 1165 by Nureddin.

A small **museum** (adult/student S£300/15; 9am-6pm Apr-Sep, to 4pm Oct-Mar, closed Tue), halfway between the Bab Baghdad and the clock tower, has some interesting artefacts from excavation sites in the area, although the best pieces have always gone to the museums in Aleppo and Damascus.

Every day but Friday, an impressively sized livestock market is held early in the morning about 2km north of Bab Baghdad. Follow the city wall to the end and ask for the 'souq ad-dawab'.

Sleeping

The options are unappealing, and unless you need to, Raqqa is a place to avoid overnighting in.

Ammar Hotel (222 612; Sharia al-Quneitra; d S£400) Just north of the clock tower, the Ammar offers the kind of accommodation people are more usually sentenced to, rather than willingly settle on by choice. Showers and toilet facilities are shared. Don't accept the kind offer of coffee or tea – it could show up on the bill at a vastly inflated price.

Hotel Tourism (220 725; Sharia al-Quwatli; s/d S£300/500) One block east of the clock tower, this place is depressingly gloomy but the rooms are at least reasonably clean and have their own showers, though don't count on hot water. Toilet facilities are shared and grim.

Karnak Hotel (210 684/5/6; Sharia Saqr Quraysh; s/d US$23/27;) A large 1970s concrete station on the western edge of town. Rooms are spartan but come with a reasonable private bathrooms. To find the hotel follow Sharia al-Malek Faisal west, crossing a main street, and curving north. Take the first left after passing a small grassy triangle and at the end of the street the hotel is visible off to the right. It's about a 10-minute walk from the clock tower.

Eating

Al-Rashid Restaurant (241 919; Sharia al-Malek Faisal; noon-midnight) Although it looks far from promising from the outside (a shabby school hall of a building approached through a ruinous garden gone wild), the food here is fine. The salad is fresh and clean, and the chicken and kebabs, plus mezze are actually very good. Beer is served. Expect to pay around S£200 per person.

Al-Waha Restaurant (Sharia ath-Thaura; ⏰ 11am-10pm) This place does a reasonable set meal known as *wajabeh*, which includes soup, rice and stew (S£100).

Al-Bustan (Sharia Hisham ibn Abdel Malek; ⏰ 6pm-midnight) Also said to be very good, it has an open-air rooftop restaurant serving traditional mezze and grilled meats, and alcohol. The entrance is down a little side alley off the main street, signed in Arabic only.

Getting There & Away
BUS
Several different companies have offices at Raqqa's central bus station, including Qadmous with four daily services to Aleppo (S£85, 2½ hours), three to Damascus (S£175, six hours) and four to Deir ez-Zur (S£60, 2¼ hours). If the times of the Qadmous departures don't suit, try one of the other companies, although note that Al-Ahliah, the other top company with offices here, does not go to Deir ez-Zur. Alternatively, take a microbus.

MICROBUS
The microbus station is across the road from the bus station. From here there are regular services west to Al-Mansoura (for Rasafa; S£15, 20 minutes), Ath-Thaura (for Qala'at Ja'abar; S£25), Aleppo (S£75) and Deir ez-Zur (S£60).

TRAIN
The train station in Raqqa does not inspire confidence. Windows are smashed, doors boarded up, and there is an awful stink coming from what we presume was the toilet block. But a guy we found sleeping in a back room assured us that a train for Aleppo came through at 4am each day and there was one for Deir ez-Zur and on to Hassake and Qamishle at 2am. To get to the station walk north up Sharia al-Quneitra and its continuation Sharia at-Tahrir for about 2km.

RASAFA   الرصافة
This ancient, long-abandoned **walled city** (adult/student S£300/15) lies 25km south of the Euphrates highway, rising up out of the

featureless desert. It's a fascinating place to explore, made all the more intriguing by its remote location. Bring a hat for protection against the sun.

History
Possibly inhabited in Assyrian times, Diocletian established a fort here as part of a defensive line against the Sassanian Persians late in the 3rd century AD. A desert road led through Rasafa from the Euphrates south to Palmyra, a trail that can be followed today by 4WD and a guide. About this time a cult to the local martyr St Sergius began to take hold. Sergius was a Roman soldier who converted to Christianity and was executed for refusing to perform sacrifices to Jupiter. By the 5th century Rasafa had become an important centre of Christian worship and an impressive basilica had been raised.

A century later the city was at the height of its prosperity. The Byzantine emperor Justinian (r AD 527–65) further fortified the growing settlement against the threat of Persian assault. Ultimately, this was to no avail as Rasafa capitulated to the eastern empire in 616.

Following the Muslim Arab invasion of Syria the city was occupied by Hisham abd al-Malek who pursued an energetic building policy, constructing a whole series of castles and palaces in Syria (including Qasr al-Heir ash-Sharqi, see p215); here in Rasafa he adorned the existing city with a palatial summer residence. Just seven years after

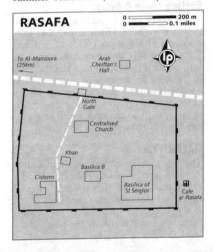

Hisham's death, the palace and city were razed by the Baghdad-based Abbasids, fierce rivals of the Umayyads. The city remained occupied but with a much reduced population. It was finally abandoned altogether when invading Mongols swept across northern Syria in the 13th century.

Sights

The walls, enclosing a quadrangle measuring 550m by 400m, are virtually all complete. The main entrance is by the **North Gate**. Once inside, you are confronted by the immensity of the place, mostly bare now save for the churches inside. Little excavation has yet been done and you should stroll around the defensive **perimeter walls** before exploring the site. At certain points it is possible to climb to the upper terrace for enhanced views.

Three churches remain standing. The grandest is the partially restored **Basilica of St Sergius**. The wide central nave is flanked by two aisles, from which it is separated by a series of sweeping arches each resting on pillars and a pair of less ambitious arch and column combinations. This and the two other churches date from the 6th century. In the southwestern corner of the complex lie huge underground **cisterns** (watch your step) that could keep a large garrison supplied with water through long sieges.

There's a small café, the imaginatively named **Cafe ar-Rasafa**, outside the east wall of the site selling snacks and drinks.

Getting There & Away

It requires patience to get to Rasafa as transport is infrequent. Catch a microbus from Raqqa to Al-Mansoura (S£15, 20 minutes). Then it's a matter of waiting at the signposted turn-off for a pick-up to take you the 25km to the ruins for about S£20, which can take a while. If you're impatient, you can ask one of the pick-up drivers lounging around here to take you there and back for an emperor's ransom – S£200 would not be unusual.

HALABIYYA   حلبيه

The town of Halabiyya was founded by Zenobia, the rebellious Palmyrene leader, in the years immediately preceding her fall in AD 272 (for more on Zenobia see p205). It was later refortified during the reign of Justinian, and it is mainly the result of this work that survives today.

The fortress town was part of the Byzantine Empire's eastern defensive line against the Persians (which failed in AD 610). The walls are largely intact, and there are remnants of the citadel, basilicas, baths, a forum and the north and south gates. The present road follows the course of the old colonnaded street.

Zalabiyya   زلبيه

Across the river and further south is the much less intact forward stronghold of the main fort, Zalabiyya. In summer, the Euphrates is sometimes passable between the town and the fort, which is what made Zalabiyya necessary.

Getting There & Away

Neither Halabiyya nor Zalabiyya is easy to get to. Halabiyya is the more interesting of the two, and at least the first stage of this hike is straightforward enough. Get a Deir ez-Zur bus from Raqqa and get out at the Halabiyya turn-off. If you don't have transport, from here you'll have to hitch a ride or, if you feel up to it, undertake the 8.5km walk. Alternatively, negotiate with a local to take you out there – this could cost you up to S£500 for the round trip.

To get to Zalabiyya, from Halabiyya head north, crossing a pontoon bridge and passing a train station en route. It's a distance of around 4.5km. The hardest bit is getting back. There aren't many buses plying the right bank of the Euphrates – if you're here in the afternoon, you'll just have to sit it out and hope for a passing truck.

DEIR EZ-ZUR   دير الزور
☎ 051

Deir ez-Zur ('Deir' to the locals) is a busy little market town by the Euphrates. On weekdays its streets are filled with colourfully dressed peasants from the surrounding countryside, in town to buy and sell produce at the small but thriving souq (market) off the main square. While it did become something of a boom town in the early 1990s with the discovery of high-grade oil in the surrounding area, this does not seem to have affected the essential character of Deir ez-Zur.

The character of the town is heavily influenced by its distance from Damascus and its proximity to Iraq. The dialect spoken here is much rougher than the Syrian Arabic spoken

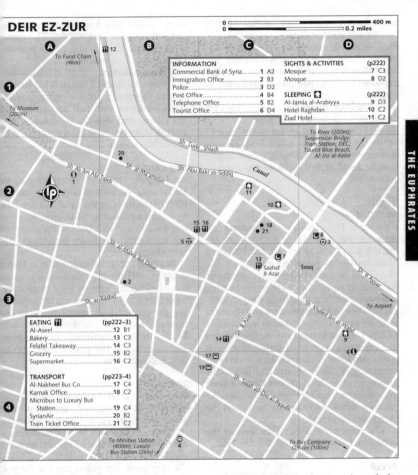

DEIR EZ-ZUR

INFORMATION	
Commercial Bank of Syria	1 A2
Immigration Office	2 B3
Police	3 D2
Post Office	4 B4
Telephone Office	5 B2
Tourist Office	6 D4

SIGHTS & ACTIVITIES	(p222)
Mosque	7 C3
Mosque	8 D2
SLEEPING	(p222)
Al-Jamia al-Arabiyya	9 D3
Hotel Raghdan	10 C2
Ziad Hotel	11 C2

EATING	(pp222–3)
Al-Aseel	12 B1
Bakery	13 C3
Felafel Takeaway	14 C3
Grocery	15 B2
Supermarket	16 C2

TRANSPORT	(pp223–4)
Al-Nakheel Bus Co	17 C4
Karnak Office	18 C2
Microbus to Luxury Bus Station	19 C4
SyrianAir	20 B2
Train Ticket Office	21 C2

PALMYRA TO THE EUPHRATES

elsewhere in the country and some of the vocabulary even differs – the standard Syrian greeting of *kifak*, in Deir becomes *shlonak*.

Many travellers find themselves stopping over in Deir en route to Qamishle or the ancient sites of Mari and Dura Europos. Although there really isn't that much to see in town, it does benefit from a pleasant riverside setting and a wonderful fragrance of jasmine, bicycles are as numerous as cars, and there's an enticing evening buzz around the pedestrianised shopping lane Sharia al-Maisat.

Orientation

The centre of town is the main square, Saahat 8 Azar, a scruffy, dusty place with the busy souq on its east side. The main north-south

road, which runs from the river through the square and down on past the new post office to the minibus station is called Sharia 8 Azar. This is bisected by the main east-west axis, which also runs through the square and is called Sharia Khaled ibn al-Walid to the east, and Sharia Ali ibn Abi Taleb to the west.

The body of water flowing just north of the square is not the Euphrates but a branch channel (p222).

Information

CBS (Sharia Ali ibn Abi Taleb; ☾ 8am-12.30pm Sat-Thu) About a 10-minute walk west of the main square. There's a commission of S£25 on travellers cheques.

Immigration Office (☾ 8am-1.30pm Sat-Thu) A good place to extend your visa; the process takes only about half an hour. You need two photos and it costs S£25. To find the office, walk south from the telephone office, then diagonally across the square turning right onto Sharia ar-Rashid; it's the low concrete building on your right.

Post Office (Sharia 8 Azar; ☾ 8am-8pm Sat-Thu, to 1pm Fri) Halfway between the main square and the minibus station.

Telephone Office (Sharia Ali ibn Abi Taleb; ☾ 8am-10pm Sat-Thu) This is 250m west of the main square.

Tourist Office (☎ 226 150; ☾ 9am-2pm Sat-Thu) In a side street off Sharia Khaled ibn al-Walid, about a 10-minute walk east of the main square. As ever, it's not particularly useful but the staff are friendly and there's often a pot of tea on the boil.

Sights
MUSEUM

Opened in 1996, Deir ez-Zur's **museum** (Saahat ar-Rais; adult/student S£300/15; ☾ 8am-6pm Apr-Sep, to 4pm Oct-Mar, closed Tue) is a fair bit better than most other museums in Syria. While the pieces in the collection may not be as valuable or striking as those in the two big national museums, thankfully the presentation of the exhibits is excellent and there are detailed explanations provided in a number of languages including English. The focus of the collection is on prehistoric and ancient Syria, and some of the most important finds from digs in the Euphrates and Jezira (the region between the Tigris and Kabur Rivers) region are on display. There are also smaller sections devoted to Classical Syria and the Arab Islamic period.

The museum is about 1km west of the centre, out along Sharia Ali ibn Abi Taleb.

RIVER

To get to the main body of the Euphrates you need to cross the branch channel and head north up Sharia 7 Nissan (the continuation of Sharia 8 Azar) for 500m. You hit the river at a point where it's crossed by a narrow 400m-long **suspension bridge**, for pedestrians and bicycle users only. It's quite an impressive structure, and a favourite place with the locals for an evening promenade. On the other side of the bridge is a small recreation ground where the local boys swim.

Sleeping
BUDGET

Al-Arabi al-Kebir (☎ 222 070; Sharia Khaled ibn al-Walid; s/d S£200/300) East of the square, this place is basic but clean. Rooms have fans and fresh

sheets, and a couple have balconies. Shower and toilets (squat) are shared. The owne speaks a little English, and this is probabl Deir's best budget option.

Al-Jamia al-Arabiyya (☎ 221 371; Sharia Khale ibn al-Walid; s/d S£200/250) Though it has shabby spartan rooms this hotel is kept reasonabl clean, equipped with fans and basin. Toi lets (squat) and showers are shared. Som English is spoken. The hotel entrance is o Sharia Maysaloun.

MID-RANGE

Hotel Raghdan (☎ 222 053; fax 221 169; Sharia Ab Bakr as-Siddiq; s/d US$14/20, with private bathroor US$17/23) Overlooking the canal this hotel ha a pleasant reception area but promising firs impressions are undermined by unappeal ing rooms that are badly maintained an very gloomy.

Ziad Hotel (☎ 214 596; fax 211 923; Sharia Abu Bak as-Siddiq; s/d US$21/27; ☒) This hotel is an abso lute blessing. It's a newly built three-store place, just west of the main square overlook ing the canal. Its 33 rooms are large an tastefully furnished (think Ikea) with hig beds with thick mattresses, air-con, fridg and satellite TV. The price includes break fast. Excellent value.

TOP END

Furat Cham (☎ 225 418; www.chamhotels.com; s/ US$160/190; ☒ ☒) Located 5km out of tow along the river, Furat Cham is the plac to rub shoulders with foreign oil-compan employees. The staff are pleasant, service i excellent and the buffet breakfast and dinne are very good. Nonguests can use the poo for S£200 a day, but phone ahead first to se if there's any water in it.

Eating

Just as accommodation options are severel limited in Deir, there isn't a lot of choic when it comes to eating, either.

Al-Aseel (Sharia Abu Bakr as-Siddiq) A small plac beside the canal, about 800m west of th centre. It has outside seating in summe and an indoor restaurant for the colde months; but most importantly, according t one longtime resident expat, it does the bes kebabs in all Syria.

DEC (☎ 220 469; ☾ 6pm-late) A large Soviet style dining hall on the north bank of th river that's quiet early on in the evening bu fills up after 10pm, DEC is particularly popular with parties and functions. Live music buoys things along. Food is the standard mezze and kebabs for around S£250 a head and alcohol is served. To get here cross the suspension bridge and as you do so you'll see the restaurant's illuminated Viking ship sign off to the right.

Layalty (☎ 226 388; Sharia Ali ibn Abi Taleb; ✆ noon-midnight) A smart new place in a converted function hall 400m west of the main square. The menu is a mix of Syrian standards plus international dishes – lots of chicken plus oddities like 'English dish'. The food's not bad at all and prices are low (and listed on the English-language menu). No alcohol.

Al-Sanabel (Sharia Ali ibn Abi Taleb; ✆ 11am-10pm) A modern, bright, gleamingly clean Syrian-style snack bar just west of the main square. Go for spit-roast chicken, shwarma, omelettes, chips and salads. Prices are fantastically cheap.

One good fallback is an excellent **felafel takeaway** (Sharia 8 Azar) about 200m south of the square. A filling sandwich will cost S£15. You can recognise the place by its red and white tiling. Otherwise, there are numerous shwarma, chicken and kebab places along Sharia Khaled ibn al-Walid.

There are also a couple of restaurants on the south bank of the Euphrates: **Tourist Blue Beach** just to the north of the suspension bridge and **Al-Jisr al-Kebir** (Big Canal) just to the south. Both are little more than open-air terraces but with excellent riverside settings that go some way to compensating for indifferent, overpriced food.

SELF-CATERING

There is an excellent little hole-in-the-wall **bakery** (✆ 5am-11pm Sat-Thu) on the southwest corner of the main square where huge flat disks of hot bread (S£5) are pulled out of the clay ovens continually. For condiments to add to your bread there's a decent **supermarket** west of the main square and a **grocery** round the corner from that, opposite the telephone office.

Entertainment

Al-Kandel (Sharia Ali ibn Abi Taleb) This is a no-frills bar just west of the town square. It's done out in a fetching colour scheme of pink, yellow and turquoise further enlivened with topless pin-ups and a poster of the Virgin and child. It's scuzzy but friendly (or in its own words 'welekoming'). Solo women should probably avoid.

Coffeehouse (Sharia Khaled ibn al-Walid) This particularly lively coffeehouse is just beyond the junction with Sharia Sobhi, and is filled most evenings with a lively crowd engrossed in high-volume games of cards, dominoes and backgammon.

Getting There & Away

AIR

The airport is about 7km east of town and the twice-weekly flight between Deir ez-Zur and Damascus costs S£742. A shuttle bus runs to the airport from the office of **SyrianAir** (☎ 221 801; Sharia al-Ma'amoun; ✆ 8.30am-12.30pm Sat-Thu).

BUS

The luxury bus station is 2km south of town, at the far end of Sharia 8 Azar. There's a local microbus service (S£5) to the airport from a stop about a five-minute walk south of the main square, on the right-hand side, otherwise a taxi (ask for 'al-karaj') will cost S£25. Several companies have their offices here and between them they offer regular services to Damascus (S£175, seven hours) via Palmyra (S£75, two hours) and to Aleppo (S£135, five hours) via Raqqa (S£60, two hours).

There's little need to book in advance – just show up and get a ticket. However, if you want to be certain of getting a particular bus, then Qadmous, Al-Furat and Raja all have town centre offices on Sharia Salah ad-Din al-Ayyubi, about 400m east of Sharia 8 Azar. None of the companies have signs in English but they are all in the block past the mosque.

Services to Hassake (S£75, two hours) and Qamishle (S£110, three hours) are less frequent, and in fact to the latter there's only one service a day, operated by Qadmous and departing at 3.30pm. Better to take a microbus.

MINIBUS & MICROBUS

The minibus station is on Sharia 8 Azar about 1km south of the main square. From here there are frequent departures for Raqqa (S£60, two hours), for Hassake in the northeast (S£75, 2½ hours) and on to Qamishle on the Turkish border (S£125), and south to Abu Kamal (S£50, two hours) for Mari and Dura Europos.

TRAIN

The train station is across the river to the north of town, about 3km from the centre. If you feel like a half-hour walk, cross the suspension bridge, continue on to the T-junction and turn right. Alternatively, catch one of the yellow shuttle buses that run from the train ticket office to the train station for S£5. These only run when a train is due to leave. The **train ticket office** (9am-1pm & 4-8pm) is in the concrete mall northeast of the main square.

The train to Aleppo leaves around 1.30am (1st/2nd class S£90/60, S£225 for a sleeper), while the Damascus service departs at 8.30pm (1st/2nd class S£155/105, S£455 for a sleeper). Several trains run to Hassake and on to Qamishle (S£60/40, three hours), although, typically, all but the 12.30pm service are in the early hours of the morning.

Getting Around

BICYCLE SPARES & REPAIRS

There's a small workshop just north of the mosque on the main square, and another slightly better stocked place on Sharia Khaled ibn al-Walid, about 300m east of the square.

SOUTHEAST OF DEIR EZ-ZUR

The route southeast of Deir ez-Zur follows the Euphrates River down to the Iraqi border, and is dotted with sites of archaeological interest. The impatient traveller with a car could visit the lot and be back in Deir ez-Zur for dinner on the same day. With a very early start, it might just be possible to do the same with a combination of microbuses and hitching.

Dura Europos تل الصالحية

The extensive, largely Hellenistic/Roman fortress city of **Dura Europos** (adult/student S£150/10) is by far the most intriguing site to visit on the road from Deir ez-Zur to Abu Kamal.

Based on earlier settlements, the Seleucids founded Europos here in around 280 BC. The town also retained the ancient Assyrian name of Dura (wall or fort), and is now known to locals as Tell Salhiye. The

DURA EUROPOS

0 _____ 200 m
0 _____ 0.1 miles

SIGHTS & ACTIVITIES	(p225)
Agora	1 B4
Bath	2 B4
Bath & Amphitheatre	3 A3
Baths	4 A3
Christian Chapel	5 A4
Houses	6 B4
Houses	7 A3
Houses & Bath	8 A4
Khan	9 A4
Military Temple	10 B3
Mithraeum	11 A3
Palace of Dux Ripae	12 A3
Redoubt Palace	13 A4
Synagogue	14 A4
Temple of Adonis	15 A4
Temple of Aphlad	16 A4
Temple of Artemis	17 B4
Temple of Atargatis	18 B4
Temple of Azzanathkona (Praetorium)	19 A3
Temple of Bel	20 A3
Temple of the Two Gads	21 B4
Temple of Zeus Dolichenus	22 A3
Temple of Zeus Kyrios	23 A4
Temple of Zeus Megistos	24 B4
Temple of Zeus Theos	25 B3

desert plateau abruptly ends in a wall of cliffs dropping 90m into the Euphrates here, making this the ideal location for a defensive installation.

In 128 BC the city fell to the Parthians and remained in their hands (although under the growing influence of Palmyra) until the Romans succeeded in integrating it into their defensive system in AD 165. As the Persian threat to Roman pre-eminence grew, so too did the importance of Dura Europos. It is famous for its reputed religious tolerance seemingly confirmed by the presence of a church, synagogue (now in the National Museum in Damascus; see p94) and other Greek, Roman and Mesopotamian temples side by side.

The Sassanian Persians seized control of the site in 256, and from then on its fortunes declined. French and Syrian archaeologists continue to work on the site.

Bring plenty of water and a hat for protection against the sun.

SIGHTS
Touring the Ruins

The western wall stands out in the stony desert 1km east of the main road; its most imposing element is the **Palmyra Gate**. You will have to deal with a gun-toting guardian here, to whom you must pay your admission fee.

Just inside the Palmyra Gate and past some houses and a bath was a Christian chapel to the right, and a synagogue to the left. The road leading towards the river from the gate passed Roman **baths** on the right, a **khan** on the left and then the site of the Greek **agora**.

Opposite the agora are the sites (little remains) of three **temples** dedicated to Artemis, Atargatis and the Two Gads. The original Greek temple to Artemis was replaced by the Parthians with a building along more oriental lines, characterised by an internal courtyard surrounded by an assortment of irregular rooms. These were added to over the years, and even included what appears to have been a small theatre for religious gatherings. In the block next door, the temple dedicated to Atargatis was built along similar lines. Precious little remains of the temple of the Two Gads, where a variety of gods were worshipped.

At the northwestern end of the city the Romans installed themselves, building barracks, baths, a small amphitheatre and a couple of small temples, one to Zeus Dolichenus. West of the **new citadel**, which commands extraordinary views over the Euphrates Valley, the Romans placed their **Palace of Dux Ripae**, built around a colonnaded courtyard of which nothing much is left.

GETTING THERE & AWAY

Any microbus between Abu Kamal and Deir ez-Zur will drop you on the highway – it takes 1½ hours to get here from Deir. Ask to be dropped off at Tell Salhiye and the site is clearly visible from the road about 1km distant.

Mari تل الحريري

The ruins of **Mari** (Tell Hariri; adult/student S£300/15), an important Mesopotamian city dating back some 5000 years, are about 10km north of Abu Kamal. The mud-brick ruins are the single greatest key serving to unlock the door on the very ancient past of Mesopotamia, but while they are fascinating for their age, they do not grab the neophyte's imagination as much as you might hope.

The most famous of Mari's ancient Syrian leaders, and about the last of its independent ones, was Zimri-Lim, who reigned in the 18th century BC and controlled the most important of the trade routes across Syria into Mesopotamia, making his city-state the object of several attacks. The Royal Palace of Zimri-Lim was enormous, measuring 200m by 120m with more than 300 rooms. Today sheltered from the elements by a modern protective roof, the palace remains the main point of interest of the whole site. The city was finally destroyed in 1758 BC by the Babylonians under Hammurabi. Before this, Mari had not only been a major commercial centre but also an artistic hothouse, to which the many fragments of ceramics and wall paintings discovered since 1933 amply attest.

Large chunks of pottery lie scattered all over the place, but most of the good stuff is on display in the museums in Aleppo and Damascus, and in the Louvre. Excavations begun in 1933, financed largely by the French, revealed two palaces (including Zimri-Lim's), five temples and the remains of a **ziggurat**, a kind of pyramidal tower peculiar to Mesopotamia and usually surmounted by a temple. Perhaps more importantly, a great many archives in Akkadian – some 25,000 clay tablets – were also discovered, providing valuable insights into the history and workings of this ancient city-state. French teams continue to work at the site.

Although attributed to Zimri-Lim, the **Royal Palace** had been around for hundreds of years by the time he came to the throne. Comprising a maze of almost 300 rooms disposed around two great courtyards, it was protected by earthen ramparts. Interpretations of what each room was used for vary. For instance, some say the room directly south of the central courtyard was a throne room, others say it was a sacred hall dedicated to a water goddess. It appears that the

AGATHA & SIR MAX

Agatha Christie's husband was Sir Max Mallowan, a noted archaeologist who in the late 1930s excavated in northeastern Syria. Between 1934 and 1939, accompanied by his already famous crime-writing wife, he spent summer seasons at Chagar Bazar, 35km north of Hassake, where they had built a mud-brick house with a beehive dome. While at Chagar Bazar, Mallowan was also digging at Tell Brak, 30km to the east, where he unearthed the remains of the so-called 'Eye Temple', the finds from which are displayed in Aleppo's National Museum. Christie spent her time here writing.

Surprisingly, given all the time spent in the country, Syria did not find its way to a starring role in any of her more famous mysteries. Instead she dreamed up *Appointment With Death*, set around Petra, where she and Mallowan had visited on one of their journeys home, and *Murder on the Orient Express*, which opens in Aleppo but then unfolds aboard the train on which Christie frequently travelled between Europe and the Middle East. The Syrian desert also features in a short story 'The Gate of Baghdad' (published as part of *Parker Pyne Investigates,* 1934), and Aleppo cameos again in *Absent in the Spring* (1944), a novel written under the pseudonym Mary Westmacott.

Her time onsite did result, however, in a substantial and humorous autobiographical work called *Come, Tell Me How You Live*. This is the tale of an archaeologist's wife, a lively account of hiring mouse-killing cats, disinterring corpses and constipation. Solving murders seems a breeze by comparison.

area to the northwest of the central courtyard served as the royal living quarters, the baths were located immediately to the right (directly north of the central courtyard).

Just to the southeast of the palace complex are the ziggurat and several temples. A temple to Ishtar stood to the west of the palace.

GETTING THERE & AWAY

There is a microbus from Abu Kamal that goes right by Mari. It leaves from a side street east of the square and takes about half an hour by a circuitous route (S£10). Alternatively, if you are coming from Deir ez-Zur, buses will drop you at the turn-off from the highway (ask for Tell Hariri). From this same spot it is normally possible to hitch a ride or pick up a passing microbus for the return trip to Deir ez-Zur.

THE NORTHEAST

Bordered by Turkey and Iraq, there are no major monuments or must-see sites in the northeastern corner of the country, but this does not mean it is empty of attractions. Perhaps the greatest is the chance to meet the Kurds, a people without a state, who have yet to give up their struggle. Only about one million of a total of some 20 million Kurds live in Syria. The rest are spread across southeastern Turkey, northern Iraq and northwestern Iran.

The area between the Kabur and Tigris Rivers, also known as the Jezira, is an increasingly rich agricultural zone, helped along by underground aquifers and the irrigation schemes born of the Lake al-Assad project on the Euphrates to the west.

The numerous tells dotted around the place are a sign that this area has been inhabited since the 3rd millennium BC, its mainstay being the wheat and cotton crops that still predominate. These tells are increasingly attracting archaeological teams and although there is generally precious little for the uninitiated to see, you can visit the sites so long as you respect the teams' work. They are generally present in spring and summer. **Tell Brak**, 45km northeast of Hassake, was excavated under the direction of Max Mallowan (see the boxed text Agatha & Sir Max, above).

Ras al-Ain أس العين

There's not a lot to this largely Kurdish town on the Turkish border (you cannot cross into Turkey here), but there is a chance you'll be invited to eat with the locals. Don't be surprised if the subject of conversation turns to politics. The Kurds are not much more pleased with their position in Syria than elsewhere. In summer the attraction is the restaurant in the main park (near the road to Hassake), where they set the tables in the shin-deep water from nearby sulphur springs. You cool your heels as you eat.

Three kilometres away is **Tell Halaf**, the site of an ancient northern Mesopotamian settlement discovered in 1899 by Baron Max von Oppenheim, a Prussian engineer overseeing the construction of the much trumpeted Berlin–Baghdad railway. Although plenty more artefacts are said by locals to be buried here, you'll see nothing other than a bald artificial hill. The bulk of what was found went to Berlin and was destroyed in WWII. Replicas were made of some artefacts and can be seen at Aleppo's National Museum (p183), including the giant basalt statues at its entrance.

GETTING THERE & AWAY

The microbus from Hassake, about 75km away, takes about 1½ hours and costs S£45. No public transport returns in the afternoon, especially on Friday and holidays; other than this you should be OK until 4pm.

Qamishle القامشلي

Situated at a crossing point on the Turkish border in the northeast, Qamishle is full of Kurds and Turks and the cheaper hotels will sometimes quote prices in Turkish lire rather than Syrian pounds.

There is nothing to see in Qamishle, but the mix of people makes it an intriguing spot. Because of its proximity to the border, be prepared for passport checks at the hotels and when getting on or off buses or trains.

The Turkish border is only about 1km from the town centre. Note, you cannot drive across the border here but must walk. Once on the other side, it's a further five minutes' walk into Nusaybin, the town on the Turkish side, where it's possible to pick up a *dolmuš* (minibus) for onward travel. The crossing is open only from 9am to 3pm.

SLEEPING & EATING

Hotel Semiramis (☎ 421 185; s/d/tr US$15/22/24) About 100m south of the microbus station, this is the town's top establishment. It's a two-star place with clean rooms with fans (foreigners prices quoted). Expatriate workers in the oilfields often stay here.

Chahba Hotel (beds S£100) Just around the corner from Hotel Semiramis, Chahba is certainly nothing to write home about. The

upstairs terrace is OK, though. Women must take a double room.

Marmar (s/d S£300/400) A block south of the Chahba, this place is better value while being a tad more expensive. The rooms featuring balconies are quite good, and there is hot water.

Hadaya Hotel (☎ 420 141; Sharia al-Wahida; s/d US$15/22) On the street which crosses the northern end of the main drag, this is not exactly the friendliest place on earth, and the rooms are certainly nothing special either. Given that there's not much choice in town it might make a good last resort if the others are full.

Across from the Chahba is a pleasant **restaurant** (meals about S£200) with an outdoor section, where you can get a good meal of kebabs and the usual side orders of hummus, *foul* (fava bean paste) and other mezze.

GETTING THERE & AWAY
Air
The airport is 2km south of town. Take a taxi or any Hassake-bound bus. The SyrianAir office is just off the main street, two blocks south of the Semiramis. There are three flights a week to Damascus (S£1200).

Bus
Pullmans and more expensive private companies operate buses from Qamishle to most major destinations. The better buses run from a station opposite the Gabriel Restaurant, southeast along Sharia Zaki al-Arsuzi, the street that runs beside the river. The trip to Damascus takes up to 10 hours and costs around S£340. For Aleppo, reckon on at least six to eight hours and S£175. More rickety buses do the same trips from another station and cost as little as S£150 and S£90 respectively.

Microbus
The microbus station is on the main street, 100m north of the Semiramis. There are departures for Hassake, Ras al-Ain and Al-Malkyer in the east.

Train
The train station is a long way from the town centre, and you'll have to catch a taxi. There is, however, a **booking office** (⊗ 8.30am-3pm & 4.30-6pm) in the centre, virtually opposite Chahba Hotel. Up to three trains go as far

as Aleppo (1st/2nd class S£132/87, S£350 for a sleeper), and one or two proceed all the way to Damascus (S£200/135 and S£560 respectively). The Damascus train, calling at all stops along the line, can take from 16 to 19 hours.

Ain Diwar   عين ديوار

In the extreme northeast corner of the country is an impressive medieval bridge over the Tigris. Unfortunately, relations between Turkey and Syria are not brilliant, and a Syrian border garrison may stop you from getting out to it – they say because the Turkish border troops tend to shoot first and ask questions later. You may have guessed that there is no border crossing here.

There are great views from the plateau (which may be as far as you can safely get), which overlooks the Tigris, northeast to the snowcapped mountains of southern Turkey and east to Jebel Zakho in Iraq (some locals call it Jebel Barzani, after one of the rebel Kurdish leaders there). On a clear day, you might just make out mountains in Iran through the gap between Jebel Zakho and the Turkish ranges.

If you want to try your luck, take a microbus from Qamishle to Al-Malkye (S£45, two hours). From there, negotiate with one of the kids to take you out on a motorbike, or just hitch. Bear in mind that there is not much traffic on this last stretch of road.

Lebanon

BETHUNE CARMICHAEL

Lebanon لبنان

LEBANON

LEBANON

0 — 20 km
0 — 12 miles

SYRIA

MEDITERRANEAN SEA

LEBANON

To Lattakia (90km)
To Krak des Chevaliers (10km)

Homs
Amrit
Aabboudiye
Aarida
Nahr al-Kabir
Quobayet
Lake Qattinah
Tell Nabi Mend
Halba
Akkar al-Atiqa
Charbiné
Al-Mina
Qubbet al-Baddawi
Nahr Abu Moussa
Tripoli (Trablous)
Qalamoun
Enfe
Zgharta
Hermel
Deir Mar Maroun
Hermel Pyramid
Balamand
Chekka
Amioun
Nahr Abu Ali
Horsh Ehden Nature Reserve
Qornet as-Sawda (3090m)
Al-Qaa
Qubba
Ehden
Batroun
Bcharré
Al-Ain
Rachana
Barzaoun & Hasroun
Douma
The Cedars
Mt Lebanon Range
Nahr al-Aasi (Orontes River)
Amchit
Laklouk
Bekaa Valley
Byblos (Jbail)
Aaqoura
Mashnaqa
Qartaba
Nahr Ibrahim
Qanat Bakiche
Fiqra
Faraya Mzaar
Talat Musa (2659m)
Jounieh
Ajaltoun
▲ Jebel Sannine (2628m)
Baalbek
ANTI-LEBANON RANGE
Jeita Grotto
Bikfaya
Baskinta
Niha
BEIRUT
Beit Mary
Zaarour
Broummana
Furzol
Aabadiye
Chtaura
Zahle
Rayak
Baabda
Qabb Elias
SYRIA
Damour
Deir al-Qamar
Aanjar
Baaqline
Beiteddine
Masnaa
Moukhtara
Majdel Aanjar
Joun
Chouf Cedar Reserve
Sidon (Saida)
Nahr al-Awali
Temple of Echmoun
Lake Qaraoun
Ghaziye
Maghdouche
Jezzine
DAMASCUS
Sarafand
Nahr Litani
Qatana
Nabatiye
Hasbaya
▲ Jebel ash-Sheikh (Mt Hermon) (2814m)
Marjeyun
Beaufort Castle
Khiam
Tyre (Sour)
Tomb of Hiram
Area Administered by Syria Under UN Supervision
Qana
Kiryat Shmona
Mansoura
Quneitra
Jordan River
Bint Jbayl
Golan Heights
Nahariya

ISRAEL & THE PALESTINIAN TERRITORIES

To Haifa; Tel Aviv; Jerusalem
To Jerusalem
To Jerusalem
To Der'a; Ramtha; Amman

Snapshot Lebanon

Converse with the Lebanese about the current state of Lebanon and the talk inevitably – and swiftly – turns to politics and economics. With the USA breathing down Syria's neck, a contentious wall being built next door in the Occupied Palestinian Territories (or Israel, depending on your sympathies), an increasingly radical Islam, and Palestinian refugee camps in Lebanon on a war footing against assassination attempts, the issue most Lebanese want to discuss is…jobs.

The unemployment rate is around 20%, so it's not surprising that making a living is a key topic of conversation, along with how the government is handling this problem. On the surface it would seem that the government's response amounts to little more than public bickering between President Émile Lahoud and Prime Minister Rafiq Hariri about issues of public spending and privatisation. While Hariri – whose shares in Solideré (see p248) and ownership of a newspaper and television station would make many a Western politician blush – is all for privatisation, Lahoud sees himself as the guardian of public assets.

The issue of the sale of assets is tied to loans that Lebanon was promised at the 'Paris II' donor conference. The privatisation program was intended to reduce Lebanon's public debt, standing at a not insubstantial US$32 billion; that it is has not proceeded as quickly as planned is raising eyebrows at both the World Bank and the International Monetary Fund (IMF). And while this difference of opinion between Lahoud and Hariri may appear to be ideological, it's also very personal. Lahoud sacked Hariri in 1988, but Hariri returned two years later and their frosty relationship sets the scene for a showdown ahead of the November 2004 presidential elections.

Another factor also comes into play here: Syria. The level of Syrian jurisdiction over Lebanon's politics is the source of much debate, and most analysts agree that there won't be a Lebanese president elected without a Syrian nod of the head. President George W Bush's signing off economic and diplomatic sanctions against Syria, the increasing pressure on Syria to clamp down on its perceived inability to stop 'terrorists' crossing over the border into Iraq, as well as its ignoring the frequent cross-border Hezbollah-Israeli confrontations from inside Lebanon's borders, will all have serious implications for Lebanon.

The 'war against terror' has caused increasing instability in the region. Even so, more Arab tourists than ever are enjoying Lebanon's hospitality. In a world where wearing the traditional Arab headdress has become an invitation to be fingerprinted and photographed by customs, tourists to Lebanon from Kuwait, the United Arab Emirates and Saudi Arabia have risen steadily since the attacks on 11 September 2001.

Unfortunately, passing these arrivals at the airport are the future members of Lebanon's diaspora. While it has become increasingly hard for Lebanese to even get near the US embassy, let alone obtain a Green Card, the economic situation still sees many of Lebanon's best and brightest making a beeline overseas, seeking a better financial return for their qualifications. Nevertheless, students are protesting about the economic and political situation, and university funding.

Lebanon faces an uncertain future, as does the whole of the Middle East. Still, one thing is certain: the Lebanese people are well used to rebounding after periods of uncertainty and strife.

FAST FACTS

Total population: around 4.4 million

Inflation: 3.5%

GDP per capita: US$4078

Unemployment rate: around 20%

Number of 'foreign workers': around one million

Population below poverty line: 28%

Average age: 26

Number of Lebanese living overseas: 10 million

Estimated number of migrants during civil war: 500,000

Lebanon might be only 85km wide, but it sports a whopping 225km-long coastline

Beirut بيروت

While Beirut may well be the capital of Lebanon, its inhabitants appear hellbent on restoring its title as party capital of the Middle East. As pretenders to the throne (such as Dubai) sought to steal its crown, Beirut shook off the cement dust after a long and vicious civil war and immediately resumed work on perfecting the art of living the good life.

Even the shortest stay in the capital, however, will reveal the enormous contrasts and contradictions that make up the unique fabric of everyday life in Beirut. In Achrafiye, beautifully restored apartment blocks stand next to shelled-out buildings – with both structures equally occupied. Carefully coiffured, mobile-phone wielding Mercedes drivers battle the tyre-squealing, horn-honking traffic chaos alongside rusted, smoke-belching Mercedes taxis of a much earlier vintage. While drinking in the hippest of the Rue Monot bars, the power will go off, lights and music stop, but conversations barely miss a beat and the drinks continue to flow courtesy of some well-placed candles.

Nevertheless, Beirutis don't seem overly concerned about this. In other countries the former Green Line would be a solemn reminder of those who lost their lives in the war. Beirutis turned a section of it into the hottest clubbing street in the Middle East. True to their long-standing reputation, Beirutis are doing their utmost to put the recent past behind them by eating well, partying hard and generally enjoying life, giving the place a buzz that is absent from almost every other city in the region.

BEIRUT

HIGHLIGHTS

- Take part in a Beirut ritual with a leisurely afternoon stroll on the **Corniche** (p246)
- Follow it up with a nargileh break at a café overlooking **Pigeon Rocks** (p247)
- Enjoy the reborn and tastefully reconstructed centre of the **Downtown area** (p247)
- Experience 6000 years of history in a couple of hours at the **National Museum of Beirut** (p242)
- Follow Beirut's young and beautiful into one of **Rue Monot's** (p263) hot clubs
- Work your way though the mezze menu of one of the city's best **restaurants** (p256)

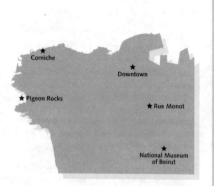

- TELEPHONE CODE: 01
- POPULATION: 1.2 MILLION

HISTORY

The earliest traces of habitation in Beirut date from the Stone Age when the area now occupied by the city was in fact two islands in the delta of the Beirut River. Later, when the river silted up, the area became one land mass. Excavations between Place des Martyrs and the port revealed a Canaanite site dating from 1900 BC. This Bronze Age city has an entrance gate of dressed stone, and nearby are the remains of Phoenician canals with sloping sides.

The first historical reference to Beirut dates from the 14th century BC, when it is mentioned in tablets with cuneiform script discovered at Tell al-Amarna in Egypt. The tablets were letters from the Canaanite king of Beirut asking the pharaoh Akhenaten for military assistance.

The original name of the city seems to have been variously Birut, Birrayyuna or Birrayat, which suggests that it was named after a well or wells (modern Arabic still uses the word *bir* for well). On the other hand, according to Philo in his *History*, Birut was the first queen of the city.

In Phoenician times, Beirut appears to have been overshadowed by Sidon, Tyre and Byblos. After Alexander the Great's conquest it is mentioned in Hellenistic sources, and excavations have revealed an extensive Hellenistic city upon which the later Roman grid was based.

It was during the Roman period that the city came into its own; the city quickly became 'Romanised' and large public buildings and monuments were erected.

In the 3rd century AD the city found fame and prestige through its School of Law, which rivalled those in Athens, Alexandria and Caesarea. The basis of the famous Justinian Code, upon which the Western legal system drew inspiration, was established. The city's importance as a centre of learning and commercial hub continued as the Roman Empire gave way to the Byzantine, and Beirut became the seat of a bishopric. In the middle of the 5th century, a series of devastating earthquakes and tidal waves almost destroyed the city and the death toll was high. The School of Law was evacuated and moved to Sidon. This calamity marked the decline of the city for centuries to come.

The Arabs came in AD 635 and took the city without much of a struggle. Their rule was uninterrupted until AD 1110 when, after a long siege, the city fell into the hands of Baldwin I of Boulogne and a Latin bishopric was established.

Beirut remained in Crusader hands for 77 years, during which time the Crusaders built the Church of St John the Baptist of the Knights Hospitallers on the site of an ancient temple (now the Al-Omari Mosque). In 1187 Saladin (Salah ad-Din) managed to wrest the city back into Muslim hands, however, he was only able to hold on to it for six years before Amoury, King of Cyprus, besieged the city once again and the Muslim forces fled. Under the rule of Jean I of Ibelin, the city's influence grew and spread throughout the Latin East, but the Crusaders lost the city again, this time for good, in July 1291 when the Muslim Mamluks took possession.

The Mamluks remained in control of Beirut until they were ousted from the city by the Ottoman army in 1516. Once part of the powerful Ottoman Empire, the city was granted semi-autonomy in return for taxes paid to the sultan. One of the emirs, Fakhreddine (Fakhr ad-Din al-Maan II), established what was in effect an independent kingdom for himself and made Beirut his favourite residence (for more information, see the boxed text Fakhreddine, p294). Fakhreddine's keen business sense led him to trade with the European powers, most notably the Venetians, and Beirut began to recover economically and regain some of its former prestige.

The 18th century presented mixed fortunes for the city. Emir Bashir Shihab II (1788–1840) injected new vigour into the city, renewing its prosperity and stability once again. However, in 1832, he entered into an alliance with Ibrahim Pasha, son of the rebellious Mohammed Ali of Egypt. Mohammed Ali's threat to the Ottoman Empire, and by extension the balance of power with Europe, alarmed the British and in 1840 the city was bombarded and subsequently recaptured for the Ottomans by the combined Anglo-Austro-Turkish fleet.

The population of Beirut at that time was only 45,000, but the booming silk trade and influx of Maronites fleeing from massacres in the Chouf Mountains and Damascus meant that the numbers doubled during the following 20 years. This was the start of the

THE REBUILDING OF CENTRAL BEIRUT

Repairing the catastrophic damage to Beirut's Central District (BCD) was one of the greatest challenges facing the government in the aftermath of the civil war. Redevelopment had a symbolic as well as a practical purpose: by re-creating the area associated with Lebanon's past prosperity the country was signalling that it was once again open for business.

In 1992 the Lebanese parliament, headed by Prime Minister Rafiq Hariri, formed the Lebanese Company for the Development and Reconstruction of the BCD, known by its French name, Solideré, a joint stock company in which pre-existing property owners were majority shareholders.

While seemingly a straightforward task, the legalities related to sorting out just who were the pre-existing property owners proved problematic. In one case, there were 4700 claimants to a single plot of land in the souq area. The solution was to give everyone with some sort of legal claim shares in Solideré equal to the value of their property holding. Altogether the value of the claimants' shares was some US$1.7 billion.

Solideré was to carry out all infrastructure projects and restore more than 200 Ottoman and French Mandate–period buildings. In return for this, Solideré itself would get some 1650 real-estate lots, worth around US$1.17 billion, in addition to investment from the state and private investors. Solideré also had to cooperate with archaeologists, handing over the excavation of archaeological sites as they were uncovered. To this end, there has been some criticism of Solideré by archaeologists who feel that Solideré has not found the right balance between historical and financial concerns.

Many say that Solideré grossly underestimated land values when distributing shares to property owners, pulling off a massive land-grab at their expense. Others criticise the project's largest stakeholder, Prime Minister Hariri, as having a conflict of interest between the project and his political position. The restoration of the old souq areas has been significantly delayed, with formal approval only coming in late 2003. With rents in the downtown area rivalling those in Paris or New York, the area has also seen a significant turnover of businesses, especially restaurants. In addition to this, many of the area's best restaurants lost a significant number of patrons with the temporary removal of the popular outdoor seating area overlooking the cardo maximus. Many find the area created by Solideré a little 'Disneyesque' and as having no real soul.

Despite the controversy, even the staunchest critics of the project have to concede that relaxing in one of the busy cafés or restaurants that line the pedestrian area of BCD has fast become a must for any visitor to Beirut.

commercial boom that resulted in Beirut being transformed from a backwater into a commercial powerhouse. It was also the beginning of European meddling in Lebanon. The massacres of the Maronites resulted in French troops landing in Beirut and ties with Europe grew in the coming decades. In 1866 Syrian and American missionaries founded the Syrian Protestant College, now known as the American University of Beirut (AUB; see p246 for details), which became one of the most prestigious universities in the Middle East.

During WWI, Beirut suffered a blockade by the Allies, which was intended to starve out the Turks. This, combined with a series of natural disasters, resulted in widespread famine, followed by plague, which killed more than a quarter of the population. A revolt broke out against the Turks and resulted in the mass hanging of the rebel leaders in what became known as the Place des Martyrs.

WWI ended Turkish rule and on 8 October 1918 the British army, including a French detachment, arrived in Beirut; on 25 April 1920 the League of Nations granted a French mandate over Lebanon (and Syria), and Beirut became the capital of the state of Greater Lebanon.

During WWII Beirut was occupied by the Allies and, thanks to its port, became an important supply centre. In 1946 the French left the city, and subsequently Beirut became one of the main commercial and banking centres of the Middle East. The 1948 Arab-Israeli War resulted in huge numbers of Palestinian refugees settling in refugee camps in the south of Beirut, where, despite massacres and great poverty, they still live today.

Beirut was the epicentre of anarchy during the civil war. The city was ruled, area-by-area, by militias loyal to one of various factions and the infamous Green Line tore the city into Christian and Muslim halves. Continual intercommunal fighting between militias, combined with shelling from Israeli fighter planes, devastated the city. The human casualties were enormous and the effect on the economy was catastrophic. By 1991 the Green Line was dismantled and while most of the physical scars have faded, the psychological scars are taking longer to heal.

The post-war government faced a daunting task in repairing the country's destroyed infrastructure. The jewel in the crown of reconstruction in Lebanon is the Beirut Central District or BCD (see the boxed text, The Rebuilding of Central Beirut, opposite, for details). While the recent economic downturn slowed progress in the last couple of years, the work has uncovered more archaeological sites, providing yet another link for Beirut to its long history.

ORIENTATION

Geographically, Beirut is actually an easy city to navigate as there are strategically located landmarks (for some good directions see the boxed text Navigating Beirut, below). There's a promontory bound by the Mediterranean Sea on the north and west coast (the headland of the promontory has dramatic cliffs falling away into the sea, while to the south the coast gives way to a sandy beach). In the west of the city, the land is very hilly, flattening out as you travel east.

For most visitors to Beirut, the Hamra district will be the hub of the city as it contains the lion's share of the city's budget and mid-range accommodation. This is where you'll find the Ministry of Tourism, major banks, travel agents and airline offices, all within walking distance of each other. Heading south from Hamra is the area commonly known as Verdun, full of high-rise apartments, and home to Beirut's upmarket shopping malls and designer clothing outlets located along Rue Verdun.

Southwest from Hamra is the Raouché area, home to Pigeon Rocks, and heading clockwise around the coastline is Ras Beirut, home of the American University of Beirut (AUB) campus. Prior to the war, both Ras Beirut and Hamra were bases for the liberal-thinking intelligentsia and artistic communities.

The newly rebuilt BCD, also called Downtown or Solidere, is the symbolic heart of the city. Further southeast is the increasingly gentrified area of Gemmayzeh and the Charles Helou bus station. Heading south (and uphill) from here is Achrafiye, with its busy restaurants, bars and nightclubs.

Affluent areas, such as Achrafiye, which have been massively reconstructed, are worlds away from those in the city's south, where the Cola transport hub, the National Museum of Beirut and, further on, the infamous Palestinian camps of Sabra-Shatila and Burj al-Barajnah are found.

NAVIGATING BEIRUT

Easy as this is to follow on a map, navigating your way around Beirut's streets can be tricky as many of the street signs are incomplete or nonexistent. The blue street signs, located on the corner buildings of each street, often only show the sector (suburb) name, sector number, and rue (street) number, with the rue name missing. Compounding this, numbered buildings are rare and often the street names are different from the name they're known as locally. When giving directions, Beirutis often launch into complicated explanations involving local landmarks or sector names that you might not be familiar with. Buildings are often known either by the name of their owner or by their function (eg the British Bank building). This sounds more confusing than it actually is and, luckily, Beirut is a manageable size so you can't get too far off track. When walking, it's advisable to use a detailed map (for more information see Maps, p239) and check every couple of streets that you're still on track. If taking a taxi (as opposed to a service taxi – see p266 for details of the differences between the two types) to a specific destination, a good tip is to have the telephone number of the destination handy and get the taxi driver to telephone and confirm the directions. If the taxi driver is not familiar with the destination and doesn't have a mobile phone, it's better to take another taxi.

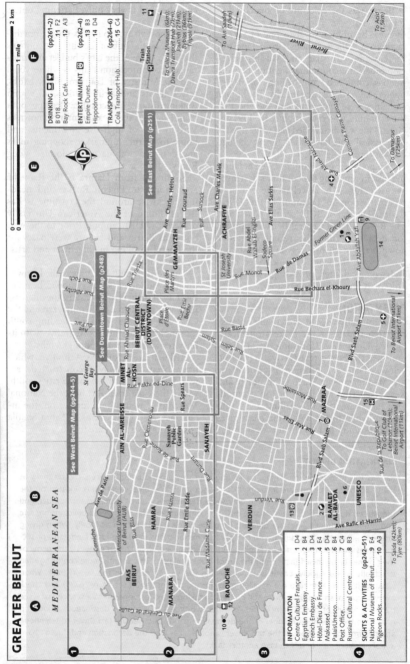

Maps

The best map of Beirut is published by GEO Projects in English, Arabic and French, and is available from major bookshops in Beirut. It publishes a dedicated Beirut map and a larger Lebanon map with one side featuring Beirut. The map of Beirut is the same scale on both maps. Be sure to get the latest edition, which at the time of writing was 2002, and keep in mind that the English version has translated the street names from French into English (eg Rue de Damas becomes Damascus St), which can be a little confusing. There is also a commercial map, published by **All Prints** (Map pp244-5; ☎ 342 009; Rue Jeanne d'Arc, Hamra), which has a good city map of Beirut on the reverse. English and French versions are available. The free map of Beirut from the **Ministry of Tourism** (Map pp244-5; ☎ 343 073; www.lebanon -tourism.gov.lb; Ground fl, 550 Rue Banque du Liban, Hamra) is also useful.

INFORMATION
Bookshops

Stocked with academic books, dictionaries, novels, travel guides and European newspapers, Beirut has a good selection of foreign-language bookshops.

All Prints (Map pp244-5; ☎ 342 009; Rue Jeanne d'Arc, Hamra)

Bookland Bookshop (Map p251; ☎ 612 345; Sodeco Square, Achrafiye)

Books & Pens (Map pp244-5; ☎ 741 975; Rue Jeanne d'Arc, Hamra) Also has extensive art supplies and stationery.

Librairie Antoine Hamra (Map pp244-5; ☎ 341 470; Rue Hamra); Achrafiye (Map p251; ☎ 331 811; Ave Elias Sarkis); Dunes Centre (Map p238; ☎ 794 950; Rue Verdun; Verdun)

Librairie International (Map pp244-5; ☎ 743 285; Block D, Gefinor Center, Rue Maamari, Hamra) Stocks many Middle Eastern political titles.

Virgin Megastore (Map p248; ☎ 999 666; Opera Bldg, Downtown) Good range of French and English titles.

Cultural Centres

The listed cultural centres are very active in Beirut, often staging art and photography exhibitions, film festivals, plays, as well as musical events, highlighting work from their respective countries. Check for details in the press, their websites or by phoning them to see what's on.

British Council (Map pp244-5; ☎ 740 123/4/5; www .britishcouncil.org/lebanon; Azzar Bldg, Rue Sadat, Ras Beirut)

Centre Culturel Français (Map p238; ☎ 615 859; Espace Des Lettres, Rue de Damas) Near the National Museum of Beirut.

Goethe Institut (Map pp244-5; ☎ 740 524; www .goethe.de/beirut; Gideon Bldg, Rue Bliss, Manara)

Instituto Cervantes (Map p248; ☎ 347 755; www .cervantes.es; Rue al Maarad, Downtown)

Italian Cultural Institute (Map pp244-5; ☎ 749 801; www.iicbeirut.org; 2nd fl, Najjar Bldg, Rue de Rome)

PalaisUnesco (Map p238; ☎ 786 680, 786 584; www .palaisunesco.gov.lb; Unesco)

BEIRUT IN...

Two Days

Start your day with a shot of Turkish coffee and a pastry on **Rue Bliss** (p259) with the AUB students. Then head for the must-see **National Museum of Beirut** (p242) before walking along the former **Green Line** (p242) to the **Downtown** (p247) area for lunch.

Late afternoon, take a stroll along the **Corniche** (p246), timing it for a sunset drink/nargileh at the **Bay Rock Café** (p259), overlooking **Pigeon Rocks** (p247).

Rest up, because your dinner reservation in **Achrafiye** (p257) or **Gemmayzeh** (p258) isn't until 9pm. After dinner, head to **Rue Monot** (p263) for the bars and clubs.

Start day two with lunch at **Casablanca** (p257) or if you overspent at the clubs, grab a hangover-curing manaeesh bi-zaatar from **Zaatar w Zeit** (p260).

Clothes shoppers should head to the **Dunes Centre** (p264), while others may opt for a walk around **Achrafiye** (Map p251) admiring the architecture. For a different night, head either to the **Blue Note** (p263) for some jazz, or the **Gemmayzeh Café** (p263) for some live oud (lute) music.

Four Days

Follow the two-day itinerary, then on day three, head to **Baalbek** (p327) for the superlative Roman ruins, visiting the **Ksara Winery** (p324) on the way back. Day four, take a trip to the ancient site of **Byblos** (p280) for the ruins or just lunch at the **Byblos Fishing Club** (p285).

BEIRUT

Russian Cultural Centre (Map p238; ☎ 790 212; Rue Verdun, Unesco)

Emergency

Ambulance ☎ 140
Fire Brigade ☎ 175
Police ☎ 112
Tourist Police ☎ 350 901

Immigration Office

General Security Office (Map pp244-5; Rue Spears; ✆ 8am-1pm Mon-Thu, 8-10am Fri, 8am-noon Sat, closed Sun)

Internet Access

Beirut is blessed with a large number of Internet cafés, many clustered around the **AUB campus** (p246). Unfortunately, Beirut is not blessed with antismoking laws, so an hour or so in many of the cafés will have you smelling like you've been out clubbing. Like many businesses in Beirut, café opening times can vary and cafés regularly open later or shut earlier than advertised. Generally, Internet speed is slow to middling, but here is a selection of the quicker and more reliable cafés in town.

Images Computer Services (Map p251; ☎ 338 933; Rue Lebanon, Achrafiye; per hr LL2000; ✆ 8.30am-10pm Mon-Fri, 8.30am-8pm Sat) Rates are competitive.

Momento Internet Café (Map pp244-5; ☎ 740 157; Rue Labban, Hamra; per hr LL3000; ✆ 7-2am) One of the best-organised cafés, in a large space with plenty of terminals. There's another branch in Downtown that charges LL6000.

Net (Map pp244-5; ☎ 740 157; Rue Mahatma Gandhi, Hamra; per hr LL3000; ✆ 9-1am) Just down from PC Club.

PC Club (Map pp244-5; ☎ 740 382; Rue Mahatma Gandhi, Hamra; per hr LL3000; ✆ 24hr) A student hang-out, thankfully with a separate games room.

Santa Computer (Map p251; ☎ 446 275; Rue Gouraud, Gemmayzeh; per hr LL2000; ✆ 9.30am-midnight) Handy to the Gouraud restaurant area.

Virgin Café (Map p248; ☎ 999 777; Opera Bldg, Downtown; per hr LL3000; ✆ noon-midnight) The most pleasant place to check your email in Beirut. Full café menu available, including alcohol. See also Virgin Megastore (p239).

Web Café (Map pp244-5; ☎ 348 880; Rue Khalidi, Ras Beirut; per hr LL4000; ✆ 9am-midnight) Plenty of terminals and good coffee.

Internet Resources

Cyberia (www.thisiscyberia.com) One of Lebanon's main Internet service providers (ISPs) and its 'portal' website is a great resource for events, cinema screening times, live music and museum details for Beirut.

Daily Star (www.dailystar.com.lb) Doesn't deliver the same content as the print edition of Beirut's high-quality English-language newspaper – it's heavy on editorial and opinion and light on 'what's on' info – but hey, it's free. If you find you really can't live without the features of the print edition, the paper now has an online subscription.

L'Orient Le Jour (www.lorientlejour.com) Makes a good fist of putting helpful information online from its print version newspaper and it's a good resource for Francophiles to see what's on in Beirut.

Monot Street (http://monotstreet.com) A website dedicated to the nightlife on Rue Monot, Beirut's party street. Besides listing the bars/pubs/clubs that are situated around Monot, it features details on DJs and new music releases.

Vibe Lebanon (http://vibelebanon.com) Follows on nicely from the Monot Street website with its Internet radio station playing the same tracks you'll hear on a night out! Besides the music-related info, it also has movie reviews and information.

Laundry

It's a good idea to pack that portable clothesline for Beirut as there are no self-service laundromats. Hotels and dry-cleaners will do laundry, but it can get expensive as they charge per piece (LL2000).

Media

The *Daily Star*, Lebanon's high-quality English-language daily newspaper, is now bundled with the *International Herald Tribune*. The newspaper has two sections, a Middle East and a Lebanon section with particularly good editorials and opinions, as well as features on Beirut, with a movie guide and gallery exhibition listings.

L'Orient-le Jour is the *Daily Star*'s French equivalent; it has up-to-date listings for local cinema and theatre performances.

The *Guide* is an extremely useful glossy monthly with extensive but selective listings of bars, cafés, restaurants, shops, films, theatres and other cultural events.

Medical Services

All medical services (including ambulances) have to be paid for. If you require medical assistance but do not need an ambulance, take a taxi to one of the hospitals listed.

American University of Beirut Hospital (Map pp244-5; ☎ 350 000, 374 374; Rue du Caire) Generally regarded as the best choice.

Hôtel-Dieu de France (Map p238; ☎ 615 300; Rue Hôtel-Dieu, Hôtel-Dieu)

Makassed (Map p238; ☎ 646 590; Rue Tariq al-Jedide, Ouzai) Near the Hippodrome.

Rizk (Map p251; ☎ 200 800; Rue Zahar, Achrafiye)
St George's Greek Hospital (Map p251; ☎ 585 700; Achrafiye) Known locally as 'Roum'.

Pharmacies

Berty (☎ 330 033; Achrafiye) A late-night pharmacy.
Mazen Pharmacy (☎ 313 362; Blvd Saeb Salam; ☉ 24hr daily) Almost opposite the post office. It offers a delivery service to 8pm; you simply telephone your order through and pay on delivery. The pharmacist speaks English and French and can advise you on what drugs you may need.
Wardieh Pharmacy (☎ 330 033) Another pharmacy offering free 24-hour home delivery.

Money

There are ATMs dispensing both US dollars and Lebanese lira outside banks everywhere around the city and this is definitely the easiest way to access cash. There are several moneychangers located on Rue Hamra between Rue du Caire and Rue Jeanne d'Arc.

Other banks and moneychangers around the city:

Abou al-Nasr Bassatni Est (Map pp244-5; ☎ 748 328; Rue Omar ben Abdel Aziz, Hamra) One of the most conveniently located moneychangers. Like most moneychangers in Hamra, its opening hours vary.
Amex (Map pp244-5; ☎ 749 574/5/6; 1st fl, Block C, Gefinor Center, Rue Maamari, Hamra; ☉ 9am-4pm Mon-Fri, 8.30am-1.30pm Sat) The actual office will replace cards if they've been stolen and will give cash advances on some, but not all, types of its card. It won't change travellers cheques, though. Your only other option when it comes to changing these is to go to a moneychanger.
Banque Libano-Français (Map pp244-5; Ground fl, Block A, Gefinor Center, Rue Maamari, Hamra) Opposite the Sogetour office. If you need to organise an over-the-counter cash advance against your Visa card or MasterCard, then it will oblige if you have a passport to prove your identity.
Sogetour (Map pp244-5; ☎ 747 111; Ground fl, Block A, Gefinor Center, Rue Maamari, Hamra; ☉ 8.30am-4pm Mon-Fri, 8.30am-1pm Sat) The best place in Beirut to exchange Amex travellers cheques in US dollars. It charges a 2% commission.

Post

DHL (Map p248; Rue Emir Bechir, Downtown)
Federal Express (☎ 345 385; Chaker Oueni Bldg, Riad El Solh Square, Downtown)
LibanPost (Map pp244-5; 2nd fl, Matta Bldg, Rue Makdissi, Hamra; ☉ 8am-5pm Mon-Fri, 8am-1pm Sat) This place is a little hard to find and the entrance is not clearly signposted – look for the Embassy Hotel opposite it. It offers the usual services including a poste restante service.

Main Post Office (Map p248; Rue Fakhr ed-Dine, Minet al-Hosn; ☉ 8am-5pm Mon-Fri, 8am-1pm Sat) Currently situated just up the road from Hotel Monroe (within walking distance of both Hamra and Downtown) while the main office on Rue Riad El Solh undergoes an extended restoration. There is also a private **post office** (Map pp244-5; ☉ 8am-4pm Mon-Fri) at the AUB.

Telephone & Fax

There is a government-run **telephone office** (Map pp244-5; ☉ 7.30am-11pm Mon-Thu & Sat, 7.30-11am Fri; Rue Banque du Liban, Hamra) in the Ministry of Tourism building in Hamra. To make a call, you go to the counter and fill in a slip of paper with the country and number you want and wait to be directed to a booth. You pay when you have finished your call.

There are several private telephone offices located on Rue Bliss and on Rue Jeanne d'Arc, near the AUB campus. These operate on a similar system as the government one, although their rates are a bit more expensive. Many of these offer fax facilities as well. An alternative is to use the large hotel business centres; these tend to be frighteningly expensive but are often open 24 hours.

Tourist Information

Beirut's **tourist information office** (Map pp244-5; ☎ 343 073; www.lebanon-tourism.gov.lb; Ground fl, 550 Rue Banque du Liban, Hamra; ☉ 8.30am-2pm Mon-Thu, 8.30-11.30am Fri, 8.30am-12.30pm Sat) is on the ground floor of the office block housing the Ministry of Tourism, on Rue Banque du Liban (an extension of Rue Hamra and Rue de Rome). Enter from Rue Banque du Liban through the covered arcade that runs under the building. The office has a series of brochures on the main archaeological and tourist sites of Lebanon in English, French and Arabic. It's advisable to take brochures for the sites you plan to visit as sometimes there aren't any brochures available at the sites. The office also has some maps and often stocks the local bus timetables. The English-speaking staff can advise you about accommodation options.

If you are unfortunate enough to be robbed, contact the **tourist police office** (Map pp244-5; ☎ 350 901; Rue Banque du Liban, Hamra), located on the opposite side of the covered arcade.

Travel Agencies

There are travel agents all over Beirut. We've listed overleaf a couple of the more long-standing travel agents around town.

Campus Travel (☎ 744 588; www.campus-travel.net; Maktabi Bldg, Rue Makhoul, Hamra) Travel agency focusing on student travel. Arranges skiing trips, tours in Lebanon and to neighbouring countries, such as Syria and Jordan.

Tania Travel (☎ 739 682/3/4; www.taniatravel.com; 1st fl, Shames Bldg, Rue Sidani, Hamra, opposite Jeanne d'Arc theatre) It has tours to Aanjar, Baalbek, Bcharré, Beiteddine, Byblos, The Cedars, Deir al-Qamar, Sidon, Tyre and one-day trips to Damascus.

DANGERS & ANNOYANCES

The most obvious hazard in Beirut is the traffic – especially for pedestrians (also see p360). Locals seem to take a fatalistic approach to crossing the road and saunter across, trusting that cars will slow down, which they usually do, only to be confronted by a motor scooter going the wrong direction. In many parts of Beirut there's also a distinct lack of usable footpaths, often forcing pedestrians to walk on the road, giving all of Beirut yet another reason to lean on their car horns. All of which can be especially annoying for those travelling with children, not the least because you will have to explain why the road rules you taught them simply don't apply here!

When walking along a footpath look out for potholes, uneven or broken paving stones, loose electrical wiring, and localised flooding from overflowing water mains. This is especially problematic at night as some areas have poor or no street lighting. On the bright side, there is a significant amount of roadwork and paving projects ongoing in Beirut that will alleviate many of these problems.

Theft in Beirut is not a great problem, but it pays to be vigilant with your bags especially at busy places, such as bus stations. Keep your wallet or purse on your body; recent reports indicate an increase in handbag robberies by scooter-mounted thieves.

Remember to always travel with your passport, especially on day trips out of Beirut, in case you come across a checkpoint.

SIGHTS

National Museum of Beirut   Map p238
المتحف الوطني

This must-see **museum** (☎ 612 295/7; www.beirutnationalmuseum.com; cnr Rue de Damas & Ave Abdallah Yafi; adult/student & child LL5000/1000; ◷ 9am-5pm Tue-Sun except some public holidays) has an impressive collection of archaeological artefacts, statuettes and sarcophagi. Situated on a strategically

important intersection of the former Green Line, the wonderful 1930s-era building was badly damaged during the civil war, but has been meticulously renovated. With a huge amount of foresight, as the war was starting the important exhibits that were too large to move were enclosed in concrete, while others were secured in the basement. The easiest way to get to the museum is to either take a 15-minute walk from Sodeco Square along Rue de Damas (part of the former Green Line), or hail a service taxi and ask for Musee or the Hippodrome.

On the left of the foyer is the museum gift shop (with some very cute reproductions of the figures from the Obelisk Temple in Byblos; see p283) and on the right is the theatrette. On the hour there is a screening of a 15-minute video of the museum's history, featuring a fascinating account of how curators saved the collection during the war, the highlight of which is the sarcophagi being 'unentombed'. Inside, the exhibits are organised in roughly chronological order, following a clockwise rotation on both floors, and take a couple hours to view at a leisurely pace. Nearly all exhibits are labelled in English, Arabic and French. Written guides are available for LL15,000.

GROUND FLOOR

This floor contains the museum's largest artefacts, including colossi, sarcophagi and mosaics from the 1st and 2nd millennia BC up to the Roman and Byzantine periods.

2nd Millennium BC

To the left of the entrance are artefacts from the 2nd millennium BC, most of which show evidence of Lebanon's close relations with Egypt. A number of faded hieroglyphic reliefs, mostly from Byblos and Tyre, sit against the left wall.

1st Millennium BC

Following the clockwise rotation, you then enter into a chamber which covers the period from the 1st millennium BC. One of the highlights of the room is beautifully preserved 5th-century BC marble sarcophagi from Ain al-Helwa, which clearly show the coming together of Egyptian, Persian and Hellenistic influences. More evidence of Egypt is seen in a pair of sphinxes and statues with Egyptian-style loincloths. At the far end is a wonderful capital with bull protomes from Sidon.

Returning to the main room, immediately to your left, is a series of Hellenistic funerary stelae. Next to these, on the back wall to the left of the entrance, is a series of Thrones of Astarte, characteristic of the Phoenician mainland. Most are from the Hellenistic period and are made of limestone.

Roman & Byzantine

On the other side of the main hall is the Roman and Byzantine section. At the far end of the room, in cases, are a series of beautifully rendered white marble baby boys from Echmoun, one of which has Phoenician inscriptions. These extremely realistic cute chubby boys were sons of Sidonian aristocrats and the statues were offered to the gods in thanks for healing the children. Dating back to the 5th century BC, the statues are also significant because they are executed in the Hellenistic style but were made some 150 years before Alexander the Great arrived in Phoenicia.

Next to the statues is a 3rd-century mosaic from Byblos depicting the abduction of Europa. At the other end of the room is another particularly beautiful 4th-century mosaic depicting the birth of Alexander.

Back out in the main entrance hall, near the exit, is a stunning Roman torso of white marble. Beside this is an enormous white marble sarcophagus from Tyre. This is the most beautifully preserved of the sarcophagi, and is topped with an imposing reclining figure of a man and a woman, the frieze around it telling the story of the legend of Achilles.

1ST FLOOR

The 1st floor houses more intricate artefacts than the ground floor, almost all of which are in glass cases and date from prehistoric times until the Islamic era. Most of the cases overlooking the main hall have sliding magnifying glasses allowing you to get a closer look at the fabulous detail of the artefacts and are worthy of closer inspection.

Prehistory & Bronze Age

Following the arrow on the staircase leading to the right, the first half of the room features an impressive array of prehistoric and Bronze Age artefacts. Upon entering the room, a series of cases shows some fascinating prehistoric implements, some dating back as far as 3200 BC. Case 3 has a number of small statues from this era, many betraying the Egyptian influence. Case 7 has some fine examples of jewellery, including a necklace with a gold medallion inlaid with carnelian and other semiprecious stones. This and other objects in the case were offerings found at Byblos, dating from between 3200 and 2000 BC.

Moving further around the room, in Case 9 you will see some fine examples of late Bronze Age amphorae in white alabaster and granite. Case 10, overlooking the ground floor, has a delicately made obsidian-handled scimitar and mirror, both funerary objects dating to between 2000 and 1500 BC and

---

WAR & PILLAGE

Amid the chaos of Lebanon's civil war, the country's archaeological treasures were subject to a degree of pillage not seen since European colonists descended on the Middle East in the 18th and 19th centuries and hauled off the region's treasures to stock their museums.

Militias stole from Department of Antiquities storerooms, ransacked archaeological sites and bulldozed entire cemeteries and ancient settlements in their search for treasure. Even sarcophagi at the National Museum of Beirut were smashed in the hope of finding treasure inside. The thieves were aided and abetted by unscrupulous middlemen and Western art dealers who turned a blind eye to the provenance of the artefacts. According to Robert Fisk (in an excellent article 'The Biggest Supermarket in Lebanon', in *Berytus,* vol. XXXIX), an astounding 11 tons of stolen Lebanese Graeco-Roman and Byzantine-era artefacts arrived at an English port in February 1991. After determining whether or not taxes were due on the shipment, British customs let them into the country and they were later sold by a British dealer.

The only thing worse than the haemorrhage of national treasure was the accompanying destruction of the ancient sites. By bulldozing through layers of history, any information that the sites may have been able to tell us about the past was lost.

WEST BEIRUT

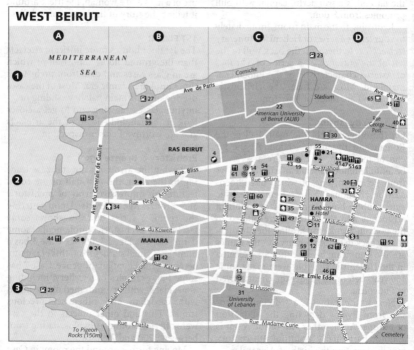

found at Byblos. On the other side of the room, Case 11 displays a stunning collection of Egyptian-influenced jewellery dating between 1500 and 600 BC. One vase in gold and obsidian has hieroglyphic inscriptions with the name of the pharaoh Amenemhet IV (1772–1763 BC). In the middle of this section, in Cases 13 and 17, are a series of

ings from Tyre in Case 33; and, in Case 38, some gold jewellery with semiprecious stones that came from the tomb of a woman near Sidon.

Hellenistic Period
Lasting from only 333 to 64 BC the Hellenistic period is represented in only a brief display, which includes a collection of funerary objects and coins as well as, in Case 43, some terracotta figurines.

Roman Period
The Roman period is well represented with some beautiful 3rd- and 4th-century jewellery in Case 45. Case 48 also has a number of glittering, gold-leaf funerary ornaments. Case 49 shows the high quality of Phoenician glassware, with tiny amphorae and glass-and-alabaster flasks. In Case 53 there are a number of masks with comic/tragic expressions derived from Greek theatre and in case 51, daily objects including a small Roman frying pan. Case 56 contains a group of bronze objects that include a Greek votive ship transformed into a lamp. An inscription says that it was dedicated to the god Zeus Beithmares in AD 232. Moving around the room, Cases 61 and 62 contain beautiful examples of Roman/Phoenician glass.

Byzantine to Mamluk
The continuation of early Christian to Islamic civilisation can be seen in this last part of the exhibit. Case 62 contains fine glassware from the Byzantine to Ottoman periods. In Case 64 there is some very beautiful Byzantine jewellery made of gold inlaid with precious stones. The Byzantine technique of granulation, in which tiny balls of gold formed part of the decoration, is carried over into the Mamluk-era jewellery in Case 65. Other exhibits in this section include coins in Cases 63 and 67, and some examples of Mamluk pottery in Cases 68 and 69.

Just before you reach the stairs visitors will note there is a small display case showing lumps of melted objects – all in all it's quite a twisted mess of metal, ivory, glass and stone. This case houses just some of the National Museum's war casualties, showing just how high the temperatures rose when a shell hit the storage area, setting it on fire.

tiny figures armed with spears and swords. The figures in Case 13 are notable for their increasing popularity as visual icons in Lebanon. Cases 19 and 20 contain some striking weaponry found at Byblos and dating back to between 2000 and 1500 BC. Particularly fine is a dagger and sheath in gold, silver and ivory. So, too, are the axe heads devoted to the war gods at Byblos.

Turning the corner, a series of cases contains more funerary jewellery and figurines, most from Byblos. Case 25 has some fascinating cuneiform tablets, notably one that has been translated into English.

Iron Age
This period, from 1200 to 333 BC, was the apogee of Phoenician civilisation, despite domination by the Assyrians, followed by the Babylonians and Persians. The influence of the conquerors can be seen in some of the artefacts on display. Highlights include (in Case 32) black, glazed Greek pottery that was traded between the 4th and 6th centuries BC; funerary offer-

BEIRUT

American University of Beirut

Map pp244-5

The American University of Beirut (AUB) is arguably the Middle East's most prestigious educational institute, and its campus and the surrounding Ras Beirut and Hamra areas are a hive of activity during semesters. The university is privately owned, nonsectarian and teaches all classes in English – hence the local students wandering around the Hamra district conversing in English as often as Arabic. Both the museum and the campus grounds are open to the public and are definitely worth a couple of hours of your time.

AUB MUSEUM

The AUB **museum** (☎ 340 549; ddc.aub.edu.lb/pro jects/museum/; AUB campus; admission free; ☒ 10am-4pm Mon-Fri except university & public holidays), just inside the university's main gate, was founded in 1868 and is one of the oldest in the Middle East. On permanent display is its collection of Lebanese and Middle Eastern artefacts dating back to the early Stone Age and a fine collection of Phoenician glass and Arab coins dating from as early as the 5th century BC. There are also terracotta statuettes, including fertility goddesses, and a large collection of pottery dating back to 3000 BC.

The museum runs regular lectures throughout the year, and hosts temporary exhibitions, as well as children's programmes. It's also involved in ongoing excavations in Lebanon and Syria. There is a museum shop selling the usual range of souvenirs.

AUB CAMPUS

Spread over 28 hectares, the **campus** (www.aub .edu) runs from Rue Bliss down to the water (yes, it even has its own beach club – see p250 for more information) and is one of the most beautiful – and enviable – university campuses to study at in the world. But even the stately charm of the campus did not escape the ugliness of the civil war, with various kidnappings and murders of university staff, including the ninth president of the university, Dr Malcolm Kerr, who was assassinated outside his College Hall office in 1984. The College Hall itself, first used in 1873, was rocked by a huge explosion in 1991, had to be demolished, but has since been rebuilt.

Hamra

Map pp244-5

While rival militias pulverised Beirut's Downtown during the war, the businesses and shops that were once clustered there moved to the Hamra district. Close to the university campus and many of Beirut's hotels, it lost some of its gloss with the re-emergence of the original downtown area and the growing popularity of Achrafiye to the east. Nevertheless, it is still one of the city's main hubs, with a varied streetlife and a good selection of clothing shops, fast-food joints, cafés, street vendors and bookshops.

Just off the eastern end of Rue Hamra is the **University of Lebanon campus**, with its 19th-century buildings and very attractive grounds. This is also where the **Sanayeh Public Garden**, one of the city's few public parks, is located.

Although most of the buildings here are forgettably modernist, there are some exceptions tucked away in the side streets. There are some restored older buildings found in the nearby areas of **Ain al-Mreisse**, close to the little fishing port inside the Corniche, and in **Minet al-Hosn**, slightly to the east.

Corniche

Map pp244-5

The Corniche (seafront) is a favourite promenade spot, especially late in the afternoon

---

ST GEORGE & THE DRAGON

The legend of St George slaying the dragon is known the world over but where it actually took place has been disputed for centuries. Libya, Cappadocia (modern Turkey) and Beirut all lay claim to the drama.

St George, born in Palestine, served in England with the Romans. He converted to Christianity and was martyred in AD 203.

According to Beirut lore, a monster terrorised the city and in an effort to appease it the town's king offered to sacrifice his daughter. St George appeared on a horse, rescued the princess and killed the dragon at a spot close to the Old City walls.

The dragon is seen as the symbol of evil, in particular of paganism. In the time of the Crusades, the Christians believed that a country could be converted to Christianity by the saint's killing of the evil – the dragon. By killing the dragon, St George saved Beirut from the evil of pagan religion.

The site of the battle with the dragon became sacred ground and in Crusader times a chapel was built here.

and on weekends. Families, couples and groups of young people dressed up saunter along its length, stopping to greet friends or to have a coffee-and-nargileh break at one of the cafés along the route. While many locals say the Corniche starts at Ras Beirut on Ave de Paris heading east and ending at the **St George Yacht Motor Club** (p250) in Ain al-Mreisse, others say it encompasses the entire waterfront area around to **Pigeon Rocks** (below).

You'll see a great cross-selection of Beiruti life on your walk, from backgammon-playing old men to teenagers dressed to impress.

Pole fishing from the Corniche is a popular pastime, especially near the steps that lead down to the front of the Corniche wall. You'll wonder how they manage to not get tangled up, not to mention wondering what they do with the tiny fish caught here! As you walk along this first section you'll no doubt notice the vendors with their handcarts of hot nuts, corn, *panini*-style bread, and *ka'ik*, the circular bread hooped around the vendors' carts. You'll also hear the clinking of coffee cups from the coffee vendors plying their trade as they walk along the Corniche. To really feel like a local, dodge the traffic and slip across to Uncle Deek and grab a takeaway coffee from this popular coffeehouse to sip as you take your walk.

While the nargileh cafés further along the Corniche are very popular, you'll no doubt notice the 'BYO' version, which entails parking your car near a bench on the Corniche, cranking the music up and lighting up your own hookah pipe to share among your closest friends. If you're visiting during the summer months, just before you reach the **AUB Beach** (p250) you will also see the teenagers risking life and limb diving off the Corniche and landing in the sea between the rock formations.

Pigeon Rocks   Map p238
These rocks are the most famous (in fact the only) natural feature of Beirut. The offshore natural rock arches of the Pigeon Rocks are spectacular and are a natural magnet for city dwellers craving something beautiful to look at, particularly at sunset. The stretch of the Corniche directly in front of the rocks is an excellent vantage point. Far more interesting is to take one of the tracks down to the lower cliffs. One track starts from the southern side of the rocks and, after a steep 100m,

you find yourself down on the lower level of chalk cliffs. Almost immediately, you can completely forget you are in the city.

The way across the rocks is quite rugged and sensible shoes are a good idea, although you see local women teetering precariously across the cliffs in high heels. Down on the lower levels, you get a good side view of the Pigeon Rocks with the city behind. If you fancy sitting for a while to watch the waves crash through the rocks, there is probably the smallest café in the world (two chairs) overlooking the scene. Further down towards the open sea there is a larger café (four chairs), where you can sit and watch the sunset.

There are a number of inlets and caves in the cliffs. During summer, small boats take people around the rocks and to the caves for a small fee.

Downtown Beirut   Map p248
In the 1970s the BCD, now called Downtown or Solidere, was exalted as the Paris of the Middle East. In the 1980s it was the centre of a war zone, and in the 1990s it became the focus of one of the world's most ambitious rebuilding programmes. Today, with much of the rebuilding finished, its spotlessly clean and traffic-free streets are so unlike the rest of the city that it has an almost surreal feel. Indeed, the whole area, though impressive, has a Disneyesque flavour, with ersatz Ottoman- and French Mandate–era architecture almost indistinguishable from the restored real thing. In defence of the architects and planners who have worked on the project, it must be said that the area is now the place-to-be-seen in the city. On weekend evenings the area around the Place d'Étoile (AKA Nejemah Square) is awash with people sitting in the outdoor cafés, drinking arak or beer and smoking nargileh.

The **Solidere information office** (☎ 980 650/60; www.solidere-online.com; Bldg 149, Rue Saad Zaghloul; ☿ 9am-3pm & 4-6pm Mon-Fri) has display models and information boards outlining the redevelopment of the area. Information officers are usually on hand to answer questions or suggest walks around the area.

If you devise your own walking tour of Downtown, make sure you don't miss the **Al-Omari Mosque** (which is currently being renovated), originally built in the 12th century as the Church of St John the Baptist of

BEIRUT

DOWNTOWN BEIRUT

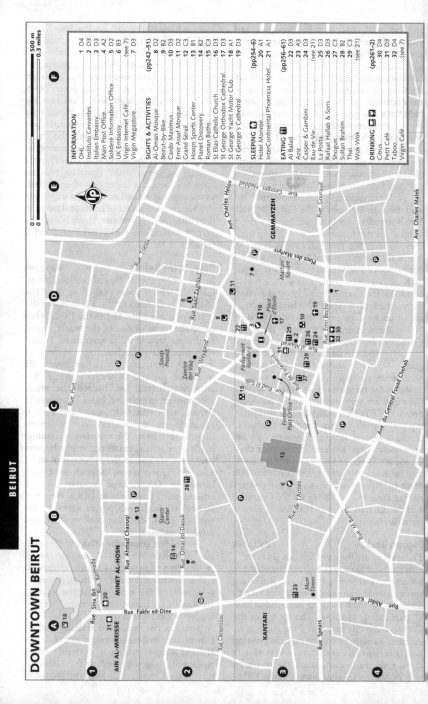

500 m
0.3 miles

BEIRUT

Ottoman- and French Mandate–era architecture along Rue al Maarad,
off Place d'Étoile (p247), Beirut, Lebanon

MARK DAFFEY

Pigeon rocks (p247), Beirut, Lebanon

MARK DAFFEY

Outdoor cafés on Place d'Étoile (p247), Downtown Beirut, Lebanon

Architecture in Downtown area (p247), Beirut, Lebanon

BETHUNE CARMICHAEL

the Knights Hospitallers and converted into a mosque in 1291; **St George's Cathedral** (☎ 561 980; services 7.15am & 6.30pm Mon-Thu & Sat, 9am & 11am Sun), a Maronite church dating back to the Crusades; the magnificently restored **Roman baths**; the **cardo maximus**, evocative remains of a Roman-era market area; and the **Grand Serail**, a majestic Ottoman-era building that has been restored to its former grandeur and now houses government offices.

Galleries

Beirut's vibrant art scene means that there are many galleries. For more on the art scene, see p49. Check local listings for exhibitions.

Agial Art Gallery (Map p244-5; ☎ 345 213, 03-634 244; 63 Rue Omar Abdel Aziz, Hamra) Close to the AUB, this is a shopfront gallery that specialises in showcasing the work of local artists.

Espace SD (Map p251; ☎ 563 114; Ave Charles Hélou, Achrafiye) Set over three levels, it exhibits contemporary Lebanese and international artists, in addition to furniture design, fashion and accessories.

Galerie Alice Mogabgab (Map p251; ☎ 336 525; 253 Rue Gouraud, Gemmayzeh) Specialises in modern art, including artists from abroad.

Sursock Museum   Map p251

Lit up at night, so that the full glory of its colourful stained glass is on show, the **museum** (Musée Nicholas Ibrahim Sursock; ☎ 334 133; Rue Sursock, Achrafiye; ☼ 10am-1pm & 4-7pm when exhibitions are scheduled) is truly an extraordinary sight.

Owned by the Sursock family, one of the country's most illustrious dynasties, the extraordinary and magnificent Lebanese-Italian architectural style of the building that houses the museum often overshadows the temporary exhibitions. The location of the museum, in a wonderful street of luxurious modern apartment blocks and beautiful Ottoman- and French Mandate–era mansions, makes a walk around the neighbourhood mandatory. The interior of the museum is equally grand with vast wood panelling and marble floors. Some of the rooms are decorated in the oriental style and the main hall has a collection of 19th-century Turkish silver. In the centre of the room is a gigantic 7th-century Abbasid jar. The former study of Nicholas Ibrahim Sursock features his portrait by Kees Van Dongen. The room also houses a small collection of icons. Unfortunately, the exhibitions of contemporary Lebanese art and photography that are held

---

SPIRITS AGAINST BULLDOZERS

In 1992 the rubble of Beirut's souqs was being cleared as archaeologists, working against the clock, tried to investigate the site before it was built over by developers. A bulldozer clearing an area in what had been Souq Tawile was scooping up debris and came up against a small, domed building. The machine suddenly stopped. The driver, wanting to finish his job, started the machine up again but when he tried to move the controls, his hand was suddenly paralysed. Later, when he was away from the site, the paralysis disappeared.

News quickly spread of the 'miracle' that saved the building, which turned out to be part of a *zawiya*, or hospice and religious school, built by 16th-century mystic and scholar, Mohammed ibn Iraq al-Dimashqi. Crowds visited the shrine and reports began to circulate of miraculous healing among the ill who had prayed there.

Muslim religious authorities erected a protective wall around the *zawiya* and announced that it would not be demolished. It is now the only Mamluk building left in Beirut and stands waiting to be incorporated into the new Downtown development.

---

here often don't live up to their surroundings. Make sure you phone ahead to confirm that the museum is open. The museum is a 10-minute walk from the Downtown area.

Cilicia Museum

This **museum's** (☎ 04-410 001; www.cathcil.org; Antelias; ☼ 7.30am-1pm Tue-Fri, 7.30am-noon Sat, 10am-1pm Sun summer; 10am-5pm Tue-Sat, 10am-1pm Sun winter) gorgeous collection of Armenian religious and cultural artefacts, including silver-bound bibles, manuscripts, embroidery, coins and carpets, is one of Beirut's best-kept secrets. And secrets play a major role in the history of this museum as most of the collection was smuggled out of what was known as Turkish Armenia by monks from the Monastery of Sis in Cilicia in 1915. Given just several days to flee the genocide by the Turks, the monks removed as much of their treasures as they could and began their dangerous overland journey, eventually arriving in Aleppo (Syria). In 1930 they finally settled in Antelias, just north of Beirut.

The museum, officially opened in 1998, covers three floors with the first containing relics and reliquaries, crosses, chalices, embroideries, liturgical vestments and stone crosses. The highlights of the 1st floor include the recently restored manuscript known as *Gospel of Bardjrberd* (1248) with its exquisite portrait of St Mark; the vast silver cauldron designed in 1817 in Constantinople for the preparation of the Holy Myrrh, which is used for baptismal rites; the Right Arm of St Gregory the Illuminator (the founder of the Armenian Church), an important reliquary with a complex history used in the consecration of the mix of Holy Myrrh; and in the smaller room of the 1st floor the pure silver chandelier (1804) that was dismantled and removed piece by piece from Armenia.

The 2nd floor showcases most of the museum's beautifully detailed medieval manuscripts. Highlights here include books printed in Venice in 1512 and 1513, and the first printed version of the *Armenian Holy Bible* (1666; Amsterdam). The open manuscripts with their extraordinarily colourful miniatures are worthy of close inspection. Notable is the frequent use of a strong red colour, the pigment extracted from worms thriving only in Armenia. The smaller hall on the same floor displays archaeological collections, carpets, tapestries and some wonderful traditional Armenian costumes.

The 3rd floor houses a changing collection of paintings and sculptures from artists of the Armenian diaspora, most notably a painting by Russian-Armenian master Ivan Aivazovsky (1817–1900). There's also a 1948 painting of the Armenian Catholicosate of Antelias (where the museum is housed), surrounded by farmland – a stark contrast to the busy location it's in now. Despite this, you'll probably have the museum to yourself as it appears most Lebanese outside the Armenian population are unaware of its existence.

To get to the museum, take the LCC bus (p266 has route details) or any minibus going north to Jounieh and Byblos via the highway, and get off near the green-coloured footbridge over the southbound highway at Antelias. From here you should be able to spot the spires of the cathedral. You can take the LCC No 2 bus that finishes its route at Antelias. Get off at the last stop and walk towards the water where you'll spot the entrance. The museum is at the left rear of the courtyard.

ACTIVITIES

Many cycling and trekking outfits operate out of Beirut, see pp356–7 for details.

Golf

The **Golf Club of Lebanon** (☎ 822 470; in Bir Hassan), located south of Ramlet al-Bayda, has been open since the 1960s and has a picturesque 18-hole course. The club also includes tennis and squash courts, swimming pool and billiard tables. Although you are supposed to be a member to play here, it sometimes allows nonmembers in.

Health Clubs

A considerable number of sports clubs are helping Beirutis keep those well-maintained bodies looking good, but many have memberships for a minimum of one month and guests are accepted on a discretionary basis. For complete club listings grab a copy of the *Guide*; see Media (p240) for details.

One club that does have daily membership is **Escape** (☎ 740 955; facing Luna Park, Manara; activities US$7 per day, gym US$5), offering aerobics, squash and tennis as well as bellydance lessons.

Swimming

Swimming is one of the most popular activities for Beirutis in summer. The only free place to swim in Beirut is the public beach, Ramlet al-Bayda, south of Raouché. Given the polluted waters, this is not recommended. If you want to swim in the city the private beach clubs are a far better option. While there's no sand, most of these clubs come with swimming pools and loads of extras, the most obvious being convenience and exclusivity. It's quite a scene: mobile phones, unnaturally sculpted bodies and designer bathing suits are the norm and the experience is as much about seeing and being seen as it is about taking a dip.

Here is a list of beach clubs:

AUB Beach (Map pp244-5) Accessible only via a tunnel from the university, this is smack in the middle of the Corniche. Canvas awnings keep things relatively private. Open to AUB students and their friends.

Riviera Beach Club (Map pp244-5; ☎ 373 210; Manara; admission LL20,000) Belonging to the upmarket Riviera Beirut Hotel and therefore free to guests, otherwise by membership only. Facilities include a marina (you too can tie up your yacht for LL1,000,000!) and the usual pools and restaurants.

St George Yacht Motor Club (Map p248; ☎ 356 350; Ain al-Mreisse; admission LL15,000 weekdays, LL20,000 Sat

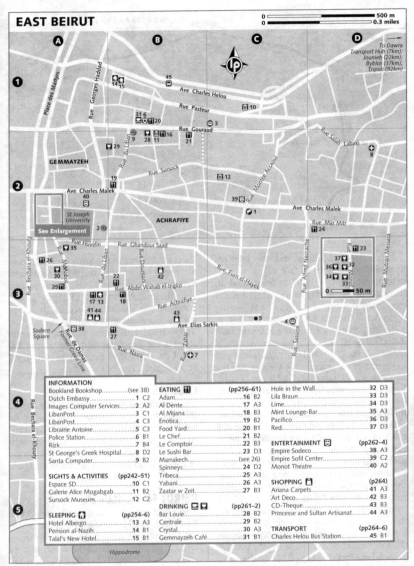

EAST BEIRUT

0 — 500 m
0 — 0.3 miles

To Dawra
Transport Hub (7km);
Jounieh (22km);
Byblos (37km);
Tripoli (92km)

GEMMAYZEH

St Joseph University

See Enlargement

ACHRAFIYE

Sodeco Square

Hippodrome

INFORMATION	
Bookland Bookshop	(see 38) C2
Dutch Embassy	1 C2
Images Computer Services	2 A2
LibanPost	3 C1
LibanPost	4 C3
Librairie Antoine	5 C3
Police Station	6 B1
Rizk	7 B4
St George's Greek Hospital	8 D2
Santa Computer	9 B2

SIGHTS & ACTIVITIES	(pp242–51)
Espace SD	10 C1
Galerie Alice Mogabgab	11 B2
Sursock Museum	12 C2

SLEEPING	(pp254–6)
Hotel Albergo	13 A3
Pension al-Nazih	14 B1
Talal's New Hotel	15 B1

EATING	(pp256–61)
Adam	16 B2
Al Dente	17 A3
Al Mijana	18 A3
Enotica	19 B2
Food Yard	20 B1
Le Chef	21 B2
Le Comptoir	22 B3
Le Sushi Bar	23 D3
Marrakech	(see 26)
Tribeca	24 D2
Yabani	25 A3
Zaatar w Zeit	26 A3
	27 B3

DRINKING	(pp261–2)
Bar Louie	28 B2
Centrale	29 B2
Crystal	30 A3
Gemmayzeh Café	31 B1

Hole in the Wall	32 D3
Lila Braun	33 D3
Lime	34 D3
Mint Lounge-Bar	35 A3
Pacifico	36 D3
Red	37 D3

ENTERTAINMENT	(pp262–4)
Empire Sodeco	38 A2
Empire Sofil Center	39 C2
Monot Theatre	40 A2

SHOPPING	(p264)
Ariana Carpets	41 A3
Art Deco	42 B3
CD-Theque	43 B3
Princesse and Sultan Artisanat	44 A3

TRANSPORT	(pp264–6)
Charles Helou Bus Station	45 B1

& Sun) A recently renovated version of what was *the* club of the 1960s. Has a marina, nice swimming pool, jet skis, restaurants and grass on which to stretch out.

Sporting Beach Club (Map pp244-5; ☎ 742 481; Manara; admission LL16,000) Open all year to members and guests of the Hotel Mediterranee, the club has two pools, scuba club, basketball courts, restaurants and steps down to the sea.

WALKING TOUR

You can start the walk anywhere from Downtown or from **Hotel Monroe** (**1**; p255). It's best to allow at least 1½ hours for the walk (which is about 5km), including people-watching – a quintessential Beirut pastime – and timing it perfectly for a sunset drink at Pigeon Rocks is ideal.

BEIRUT

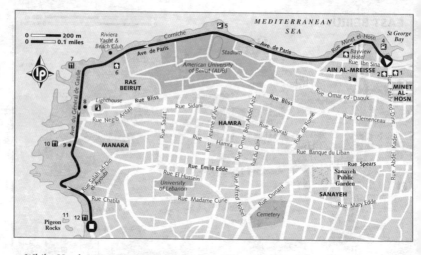

While Hotel Monroe and the **InterContinental Phoenicia Hotel (2)** face off in a competition for the best hotel to be spotted at, the shell of the **Holiday Inn (3**; p253) behind the InterContinental remains a towering reminder of the war. On the seaward side, at a stretch you can see into the **St George Yacht Motor Club (4**; p250,), the renovated version of *the* club of the 1960s and one of the claimants as the site of the legend of St George and the Dragon (see the boxed text, p246 for details). Further along with the Bayview Hotel on the landward side and the restaurant complex on the seaward side, the *corniche* proper begins.

At the end of the next stretch after the **AUB Beach (5**; p250), you'll spot the **Riviera Beirut Hotel (6**; p256) on the landward side and its yacht and beach club on the seaward side. By now, wind permitting, you should note the sweet apple nargileh smell emanating from the **Manara Palace Café (7**; p259). In front of the old lighthouse, located up on the hill on the seaward side, you should see a wonderful pink **Ottoman-style mansion (8)**, a reminder of days gone by. As you approach **Luna Park (9**; Map pp244-5) there is a driveway leading to **Al-Raouda café (10**; p259), another popular nargileh stop. While Luna Park itself is not really noteworthy, the nargileh café at the front of it often has a live singer and band entertaining the crowds, visible from the street.

As you negotiate the least picturesque section of the walk, up the reverse s-shaped hill, don't be tempted to take the well-worn short cut leading to the army lookout, complete with barbed wire and APCs (Armored Personnel Carriers). By now you should be able to spot **Pigeon Rocks (11**; p247), and don't be too shocked to see locals jumping the Corniche guard rail to get the best happy-snap! Follow the road as it curves around the headland and stop at the **Bay Rock Café (12**; p259) for that sunset drink and nargileh. You've earned it.

COURSES

The **American Language Center** (☎ 366 002, 03-602 871; www.alc.edu.lb; 1st fl, Choueiry Bldg, Rue Bliss, Ras Beirut) offers monthly, colloquial (spoken) Arabic courses for beginners, intermediates and advanced students over a period of a month (25 hours). The centre also runs courses in Tripoli and Zahlé.

BEIRUT FOR CHILDREN

The good news for families travelling to Beirut is that all Lebanese love children. Indeed couples of almost any age who travel without children around Lebanon will be endlessly questioned about their offsprings' whereabouts. The not-so-good news is that Beirut has a reputation for not being a particularly child-friendly destination in terms of activities, but with a little planning you can find enough activities to satisfy the most demanding youngsters.

Baby-sitting services for visitors to Beirut are scarce as the locals put to use their extended families (or live-in nannies, wealth

---

THE HOLIDAY INN

While visiting Beirut, you will notice many reminders of the war, but none is so visible as the massive Holiday Inn (Map pp244-5), located behind the InterContinental Phoenicia Hotel. Opened only shortly before the war, the hotel became a prime sniper position, and in turn attracted firepower of all calibres, which left it in its current bullet-riddled state. Designed to withstand an earthquake, the building is apparently still structurally sound and there are plans to restore the hotel to its former glory. It will be with mixed feelings that Beirutis again enjoy its revolving restaurant and superb views, but it will be a significant step in healing the still-visible wounds of the civil war.

---

permitting), but the larger chain hotels, such as the **InterContinental Phoenicia Hotel** (☎ 369 100), offer baby-sitting. Restaurants are generally family-friendly (except those on Rue Monot) and have high chairs and staff who are well versed in children's needs.

Some sights that are great for children include investigating the action on Beirut's **Corniche** (p246). Older children will appreciate the **National Museum of Beirut** (p242), while the younger kids can let off steam at the small **playground** at the Al-Raouda café (p259). While Beirut has a dearth of parks, the **Sanayeh Public Garden** (Map pp244-5) has bike hire and paved paths perfect for in-line skating. Bike rentals outside the confines of a park might sound a little scary given Beirut's traffic, but the Downtown area is pedestrian only on Sundays. You can hire bikes from **Beirut-by-Bike** (Map p248; ☎ 03-435 524, 03-603 498; Rue Omar ed-Daouk, facing Planet Discovery). Nearby, for those kids who like round-ball sports, there's **Hoops Sports Center** (Map p248; ☎ 371 713; near Starco Center) offering activities such as basketball, soccer and volleyball.

There's always the stunning series of caverns of the **Jeita Grotto** (p277) to explore.

For more cerebrally stimulating activities, a trip to **Planet Discovery** (Map p248; ☎ 980 650, 980 660; Rue Omar ed-Daouk, Minet al-Hosn; adult & child LL5000; ☼ 9am-6pm Mon-Fri, 10am-8pm weekends & public holidays) is a great option that kids will love. An interactive science museum especially designed for three- to 12-year-olds, it

also holds cultural and artistic workshops. Three- to 14-year-olds will be in seventh heaven if you take them to **Rainbow Island** (☎ 05-956444; www.rainbowislandjunior.com; Faubourg St Jean, cnr Damascus Hwy & Presidential Palace Rd, Hazmieh; weekdays/weekends LL8000/10,000; ☼ 10am-8pm), an enormous indoor playground with learning activities. There's a nursery school here on weekdays.

During the warmer months, especially if you're staying in a hotel without a pool, you'll be begged to head to one of Lebanon's water parks, such as **Waves Aqua Park** (☎ 04-533 555; www.wavespark.com) in the Metn area, **Splash Mountain** (☎ 04-531 166; www.splashmountainlb.com; LL20,000; ☼ 10am-6pm) in Beit Mery, or **Rio Lento** (☎ 04-915 656; www.riolento.com) in Nahr al-Kalb (p276). All of these parks are within an hour of Beirut (traffic permitting, of course) so a day trip could be based around an activity in the morning (such as the Jeita Grotto) with a splash in the afternoon.

If you're visiting during winter, consider a day trip to **Faraya Mzaar** (p273), where children under five have free access to the ski slopes and lessons are tailored for the little ones.

TOURS

Beirut is easily managed without taking an organised tour, and is small enough, particularly if you follow the suggestions in the boxed text Beirut in… (p239), and the Walking Tour (p251). If time is important contact the travel agents listed (pp241-2) for more information of tours around Beirut. But if you wish to pack as much sightseeing as you can into your trip around Lebanon, see also Local Tour Operators, p388.

FESTIVALS & EVENTS

Given the size of the country, any festival in Lebanon is easily accessible. Bookings for these are advisable and tickets can be purchased online from www.tradingplaces .com.lb. For a complete list of festivals and events for Lebanon see p363.

Beirut International Marathon (www.beirutmarathon .org) Held in early October, it includes wheelchair events, a 10km-long run, a minimarathon, and other marathon events.

Mid East Film Festival Beirut (www.beirutfilmfounda tion.org) Also held in October, this festival showcases films from Lebanon and the Middle East, and aims to encourage co-productions between the Arab and international communities.

GAY & LESBIAN BEIRUT

Homosexuality is illegal in Lebanon, however there is a clandestine gay scene in Beirut – and it's clandestine for a very good reason. Any openly gay establishment is likely to be frequently raided and its patrons harassed. In a now legendary case, a US-based doughnut chain even refused to serve a 'gay-looking' patron on the pretext that it was a family establishment. While Lebanon prides itself as the most liberal of the Middle Eastern countries, its attitude towards sexuality (at least in law and on the surface of society) is decidedly heterocentric. All men and women in Lebanese society are expected to get married and have children and there is enormous pressure to comply. Being openly gay is rare – having an openly gay relationship even rarer.

There are signs that there may be more acceptance forthcoming. During a protest in the lead-up to the invasion of Iraq in 2003, a small group of gay protesters marched with the rainbow flag in Beirut. Both Acid (p263) and B 018 nightclubs (p263) are very gay-friendly establishments. A couple of the beach clubs in Beirut are great places to meet new people. The hammams provide opportunities for men to meet. An evening walk along the Corniche (p246) is popular. But entrapment is not unheard of (as is robbery under these circumstances) and you will be arrested if caught having sexual relations that are 'contradicting the laws of nature'. At the clubs pay careful attention to the behaviour of other patrons and if people start dancing 'apart' suddenly, there's probably a very good reason – raids do occur.

Given this, as a gay visitor to Beirut, your best option is to make some contacts before you arrive. The following websites are a good place to start.

http://legal.20m.com

www.bintelnas.org A good website for lesbian-specific information.

www.gaymiddleeast.com

www.travelandtranscendence.com

SLEEPING
Budget

Cheap accommodation isn't plentiful in Beirut. The only places offering rooms under US$20 per person per night are found in Ain al-Mreisse and near Charles Helou bus station – of the two, Ain al-Mreisse is the more pleasant location, though the area around Charles Helou is closer to Rue Monot and Rue Gouraud, the city's main nightclub and eating strip.

Talal's New Hotel (Map p251; ☎ 562 567; ZSAL72 TNH@yahoo.com; Ave Charles Hélou, Gemmayzeh; dm/s/d with air-con US$6/12/14, without air-con US$4/8/10; ✗ 🖳) A clean, friendly place near Charles Helou bus station offering beds at bargain-basement prices. The rooms are slightly claustrophobic, but at these prices, who's complaining? All rooms have satellite TV and hot showers are free. There's a communal kitchen, laundry facilities (LL3000 per load) and Internet access (first 15 minutes free, LL1500 per hour after that).

Pension al-Nazih (Map p251; ☎ 564 868, 03-475 136; www.pension-alnazih.8m.com; Ave Charles Hélou; dm/s/d US$6/8/12, d with bathroom & air-con US$20; ✗ 🖳) Pension al-Nazih is a budget place near the bus station. Lonely Planet has heard from one female traveller that she was assaulted in her room at this pension.

Pension Home Valery (Map pp244–5; ☎ 362 169; homevalery@hotmail.com; Saab Bldg, Rue Phoenicia, Ain al-Mreisse; dm/s US$6/8; 🖳) Probably the most well-known pension in Beirut, it's clean, has pleasant English-speaking staff and is a good, reliable budget choice. It has free hot showers, cooking facilities and fans in all rooms. It's located on the 2nd floor of the building next to the Wash Me car wash, and this building now houses several pensions, each on different floors. To find them, go into the dingy hallway and walk to the rear of the building where the lift and stairs are located. Confusingly, there is a 3rd-floor pension with the **same name** (☎ 364 906), prices, facilities and general friendliness levels are on par, although it doesn't offer Internet access or dorms. Pensions on the other floors are currently not recommended.

Regis Hotel (Map pp244–5; ☎ 361 845; Rue Razi, Ain al-Mreisse; s/d with bathroom US$17/20) It might be located in one of the less reconstructed streets of Ain al-Mreisse, but it's fine for those looking for more privacy than a dorm room offers. Rather basic but reasonably clean rooms have air-con or fan, plus a fridge and TV. Discounts are offered for stays of three or more nights, and for stays during October to May.

Mid-Range

Beirut's mid-range accommodation options are generally located in the Hamra and Ras Beirut areas. Many of these hotels are set against the backdrop of Hamra traffic chaos and can be noisy – something to consider if you've had a late night on Rue Monot! Prices can drop significantly out of season (up to 40% for some hotels) and the rates quoted here are standard rack rates.

University Hotel (Map pp244-5; ☎ 365 391; 19 Rue Bliss, Ras Beirut; s/d/ste with bathroom US$32/44/57; ☒) Well situated just near the main gate of the AUB, it's located up a laneway next to Mc-Donald's – just look for the bored soldiers standing guard. While recent renovations and a resulting price hike moved it out of the budget category, most of its small rooms are still rented by students from the university, making it hard to get a room during semesters. All rooms have satellite TV and fridge and several have balconies with sea views.

Cedarland Hotel (Map pp244-5; ☎ 340 233/4; cedarland_lb@yahoo.com; Rue Omar ben Abdel Aziz, Hamra; s/d/ste with bathroom US$33/39/50; ☒) While it's adjacent to a particularly bustling intersection in Hamra, making its rooms quite noisy, it's spotlessly clean – and reassuringly popular with student doctors from the nearby AUB Hospital. It also has some roomier 1960s-style suites (ask when you book) and all rooms have satellite TV and fridge. Breakfast is US$5, but most guests choose to eat on the run. It offers good discounts for long-term stays.

Seaside Furnished Flats (Map pp244-5; ☎ 363 200/1; www.beirutflats.com; Rue George Post St, Ain al-Mreisse; apt with/without sea views US$65/50; ☒ ▢) These one-bedroom apartments are a good option for a long-term stay in Beirut. While they resemble student digs tidied up for a landlord visit, they are clean and each has a balcony (most with sea view), kitchen and lounge with satellite TV. The apartments are close to the AUB and the Corniche.

Marble Tower Hotel (Map pp244-5; ☎ 354 586, 346 260; marble@marbletower.com.lb; Rue Makdissi, Hamra; s/d/ste LL130,000/149,000/290,000; ☒) Located smack-bang in the centre of Hamra it's a long-standing favourite for many travellers

familiar with Beirut. Its well-worn though spotlessly clean rooms can be a bit noisy but the service is excellent, the price includes breakfast, the beds are comfortable and the suites are great value.

Lord's Hotel (Map pp244-5; ☎ 740 382; fax 740 385; the Corniche, Manara; basic s/d US$35/50, renovated with sea views US$65/75; ☒) Another hotel with that frayed-around-the-edges charm. Clean and serviceable, its selling point is its excellent proximity to the Corniche, making it a particularly good summer choice.

Mayflower Hotel (Map pp244-5; ☎ 340 680; www.mayflower.com.lb; Rue Neamé Yafet, Hamra; s/d/ste LL120,000/140,000/230,000; ☒ ☒ ▢ ☒) A Hamra institution, this hotel was a popular post-war hang-out for journalists. Today it's a comfortable, old-fashioned hotel, with spotlessly clean rooms and excellent service – with the added bonus of a hotel pool. To really soak up the history, imbibe at the hotel's Duke of Wellington bar. Prices go up by 30% during the high season and are 40% less during the low season.

Hotel Cavalier (Map pp244-5; ☎ 353 001; cavatel@dm.net.lb; Rue Hamra, Hamra; s/d US$60/70; ☒ ▢) This venerable hotel may have lost a little of its charm in its recent renovation, but prices out of season make it four-star quality at three-star prices. Well situated in the Hamra area, its double-glazed windows block out the traffic chaos. Its comfortable rooms are well appointed and the hotel does a great breakfast.

Top End

There are quite a few quality (but bland) chain hotels in Beirut competing for your lira, but they leave you feeling that you could be staying at any capital city around the world. The hotels listed below offer you something a little different in the same price bracket.

Hotel Albergo (Map p251; ☎ 339 797; www.albergobeirut.com; 137 Rue Abdel Wahab el-Inglizi, Achrafiye; d/ste US$270/308; ☒ ▢ ☒) This is one of our favourites. Read the boxed text The Author's Choice (p256) to find out why.

Hotel Monroe (Map p248; ☎ 371 122; www.monroebeirut.com; Rue Kennedy, Minet al-Hosn; s/d/ste US$135/155/210; ☒ ▢ ☒) This hotel opened to a huge sigh of relief from clients looking for a stylish, but not too expensive, alternative to the four- and five-star chain hotels. While not really living up to the initial hype – the restaurants are disappointing – its attitude is friendly rather than pretentious and the

THE AUTHOR'S CHOICE

Hotel Albergo (Map p251; ☎ 339 797; www .albergobeirut.com; 137 Rue Abdel Wahab el-Inglizi, Achrafiye; d/ste US$270/308; 🍽 🖳 🛋) This is the kind of hotel you never want to check out of. Its 33 rooms of individual and effortless opulence are not for fans of minimalism, but they'll still be impressed by the exemplary and discreet service, not to mention the extraordinary rooftop pool and bar. The themed rooms – take your pick of Orientalist, European, Colonial and Mediterranean styles – could have been a disaster in less sure hands, but a Relais & Châteaux hotel rarely gets the details wrong. Located in one of the prettiest areas of Achrafiye, it's close to some of Beirut's most stylish eating establishments, so when you're tired of the Italian gastronomic delights at its Al Dente restaurant (p258) next door, you'll have other restaurants to explore when you extend your stay by a couple of days.

rooms, though small, are among the most comfortable in town.

Riviera Beirut Hotel (Map pp244-5; ☎ 373 210; www.meliariviera.com; Ave de Paris, the Corniche, Manara; s/d with garden views US$164/189, with sea views US$214/ 220; 🍽 🖳 🛋) This hotel is simply *the* best Beirut summer option. While several other hotels also have sea views, similar service and comfort levels, the Riviera has the advantage of having the best (and most lively) hotel beach club (p250) in Beirut, as well as a gorgeous garden and good restaurants. Breakfast is an extra US$16.

InterContinental Phoenicia Hotel (Map p248; ☎ 369 100; www.ichotelsgroup.com; Rue Fakhr ed-Dine, Minet al-Hosn; d/ste US$190/240) Beirut's most prestigious pre–civil war hotel, it has now been redeveloped in a rather glitzy style with acres of marble and huge ceilings. It does have the best amenities in town and has once again become the favourite of Beirut's moneyed set.

EATING

Beirut is famous for its eating places, and no wonder – from its local food stalls through to its stylish restaurants, good food beckons at every turn. While the street food is relatively cheap (not to mention surpassing the Western fast-food chains for taste as well as value) the top-end restaurants are expensive – often

to pay for the lavish interiors! But Beirut takes its food seriously and even those on a tight budget will be tempted to dip into the emergency money at least once to indulge in the favourite pastime of most Beirutis – good conversation while unhurriedly indulging in a sumptuous and totally delectable array of mezze and grills. A meal taken this way is a short cut to understanding an essential aspect of Beirut's character. Those travelling with children will find most restaurants are well used to catering for the little ones, especially those with outdoor eating areas.

Restaurants

There are so many wonderful restaurants in Beirut that it seems a sin to single out a few. Those wanting to sample what's on offer should note that Beirutis are usually immaculately attired and eat quite late: most diners won't arrive at the restaurant until 9.30pm for dinner, except in the Downtown area where many an after-work drink and nargileh turns into an impromptu dinner. Besides wonderful Lebanese (mezze are great for vegetarians) and Middle Eastern cuisine, French, Italian and, more recently, Japanese restaurants are in abundance. Most of the options listed here accept credit cards and serve alcohol – exceptions are noted. Most good restaurants in Beirut are aimed at the moneyed middle-class and are priced accordingly, but you can still dine in style by skipping entrée or sticking to mezze.

ASIAN

Thai (Map p248; ☎ 999 944, 999 955; Rue Toubia Aoun, Downtown; Thai salads LL7500, curries LL10,500; 😋 11am-late) A welcome addition to the Downtown eating scene, this small restaurant serves good-quality, authentic and reasonably priced Thai, only let down by the fact that it presently doesn't serve alcohol. If you can eat Thai food without washing it down with a Singah beer, it's a good choice for a break from endless mezze.

Shogun (Map p248; ☎ 997 888; Rue de Parlement, Downtown; sushi & sashimi around LL8000 per serve; 😋 11am-late, closed Sun) Widely considered to have the best-quality sushi and sashimi around, it keeps its enviable reputation intact with twice weekly deliveries from Japan. Needless to say, it's not cheap (good sushi rarely is), so if you're with a group go for the 'special sets'. Aficionados will spot fatty tuna and kobe beef on the menu as they sip a Sapporo beer – yes, it's the real thing.

Yabani (Map p251; ☎ 211 113, 03-503 222; Rue de Damas, Achrafiye; tempura LL9500, mixed sushi LL19,500; ☽ 12.30-3.30pm & 8.30-11.30pm, closed Sun lunch) A very different Japanese experience to Shogun – as you'll realise when you see the glass lift transporting diners underground to both Yabani and to Marrakech (p259). Thankfully the food is as superb as its futuristic interior with especially good tempura and noodles, as well as a wide selection of sushi and sashimi.

Other recommended Asian restaurants:

Le Sushi Bar (Map p251; ☎ 338 555; Rue Monot, Achrafiye; sushi around LL4500 per serve; ☽ noon-4pm & 7pm-midnight)

Wok Wok (Map p248; ☎ 369 100; InterContinental Phoenicia Hotel, Minet el Hosn; meals around LL25,000 per person; ☽ noon-midnight)

FRENCH

Aziz (Map p248; ☎ 358 000; near Murr Tower, Kantari; entrées & mains around LL40,000 per person excl wine; ☽ 12.30-3.30pm & 8.30-11.30pm, closed Sun evening) A long-standing name in the French dining scene in Beirut, this stylish but relaxed restaurant up the hill from Hotel Monroe doesn't disappoint. The frequently changing menu, wonderful presentation and extensive French wine list make this the most satisfying French dining experience in Beirut. The downstairs deli is a gourmand's delight.

Eau de Vie (Map p248; InterContinental Phoenicia Hotel, Minet el Hosn; meals per person around LL40,000; ☽ lunch & dinner until late) The sophisticated Eau de Vie restaurant was around in the Phoenicia pre–civil war and has made a welcome return with the hotel's reincarnation. For diners wanting classic French food there's an à la carte menu with the usual dishes, and for the more adventurous there's an interesting chef's menu. A good choice for avid Francophiles and foodies alike.

INTERNATIONAL

Adam (Map p251; ☎ 560 353; Rue Gouraud, Gemmayzeh; entrées around LL8000, mains around LL18,000; ☽ noon-4pm & 7pm-midnight, closed Sun) With its hip retro-funky interior, well-prepared and well-presented dishes and good house wine, this addition to the burgeoning Gemmayzeh eating scene has quickly developed a following. The small and seasonal menu covers enough territory to please most palates, including vegetarians, and the desserts (LL7000) are worth saving room for. Bookings preferred.

Casablanca (Map pp244-5; ☎ 369 334; Rue Ain al-Mreisse, Ain al-Mreisse; entrées around LL16,000, mains around LL22,000; ☽ 12.30-4pm & 8pm-1.30am Tue-Sat, 11am-4pm & 8pm-1.30am Sun) Housed in a stylishly renovated Ottoman villa overlooking the Corniche, Casablanca is a long-established favourite for the ultrafashionable to take a weekend lunch. The eclectic East/West menu suffers from a bit of an identity crisis and not every dish

---

HOOKAH HISTORY

There are several common names for the water pipe that first emerged from Turkey in the 16th century. Sheesha, hubble-bubble and hookah are some of the ones you'll hear across the Middle East, but in Lebanon the most common name is nargileh (narg-ee-*leh*). While it is thought that the original idea of smoking substances by passing the smoke through cooling liquid (not always water), came from either Persia or India, it was in Turkey that the water pipe was fashioned and became an *objet d'art*, with coloured glass bases and heavily decorated beaten shafts of silver or gold.

The tobacco and molasses mix that is used (called sheesha or shisha in Arabic) is commonly flavoured with apple, strawberry, melon, cherry or mixed fruit and whether you're Downtown or strolling along the Corniche, you'll soon notice the sweet smell of sheesha in the air. When you order a nargileh in Beirut, don't worry if you're a novice, just choose your flavour and the waiter will help you get started and periodically check that the coals are still burning. It's important to take a puff every now and then to keep the coals hot.

While less harmful than smoking cigarettes, smoking sheesha is still bad for your health. The first couple of times you smoke you'll probably get dizzy, but that's part of the appeal! And yes, you can smoke other substances with a water pipe, but most connoisseurs would never use the one water pipe for different substances. Remember, the saying goes that it's not what's in the pipe that counts, it's who you share the experience with that's important.

THE AUTHOR'S CHOICE

Food Yard (Map p251; ☎ 03-477 336; Rue Gouraud, Gemmayzeh; entrées around LL10,000, mains around LL17,000; ⏱ 11.30am-3pm & 7pm-midnight, closed Sun) Instead of blowing huge sums of money trying to compete with the excessive interiors and 'con-fusion' menus of some of Beirut's newer establishments, the owners of Food Yard have created a deliberately casual neighbourhood eatery. While it *is* funky (and plays great music), the result of spending more time working on the menu than the décor means that Beirut now has an eatery that can put tuna tartare and duck *confit* on the one menu and deliver both with ease. Situated in Gemmayzeh, a wonderful neighbourhood full of Ottoman- and French Mandate–era buildings, it's already attracted the attention of other restaurateurs wanting in on the local scene. But just as the now-closed Otium spawned a host of competing restaurants that paid homage to its modus operandi, at least this time the revolution will have reasonably priced menus and affordable wines. Bookings advisable.

works, but listen to the waiter for the daily specials. Bookings are recommended.

Food Yard (Map p251; ☎ 03-477 336; Rue Gouraud, Gemmayzeh; entrées around LL10,000, mains around LL17,000; ⏱ 11.30am-3pm & 7pm-midnight, closed Sun) This restaurant is the best thing to come out of the closure of Beirut's most talked about restaurant, Otium. Read the boxed text The Author's Choice (above) to find out why.

ITALIAN

Pasta di Casa (Map pp244-5; ☎ 366 909, 363 368; Ashkar Bldg, just off Rue Clemenceau, Ras Beirut; mains around LL10,000; ⏱ noon-midnight) An unpretentious local Italian place that's only a short walk from most Hamra accommodation options. Friendly staff and good home-made pasta make it a welcoming place for a pasta fix. It only has 10 tables, doesn't accept credit cards and can get very busy for dinner.

La Posta (Map p248; ☎ 970 597; Rue al Maarad, Downtown; entrées & pastas around LL12,000; ⏱ noon-midnight) While delivering tried and true Italian staples, the combination of a great Italian chef and fresh ingredients sourced from Italy set this fashionable Downtown

restaurant apart from the competition. The rear section of the restaurant is where the action is – usually with a table or two of besuited VIPs working their way through several courses. However, you can just have one pasta course or a pizza (both recommended) and still have that superb view of the cardo maximus.

Al Dente (Map p251; ☎ 202 440, 333 333; 137 Rue Abdel Wahab el-Inglizi, Achrafiye; mains around LL28,000; ⏱ 12.30-3pm & 8.30-11pm Mon-Fri, 8.30-11pm Sat) Attached to the Hotel Albergo (p255), this formal Italian restaurant's suitably lavish décor and lengthy wine list make it a Beirut establishment favourite – for everyone else it's a special occasion restaurant. Nevertheless, with great pastas and sublime risottos, eating here is a special enough occasion in itself. Bookings essential.

Fennel (Map pp244-5; ☎ 363 792; Weavers Centre, Rue Clemenceau, Kantari; entrées around LL14,000, pastas around LL17,000; ⏱ 11-2am Tue-Sun) A groovy, soft-lit creamy-coloured restaurant offering simple but excellent Italian food – try the saffron risotto –and a decent wine list. It also has an outdoor area popular for lunch and a cocktail bar upstairs.

LEBANESE/MIDDLE EAST

Abou Hassan (Map pp244-5; ☎ 741 725; Rue Salah Eddine el-Ayoubi, Manara; ⏱ noon-midnight) A cosy neighbourhood eatery with only six tables, serving honest food at bargain-basement prices. Choose from the ultrafresh range of dips and grills on display and you'll be in seventh heaven. Expect to pay LL12,500 for mezze, grill and beer. No credit cards.

Le Chef (Map p251; ☎ 445 373, 446 769; Rue Gouraud, Gemmayzeh; 2-course meals around LL10,000; ⏱ 6am-6.30pm Mon-Sat) A Beirut institution, some other chefs say the food is similar to that served in an institution. Nevertheless, while the Rue Gouraud eating scene develops around it, this daytime 'workers' café' keeps faithfully dishing out huge plates of home-style Arabic food at great prices. Ask the helpful waiters about the daily specials. No credit cards or alcohol.

Restaurant Istambuli (Map pp244-5; ☎ 352 049, 353 029; Rue Commodore, Hamra; mezze around LL3500, grills around LL8000; ⏱ 12.30pm-midnight) Traditional Lebanese food that's extremely good value and good quality sees this place always jam-packed with local families. Make sure you try the delicious cheese pastries.

Al Balad (Map p248; ☎ 985 375; Rue Ahdab, Downtown; mezze around LL5000; ☽ noon-midnight) While located in the quieter restaurant area north of Place d'Étoile, this place offers the best Lebanese mezze in the Downtown area. The standard mezze are all beautifully prepared, but dishes such as the red hummus and delicious deep-fried potatoes set it apart from the competition.

Marrakech (Map p251; ☎ 212 211, 03-502 444; Rue de Damas, Achrafiye; entrées around LL10,000, mains around LL20,000; ☽ 8.30pm-late, kitchen closes midnight, closed Mon) Boasting one of the best interior designs in Beirut, this stylish restaurant is situated directly below another of the city's best, Yabani (p257), which you'll gawk into on your way past in the glass lift. The food is typical Moroccan, thankfully sticking to the classics, such as tagine and pastilla, but it can't compete with the gorgeously low-lit room. Don't arrive before 10pm, or you'll dine alone.

Al Mijana (Map p251; ☎ 328 082, 334 675; Rue Abdel Wahab el-Inglizi, Achrafiye; mezze around LL5500, grills LL11,000; ☽ noon-3pm & 8-11.30pm Sun-Fri, 8-11.30pm Sat) Housed in a restored and opulently decorated Ottoman house with both indoor and large outdoor eating areas, this restaurant serves traditional Lebanese food at its best. The à la carte menu is better value than the set menus, and while the food's reasonably priced, a bottle of Château Ksara will set you back LL52,000.

Sultan Brahim (Map p248; ☎ 989 989; near Starco Center, Downtown; mezze around LL5500, fish market price; ☽ noon-3pm & 8-11.30pm Sun-Fri, 8-11.30pm Sat) These long-standing Lebanese seafood restaurateurs have really hit the mark with their new branch. Despite its location in a less-visited Downtown area, when the weather's fine the terrace is packed with diners enjoying the local seafood – you select your own – and excellent mezze. Be sure to book ahead.

Cafés

Beirutis are dedicated to the art of drinking coffee. Whether it's a small stand-up with tiny espresso machine, a street vendor clinking cups to attract customers, a roadside van with an espresso machine poking out the back, or a stylish café offering 10 different coffee blends, it's an integral part of Beiruti life. The city has a wealth of places where it's possible to – indeed, almost obligatory – to

while away hours over a coffee and pastry or nargileh. The most pleasant of these are along the waterfront or overlooking the cardo maximus downtown. At most places listed here an Arabic coffee costs between LL1500 and LL4000, pastries around LL3000 and a nargileh between LL8000 and LL15,000.

Al-Kahwa (Map pp244-5; ☎ 362 232; Al-Kanater Bldg, Rue Bliss, Ras Beirut; ☽ 10-1am) A popular hang-out with students from the AUB. Its friendly atmosphere, and good, reasonably priced Western and Arabic menu make it a reliable choice for breakfast, lunch or for dinner. An Arabic breakfast here costs LL6000, cooked English breakfast is LL6000, a club sandwich with fries is LL6500, and a Caesar salad is LL5000.

Taj Al Moulouk (Map pp244-5; ☎ 370 096; Rue Bliss, Ras Beirut; ☽ 5.30-1.30am) Great Turkish coffee and an amazing array of pastries make a visit here essential. This branch has a terrace and indoor café, so it makes a welcome pit stop when walking the length of the Corniche; the other branch on Rue Bliss, is sit-down in its ice-cream parlour only.

Manara Palace Café (Map pp244-5; ☎ 03-753 887; the Corniche, Manara; ☽ 24hr) With a super location right on the water, this café is a pleasant place to drink coffee or have a snack. There's an outdoor terrace and there's live Arabic music after 10pm each night.

Al-Raouda (El Rawda; Map pp244-5; ☎ 743 348; the Corniche, Manara; ☽ 8am-midnight) A waterfront favourite with local families (it has a small playground), this place is packed on weekends. It's a little hard to find – walk down the lane right next to the Luna Park entrance and you'll spot the misspelt 'El Rawda' sign.

Bay Rock Café (Map p238; ☎ 796 700; Ave du Général de Gaulle, Raouché; ☽ 7-2.30am) A fabulously situated café overlooking Pigeon Rocks. Meals, snacks, coffee and drinks are a bit pricey, but the outdoor terrace is a particularly attractive place to watch the sunset with a beer or a nargileh.

Tribeca (Map p251; ☎ 339 123; Rue Abdel Wahab el-Inglizi, Achrafiye; bagels LL5000-10,000; ☽ 8-1am) This café is most notable for its home-made bagels that are good enough to stand up and be counted in New York. A good place for brunch if you're in the area.

Ristretto (Map pp244-5; ☎ 739 475; Rue Mahatma Gandhi, Hamra; ☽ 7am-8pm Mon-Sat) As its name implies, this small café serves good strong espresso shots. It also serves some of the best breakfast eggs and pancakes in town, and is an excellent place to cure that Rue Monot–induced hangover. It also has a decent lunch menu.

Wimpy Movenpic (Map pp244-5; ☎ 345 440/1; Rue Hamra, Hamra; ⏲ 7.30am-11.30pm) Notable for being one of the last of the popular cafés left on Rue Hamra where you'll find older gentlemen sipping their Turkish coffee and reading the newspaper. Located on the busiest intersection of the area, it's a great vantage point from which to watch the Hamra chaos. Those who desperately need a 'white chocolate double decaf mocha' can go across the road.

Casper & Gambini (Map p248; ☎ 983 666, 03-423 777; Rue al Maarad, Downtown; ⏲ 9-1am) One of the first cafés to start up in the Downtown area, it's still serving some of the best coffee, gourmet sandwiches and desserts around. Hopefully by the time you read this it will have its popular terrace overlooking the cardo maximus back.

Rafaat Hallab & Sons (Map p248; ☎ 444 411, 03-331 229; Rue al Maarad, Downtown; ⏲ 5am-11pm) Tripoli's favourite sweets-maker (see p308 for more information) now has a Downtown Beirut branch offering the usual range of sweets such as baklava and *borma* (birds' nest pastry shaped into cylinders and filled with a mixture of nuts) served up on the outdoor terrace. To keep Beirutis fitting into those tight clothes it even has low-fat and sugar-free creations.

Cheap Eats

Every suburb has a multitude of stalls offering felafel, *manaeesh bi-zaatar*, kebabs, *foul*, fresh juices, *fatayer bi-sbanikh* (spinach parcels) and shwarma; the best way to get a feel for where to eat is to wander around and choose the busy ones, as they are likely to be offering the freshest food. Most of these places work to a system whereby you choose what you want, tell the cashier, pay and then take your receipt to the food counter to collect your meal or snack. Prices are on a par: a felafel will cost around LL2500, a *manaeesh* LL2000, a kebab LL3000, a large fresh juice LL3000 and a shwarma LL3000. Sit-down places are both harder to find and, in many cases, less satisfying; some of the better ones are listed here with a few of the city's most-famous street-food stands.

Bliss House (Map pp244-5; ☎ 756 657; Rue Bliss, Ras Beirut; ⏲ 7-5am) This is one of the most popular takeaways in Beirut and is always packed with AUB students grabbing a quick snack on their way to/from class. Its three shop fronts offer cheap and filling shwarma, kebabs, fresh juice and ice cream.

Japanese Please! (Map pp244-5; ☎ 361 047; Rue Bliss, Ras Beirut; ⏲ 11am-4pm & 7-11pm Mon-Sat) This tiny sushi bar is a welcome oddity among the fast-food franchises of Rue Bliss. Customers can take away, eat at the bar, or take advantage of the free delivery service. Reasonable prices.

Marrouche (Map pp244-5; ☎ 743 185/6; Rue Sidani, Hamra; ⏲ 24hr) Specialises in very tasty *shish tawouq* (marinated grilled chicken on skewers) and chicken shwarma.

Pizza Hiba (Rue de Rome, Hamra; ⏲ 7am-7pm Mon-Sat) This tiny food stand serves up good, fresh *manaeesh* and *fatayer bi-sbanikh* for local workers. Just up the street opposite the tourist information office is the just-as-popular **Pizza Hamda** (Map pp244-5; Rue de Rome, Hamra; ⏲ 7am-7pm Mon-Sat), serving the same.

Al-Tazaj Fakieh (Map pp244-5; ☎ 363 800; the Corniche, Ain al-Mreisse; ⏲ noon-late) Another popular choice, its pleasant outdoor terrace is a great place to sit and eat the extra-tasty BBQ chicken on offer while watching Beirutis promenade along the Corniche.

Kabab-ji (Map pp244-5; ☎ 351 346; Rue Hamra, Hamra; ⏲ 8-2am) A long-standing branch of the Lebanon-wide chain. It's a little more stylish than most kebab shops and an extremely popular place to sit and sample fresh and delicious kebabs.

Barbar (Map pp244-5; ☎ 379 778/9; Rue Spears, Hamra; ⏲ 24hr) The granddaddy of them all. This phenomenally popular chain sells *manaeesh*, shwarma, pastries, mezze, kebabs, ice cream and fresh juice. Join the hordes of people gobbling their snacks on the street in front, or organise to have food delivered to your hotel or apartment.

Zaatar w Zeit (Map p251; ☎ 614 302, 03-614 302; Rue Nasra, Sodeco, Achrafiye; ⏲ 24hr) This branch is busiest late at night when patrons from the nearby clubs flock here to re-energise over cheap and delicious *manaeesh* with a multitude of toppings. There is another branch on Rue Bliss (Map pp244-5) that is popular by day and night.

Mino (Map pp244-5; ☎ 365 632; Rue Bliss, Hamra; ⏲ 11am-late) This tiny shwarma stand really sells only four things – meat and chicken shwarma in two sizes. But what it does, it does well, and it beats waiting at Bliss House when it's packed with students.

Self-Catering

Beirut is packed with small neighbourhood grocery shops selling the basics, including items such as milk and bread and usually a small range of fruit and vegetables. If you're doing day trips outside Beirut you'll find that fresh fruit and vegetables are available at roadside stalls, sometimes directly in front of the land where the produce was grown. The best of the larger Hamra supermarkets is the **Consumers Co-op** (Map pp244-5; Rue Makdissi, Hamra; ☾ 7am-11pm). Look out for **Charcuterie Bayoud** (Map pp244-5) just outside the Co-op, which is more popular for its beer, wine and spirits than meats. Excellent vintage Lebanese and imported wines can be sourced at **Enotica** (Map p251) and **Le Comptoir** (Map p251) in Achrafiye.

If you're planning a picnic to sample those wines, try the wonderful deli at **Aziz** (Map p248; ☎ 358 000; near Murr Tower, Kantari), which stocks all sorts of French gourmet goodies. If you're staying in Beirut long-term and need to undertake a more serious shopping expedition, try the **Spinneys** (Map p251; Rue Alfred Naccache) supermarket in Achrafiye.

DRINKING

Beirut has an embarrassment of riches when it comes to bars. While this is great for patrons, for bar-owners the competition is fierce and bars open, close, change names, venues, décor and style with monotonous regularity. On top of this, the bar/club/restaurant lines are blurred – the same table you were eating at an hour ago may now be an impromptu dance floor.

With dinners booked from 9.30pm onwards, bar-hopping is a nocturnal pastime. Beirutis don't like waiting in line or being turned away from a bar or club so generally they book a table or space at the bar they wish to visit after dinner. If you arrive early at one of the hottest bars, you'll probably get a space (and get to check out the ultrahip interior), but you might be asked to move just as the night starts hotting up. Thursday, Friday and Saturday nights are by far the most popular and arriving at Rue Monot at midnight on Saturday night will have

you wishing you had booked ahead! The bars where you should book are noted. For a drink in the afternoon or early evening, head to the cafés on the Corniche or the Downtown area.

Note that closing time of 'late' means that closing depends on whether there is a good crowd or not.

Petit Café (Map p248; ☎ 976 060; Rue al Maarad, Downtown; ☾ 8-3am) This café is arguably the most popular place for nargileh on the Downtown strip. Skip the food menu, select your nargileh flavour, and puff away with the rest of Beirut. Gets superbusy as the night goes on, especially on weekends.

Virgin Café (Map p248; ☎ 999 777; Opera Bldg, Downtown; beers LL4500; ☾ noon-midnight) Head upstairs from the indoor café to the rooftop for one of the best terraces in Beirut. Take in the fantastic view while relaxing over a nargileh (LL13,000), glass of wine or a beer. From here you can check out the coastline north of Beirut and the snowcapped Jebel Sannine (season permitting) to the northeast.

Mint Lounge-Bar (Map p251; ☎ 339 637, 03-921 888; Rue Monot, Achrafiye; ☾ 5pm-late) The perfect place for sipping a Martini while listening to the in-house DJ and checking out the décor. This small and stylish bar also has guest DJs – look for the posters and flyers around Hamra and Monot advertising the nights.

Pacífico (Map p251; ☎ 204 446; Rue Monot, Achrafiye; local beers LL6000; ☾ 7pm-late) This Latin-themed bar is the long-standing number one with the local 30-something crowd. Happy hour is between 7pm and 8pm.

Lime (Map p251; ☎ 03-348 273; Rue Monot, Achrafiye; local beers LL5000; ☾ 7.30pm-late) A popular drinking spot with an outdoor terrace. Ambience outweighs attitude here, which is a nice change on Rue Monot. The local beer is reasonably priced.

Hole in the Wall (Map p251; Rue Monot, Achrafiye; ☾ 7pm-late) For those wanting a break from cool interiors and guest DJs and needing a beer poured into a glass with a handle, this one's for you. It's a great little pub smack bang in the centre of Rue Monot, and it's a regular stop for expats. Mind you, that doesn't stop it from charging the same as everyone else, but at least you don't have to know the doorman.

Lila Braun (Map p251; ☎ 331 662; Rue Monot, Achrafiye; ☾ 8pm-late) One of the favourites of the

---

COFFEE CRAZE

Coffee should be black as hell, strong as death, and sweet as love.

Turkish Proverb

In 1526, Ali, son of pious mystic Mohammed ibn Iraq al-Dimashqi, learned that his father had died in Mecca. The distraught son departed for Arabia immediately and spent almost 15 years in the holy city, where he adopted some of the local customs, including the drinking of coffee, then unheard of in Beirut. Unable to kick the habit, he returned to his home town with sacks of beans and is credited with single-handedly creating generations of caffeine addicts.

When at a café in Beirut, coffee or *café* on the menu is generally Turkish coffee brewed in a pot with a handle (generally called an *Ibrik*). Sometimes this coffee is mistakenly called 'Arabic coffee', which has far more cardamom than its Turkish cousin. The coffee beans for Turkish coffee are ground down to a fine powder not unlike the consistency of baby powder. Sugar is included at the time of brewing, so you need to tell the waiter how you would like it: without sugar (*bidoon sukkar*), a little sugar (*sukkar qaleel*), medium (*maDbooTah*) or very sweet (*sukkar katheer*). You drink the coffee out of small porcelain cups – remember to not gulp down the last mouthful or you'll be drinking mud, which is the ground coffee sitting in the bottom of the cup!

Those who haven't acquired the taste for Turkish coffee will find menus usually have espresso (and the variants thereof) listed separately, as well as 'Nescafé', which is instant coffee.

Monot scene, it's a two-storey restaurant-bar with a cool red and white interior, with a DJ upstairs. Can be a bit hit-or-miss though, and by 1am doesn't let people in because it's either full or closed.

Bar Louie (Map p251; ☎ 03-477 336; Rue Gouraud, Gemmayzeh; ☺ 11am-late) Brought to you by the same folks who own Food Yard (p258), one suspects that they opened it to stop people hanging around their restaurant listening to its music. A deliberate step away from the increasingly youth-oriented Rue Monot scene, Bar Louie features an eclectic range of guest musicians and succeeds in creating an earthier atmosphere than the bars up the road.

Centrale (Map p251; ☎ 575 858, 03-915 925; Rue Mar Maroun, Achrafiye; ☺ 8pm-12.30am kitchen, bar open till late) Sporting one of Beirut's most handsome interiors, Centrale epitomises the new Beirut – once you've managed to find the entrance, that is (look for the landing lights). Once inside head upstairs to the bar, soak up the atmosphere and (weather permitting) the view. Call first on weekends.

Red (Map p251; ☎ 326 484; Rue Monot, Achrafiye; ☺ 10pm-late) As its name implies, it's very red, plush and a great place to settle back with a stiff vodka. While it's a lounge-bar, it doesn't seem to stop people dancing, especially on the weekends and on the tables. Book some space in advance.

ENTERTAINMENT

The best sources of 'what's on' information are the daily newspapers and the monthly *Guide*; check out Media (p240) for more information.

Cinemas

Cinemas in Beirut tend to play it safe, screening the same Hollywood movies that play almost simultaneously worldwide. All is not lost however – Beirut's cultural centres (p239) organise screenings that showcase current and classic films that cost less than the promotional budget of one Bruce Willis film, but pack 20 times the emotional resonance. There are also film festivals during the year, in particular the Mid East Film Festival Beirut (p253). For daily listings, consult the *Daily Star* newspaper (p240).

There is no dedicated 'art' cinema venue in Beirut – the cinemas listed play the same films you could see, well, anywhere.

Concorde (Map pp244-5; ☎ 738 439; Rue Dunant, Hamra)
Empire Dunes (Map p238; ☎ 792 123; Dunes Centre, Verdun)
Empire Sodeco (Map p251; ☎ 616 707; Sodeco Square)
Empire Sofil Center (Map p251; ☎ 328 806; Sofil Center, Ave Charles Malek, Achrafiye)

Live Music

There are really only a couple of dedicated live-music venues in Beirut that are worth mentioning, but the cultural centres (p239) once again come to the rescue with programmes of visiting musicians and singers. Festivals also offer extensive opportunities to see live performances; some cafés have musical guests and posters advertising them often go up around Hamra.

Blue Note (Map pp244-5; ☎ 743 857; www.bluenote cafe.com; Rue Makhoul, Hamra; admission LL8000-20,000 depending on artist; ☒ 11-1am) This is *the* place to hear live jazz. Generally Thursday, Friday and Saturday are the only nights when the music is live, and these are definitely the best nights to visit. There's a very good food menu if you want to do dinner first, but live jazz is the main course here. Aficionados should phone or check the website to see who's playing before booking as it sometimes books non-jazz acts.

Gemmayzeh Café (Map p251; ☎ 580 817; Rue Gouraud, Gemmayzeh; ☒ 8-3am) This Beirut institution is one of the best places to hear live Arabic music in Beirut. Generally consisting of an oud (lute) player and singer, you should make a booking for the live music and dinner – the café has a great mezze menu, but it's worth popping in here any time of day for a coffee and to check out the charming building.

Nightclubs

Make sure you're well rested as a stay in Beirut is incomplete without devoting at least one evening to the art of the Beiruti nightclubbing. Keep in mind that visiting one of the nightclubs listed is usually preceded by dinner generally finishing no earlier than 11pm, followed by a spot of bar-hopping. Acid and B 018 in particular don't get going until after 1am.

Acid (☎ 03-650 904, 03-714 678; Sin el Fil, south of the Sin el Fil roundabout; admission free for women before midnight, men US$20 incl open bar; ☒ 9pm-late) A huge club playing house and Arabic music that's popular with a mixed crowd, although more women seem to go on Friday than Saturday nights. Ring and book a taxi to get there as many service taxis don't know where it is.

B 018 (Map p238; ☎ 580 018, 03-800 018; Beirut-Jounieh Hwy at La Quarantaine; admission free; ☒ 9pm-late) This venerable club is easily the most famous in town. Known for its particular décor as much as its music, it's situated underground in a car park a few kilometres north of central Beirut. With its mock-horror baroque interior complete with coffins for seats, B 018

is certainly memorable. Those suffering from claustrophobia needn't worry – the roof is always opened at some stage during the night. Its liberal reputation means that gays and lesbians will feel comfortable here. You'll find it about 10km from the BCD; ask a taxi driver for the club or for the Forum de Beyrouth.

Citrus (Map p248; ☎ 972 100; Azarieh Bldg, Rue Emir Bechir, Downtown; admission free; ☒ 9pm-late) Arrive here after midnight on a busy night and you'll find yourselves the only people with their feet on the floor – everyone else is up on any available space in the room dancing to the latest Arabic dance-floor hits. It's infectious – after a cocktail, you'll find yourself looking for a space to join them.

Crystal (Map p251; ☎ 332 523; 243 Rue Monot, Achrafiye; admission free; ☒ 8.30pm-late) Formerly known as Circus, this place is still one of the city's most popular nightclubs. It's a great space with a good, fun atmosphere where the well-heeled clientele generally book a large table with friends (for dinner) and settle in for the night. You might get a seat at the bar, but don't expect to get a table if you haven't booked.

Taboo (Map p248; ☎ 03-225 555; Rue Emir Bechir, Downtown; admission free; ☒ 9pm-late) Located virtually next to Citrus, this is another Downtown club playing commercial dance-floor hits accompanied by a wild dancing crowd. While it's busy during the week, on weekends you should book. At the time of writing it was *the* in spot of the Downtown scene.

Spectator Sports

Football (soccer) is by far the most popular spectator sport and Beirut's most popular teams are Beirut Nejmeh, Beirut Ansar and Olympic Beirut. If you want to catch a match, you should check the *Daily Star* (see p240) for listings.

If you have an interest in horse racing, just behind the National Museum of Beirut the racecourse or **Hippodrome** (Map p238; ☎ 632 515; admission LL5000-15,000) is one of the only places in the Middle East where you can legally place a bet. Horse racing has always been wildly popular with the Lebanese; in the old days the Hippodrome was the place to go at weekends. Races are held at 1pm April to September and 11am October to March on most Sundays. Entry costs vary, depending on seating.

Theatre

There are several excellent theatres in Beirut that sometimes stage non-Arabic productions. Listings for what's on at individual theatres can be found in the local daily newspapers and in the *Guide* (see p240 for details).

Al-Medina Theatre (Map pp244–5; ☎ 371 962; Rue Justinien, Clemenceau) Shows modern Lebanese plays in Arabic, French and sometimes English.

Monot Theatre (Map p251; ☎ 202 422; next to St Joseph's Church, St Joseph University, Achrafiye) Regular programme of French-language theatre.

Théâtre de Beyrouth (Map pp244–5; ☎ 363 466; Rue Graham, Ain al-Mreisse) Small theatre hosting cutting-edge productions and performances from Lebanon and abroad, in Arabic, English and French.

SHOPPING

High-quality oriental souvenirs found across much of the Middle East, including colourful caftans, satin slippers, wooden boxes, backgammon sets, ceramics and Phoenician figurines all make memorable souvenirs, and can be found in Beirut. Although you will find few things to buy that are exclusive to Lebanon, you will see goods that are a bit different in wonderful stores, such as the **Artisans du Liban et d'Orient** (Map pp244–5; ☎ 998 811; the Corniche, Ain al-Mreisse) and the **Princesse and Sultan Artisanat** (Map p251; ☎ 611 413; 155 Ave Elias Sarkis, Sodeco). The latter has a unique gift in its sets of arabesque drink coasters inspired by the floor tiles in Lebanese houses.

Traditional Palestinian embroidery can be purchased from **Al-Badia** (Map pp244–5; ☎ 746 430; 78 Rue Makdissi, Hamra), which sells colourful dresses, cushion covers, shawls and scarves made by refugee women. Proceeds go to Palestinian refugees in Lebanon. If you don't have room for a carpet, you can find cushion covers made out of kilims at carpet shops, such as **Ariana Carpets** (Map p251; ☎ 614 319; Ave Elias Sarkis, Sodeco).

Nearby, a number of interesting antique stores are scattered around Achrafiye. **Art Deco** (Map p251; ☎ 338 785; 79 Rue Trabaud, Achrafiye) is a regular treasure trove. After admiring the original Art Deco furniture and French Deco–inspired copies, you can rummage around the back-room shelves for smaller decorative gifts. For something more modern, or rather post-modern, cool books on Middle East photography, visual culture and cultural studies can be found at **CD-Thèque** (Map p251; ☎ 321 485; Ave Elias Sarkis, Achrafiye), along

with an enormous range of excellent DVDs, videos and CDs from the region, in all genres and styles.

Heading south from Hamra, in Verdun you'll find Beirut's upmarket shopping malls, including the Dunes Centre, and designer clothing outlets along Rue Verdun.

GETTING THERE & AWAY

For information about getting to Syria from Beirut, see Travel Between Syria & Lebanon (p387). Buses, minibuses and service taxis to destinations north of Beirut leave from Charles Helou bus station (Map p251) and the Dawra (aka Dora) transport hub (7km northeast of town). To the south and southeast they leave from the Cola transport hub (Map p238) on the opposite side of town, south of Blvd Saeb Salam. See the relevant town and city sections for further details.

Air

Beirut has the only airport in the country, **Beirut International Airport** (BEY; ☎ 628 000; www .beirutairport.gov.lb). See opposite for details.

AIRLINE OFFICES

Most airlines have offices in the **Gefinor Center** (Map pp244–5; Rue Maamari, Hamra). For details of major airlines flying to and from Beirut, see p381.

Bus & Microbus

Buses and microbuses travel between Beirut and Lebanon's major towns. There are three main bus hubs in Beirut:

Charles Helou bus station (Map p251) Just east of Downtown, for destinations north of Beirut (including Syria).

Cola transport hub (Map p238) This is in fact a confused intersection that is sometimes called Mazraa. It is generally for destinations south of Beirut.

Dawra transport hub East of Beirut, and covering the same destinations as Charles Helou, and is usually a port of call on the way in and out of the city.

Charles Helou is the only formal bus station and is systematically divided into three signposted zones:

Zone A For buses to Syria.

Zone B For buses servicing Beirut (where the route starts or finishes at Charles Helou).

Zone C For express buses to Jounieh, Byblos and Tripoli.

Zones A and C have ticket offices where you can buy tickets for your journey.

Cola is not as well organised as Charles Helou but if someone doesn't find you first (which is what usually happens) ask any driver where the next bus to your destination is leaving from. Buses usually have the destination displayed on the front window or above it in Arabic only. There are also a growing number of microbuses covering the same routes, which are slightly more expensive than regular buses, but a lot cheaper than service taxis. Microbuses are operated by individuals. The advantage is that they are small, comfortable and frequent, but you'd be taking your chances regarding the driver's ability. You pay for your ticket on the microbus, at either the start or the end of your journey.

Service Taxi & Taxi

Taxis to Syria depart from the Charles Helou and Cola bus stations and operate on the usual system of waiting until the vehicle fills up before leaving. They have an advantage over the buses in that you don't have to wait around too long to depart, but the disadvantage is that they can be a bit of a squash, especially on a long journey. If you want the taxi to yourself, you will have to pay for all five passenger seats. See Service Taxi & Taxi (p266) for more information.

GETTING AROUND
To/From the Airport

Beirut International Airport (BEY; ☎ 628 000; www.beirutairport.gov.lb) is approximately 10km south of Beirut city centre. From here it's theoretically possible to catch a bus into the city, but the fact that the airport bus stop is at the roundabout at the airport exit, a 1km walk from the terminal, is a major pain. The red-and-white LCC bus No 1 will take you from the airport roundabout to Rue Sadat in Hamra; bus No 5 will take you to Charles Helou bus station. The blue-and-white OCFTC buses No 7 and 10 also stop at the airport roundabout en route to the city centre; bus No 10 goes to Charles Helou bus station and bus No 7 goes to Raouché, from where you can take bus No 9 to Hamra. Fares are LL500. The buses operate between 5.30am and 6pm and the maximum wait should be 10 minutes.

Taxis from the airport are notoriously expensive, with drivers usually attempting to extort US$25 for the trip into town. It's possible to bargain this down to as little as US$10, but only if the supply of taxis is greatly outstripping demand when you walk out the front of the airport terminal. A cheaper option is to walk 1km to the highway and hail a service taxi into town for LL2000. Alternatively, if you have arranged your hotel before you arrive, ask it if it can provide transport from the airport. This will save a lot of hassle and some smaller hotels do it for as little as US$10, sparing you a theatrical performance to get the price down this far outside the terminal.

On a brighter note, it's cheaper to catch a taxi from Beirut to the airport; the average fare is LL10,000. Make sure you confirm this price with the driver before you get into the taxi.

Car & Motorcycle

For general information on hiring a car or motorcycle, please see p391. Following is a selection of car-rental companies.

Advanced Car Rental (☎ 482 424; www.advancedcarrent.com)
Avis (☎ 367 124; www.avis.com.lb)
Budget (☎ 740 741; www.budget-rental.com)
City Car (☎ 803 308; www.citycar.com.lb)
Lenacar-Europcar (☎ 480 480; www.lenacar.com.lb)
Sixt (☎ 803 308; www.sixt.com.lb)
Thrifty Car Rental (☎ 510 100; www.thrifty.com.lb)

Public Transport

Beirut is well serviced by its network of buses. The red-and-white buses are run by the privately owned Lebanese Commuting Company (LCC) and the large blue-and-white OCFTC buses are government owned. Sometimes the **tourist information office** (Map pp244-5; ☎ 343 073; www.lebanon-tourism.gov.lb; Ground fl, 550 Rue Banque du Liban, Hamra; ☻ 8.30am-2pm Mon-Thu, 8.30-11.30am Fri, 8.30am-12.30pm Sat) has free LCC route maps available.

Buses operate on a 'hail-and-ride' system: wave to the driver and the bus will stop. The only official bus stops are where the bus starts and finishes. There are no timetables, but buses come frequently during the day. Both companies stop their services in the early evening.

The buses can be excruciatingly slow but handy if you're on a time-rich–cash-poor stay. They're especially good value for trips to places such as Brummana (p271) and Beit Mery (p269).

BEIRUT

The bus routes most useful to travellers are listed here. A trip will almost always cost LL500.

LCC BUSES

No 1 Hamra – Khaldé: Rue Sadat (Hamra), Rue Emile Eddé, Hotel Bristol, Rue Verdun, Cola roundabout, Airport roundabout, Kafaat, Khaldé

No 2 Hamra – Antelias: Rue Sadat (Hamra), Rue Emile Eddé, Radio Lebanon, Sassine Square, Borj Hammoud, Dawra, Antelias

No 5 Ain al-Mreisse – Hay as-Saloum: Manara, Verdun, Yessoueiye, Airport roundabout, Hay as-Saloum

No 6 Dawra – Byblos: Antelias, Jounieh, Jbail (Byblos)

No 7 Museum – Baabdat: Museum, Beit Mery, Brummana, Baabdat

No 13 Charles Helou – Cola: Place des Martyrs, Riad al-Solh Square, Cola roundabout

OCFTC BUSES

No 1 Bain Militaire – Khaldé: Bain Militaire, Unesco, Summerland, Khaldé

No 4 Dawra – Jounieh: Dawra, Dbayé, Kaslik, Jounieh

No 5 Ministry of Information – Sérail Jdeideh: Ministry of Information, Sodeco, Borj Hammoud, Sérail Jdeideh

No 7 Bain Militaire – Airport: Bain Militaire, Summerland, Borj Brajné, Airport

No 8 Ain al-Mreisse – Sérail Jdeideh: Ain al-Mreisse, Charles Helou, Dawra, Sérail Jdeideh

No 9 Bain Militaire – Sérail Jdeideh: Bain Militaire, Rue Bliss, Rue Adbel Aziz, Rue Clemenceau, Rue Weygand, Tabaris Square, Sassine Square, Hayek roundabout, Sérail Jdeideh

No 10 Charles Helou – Airport: Charles Helou, Shatila, Airport roundabout

No 15 Ain al-Mreisse – Nahr al-Mott: Ain al-Mreisse, Raouché, Museum, Nahr al-Mott

No 16 Charles Helou – Cola: Charles Helou, Downtown, Cola

No 23 Bain Militaire – Dawra: Bain Militaire, Ain al-Mreisse, Charles Helou, Dawra

No 24 Museum – Hamra: Museum, Barbir, Hamra

Service Taxi & Taxi

Service taxis are plentiful and cheap in Beirut. Most routes around the capital are covered and you can hail one at any point

on the route. The only way to find out if the driver is going where you want is to hail him and ask. If the driver is not going where you want he'll (and it's nearly always a 'he') respond by driving off. If he's going in your direction the acknowledgment to get in may be as imperceptible as a head gesture. You can get out at any point along their route by saying 'anzil huun' (I get out here), to the driver. Occasionally when the drivers have an empty car they will try and charge you a private taxi fare. To let him know that you want to take the taxi as a service taxi, be sure to ask him 'servees?'. Taxis are usually an elderly Mercedes with red licence plates, generally with a taxi sign on the roof and smoke belching from both the interior and the exhaust. The fixed fare for all routes in central Beirut is LL1000. The fare to outlying suburbs is LL2000. Try and pay at the earliest opportunity during your trip. It's a good idea to keep a few LL1000 notes handy for these trips.

If you do wish to take a service taxi as a private taxi, make sure the driver understands exactly where you are going and negotiate a price before you get in. Most destinations in the centre of Beirut cost LL5000 to LL7000, however it's not uncommon for drivers to ask for LL10,000, and grudgingly settle for LL7000. If you think the driver is asking too much, just wave him on and wait for another one.

You can also telephone for a taxi from a number of private hire firms. They charge a bit more, but are safer at night. Remember to ask the fare over the phone.

Some of the better-known companies:

Allo Taxi (☎ 366 661)
Auto Tour (☎ 888 222)
Beirut Taxi (☎ 805 418)
City Taxi (☎ 397 903)
Dabour Taxi (☎ 346 690/1)
Lebanon Taxi (☎ 353 152/3)
Radio Taxi (☎ 804 026, 352 250)
TV Taxi (☎ 862 489, 862 490)

Mt Lebanon & the Chouf Mountains

جبل لبنان وجبال الشوف

Mt Lebanon & the
Chouf Mountains

Mt Lebanon is the heartland of modern Lebanon. In medieval times the name referred to the mountain range between Byblos and Tripoli, the traditional stronghold of the Maronites. Today, however, Mt Lebanon is an administrative district incorporating the coast from Beirut almost as far north as the town of Batroun (included in this chapter), as well as the steep mountains around the city. Highly urbanised as the coastal stretch is, hidden among the concrete chaos is ancient Byblos, one of Lebanon's important historical gems, as well as some decent beaches that are popular in summer.

The proximity of Mt Lebanon's steep coastal mountains to Beirut has seen much of the mountain areas urbanised as well, with high-rise buildings perched precariously on their sides. Here you'll find the resort towns where Lebanese families spend the summer months escaping the heat and humidity of the coast. Further on are Lebanon's most famous ski resorts, and even further afield, the wild and beautiful Adonis Valley.

The Druze stronghold of the Chouf Mountains lies southeast of Beirut and forms the southern part of the Mt Lebanon Range. In places, the mountains appear untouched; in others they are peppered with small villages and terraced for easy cultivation. Numerous springs and wells feed the main crops of olives, apples and grapes. Most people travel here to see the village of Deir al-Qamar and the nearby Beiteddine Palace, but it is also pleasant to simply wander among the mountain villages of the area.

HIGHLIGHTS

- Absorbing over 7000 years of history at the ruins at **Byblos** (p281), followed by 40 years of history at the **Byblos Fishing Club** (p286)
- Remembering how to tell your stalactites from your stalagmites at the spectacular **Jeita Grotto** (p277)
- Taking a heart-stopping ride on the **Téléférique** (p278) for a wonderful view of Jounieh
- Checking out how the Beirut party scene seamlessly transforms into the **Faraya Mzaar** (p273) après-ski scene during winter
- Admiring the palaces, khans and awesome views from the traditional village of **Deir al-Qamar** (p292)
- Getting back to nature with a hike among the cedars at the **Chouf Cedar Reserve** (p297)

THE METN & KESROUANE
المتن وكسروان

The Metn is the mountainous area east of Beirut and was the frontline between the Christians and the Druze during the civil war. These days it's a popular summer getaway for middle-class Beirutis escaping the stifling heat and humidity in the city. Outside the summer months it can be very quiet, but the wonderful views and clean air offer a welcome respite from the chaos and pollution of Beirut. Brummana is the main resort area with lots of accommodation and restaurants, while Beit Mery has Roman and Byzantine ruins. Both can be done as an easy day trip from Beirut, keeping in mind that on the trip up and down the mountain you'll experience some of the most hair-raising driving in Lebanon – no small feat!

The Kesrouane is the *caza* (district) adjoining the Metn and lies above Jounieh. Historically, Shiites inhabited the Kesrouane but in the 13th and 14th centuries the area's Mamluk overlords settled Sunni Muslim Turkoman clans to police the territory. It was from these Turkomans that the dominant Assaf dynasty emerged, and under the Ottomans the Assafs in turn encouraged Maronite emigration to the Kesrouane to keep the Shiites under control. This they did with such efficiency that by the 18th century most of the original Shiites had been driven out of the area and it became primarily Maronite. Nowadays, it is famed for its spectacular vistas and ski resorts.

BEIT MERY
بيت مري
☎ 04

This popular summer retreat is 17km from Beirut centre and 800m above sea level. The views from the town are wonderful with Ras Beirut jutting out into the sea on the west and the deep valley of Nahr al-Jamani blocked to the east by the Sannine massif. The original village has grown into a small town: many of the villas have been built in strategic positions to take advantage of the views, with little concern for aesthetics.

Sights
The **ruins** that remain here date from the Roman and Byzantine periods. Worth seeing in particular are the fine **mosaics** on the floor of the AD 5th-century Byzantine church. The remains of a number of small **temples** surround the mosaics, including one dedicated to Juno that was built in the reign of Trajan (AD 98–117). There is also a fairly well-preserved public bath, where you can see the original hypocaust tiles that acted as the heating system.

Nearby is the Maronite monastery of **Deir al-Qalaa**, built in the 17th century on the remains of a Roman temple, which in turn was probably built on an earlier Phoenician temple. As at Baalbek (see p327), the Roman temple was dedicated to Baal, known here as Baal Marqod. Although the site was heavily damaged in the civil war, you can still see a Roman column built into one of the monastery walls. At the time of writing, however, the monastery was being restored and was out of bounds. To reach the ruins (coming from Beirut), turn right at the small roundabout after the start of Beit Mery and head up the hill. A large red-and-white communications tower adjacent to the monastery is visible from both directions.

Other than visit these sites, there is little to do in Beit Mery except walk around and enjoy the views, which is a pleasant enough way to pass a couple of hours.

Festivals & Events
Music lovers should note that there is an annual international music festival, **Al Bustan Festival** (www.albustanfestival.com), which starts in mid-February and runs for about a month. Check out the website for more information.

Sleeping & Eating
Hotel al-Bustan (☎ 972 980/1/2; www.albustanhotel.com; s/d/ste from US$160/192/247, breakfast from US$13; ☒ ☐ ☒) This privately owned luxurious hotel is the only useful one in town. It has an arty feel in keeping with its running of Al Bustan Festival. The rooms, service, food and views are first rate but if the price makes you flinch, just pop into the Scottish Bar for a drink and check out the spectacular view. There are two well-regarded restaurants here, **Il Giardino** (per person US$25-30), an Italian trattoria, and the French **Les Glycines** (per person from US$50).

Tigre (meals around US$12) Near Deir al-Qalaa and serving traditional Lebanese food, this place has breathtaking views without a breathtaking price.

MT LEBANON & THE CHOUF MOUNTAINS

Al Janna (☎ 873 120/1; meals around US$25) On the main road to Brummana, above the turn-off for Deir al-Qalaa, 'al-janna' is Arabic for paradise. It's a popular place with two restaurants: Kan Zaman with the usual mezze and grills; and an outside Brazilian restaurant, El Diabolo. It also has a pub, a nightclub and Turkish baths.

There are many other restaurants between Beit Mery and Brummana – for more details see p269).

Getting There & Away

From Beirut you can catch a service taxi to Beit Mery (LL2000) at Dawra bus station or at the National Museum of Beirut. Taxis stop on the main roundabout in the town and you can easily walk around the whole town from there. Two buses, the No 17 OCFTC or the No 7 LCC, also head up here from opposite the National Museum.

BRUMMANA برمانا
☎ 04

Around 4km northeast of Beit Mery, the resort town of Brummana is packed with hotels, cafés, shops and nightlife. Recently officially declared a city, Brummana has nothing as serious as ancient monuments to distract you from the pleasures of eating, drinking and all-round partying. During summer the place is crowded to bursting point and on weekends the traffic can be quite horrendous. Things are particularly busy during the national tennis tournament, held in August.

If visiting out of season, things are much quieter – and many of the hotels considerably better value – but it lacks the buzz of the busy summer months. Nonetheless, the views down to Beirut and the Mediterranean are even better than at Beit Mery, and there is a pleasant walk past the Mounir restaurant (p272), down the pine-studded hillside.

Information

Internet access is available in the centre of Brummana, but the addresses change every summer and your best bet is to walk along the main street or ask at a hotel. **Credit Libanais** has an ATM in the main street and there are a couple of moneychangers there as well. Other banks have ATM machines inside. The **post office** (◷ 8am-5pm Mon-Fri, 8am-noon Sat) and **telephone offices** (◷ 7am-midnight) are in the same building on the main street.

Sleeping

Brummana is geared towards well-off Lebanese and Middle Eastern clients, with a distinct shortage of cheap and even mid-range accommodation. The flip side is that outside the summer months, prices drop dramatically; some of the cheaper hotels do close for the winter.

Kanaan Hotel (☎ 960 025; fax 961 213; s/d US$35/40 low season, US$40/60 high season) One of the less-expensive hotels open all year, this place is small, friendly and family run. Its rooms are simple but all have attached bathrooms and balconies with views of the Mediterranean. The lounge is decorated with old Lebanese objets d'art, oil paintings and chandeliers. On the main street, opposite Brummana High School.

Garden Hotel (☎ 960 203; www.gardenhotellb.com; s/d/ste low season US$45/50/75, US$70/80/120 high season) Another friendly family-run hotel that's particularly good value in the off season. The rooms are a little old-fashioned but are well appointed with a minibar and satellite television. The hotel also has its own bar and a restaurant; it's on the main street, near Printania Palace Hotel.

Hotel Le Crillon (☎ 865 555; www.lecrillon.com; Rue Centrale; s/d/ste US$54/60/72 low season, US$90/120/150 high season;) This comfortable hotel has great views, from most of its rooms, towards Jebel Sannine. Its quaintly furnished rooms and reception are at odds with the pool area and exterior, but extras such as a gym and a health club make it a good low-season option.

Printania Palace Hotel (☎ 862 000; www.printania .com; Chahine Achkar St; s/d/ste US$120/130/240 low season, US$150/160/280 high season;) For many years this was the most luxurious hotel in Brummana – a claim now made by Grand Hills Hotel & Spa Hotel. It still has plenty of old-fashioned charm and all the accoutrements you would expect, with particularly pleasant rooms, an attractive garden, a French restaurant and a Lebanese restaurant.

Grand Hills Hotel & Spa Hotel (☎ 862 888; www .grandhillsvillage.com; s/d/studio US$187/198/297 low season;) This hotel has to be seen to be believed. It is part of Grand Hills Village, a lavish residential compound set on a huge chunk of prime Brummana real estate, that is owned by Robert Mouawad, a well-known international jeweller. The hotel exhibits the same attention to detail as one of his famous jewellery pieces with the 118 rooms and suites exquisitely decorated in 25 different themes – all positioned to take advantage of the great views. After a relaxing day at the spa and a wander around the gardens, you'll find yourself wanting to sell your own jewellery to stay an extra night. In the high season add about US$100 extra per room.

Eating & Drinking

Brummana has a great range of eating options in all price brackets. All those listed here are along the main road, where there are also the usual shwarma joints.

Tonino Crepes & Bakery (☎ 862 472) Serves crepes, pizza, salads, burgers, sandwiches and *manaeesh* at cheap prices. Also good value and with a similar menu is **Farrouj El Achkar** (☎ 862 443). You can also try **256 Pizza & Snack** near Cheers Cave restaurant.

Crepaway (☎ 964 347) This chain outlet is a bit further up the price scale, serving burgers and pizza as well as savoury French-style crepes.

Manhattan (☎ 961 967) This popular and more upmarket American-style diner serves burgers, pizza and French food.

Le Gargotier (☎ 960 952; meals from US$20; noon-3pm & 7pm-midnight, closed Fri) and its sister restaurant **La Garote** (☎ 960 096) both serve good traditional French food in traditionally French surroundings.

Burj al-Hamam (☎ 960 058; à la carte meals from around US$35; noon-late) A popular upmarket Lebanese restaurant famous for its mezzes and seafood, it has a huge terrace that's packed in summer with well-dressed Beirutis enjoying the excellent views over the mountains, while lingering over a long lunch. Bookings advised.

Mounir (☎ 873 900) In a similar vein as Burj al-Hamam, Mounir has fabulous views towards the Mediterranean. The expansive mezze menu lives up to the restaurant's lofty reputation and for those who can manage to move on to main courses, the grills and fresh seafood are beautifully cooked. The restaurant also has a wonderful garden and a children's playground, perfect for those families settling in for a (recommended) long afternoon. Bookings are essential, especially if you want a table with a view in summer.

Moods Pub (☎ 960 616) and the popular **Oaks Pub** (☎ 03-819 243, 03-874 407) are both good for drinks.

Getting There & Away

Perhaps the best way to enjoy the two towns is to catch a bus or service taxi to Brummana, spend an hour or so there, and then walk or catch a service taxi (LL1000) to one of its restaurants. You could then follow up with a walk into Beit Mery and a leisurely look at the ruins and monastery before making your way back to Beirut. Service taxis from the National Museum or Dawra charge LL2000 to Beit Mery or Brummana. The No 7 LCC bus (LL500, 40 minutes) leaves from just east of the National Museum.

JEBEL SANNINE ﺟﺒﻞ ﺻﻨّﻴﻦ

This impressive mountain (2628m) is worth climbing in the summer for the unparalleled views of Lebanon from its summit. There are actually two summits: the higher one is less interesting and it is the slightly lower peak that affords the spectacular views. To make the climb, head for the village of **Baskinta**, which is east of Bikfaya. From there, continue 6km to the hamlet of **Nebaa Sannine**, where there is a spring that feeds **Wadi Selle ash-Shakroub**, the starting point for the climb. It is best to make the climb from the most southerly slopes rather than tackling the slopes that overlook the hamlet. It is a moderately steep climb and should not take more than three hours. The last part of the climb is easier: there is a path that runs like a ledge around the top of the mountain.

From the top you can see Qornet as-Sawda, Lebanon's highest peak at 3090m to the north, and Jebel ash-Sheikh (Mt Hermon; 2814m) to the south. The Bekaa Valley and the Anti-Lebanon Range are clearly visible to the east and in the foreground are Jebel Keniseh (880m) and Jebel Barouk (1980m). To the west you can see the foothills of the Mt Lebanon Range slope all the way down to Beirut. Choose a clear, fine day to make this ascent; you will also need to be well shod and reasonably fit.

Getting There & Away

If you do not have your own transport, the only practical solution would be to take a taxi to Nebaa Sannine and arrange to be picked up at a specific time and place. Failing that, you would have to make the walk back to Baskinta, about 6km, and pick up a service taxi from there. It would be a wise idea to

nform someone (your hotel or friends) of
our plans and what time you expect to
eturn.

QANAT BAKICHE & ZAAROUR
قناة بكيش والزعرور

Qanat Bakiche and Zaarour sit on the slopes
of Jebel Sannine and are Lebanon's two small-
st ski resorts. Both are set in spectacular
ocations but were heavily damaged during
he war. These days Zaarour has by far the
etter facilities both on and off the slopes,
ut operates as a private club. However you
an contact the resort and ask about access
uring off-peak periods (generally during
he week).

Qanat Bakiche has not recovered as well
nd there's really only the resort owners'
now Land Hotel (☎ 03-340 300; www.snow-land.com)
or accommodation, equipment and lessons.
More adventurous skiers and snowboarders
vill be happy to note that the resort has
snowcat for trips to the back country, as
vell as Skidoos for hire.

The ski resorts can be a little difficult to
each without a car. The best way to get to
Qanat Bakiche from Beirut, is to head north
along the coast to Antelias, and then turn
up towards Bikfaya, then Baskinta village
just below Qanat Bakiche. From here, take
a sharp left turn and follow the signs for
'Snow Land'. You can also reach Faqra resort 4km away (see p275) by continuing on
past Snow Land. To get to Zaarour you can
go via Brummana and continue through
Bikfaya, Dour Ech-Choueir and Mrouj. Alternatively, you can follow the directions for
Qanat Bakiche via the coast road and follow
the directions from Bikfaya as above.

FARAYA & FARAYA MZAAR (OUYOUN AL-SIMAAN)
فاريا وفاريا المزار (عيون السيمان)

☎ 09

Better known for the ski resort, Faraya
Mzaar, lying 6km above it, Faraya itself
is a sleepy village that comes alive from
December to March every year with the
annual invasion of ski-toting Beirutis. Most
skis, however, spend more time facing sky-
ward in front of the cafés than facing down
the well-groomed slopes, and the après-ski
activities start early in the afternoon and end
late in the evening. Thankfully Faraya Mzaar
has more to offer than just partying; with the
fastest and most extensive lift system, decent
annual snowfall and the best variety of slopes
for all abilities, it's by far the best resort in
Lebanon. The slopes themselves consist of
three separate areas, Refuge, Jonction and
Wardeh, which are linked. There are also a
few cross-country skiing trails. In the summer, most of the larger hotels stay open and
offer mountain biking and hiking. For more
information on the resort, see the boxed text
Ski Facts: Faraya Mzaar (p274).

Sights & Activities
The main attraction of the area is its natural
beauty. If you're not there for the snow, then
there are some beautiful **walks** – it's possible
to walk to Faqra (6km) and back in a couple
of hours. One of the most famous natural
features of the area is the **Faraya Natural Bridge**
(Jisr al-Hajar). It is easy to spot from the
road, if you look to the right while heading
from Faraya to Faqra, and there's a place to
park just off the road. You can take an interesting but steep walk down to the bridge
itself. Centuries ago the bridge was thought
to be a work of human construction, but it
is in fact entirely a freak of nature.

SKI FACTS: QANAT BAKICHE & ZAAROUR

- **Altitude** 1904–2250m (Bakiche)
  1651–2000m (Zaarour)

- **No of Lifts** Bakiche has one beginner
  and two medium/advanced; Zaarour
  has three beginner, two medium, two
  advanced

- ☉ 8am-3.30pm Mon-Fri, 8am-4pm
  Sat & Sun

- in Bakiche ☎ 03-340 300 , in Zaarour
  04-310 010

- **Adult Day Pass** Bakiche US$18
  (Sat & Sun); Zaarour (private) US$27

With Zaarour being a private resort and
Qanat Bakiche lacking extensive facilities,
these resorts don't seem to offer much for
snow-sports enthusiasts. However if you
can get into Zaarour, or you don't mind
the extra work to get the fresh stuff at
Qanat Bakiche, both have awesome views
and uncrowded slopes.

MT LEBANON & THE
CHOUF MOUNTAINS

SKI FACTS: FARAYA MZAAR

- **Altitude** 1850–2465m
- **No of Lifts** 17
- (🕐) 8am-3.30pm Mon-Fri, 8am-4pm Sat & Sun
- ☎ 09-341 502
- **Adult Day Pass** US$17-25 Mon-Fri, US$28-45 Sat & Sun

Faraya Mzaar is the best (some say only!) ski resort in Lebanon. It's by far the best-equipped and most-popular resort and on a good weekend it looks like all of Beirut is on the slopes at once. Unfortunately, the Lebanese tend to ski like they drive – with the same disregard for the rules – so it can be dangerous. Weekdays are far quieter (and less expensive) and after a good dump of snow it can be a magical place to ski or snowboard.

Many coming to the resort take the après-ski activities far more seriously than the skiing and the resort has a hard-partying reputation. This is not to say that it's not a family-friendly resort – children under five have free access to the slopes. Ski and snowboard equipment can be rented from a number of places for between US$15 and US$20 per day, and there are rescue and Red Cross teams on hand.

The drive up to the area is also very scenic. There are two routes up to the ski resorts of Faraya Mzaar and nearby Faqra: one from Jounieh via Harissa and the other via the road to Jeita Grotto. The latter is the most picturesque route. While the first few kilometres along this route is solidly developed with shops, restaurants and apartments, at **Ajaltoun** the views of the coast and Beirut are lovely. When you reach Raifoun, you come to a roundabout; take the left exit, which leads up to **Faytroun**, where there are several ski-hire shops. Past Faytroun there are some dramatic rock formations in the dolomite limestone. Visible from the road, these are known by the locals as the 'House of Ghosts' and are actually **rock tombs** cut into the side of the hills. The Faqra ruins are also nearby (see p275).

Sleeping

Most of the accommodation in the Faraya Mzaar area consists of private apartments and chalets that are rented out for the entire ski season. Accommodation bookings are heaviest just before Christmas and it can be busy through to the end of March depending on snow conditions. Hotels are nearly always booked well in advance for the weekends but you can usually find somewhere to stay during the week. The sleeping options are listed in order from the town of Faraya up to the resort, which basically get more expensive as you approach the slopes.

Coin Vert Hotel (☎ /fax 720 812, 03-724 611; s/d US$30/40/50) This friendly, family-run hotel is on the main road of Faraya village just before the roundabout. It's a small, simple but clean one-star hotel that's open all year. It has a restaurant serving European and Lebanese dishes (with an average cost of US$10 for lunch or dinner) and a bar that's popular during the ski season. There's also a ski shop where you can rent equipment.

Tamer Land Hotel (☎ 321 268, 03-818 981; f 321 268; s/d/ste US$40/50/70) Another friendly family-run hotel in the centre of the village (up past the roundabout), with a choice of regular rooms or suites suitable for families. It's reasonably clean and all rooms have a private bathroom and satellite TV. The hotel also has a restaurant and a bar.

Chateau d'Eau (☎ /fax 341 424; s/d/tr US$45/50/70) This cosy hotel is about 5km beyond Faraya along the road to the snowfields. It's very comfortable with a nice clubby atmosphere and, like most places in Faraya, a lively après-ski scene with plenty of partying. There's a good restaurant and bar, plus a great open fireplace to sit around and swap ski stories.

Merab (☎ 341 341; merab@cyberia.net.lb; s & d from US$90; ❄ 🖵) A small hotel right in the middle of the resort, it has snug but nicely furnished rooms with minibar, central heating and room service. Downstairs from the hotel is the restaurant, Chez Mansour (see p275).

Mzaar 2000 (☎ 340 100; s/d from US$130/160 ❄ 🖵 🛗) A huge InterContinental resort and spa that opened in the winter of 2006. Mzaar is the most expensive hotel in Faraya. It has a superb location and all the usual five-star amenities, including equipment rental. With direct access to the slopes and an excellent fondue restaurant, it offers the full-on winter experience.

Eating & Drinking

There is plenty of choice when it comes to restaurants, but they fill quickly and it's worth booking a table. On the slopes, food is available at both Jonction and Refuge.

Chez Mansour (☎ 341 341) This shopping and restaurant complex is at the heart of the resort. Less glitzy than many of the other offerings around here, it has reasonably priced, unpretentious food that matches its atmosphere. Expect to pay about LL7000 for a cheeseburger, fries and a salad.

Jisr al-Qamar (☎ 03-877 993) Its name meaning 'Bridge of the Moon', this is a good Lebanese restaurant near the Coin Vert Hotel. If you go in for grills as well as mezze, expect to spend between US$25 and US$30 per person.

During the ski season Faraya's nightlife rivals Beirut's.

Igloo (☎ 640 067) This long-standing hot spot is in a white, conical-shaped building in the resort. In Rue Monot style, it's a restaurant early in the evening (pasta around LL15,000) and turns into a full-on bar/club once the food is cleared away.

L'Interdit (☎ 03-822 283) This is another popular restaurant-nightclub with a dance floor surrounded by tables. The menu is mostly French, expensive, and a drink will set you back US$10, but if you want to dance there's everything from techno to funk and soul.

Stars (☎ 340 100) Attracts a well-heeled crowd to the Mzaar 2000 resort with a mix of music, but it's not as hip as the others mentioned here.

Getting There & Away

You should be able to pick up a service taxi all the way to Faraya from Beirut's Dawra bus station, but only in the busy winter season, when there are plenty of people coming and going. Unfortunately Faraya is not on the main route to anywhere else. More likely you will have to go by service taxi to Jounieh and get a taxi from there. If you haggle, you will probably get a taxi to take you for US$15 for the 30-minute ride from Jounieh. When you leave, you will either need to get the hotel to call a taxi for you or, if you are lucky, find one in the main street in the Faraya village on its way back to Jounieh or Beirut. If you're staying at one of the better hotels they offer transfers to and from Beirut.

FAQRA فقرا

Faqra, 6km beyond Faraya, is one of the world's first private resorts and you can only ski here if you stay at the exclusive hotel, or are invited by a member who has one of the chalets within the grounds. If you do manage to get invited or are lucky enough to stay at the hotel, the ski slopes are well run and maintained with good medical facilities. There are three lifts plus a baby lift and a reasonable ski area, though snow coverage is a little patchier than at Faraya.

The main reason to come here, apart from skiing, is to see the **ruins** (☸ 8am-5pm; LL3000). These date from the Greek era, look dramatic when covered with snow, and lie very picturesquely on the side of a hill overlooking the valley below.

There is a heavily restored large temple with six Corinthian columns that feature widely on postcards of Lebanon. The temple is dedicated to Adonis, the 'very great god', and sits in the middle of a labyrinth of rocks. A rectangular court cut out of the rock precedes it and nearby are a couple of altars, one dedicated to Astarte (the great goddess of fertility), the other to Baal Qalach.

Just down the hill from here is another smaller temple that was originally dedicated to the Syrian goddess Atargatis, and later to Astarte. In the 4th century AD it was transformed into a church, and a Byzantine-style cross can still be seen on one of the fallen stones in what was the nave.

Surrounding the larger temple are some rock-cut tombs and to the north is a ruined cube-shaped base known as the **Claudius Tower**. According to an inscription above the entrance it was rebuilt by the Emperor Claudius in AD 43–44, but is likely to date back even further. It is thought to have been dedicated to Adonis. The base was originally covered with a step pyramid, perhaps like the one near Hermel (p332). Inside there are steps leading up to the roof. Beside the base there are two altars. One has been restored and has 12 tiny columns supporting its table top.

Sleeping & Eating

L'Auberge de Faqra (☎ 300 600; www.faqraclub.com; d US$125, US$230 Dec-Apr & Jul-Sep; ☒ ☐ ☲) The only place to stay in Faqra is this ultrasmart hotel, which is part of the large sports and leisure development. Hotel guests can use facilities such as the swimming pool, and tennis and squash courts, although there is a small extra charge. The rooms and service are of a very high standard and there's a ski lift to the most challenging ski area right outside the door. The resort is open in the summer and hires out mountain bikes.

Chez Michel (☎ 03-694 462; mezzes around LL4000) The exclusive Chez Michel is at the top end of the scale. It is just off the main road before Faqra Club. By far the most famous restaurant in the area, it serves great mezzes and grills, and has an excellent Lebanese-wine list. While it's open all year round, Saturday nights during the ski season usually end with some wild partying. If you can pull yourself away from the log fire, there are also fantastic views. Reservations are essential.

On the road above the village, next to a petrol station, Highland Snack is a small restaurant that offers the only cheap meals around. Further down near the ruins, Restaurant Faqra is a bit more expensive. About 1km past the village, Restaurant Kanater is also quite good.

THE COAST

Heading north along Lebanon's coast, the division between Beirut and the coastal towns is somewhat blurred by concrete, billboards and breakneck traffic. But taking an exit from the freeway will reveal good beaches, one of the world's most visually stunning sets of caves, sumptuous seafood restaurants and one of Lebanon's most significant and picturesque ruins. Making the region even more tempting, the area's proximity to Beirut makes it a comfortable day trip from the capital.

NAHR AL-KALB   نهر الكلب

The mouth of **Nahr al-Kalb** (Dog River; the Lycus River of antiquity) is on the coast road, heading north between Beirut and Jounieh. Prior to the building of the huge highway that now crosses the river, the steep-sided gorge was very difficult for armies to traverse, forcing them to cross in single file and leaving them vulnerable to attack. To give thanks for their successful crossing, conquering armies have, in the past, left a plaque or memorial carved into the sides of the gorge, with the most recent

inscriptions left by Christian militias during the civil war.

Apart from the earlier Assyrian carvings there are **stelae** in Latin, Greek, Arabic, French and English. All of these, except for the stele of Nebuchadnezzar II, are on the left bank, following the ancient courses of the steep roads carved along the slopes of the gorge.

Some of the oldest stelae have eroded to almost nothing, but some of the later inscriptions are still visible, if not always clearly.

Riverside Inscriptions

Starting from the motorway, the first bridge is the old 'modern' road. A hundred metres past that you see the charming, triple-arched old **Arab bridge** which now serves as a crossing point to a restaurant.

All inscriptions before 1920 have Roman numerals, and run as follows:

I Engraved by Nebuchadnezzar II on the rocky wall on the right (north) bank near the junction of the motorway and the old 'modern' road is a cuneiform inscription from the 6th century BC recording the campaigns of Nebuchadnezzar II in Mesopotamia and Lebanon. This is very overgrown and hard to see. All the other inscriptions are on the left bank starting near the Arab bridge and following the bank of the river to the main road, then continuing up the side of the gorge. Follow the stairs up until you are on top of the motorway tunnel. The ancient Egyptian and Roman roads continue and there are further inscriptions.

II This is an Arabic inscription lying almost at water level opposite the Arab bridge and commemorating its construction. It dates from the 14th century and was inscribed on behalf of Sultan Seif ad-Din Barquq by the builder of the bridge, Saifi Itmish.

III few metres downriver there is a Latin inscription from the Roman emperor Caracalla (Marcus Aurelius Antonius, AD 198–217) describing the achievements of the 3rd Gallic Legion. Just above the Roman inscription is a modern obelisk, which marks the French and Allied armies' arrival in Lebanon in 1942, while beyond it is another modern inscription commemorating the 1941 liberation of Lebanon and Syria from Vichy forces.

IV A French inscription marks the French invasion of Damascus on 25 July 1920 under General Gouraud. Not far from this is a plaque with Arabic script and the date 25/3/1979; next to this, another plaque with the engraving of a cedar tree and another Arabic inscription commemorates the withdrawal of French troops from Lebanon in 1946.

V The original stele showing an Egyptian pharaoh and the god Ptah has been covered by a later inscription by the French army commemorating its 1860 expedition in the Chouf.

VI An Assyrian king, depicted wearing a crown with his right hand raised, is badly preserved.

VII Next to VI, another Assyrian figure, which is now almost impossible to make out.

VIII Further along, another Assyrian stele, which again is in a very bad state of preservation.

IX Above VI and VII, a commemoration of British-led Desert Mountain Corps' and its 1918 capture of Damascus, Homs and Aleppo.

X Right by the motorway, a British commemorative plaque dating from 1918 marks the achievements of the British 21st Battalion and the French Palestine Corps. Beside this, steps lead up the mountainside and over the motorway, leading to the other inscriptions.

XI A weathered Greek inscription.

XII Another Greek inscription, but it is very worn. Just past this and to the right is the white rock plinth where the wolf statue once stood.

XIII About 30m further on, a stony path climbs sharply, just after some cedars carved into the rock by Phalange fighters. This next stele shows an Assyrian king in an attitude of prayer.

XIV Next to XIII is a rectangular tablet showing Pharaoh Rameses II of Egypt (1292–1225 BC) sacrificing a prisoner to the god Harmakhis. This is the oldest inscription at Nahr al-Kalb.

XV A little higher and only a few metres away on a dead-end path is another inscription of an Assyrian king.

XVI About 25m further up the slope, you come to the road at the top. There you'll see a rectangular stele, which shows Ramses II again, this time sacrificing a prisoner to the sun god Amun by burning him to death.

XVII The last stele is Assyrian and shows Esarhaddon with cuneiform text describing his victory against Egypt in 671 BC.

While viewing the inscriptions, or on the way to the Jeita Grotto, you will see the nearby Catholic retreat of **Deir Luwaizeh** on the north side of the gorge. It has a huge statue of Christ, which stands on top of the building, with arms outstretched.

Getting There & Away

Given its proximity to both Jounieh and Beirut, Nahr al-Kalb is best visited on a day trip (including the Jeita Grotto) or when going or coming back from a trip up the coast.

Nahr al-Kalb is simple to get to as it's on the highway. You can take a service taxi (LL2000) or a minibus that is going to Jounieh from Beirut's Dawra or Charles Helou bus stations, and get it to drop you off. The river mouth is just past the long tunnel on the highway and is easy to spot. When you leave, it is easy to flag down a service taxi or minibus going in either direction on the highway. Another alternative if you are staying in Jou-

nieh (or Byblos), is to negotiate a price for a taxi to Nahr al-Kalb and Jeita Grotto and get the driver to wait for you while you visit. This should cost around LL20,000 from Jounieh, if you bargain hard.

JEITA GROTTO مغارة جعيتا

A stunning series of caverns, **Jeita Grotto** (☎ 09-220 840/3; www.jeitagrotto.com; adult/child aged 4-11 LL18,150/10,175; ☻ 9am-6pm Mon-Fri, 9am-7pm Sat & Sun Jul-Aug; 9am-6pm Tue-Fri, 9am-7pm Sat & Sun May-Jun & Sep-Oct; 9am-5pm Tue-Sun Nov-Apr; closed approximately 3 weeks Jan & Feb) contains one of the world's most impressive agglomerations of stalactites and stalagmites. Stretching some 6km back into the mountains, these caves are the source of the Nahr al-Kalb and in winter the water levels rise high enough to flood the lower caverns. During the civil war, the caves were used as an ammunitions store, but they were cleared and reopened to the public in 1995 and have become one of the country's biggest tourist attractions. Allow at least a couple of hours to visit the Grotto.

The upper cavern is home to some extraordinary stalactites and stalagmites, visible as you first enter the cavern. As you walk further along the (often slippery) cement path, however, the cavern opens up to reveal its astonishing size. It's quite breathtaking. The lower cavern, explored by a short and quiet (thanks to electric outboard motors) boat ride, is beautifully lit, but keep in mind it's often closed in the winter because of high water levels. Regardless of what time of year you visit, however, the upper cavern is the highlight of the show.

And show is the operative word, because in order to view the caverns you must endure the unnecessary and unsympathetic additions such as a cable car (which would be better utilised at one of Lebanon's ski resorts), piped outdoor music, a tragic bird 'zoo', and a Disney-style toy train to transport you from the upper to lower caverns. Despite the additions, the grotto is amazing, most definitely worth a visit, and children will love it. There is strictly no photography allowed inside the caves, and cameras must be placed in the lockers provided before you proceed into either cavern.

The road to the caves is the first turn on the right past Nahr al-Kalb, if you are heading north. You can catch a service taxi to Nahr al-Kalb and either walk from there (if you're fit – it's close to a one-hour uphill slog), or catch a taxi to take you up from the highway – not many service taxis go up this road. It is about 5km from the highway to the grotto. A return trip to the caves from Nahr al-Kalb will set you back at least US$10. The turn-off to the grotto is clearly signposted on the highway from both directions.

JOUNIEh   جونيه
☎ 09

Prior to the war, Jounieh, 21km north of Beirut, was a sleepy fishing village. But with Beirut sliced in half by the conflict, wealthy Christian Beirutis wanted a place to escape from the shells and so Jounieh became the place to party their troubles away. While the old Centre Ville retains some charm, the frenzied haste in which construction progressed during the war has resulted in a high-rise strip mall hemmed in by the sea on one side and the mountains on the other. Not content with building on every square metre of land next to the sea, developers moved up the mountain and plonked high-rise buildings gravity-defyingly high up the steep mountainside. With much of the nightclub action returning to Beirut, Jounieh's reputation as *the* party town in Lebanon has diminished somewhat, but still remains popular in summer with expat Lebanese returning for their holidays, tour groups, and visiting Gulf Arabs escaping the summer heat.

Orientation

The town is roughly divided into three parts; viewed from the south they are Kaslik, Centre Ville and Maameltein. Kaslik is home to designer clothing, cinema complexes, fast-food outlets and some clubs. Heading north, about 20 minutes' walk downhill from central Kaslik is Centre Ville, concentrated on Rue Mina. Here you'll find a large supermarket, banks, cafés, some carpet shops and the taxi stand. North of the municipality building, Rue Mina becomes Rue Maameltein, and is the start of the Maameltein area, home to some hotels, most of the 'super' nightclubs, the Téléférique station and the casino.

Information

Blues Club Net (Rue Mina; per hr LL2000; ⊙ 2-11pm) Good Internet facilities right in the middle of Centre Ville.

Post Office (⊙ 7.30am-5pm Mon-Fri, 8am-1pm Sat) There's also a telephone office in the same building opposite the municipality building.

Sights & Activities

Other than taking a dip in the often less than perfect waters, sipping an overpriced drink in front of a bored Eastern European dancer at a 'super' nightclub, or having a long seafood meal, Jounieh doesn't offer much to keep you there too long. However a walk along Rue Mina in Centre Ville checking out the traditional houses is obligatory; a stroll along its entire length won't take more than about an hour.

If you do want to swim, you can go to any of the resorts that surround the bay. You'll pay between US$5 and US$10 depending on the facilities offered. Most have windsurfing equipment and body boards for hire.

Once you have exhausted the swimming, eating and drinking possibilities, it's time to take on the **Téléférique** (التفريك; ☎ 914 324, 93 075; www.teleferiquelb.com; adult/student/child aged 4-1 return ticket LL7500/6000/3500; ⊙ 10am-11pm Jun-Oc 10am-7pm Nov-May, closed Mon, Christmas Day & Good Fri), cable car travelling from the centre of town up to the dizzying heights of Harissa (see p280) This ride, dubbed the Terrorifique by some takes about nine minutes with the second half of the trip living up to its nickname. If you suffer from vertigo, avoid. Voyeurs will enjoy the bizarre views into people's flats as you ascend between huge apartment blocks.

Sleeping

Options are limited to only one hotel for those on a tight budget. Those looking for mid-range accommodation should note that off-season rates are significantly lower so ask for the best price.

Hotel St Joseph (☎ 931 189; Rue Mina; basic/large r US$20/30) Located in the old part of town about 70m north of the municipality building, this increasingly shabby pension is no hotel. However, it's well positioned and the building itself retains some of the charm of its former life as a mayor's residence. The basic rooms (for one to two people) and the larger ones (for two to three people) all have showers and toilets. There is also a common lounge kitchen and lovely outdoor terrace Book ahead for the summer months.

La Medina Hotel (☎ 918 484, 03-274 011; www. medinahotel.com; Rue Maameltein; s/d US$65/90; 🏊 🅿)

The rooms are clean and decorated in various degrees of kitsch (some with mirrored bed heads!), but they're no match for the foyer, which is on another planet. Along with the Holiday Suites Hotel, it's one of only two real waterfront hotels worth considering in town.

Mercure Hotel Beverly Beach (☎ 643 333, 639 999; everly@inco.com.lb; Rue Maameltein; s/d US$60/80; 🅿 🅡) Currently the best hotel in Jounieh, it's in the middle of the Maameltein strip, and has real comfortable, well-appointed rooms. Make sure you get one of the sea-facing rooms, with their large balconies and superlative views. The hotel has the added bonus of being virtually opposite Chez Sami, so it's not far to walk back for a nap after a seafood feast.

Holiday Suites Hotel (☎ 933 907; www.holidaysuites .com; Rue Mina; s/d/ste US$65/75/95; 🅿 🖳 🅡) Opposite the municipality building, this hotel is very friendly with some worn-looking but clean-enough rooms overlooking the sea. The main attraction, however, is its absolute waterfront location and swimming pool. This makes the hotel popular with tour groups, so book ahead, even out of season.

Eating

Jounieh has the ubiquitous tiny felafel-type stalls, juice bars and cafés. Rue Mina also has a couple of new places serving burgers and nachos. Chez Sami stands in a class of its own, while up in Kaslik there are the usual Western-style fast-food chains, but nothing really worth a walk or taxi ride, unless you're shopping as well.

Makhlouf (☎ 645 192; Rue Maameltein; shwarma LL3500, mains LL11,000, large fresh juice LL3000; ☽ 24hr) A branch of the popular Lebanese chain, this is always packed with locals. It has a great outdoor terrace overlooking the sea and is perfect for a sunset nargileh or an inexpensive dinner.

Algouna (Rue Mina; burgers LL5000; ☽ noon-late) A café in one of Rue Mina's restored shops with a good burger/nachos menu and indoor-outdoor seating. It's popular at night with locals not taking in the nightlife scene. Also popular is the similar Café Toni, next door.

Chez Sami (☎ 910 520, 03-242 499; Rue Maameltein; meals around US$30; ☽ noon-midnight) Simply one of the best fish restaurants in the country, Chez Sami is set in a wonderful old stone house. It sports a very stylish interior, but it's the two outdoor terraces overlooking the beach that are the focus of attention. Besides the fresh fish and excellent service, it's also famous for its mezze, the highlight of which is the squid in its own ink. The restaurant is no secret though, so book ahead. If you're keen to move on elsewhere for coffee and dessert, Patisserie Rafaat Hallab & Fils, a branch of the famous Tripoli sweet makers, is conveniently located directly opposite.

Fahed Supermarket (☽ 8.30am-8pm Mon-Sat, 9am-1.30pm Sun) This large supermarket is great for self-catering and sells wines and spirits.

Entertainment

While Jounieh was famed for its nightlife, Beirut's renaissance has seen most of the action move back to Rue Monot or the Downtown area. What's left, especially in Maameltein, are the 'super' nightclubs with tacky floorshows, over-priced drinks and lots of single women who seem to know the manager.

Oliver's (☎ 934 616; Rue Maameltein) One exception on this stretch, Oliver's is a popular venue for young locals and has good food, drink and music, as well as a lively atmosphere.

Casino du Liban (☎ 855 888, 853 222; ☽ slot-machine area noon-4am, gaming rooms 8pm-4am) This is Jounieh's most famous nightspot. Overlooking the northern end of Jounieh bay, it opened in 1959 and was the symbol of Beirut's decadence in the 1960s. The rich and famous flocked here to see extravagant floorshows, hang around the gaming tables, à la James Bond, and patronise the restaurants and bars. Closed during the war, it reopened with much fanfare in 1996. Those heady days of the '60s are long gone, but if you don't mind throwing away lots of money for the sake of kitsch or curiosity, it could be worth a visit to one of the 60 gaming tables or six restaurants, the 1200-seat theatre or any of the other facilities on offer. You'll need to be over 21 and wearing smart casual gear (no jeans or sports shoes) for the slot-machine area, and a suit and tie (men) and evening dress (women) for access to the main gaming rooms.

Getting There & Away

You can get to Jounieh by bus (see p387) for LL1000. Service taxis leave from Beirut's Dawra bus station and cost LL2000. If you catch a taxi that is going further north, you will be dropped off on the highway. Ask to be let out near the Téléférique, where there is a pedestrian bridge across the highway, which leads to the centre of town (about a five-minute walk). A private taxi from Jounieh to Hamra (Beirut) costs LL20,000.

HARISSA   حريصا

High above Jounieh bay is the gigantic white statue of the **Virgin of Lebanon** with her arms outstretched, where she has stood since the end of the 19th century. Around her are the churches and cathedrals of various denominations, the latest being the modernist Maronite cathedral whose outline can be seen from Jounieh below.

During religious festivals, such as Easter, there are often rather colourful **religious parades** that attract the crowds. At other times, pilgrims climb the spiral staircase around the statue's base. Others just enjoy the fantastic view from the top. There is a good restaurant, **Panorama – Harissa** (☎ 09-263 915) at the Téléférique terminus that serves mezze, grills, and great views for about US$15 per person.

The most common way to get to Harissa is by the (somewhat frightening) **Téléférique** (cable car) – see p278. If you want to catch a taxi up to Harissa (around LL7000), go to the main taxi stand in Jounieh's Rue Mina.

BYBLOS (JBAIL)   بيبلوس (جبيل)
☎ 09

With its picturesque ancient fishing harbour, Roman site, Crusader castle and restored souq area, visitors fall in love with Byblos. In existence before the great civilisations of the Middle East were even thought of, Byblos is one of the world's oldest continually inhabited towns. Although it is only around 40km from Beirut, the section of town around the harbour remains relatively unspoiled and it's a great place to visit overnight or on a day trip.

In its heyday before the civil war, Byblos was a favourite watering hole for the crews of visiting private yachts, international celebrities, and the Mediterranean jet set. These days, however, visitors come to absorb history, rather than make it. A wander around the ruins, a succulent seafood feast, and a lazy afternoon admiring the shimmering harbour is one of the most memorable experiences of a trip to Lebanon.

History

The earliest known occupation of Byblos dates from the 5th millennium BC, when the first settlers fished and tended their animals.

This was the era of early agriculture and the remains of cultivated grains have been found at a partially excavated site on the promontory. Tools and primitive weapons discovered there are now at Beirut's National Museum (see p242). By around the 4th millennium BC, the use of metals and ceramics was commonplace and large numbers of distinctive terracotta storage jars found at the site were used by the Chalcolithic-period inhabitants to bury their dead.

By the middle of the 3rd millennium BC, the city-state of Byblos was colonised by the Phoenicians, becoming a significant religious centre. The temple of Baalat Gebal, probably built on the site of a sacred grotto, was famous in antiquity.

Close links with Egypt encouraged the cultural and religious development of Byblos, with the temple receiving generous offerings from several pharaohs. During this flourishing period, Byblos evolved its hybrid style of art and architecture – part Egyptian, part Mesopotamian, and later showing some Mycenaean influences.

Around 2150 BC the Amorites, a hardened Semitic-speaking people, invaded the city and ruined much of its well-ordered layout and prosperity. This is the period of the underground royal tombs and of the Obelisk Temple dedicated to Resheph, god of burning and destructive fire.

The Amorite occupation ended in 1725 BC with another invasion, this time by the warlike Hyksos from western Asia, who arrived with horses and chariots, hurling javelins and carrying lances, all new to the people of this region. The Egyptians, also suffering from a Hyksos invasion, soon retaliated and from 1580 BC claimed the Phoenician coast. A long period of trade and development followed, during which time the kings of Byblos were subservient to their Egyptian masters. Many Egyptian customs were adopted, with temples and burial chambers decorated in the Egyptian style.

The linear alphabet, perhaps the most significant achievement of the Phoenicians, was developed during this period. Thought to have originated in Byblos, it was invented as a more practical way of recording trading transactions than the cuneiform script and quickly spread throughout the civilised world.

The Egyptian-dominated period of prosperity did not last and between 1100 and 725 BC Byblos was eclipsed by Tyre as the most important Phoenician city-state. Byblos then became a pawn in the power struggle between the Greeks and Assyrians (725–612 BC), eventually being ruled by the Assyrians and then the Neo-Babylonians.

Following the conquest of Babylon by Cyrus the Great in 539 BC, Byblos was regenerated as a trading link to the east under the Persian Empire. During the Hellenistic period, Byblos, unlike Tyre, voluntarily became an ally of Alexander and continued to flourish under its own royal dynasty.

When the Greek Empire waned and the Roman Empire waxed, Byblos concentrated its trading efforts to the west. From 63 BC onwards, the Roman Empire became a market for Phoenician goods and the city boasted lavish public architecture and suburban farming developments. Unfortunately, Byblos had sowed the seeds of its own downfall by not regulating the pace of deforestation – the very resource that had made this boom town wealthy was in short supply. When the Roman Empire split into east and west in AD 395, Byblos allied itself to Constantinople and became increasingly important as a religious centre. Pagan religion gradually gave way to Christianity and the city became the seat of a bishopric under Emperor Diocletian, protected by the Eastern Roman Empire until the Islamic invasion in 636.

Under the Muslims the focus turned eastward and Byblos' sea port dwindled into insignificance along with the city's defences. Byblos, by now known as Jbail, was left vulnerable. During the Crusader offensive, which began in 1098, Jbail fell to the Count of Tripoli, Raymond de Saint-Gilles. Despite resuming trade with Europe, the city never regained its former power. The subsequent struggles between the Crusaders and the Muslim forces continued until August 1266 when Emir Najibi, lieutenant of the Mamluk sultan, Beybars, laid siege to the town.

The next few centuries were relatively uneventful; the Turks took control of the city in 1516 and Byblos passed into insignificance until Ernest Renan, a French historian and philosopher, began to excavate the site in 1860. Excavations came to a standstill during the civil war and have yet to resume.

PAPYRUS CITY

Byblos was called Gebal in the Bible and Giblet by the Crusaders. Today, in Arabic, it is known as Jbail. However, its ancient name, Byblos, is thought to derive from *bublos*, the Greek word for papyrus. In Phoenician times the town was a stopping-off point for papyrus shipments en route from Egypt to Greece. A collection of papyrus sheets was called *biblio* (book), and from the Greek *ta biblia* (the books), the English word 'Bible' was derived.

Orientation

The medieval town, which is where most travellers spend their time, stretches north from just outside the perimeter of the ruins, which are flanked to the north by Rue al-Mina and to the west by the harbour. Scattered around the edge of the harbour are several restaurants. The modern town, where you'll probably arrive, is centred on Rue Jbail, where the buses and taxis congregate and most of the fast-food outlets and banks are located.

Information

Banque Libanaise pour le Commerce (Rue Jbail) Has an ATM.
Byblos Bank (Rue Jbail) Has an ATM.
Byblos Sur Mer (☎ 548 000; Byblos harbour) Money can be changed at this hotel.
CD Master (cnr Rue Jbail & Rue al-Mina; per hr LL2000; ☺ 24hr) The most-reliable option in town for Internet access, and even offers wireless access. Its other branch, near the ruins, has more-limited opening hours.
Medical Emergency (☎ 140)
Police (☎ 112)
Post Office (☎ 540 003; ☺ 7.30am-5pm Mon-Fri, 8am-1pm Sat) Turn into the street, off Rue Jbail, with Diab Brothers on the corner; it's 20m up the hill on your right, on the 2nd floor of the building.
Standard Chartered Bank (Rue Jbail) Has an ATM.
Tourist Office (☎ 540 325; ☺ 8.30am-1pm Mar-Nov, closed Sun Dec-Feb) Located near the archaeological site entrance, in the souq area, it has the official Ministry of Tourism brochure for Byblos, but no town map.

Sights
THE RUINS

This ancient **site** (adult/student & child LL6000/1500; ☺ 8am-sunset) is entered through the restored Crusader Castle and has guides who speak English, French, German, Italian or Japanese.

BYBLOS (JBAIL)

MEDITERRANEAN SEA

They rely on gratuities, but if you don't like to negotiate these things up front, figure on paying at least LL10,000 (up to LL20,000 or more if there are several of you). If you have time before visiting the ruins, scour the souvenir shops in the souq for a copy of Bruce Conde's *Byways of Byblos*, published in the 1950s and a charming pocket guide to Byblos. Many of the artefacts originally located on the site are now housed at the National Museum of Beirut (p242), so a visit there, either before or after visiting the ruins, is recommended.

CRUSADER CASTLE

The most dominant monument at the archaeological site is the castle built by the

Franks in the 12th century and constructed out of monumental blocks, mostly pillaged from the Roman ruins. Some of the blocks are the largest used in any construction in the Middle East (apart from one or two at Baalbek – see p330). The castle measures 49.5m by 44m, with a deep moat around it. You can see the nearby Phoenician ramparts on either side of the entrance. The structure has some points of interest, for example, the whole basement area is a huge water cistern that is largely intact. Unless you're passionate about Frankish architecture, however, the best part of visiting the castle is the commanding view of Byblos from the top of the ramparts, which gives you a clear idea of the layout of the ancient city. It's worth noting that because of the many layers contained in the small site, later monuments were moved and reconstructed in order to gain access to those underneath. So while the Roman theatre is now at the western edge of the site, it was originally located between the town's northeast entrance and the Temple of Resheph. Access to its roof is via a staircase.

CITY RAMPARTS

The defences of Byblos have been maintained and added to since the city's foundation. They date from the 3rd and 2nd millennia BC. Six different constructions have been discovered forming a 25m-thick wall. The ramparts curve around from the castle to the shore and on the opposite side of the castle curve west and then south, blocking access to the promontory where the original city was confined.

TEMPLE OF RESHEPH

This 3rd-millennium-BC temple was burned and rebuilt during the Amorite occupation. The later temple, known as the Obelisk Temple, was moved to a nearby site so that Maurice Dunand, the resident archaeologist, could excavate the original structure. It consists of a sacred enclosure. In the middle is a tripartite sanctuary facing east.

TEMPLE OF BAALAT GEBAL

This is the oldest temple at Byblos and dates back to the 4th millennium BC. The temple underwent major rebuilding after being destroyed by fire during the Amorite period. A few centuries later the site was levelled and a new sanctuary built. It later became a

symbol of the close relations between Egypt and Byblos. Numerous alabaster fragments of votive vases, many inscribed with the names of Old Kingdom pharaohs, were discovered here and can be seen in Beirut's National Museum. The temple remained an important religious centre through the centuries. A colonnade of six standing columns from around AD 300 lines the route to the temple and testifies to its use in Roman times, when it was thought to have been dedicated to the goddess Astarte.

OBELISK TEMPLE

The temple, rebuilt on this site, consists of a forecourt and courtyard that houses the slightly raised sanctuary. The cube-shaped base of an obelisk stands in the middle of the sanctuary and is thought to have been a representation of Resheph. In the courtyard is a collection of standing obelisks, including one built at the command of Abichemou, king of Byblos at the end of the 19th century BC. The obelisks were thought to have originally been 'God boxes', where the gods would live and be worshipped. Several votive offerings have been found here, including the wonderful bronze figurines now housed at the National Museum. Other schools of thought suggest that they may be connected to the rites of Adonis and Astarte.

KING'S WELL

In the centre of the promontory is a deep depression, which is the site of the King's Well (Bir al-Malik). According to legend, Isis sat weeping here when she came to Byblos to search for Osiris. Originally a natural spring, the well supplied the city with water until the end of the Hellenistic era. By Roman times it was used only for religious rituals as the city's water came from the surrounding mountains and was transported through a network of earthenware pipes. The stone walls were built because the rising ground level threatened to close over the spring.

ROMAN THEATRE

This charming reconstruction of the theatre is only one-third its original size and has been sited near the cliff edge, which gives it marvellous views across the ocean. First built in AD 218, its orchestra had a fine mosaic floor depicting Bacchus, now at the National Museum. One notable feature is the series of miniature porticoes situated in front of the stage.

ROYAL TOMBS

Nine royal tombs are cut in vertical shafts deep down into the rock and date from the 2nd millennium BC. These well tombs are not found elsewhere and attempts to protect them from plunder proved fruitless – all have been raided for treasure. The most important tomb is that of King Hiram (1200 BC), who was a contemporary of Ramses II of Egypt. The shaft containing his grave was inscribed with early Phoenician script that said 'Warning here. Thy death is below'. Hiram's sarcophagus is now a highlight of the National Museum. There are steps leading down into one of the tombs, and a tunnel leads to another containing a stone sarcophagus of a 19th-century-BC prince, Yp-Shemu-Abi.

EARLY SETTLEMENTS

To the south of the site are Neolithic (5th millennium BC) and Chalcolithic (4th millennium BC) enclosures, houses and huts, of which only the crushed limestone floors and low retaining walls remain. Throughout this area, large burial jars were found in which the bodies were curled up in a foetal position. In the earlier period the dead were buried beneath the floors of the houses. Dominating the ruins here is an **Ottoman-era house**. There is also a reasonably well-preserved Early Bronze Age residence and building foundations.

THE MEDIEVAL TOWN
Church of St John the Baptist

In the centre of this Crusader town is the Romanesque-style Church of St John the Baptist, which was begun in 1115 but badly damaged by an earthquake in 1170. Ancient columns were used in the doorways, and the heavy buttressing on the western side is thought to have been an effort to prevent further damage. One of its most unusual architectural features is the open-air baptistry, which sits against the north wall. Its arches and four supporting pillars are topped by a dome.

The church also has an unusual layout: the apses are facing northeast, but a sharp change in direction brings the northern half of the church back into its more conventional east–west alignment. Apparently, this is because a mistake in orientation was only

discovered after the apses had been built and was corrected halfway through construction. The south portal is purely Romanesque, but the north doorway is of an 18th-century Arab design.

To the west of the church is a single standing column and overgrown mosaic floor, remnants of an earlier Byzantine church.

Wax Museum

Almost opposite the Church of St John is this **Wax Museum** (☎ 540 463; LL5000; ☼ 9am-5pm) containing wax figures in various tableaux representing the history of Byblos from earliest times – high kitsch and only worth visiting if you really like this sort of thing.

Souq Area

The medieval part of the city has a beautifully restored souq area that houses a range of souvenir shops. You'll find the usual 'antiques', brass goods, T-shirts etc, but the highlights include the kitsch 1950s-era postcards, and **Mémoire Du Temps** (☎ 547 083; www.memoryoftime.com; ☼ 8.30am-5.30pm). Here you can buy ancient fossilised fish remains, set in the rock in which they were found, for as little as US$10. Excavated from a site near Hjoula, in the mountains above Byblos, the sale of the fossils is legal. You'll even get a certificate of authenticity.

The Harbour

It seems hard to believe that this peaceful little harbour was once a nerve centre of world commerce, but it was from this small port that the cedar and other wood, for which Byblos was famous, was shipped to the capitals of the ancient world. Much later the Crusaders left their mark here, building defensive towers on either side of the harbour mouth. A chain between the towers could be raised to prevent boats from entering. The northern tower was restored in Mamluk times and is still in fairly good condition. From the top you can look down and see the remains of ancient quays in the clear water below.

Activities
SWIMMING

If you don't mind a stony beach, there's the aptly named **Pebble Beach**, just to the north of the harbour beyond the Byblos Sur Mer hotel. A better place to swim, however, is **Tam-Tam Beach**, which turns into **Paradise Beach** (a well-known gay hang-out) at its northern end. Tam-Tam Beach is about 1km south of the centre of town. Follow the road that runs parallel to the coastal highway and look for the hand-painted sign on the right. There is a small road leading down to a car park. It can get very crowded (and very noisy) with young Beirutis on summer weekends, but surveying the scene is part of the fun. There are a couple of snack stands selling food, drinks and beer. To use the beach costs LL1000, and if there's some swell around you can even hire surfboards. Take care when swimming, though; thanks to a strong undertow, lifeguards regularly pluck people out of the water. A taxi fare from the centre of town is about LL2000. If you want to brave the traffic, you can also get the bus or service taxi to/from Beirut to drop you off on the main highway.

BOATING
A cluster of long motorboats in the harbour takes visitors on 15-minute rides (LL5000 per person) from spring until autumn. If you want to experience the tough life of a local fisherman (at least for a few hours), **Esprit-Nomade** (☎ 03-233 552; www.esprit-nomade.com; 6.45pm; per person all-inclusive US$15) holds moonlight fishing trips with Byblos fishermen every Friday night.

WALKING TOUR
Byblos is ideal to explore on foot. Starting at the **taxi stand** on Rue Jbail, head north and veer left onto Rue al-Mina, which follows the medieval walls. As you reach the water check out the view north past the public **Pebble Beach** on your right. The road then curves around to the left and the swimming pool area of the **Byblos Sur Mer** hotel is in front of you, as well as a great view of the harbour. A stroll of the harbour brings you to a turn on your left leading uphill. Take this road, which leads up to the **Church of St John the Baptist**. Half a block up the road on the opposite side of the street is the **Wax Museum**, with its rather kitsch tableaux of Lebanese culture. From here, turn right and walk through the **souq**. You will see the entrance to the **archaeological site** ahead of you, slightly to the left. You'll need at least a couple of hours to explore the site. When you leave by the same entrance, head back to the small souq area and check out the (legal) fossil souvenirs at **Mémoire du Temps**. Next, head west back down to the harbour and end up at the

Byblos Fishing Club (see p286) for a well-earned drink and a look at the wonderful photos of Byblos, and Pepe (see the boxed text Pepe the Pirate, p286), in their heyday.

Sleeping
Camping Amchit Les Colombes (☎ 540 322, 943 782; camp sites US$3, 'tungalows' US$20, 3–4-person chalets with/without air-con US$27/30) Commonly known as 'Camping Amchit', this complex is 3km north of Byblos on a promontory overlooking the sea. It has all the necessary amenities, including showers, toilets, kitchen with gas burners, and electrical points for caravans (220V), although these aren't as well maintained as they could be. In addition to tent and caravan sites, there are also fully furnished chalets and 'tungalows' (claustrophobic bungalows in the shape of a tent, with two beds and a Portaloo-type shower and toilet) sleeping two people. The camping ground is set on a wooded cliff top, with steps down to its own rocky beach and the chalets and tungalows have fabulous views. It's a 25-minute walk from Byblos; a service taxi costs LL1000.

Motel/Restaurant Abi-Chmou (☎ 540 484; Nassib Eid Bldg; s/d/tr US$30/40/50) This is the best-value sleeping option in town. All rooms, except one, have views of the ruins, and run off a huge communal living area with a TV. There's also a spotlessly clean kitchen and shared bathroom. The owner likes to rent out the rooms off the living area to groups, and the double room (which you can take as a single) has a private shower. The motel is near the tourist office.

Hotel Ahiram (☎ 540 440; www.ahiramhotel.com; s/d/tr US$50/65/75; 🔀) This hotel has most certainly seen better days. Its none-too-clean rooms have air-con, balcony with sea views and a small bath. Still, it has a great position behind the Pebble Beach, just north of Byblos harbour. Prices include breakfast and are lower outside the summer season.

Byblos Sur Mer (☎ 548 000; www.byblossurmer .com.lb; s/d/ste US$66/76/103; 🔀 🖭) This long-established hotel has comfortable, smallish rooms with wonderful views over Byblos harbour and its seafront swimming-pool area. There's no denying that its position is sensational and the staff are friendly, but the rooms are a little tired and overpriced. The hotel has its own restaurant on the 1st floor and operates **L'Oursin restaurant** (Apr-Oct) across the road, and by the sea.

PEPE THE PIRATE

Widely known as the Pirate of Byblos, Pepe Abed has long been a Byblos tourist attraction in his own right. Born in Mexico to Lebanese parents, he has worked as a jewellery designer and marine archaeologist, but Pepe is perhaps better known for his ability to throw a party, attracting the beautiful people of the prewar jet set to his bar, the Fishing Club, which opened in 1963. While the evidence of those heady days is writ large on the walls of the Club as well as on the face of the now elderly Pepe, the twinkle in his eyes still suggests that he doesn't need to look at the photos of the likes of Marlon Brando, David Niven, Brigitte Bardot and Anita Ekberg to remember the good times.

But there were bad times as well. The civil war saw Pepe back in Mexico while his local Lebanese businesses closed. When he returned to Lebanon he once again worked designing jewellery, saving enough money to get the Fishing Club back on its feet. The beautiful people, never known for their long memories, didn't materialise, and while the Fishing Club is an institution, it has become more of a museum, less of a restaurant. Indeed the collection of artefacts that Pepe collected over the years now forms the basis of the Pepe Abed Foundation. These days Pepe, nearing 90 years of age, is more likely to have a blanket on his lap than an actress, but having already achieved legendary status, he has nothing left to prove.

Eating & Drinking

Byblos Fishing Club (☎ 540 213; Byblos harbour; meals around US$25; ☽ 11am-midnight) This place is famed for the stream of film stars, politicians and beauty queens, who have passed through over the decades, as well as for its owner Pepe (see Pepe the Pirate, above). While the charm of the place is still palpable, Pepe doesn't have the presence he once did and the staff appear bored and inattentive. But on a busy weekend in front of a glistening harbour, you can almost imagine it's the 1960s, your speedboat's out front, and Bardot and Brando are holding court at the next table.

Bab El Mina (☎ 540 475; Byblos harbour; ☽ 11am-midnight) Next to the Fishing Club is Bab El Mina, and while it doesn't have the history of its more famous neighbour, it certainly has the edge when it comes to the food. The fried calamari and mezze are good, and the 'fisherman basket' (LL45,000 for two) is great value. Make sure you book.

El Molino (☎ 541 555; meal with 2 margaritas about LL35,000; ☽ noon-midnight Tue-Sun) For authentic Mexican food in a good, fun atmosphere, which possibly has something to do with the excellent margaritas, try El Molino. Accordingly, it gets very busy so you should book, especially for weekend nights when it's worth staying on late as there are no real bars in town.

There is no shortage of small places selling shwarma sandwiches and felafels, as well as the usual pizza and burger joints, along Rue Jbail. **Rif Grill** (☎ 545 822; off Rue Jbail) is the best of these joints: a modern place serving burgers (around LL3000), BBQ chicken, and pizza (around LL8000), including vegetarian. You could also try Restaurant Rock or Kaddoum Centre, next to each other on Rue Jbail and extremely popular with locals.

Getting There & Around

The service-taxi stand in Byblos is near the Banque Libanaise pour le Commerce. A service taxi to/from Beirut (the hub in Beirut is Dawra) costs LL3000. You can also take an express bus heading for Tripoli from Charles Helou (LL1000, around 50 minutes) and ask the driver to stop at Jbail. The LCC bus No 6 (LL500, around one hour) and minibuses (LL1000) also leave from Dawra and travel regularly along the coast road between Beirut and Byblos, stopping on Rue Jbail. It's a scenic and pleasant trip – traffic permitting.

Within Byblos everything is easily reached on foot, but if you need to use a taxi, they congregate at the junction of Rue Jbail and the road down to the harbour, and also at a point halfway along Rue Jbail heading east towards the highway. A short ride of up to 5km will cost around LL7000, to destinations within the town, LL5000. The local service taxis, which leave from the same places, charge from LL1000 to LL2000, depending on your destination, or you can flag one down on the highway, which is a five-minute walk from the centre of town.

AMCHIT عمشيت

 09

The town of Amchit, 3km north of Byblos, is a well-preserved relic of Lebanon's past. Do not let the general view of low-rise concrete chaos put you off. Amchit is famous for its collection of **traditional town houses**, which were built by wealthy silk merchants in the 19th century. They are now nearly all privately owned – some are fully restored, others are in need of work.

There are 88 old houses in total, which are now under a preservation order. The houses were constructed using the old stones of the area and you can often spot an ancient piece of carving being used as a lintel. The architecture is influenced by both the Oriental and Venetian styles, with double-arched mandolin windows and covered courtyards. This Italian influence was due to the trade agreement between Lebanon and the Duke of Tuscany.

A service taxi from Byblos costs LL1000. The highway dissects the town and the town houses are on the upper part of the town, away from the sea.

RACHANA رشانا

About 17km north of Amchit is the turn-off to Rachana, the 'Museum Village'. Situated high on a hill it's easily recognised by the wonderful **modern sculptures** lining the road. This is the work of the Basbous brothers, who have created an extraordinary artistic community in the village. Of the three brothers – Michel, Alfred and Yusuf – only Alfred is still alive, and he has a gallery in the village where you can purchase some of his works.

One of the highlights of the village is Michel's house, which is built in organic shapes, reminiscent of the work of Gaudi. He used all manner of found materials, such as the curved windscreen window. There is also an outdoor sculpture park, where entries in the annual sculpture symposium are displayed.

To find the studios, turn left at the junction of the main street in Rachana, by a small shop selling cold drinks. A few hundred metres along the road you will come to a bend and Yusuf's house. Alfred's house is a short distance around the corner.

The turn-off to Rachana is about 5km south of Batroun at a Lebanese army post.

The village is a further 3km to the northeast. If you do not have your own transport, you will need to get a taxi from Amchit or Byblos and get it to wait for you while you visit the studios. The return trip will cost about US$15.

BATROUN البترون

 06

Batroun is a small Maronite town located on the coast approximately 22km from Byblos and 56km north of Beirut. This was the Graeco-Roman town of Botrys, but it was founded much earlier than this. It is mentioned in the Tell al-Amarna tablets (Tell al-Amarna is the modern name of Akhetaten, an ancient Egyptian city) as a dependency of the king of Byblos. Called Butron in medieval times, it fell under the diocese of the County of Tripoli and was famous for its vineyards.

Today, behind the coastal sprawl, the town has a small fishing port with two interesting old churches.

ERNEST RENAN (1823–92)

The name of Ernest Renan turns up frequently in Lebanon. His early life in France prepared him for a career as a Roman Catholic priest, but he later broke away from the church. He is famous as a theological writer and critic.

His best-known work, *Vie de Jésus* (Life of Jesus), was published in 1863 and formed part of an eight-volume work *History of the Origins of Christianity*. More relevant to Lebanon, he published the *Mission de Phénicie*, a painstaking survey of Phoenician ruins in Lebanon (reprinted in Beirut by Terre du Liban et Cellis in 1998), as well as numerous philological works that have earned him the not-entirely complimentary designation as one of Orientalism's founding fathers.

He lived in Amchit with his beloved sister, Henriette, during his research of the site at Byblos. She died after an illness and is buried in the churchyard in Amchit, where you can see her mausoleum. Renan described the spot in his preface to *Vie de Jésus*: 'beneath the palms of Amchit near sacred Byblos, not far from the river Adonis to which the women of the ancient mysteries came to mingle their tears...'

Sights & Activities

St Georges Orthodox Church is just behind the harbour and was built in the late 18th century. It has 21 fine, painted panels and carved, wooden doves above the altar screen. Close by is the larger **St Estaphan (Stephen) Church**, also known as the fisherman's church. Its old stonework has recently been restored.

The **old harbour** has a small section of an extraordinary natural sea wall, creating a pool on the land side. The Phoenicians reinforced this natural feature and the remains of their harbour are visible. Around the old harbour is a small area of well-preserved Ottoman-era stone houses and souqs, which make for a pleasant walk.

In the garden of a private house northeast of the town centre are the remnants of a **Roman theatre**. Visitors are welcomed, or you can just look over the wall. To find it, head north along the main street, Rue Principe, walk 200m past the Badawni Restaurant and turn right at the pharmacy. The theatre is about 50m along on your right near a restaurant called Studio Jamal.

Just south of Batroun is **White Beach**. Although covered with fine white pebbles (hence the name) rather than sand, it is spotlessly clean and the water is crystal clear. There is also a beachside café and a restaurant. Entry costs LL5000, but be warned: it gets crowded on summer weekends. This stretch of beach is also known as one of the best spots in Lebanon for **windsurfing** and **surfing**.

Sleeping & Eating

All the hotels are resort-style complexes along the beach, just south of the town centre.

San Stephano Beach (☎ 740 366; d US$70) This resort complex has a large swimming pool, a restaurant and a beach snack bar. It also houses the popular **VIP** nightclub.

Aqualand (☎ 742 760; d US$90) This is the newest resort along the strip and, architecturally, is slightly more tasteful than the others. It has all the resort staples; prices don't include breakfast.

Restaurant al-Mina (☎ 740 188; meals US$15) In a restored Ottoman house overlooking the old harbour, Al Mina has mezze starting at LL2500, and fish sold by weight.

Maracina Restaurant (☎ 744 343) Almost next door to Restaurant al-Mina, this is in another wonderful Ottoman-era house.

White Beach Restaurant (☎ 742 404) Beside the sea just south of Batroun this is a very pleasant lunch place offering traditional mezze and seafood meals for about US$15 or US$20 per person.

A local speciality of Batroun is lemonade, made using water soaked in fresh lemon peel. You can find it at the several juice shops and cafés along the main street. Mango's Cocktail, on Rue Principe, is a good fruit-juice place. Further north along Rue Principe, close to the souq area, try **Chez Hilmi** (☎ 640 068) for the traditional lemonade – the original and the best. It also sells great sweets.

Castello (☎ 03-910 710) This stylish place is good to drop into for a drink. It's in a wonderful building on the main street.

Getting There & Away

As Batroun is a coastal town just off the highway, you could easily get a service taxi from Beirut or Byblos that's heading for Tripoli to drop you at the turn-off and walk the short way into town. The cost from Beirut should be LL4000. Alternatively take the Tripoli bus from Beirut and get the driver to drop you off. The price will be the full fare to Tripoli, LL2000.

MOUSSALAYHA CASTLE قلعة المسيلحة

About 3km beyond Batroun, in the narrow valley at Ras ech-Chekka, is the fairytale Moussalayha Castle, which used to defend the only land route between Beirut and Tripoli. Unfortunately the highway runs right beside it, diminishing the drama of its craggy setting. It stands on a rocky outcrop and is built on the summit in such a way as to look like part of the living rock. Although dramatic-looking, it is restricted by its rocky foundation and its proportions are almost miniature. The entrance is at the top of a steep, rock-cut stairway.

Although the site is very ancient (it is probably the ancient Gigarta mentioned by Pliny), the castle probably dates to the 16th century. It seems that the site was abandoned until the present Moussalayha Castle was constructed. Beneath the castle runs a small river with an ancient stone bridge crossing it.

If you are using a service taxi heading for Tripoli, simply get it to drop you off at Moussalayha and then flag down another service taxi when you want to continue your journey (there are plenty of service taxis serving this route). The castle is within easy walking distance from the highway. If you have a taxi to yourself, it's best to get it to wait for you. To drive down, take the small dirt track to the right of the highway, just before you can see the castle.

ADONIS VALLEY & JEBEL TANNOURINE
جبل تنّورين ووادي أدونيس

Famed for its romantic legends as much as for its dramatically beautiful scenery, the Adonis Valley is a deep, jagged cut forged in the coastal mountains by the Nahr Ibrahim (Adonis River) as it flows out to sea. The river's source, the Afqa Grotto, is at the head of the valley, and in ancient times its northern side was a pilgrimage route. Now the road is dotted with ancient remains as well as breathtaking views. To the north lie villages perched on the side of Jebel Tannourine and the ski resort of Laklouk. The entire area can be visited on a day trip from Beirut. If you don't have your own car, it would be worth getting a group together and renting one, or a taxi, for the day.

AFQA GROTTO
مغارة أفقا

This huge cavern dominates the rocky mountainside at the head of the valley and is best seen after winter, when water roars down under a stone Roman bridge before snaking its way towards the sea. This is the sacred source of the Nahr Ibrahim where, mythology tells us, Adonis (or Tammuz to the Phoenicians) met his death; he was gored by a wild boar while out hunting. The grotto is also intertwined with the legendary love story of Adonis and Aphrodite (see the boxed text Lovers Forever, p289). Legend has it that this is where they exchanged their first kiss, and the Greek word for kiss, *aphaca*, would appear to reinforce the romantic connection.

The area is rife with ancient shrines and grottos dedicated to this tragic tale. Adonis' story has come to symbolise life, death and rebirth, the theme echoed in the stories of Osiris and Christ. Each spring the river runs red, and in antiquity this was believed to be the blood of Adonis. In reality, the force of the water flowing down the valley picks up ferruginous minerals from the soil and stains the water the colour of red wine.

After winter a torrent rages down from the grotto 200m above. When the flow isn't too strong, you can enter the cave by walking up a set of steps on the right-hand side

---

LOVERS FOREVER

According to Greek mythology, Adonis was the most beautiful baby in the world, the fruit of an incestuous union between King Cinyras and his daughter Myrrha (who was turned into the myrrh tree for her sin). The goddess Aphrodite (Venus to the Romans) took the baby and left him in the care of Persephone, goddess of the underworld. When she gazed upon Adonis' beauty, Persephone refused to return the child. Zeus mediated between the two goddesses and decreed that Adonis was to spend half the year with Aphrodite, and the other half in the underworld.

Aphrodite and Adonis eventually became lovers, incurring the wrath of Aphrodite's husband, Ares, who turned himself into a boar and attacked Adonis at Afqa. Aphrodite tried in vain to heal his wounds but her lover bled to death in her arms. In the places where his blood fell to the ground, red anemones sprang up. But the decree of Zeus remained in force and Adonis was permitted to return to his love every six months. Each spring the red anemones (*naaman* or 'darling' in Arabic – also an epithet for Adonis) return, symbolising his return to the world.

Apart from being a racy tale of incest, jealousy, sex, murder and the triumph of true love, the Adonis and Aphrodite myth symbolises those most ancient of themes: fertility and rebirth. In the myth's earlier Semitic form, Aphrodite was Astarte, the great goddess of fertility; her lover was Tammuz (called 'Adon' by his followers, transformed into Adonis by the Greeks), a god associated with vegetation who journeyed to the underworld each year. Astarte would follow to retrieve him, and while she was gone the world would become barren, reproduction would stop and life itself would be threatened. Followers of Adonis would spend seven days lamenting his death; on the eighth day, in a practice echoed in Christianity, his rebirth was celebrated.

of the bank of the river (steep but not too difficult). Inside, the cave is enormous and the freezing water surges out of an unseen underground source. When the flow of water slows in the summer it is possible to explore the extensive tunnels and caverns further into the mountain.

At the foot of the main fall is a Roman bridge. If you walk down beneath the bridge, there is a café on a terrace, with soothing views of the water as it crashes and tumbles over the rocks (or, in summer and autumn, slowly trickles) to the river below.

On a raised plateau nearby, above the left bank and just below the village of Khirbet Afqa, are the ruinous remains of a **Roman temple** dedicated to Astarte. Its broken columns are made of granite from the famous Pharaonic-era quarries at Aswan in Egypt. The cost involved in bringing the stone hundreds of kilometres down the Nile, shipping it to the Lebanese coast and then dragging it up the valley must have been astronomical, and is a testament to the temple's importance as a pilgrimage site. In the foundations, on the riverside, is the entrance to a sort of tunnel that is thought to have carried water into a sacred pool in the temple, into which offerings may have been thrown, or in which devotees carried out their ablutions. Constantine destroyed the temple because of its licentious rites, but the power of legend has stayed. Both Christians and Shiite Muslims attribute healing powers to the place, and strips of cloth are still tied to the nearby fig tree in a ritual that dates back to antiquity.

Sleeping & Eating

Just after the turn-off to Afqa is **La Reserve** (☎ 01-498 744/5/6; www.lareserve.com.lb). This well-appointed camping ground and ecoresort encompasses hundreds of square kilometres in the mountains surrounding the Adonis Valley. It organises a huge range of outdoor activities all over Lebanon, including rafting, caving, hiking, mountain biking and horse riding (check out its website for more information and the prices of individual activities). Accommodation in canvas tents, sleeping up to four people, costs US$10 per person. Mattresses and pillows are provided but you will need your own sleeping bag. In the summer La Reserve organises a 12-day summer camp for children aged six to 15.

The **café-restaurant** (◷ spring-summer; lunch US$6-8) beneath the bridge is the only place to eat. It serves tea, coffee and cold drinks (including beer). Light meals and snacks of the kebab-and-chips variety are available quite cheaply.

Getting There & Away

Without a private car, the only way to get to Afqa is by taxi. It is not on a service taxi route, so this will cost around US$20 from Byblos.

AAQOURA العاقورة

Aaqoura is famous for its spectacular location, its devotion to Maronite Christianity and its cherries. Reputed to be one of the first villages in the area to convert to Christianity, some 42 churches lie within its confines. The most famous is **Mar Butros** (St Peter), which sits in a grotto in the towering cliffs that surround the village and can be reached by steps carved out of the rock. The hollowed-out tombs inside the grotto may originally have been part of a Roman necropolis, but what is particularly noteworthy here is the faint traces of writing at the back of the cave. This is thought to be a rare extant example of a Chinese-influenced vertical Syriac script brought back by Christian missionaries to China in the 7th century. Down in the village there are also the remains of a Roman road, which was part of the pilgrimage route that would lead devotees of the Adonis cult over the mountains and into the Bekaa Valley. Note that the mountains around Aaqoura were heavily mined during the war, and hiking without a local guide is not advised.

LAKLOUK اللقلوق
☎ 09

Laklouk is a popular ski resort set in an attractive rocky location, 1920m above sea level, 28km east of Byblos. Family-oriented, with gentle to medium slopes and good cross-country skiing opportunities, it's a relaxed and low-key alternative to Faraya Mzaar (see p273). It is also a very pleasant area to visit in summer. The place consists of a few hotels and restaurants – there isn't a village as such and this adds to the area's peaceful air.

Sights & Activities

Apart from enjoying the scenery, there are a few places of interest nearby. About 2km from the resort on the Chatin–Balaa road are the unusual **Balaa rock formations**,

---

SKI FACTS: LAKLOUK

- **Altitude** 1650–1920m
- **No of Lifts** Nine
- ⏱ 8am-3.30pm Mon-Fri, 8am-4pm Sat & Sun
- ☎ 03-256 853
- **Adult Day Pass** US$10 (Mon-Fri), US$20 (Sat & Sun)

Originally one of Lebanon's smaller ski resorts, Laklouk was expanded in 1996. There are now three chairlifts, three ski lifts and three baby lifts. It is also possible to do cross-country skiing and snowshoeing here. More family-oriented than some of the ski resorts closer to Beirut, Laklouk is best suited to beginner and intermediate skiers, although there is one slope that has been approved by the International Ski Federation for international competitions.

---

which consist of several houses or chapels carved into the rock. They are known as the 'bishop's house'. The landscape here, with its otherworldly shapes, is reminiscent of Cappadocia in Turkey.

Further along the same road, about 6km from Laklouk, is **Balaa Gorge**. There is a small turning on the left, if you are coming from Laklouk, and, after about 400m, the road ends. This is the beginning of the descent on foot to the gorge. The walk down is easy and takes about 15 minutes. At the bottom is an extraordinary natural rock formation – a rock bridge spans the chasm and a waterfall crashes down into a deep hole behind. It is well worth the effort to visit, but be warned: there are no fences or barriers and the drops are sheer. The return walk takes approximately 25 minutes.

Sleeping & Eating

Shangrila Hotel (☎ 03-430 005; s/d/tr US$50/60/75; 🏊) This pleasant, traditional hotel built in the 1950s is right in the centre of the resort and close to the ski lifts. It is open all year and in summer has a sunroom and a pool. Staff can organise horse-riding excursions and there are mountain bikes for hire. The price includes breakfast, and the restaurant serves a range of European and Lebanese dishes.

You will find rooms slightly cheaper at the Nirvana Hotel, which is part of the Shangrila, but only open when the Shangrila is fully booked.

Motel La Vallade (☎ 904 140, 03-205 901; d US$45; 🏊) This motel is on the left as you enter Laklouk. It is open all year and has a swimming pool and tennis courts that open in the summer. It's large rooms can sleep up to six, and there are chalets.

For cheap eats, there are a couple of simple snack places close to the slopes (only open in winter). Other than that you are limited to the hotel restaurants.

Getting There & Away

Laklouk is not on any bus or service-taxi route, so you'll need your own transport or to pay for a taxi from Byblos (around US$25 one way).

DOUMA   دوما

☎ 09

This is another traditional, but very well-preserved red-roofed village, famous for being in the shape of a scorpion, seen from the hillside overlooking the village. About 22km northeast of Byblos, it is a quiet and peaceful place that is said to have been named after the wife of Roman Emperor Septimus Severus, who came here to escape the summer heat on the coast. Under the Ottomans it was famous for the production of swords and guns, a lucrative business in always-troubled Lebanon, and this paid for the grand houses that can be seen around the village.

The main square has a **Roman sarcophagus** and there are two churches. Above the village there are some Roman inscriptions from the reign of Hadrian. There is a small souq in the village.

The Douma Hotel arranges hiking expeditions – there are eight different walks from Douma of varying difficulty.

Sleeping & Eating

Douma Hotel (☎ 520 202; s/d/ste US$35/50/70) About 1km from the main square, along the main road, this is only hotel around. Open year-round, it's a pleasant enough place and its 36 rooms each have a TV and bath. There is **restaurant** (per person US$15-$20) serving Lebanese or Continental food.

There are a number of snack bars and cafés around the village square.

Getting There & Away

There are no buses to Douma and very few service taxis from Byblos. You can take a service taxi to Batroun on the coast and pick up a taxi from there (about US$15), or from Byblos (around US$25).

THE CHOUF MOUNTAINS

DEIR AL-QAMAR   دير القمر

☎ 05

In the Middle Ages, Lebanon was divided into fiefdoms, each ruled by an emir. By the early 17th century, Fakhreddine (Fakhr ad-Din al Maan II – see the boxed text Fakhreddine, p294), the Druze governor of Lebanon, had extended his power throughout the territory, which roughly corresponded to modern Lebanon, and united the small fiefdoms into one. His first capital was at Baaqline, but because of water shortages, he moved to nearby Deir al-Qamar, which is fed by numerous springs. Three centuries later the village is one of the best-preserved examples of 17th- and 18th-century provincial architecture in the country. It's an extremely picturesque spot to spend a couple of hours, even though it is strangely devoid of any real activity besides tourism. The focal point of the old town is a large square with a fountain, around which most of the historic buildings are grouped.

Sights
MOSQUE OF EMIR FAKHREDDINE MAAN
جامع الامير فخرالدين المعني

To the west of the fountain is the mosque of Fakhreddine, with its distinctive octagonal-shaped minaret. The original building dates to 1493, but it was restored under the name of Fakhreddine. Built in Mamluk style, the mosque has a vast square room with high arches resting on a central pillar. Quranic verses, along with the date of construction, are carved into the western façade.

Steps behind the mosque lead up to what was once the town's **souq**, still housing a few shops and a café.

PALACE OF YOUNES MAAN   قصر يونس معن
Younes Maan governed Deir al-Qamar when his brother, Fakhreddine, was in exile in Italy. Younes Maan's palace dates to the 18th century, but is now a private house and

closed to visitors. However, the elaborate entrance is particularly fine and definitely worth a look.

SILK KHAN
Dominating the main square is the huge silk khan (travellers' inn) and its warehouse. It dates to 1595 and takes the form of a huge rectangle, incorporating an open courtyard surrounded by arcaded galleries that were once used as stables and servant quarters. Part of the 1st floor, which originally housed the main part of the khan, is now the **Centre Culturelle Français** and can be visited.

PALACE OF FAKHREDDINE   قصر فخر الدين
Next to the silk khan and warehouse is Fakhreddine's palace, dating to 1620. It is built on the site of an earlier palace that was destroyed during a battle with Youssef Sifa, Pasha of Tripoli, in 1614. According to local lore, Fakhreddine vowed his revenge and took Youssef's castle at Akkar near Tripoli. He tore down the castle and brought the stones back to Deir al-Qamar. He then brought in Italian architects, who rebuilt the palace in an Italian Renaissance style.

The palace has been converted, by its present owners, the Baz family, into the **Marie Baz Wax Museum** (☎ 505 094; adult/child LL6000/4000; ⏰ 8am-10pm summer, 9am-5pm winter). The collection is an eclectic jumble of figures relating to Lebanese history, including Lady Hester Stanhope flanked by the French poet Lamartine. The modern-history section includes a jovial-looking George Bush (senior) standing next to a grim-looking General Aoun. Unfortunately, apart from tantalising glimpses of other parts of the palace from the pleasant cafeteria in the courtyard, only four rooms are accessible and the 10 minutes or so it takes to view the waxworks hardly make the museum worth the price of admission.

SERAIL OF YOUSSEF CHEHAB   سراي يوسف شهاب
On the lower (south) side of the square is the Serail of Youssef Chehab, which is built on the hillside on several levels. Built in the 18th century, it has a somewhat grisly past: not only did Emir Youssef Chehab assassinate several of his relatives here, but the central courtyard was the site of a massacre

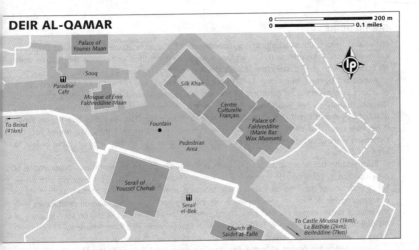

DEIR AL-QAMAR

Map labels:
- Palace of Younes Maan
- Souq
- Paradise Cafe
- Mosque of Emir Fakhreddine Maan
- Silk Khan
- Centre Culturelle Français
- To Beirut (41km)
- Fountain
- Pedestrian Area
- Palace of Fakhreddine (Marie Baz Wax Museum)
- Serail of Youssef Chehab
- Serail el-Bek
- Church of Saidet at-Tallé
- To Castle Moussa (1km); La Bastide (2km); Beiteddine (7km)
- 0 — 200 m
- 0 — 0.1 miles

during the anti-Christian violence in 1860. Nowadays the building is noteworthy for its beautiful stonework. Just above the entrance there are two carved lions, symbolising, ironically enough, justice. Beyond the massive doorway is a large central courtyard. On the south side, overlooking the valley, is the former royal apartment, which has an elegance that belies the ruthlessness of some of its former inhabitants. There is a dome above the centre of the room, and a beautifully restored, painted wooden ceiling to the side. It houses **municipal offices** (8am-1pm Mon-Sat), and visitors can wander through some parts of the building during office hours.

CHURCH OF SAIDET AT-TALLÉ   كنيسة سيدة التلة
The words *deir al-qamar* mean 'monastery of the moon', and the lunar motif can be seen carved in stone on a figure of the Madonna in the Church of Saidet at-Tallé, which sits on the lower slopes of the town. The crescent moon was a symbol of Phoenicia's pagan cult and the Madonna standing on it could be taken as a symbol of Christianity superseding the pagan religion; on the other hand it could simply be incorporating the old religion into the new. The original church was built in the 7th century on a temple dedicated to Astarte, but was destroyed by an earthquake a century later. Fakhreddine reconstructed the building in the 16th century and it was enlarged again in the 17th century.

CASTLE MOUSSA   قلعة موسى
About 1km out of town in the direction of Beiteddine is the extraordinary **Castle Moussa** (☎ 500 106, 501 660; LL5000; ⏰ 8am-8pm summer, 8am-6pm winter), the fulfilment of the life-long quest of Mr Moussa, who as a child was beaten by his teacher for dreaming of living in a castle. After becoming a successful businessman he went about building this castle to realise his fantasy. He then filled it with wax models depicting scenes from traditional Lebanese life as well as one of himself as a child being beaten by his teacher – all enhanced with mechanical movement. Sadly Mr Moussa's teacher died before he could witness the kitsch result, which is probably just as well given he was an art teacher. Very popular with Lebanese groups, who visit by the bus load.

Sleeping & Eating
There is no accommodation in Deir al-Qamar itself.

La Bastide (☎ 505 320, 03-643 010; tw US$60) is about 2km past the town, on the way to Beiteddine. It is clean with a variety of pleasant rooms, some with kitchenette. Front rooms have wonderful views across to Beiteddine

Next to Castle Moussa, **Restaurant Farah** (☎ 500 509; lunch & dinner US$15-20) serves mezze and has spectacular views.

Paradise Cafe sells simple meals and snacks, and there is another pleasant café below the old souq. Serail el-Bek restaurant, next to the Serail of Youssef Chehab, has a good menu of mezze and agreeable outdoor seating.

FAKHREDDINE

Nationalist hero, brilliant administrator, connoisseur of fine architecture and all-round Ottoman-era gentleman, Fakhreddine (Fakhr ad-Din al Maan II) is credited with being the first to unify Mt Lebanon with the coastal cities, foreshadowing the modern state of Lebanon.

Appointed by the Ottomans in 1590 to pacify the unruly Druze of the Chouf Mountains (many of whose ringleaders were members of his own family, the Maans), he proved more than up to the job. Initially his fief was confined to the district of Sidon and the Chouf, but he was soon granted Beirut and eventually extended his rule to include the Qadisha Valley and Tripoli. While it became clear that their governor was not the subservient puppet they had hoped for, the Ottomans were occupied with revolt in Anatolia and Persia and initially left him more or less to his own devices.

Fakhreddine did more than simply grab territory. He began an ambitious programme of development in Lebanon. He was exiled to Tuscany from 1613 to 1618, for entering into an alliance with one of the Medicis. Fakhreddine returned, inspired by his time abroad, and set about modernising his dominions, developing a silk industry and upgrading olive-oil production with the help of Italian engineers and agricultural experts. Their influence can still be seen in some of his buildings in Deir al-Qamar. Trading links with Europe were also strengthened and European religious missions were allowed to settle in the areas under his control.

Consolidating his power at home, Fakhreddine developed links with the Maronite Christians in the north and encouraged their migration to the south, where they provided labour for silk production. He modernised the ports of Sidon and Beirut, turning them into busy trading centres. In all, the economy flourished under his rule and his power grew to the extent that he controlled areas of what are now Jordan and Israel.

Alarmed at their vassal's growing independence, the Ottomans reacted, sending their Syrian and Egyptian governors to attack his territory and bring it back under İstanbul's control. After fleeing to a nearby cave, Fakhreddine was captured in 1633 and taken to İstanbul. Two years later he was executed.

Getting There & Away

Service taxis en route to Beiteddine go through Deir al-Qamar and can drop you off there. The fare from Beirut's Cola bus station is LL4000. If you are planning to visit both places in the same day (a good idea), you could continue to Beiteddine and then walk back (6km) to Deir al-Qamar, a pleasant, downhill walk. Keep in mind that service taxis are scarce after dark.

BEITEDDINE   بيت الدين
☎ 05

Some 50km southeast of Beirut, Beiteddine is the name of both a village and the magnificent palace complex that lies within it. The palace, former stronghold of the 18th-century governor, Emir Bashir, can be seen from across the valley as you approach, and looks almost like a vision from a fairy tale. The style is a cross between traditional Arab and Italian baroque (the architects were, in fact, Italian) with its grounds descending over several terraces planted with poplars and flowering shrubs.

There were three other palaces in the vicinity, built for Emir Bashir's sons. Of these only one, **Mir Amin Palace**, still stands and is now a luxury hotel above the main part of the village (see p296). Nearby is Emir Bashir's **country house**, which now houses the archbishopric. There are still some remains of the original building including a beautiful stone doorway, which leads onto a roof shaped like a Chinese pagoda.

Sights
BEITEDDINE PALACE   قصر بيت الدين
This restored early-19th-century **palace complex** (☎ 500 045/78; adult/student LL7500/2000; 9am-6pm summer, 9am-4pm winter) was built over a period of 30 years, starting in 1788, and became the stronghold of Emir Bashir, the Ottoman-appointed governor and leading member of the Shihab family. It is the greatest surviving achievement of 19th-century Lebanese architecture and an impressive symbol of Bashir's power and wealth. Note that many rooms of the palace are locked but there are guides – with keys –who can

be hired to tour the palace (price dependent on your negotiating skills, but expect to pay at least LL10,000). This magically gains you access to areas that are usually kept locked and it's a worthwhile undertaking.

The name Beiteddine means 'house of faith' and the original site was a Druze hermitage, which was incorporated into the complex. The palace was built after the Shihab family took over from the Maan dynasty. Partly due to family disagreements, Emir Bashir decided to move from Deir al-Qamar and build his own palace, which would reflect the increasing power and glory of his reign. Architects from Italy, and the most highly skilled artisans from Damascus and Aleppo, were hired and given free rein to try out new ideas. The result was a huge edifice, over 300m long, built high on a mountain overlooking the valley. The grounds below the palace are terraced into gardens and orchards.

During the French Mandate the palace was used for local administration, but after 1930 it was declared a historic monument and placed under the care of the Department of Antiquities, which set about restoring it. In 1943 Lebanon's first president after independence, Bishara al-Khouri, made it the official summer residence and brought back the remains of Emir Bashir from Istanbul, where he'd died in 1850.

The palace suffered tremendous losses following the Israeli invasion, when as much as 90% of the original contents are reckoned to have been lost. Once the fighting ended after 1984, the Druze leader, Walid Jumblatt ordered its restoration and declared it to be a 'Palace of the People'. As such, it contains several museums housing various collections, including some magnificent mosaics and a small exhibition dedicated to Walid Jumblatt's father, Kamal, who was assassinated – many say by the Syrians – in 1977. Most of the items on display are there courtesy of the Jumblatt family (see the boxed text Mrs Jumblatt, p296).

The palace consists of three main courts: Dar al-Baraniyyeh (the outer courtyard to which passing visitors were admitted freely), Dar al-Wousta (the central courtyard, which housed the palace guards and offices of the ministers) and Dar al-Harim (the private family quarters). Beneath Dar al-Wousta and Dar al-Harim are huge vaulted stables, which held 500 horses

and their riders, in addition to the 600 infantry that formed the emir's guard. Part of the stables now houses the mosaic collection.

From the entrance to the palace, you pass through a passage that leads into the small Kamal Jumblatt Museum. The former Druze leader was born in 1917 and established the Progressive Socialist Party in 1949. Exhibits include photographs, some personal possessions and documents chronicling his life.

The museum exit leads into a 60m-long courtyard where public festivals and gatherings took place. It was from here that the emir would leave for his hunting expeditions or to fight wars. Along the north side of this courtyard are the guest apartments. It was the custom of noble houses to offer hospitality to visitors for three days, before asking their business or their identity.

The restored upper floor of this wing is used to exhibit the Rachid Karami Ethnographic Collection. This large collection includes pottery from the Bronze and Iron Ages, Roman glass, Islamic pottery, lead sarcophagi and gold jewellery. There is also a scale model of the palace and, in other rooms, a collection of weapons and costumes.

At the far end of the outer courtyard is a double staircase leading up to the entrance of the central courtyard. It's known as the 'tumbling staircase' because of the tale of a sheep that escaped the butcher's knife and headbutted an eminent pasha down the stairs.

Through an arched passageway is the central courtyard. The entrance is decorated with an inscription of welcome and a decorative marble portal. Inside is a charming courtyard with a fountain; the open side overlooks the valley. The apartments and offices off the courtyard are set along graceful arcades. The rooms are luxurious and richly decorated with marble, mosaics and marquetry, with furnishings in traditional Oriental style. The walls and ceilings are of painted, carved cedar wood embellished with Arabic calligraphy. In the richly decorated room on the south side of the courtyard an inlaid marble water fountain is built into the wall, which both cools the room and makes conversation inaudible to eavesdroppers.

The entrance to the third court is a beautiful façade that leads through to the lower court (the kitchens and hammam) and the upper court (the reception rooms). The rooms are lavishly decorated. On the ground floor, immediately beyond the entrance is the waiting room, known as the **room of the column**, named for the single column supporting the vaulted ceiling. Beyond this is a two-level **reception room** (salaamlik) with a mosaic floor and inlaid marble walls.

The huge **kitchens** are also well worth a look. In their heyday they catered for 500 people a day. Endless trays of food would have been carried out to set before the divans and sofas of the court and their visitors. To the north of the kitchen is the large **hammam**, a series of domed rooms luxuriously fitted out in marble with carved marble basins and fountains. Bathers would move between the cold, warm and hot chambers before reclining to rest in the anteroom. In a small shaded garden to the north of the hammam is the **Tomb of Sitt Chams**, the emir's first wife. The ashes of Bashir are also reported to be in the tomb.

In the lower part of the palace is one of the most spectacular collections of **Byzantine mosaics** in the eastern Mediterranean, if not the world. These were mostly excavated from a former church at Jiyyeh, the ancient city of Porphyrion, which was discovered by workers digging on the coast in early 1982. The area was then under the control of Walid Jumblatt, who had the well-preserved mosaics brought to him, so he could keep them safe from looters throughout the war. The magnificent collection includes some 30 room-sized mosaics and many smaller ones. The designs are often

---

MRS JUMBLATT

The Jumblatts have long been prominent in the Chouf and have headed the Druze community in Lebanon for the past century. Back in the 1920s their position was threatened when Fouad Jumblatt, great-grandfather of Walid Bey, was assassinated. His son, Kamal, was too young to assume power and the Druze community came to Fouad's wife to help them decide what to do. She took the initiative and assumed leadership of the community herself until Kamal came of age. The unprecedented spectre of a woman leader was difficult for many to accept (particularly close male relatives), but eventually she won them over and remained in power until Kamal grew up.

---

geometric and stylised, reflecting the austere nature of early Christianity in the area. There are also depictions of animals, including leopards, bulls, gazelles and birds, as well as religious figures. Set among the graceful stone arches and vaulted ceilings of Beiteddine's former stables, and along the walls of the palace's lower gardens, the mosaics are a stunning visual treat.

Festivals & Events

A **festival** is held in Beiteddine every summer in July and August. It features an eclectic mixture of international and Arab musicians, singers, dancers and actors. Contact the **Beirut tourist-information office** (☎ 01-343 073; www.lebanon-tourism.gov.lb) for further details.

Sleeping & Eating

There are no cheap-hotel options in the area and if you are looking to stay nearby, the best bet is **La Bastide** in Deir al-Qamar (see p293).

Mir Amin Palace (☎ 501 315/6/7/8; miraminpalace.com; s/d US$108/136; ❄ ☐ ☎) The only hotel in Beiteddine itself is the luxurious Mir Amin, set on the hill overlooking Beiteddine Palace. It is the restored palace of Emir Bashir's eldest son. There are 24 individually and beautifully decorated rooms and even if you're not staying here, it's still well worth dropping by for a drink on the terrace, where views are spectacular. The hotel also has a couple of good restaurants with Lebanese and Continental cuisine where you can expect to spend at least US$30 to US$40 per person for a meal. Rates are cheaper during the low season.

Down in the town there are a few unimpressive cafés and snack places. Near the main square, Hatemia Restaurant has pizza and burgers starting at about US$5. Snack Vieux Moulin serves up the usual Lebanese menu and snacks.

Restaurant New Garbatella (☎ 301 411; pizza from LL6500, steaks from LL11,000), in the village of Baaqline, just off the road to Mir Amin, has good views over the valley, a selection of European-style food and a few mezze choices. To get there, take the right fork just before the turn-off to Mir Amin and follow the road for about 1km.

Getting There & Away

The route to Beiteddine runs south from Beirut along the coast to Damour and then east. Service taxis from Beirut's Cola bus station

Local man at the historic town of
Deir al-Qamar (p292), Lebanon

BETHUNE CARMICHAEL

MARK DAFFEY

Ski resort at The Cedars (p314),
Lebanon

Boats on the waterfront, Byblos (p285), Lebanon

JANE SWEENEY

Street scene, Tripoli (p300), Lebanon

Bcharré (p312), Qadisha Valley, Lebanon

serve the route and the fare to Beiteddine is LL4000.

It is feasible to visit several places and be dropped off along the way, hailing a passing service taxi when you want to move on, but along the quieter stretches you may have a bit of a wait. The service-taxi stand in Beiteddine is close to the palace on the main square. Keep in mind that you're unlikely to find service taxis running after dark. If you hire a taxi or have a hire car, Beiteddine, Deir al-Qamar and the Chouf Cedar Reserve (see p297) make a good full-day trip from Beirut.

MOUKHTARA المختارة

About 9km south of Beiteddine is the town of Moukhtara. This is the seat of the Jumblatt family and de facto capital of the Chouf. The Jumblatt's 19th-century stone palace dominates the town. Consisting of three large buildings, it has its own hammam, a garden with a collection of Roman sarcophagi and a waterfall that tumbles into an ornamental pool. There are public reception rooms that are open to visitors.

Each weekend that he is in residence, Walid Jumblatt, head of the family and leader of the Druze, spends his mornings listening to the complaints of his mostly Druze followers. If you happen to be there then, you will see the long line of petitioners as they wait to see their leader.

Apart from the overwhelming Jumblatt presence, the town is picturesque and has a number of traditional red-tiled buildings that make for a pleasant wander.

Getting There & Away

Service taxis to Moukhtara leave from Beirut's Cola bus station and cost LL5000 each way. Keep in mind, especially when planning your return trip, that service taxis can be infrequent.

CHOUF CEDAR RESERVE محميّة ارز الشوف

The largest of Lebanon's three natural protectorates, the **Chouf Cedar Reserve** (☎ 05-311 230, 03-682 472; www.shoufcedar.org; LL5000; 9am-7pm) represents a quarter of the remaining cedar forests in the country and 5% of Lebanon's entire area. The reserve marks the southernmost limit of Lebanese cedar *(Cedrus libani)* growth, and incorporated within the protectorate are six cedar forests, of which the Barouk and Maaser ech-Chouf forests have the largest number of ancient trees – some are thought to date back 2000 years. Hunting and livestock-grazing bans are strictly enforced and a number of species of flora and fauna have returned to the area in recent years. More than 200 species of birds and 26 species of wild mammal (including wolves, gazelles and wild boar) either live in or pass through the area.

Also within or just outside the reserve's boundaries are a number of historical sites. These include the remains of the rock-cut fortress of **Qab Elias** and **Qala'at Niha**, in addition to the **Shrine of Sit Sha'wane**, a woman saint venerated by the Druze and still a site of pilgrimage for local residents.

Apart from the outstanding hiking, the reserve's **trails** are also ideal for mountain biking and, in winter, snowshoeing. **Esprit-Nomade** (www.esprit-nomade.com) organises these activities with an eye towards minimal damage to the environment.

Getting There & Away

The reserve can be reached either from the road leading from Beiteddine to Sofar, or via Ain Zhalta from the Beirut–Bekaa Hwy. There are three entrances into the reserve, although only two, near the villages of Barouk and Maaser ech-Chouf, can be accessed without calling ahead. The latter is the best place to view the old-growth cedars, and is marked by a small visitors centre that sells delicious local produce, including honey, dried fruit and jam. Because both villages are out of the way, you're unlikely to find frequent service taxis there. If you don't have your own vehicle, the best way is to get a taxi from Beiteddine, some 10km away. If you have a 4WD vehicle, there is also a track that leads from Maaser ech-Chouf through the mountains and down to the village of Kefraya in the Bekaa Valley. In winter it can sometimes be blocked with snow, so check accessibility with the Chouf Cedar Reserve office.

Tripoli & the North

CONTENTS

Northern Lebanon is dominated by the city of Tripoli, with its well-preserved and bustling medieval souqs, myriad historic buildings and busy port of Al-Mina. Lebanon's second city, it was at one stage slated to become the capital, but today the city appears happy to retain its distinctly less-Westernised feel. In the mountains behind Tripoli lies one of the most beautiful areas of Lebanon, the Qadisha Valley. A long deep gorge, the valley starts near Batroun in the west and rises dramatically to its head just beyond the town of Bcharré. On route to Bcharré is Ehden, located on the northern rim of the Qadisha Valley. This summer resort is a popular escape from the heat with its picturesque old centre, lively main square and hillside restaurants.

The trip onwards to Bcharré takes you through some of the most beautiful scenery in Lebanon. The road winds along the mountainous slopes, continuously gaining in altitude and offering spectacular views of the Qadisha. Bcharré is the traditional home of one of Lebanon's favourite sons, the famous poet and artist Khalil Gibran, and a museum there pays tribute to his life and work.

Below Bcharré is the World Heritage–listed Qadisha Valley, where a walk down to the valley floor takes you past centuries-old monasteries and chapels. Above Bcharré is the Cedars, where visitors can check out the small grove of historically significant cedars before heading up further to Lebanon's first and highest altitude ski resort.

HIGHLIGHTS

- Discover why Khalil Gibran is more than just a world-famous writer at his **museum** (p312) in Bcharré

- Work your way through a sampling of **Tripoli's famous sweets** (p308)

- Work off sweets-induced calories with a wander around Tripoli's **medieval souqs** (p305)

- Marvel at the grottoes and rock-cut monasteries of the World Heritage–listed **Qadisha Valley** (p310)

- Carve the snow-covered slopes of Lebanon's highest **ski resort** (p314) at the Cedars

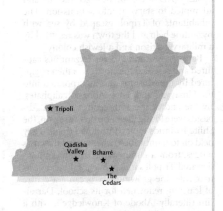

TRIPOLI (TRABLOUS)

طرابلس

☎ 06

Tripoli (Trablous in Arabic), 85km north of Beirut, is Lebanon's second-largest city and also the main port and trading centre for northern Lebanon. Famous for its medieval Mamluk architecture, including a large old-city souq area acknowledged as being the best in Lebanon, it's a great point from which to explore northern Lebanon. Tripoli is also famous as the sweets capital of Lebanon, so any trip to the city is not complete without a visit to one of its Arabic sweet shops.

HISTORY

While there is some evidence of a settlement in Tripoli as far back as 1400 BC, its past is likely to go back even further. By the 8th century BC, what had been a small Phoenician trading post by the sea grew with the arrival of traders from Sidon, Tyre and Arwad (Aradus, which became Tartus in Syria). Each community settled within its own walled area, giving rise to the Greek name Tripolis, which literally means 'three cities'.

During the rule of the Seleucids, and later the Romans, Tripoli prospered but a huge earthquake in AD 543 changed the geography of the port area completely and destroyed most of the town. It was quickly rebuilt but, by AD 635, a general of Mu'awiyah, the governor of Syria and founder of the Umayyad dynasty (AD 661–750), besieged the city and attempted to starve it into submission. The inhabitants of Tripoli escaped by sea with Byzantine help and the town was resettled by a military garrison and a Jewish colony.

Between 685 and 705 the Byzantines captured and resettled the city. It was then recaptured by the Muslims and incorporated into the Umayyad and, later, Abbasid caliphates. By the end of the 10th century, as the Abbasids were losing their grip on the region, the Shiite Fatimids took control of Tripoli. They held on to it until 1069, when one of the city's judges, from a family named Banu Ammar, declared Tripoli's independence. Under Ammar rule, the growing city became a centre of learning renowned for its school, Dar al-Ilm (literally 'Abode of Knowledge'), with a library containing some 100,000 volumes.

When the Crusaders, led by Raymond de Saint-Gilles of Toulouse, first arrived in 1099, the Ammars persuaded them to bypass Tripoli, bribing them with lavish presents. However, Tripoli's agricultural wealth was too glittering a prize and Raymond returned some three years later. Tripoli's rulers brought in reinforcements from Damascus and Homs, but Raymond defeated the three armies with only 300 men. He then built a fortress, the Citadel of Raymond de Saint-Gilles, on a hill inland from the busy port area and controlled land trade coming into the city.

Tripoli's leaders launched repeated raids on the fortress, eventually mortally wounding Raymond. Just before he died he signed a truce guaranteeing safe passage in and out of the city for its inhabitants and this lasted until his successor, Guillaume Jourdain, took over and once again imposed the blockade with the assistance of the Genovese fleet, which blocked the city from the sea. After four increasingly desperate years under siege, the city finally fell to the Crusaders in June 1109. The victors sacked the city and set fire to the magnificent library at Dar al-Ilm.

Tripoli became the capital of the County of Tripoli and the Crusaders managed to hang on to the city for 180 years, during which time the economy, based on silk-weaving

---

THE TRAGEDY OF MELISINDA

One of the most romantic and tragic figures who lived in the Saint-Gilles citadel was the beautiful sister of Raymond de Saint-Gilles, Melisinda. Hearing about her charm and beauty, the emperor of Constantinople asked for her hand and Raymond delightedly accepted. It was to be a very advantageous alliance. A splendid dowry was prepared and 12 galleys were made ready to conduct Melisinda to Byzantium, in a manner befitting a future empress.

At the last minute the emperor decided it was more politically fitting to ally himself with the house of Antioch and asked Maria, sister of Prince Bohemond I, to marry him instead. Raymond was furious at the insult to him and his sister. He loaded the 12 galleys with thugs and sent them to pillage the emperor's territories. Meanwhile, Melisinda was heartbroken and died soon afterwards of grief.

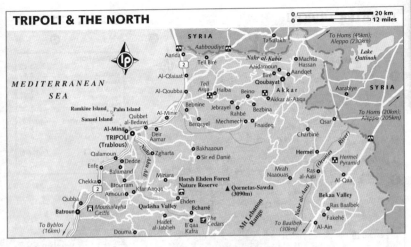

TRIPOLI & THE NORTH

and glass-making, prospered. Academic traditions were revived too, although this time it was Christian schools, rather than Islamic ones, that led the way.

The Mamluk sultan, Qalaun, took the city of Tripoli in 1289, massacring most of the population and razing the port city. Qalaun built his new city around the Citadel of Raymond de Saint-Gilles and once again the area flourished: the souqs, mosques, madrassas (theological schools) and khans (inns) that form the bulk of present-day Tripoli's monuments are testament to the city's economic and cultural prosperity in Mamluk times. The Turkish Ottomans took over the town in 1516 under the ruling sultan, Selim I. When the *mutasarrifa* (administrative district) of Mt Lebanon was created in 1860, Tripoli was still ruled by the Ottomans; however, it fell within the boundaries of the French Mandate of Greater Lebanon in 1920.

Since independence in 1946, Tripoli has been the administrative capital of northern Lebanon. Conservative and predominantly Sunni Muslim, it was perhaps natural that the pro-Arab nationalist forces, led by Rachid Karami, based themselves here in the civil war of 1958. The labyrinthine old city was almost impossible for outsiders to penetrate and Karami's men held out for several weeks.

In the 1975–91 round of fighting, Tripoli suffered a lot of damage – especially during the inter-Palestinian battles of 1983 – but it still fared better than the south. Both during and after the war, the city's population grew rapidly, swelled by refugees, including large numbers of Palestinians. Today it is concentrating on rebuilding its industry and business sectors, and looking to tourism as a source of future income.

ORIENTATION

There are two main parts to Tripoli: the city proper, which includes modern Tripoli and the old city; and Al-Mina (the port area), a promontory 3km to its west. The geographical centre of town is Sahet et-Tall (at-tahl), a large square by the clock tower where you'll find the service-taxi and bus stands, as well as most of the cheap hotels.

The old city sprawls east of Sahet et-Tall, while the modern centre is west of the square, along Rue Fouad Chehab. Between Rue Fouad Chehab and Al-Mina are broad avenues with residential buildings, modern shopping malls, Internet cafés, and restaurants. In Al-Mina you'll find the pleasant waterfront, shops and some of the city's best restaurants and cafés.

INFORMATION

EMERGENCY

Ambulance (☎ 602 510, 610 861)
Fire (☎ 431 017)
Police (☎ 430 950/1/2/3)
Red Cross (☎ 602 510)

INTERNET ACCESS

There are Internet cafés scattered around the new part of town. There are a couple in the

TRIPOLI & THE NORTH

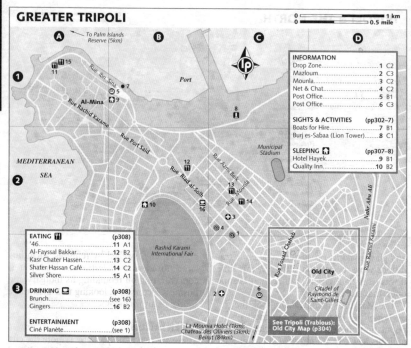

GREATER TRIPOLI

0 ————————— 1 km
0 ————————— 0.5 mile

To Palm Islands
Reserve (5km)

Rue Ibn Sina

Port

Rue Rachid Karame

Al-Mina

MEDITERRANEAN
SEA

Rue Port Said

Rue Riad al-Solh

Rue Azmi Beik

Municipal
Stadium

Rue Mounla

Rashid Karami
International Fair

Nahr Abu Ali

Rue Rachid Karami

Rue Fouad Chehab

Old City

Citadel of
Raymond de
Saint-Gilles

See Tripoli (Trablous):
Old City Map (p304)

La Mounia Hotel (1km);
Chateau des Oliviers (3km);
Beirut (84km)

INFORMATION
Drop Zone................................1 C2
Mazloum.................................2 C3
Mounla..................................3 C2
Net & Chat..............................4 C2
Post Office..............................5 B1
Post Office..............................6 C3

SIGHTS & ACTIVITIES (pp302–7)
Boats for Hire...........................7 B1
Burj es-Sabaa (Lion Tower)..............8 C1

SLEEPING (pp307–8)
Hotel Hayek.............................9 B1
Quality Inn.............................10 B2

EATING (p308)
'46.....................................11 A1
Al-Fayssal Bakkar.......................12 B2
Kasr Chater Hassen......................13 C2
Shater Hassan Café......................14 C2
Silver Shore............................15 A1

DRINKING (p308)
Brunch...............................(see 16)
Gingers................................16 B2

ENTERTAINMENT (p308)
Ciné Planète..........................(see 1)

old city, but they've more or less surrendered to game-playing kids.

Drop Zone (Map above; Rue Riad al-Solh; per hr LL2000; 10.30am-11pm) In the half-empty City Complex; it has good connection speeds.

Net & Chat (Map above; per hr LL2000; 10am-midnight) Turn off Rue Riad al-Solh at Pain d'Or and walk one block; it's on the northwest corner.

MEDICAL SERVICES

Mazloum (Map above; ☎ 628 303) and **Mounla** (Map above; ☎ 210 848) are good private hospitals. Pharmacies are scattered along the length of Rue Tall and in Al-Mina.

MONEY

Most of the large banks have ATMs. Change US-dollar travellers cheques into any denomination at the **Walid M el-Masri Co Exchange** (Map p304; Rue Tall) for US$2 per cheque.

POST

There are two post offices in Tripoli. The main **post office** (Map above; Rue Fouad Chehab; 8am-5pm Mon-Fri, 8am-noon Sat) is near the Bank of Lebanon building, just south of Abdel Hamid Karami Square, and the other **branch** (Map above; Rue ibn Sina) is in Al-Mina.

TELEPHONE

There is a public telephone at both post offices and a **public telephone office** (Map p304) on a side street running between Jamal Abdel Tell Square and Rue Fouad Chehab.

TOURIST INFORMATION

Tourist office (Map p304; ☎ 433 590; 8am-5pm Mon-Sat) Has a few brochures and perhaps the largest and silliest tourist map ever produced. The staff are friendly but don't all speak English. They can help with the permit to visit the Palm Islands Reserve (p307).

SIGHTS & ACTIVITIES
Old City

The old city mostly dates from the 14th and 15th centuries (the Mamluk era) and is a maze of narrow alleyways, colourful souqs, hammams (bathhouses), khans, mosques and madrassas. Some monuments were damaged during the civil war, others have suffered greatly from neglect over the years. Still, it's a very lively place where artisans, including jewellers, tailors and coppersmiths, continue to work as they have done for centuries.

There are 40 listed monuments in Tripoli, almost all in the old city, and they have numbered plaques. Some monuments are completely ruined, some are being squatted in and many are locked, but a key is usually kept in a nearby shop or house – just ask.

CITADEL OF RAYMOND DE SAINT-GILLES

The city is dominated by the vast **citadel** (Map p304; Plaque No 1; ☼ 8am-6pm, closes earlier in winter; adult/student LL7500/3750), known as Qala'at Sanjil in Arabic. In AD 1102 Raymond de Saint-Gilles occupied the hill which overlooks the valley, the town and the coast. He decided to transform this position, which he called Mont Pelerin (Mt Pilgrim), into a fortress. The original castle was burnt down in 1289, as well as on several subsequent occasions. It was rebuilt (1307–08) by Emir Essendemir Kurgi, and was added to right up until the 19th century. As a result, only the foundation stones remain of the original construction.

The first entrance is a huge Ottoman gateway, over which is an engraving from Süleyman the Magnificent, who ordered the restoration (yet again) of 'this blessed tower, that it may serve as a fortified position until the end of time'. After this there is a bridge across a moat dug by the Crusaders. Inside the castle is a confusing mixture of architectural styles and features that reflect the different occupants and stormy history of the city.

When you have explored the castle, walk down to the bridge and cross the river. The east bank is the best place to view the castle with its sheer walls and picturesque Arab buildings nestling at the foot of the mount.

MADRASSAS

From the top of the citadel, walk down the set of steps directly in front to the street, turn left and first right and walk along Rue Rachid Rida. Take the first right and soon you'll see the 14th-century **madrassas of Al-Machhad and Al-Shamsiyat** (Map p304), adjacent to the entrance of the Great Mosque. Opposite the entrance are two more 14th-century madrassas, **Al-Khairiah Hassan** and **Al-Nouriyat**. The latter is still in use and has distinctive black-and-white stonework around its doors and windows, and a beautiful inlaid mihrab (prayer niche).

GREAT MOSQUE الجامع الكبير

Construction of the **Great Mosque** (Map p304; Plaque No 2) was begun in 1294 and completed 21 years later. It was built on the ruins of a 12th-century Crusader cathedral, St Mary of the Tower, which was destroyed by the Mamluks. The mosque's northern entrance and the minaret, a distinctive Lombard-style tower, are likely remnants of the original building. Inside, a large courtyard is surrounded by porticos on three sides, and a domed and vaulted prayer hall on the fourth.

Women are expected to wear a gown (provided) and have their heads covered to visit the Great Mosque. You might be lucky to find **Ali Khawaja**, a very knowledgeable local guide, who can help with a gown that's been washed in this century.

MADRASSA AL-QARTAWIYYA
المدرسة القرطاوية

Attached to the east side of the Great Mosque is **Madrassa al-Qartawiyya** (Map p304; Plaque No 3), which was built by a Mamluk governor of the same name between 1316 and 1326. Famed for its fine workmanship, the madrassa has an elegant façade of black-and-white stone facings, topped by a honeycomb-patterned half-dome above the portal. The back wall is also made with black-and-white stone and has some beautiful Arabic inscriptions. Inside, the prayer hall is topped by Tripoli's only oval dome and has a finely decorated south-facing wall and minbar (pulpit).

HAMMAM AL-NOURI حمام النوري

Back opposite Al-Khairiah Hassan and Al-Nouriyat madrassas, look right and you should see the entrance to **Hammam al-Nouri** (Map p304), a large public bath built around 1333. The entrance to the hammam is behind a juice stand – the vendor will let you past. Once inside, if you go right from the main sitting room, you have access to an outside ladder (among the garbage) up to the roof. While it's not safe to walk across, you can observe the once wonderful domes of the hammam roof.

MADRASSA AL-TUWASHIYAT
المدرسة الطويشية

Back out on the street, **Madrassa al-Tuwashiyat** (Map p304; Plaque No 9), a law school with

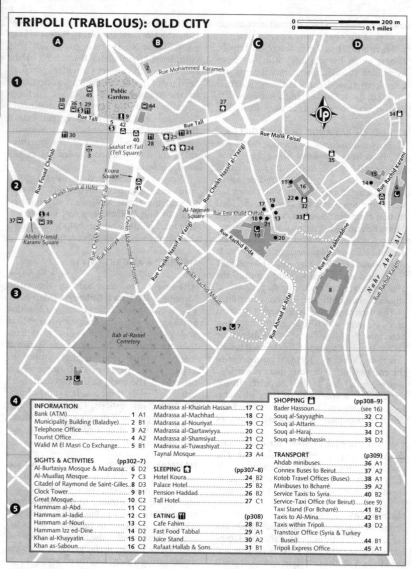

TRIPOLI (TRABLOUS): OLD CITY

0		200 m
0		0.1 miles

INFORMATION
Bank (ATM).....................................	**1** A1
Municipality Building (Baladiye)......	**2** B1
Telephone Office............................	**3** A2
Tourist Office.................................	**4** A2
Walid M El Masri Co Exchange.......	**5** A1

SIGHTS & ACTIVITIES (pp302–7)
Al-Burtasiya Mosque & Madrassa..	**6** D2
Al-Muallaq Mosque........................	**7** C3
Citadel of Raymond de Saint-Gilles..8	D3
Clock Tower...................................	**9** B1
Great Mosque................................	**10** C2
Hammam al-Abd.............................	**11** C2
Hammam al-Jadid...........................	**12** C3
Hammam al-Nouri...........................	**13** C2
Hammam Izz ed-Dine......................	**14** D2
Khan al-Khayyatin..........................	**15** D2
Khan as-Saboun.............................	**16** C2

Madrassa al-Khairiah Hassan.......	**17** C2
Madrassa al-Machhad..................	**18** C2
Madrassa al-Nouriyat...................	**19** C2
Madrassa al-Qartawiyya...............	**20** C2
Madrassa al-Shamsiyat.................	**21** C2
Madrassa al-Tuwashiyat................	**22** C2
Taynal Mosque.............................	**23** A4

SLEEPING (pp307–8)
Hotel Koura................................	**24** B2
Palace Hotel...............................	**25** B2
Pension Haddad..........................	**26** B2
Tall Hotel...................................	**27** C1

EATING (p308)
Cafe Fahim.................................	**28** B2
Fast Food Tabbal.........................	**29** A1
Juice Stand.................................	**30** A1
Rafaat Hallab & Sons...................	**31** B1

SHOPPING (pp308–9)
Bader Hassoun............................(see 16)
Souq al-Sayyaghin......................	**32** C2
Souq al-Attarin...........................	**33** C2
Souq al-Haraj.............................	**34** D1
Souq an-Nahhassin.....................	**35** D2

TRANSPORT (p309)
Ahdab minibuses.........................	**36** A1
Connex Buses to Beirut................	**37** A2
Kotob Travel Offices (Buses)........	**38** A1
Minibuses to Bcharré...................	**39** A2
Service Taxis to Syria..................	**40** B2
Service-Taxi Office (for Beirut)....(see 9)
Taxi Stand (For Bcharré)..............	**41** B2
Taxis to Al-Mina..........................	**42** B1
Taxis within Tripoli......................	**43** D2
Transtour Office (Syria and Turkey Buses)...................................	**44** B1
Tripoli Express Office...................	**45** A1

an attached mausoleum that dates back to the early 1470s, is on the main street of the gold souq (Souq al-Sayyaghin). The Madrassa al-Tuwashiyat is built of sandstone in alternating black-and-white patterns, and it has an unusual, finely decorated portal that towers above the entire building's ornate façade.

HAMMAM AL-ABD حمام العبد

Close by the Madrassa al-Tuwashiyat is Tripoli's only functioning bathhouse, **Hammam al-Abd** (Map above; 8am-11pm; basic bath LL10,000), built around 1700. For those travelling in Lebanon only (not visiting Syria), this is perhaps your best bet to try the hammam experience. Unfortunately, you have to be male to indulge, unless you can get a group of women together and book the entire place in advance. Pay at least LL6000 extra if you want a scrub and rub. It's easy to miss the entrance – look for the sign marked 'Sona-Massage' and it's right down the end of the laneway.

KHAN AS-SABOUN

Virtually next door to the hammam is **Khan as-Saboun** (خان الصابون; Map opposite; Plaque No 10), which was built in the 16th century and first used as an army barracks. After 70 years it was abandoned and later came back to life as a market where local farmers sold their olives and olive-based products – soap in particular – from the small shops surrounding the courtyard. The khan became famous for its high-quality scented soaps and when the soap industry took off in the 18th century (see the boxed text A Tripolian Soap Opera, p306) the khan was at its centre. Now the khan is occupied by only about five shops, including **Bader Hassoun** (☎ 03-438 369), where the English-speaking soap entrepreneurs will show you around.

HAMMAM IZZ ED-DINE   حمام عز الدين

Izz ed-Dine Aybak was the Mamluk governor of Tripoli at the end of the 13th century, and he not only donated this **bath** (Map opposite; Plaque No 11) to the city but gave orders to be buried beside it (his mausoleum can be seen next to the hammam). The building incorporates remains from an earlier Crusader church and hospice. It was heavily damaged during the civil war and slated for restoration, but the beauty of the entrance is still visible.

KHAN AL-KHAYYATIN   خان الخياطين

Beside Hammam Izz ed-Dine is the beautifully restored **Khan al-Khayyatin** (Tailors' Market; Map opposite; Plaque No 12), which was built in the first half of the 14th century, making it one of the city's oldest khans. It was probably built on top of an earlier Byzantine and Crusader building that was part of the commercial suburb built by Raymond de Saint-Gilles to control trade into the area.

KHAN AL-MISRIYYIN   خان المصريين

On the northern side of the old city **Khan al-Misriyyin** (Khan of the Egyptians; Map opposite; Plaque No 14) is in need of restoration; it is thought to have been built at the beginning of the 14th century. Used by Egyptian merchants, the building has a traditional khan design, with two arcaded storeys built around an open courtyard.

If you proceed upstairs, you can observe one of Tripoli's only real soap-makers, **Mhamoud Nasser Charkass**, who makes soap by hand, using the methods his family has used for centuries.

SOUQ AL-HARAJ   سوق الحرج

At the northern end of the old town is **Souq al-Haraj** (Map opposite; Plaque No 21), which is thought to have been built on the site of a Crusader church. Its high, vaulted ceiling is supported by 14 granite columns, two of which are in the centre and the other 12 around the side, which probably came from the earlier structure. Today the souq specialises in mats, pillows and mattresses.

Khan al-Askar   خان العسكر

Just around the corner from Souq al-Haraj is **Khan al-Askar** (Soldiers' Khan; Map opposite; Plaque No 33), which consists of two buildings joined by a vaulted passage. It is thought to have been built in the late 13th or early 14th century, and was restored in the 18th century.

Other Sights & Activities

AL-MUALLAQ MOSQUE   جامع المعلق

To the south of the Great Mosque is **Al-Muallaq Mosque** (Hanging Mosque; Map opposite; Plaque No 29). It's a small, 14th-century mosque that is unusual because it is built on the second floor of the building. It has a simple interior and leads down to a courtyard garden.

HAMMAM AL-JADID   حمام الجديد

The **Hammam al-Jadid** (New Baths; Map opposite; Plaque No 30) is almost opposite Al-Muallaq Mosque. While certainly not new – it was built around 1740 – it was in use until the 1970s and is the city's best-preserved and largest hammam (with the exception of the still-functioning Hammam al-Abd). It was donated as a gift to the city by As'ad Pasha al-Azem of Damascus and no expense was spared in its construction. Draped over the portal is a 14-link chain carved from a single block of stone. A huge, glass-pierced dome dominates the main chamber and brings a dim light to the pool and fountain below.

A TRIPOLIAN SOAP OPERA

Tripoli's Khan as-Saboun may only have one or two traditional soap-makers nowadays but historically soap was an important part of the city's economy. Some local patriots claim that soap was invented here, but whether or not this is true, by the 18th century Tripoli soap was a prized product in Europe.

Soap was traditionally made with olive oil, honey, glycerine and other natural ingredients, which were melted together in a huge vat, coloured with saffron and other natural dyes, and scented with essential oils. The soap supplied the local hammams as well as households. A collection of differently shaped soaps, symbolising purity, would also be given to brides as part of their trousseau.

Cheap mass-produced soap almost killed traditional soap-making in Tripoli a generation ago, but now the handmade soaps are making quite a comeback aided by the Musée du Savon in Sidon (p341) and orders from boutique hotels. Tourism in the souqs is also seeing the soaps rebranded and repackaged, betting that the trend for all-natural, handmade beauty products in the West will result in higher sales.

The floor and fountain are laid with slabs of marble in contrasting colours. Several smaller chambers, also with glass-pierced domes, lead off the main room.

BURTASIYA MOSQUE & MADRASSA
جامع ومدرسة البرطاسية

Situated by the river, across the street from the eastern entrance to the Khan al-Khayyatin, is **Burtasiya Mosque and Madrassa** (Map p304; Plaque No 19). Built by the Kurdish prince, Sharafeddin Issa ben Omar al-Burtasi, in 1315 its square, tower-like minaret and black-and-white stonework are particularly fine. Inside, the intricately decorated and inlaid mihrab makes the visit worthwhile. Look for the mosaic in its half-dome.

TAYNAL MOSQUE
جامع تينال

Standing on its own to the southeast of the cemetery, but well worth the few minutes' walk it takes to get there, **Taynal Mosque** (Map p304; Plaque No 31) is one of the most outstanding examples of Islamic religious architecture in Tripoli. Built in 1336 by Sayf ed-Din Taynal, on the ruins of an earlier Carmelite church, it still has a partially preserved Carmelite nave in the first prayer hall. Other recycled elements, including two rows of Egyptian granite columns topped with late-Roman capitals, were taken from an earlier monument. The simplicity of the bare stone walls contrasts beautifully with some of the Mamluk decorative elements, in particular the entrance to the second prayer hall, a masterpiece of alternating black-and-white bands of stone with Arabic inscriptions, marble panels with geometric designs and a honeycomb-patterned half-dome.

Al-Mina
الميناء

The district of Al-Mina covers the headland and its three main avenues run from the old part of Tripoli down to the port. Until a few decades ago the avenues ran between orange groves, but these have now been built over, testament to the city's rapidly expanding population. Although the history of the port area stretches back far further than the medieval city, there is almost nothing of this earlier occupation left today. Instead, the area has a seaside air, with families promenading along the Corniche in the early evenings.

BURJ ES-SABAA (LION TOWER)
برج السبع

The only monument of any interest in Al-Mina is the **miniature fortress** (Lion Tower; Map p302) at the far eastern end of the harbour. Named after the bas-relief decorations of lions that used to line the façade, the building dates from the end of the 15th century and was probably built by the Mamluk sultan, Qaitbey. It is an exceptional example of Mamluk military architecture with a striking black-and-white striped portico. The whole of the ground floor is one vast chamber that used to be decorated with paintings and armorial carvings, traces of which you can still see.

BOAT RIDES

Along the seafront there are many **boats** (Map p302) available to take people to the small islands just offshore. A return trip takes about two hours (with enough time for a swim) and costs LL5000. If there is a group, you can hire the entire boat (between 10 and 12 people) for LL50,000. A trip to the

Palm Islands Reserve needs to be negotiated separately.

PALM ISLANDS RESERVE

The Palm Islands Reserve consists of three islands, Palm, Sanani and Ramkine, which lie 5km off the shore of Al-Mina. The protected area covers almost 5 sq km of land and sea and represents an eastern-Mediterranean marine ecosystem. The site is particularly significant as a resting and nesting place for migratory birds. Over 300 species have been observed here, including seven that are threatened worldwide, and 11 others that are rare in Europe. In recent years, the threatened Mediterranean turtle has also come here to lay eggs.

On Palm Island there are some 2500 palm trees, and paths have been laid out for visitors. There are also beaches and you can swim from one island to the other, or have a picnic while you watch the birds and wildlife.

The islands are open to the public from July to September and you need a (free) permit, which you can get from the tourist office. You have to negotiate with one of the boat owners for the trip; expect to pay at least LL20,000 return.

SLEEPING

While there's plenty of budget accommodation in Tripoli, there's no decent mid-range accommodation and the top-end hotels are located a little to a long distance from the action.

Budget

Pension Haddad (Map p304; ☎ 624 392, 629 972; haddadpension@hotmail.com; off Rue Tall; dm/s/d US$7/10/16) Using the advertising slogan 'Miss your Grandma? Stay with us!', the spotlessly clean rooms, solicitous owners and plethora of doilies show that they're not kidding. The pension provides dinner (LL5000) if requested, does laundry (small/large load LL500/1000), has a satellite TV and offers free tea. To find it, look for the inconspicuous stencil of its name high on the building, go past the stationer and to the back stairs, when you reach the 1st floor.

Tall Hotel (Map p304; ☎ 628 407; Rue Tall; s/d LL13,000/25,000, with bathroom LL30,000/30,600; ⊠) All rooms have TV. It's reasonably clean but not as welcoming as the other budget options listed here. It's a little difficult to spot

the entrance – look for the red 'tell hotel' stencilled high on the building.

Hotel Koura (Map p304; ☎ 03-371 041, 03-326 803; off Rue Tall; s/d/tr with bathroom US$20/30/45, dm/d without bathroom US$10/15; ⊠) A spotless, small hotel opposite Pension Haddad and run by a charming brother and sister. The nicely renovated rooms are available in different configurations depending on how many guests they have staying. There's a central shared lounge area, breakfast is included in the price and the owners can organise day trips.

Palace Hotel (Map p304; ☎ 432 257; Rue Tall; s/d/tr US$15/25/30; ⊠) Located in a beautiful old building with high ceilings and stained glass windows. The inside doesn't quite live up to the exterior's promise, but still it's well positioned and adequate, if you're out all day sightseeing.

Hotel Hayek (Map p302; ☎ 601 311; Rue ibn Sina; dm/s/d/tr with breakfast US$15/20/30/35) A friendly, family-run business in Al-Mina, offering clean, basic rooms with sea views. The hotel is above a billiard parlour–café on a street running parallel behind the Corniche. The entrance is at the back of the building.

Top End

La Mounia Hotel (☎ 401 801; s/d with breakfast US$80/100; ⊠ ☐ ☑) This hotel offers five-star service and amenities for four-star prices, probably because it's located in Kalamoun, a seaside suburb 2km to the south of Tripoli. There's a restaurant, bar and pool, all of which are popular with the package groups that stay here. Travellers without their own transport will find it difficult to stay here and commute into Tripoli.

Quality Inn (Map p302; ☎ 211 255; www.qualityinn .com; Rashid Karami International Fair; s/d/ste US$76/101/126; ⊠ ☐ ☑) Adjacent to the Oscar Niemeyer–designed fairgrounds, this hotel – easily the best in town – is strategically situated between Al-Mina and the old city. Rooms are large, clean, and very well appointed. Like La Mounia, it offers five-star service at a four-star price, and yes, that really is an original Dali sculpture in the foyer.

Chateau des Oliviers (Villa Nadia; ☎ 411 170, 03-634 546; www.chateau-des-oliviers.com; d from US$100; ⊠ ☑) This modern mansion was converted into a hotel by its owner Nadia Dibo. Set high on a hill a few kilometres south of the city in the Haykalieh region, it has some rather uniquely decorated – to say the least – rooms and open areas. However, the reason many come here is the charming Madame Nadia herself. From the Beirut–Tripoli highway a few kilometres before Tripoli, turn into the Haykal road at the Hypermarket, it's up past the Haykal hospital.

EATING

Cafe Fahim (Map p304; Rue Tall) This is the most atmospheric café in town, with its extraordinary vaulted interior and crowd of local men smoking nargileh and playing backgammon. It has an outdoor terrace and charges LL1500 for a tea.

Rafaat Hallab & Sons (Map p304; Rue Tall) This is the best place to sample Tripoli's famous sweets. There are branches near the fairgrounds, on Riad al-Solh, and at Aboullaban, on Rue Fouad Chehab. Both have sit-down areas where you can enjoy a tea or coffee with your sweets.

Al-Fayssal Bakkar (Map p302; ☎ 202 203; mezze around LL2000, grills around LL5000; ☽ noon-midnight) A large, family-style restaurant that's very popular with locals, who come for the good food, reasonable prices and friendly staff. It's a good option, although ordering can be a challenge (staff speak Arabic only). You'll find it heading towards Al-Mina. Look for the mosque and the garden island in the middle of the road – Al-Fayssal Bakkar is on the opposite side of the mosque.

Kasr Chater Hassen (Map p302; ☎ 208 208; Rue Mounla; meals around LL40,000; ☽ noon-midnight) While the Lebanese food on offer can't possibly match the truly over-the-top exterior, a meal here is recommended nonetheless. Head towards Al-Mina, along Rue Riad al-Solh and turn right at Rue Mounla. Kasr Chater Hassen is in front of you on the left-hand side. Just look for the Vegas-style exterior lighting. No credit cards.

'46 (Map p304; ☎ 212 223; the Corniche, Al-Mina; mains LL16,500; ☽ 7-1am Tue-Sun) Named after the year 1946, when the current owner's father opened the restaurant, it has a great Italian/international menu. The very friendly waiters, stylish interior and big windows overlooking the Corniche make it a very pleasant dining experience. The restaurant is near the public gardens; enter from the rear of the building rather than from the Corniche.

Silver Shore (Map p302; ☎ 601 384/5; the Corniche, Al-Mina; meals around US$35; ☽ 11am-8pm) Easily the best seafood restaurant in town, it specialises in dishes accompanied by a special-recipe hot sauce. Oddly, it closes early in the evening, but it makes a great place to visit for a late weekend lunch. Owned by the same people as '46, you'll find it right next door. Make sure you book.

There are a number of fast-food places located around Sahet et-Tall. The best is probably **Fast Food Tabbal** (Map p304), which serves good felafel (LL1000) and has tables to sit at. Another popular sit-down fast-food option is **Shater Hassan Café** (Map p302; ☎ 210 597; ☽ 6-1am), which is like a hybrid of McDonald's, Pizza Hut and KFC. Situated in the new part of town, it's extremely popular with young Tripolitanians, who go for the pizza (LL9000) and burgers (LL4000). Heading towards Al-Mina, turn right into Rue Nadimal Jisr (just past the City Complex) and take the third street on your left; it's on the right-hand side a little down the street.

DRINKING

A conservative town, Tripoli, by Beirut's standards, is pretty dead at night. But there is a 'scene' of sorts, revolving around the cafés on Rue Riad al-Solh, heading towards Al Mina, just before the communication tower. Weather permitting, by 7pm the outdoor seating at both **Gingers** (Map p302; ☎ 204 780) and **Brunch** (Map p302; ☎ 204 780) in particular, is full of young Tripolitanians smoking nargileh and checking each other out.

ENTERTAINMENT

If people-watching doesn't appeal, you can always check out the latest-release English-language movies at **Ciné Planète** (Map p302; ☎ 442 471; City Complex, Rue Riad al-Solh; tickets LL10,000) with half-price tickets on Monday and Wednesday, and at all afternoon sessions.

SHOPPING

Exploring the old souqs is the best way to shop in Tripoli. If you are looking for jewellery, there is a whole souq devoted to gold, **Souq as-Sayyaghin** (Map p304). If you are looking for a more modest souvenir, then head for **Souq an-Nahhassin** (Map p304), the brass souq. Even if you don't want to buy, it is well worth a visit just to see the metalworkers making pieces by hand in the same way that they have done for centuries. For traditional handmade soap, head to **Khan** as-Saboun (Map p304) or upstairs at **Khan al-Misriyyin** (Map p304). Note that many shops in the souqs close on Friday.

GETTING THERE & AROUND
To/From Beirut

There are several companies running coach services from Beirut to Tripoli. All three services leave from Zone C of Charles Helou bus station, where there's a dedicated ticket booth. There's no need to book ahead.

Ahdab Runs minibuses from Tripoli to Beirut (LL1000, around two hours, every 10 minutes 6am to 6pm). They depart from Rue Fouad Chehab and Rue Tall.

Connex (☎ 611 232/3, 587 507) Runs daily express 'luxury coaches' from Beirut (LL2000, 90 minutes, every 30 minutes 7am to 8.30pm); and from Tripoli (every 30 minutes 5.15am to 5pm).

Kotob Runs older buses (it takes longer but is cheapest) from Beirut (LL1500, up to two hours, every 15 minutes 6am to 6.30pm), stopping to let passengers off and on at Jounieh (LL1500, 30 minutes), Byblos (LL1500, one hour) and Batroun (LL1500, 90 minutes); and from Tripoli (every 15 minutes 5am to 5.30pm) it makes the same stops.

Tripoli Express Runs smaller buses from Beirut (LL2000, 90 minutes, every 20 minutes 7am to 8.30pm); and from Tripoli (every 15 minutes 5.30am to 5.30pm; the 6.30am, 7.30am and 9am services are on larger buses).

Service taxis heading to Beirut (LL4000) leave from just outside the clock tower.

To Bcharré, the Cedars & Baalbek

Minibuses leave from outside the travel agency near the tourist office for Bcharré (LL2500, 80 minutes, at 7.30am, 8.30am and 10am, then hourly until 4pm); and from Bcharré (hourly 6am to 2pm). Those wanting to travel on to the Cedars will need to organise a taxi at Bcharré (LL15,000).

Service taxis heading to Bcharré (LL6000) and the Cedars (LL10,000) leave from Al-Koura Square.

When there's no snow or ice and the mountain road is open (usually early April to mid-December) it's possible to get a taxi from Bcharré to Baalbek (around US$40, 90 minutes).

To Syria, Turkey, Jordan & Saudi Arabia

Kotob runs buses for Aleppo in Syria (LL8000, almost four hours, every 30 minutes 9am to midnight daily), stopping in Homs (LL6000, two hours). It also runs a bus to Riyadh in Saudi Arabia (daily at 3am), stopping in Damascus (US$5, four hours) and Amman in Jordan (US$25, 10 hours).

Transtour (☎ 03-411 015) runs buses to Aleppo in Syria (US$5, almost five hours, hourly 9am to midnight daily); to Homs (LL5000, two hours, hourly 5am to midnight); to Damascus (LL7000, four hours, twice daily at 5am and 3pm), and to İstanbul in Turkey (US$45, once daily).

Service taxis to Homs (LL7700), Hama (LL3000) and Aleppo (LL15,000) leave when full from Sahet et-Tall. Service taxis don't go to Damascus.

Around Town

Service taxis travel within the old and new parts of Tripoli (LL1000) and to Al-Mina (LL2000).

AROUND TRIPOLI

ENFE   انفه
☎ 06

On the coast 15km south of Tripoli is the village of Enfe (the name means 'nose' in honour of the shape of the coastline). Nowadays this is a largely Greek Orthodox town, but during the Crusades this was the town of Nephim, a fief of the County of Tripoli. The lords of Nephim played an important role here and later moved to Cyprus in the 13th century. There is very little left of the Crusader castle, except for a few ruined stone walls. Several vaults carved into the rock remain, and the most interesting relics are two **Crusader moats**, one of which is over 40m long.

The castle had a sadistic history: the lord of Nephim, Count Bohemond VII, walled up his rivals, the Embiaci, in the castle. This grisly scene was later recalled in Edgar Allan Poe's story, *The Cask of Amontillado*.

There are also four **churches**, one of which is Byzantine and has the remains of painted murals. It is romantically named Our Lady of the Wind. The Church of the Holy Sepulchre dates from the time of Bohemond in the 12th century and is still very much in use.

As the coast is clean and attractive in this part of Lebanon, it has not escaped the developers' meddling. **Marina del Sol** (☎ 541 301, 03-331 466/77; apt per night US$125) is one of the big resorts, with apartments that are rented or leased, usually by the season. Nearby is

Las Salinas (☎ 540 970) with the same resort facilities at similar prices.

Enfe is on the service-taxi route between Tripoli, Byblos and Beirut, so it is easy to get to; simply ask the driver to drop you at the turn-off. You will probably be charged the full service-taxi fare to Tripoli (LL5000). Alternatively, a taxi from Tripoli will cost about LL7000.

BALAMAND   بلمند
☎ 06
High above the village of Qalamoun, overlooking the old Tripoli–Beirut road, is the Greek Orthodox abbey of **Balamand** (Belmont; ☎ 400740, 400742). This started out as a Cistercian abbey and was founded in 1157. It is possibly even older than this, as it was built on the site of a Byzantine monastery. The Cistercians either abandoned it or were driven out, possibly in 1289 when the Mamluk sultan, Qalaun, took Tripoli.

The monastery underwent major restoration work several centuries ago and the Crusader buildings were all but lost to later designs. The Church of Our Lady of Balamand is very pretty, and its bell tower is still intact. The church interior has been carefully restored and is worth seeing for the fine icons set into a carved screen behind the altar.

These days the abbey is a university as well as a cultural and religious centre. Balamand is 12km south of Tripoli. Taxis leave from the main stand on Rue Tall.

QADISHA VALLEY
وادي قاديشا

One of the most beautiful spots in Lebanon, the Qadisha Valley is a long deep gorge that starts near Batroun in the west and rises dramatically to its head just beyond the town of Bcharré. Villages with red-tiled roofs perch atop hills, or cling precariously to the mountain sides. The Qadisha River (Nahr Abu Ali), with its source just below the Cedars, runs along the valley bottom while Lebanon's highest peak, Qornet as-Sawda, towers overhead.

The word 'qadisha' comes from the Semitic root for 'holy' and the valley's steep, rocky sides have made it a natural fortress for persecuted religious minorities for millennia. From the 5th century onwards, the Maronites made this area their refuge and the valley is scattered with rock-cut monasteries, hermitages and churches. Today, the villages perched atop the cliffs surrounding the valley are almost exclusively Maronite.

Because of its natural beauty and unique history the Qadisha Valley has been recognised as a World Heritage site by Unesco, although this hasn't prevented its environment from coming under threat. Until recently, hunting was a major problem, garbage was often dumped in the area and sewage was pumped into the river from surrounding villages. The construction of a waste-water

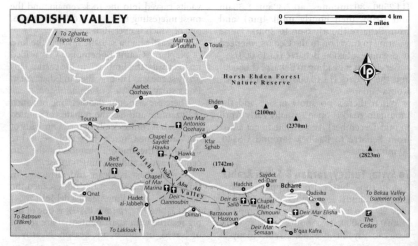

QADISHA VALLEY

0 ——————— 4 km
0 ——————— 2 miles

To Zgharta; Tripoli (30km)

Mazraat al-Touffah   Toula

Horsh Ehden Forest Nature Reserve

Aarbet Qozhaya

Seraal   Ehden

Tourza   (2100m)   (2370m)

Deir Mar Antonios Qozhaya

Chapel of Saydet Hawka   Kfar Sghab   (2823m)

Beit Menzer   Hawka

Chapel of Mar Marina   Blawza   (1742m)

Qnat   Saydet ed-Darr   Bcharré

Hadet al-Jabbeh   Deir Qannoubin   Hadchit   To Bekaa Valley (summer only)

Deir as-Salib   Chapel Mart Chmouni   Qadisha Grotto

To Batroun (38km)   (1300m)   Diman   Barzaoun & Hasroun   Deir Mar Elisha

To Laklouk   Deir Mar Semaan   B'qaa Kafra   The Cedars

treatment plan, enforcement of hunting bans and clean-up efforts are all paying off.

Although the valley is nearly 50km long, the main area of interest is the higher 20km section from Tourza up to the Qadisha Grotto. This is a hiker's paradise with numerous waterfalls, rock-carved tombs and monasteries, and stunning scenery.

EHDEN   اهدن

☎ 06

On the northern rim of the Qadisha Valley, around 30km from Tripoli, Ehden is easily reached via a brief stretch of highway that runs as far as Zgharta. This popular summer resort has a picturesque old centre that's dominated by a lively main square lined with cafés.

Opposite the square, a small street leads up to St George's Church, where there is an equestrian **statue of Youssef Bey Karam**, a 19th-century nationalist hero who led rebellions against Ottoman rule with the support of other religious communities, as well as his fellow Maronites. He was killed by the Turks near Ehden and his mummified body, dressed in a traditional gold-braided costume, lies in a glass-topped sarcophagus against the southern wall of St George's Church. His descendants remain prominent in the area.

Northwest of the village, on a hill, there's a tiny **chapel** of Our Lady of the Castle, which is thought to have originally been a Roman look-out post. Now the chapel is dwarfed by the enormous modernist eyesore of the same name that dominates the skyline.

Sleeping & Eating

Most people who visit the Qadisha Valley stay in either Bcharré or the Cedars, but there are alternatives in Ehden – keep in mind that it's very quiet outside summer.

Belmont (☎ 560 102; d from US$50) This old-style hotel on the western entry to the town offers a variety of clean rooms, some with views and balconies.

Grand Hotel Abchi (☎ 560 001; d/ste US$54/80) This is a large modern hotel with an inexplicable UFO-like disco, overlooking the village from the west.

Hotel La Mairie (☎ 560 108; Rue Dawalib; s/d with breakfast US$50/60) On the main road of the village, this hotel is open all year.

Ehden is rather famous for its restaurants that overlook Nebaa Mar Sarkis (Mar Sarkis

Spring) as it emerges from the hillside to the northeast of the village. About four restaurants cluster around the source, and they all serve traditional Lebanese food with huge mezze spreads.

The most famous are **Al-Arze** (☎ 560 226) and **Nabeh Mar Sarkis al-Asmar** (☎ 560 150; dishes around US$20). On summer evenings, many restaurants also lay on live music and dancing. There are several other cheaper restaurants. Both **Au Pére Loup** (☎ 662 413; Dawalib St) and **Restaurant al-Rabiah** (☎ 661 806; Rue Dawalib) serve Lebanese food for slightly less (US$10 to US$20) than the restaurants overlooking Nebaa Mar Sarkis; Al-Rabiah also offers entertainment during the summer months.

For Lebanese fast food, there are a number of cafés around the main square in the old part of town, where you can sit under the trees and order *lahma bi ajeen* (spicy meat pizza) or shwarma for about LL1500, while you sip tea or beer.

THE DARKER SIDE OF EDEN

With its well-kept buildings, bustling square and beautiful scenery, Ehden and its environs do not bring mafia-style violence to mind. Yet the pastoral bliss of the Qadisha can be deceptive. Although the Maronites may have sheltered here from the persecution visited on them by other sects, both Christian and Islamic, they have recently managed to visit some pretty impressive violence upon themselves, too, based upon the local proverb 'the enemy of my grandfather can never be my friend'.

In one of the most notorious events of the civil war, Samir Geagea of Bcharré amassed several hundred militiamen, went into the home of Tony Franjieh (son of President Suleiman Franjieh) in Ehden and proceeded to kill him and his entire family as they slept. While this was explained by political differences between the two families, in fact it had its roots in a feud between the Geageas and the Franjiehs, which dates back to the 19th century. At that time, according to local (Bcharré) lore, a Geagea woman was killed by two Ehden men after offering them water and food. In response Bcharré's residents burned down the town of Ehden and killed many of its inhabitants.

Getting There & Away

If you are taking a service taxi from Tripoli to Bcharré, ask the driver to drop you at Ehden or any other point en route along the north side of the valley. If you want to get to the south side of the valley, you will have to go to Bcharré and get a taxi from there. A service taxi to any point from Ehden to Bcharré will cost LL5000. There are also microbuses that ply the rim of the valley; they pass by about six times a day and cost LL2500.

It is easier to explore this part of Lebanon with your own transport. If you don't have a car, it might be worth hiring a car and driver for the day. Your hotel can arrange this. Expect to pay between US$70 and US$100 for a whole day, which is not too bad if there are a few of you to share the cost.

HORSH EHDEN FOREST NATURE RESERVE   محميّة حرش اهدن

Just over 3km from Ehden is the nature reserve of Horsh Ehden, a 17-sq-km mountainous ecosystem. You can arrange a visit by contacting the **Friends of Horsh Ehden** (☎ 06-561 800; fohe@cyberia.net.lb).

Although the reserve covers less than 1% of Lebanon's total area, some 40% of the country's plant species have been found within its borders. There are 1058 species of plants, 12% of which are threatened. The reserve also has one of Lebanon's largest stands of native cedar, mixed with varieties of juniper, conifer, wild apple and others.

The area is a nesting place for birds and provides a refuge for some of Lebanon's endangered mammals. Wolves and hyenas have also been spotted here, as have wild boars.

KFAR SGHAB   كفر صغاب

The small village of Kfar Sghab is 4km east of Ehden. Australians, particularly Sydneysiders, passing through here might be surprised to see a sign announcing 'Parramatta Rd' on the main street. More surprising still, if you say hello to almost any of the 750 inhabitants of the village you're likely to hear 'g'day mate' thrown back at you. There's even a Para Cafe just off the main road in the centre of the village. The reason for this surreal connection between the village and a used-car strip in Sydney? A staggering 15,000 Australian Lebanese trace their roots back to this area. Many have returned to Lebanon since the war ended and are building summer homes here.

BCHARRÉ   بشرّي
☎ 06

The trip to Bcharré takes you through some of the most beautiful scenery in Lebanon. The road winds along the mountainous slopes, continuously gaining in altitude and offering spectacular views of the Qadisha Valley: villages of red-tile-roofed houses perch atop hills or cling precariously to the mountainsides; the Qadisha River, with its source just below the Cedars, runs along the valley bottom; and Lebanon's highest peak, Qornet as-Sawda (3090m), towers overhead. It's a truly magnificent area.

Bcharré is the main town in the Qadisha Valley. Famous as the birthplace of Khalil Gibran and the stronghold of the right-wing Maronite Christian Phalange party, it's a very relaxing place to spend a couple of days.

Orientation & Information

The town itself, dominated by the St Saba Church in the main street, is quite small. Heading east on the main road are some small supermarkets and a moneychanger. A block north of the main road, there's a **post office** (⌚ 8am-1pm), which has a **public telephone bureau.**

L'Intime is both a private telephone office (overseas calls US$1 per minute) and an Internet café.

Sights & Activities
GIBRAN MUSEUM

Fans of the famous poet and artist Khalil Gibran (1883–1931) will no doubt love this **museum** (☎ 671 137; adult/student LL3000/2000; ⌚ 9am-5pm, closed Mon Nov-Mar). In keeping with his wishes, Gibran, who emigrated to the USA in the 19th century and published his most famous work, The Prophet, in 1923, was buried in a 19th-century monastery built into the rocky slopes of a hill overlooking Bcharré. The museum, which has been set up in this monastery, houses a large collection of Gibran's paintings, drawings and gouaches, and also some of his manuscripts. His coffin is in the monastery's former chapel, which is cut straight into the rock. The views of the valley from the museum's terrace are quite amazing. Also see the boxed text, p314.

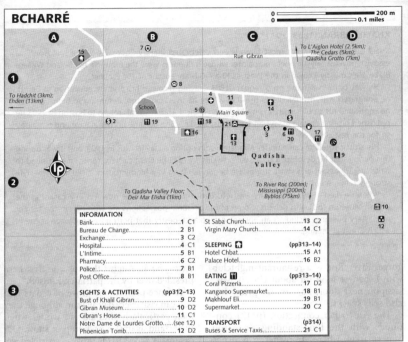

BCHARRÉ

To L'Aiglon Hotel (2.5km);
The Cedars (5km);
Qadisha Grotto (7km)

Rue Gibran

To Hadchit (3km);
Ehden (13km)

School

Main Square

Qadisha
Valley

To Qadisha Valley Floor;
Deir Mar Elisha (1km)

To River Roc (200m);
Mississippi (200m);
Byblos (75km)

INFORMATION	
Bank	1 C1
Bureau de Change	2 B1
Exchange	3 C2
Hospital	4 C1
L'Intime	5 C2
Pharmacy	6 C2
Police	7 B1
Post Office	8 B1

SIGHTS & ACTIVITIES	(pp312–13)
Bust of Khalil Gibran	9 D2
Gibran Museum	10 D2
Gibran's House	11 C1
Notre Dame de Lourdes Grotto	(see 12)
Phoenician Tomb	12 D2

St Saba Church	13 C2
Virgin Mary Church	14 C1

SLEEPING	(pp313–14)
Hotel Chbat	15 A1
Palace Hotel	16 B2

EATING	(pp313–14)
Coral Pizzeria	17 D2
Kangaroo Supermarket	18 B1
Makhlouf Eli	19 B1
Supermarket	20 C2

TRANSPORT	(p314)
Buses & Service Taxis	21 C1

NOTRE DAME DE LOURDES GROTTO

مغارة سيدة لورد

Part way up a small path near the museum
is a small cave with a spring dedicated to
the Virgin Mary. Local legend has it that she
took pity on a Carmelite gardener-monk,
who had to carry water up to the monastery
each day to water his vegetable patch. Small
candles and statuettes sit on an altar that has
been built around the spring.

PHOENICIAN TOMB

Just up the hill from the grotto is a large stone
obelisk thought to date back to 750 BC. At
the base of the obelisk is a burial chamber
and ledges for four coffins.

QADISHA GROTTO

مغارة قاديشا

This small **grotto** (admission LL4000; 8am-5pm,
June until first snow) extends about 500m into the
mountain and has great limestone formations. Not as extraordinary as Jeita Grotto
(p277), but it's still spectacular. The grotto is
a 7km walk from Bcharré; follow the signs
to the L'Aiglon Hotel (p315) and then take
the footpath opposite. It's then a very picturesque 1.5km walk to the grotto.

Sleeping & Eating

Palace Hotel (671 460; s/d/tr US$30/40/48;) In
the centre of town, this is a smallish place;
all rooms have a bath. Breakfast is an extra
US$4.50.

Hotel Chbat (671 237, 671 270; s/d/tr with breakfast
US$74/89/100;) Built in 1955 on the side of
a hill in the upper part of Bcharré, this is
the best hotel in town with views across
the Qadisha Valley. It has a relaxed, homely
atmosphere with open fires and a Lebanese
cook, who's been with the hotel since it
opened. The hotel also has a couple of
dormitories for groups, popular with school
skiing groups in winter. In summer there's a
swimming pool.

There are a couple of restaurants in town.
Makhlouf Elie, on the western side, is a small
restaurant with a roof-top terrace and fantastic views. It serves mezze and sandwiches
for about US$5. Coral Pizza is an outdoor
cafeteria just below the waterfall at the eastern edge of town and has pizza and snacks
(summer only).

Along the road at the head of the valley,
just outside Bcharré, are several restaurants
that take advantage of the views along the

KHALIL GIBRAN (1883–1931)

Khalil Gibran is Lebanon's most famous and celebrated literary figure. He was a philosophical essayist, novelist, mystic poet and painter whose influences were the Bible, Nietzsche and William Blake. He's mostly known in the West as Khalil Gibran, author of *The Prophet*.

He was born in Bcharré on 6 January 1883. Having received his primary education in Beirut, he emigrated with his parents to the USA where he lived in Boston. Returning to Beirut in 1898 he continued his studies with an emphasis on classical Arabic. On his return to Boston in 1903 he published his first literary essays and met Mary Haskell. She became his benefactor and remained so for the rest of his life.

His artistic tutelage came under Auguste Rodin during a stay in Paris in 1909, and it was during this period that he developed his visual-art skills. In 1912 he went to New York and continued to write literary essays and short stories. He began painting in a highly romanticised, mystical style strongly reminiscent of William Blake.

When he died in 1931, his body was returned to Lebanon and he now lies in a casket at the Gibran Museum (p312) in Bcharré. Some of his personal possessions are with him in the former monastery building, including an ancient Armenian tapestry that portrays a crucifixion scene in which Christ is smiling.

gorge. River Roc is a restaurant-nightclub with Lebanese food for about US$20. Mississippi, next door, has similar prices but also sells snacks.

The Australian connection (p312) continues with the long-standing Kangaroo Supermarket, where the owner, a returnee from Sydney, stocks a few Australian specialities. There's another supermarket further down the road past the Main Square.

Getting There & Away

The bus and service-taxi stop is outside the St Saba Church in the centre of town. For details about getting to Bcharré from Tripoli, and from Bcharré to Baalbek, see Getting There & Around on p309.

THE CEDARS الأرز

☎ 06

'The Cedars' is a name used for both the small grove of trees that stands at an altitude of more than 2000m on the slopes of Jebel Makmel, and the ski resort a couple of kilometres further up the road. The famous trees, about 4km from Bcharré, are the remnant of a vast forest of cedar that once covered the mountains of Lebanon (see the boxed text The Cedar Tree, p318).

A few of these slow-growing trees are very old and it's thought that some may reach an age of 1500 years. Known locally as Arz ar-Rab (Cedars of the Lord), they are under the protection of the Patriarch of Lebanon, who built a chapel in the cedar grove in 1848.

Each year in August there is a festival here presided over by the patriarch himself.

A fence protects the grove of cedars and you can visit every day all year, although they look particularly dramatic in winter when they stand against a backdrop of snow. Occasionally access to the grove is restricted, eg, when the snow is melting and the ground is soft, so that roots are not damaged by people walking on them.

About 2km further up the road is the ski station, which has a small village of shops and hotels around the ski lifts. There are also equipment-hire shops. See the boxed text Ski Facts: The Cedars for more details. The road continuing beyond this point leads to the Bekaa Valley, but it's only open outside of the winter season. Also outside winter, paragliders take off from next to this road.

Hiking

During the summer months you can hike to Lebanon's highest peak, Qornet as-Sawda (3090m), starting at the army-maintained ski lift situated on the far left as you face the mountain at the ski-fields entrance. To get to the top and back takes the good part of the day, and you'll obviously need to be relatively fit. The first part of the trip to the top of the ski lift takes about two hours; from here hike north along the path for another hour to reach the peak. The views are spectacular and the hiking isn't too difficult, although sometimes the path is not as clear as it should be. Also, the signs for each peak

SKI FACTS: THE CEDARS

- **Altitude** 1950–3087m
- **No of Lifts** Eight (five beginner)
- ☽ 8.30am-3.30pm (until 4pm Sat & Sun)
- ☎ 03-399 133
- **Adult Day Pass** US$17 (Mon-Fri), US$24 (Sat & Sun),

People first started coming to ski at the Cedars in the 1920s and the first lift was installed in 1953, making it Lebanon's oldest ski resort. While it is less developed than many of the other resorts, it is the second-most popular, particularly for those who actually ski (rather than pose). The runs are longer here and the season usually starts earlier (mid-December) and finishes later (April) than the other resorts. There are also numerous off-piste opportunities for the more adventurous types. Equipment can be rented from a number of locations and there are Red Cross teams on hand at weekends.

have blown off and only the posts remain. Remember to dress warmly – the peaks are windy and there can be snow up here as late as May. For those who think this sounds like far too much effort, take a vehicle along the road to the right of the ski fields, then when the road splits off for Baalbek, continue to the left up the mountain. The road leads over Dahr el-Qadib and the view is quite magnificent.

Sleeping & Eating

L'Aiglon Hotel (☎ 671 529; d with breakfast US$30) Opposite the entrance to the Qadisha Grotto (p313) between Bcharré and the Cedars, this hotel offers reasonable rooms and wonderful views. It can organise transport, equipment and lift tickets.

Alpine Hotel (☎ 671 517; US$30) Also on the road between Bcharré and the Cedars, this is cosy and quite simple. If you are staying a few days, the Alpine offers half board for US$40 per day. Lunch or dinner cost between US$10 and US$15.

St Bernard Hotel (☎ 03 289 600; s/d with breakfast US$84/115) This hotel is right by the forest

grove. Outside the ski season, room rates are cheaper. There's a free shuttle service to the slopes.

Hotel La Cabane (☎ 03-321575; r from US$24) Handy for the slopes, Hotel La Cabane has a restaurant and a bar.

Hotel Mon Refuge (☎ 671 438; s/d/apt US$15/30/120) This hotel has pleasant rooms, and apartments that sleep twelve (the apartments have a fireplace). Breakfast is US$5 extra. Downstairs is a **restaurant-bar** (meals US$8-15) that serves a mixture of Lebanese and Western food.

Centre Tony Arida (☎ 671 195) Next door, this place has everything from apartments that sleep up to eight people for US$300 per night (half price in spring and autumn) to a nightclub, restaurant and a large selection of ski equipment for hire. Tony is a former-ski-champion-turned-jovial-host, and he presides over his empire with good-natured gusto.

L'Auberge des Cèdres (☎ 678 888; www.sm resorts.net; s/d US$90/170) is also recommended. See the boxed text (p316) for details.

Getting There & Away

There are service taxis to Bcharré (LL6000) and the Cedars (LL10,000) from the Rue Tall taxi stand in Tripoli. Outside the ski season there are only a few service taxis to Bcharré and you will have to take a regular taxi from there to the Cedars. The fare is about LL15,000 but you may be able to haggle the price down. In Bcharré, the taxis congregate by St Saba Church and charge US$20 for a half-day tour around the Qadisha. There is a minibus at 7am to Beirut's Dawra bus station for LL4000 (double-check beforehand). When the road is open you can also get a taxi to take you to Baalbek (US$40)

THE QADISHA VALLEY FLOOR

The best way to hike into this valley (which is on the World Heritage list) is to take one of the steep goat tracks that leads out of Bcharré and into the valley below. If that's too strenuous, you can drive a car to Deir Mar Elisha and park it there while you walk along the valley floor. A hike from Bcharré to Deir as-Salib takes about six hours, there and back. A hike from Bcharré to Deir Mar Antonios Qozhaya will take the whole day. Remember to bring plenty of water; the river water is not clean enough to drink.

THE AUTHOR'S CHOICE

L'Auberge des Cèdres (☎ 06-678 888; www.sm resorts.net; s/d US$90/170) For those wishing to come back to their own open fireplace and a gourmet dinner (rather than a sleeping bag and a slice of pizza) after a day on the slopes – this one's for you. Positioned high in the Cedars village, it's your own slice of Megève or Cortina in Lebanon. Good rooms (the premium suites are a must), warmly furnished open areas, a great bar and mountain-facing sundeck terrace will make it hard to even bother putting on your boots in the morning. If you do manage to leave, the restaurant has a great menu specialising in locally sourced natural ingredients that will have you back at the hotel before sundown.

If you seek even more privacy, the hotel now has bungalows, as well as La Petite Ourse (self-contained log cabins) and Le Grande Ourse Chalets, suitable for large families or groups.

Having now brought a slice of European winter style to the lodgings, if they could just manage to get the ski area expanded and install some more ski lifts…

Deir Mar Elisha ‏دير مار شعيا‎

Dramatic and beautiful, the monastery of Mar Elisha (St Eliseus) is built into the side of the cliffs below Bcharré. The Lebanese Maronite Order, the first order to be officially recognised by the Roman Catholic Church, was founded here in 1695. The building goes back much further – by the 14th century it was already the seat of a Maronite bishop. It was restored in 1991 and turned into a museum, where there are displays of books and other artefacts relating to the monastery's history. The museum is on two storeys and to the right is a chapel containing the tomb of the Anchorite of Lebanon, François de Chasteuil (1588–1644).

You can get to the monastery from one of the tracks below Bcharré or take the main road heading east from Bcharré and, after 3km, turn off at the small blue sign for the Qadisha Valley. A narrow road winds down to the monastery.

If you follow the track west through the lush vegetation, after about 20 minutes you'll come to a picturesque riverside restaurant,

Greenland (sign in Arabic only) that is only open during the summer months.

Chapel of Mar Chmouni ‏كنيسة مار شموني‎

Built under a rocky ledge in the Middle Ages, this chapel has two constructed naves, one in a natural rock formation. Sadly the 13th-century paintings that adorn the walls have been covered with a layer of plaster.

The chapel is at the eastern end of the valley at the point where Wadi Houla (Houla Valley) and Wadi Qannoubin meet. You can follow a steep path down from Hadchit or you can get there along a path on the valley floor.

Deir as-Salib ‏دير الصليب‎

This rock-cut monastery can be reached by a steep path to the right from the valley floor or from the village of Hadchit. As well as a chapel, there are a number of caves that were used as hermits' cells. Derelict and increasingly ruined, there are nevertheless still traces of Byzantine-era frescoes inside these.

Deir Qannoubin ‏دير قنوبين‎

Continuing along the valley bottom, you will eventually come to a track to the left with a signpost to Deir Qannoubin. The name Qannoubin is derived from the Greek *kenobion*, which means 'monastery'. This is a very ancient site. Some sources say that it was founded by Theodosius the Great in the late 4th century.

Local legend has it that at the end of the 14th century, the Mamluk sultan, Barquq (who was briefly overthrown in 1389), escaped from imprisonment in Karak Castle (now in Jordan) and sought refuge in the Qadisha before returning to Egypt to reclaim his throne. Such was the hospitality shown him that he paid for the restoration of the monastery. From 1440 through to the end of the 18th century, Deir Qannoubin was the Maronite patriarchal seat. Nowadays it is a working convent.

The church is half-built into the rock face and is decorated with frescoes dating from the 18th century. Near the entrance is a vault containing the naturally mummified body thought to be that of Patriarch Yousef Tyan. Deir Qannoubin can also be reached by a path leading from the village of Blawza, on the valley's northern rim, and takes about an hour each way.

Chapel of Mar Marina   كنيسة مار مارينا

Just to the west of the monastery is the chapel-cave of Mar Marina, where the remains of 17 Maronite patriarchs are buried. The chapel is dedicated to St Marina, born in Qalamoun, who lived her life at Deir Qannoubin. See the boxed text The Marina Grotto for more information.

CHAPEL OF SAYDET HAWKA   كنيسة سيدة حوقا
Continuing on the main track past the signpost for Deir Qannoubin, and bearing right at the fork, you will eventually see Chapel of Saydet Hawka (Deir Saydet Hawka) on the right. This is a small monastery, thought to date from the 13th century, which consists of a chapel and a few monks' cells within a cave. It is associated with an attack by armed Mamluks against the natural fortress of Aassi Hawka, which is in a cave high above the monastery. The cave is only accessible to experienced rock climbers.

The monastery is deserted for most of the year but is used to celebrate the Feast of the Assumption of the Virgin with a high mass on the evening of 14 August. You can get there via a path from Hawka (about 30 minutes one way) or via the valley-floor path.

DEIR MAR ANTONIOS QOZHAYA   دير مار انطونيوس قزحيا
Continuing on the main track, you will eventually come to Deir Mar Antonios Qozhaya. This hermitage is the largest in the valley and has been continually in use since it was founded in the 11th century. It is famous for establishing, in the 16th century, the first-known printing press in the Middle East.

The **museum** houses a collection of religious and ethnographic objects as well as an old printing press that was used to publish the Psalms in Syriac, a language still used by the Maronites in their services. A popular place of pilgrimage, the hermitage also has a souvenir shop which sells all manner of kitsch religious knick-knacks. To see the museum you need to knock at the main building and get one of the monks to open it up for you.

Near the entrance to the monastery is the **Grotto of St Anthony**, known locally as the 'Cave of the Mad', where you can see the chains used to constrain the insane or possessed, who were left at the monastery in the hope that the saint would cure them.

If you're not hiking, you can reach the monastery by car from Aarbet Qozhaya on the northern-valley rim.

B'QAA KAFRA   بقاع كفرا
Back up above the valley, on the road between Bcharré and Hasroun, is B'qaa Kafra, the highest village in Lebanon (elevation 1750m) and the birthplace of St Charbel. The saint's house has been turned into a **museum**, which commemorates the saint's life in paintings. It is open daily, except Monday, and there is a shop and café at the entrance. The village now has a new convent named after St Charbel and there is a church, Notre

---

THE MARINA GROTTO

Just 4km north of Enfe, past the village of Qalamoun, is the Marina Grotto. It is about a 20-minute walk to the east of the village over stony slopes (you may need to ask for directions). The grotto, with its orange-coloured rear wall, stands out against the grey rock of the rest of the escarpment.

The grotto was a sanctuary and has painted murals from two periods; the older inscriptions are in Greek. The pictures show scenes from the life of St Marina, whose story is a curious one.

Legend has it that St Marina was raised as a boy in a Maronite monastery, where her father, a widower, became a monk. She grew up with the name Marinos and only her father and the abbot knew that she was female. When they died, she remained in the monastery as a monk. When a local girl bore a child (fathered by one of the monks), Marinos was accused of being responsible and was then banished from the monastery. She kept silent and took the abandoned child to live in the grotto, where she miraculously nursed the child with her own milk. When Marinos died, the truth of her sex became known and she was canonised. Her body was taken for burial in Constantinople, where it lies in the Chapel of Mar Marina.

The grotto became a place of pilgrimage for women who could not nurse their children and it's known locally as the Milk Grotto.

THE CEDAR TREE

There are three or four species of cedar tree (Cedrus libani) throughout North Africa and Asia. The most famous of these is the Cedar of Lebanon, which was mentioned in the Old Testament, although today only a few of the original groves still exist. In antiquity the cedar forests covered great swathes of the Mt Lebanon Range and provided a source of wealth for the Phoenicians, who exported the fragrant and durable wood to Egypt and Palestine.

The original Temple of Solomon in Jerusalem was built of this wood, as were many sarcophagi discovered in Egypt. A slow-but-sure process of deforestation took place over the millennia, and although new trees are now being planted, it will be centuries before they mature.

Of the few remaining ancient trees, most are in the grove at the Cedars, above Bcharré, and in Barouk, in the Chouf, south of Beirut. Some of the trees at the Cedars are thought to be well over 1000 years old. Their trunks have a huge girth and their height can reach 30m. Naturally, there are strict rules about taking any timber from these remaining trees and the souvenirs for sale nearby are made from fallen branches.

Dame, across the way from the museum. St Charbel's Feast is celebrated on the third Sunday of July.

DEIR MAR SEMAAN ديـر مـار سمعان

Just past the turn-off for B'qaa Kafra, as you head east, is a small path leading to Deir Mar Semaan, a hermitage founded in 1112 by Takla, the daughter of a local priest called Basil. Concrete paths lead down to the spartan four-room hermitage carved into the rocks, where Mar Samaan (St Simon) supposedly lived. Access to the caves involves squeezing through doorways. Inside there are votive candles and offerings. There are also traces of frescoes, and remains of water cisterns. The walk takes about 15 minutes.

DIMAN ديمان

In Diman, on the south side of the valley, is the summer residence of the Maronite Patriarchy, which took over from Deir Qannoubin in the 19th century. You can't miss it – it is a large modern building on the valley side of the road. The church is not old but is well worth a look for its panoramic paintings of the Qadisha Valley and religious scenes by the Lebanese painter, Saliba Doueihy. These date from the 1930s or '40s,

when the spire of the church was built. The grounds behind the building lead to the edge of the gorge and have views across the valley.

AMIOUN أميون

Back down towards the coast, Amioun stands above the highway to/from Chekka. It is easily noticeable from the road because of the rock-cut tombs that have been hewn out of its southern cliffs. These are either Phoenician or Roman burial vaults. Perched atop these cliffs is the old part of the village, a beautiful mixture of Ottoman stone buildings and narrow winding streets.

High up in the centre of the village is the 15th-century Cathedral of St George, which was built on the ruins of a Roman temple (itself built on Neolithic remains). The site was an important place of worship under the Romans, and pagan rites were reputedly practised well into the Christian era. An earthquake destroyed the temple in the 4th or 5th century AD but elements, including a couple of columns, have been incorporated into the church. A stone iconostasis (screen), with fine painted icons, contrasts with the plain vaulted interior of the church.

The Bekaa Valley وادي البقاع

Despite its name, the Bekaa Valley is actually a high plateau between the Mt Lebanon and Anti-Lebanon Ranges. For millennia the Bekaa, dubbed 'hollow Syria' by the Greeks and Romans, was a corridor linking the Syrian interior with the coastal cities of Phoenicia. The many invading armies and trading caravans that passed through left traces of their presence, which can be seen in a host of small sites around the valley, but particularly at the Umayyad city of Aanjar and the magnificent temples at Baalbek.

The Bekaa has always been an agricultural region, fed by the Nahr al-Aasi (Orontes River) and the Nahr Litani. In Roman times it was an important grain-producing region, and was one of Rome's 'breadbaskets'. Today the Bekaa is nowhere near as productive as deforestation and poor crop planning have reduced the fertility of the land.

This didn't stop one crop – cannabis – from flourishing before and during the civil war. Until quite recently 'Red Leb' was the country's most famous (or infamous) product. These days the farmers of the Bekaa have mostly cleaned up their act and potatoes, tomatoes and grapes are the crops of choice. The dry climate and fertile soil also make the valley perfect for wine-making – the Bekaa is the centre of Lebanon's burgeoning wine industry.

Perhaps because of its agricultural character, the Bekaa is also known for its good food, and regional specialities include fresh trout, Armenian specialities (in the Aanjar area) and hearty mezzes – traditionally washed down with local arak.

HIGHLIGHTS

- Marvel over the spectacular temple complex at **Baalbek** (p329)

- Walk down the main street of **Aanjar** (p325), the Middle East's only remaining Umayyad town

- Learn to like arak and mix your mezze at Lebanon's favourite **riverside restaurants** (p323) in Zahlé

- Puzzle over the mysterious 27m-high **pyramid tomb** (p333) near Hermel

- Smell the bouquet and sip the wine at the **Ksara Winery** (p324), Lebanon's most famous vineyard

CHTAURA   شتورة
☎ 08

Chtaura (44km from Beirut) is the transport hub of the Bekaa, with roads heading north to Baalbek and Homs (Syria), south to Lake Qaraoun and on to Marjeyun, and east to Damascus and Jordan. The town is really just a crossroads – its function as a stopover is clear from the many cheap restaurants that line the main road. These restaurants however are friendly and traditional, often serving local produce such as cheese and yogurt or the famous local syrups – try the almond syrup with iced milk.

Sleeping & Eating

Hotel Khater (☎ 540 133; per person US$15) The only cheap option is found on the main road above a shop-cum-café. The rooms are simple and fairly clean, but there is no restaurant and you will have to wander down to a nearby café for breakfast.

Massabki Hotel (☎ 544 644; fax 540 912; s/d US$110/138; ✷) Located on the main road in the centre of the town, this comfortable accommodation option has lovely gardens and a well-regarded restaurant.

Chtaura Park Hotel (☎ 540 011; s/d US$145/184; ✷ ☐ ☎) Tipping the top end of the scale, this super-luxury hotel has all the usual five-star amenities. While the exterior is a little bland, it's quite elegant inside, and often hosts heads of state and high-level meetings. Outside summer (and VIP visits) ask for a discount.

Akl Restaurant (☎ 540 699; mezze & mains from US$20) This is the best place in town, with its two venues (indoor and outdoor) close together on the main road. This long-established restaurant specialises in mezze dishes and also has a good-value set menu.

Another traditional Lebanese restaurant worth trying is the **Restaurant Moutran** on the main road near the Hotel Khater.

There are also a number of snack places lining the main street.

Getting There & Away

There are frequent service taxis to/from Beirut (LL4000). They congregate on both sides of the main street and you can easily get connections onward to Zahlé (LL1000), Baalbek (LL2000) and Damascus (LL6000), as well as to some of the smaller places along

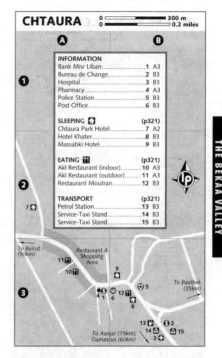

CHTAURA   0 — 300 m   0 — 0.2 miles

INFORMATION	
Bank Misr Liban	1 A3
Bureau de Change	2 B3
Hospital	3 B3
Pharmacy	4 B3
Police Station	5 B3
Post Office	6 B3

SLEEPING	(p321)
Chtaura Park Hotel	7 A2
Hotel Khater	8 B3
Massabki Hotel	9 B3

EATING	(p321)
Akl Restaurant (indoor)	10 A3
Akl Restaurant (outdoor)	11 A3
Restaurant Moutran	12 B3

TRANSPORT	(p321)
Petrol Station	13 B3
Service-Taxi Stand	14 B3
Service-Taxi Stand	15 B3

To Beirut (50km)
Restaurant & Shopping Area
To Baalbek (35km)
To Aanjar (15km); Damascus (60km)

the Bekaa Valley. Microbuses are cheaper from Beirut's Cola bus station, and pick up and drop off at Chtaura. To take one on to Zahlé or Baalbek costs LL500.

ZAHLÉ   زحله
☎ 08

Zahlé is an attractive resort town 7km northeast of Chtaura. Known locally as Arousat al-Beqa'a (Bride of the Bekaa), it is set along the steep banks of the Birdawni River (locally it's known as 'Bardouni'), which tumbles through a gorge from Jebel Sannine. Zahlé is a predominantly Greek Catholic town with a number of its Ottoman-era houses still intact despite heavy bombardment during the civil war. The town is famous for its open-air restaurants, which line the river's edge in the upper part of the town. During summer weekends and evenings, these are full of locals and Beirutis enjoying some of the finest Lebanese cooking in the country, washed down with arak (see the boxed text Arak, p326).

In the 19th century, Zahlé was involved in the communal fighting between the Druze

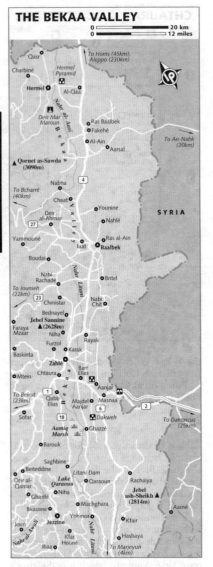

THE BEKAA VALLEY

they sent remittances, further increasing the town's prosperity. Zahlé's gracious stone houses date from this time.

Keep in mind that from November to April, most of the restaurants are closed and the town is quiet. In summer, it makes a pleasant lunch stop en route from Beirut to Baalbek, and is an ideal place to stay if you intend to spend a few days exploring the valley.

Orientation & Information

Most of Zahlé's amenities are scattered along the main road, Rue Brazil, and Rue St Barbara running parallel. This is where the banks, bureaux de change and the **post office** (8am-5pm Mon-Fri, 8am-noon Sat) can be found.

Ambulance (☎ 804 892)
Centre Culturel Francais (Rue Brazil) Has a small library and organises cultural events.
Dataland Internet (☎ 814 825; Rue Brazil; 8am-midnight; per hr LL5000) The only Internet café that's permanently open.
Hospital On Rue Brazil towards the head of the valley.
Police (☎ 803 521)
Tourist Office (☎ 802 566; 8.30am-1.30pm Mon-Sat) Signposted about 1km from the highway turn-off; on the 3rd floor of the Chamber of Commerce building, just off Rue Brazil.

Sleeping & Eating

Hotel Akl (☎ 820 701; Rue Brazil; s/d US$17/20, d/tr with bathroom US$33/40) Without a doubt this is the best budget choice in town. In a dilapidated but character-filled old house, its clean rooms have balconies and loads of natural light. The rooms at the rear overlook the river. There's a large communal lounge with TV and a piano, and the manager is very helpful.

Arabi Hotel (☎ 821 214; sarabi@inco.com.lb; s/d US$55/66; Apr-Oct) Right at the heart of the outdoor eating scene on the Birdawni River, the rooms here are quite noisy in summer. The price includes breakfast. The attached **restaurant** (meals US$20-40) is one of the most famous in Zahlé. A mezze on its outdoor terrace is a wonderful way to spend an afternoon or evening.

Hotel Monte Alberto (☎ 810 912/3/4; www.montealberto.com; d/tr US$55/66;) Located high above town, this hotel commands amazing views. To make the trip between the town and the hotel there is a funicular – complete with amusingly fake 'wagon wheels'. The rooms are clean and comfortable, and the price

and Christians and many of its inhabitants were killed in the 1860 massacre. Some 25 years later, the opening of a railway line between Beirut and Damascus (which is no longer operating) brought some prosperity to the town. At around the same time, more than half the town migrated to Brazil (after which the main street is named), from where

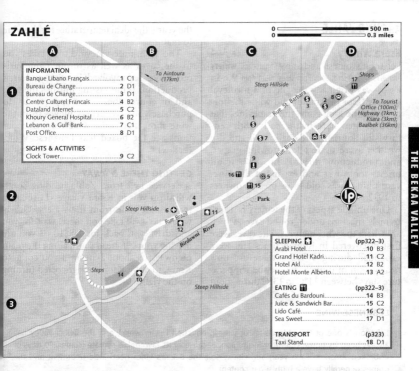

ZAHLÉ

0   500 m
0   0.3 miles

INFORMATION
Banque Libano Français................1 C1
Bureau de Change........................2 D1
Bureau de Change........................3 D1
Centre Culturel Francais.................4 B2
Dataland Internet.........................5 C2
Khoury General Hospital...............6 B2
Lebanon & Gulf Bank....................7 C1
Post Office...................................8 D1

SIGHTS & ACTIVITIES
Clock Tower.................................9 C2

SLEEPING	(pp322–3)
Arabi Hotel.................................10	B3
Grand Hotel Kadri.......................11	C2
Hotel Akl..................................12	B2
Hotel Monte Alberto...................13	A2

EATING	(pp322–3)
Cafés du Bardouni.......................14	B3
Juice & Sandwich Bar..................15	C2
Lido Café..................................16	C2
Sea Sweet.................................17	D1

| TRANSPORT | (p323) |
| Taxi Stand.................................18 | D1 |

To Aintoura (17km)
Steep Hillside
Rue St. Barbara
Shops
To Tourist Office (100m); Highway (1km); Ksara (3km); Baalbek (36km)
Rue Brazil
Park
Steep Hillside
Steep Hillside
Rue Brazil
Birdawni River
Steps

THE BEKAA VALLEY

includes breakfast. There's also an enormous **restaurant** (per person incl drinks US$15-25) with an outdoor terrace, serving up mezze feasts with the best views in town.

Grand Hotel Kadri (☎ 813 920; www.kadrihotel .com; Rue Brazil; s/d/ste US$110/137/165; ❂ ❑ ❑) The most sophisticated of Zahlé's hotels is located along the Rue Brazil strip and can get a little noisy on summer nights. Significant discounts are available in winter and special weekend rates (outside summer), which make the hotel good value. Prices include breakfast, and hotel facilities include a health club, tennis court, nightclub and four restaurants.

The restaurants on the river – look for the sign 'Cafés du Bardouni' – are open during summer only, and are further along the river than the one at the Arabi Hotel, which is worth trying first.

Lido Café (☎ 818 656; cnr Rue Brazil & Rue St Barbara; pasta LL7000, mains 14,000; ❂ 7am-late) Back in the centre of town, near the clock tower, this is a good eating option. Not as expensive as the riverside places, its pasta dishes make a good change for those suffering mezze overload.

Along Rue Brazil are a number of good juice bars and snack places that serve breakfast for a few dollars.

Sea Sweet (Rue Brazil) This has delicious Lebanese pastries to take away.

Getting There & Away
Minibuses from Beirut to Zahlé (LL2000, 90 minutes) leave from the southwest side of the roundabout at the Cola transport hub. Service taxis (LL5000) leave from the same spot. Both will drop you off at the highway turn-off, which is just over 1km from the centre of town. If you want to be dropped at the centre of town, you'll need to get off at Chtaura (LL2000, one hour) and catch a service taxi (LL1000); specify that you want to be dropped in town and not at the highway turn-off.

To get to Baalbek from Zahlé by government bus, take OCFTC bus No 4 or 5 (LL500, 30 minutes) from the bus stop just below the car park midway along Rue Brazil. Take a service taxi to Baalbek (LL2000, 30 minutes) from the main taxi stand on a square off Rue Brazil.

AROUND ZAHLÉ

☎ 08

Ksara Winery   كسارة

Lebanon's oldest and most famous **winery**
(☎ 813 495; Ksara; 9am-7pm daily, 9am-4pm Mon-Sat
winter) was originally the site of a medieval
fortress (*ksar* in Arabic) and while the fortress may be long gone, the grapevines that
were planted here in the early 18th century still flourish. The chalky soil and dry
weather were perfect for growing grapes,
and production thrived. In 1857, Jesuit
priests took over and expanded the vineyard until it was sold to its present owners
in 1972.

One unique aspect of the winery is its extremely spacious underground caves, which
are where the wine matures. The caves were
first discovered in Roman times and were
expanded during WWI – there are now
nearly 2km of tunnels, where the temperature stays between 11°C to 13°C throughout
the year – the ideal temperature for the wine
to mature.

The 45-minute vineyard tour takes you
to the caves as well as through the various processes involved in wine and arak
production. Wine-tasting finishes the tour
and of course there's an opportunity to
purchase your favourite vintages from the
wine shop. For some wine recommendations see the boxed text Lebanese Wine,
(below).

GETTING THERE & AWAY

A service taxi from Zahlé heading south
will drop you in Ksara village (LL1000), a
five-minute walk from the winery. Otherwise a taxi will take you there, wait for you
and drive you back for US$10. If you are
driving yourself, head south along the main
highway for about 2km until you come to
Ksara, then look for the signposted turning
on the right.

LEBANESE WINE

Lebanon is one of the oldest sites of wine production in the world, and the Bekaa Valley has
always been its prime vine-growing region. Because of its favourable climate (some 240 days of
unbroken sunshine each year) and chalky soil, the Bekaa's vines need little treatment and the
grapes generally have a high sugar content.

During the war, domestic demand for wine was reduced in favour of the stronger arak (no
doubt more efficient for calming jangled nerves). However wine consumption is on the increase
again. Lebanon produced approximately six million bottles in 2002, 40% of which was exported
(with export earnings worth US$6.7 million).

Ksara

The oldest commercial Lebanese wine is the Ksara vineyard (above). It produces an excellent
chardonnay made from 100% chardonnay grapes. **Château Blanc de Blancs**, the pick of the
whites, is a blend of sauvignon, sémillon and chardonnay, and matured in French-oak casks for
a few months before bottling. The lightest red is **Rosé de Ksara** made from a blend of cinsault,
cabernet-sauvignon and syrah grapes. The red worth cellaring is **Château Ksara**, made from
cabernet-sauvignon, merlot and petit verdot, aged in oak for 18 months, and then bottle-aged
before hitting the market.

A quick guide:

best whites 1999 Chardonnay (drink now), 2000 Blanc de Blancs (keep)
best reds 1999 Réserve du Couvent (drink now), 1998 Cabernet-Sauvignon (keep), any vintage Château Ksara (keep)

Kefraya

The Kefraya vineyard, which is 20km south of Chtaura and can be visited, is the largest producer
of wine in Lebanon, turning out over a million bottles a year. Since it began production in 1979
it has won dozens of prizes for its wine, many awards for its Lacrima d'Oro, a fortified white wine,
and its heavier reds. The estate produces an early drinking rosé (made from 100% cinsault) but
the Château vintages are a far more complex (and quite heady) bunch. For example, the 1991

AANJAR & AROUND
☎ 08

Only 15km from Chtaura, **Aanjar** (عنجر; Haouch Moussa) is a small, predominantly Armenian town founded by refugees fleeing genocide in Turkey.

The discovery of this astonishingly well-preserved early-Islamic town came about by accident. In the late 1940s archaeologists were digging here in the hopes of discovering the ancient city of Chalcis, founded around 1000 BC. Instead, they uncovered a walled town with a Roman layout that dated from the first centuries of Islam. Almost all periods of Arab history have been preserved at other sites in Lebanon – but traces of the Umayyads are strangely absent, so Aanjar has great historical significance.

It is a rare example of a Lebanese inland trading city, and the only site that is from a single period. Set against the backdrop of the Anti-Lebanon Range, it is a fascinating and picturesque place to visit.

Umayyad City   المدينة الاموية
This **city** (admission LL6000; ☯ 8am-sunset) is thought to have been built by the sixth Umayyad caliph, Walid I (AD 705–15). It is a walled and fortified city cut into four equal quarters, separated by two 20m-wide avenues, the cardo maximus and the decumanus maximus. Because it was built in the early days of Muslim rule, the influence of previous cultures was still strong and the layout is typically Hellenistic-Roman. Other influences include the reuse of columns and capitals in the colonnades lining the streets. The **tetrapylon**, a four-column structure placed where the two streets intersect, is another Roman element, although the stonework, with its alternating layers of large blocks and narrow bricks, is typically Byzantine.

THE BEKAA VALLEY

Le Château Kefraya is a blend of cabernet-sauvignon, syrah, mourvédre, grenache, cinsault and carignan weighing in at 14.5% alcohol.

A quick guide:

best whites 2002 or 2003 Le Blanc De Blancs Du Château Kefraya (drink now), 1995 Lacrima d'Oro (keep)
best reds 2002 Les Breteches Du Château Kefraya (drink now), 1998 Le Château Kefraya (keep)

Château Musar
While the smallest of the commercial producers, the Musar name is the one recognised by most wine buffs. It is also the only winery not working out of the Bekaa (the winery is in Ghazir, above Jounieh), and its grapes are grown in the valley and transported there by truck. The premium Château Musar range (red, white, rosé) is aged a minimum of 12 months in oak and blended before being bottled and cellar-aged for four years. While owner-winemaker Serge Hochar's wines may receive medals the word over, we should raise our glasses to him for having the tenacity to produce vintages through the civil war. The winery also now produces a range of second wines that are not oak-aged, hoping to make inroads in the domestic market.

A quick guide:

best whites Musar Cuvée Réservée Blanc (drink now), Château Musar White 1996 (keep)
best reds Musar Cuvée Réservée Rouge (drink now), 1998 Château Musar Red (keep)

Massaya
A recent addition to Lebanon's wine producers, Massaya is well known in Lebanon as a brand of excellent arak served in distinctive, tall blue bottles (see the boxed text Arak, p326). Given the response to its first vintages they may well become better known for their wines. A French-Lebanese collaboration, the first vintage (1999) sold out, with 80% going to export. There are currently three reds (Classic, Selection and Reserve) and two whites (Classic and Selection) as well as a rosé.

A quick guide:

best whites Classic Blanc 2002 (drink now), 2001 Selection Blanc (keep)
best reds 2001 Selection Rouge (drink now), 2001 Reserve (keep)

ARAK

If there is a national drink of Lebanon, or indeed the Middle East, then this is it. An acquired taste for some Westerners, this aniseed-flavoured drink has become a universal favourite in the eastern Mediterranean under several guises – ouzo in Greece, raki in Turkey – but all are fundamentally the same thing. Like a holiday romance, it doesn't feel the same when you get home and away from the sunny climes of the Mediterranean, you'll probably find the magic is gone.

Arak is also curiously classless – sipped at both the smartest dinner and the humblest café. It manages to be available at both ends of the alcohol market (US$4 to US$20). Experts say the best way to tell the difference, is by the way you feel the next morning.

Somewhat surprisingly, given that it doesn't have the least hint of 'grapiness' to its flavour, arak is a by-product of wine-making. It's a brandy, made from the bits left over from the wine press – the red grape skins and pips, much like the Italian grappa, but with the additional flavour of aniseed.

Diluted with ice and water, arak makes a good partner for Lebanese mezzes, with the flavour helping to cleanse the palate between the different dishes. So overcome any 'araknaphobia' and try it with your next mezze – you could easily become converted. If you want a bottle to take home, try Arak El Massaya, in its trademark tall and elegant blue bottles.

The Roman effect can also be seen in the **public baths**, just inside the entrance. As with all Roman baths and many later hammams, these contain three main sections: a place to change; the bathing area (consisting of chambers with cold, warm and hot water); and an area to relax and chat. In the bathing area to the left of the entrance there are two faded but reasonably intact **mosaics**.

In the southwestern corner of the site is a warren of foundations that are thought to be the remains of the **residential quarters**. Across the cardo maximus from them is Aanjar's most striking building, the **great palace**, which has had one wall and several arcades reconstructed. Also interesting is the **little palace**, where you can find Greek stone carvings of leaves, shells and birds.

Because it sits on a main east–west trade route, historians have speculated that Aanjar was a commercial centre. About 600 **shops** have been uncovered here (you can still see some of them lining the southern part of the cardo maximus). Other theories suggest that because there were two palaces and public baths here, it could also have been an imperial residence or strategic post.

Despite the obvious wealth that was behind Aanjar, it flourished for only 50 years before it was abandoned in the face of defeat by the Abbasids.

Majdel Aanjar   مجدل عنجر

The village of Majdel Aanjar is several kilometres south of Aanjar. Above the village on a hill are some **Roman ruins**, including a temple

and some fortifications. The cella is still intact, but the stones are heavily worn and underground passages have opened up. The temple is thought to date from the 1st century AD and in the 7th and 8th centuries it was converted to a fortress by the Abbasids.

The site is rarely visited, despite some half-hearted restoration efforts. To get there, pass through the village of Majdel Aanjar (note the 13th-century square minaret as you pass) and follow the road (and signs) to the top of the hill. While the last part is extremely steep and best undertaken on foot, the views are worth the effort.

Eating

The area around Aanjar is famous for its Armenian food and, thanks to trout farms, its fresh fish. One of the best is the **Shams Restaurant** (08-620 567), on the road to Aanjar, about 500m from the main Damascus highway. In addition to the fresh fish, there's the usual selection of mezzes and grills available. A meal without fish costs between US$8 and US$15; with fish it's considerably more. There are a few shops nearby where you can buy water and snacks, and the main Damascus highway is dotted with fast-food stalls.

Getting There & Away

If you are taking a service taxi heading south or to the Syrian border from Chtaura, you will have to get out at Aanjar town and walk from the highway (about 2km) to the site. If you follow the signs you'll see the Shams Restaurant on your right. After this, take the first left which takes you to the site entrance. If you don't have your own car, negotiate a return trip from Chtaura with a taxi driver who will wait for you (allow one hour for a visit – two if you are very thorough). A one-hour stay should cost about US$10.

LAKE QARAOUN & LITANI DAM
بحيرة القرعون وسدّ الليطاني

☎ 08

Way down south in the Bekaa Valley is the Litani Dam (also known as Lake Qaraoun Dam). Built in 1959 it has created a lake of 11 sq km. The Litani is the longest river in Lebanon – it rises in the north of the Bekaa, near Baalbek, and flows into the sea near Tyre. Although the dam was built for the practical reason of producing electricity and providing irrigation, it is an attractive spot to visit. Keep in mind that the waters are not safe for swimming. It's at its best in the spring and early summer, when the water level is highest.

There is a visitor centre at the southern end of the lake (the dam end) on the eastern side. Also on the eastern side of the lake, a few kilometres further along the road north, is the small town of **Saghbine**. From here the views of the lake are quite extraordinary and the **Macharef Saghbine Hotel** (☎ 671200; s/d/ste US$35/45/60; ⚙ ⚖) takes great advantage of it. It's a modern hotel with large rooms, a restaurant, a bar and a swimming pool. Open all year, it makes a great stopover if you're on a self-drive trip.

Aamiq Marsh
عميق

Halfway between Chtaura and Lake Qaraoun, at the foot of the eastern slopes of Jebel Barouk, lies Aamiq Marsh, Lebanon's last major wetland formed by the Nahr al-Riachi (Riachi River) and its underground source. Covering some 270 hectares, it consists of marshes, ponds, willows and mud flats. The area is a haven for migrating and aquatic birds, and more than 135 species have been observed here. The wetland was in an increasingly perilous state until recently, but a Christian nature-conservation organisation, **A Rocha** (http://en.arocha.org/lebanon/index.html), has been working with local landowners to improve the area.

There are plans for an eco-tourism facility, but until then you can only visit as an organised group. Check the website for details.

It is difficult to get a service taxi to the far south of the Bekaa, so you will have to negotiate hard with a taxi driver to take you. Hitching is possible, but really you need your own car.

BAALBEK
بعلبك

☎ 08

Baalbek, the 'Sun City' of the ancient world, is the most impressive ancient site in Lebanon and arguably the most important Roman site in the Middle East. It enjoyed a reputation as one of the wonders of the world and mystics still attribute special powers to the courtyard complex. Its temples were built on an extravagant scale that outshone anything in Rome, and the town became a centre of worship well into the Christian era.

Standing dwarf-like under the temple's colossal columns and watching the setting sun turn the stone a rich orange rates as a highlight of any visit to Lebanon.

Modern Baalbek is the administrative centre of northern Bekaa Valley. Until recently the fame of its Roman temples was eclipsed by its notoriety as the seat of Hezbollah (Party of God), and its former association with hostage-taking, and still radical anti-Western politics. There are numerous reminders of Hezbollah's supremacy here (their yellow and green flags are everywhere), but people are friendly and welcoming to tourists. It is a conservative region of Lebanon however, and it's prudent (and considerate) not to wander around in shorts – men and women – or any other kind of revealing clothing.

The internationally famous arts event, **Baalbek Festival** (www.baalbeck.org.lb), takes place here every summer (July and August) and features opera, jazz, poetry and theatre.

History

The site was originally Phoenician and settlement here is thought to have dated back as far as the end of the 3rd millennium BC. During the 1st millennium BC a temple was built here and dedicated to the god Baal (later Hadad), from which comes its name. The site was chosen for its nearby springs and ideal position between the Litani and Al-Aasi Rivers. It was also located at the crossroads of the main east–west and north–south trade routes.

The temples at the site were a focus for all manner of sexual and licentious forms of worship. Sacred prostitution, coupled with an insatiable bloodlust, featured in the cults

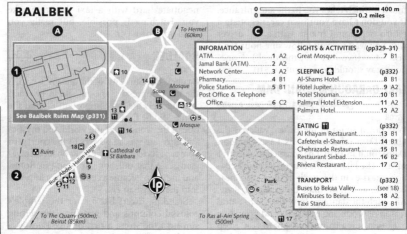

BAALBEK

0 _____ 400 m
0 _____ 0.2 miles

INFORMATION
ATM..............................1 A2
Jamal Bank (ATM)...........2 A2
Network Center................3 A2
Pharmacy.......................4 B1
Police Station..................5 A2
Post Office & Telephone
    Office........................6 C2

SIGHTS & ACTIVITIES (pp329–31)
Great Mosque..................7 B1

SLEEPING (p332)
Al-Shams Hotel................8 B1
Hotel Jupiter...................9 A2
Hotel Shouman...............10 B1
Palmyra Hotel Extension....11 A2
Palmyra Hotel................12 A2

EATING (p332)
Al Khayam Restaurant........13 B1
Cafeteria el-Shams...........14 B1
Chehrazade Restaurant......15 B1
Restaurant Sinbad...........16 B2
Riviera Restaurant............17 C2

TRANSPORT (p332)
Buses to Bekaa Valley........(see 18)
Minibuses to Beirut..........18 A2
Taxi Stand....................19 B1

See Baalbek Ruins Map (p331)

Ruins

Cathedral of St Barbara

Rue Abdel Halim Hajar

Ras al-Ain Blvd

Park

To Hermel (60km)

Mosque

Souq

Mosque

To The Quarry (500m); Beirut (85km)

To Ras al-Ain Spring (500m)

that practiced here. According to ancient tablets from Ugarit, which describe the practices of the Phoenician gods in a gruesome way, Anath, the sister and wife of Baal:

…waded up to the knees, up to the neck in human blood. Human heads lay at her feet, human hands flew over her like locusts. She tied the heads of her victims as ornaments on her back, their hands she tied upon her belt… When she was satisfied she washed her hands in streams of blood before turning again to other things.

Following the conquest of Alexander the Great, Baalbek became known as Heliopolis (City of the Sun), a name that was kept by the subsequent Roman conquerors. In 64 BC, Pompey the Great passed through Baalbek and was intrigued by its gods. A few years later, in 47 BC, Julius Caesar founded a Roman colony here because of its strategic position between Palmyra, in the Syrian desert, and the coastal cities. He named the new colony after his daughter Julia. The town became occupied by Roman soldiers and building works began. Baalbek was soon recognised as the premier city in Roman Syria.

The construction of the temples was a massive undertaking. Work is thought to have begun in 60 BC and it is known that the great Temple of Jupiter was nearing completion in AD 60 during the reign of Nero. Later, under

Antonius Pius (AD 138–61), a series of enlargements was undertaken, including work on the Great Court complex and the Temple of Bacchus. His son, Caracalla, completed them, but building was still going on when Rome's rulers adopted Christianity. It has been estimated that over the centuries some 100,000 slaves worked on the project.

The building of such extravagant temples was as much, if not more, a political act than a spiritual one. The Romans made efforts to integrate the peoples of the Middle East by appearing to favour their gods, while in fact building the most awe-inspiring structures possible in order to impress the worshippers with the strength of Roman political rule and civilisation. Even so, the deciding factor in building on such a massive and expansive scale at Baalbek was probably the threat of Christianity, which was beginning to pose a real threat to the old order. So, up went the temples in an attempt to 'fix' the religious orientation of the people in favour of pagan worship. By this time there were no human sacrifices, but temple prostitution remained.

When Constantine became emperor, the pagan world was under threat and building work was suspended. However, when Julian the Apostate became emperor in 361, he reverted to paganism and tried to reinstate it throughout the empire. There was a terrible backlash against Christians, which resulted in mass martyrdom. When the Christian emperor, Theodosius, took the throne in 379, Christianity was once again imposed

JEAN-BERNARD CARILLET

Umayyad city ruins (p325), Aanjar, Bekaa Valley, Lebanon

Drink vendor, Baalbek (p327), Lebanon

BETHUNE CARMICHAEL

CHRISTOPHER WOOD

Detail of frieze decorated with carved lion, Temple of Bacchus (p330), Baalbek, Bekaa Valley, Lebanon

Window architecture, Sidon (p337),
Lebanon

Fruits and vegetables for sale at a souq (p341),
Sidon, Lebanon

Mending a fishing net at the fishing harbour (p348), Tyre, Lebanon

upon Baalbek and its temples were converted to a basilica. Nevertheless, the town remained a centre of pagan worship and was enough of a threat to warrant a major crackdown by Emperor Justinian (r AD 527–65), who ordered that all Baalbek's pagans accept baptism. In an attempt to prevent any secret pagan rites, he ordered parts of the temple be destroyed, and had the biggest pillars shipped to Constantinople, where they were used in the Aya Sofya.

When the Muslim Arabs invaded Syria, they converted the Baalbek temples into a citadel and restored its Syriac name. For several centuries it came under the rule of Damascus and went through a period of regular invasions, sackings, lootings and devastation. The city was sacked by the Arabs in 748 and by the Mongol chieftain Tamerlane in 1400.

In addition to the ravages caused by humans, there was also a succession of earthquakes (1158, 1203, 1664 and most spectacularly in 1759), which caused the fall of the ramparts and three of the huge pillars of the Temple of Jupiter, as well as the departure of most of the population. Most of what remains today lies within the area of the Arab fortifications; the Temple of Mercury, further out, is virtually gone. By erecting walls around some of the buildings,

the Arabs unwittingly preserved the temples inside the sanctuary.

Kaiser Wilhelm II visited Baalbek in 1898 while on a tour of the Middle East and immediately contacted the Sultan of Turkey for permission to excavate the site. For the next seven years a team of archaeologists recorded the site in detail. By this time Baalbek was frequently visited by tourists, who helped themselves to sculptures and inscriptions.

After the defeat of Turkey and Germany in WWI, Baalbek's German scholars were replaced by French ones and they, in turn were replaced by Lebanese. Over a period of decades all the later masonry was removed and the temples restored as close as possible to their 1st-century splendour.

Orientation & Information

The town of Baalbek is small and thus easily explored on foot. From Zahlé or Beirut, you enter the town via the main road, Rue Abdel Halim Hajjar. It's also the street on which you'll find the town's two banks. It intersects with the other main road, Ras al-Ain Blvd.

Jamal Bank (Map p328) Has an ATM, and there's another ATM next to the Palmyra Hotel. There's nowhere in town to cash travellers cheques and none of the hotels or restaurants seem willing to accept credit cards.

Network Center (Map p328; ⏰ 9–1am; per hr LL3000) It's up a side street near the Palmyra Hotel.

Post Office (Map p328; ⏰ 8am-5pm Mon-Fri, 8am-2pm Sat) Heading along Ras al-Ain Blvd, it's up a side street before the Riviera Restaurant; the post office also has a **telephone office** (Map p328; ⏰ 24hr).

Sights

BAALBEK RUINS   Map p331

The **site** (⏰ 8.30am–30 min before sunset; adult/student LL12,000/7000, children under 8 free) also houses a free **museum**. Multilingual guides can be found (or will find you) outside the ticket office and charge US$14 for one hour. Numerous souvenir sellers and peddlers congregate around the entrance.

The entrance to the main site is at the southeastern end of the temple complex. After passing the ticket office, you enter the ruins via the monumental staircase leading up to the **propylaea** that has a portico flanked by two towers and a colonnade along the façade. This would originally have been covered by a cedar roof and paved with mosaics. The

WINE, SEX & SONG

Baalbek's enthusiasm in its worship of Baal's consort, Astarte (later called Venus or Aphrodite), appears to have shocked some contemporary visitors to the town. The Roman chronicler Eusebius disapprovingly wrote in the early 4th century:

At Heliopolis in Phoenicia, the cult of Venus has given birth to luxury habits. Men and women clasp together to honour their goddess; husbands and fathers allow their wives and daughters to prostitute themselves publicly to please Astarte.

The other god associated with Baal may have been Bacchus, who added wine and song to the 'luxury habits'. All-night Bacchanalian festivals of singing, dancing and sex were accompanied by drums and flutes. No wonder Baalbek held out against Christianity for so long.

column bases supporting the portico bear the inscription 'For the safety and victories of our lord, Caracalla'.

Through a central door you move into the **hexagonal court**. There is a raised threshold, which separates the propylaea from the sacred enclosure. This courtyard is about 50m deep. It used to be surrounded by a columned portico and to the north and south four exedrae opened symmetrically onto the portico, each with four columns. These rooms were decorated with niches that had either triangular or round pediments. To the north of the court is a famous bas-relief of Jupiter Heliopolitan that was found near the Lejuj Spring, 7km from Baalbek.

Beyond the hexagonal court is the **Great Court** (Sacrificial Courtyard). It was richly decorated on its north, east and south sides and had a double row of niches surmounted with pediments. There are a number of exedrae: four semicircular and eight rectangular. Between the exedrae there are niches, which also held statues. Covering all of these was an arcade supported by 84 granite columns. To either side of the courtyard were two pools, which still have some highly decorative carving on their sides showing Trions, Nereids, Medusas and Cupids riding sea creatures. In the centre of the courtyard there once stood a Byzantine basilica, which was dismantled by French archaeologists, revealing the foundations of a huge altar.

The **Temple of Jupiter** was built on an immense substructure over 300m long, and was approached by another monumental staircase that rose high above the surrounding buildings. It consisted of a cella in which the statue of the god was housed and a surrounding portico of 10 columns along the façade and 19 columns along the side, making for 54 columns in all. These columns are the largest in the world – 22.9m high with a girth of 2.2m. Today only six of these remain standing with the architrave still in position. It was thought in the old days that Baalbek had been constructed by giants and a quick look over the side of the temple to the foundation stones beneath reveals some of the largest building blocks to be found anywhere on earth. One of these megalithic blocks measures 19.5m by 4.3m and is estimated to weigh over 1000 tonnes – how it was moved and positioned so precisely remains a mystery.

From the south side of the temple is a wonderful view of the so-called **Temple of Bacchus**. This was in fact dedicated not to Bacchus but to Venus/Astarte, and is the most beautifully decorated temple in the Roman world. Completed around AD 150, it is also in a great state of preservation. While it wasn't built on the scale of the Temple of Jupiter, it more than makes up for this with style and decoration. Ironically it was called 'the small temple' in antiquity, although it is larger than the Parthenon in Athens. The entrance is up a flight of 30 stairs with three landings. It has a portico running around it with eight columns along the façade and 15 along the sides. They support a rich entablature; the frieze is decorated with lions and bulls. This supports a ceiling of curved stone, which is decorated with very vivid scenes: Mars; a winged Victory; Diana taking an arrow from her quiver; a Tyche with a cornucopia; Vulcan with his hammer; Bacchus; and Ceres holding a sheaf of corn.

The highlight of the temple is the doorway, which has been drawn and painted by many artists, its half-fallen keystone forever a symbol of Baalbek. Inside, the cella is richly decorated with fluted columns. The 'holy place' was at the back of the cella, which is reached by another staircase with two ramps. When the temple was in use, this would have been a dark and mysterious place, probably lit dramatically by oil lamps with piercing shafts of daylight falling on the image of the god or goddess.

In the southeastern corner of the Great Court is the **museum** (entered from the parking area, near the ticket office), housed in a large vaulted tunnel that may originally have been storerooms or housing for pilgrims. As well as some beautiful artefacts from Baalbek, the well-lit exhibits give a thorough history of the temple under loosely grouped themes. One fascinating display explains Roman building techniques, showing how the massive stone blocks used in the Temple of Jupiter were manoeuvred into place.

In a side room is a foray into Baalbek's more recent history, with a description of Emperor Wilhelm II's visit. More interesting are the photographs of the German photographer Herman Burckhardt, who visited Baalbek at the turn of the 20th century. His pictures are an invaluable record of daily life at the time.

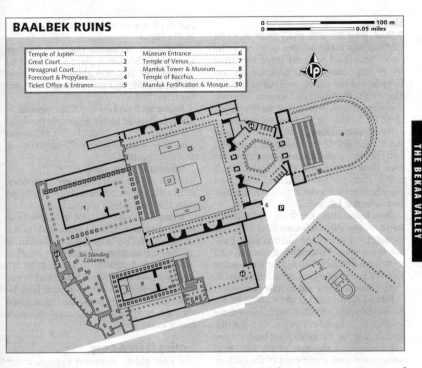

BAALBEK RUINS

0 — 100 m
0 — 0.05 miles

Temple of Jupiter............................1	Museum Entrance.........................6	
Great Court......................................2	Temple of Venus............................7	
Hexagonal Court.............................3	Mamluk Tower & Museum............8	
Forecourt & Propylaea...................4	Temple of Bacchus........................9	
Ticket Office & Entrance...............5	Mamluk Fortification & Mosque....10	

Six Standing Columns

OTHER SIGHTS

Near the main ruins, about 300m from the acropolis, is the tiny exquisite **Temple of Venus** (Map p331) – probably dedicated to Fortuna rather than Venus – a circular building with many fluted columns. Inside, it was decorated with tiers of tabernacles and covered with a cupola. During the early Christian era it was turned into a basilica and dedicated to St Barbara (who joined the saintly ranks when her pagan father tried to kill her for converting to Christianity – he got his comeuppance when a bolt of lightning reduced him to a smouldering heap). A copy of this gem of a temple was constructed in the 18th century in the grounds of Stourhead in Wiltshire, England.

To the east of the propylaea stands the ruined Umayyad or **Great Mosque** (Map p331), which was built from the stones of the temples using many styles of columns and capitals. Lebanon's only Umayyad ruin, outside Aanjar, it was built between the 7th and 8th centuries. There is an ablution fountain surrounded by four columns in the centre of the courtyard. On the right,

immediately after the entrance, are rows of arched colonnades with Roman columns and capitals, clearly taken from the temple complex. At the northwestern corner are the ruins of a great octagonal minaret on a square base.

To the southeast of Baalbek's centre is the source of the **Ras al-Ain spring**. The area has pleasant, shady parks along the spring and is the site of occasional festivities with horses and camels and side stalls. At the head of the spring is a ruined early **mosque**, which at some point was thought to be the Temple of Neptune.

About 1km south of the centre of Baalbek, on Sheikh Abdullah Hill, is the **quarry** where the huge temple stones originated. Here you can see the largest cut stone in the world (measuring 21.5m by 4m by 4.5m) lying on its side, partially submerged in the earth. The Arabs call this stone Hajar al-Hubla (Stone of the Pregnant Woman), which came about as a corruption of its original name, Hajar al-Qubla (Stone of the South). Even so, local folklore has it that women can touch the stone to increase their fertility.

Sleeping

Al-Shams Hotel (Map p328; ☎ 373 284; fax 370 305; Rue Abdel Halim Hajjar; bed in 5-bed r US$6, bed in 2-bed or 3-bed r US$6) This hotel has only three very basic rooms with washbasins. Beds are uncomfortable and the overall impression is dusty. There's a shared toilet and shower. Enter via a stone staircase next to the mobile-phone shop; the hotel is on the 1st floor.

Hotel Shouman (Map p328; ☎ 03-796 077; Ras al-Ain Blvd; dm/d LL10,000/20,000) Close to the ruins, this hotel has the added advantage of great views from three of its rooms. There are hard beds and a simple-but-clean shared toilet and shower. Enter via a stone staircase; the pension is on the 1st floor.

Hotel Jupiter (Map p328; ☎ 376 715, 370 151; Rue Abdel Halim Hajjar; s/d/tr with bathroom US$10/20/25) This friendly place is the latest addition to the Baalbek hotel scene. Entered via an arcade next to Restaurant Chich Kabab near the Palmyra Hotel, it has large rooms off a central courtyard. These are light and all have fans.

Palmyra Hotel (Map p328; ☎ 376 101/2/3, 370 011; Rue Abdel Halim Hajjar; s/d/tr US$40/56/66) One of those wonderful colonial-era relics that dot the Middle East, the Palmyra's guest book is more impressive than the state of the hotel and some of the food coming out of the kitchen. Opposite the ruins, it's set in shady gardens and has a number of rooms with balconies overlooking the ruins. It still has an air of faded grandeur, hinting at its former luxury and quite a history. During WWI it was used by the German army, and in WWII it was the British-army headquarters in the area.

The 1st-floor terrace overlooking the temple is a great place for a sundowner, and the hotel has a lovely garden terrace dotted with antique bits of masonry and shaded by jasmine trellises. It's worth stopping by for a drink even if you aren't staying.

For those less interested in sleeping with the ghosts of Jean Cocteau or General de Gaulle, and more interested in a good night's sleep, the hotel has a new, comfortable, and quite beautiful extension a few doors down. Rooms are slightly more expensive (US$75), but are lavishly furnished and have ultra-comfortable beds.

Eating

The restaurant scene is not particularly noteworthy in Baalbek as most tourists come here on a day trip and don't stop for lunch. Your best bet is the cheap eateries on Rue Abdel Halim Hajjar.

Al Khayam Restaurant (Map p328; Rue Abdel Halim Hajjar) This small place is the best of the cheapies. It serves absolutely delicious felafels (LL750) and *shwarma* (LL1500) and has a few tables.

Restaurant Sinbad (Map p328) Opposite Al Khayam, Sinbad serves up simple meals.

Further up Rue Abdel Halim Hajjar are a number of shops selling delectable sweets and meat pastries.

Cafeteria el-Shams (Map p328) This spotlessly clean place with tables serves pastries, filled rolls, sweets, coffee and tea. You'll find it on the souq side of the road.

Riviera Restaurant (Map p328; ☎ 370 296; Ras al-Ain Blvd; mezze around LL2000) On the way to the spring, this serves basic but tasty food in its outdoor eating area in the summer months.

Chehrazade Restaurant (Map p328; ☎ 371 851; top fl, Centre Commercial de Yaghi & Simbole, souq) While the food is your standard Lebanese fare, the views of the ruins are awesome. It is accessed via a lift at the rear of this small shopping centre in the souq.

Getting There & Away

The only public transport options to get yourself from Beirut to Baalbek are the minibuses (LL3000, two hours) and an array of service taxis (LL5000) from the Cola transport hub. Be warned that the drive over the Mt Lebanon Range can be a totally hair-raising experience, particularly in the winter months. The bus stop in Baalbek is just down from the Palmyra Hotel and the service-taxi office is in the souq area.

For information about how to get to Baalbek from Zahlé, see p323. For information about how to get to Baalbek from Bcharré, see p309. Keep in mind that the road across the mountains to The Cedars and Bcharré is closed during winter.

HERMEL الهرمل

Hermel is the northernmost town in the Bekaa. The main economy is agriculture and it's not really for the casual visitor. If you do not have your own vehicle, this is a good place to negotiate a taxi to take you around the district.

If Hermel ever gets properly excavated, it could turn out to be quite an important historical site; ancient remains have been found, the most interesting being an altar dedicated to Jupiter Heliopolitan.

Sleeping & Eating

There are no hotels in Hermel; the nearest place to stay is Hotel Asamaka on Nahr al-Aasi (right). Along the main road, just past the taxi stand, there are a few cafés and *shwarma* stands selling snacks and sandwiches. There are also one or two grocery stores selling cold drinks and so on. There are no proper restaurants in Hermel.

Getting There & Away

You can get service taxis from Beirut to Hermel (LL10,000), while services run north from Baalbek to Hermel (LL3000). There are also local buses that circle the northern valley and pass on the main road almost hourly (until sunset) and cost LL500 (p321).

AROUND HERMEL
Hermel Pyramid هرم الهرمل

Ten kilometres south of the town of Hermel, in the middle of nowhere, is a 27m-high monument sitting on the crest of a small hill. It can be seen for miles around and the turn-off is signposted from the main road. It is a solid square-base construction with a pyramid on top. Large sections have been restored recently but on the original stone you can see very worn depictions of hunting scenes showing stags and boars being attacked by mastiffs. One side shows a bull being attacked by wolves or bears. Nobody is quite sure what this strange monument is meant to be or why it is standing alone. It closely resembles some of the tower tombs at Palmyra (p212) to the east in Syria. Probably a Syrian royal tomb, its age is estimated at around 2000 years. Unfortunately the inscriptions are gone (and sadly marred by some graffiti), so the pyramid remains an enigma.

GETTING THERE & AWAY

If you don't have your own car, then you can hire a taxi in Hermel to take you there and back. A short tour of the Hermel Pyramid and Deir Mar Maroun, and back to Hermel, should cost about US$10. It is about 1km from the main road to the monument along a track, which is easy to spot. If you are driving, the track is fine for a car.

Nahr al-Aasi نهر العاصي
☎ 08

Near a bridge that crosses the Nahr al-Aasi (Orontes River), are restaurants specialising in trout, and a couple of hotels. The bridge is about 7km southeast of Hermel and is near the only accommodation in the area. It is a good base to begin a walk along the river to the waterfalls about 5km or 6km to the north (ie downstream as the river actually flows into Lake Homs, in Syria). These **waterfalls** are called Shilal Heira, Derdara and Shilman. It is about a one-hour walk in the other direction to the source of the river: a large basin called **Ain ez-Zerqa** (Blue Spring).

SLEEPING & EATING

Hotel Asamaka (☎ 883 024; d & tr US$30) Right by the river, about 100m from the bridge, Asamaka is clean and not too expensive. Its restaurant, shaded by awnings, overlooks the water and serves mezze, and trout fresh from a pool (about US$15). It also serves alcohol.

Al-Fardos Hotel (☎ 670 138; s/d US$15/20) The recently built Al-Fardos offers similar standards to the Asamaka.

Casino Restaurant Just by the bridge, this serves much the same sort of menu as the Asamaka restaurant at similar prices.

Shalalit al-Dardara (☎ 828 880) This overlooks the Derdara waterfalls and also serves trout and mezze (about US$20).

GETTING THERE & AWAY

This bridge is about 7km southeast of Hermel. A service taxi from Hermel costs around LL2000.

Deir Mar Maroun دير مار مارون

Overlooking Nahr al-Aasi, about 200m from Ain ez-Zerqa, sits the ancient rock-cut monastery of Mar Maroun. To reach it you can either take a 3km hike or a 12km-long drive from Hermel. Inside the monastery are several tiers of cave-like cells connected with spiral staircases.

The monastery was established in the 5th century by St Maron, the founder of the Maronite church, and was destroyed by Justinian II in the 7th century – hundreds were put to death as heretics. The survivors of this persecution fled up to the mountains and across to the Qadisha Valley (p310).

If you don't have your own car, then you can hire a taxi in Hermel to take you there

HASHISH HARDSHIP

The Bekaa Valley was once the centre of Lebanon's infamous hashish production. These days however, many of the farmers have turned their talents to growing legal crops.

In the early days of the civil war, an estimated 10,000 tonnes of hashish were exported from Lebanon each year. The lucrative trade was controlled by a cartel of about 30 Lebanese families. When the Syrians arrived on the scene, they got in on the act too, and used their tanks and artillery to protect the fields.

In their bid for American respect, around the time of the Gulf War, the Syrians tried to put an end to the industry. Farmers were discouraged from growing the crop and most now produce tomatoes, tobacco, potatoes and grain. Ironically, most of their produce cannot compete with cheaper Syrian vegetables, and farmers' incomes have plunged. Not surprisingly, some farmers have not left the industry, and in December 2003 the Lebanese army and Internal Security Forces staged a very public raid in the Bekaa using over 3000 men to arrest a few dozen people. While this has been seen by some as an attempt to show that the Lebanese officials are willing to take a tough stand on growers and dealers, it also serves to highlight statistics showing that drug use among Lebanon's youth is on the rise.

and back. A short tour of Deir Mar Maroun and the Hermel Pyramid and back to Hermel should cost about US$10.

Al-Jord Ecolodge الجرد

Jord is an Arabic word meaning a mountain area 'beyond the last villages'. Al Jord is the name given to the mountains between Hermel, Akkar and Tripoli.

Al-Jord Ecolodge (☎ 03-235 303; www.aljord.org; closed winter) is a community-based private company offering a range of environmental activities centred around an ecolodge in one of this country's most remote and stunningly beautiful areas. From the lofty 50-hectare site one can view the cedar forests of Wadi Jehannam and Fneideq, the summit of Qornet as-Sawda and, far below, the plain of Akkar and the shimmering Mediterranean. Check the website for more information.

GETTING THERE & AWAY

To visit the lodge, you should book in advance as guests are generally picked up from a parking area near Hermel.

The South

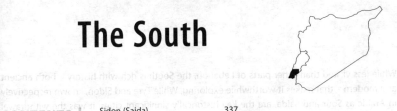

While less visited than the parts of Lebanon the South is rich with history. Both ancient and modern times live while exploring. While Tyre and Sidon have respectively an Arabic as Sion and Sida, are the two historically significant sites, it was the major of Israeli forces from the last southern border town and this southern Israeli prison mainly withdrawn that Israel brought the South region in

The northern part of Lebanon suffered greatly from the civil war and subsequent occupation, only to emerge as tourist Beirut. Being a powerful place, and it is still getting back on its feet. While this necessitate to a certain limited choice of accommodation and restaurants, even restaurant must. And medieval remains, the resort of historical significance of the area as well as crusaders beaches and good oriental souqs offer an experience a world away from the chaos of Beirut.

THE SOUTH

The South

While less visited than other parts of Lebanon, the South is rich with history – both ancient and modern – that makes it worthwhile exploring. While Tyre and Sidon, known respectively in Arabic as Sour and Saida, are the key historically significant cities, it was the withdrawal of Israeli forces from the far south in May 2000, and the release of detainees from Al-Khiam prison during this withdrawal, that has brought the South recent attention.

The southern part of Lebanon suffered greatly from the civil war and subsequent occupation (not to mention an historic lack of interest by Beirut's powerbrokers) and is still getting back on its feet. While this translates to an often-limited choice of accommodation and restaurants, the extensive ancient and medieval remains, the recent historical significance of the area, as well as clean beaches and good oriental souqs, offer an experience a world away from the chaos of Beirut.

THE SOUTH

HIGHLIGHTS

- Get lost in the old **Sidon souqs** (p341), while snacking on a fresh *sanioura*, the local delicacy

- Visit the sobering museum at the former **Al-Khiam Detention Camp** (p353)

- Lighten the mood before leaving the museum, with a **Hezbollah** souvenir (p353)

- Take a dip at one of Tyre's wonderful **beaches** (p349) after doing a lap of the **Roman hippodrome** (p348)

- While admiring the view, place yourself in the shoes of those who fought at the **Beaufort Castle** (p352)

- Ponder why there isn't a hotel that provides the same touristic experience as the **Musée du Savon** (p341) in Sidon

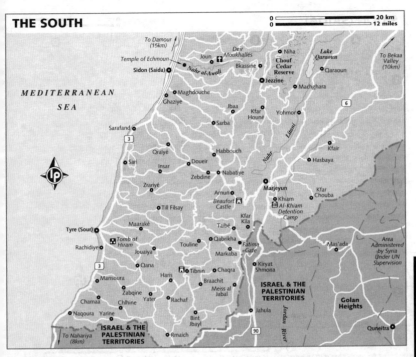

THE SOUTH

0 _____ 20 km
0 _____ 12 miles

MEDITERRANEAN
SEA

To Damour (15km)
Temple of Echmoun
Sidon (Saida)
Nahr al-Awali
Deir Moukhalles
Joun
Bkassine
Niha
Chouf Cedar Reserve
Lake Qaraoun
To Bekaa Valley (10km)
Qaraoun
Jezzine
Machghara
Maghdouche
Ghaziye
Jbaa
Kfar Houné
Yohmor
Litani
Sarafand
Sarba
Qraiyé
Habbouch
Kfair
Sari
Douier
Hasbaya
Insar
Nabatiye
Zebdine
Zrariyé
Arnun
Beaufort Castle
Marjeyun
Kfar Chouba
Till Filsay
Khiam
Al-Khiam Detention Camp
Kfar Kila
Taibé
Tyre (Sour)
Maaraké
Tomb of Hiram
Qabrikha
Fatima Gate
Mas'ada
Rachidiye
Jouaiya
Touline
Markaba
Area Administered by Syria Under UN Supervision
Qana
Tibnin
Chaqra
Kiryat Shmona
Golan Heights
Mansoura
Haris
Braachit
Meiss al Jabal
ISRAEL & THE PALESTINIAN TERRITORIES
Chamaa
Zabqine
Yater
Rachaf
Chlhine
Naqoura
Yarine
Bint Jbayl
Jahula
Jordan River
Quneitra
To Nahariya (8km)
Rmaich
ISRAEL & THE PALESTINIAN TERRITORIES

THE SOUTH

SIDON (SAIDA)   صيدا

☎ 07

The small port city of Sidon (Saida in Arabic) is set amid citrus orchards and banana groves 40km south of Beirut. At least 6000 years old, it was once a prominent and wealthy Phoenician city. With its charming Crusader Sea Castle and its fine mosques, khans and vaulted souqs, it is one of the most attractive and historically significant towns in Lebanon. Easily visited on a day trip from Beirut, it should be high on every traveller's 'must-see' list.

History

The ancient town of Sidon, the largest city in southern Lebanon, was settled as early as 4000 BC, or 6800 BC according to some claims. In the Old Testament, Sidon is referred to as 'the first born of Canaan', which may have originated from the town's possible founder, Saidoune ibn Canaan. The word for 'fishing' or 'hunting' is *sayd* in modern Arabic.

As early as the 14th and 15th centuries BC, Sidon had a reputation as a commercial centre with strong trade links with Egypt.

The city rose in prominence from the 12th to 10th centuries BC, its wealth generated from trading murex, a mollusc that produced a highly valued purple dye (see the boxed text Murex, p341). Geography helped too: like many Phoenician cities, Sidon was built on a promontory with an offshore island, which sheltered the harbour from storms and provided a safe haven during times of war.

In common with the other Phoenician city-states, Sidon suffered from conquest and invasion numerous times. In 1200 BC the Philistines destroyed the city and its fleet of trading ships, allowing Tyre to eclipse Sidon as the most important Phoenician centre. Although often under Tyre's control, or forced to pay tribute to the Assyrians, Sidon recovered its status as a trading centre, only to be destroyed in 675 BC by the Assyrian king Esarhaddon.

The city's golden age came during the Persian Empire (525–332 BC) when the city was capital of the Fifth Province, covering Syria, Palestine, and Cyprus. Apart from murex, Sidon was known for its glass-making, which was considered the best in

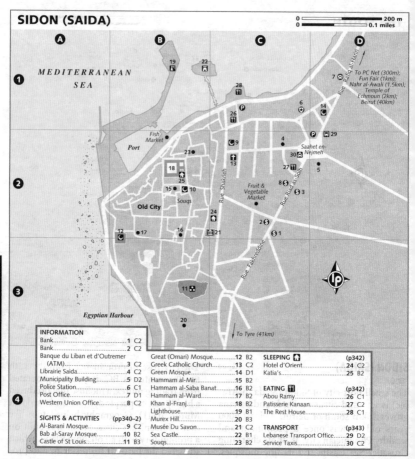

SIDON (SAIDA)

MEDITERRANEAN SEA

the world. During this period the Temple of Echmoun, about 2km northeast of the city, was built. Inscriptions found there reveal that Phoenician Sidon was built in two sections: the maritime city, Sidon Yam; and the upper part, Sidon Sadeh, which was built on the lower spurs of the Mt Lebanon Range, upwind from the noxious smell of the murex dye works.

Sidon also became known for shipbuilding and provided experienced sailors for the Persian fleet. The king of Sidon was admiral for the fleet and successful in campaigns against the Egyptians in the 6th century BC, and later against the Greeks, giving Sidon a degree of independence over its Persian overlords. This lasted until the middle of

the 4th century BC, when Phoenician rebellion, centred in Sidon, incurred the wrath of the Persians. Heading a huge army, King Artaxerxes Ochus, arrived to beat the Sidonians into submission. According to Greek historian, Diodorus, the Sidonians locked the city gates and set fire to the city rather than hand it over. More than 40,000 people died in the inferno, and this weakened the city to such an extent that when Alexander the Great marched through in 333 BC, the Sidonians were in no position to resist him and surrendered without a struggle.

Under the Greeks, Sidon enjoyed relative freedom and a sophisticated cultural life. Later the city came successively under the control of the Seleucids and the Ptolemies.

Augustus put an end to Sidon's independence and brought it under direct Roman rule.

During the Byzantine period, the earthquake of AD 551 destroyed most of the cities in Phoenicia. Sidon fared better than most and became the home of Beirut's famous School of Law when that city was badly damaged. In 667 the Arabs invaded and the city took the Arabic name Saida and remained a wealthy centre, administered from Damascus.

In 1110 Baldwin I, King of Jerusalem, besieged the city and the Sidonians gave up after 47 days of resistance. In 1187 Saladin took the city and razed the ramparts to the ground in an attempt to render it useless as a Crusader base. It failed to deter the Crusaders, however, and they recaptured it. Subsequent battles for control saw Sidon passed between the two sides as many as five times, before finally falling to the Mamluks after the fall of Acre in 1291.

Sidon's fortunes rose in the 15th century when it became a trading port of Damascus. While the city flourished again in the 17th century under the rule of Fakhreddine (Fakhr ad-Din al-Maan II), prosperity was temporary. In 1791, the Ottoman pasha of Acre, Ahmed Jazzar, drove the French from the town and Beirut took over as the centre of commerce. An earthquake in the 1830s, followed by bombardment during the Ottoman-European campaign to remove Bashir Shihab II, helped ensure the city's fall into relative obscurity.

In the early part of the 20th century the area around Sidon was developed for agriculture, particularly fruit. During the civil war Sidon was fought over by the Palestinians, Syrians, Israelis, Hezbollah and Amal, and suffered greatly. In the postwar period, it has benefited from being the birthplace of Prime Minister Rafiq Hariri, who has used his eponymous foundation to channel huge amounts of money into reconstruction. Other wealthy Sidon financiers, such as the Audi family, are sponsoring the ongoing restoration of the souqs.

Orientation

The centre of town is around Saahat en-Nejmeh, where you'll find the bus and service-taxi stands, the municipality building and the police station. Rue Riad as-Solh, which runs south off Saahat en-Nejmeh (in reality a huge roundabout), has banks, moneychang-

ers, shops and travel agencies. The old city, harbour, Sea Castle and only hotel are west of Saahat en-Nejmeh and Rue Riad as-Solh, while the city's modern shopping centres and residential buildings are on the eastern side. There's no tourist information office in town, but the Audi Foundation (see Musée Du Savon, p341) provides free maps of the old city listing many of Sidon's heritage buildings.

Information

EMERGENCY
Ambulance (☎ 722 131)

INTERNET ACCESS
PC Net (☎ 03-464 985; Rue Rafiq al-Hariri; per hr LL2000; ⊗ 24hr) The best Internet café in town.

LIBRARIES
Librairie Saida A small bookshop and stationers with magazines and postcards.

MONEY
Banks with ATMs are clustered on Rue Riad as-Solh, close to Saahat en-Nejmeh. In the old souqs are several moneychangers offering reasonable rates.

WARNING

During their 20-year-plus occupation, the Israelis, their South Lebanon Army (SLA) allies and the various Lebanese resistance organisations littered the occupied zone with land mines. While demining is ongoing in the region, the area remains full of unexploded ordnance. This is especially true in the lesser built-up areas, which are not a priority for mine-clearing. Do NOT wander off roads or even walk on paths in the area without being absolutely sure that the terrain is safe.

At the time of writing the situation in the former occupied zone, close to the Israeli border, was relatively stable; however, permission from the army was required to visit areas such as Beaufort Castle and Al-Khiam Museum. Before attempting trips to this part of the South, it's best to keep up to date with the situation by reading the *Daily Star* and, if travelling from Tyre, talk to some of the United Nations Interim Force in Lebanon (Unifil) personnel at the base there.

POST
Post office (☎ 721 604, 722 813; Rue Rafiq al-Hariri; ⏱ 7.30am-5pm Mon-Fri, 8am-1pm Sat) In a large white building with a huge antenna on the roof.

TELEPHONE
Telephone Bureau At the post office.

Western Union Office (Rue Riad as-Solh; ⏱ 9am-midnight) Acts as a private telephone office with overseas calls for LL3000 per minute.

Sights

SEA CASTLE
قلعة البحر

Built by the Crusaders in 1228, the **Sea Castle** (Qalat al-Bahr; LL4000; ⏱ 9am-6pm, closes earlier in winter) sits around 80m offshore on a small island that was formerly the site of a temple to Melkart, the Phoenician Hercules. It is connected to the mainland by an Arab fortified stone bridge (of a later date). One of many coastal castles built by the Crusaders, it was largely destroyed by the Mamluks to prevent the Crusaders from returning to the region. Fortunately, its substantial renovation was ordered by Fakhreddine in the 17th century.

The building consists of two towers joined together by a wall. The west tower, to the left of the entrance, is the best preserved. Rectangular in shape, it measures 21m by 17m, and has a large vaulted room scattered with old carved capitals and rusting cannonballs. A winding staircase leads up to the roof, where there is a small, domed Ottoman-era mosque. From the roof there is a great view across the old city and fishing harbour. The east tower isn't as well preserved and was built in two phases; the lower part dates to the Crusader period, while the upper level was built by the Mamluks, as testified by a marble inscription over a window looking into the interior hall.

In the clear, shallow water surrounding the castle, you can see many broken columns of rose granite lying on the sea floor. Preliminary archaeological work carried out before the civil war showed extensive underwater remains off Sidon's coast, some dating back to the Persian period.

KHAN AL-FRANJ
خان الفرنج

The largest and best preserved of the many khans built by Fakhreddine during his 17th-century reign is **Khan al-Franj** (Khan of the Foreigners; ⏱ Mon-Sat). The khans all followed the same basic design, with a large rectangular central courtyard, fountain, covered arcades (used for stables and storage) and a galleried second storey providing accommodation for merchants and travellers.

The Khan al-Franj was the principal khan in the 19th century and the centre of economic activity in the city. It also housed the French consul and remains the property of the French government, as described at the building's entrance. Today its painstaking restoration, funded by the Hariri Foundation, is complete and the khan will house Sidon's cultural centre. There is a café and handicrafts store on the ground floor.

GREAT MOSQUE
الجامع الكبير

Facing the northern tip of the harbour is the **Great (Omari) Mosque**. Originally a fortified structure built in the 13th century by the Knights Hospitaller, its sheer stone façade still has an air of impregnability when seen from the road. Converted to a mosque after the Crusaders were driven out of the Holy Land, its sandstone minaret was rebuilt after its destruction during the 1982 Israeli invasion. The main prayer hall once housed the Church of St John of the Hospitallers and its original walls can still be seen. There are two entrances to the mosque: one down a maze of covered streets in the souqs; the other on the eastern side of the building (once the site of a palace built by Fakhreddine). Inside is a large courtyard surrounded on three sides by arched porticos and bordered on the fourth side by the prayer hall. There are two mihrabs (niches indicating the direction of Mecca) on the southern wall of the prayer hall, with a modern minbar (pulpit) in-between. You can visit the mosque outside of prayer time (see the boxed text The Call for Prayer, p42).

BAB AL-SARAY MOSQUE
جامع باب السراي

The oldest mosque in the city is **Bab al-Saray Mosque**, which dates back to 1201. Located just east of the old Bab al-Saray (Saray Gate), it boasts the largest dome in Sidon and an enormous supporting column made from black stone, allegedly imported from Italy. The beautiful stonework has just been restored through a waqf (religious endowment). The mosque sits in the corner of a square, which has a pleasant café built on the site of the original saray (palace). If you look inside you can still see stone remnants of the old building. Remember to dress appropriately for the mosque.

MUREX

The famous purple dye of Phoenicia comes from the murex, a type of mollusc, which grew in abundance in the coastal waters off Sidon and Tyre. There were in fact two kinds of mollusc used in the dye process: the murex and the *buccinum* (sometimes known as a whelk or trumpet shell). Both have a long sac or vein filled with a yellowish fluid that turns purple when exposed to light. The discovery of this natural source of purple dye made the fortunes of many merchants in Sidon and Tyre.

The origins of the discovery are lost, but a myth remains that the god Melkart was walking on the beach one day with his lover, a nymph called Tyrus, and his dog. The dog bit into one of the murex shells and its muzzle became stained with a purple dye. When she saw the beautiful colour, Tyrus demanded that Melkart make her a garment of purple. So Melkart gathered a quantity of the shellfish to dye a gown, which he presented to her.

This romantic tale hides the fact that the production of dye was a smelly, messy business that involved a great deal of hard work. The molluscs were gathered in deep water by dropping narrow-necked baskets baited with mussels and frog meat. Once harvested the shellfish were hauled off to dye pits where their sacs were removed, pulped and heated in huge lead vessels. All the extraneous matter was skimmed off and the resulting dye fixed.

The dye pits were placed downwind of the residential areas to avoid the noxious smell. With practice, the dyers could produce a variety of colours from pale pink to deep violet by mixing the murex and buccinum fluids in different quantities. The dye industry was on such a large scale that the molluscs were farmed to extinction.

SOUQS الأسواق

The old covered **souqs** and medieval heart of Sidon lies between the Sea Castle and the Castle of St Louis. This is the medieval heart of the city where, in labyrinthine alleyways, shopkeepers ply their trades in workshops the same way they have done for centuries. Officially there are some 60 listed historic sites here, many of them, including several under preservation order, are in ruins, destroyed during the civil war, however much of the souq is undergoing renovation.

Scattered throughout the souqs are several coffeehouses, where men meet to smoke nargileh (water pipe) and while away the afternoon. In the souqs there are a huge number of pastry shops where you can buy hot bread and biscuits. The utterly delicious *sanioura* (a light crumbly biscuit) is a speciality of Sidon. The souqs are also famous for producing orange-blossom water.

MUSÉE DU SAVON (SOAP MUSEUM) متحف الصابون

Although Tripoli may take credit for being the centre of the traditional soap-making industry, it is Sidon that has Lebanon's first **museum** (Soap Museum; ☎ 733 353; Rue al-Moutran; ☉ 9am-6pm Sat-Thu) dedicated to the craft. Located in the old city in the Khan al-Saboun, a 13th-century stone building adapted for use as a soap factory in the 19th century, it produced soap to meet the needs of the hammams (bathhouses). The whole complex has been painstakingly restored with funds by the Audi Foundation and also houses the Audi family residence.

The museum's curators have assembled all the accoutrements of soap making, and the welllaid-out galleries and trilingual (Arabic, English, French) explanations take you through the entire soap-making process, from the massive stone tub where the raw ingredients were mixed together to the shaping and cutting of the still-warm liquid. Towers of soap (ironically brought here from Tripoli) show how the finished product was dried before being packaged for sale.

Also interesting is a small but fascinating display of hammam accessories, including *saflin* (small seeds used as toothpicks) and *kiyaas hammam* (goat-hair bags used as loofahs). The museum has a stylish café and a boutique selling soap and bath products that make great gifts.

CASTLE OF ST LOUIS قلعة المُعِزّ

The ruins of this once-impressive **castle** stand on a mound to the south of town. The present structure dates back to the Crusaders, who built on the site of an earlier Fatimid fortress – as reflected in the local name, Qala'at al-Muizz (Fortress of Al-Muizz) after the Fatimid caliph Al-Muizz li-din Allah, who fortified the site. The English-French name comes from Louis IX, who rebuilt and then occupied the fortress when he retook Sidon from the Ayyubids in 1253. After the Arabs retook the city it was restored, but it later suffered at the hands of the Mamluks. This, coupled with centuries of pilfering, has left the structure in poor condition.

The hill on which the castle is situated is thought to have been the ancient acropolis of Sidon. Archaeologists have uncovered remains of a theatre here, but the site remains largely unexcavated. There is a low wall around the base of the hill and a locked gate. The site is usually unattended.

MUREX HILL

Just south of the Castle of St Louis is an artificial hill, **Murex Hill**, about 100m high and 50m long, partially covered by a cemetery. This is Sidon's ancient garbage dump, largely formed from the crushed remains of hundreds of thousands of murex shells, the by-product of the city's famed dye. Traces of the shells can be seen on the embankment heading south from the castle.

Activities
HAMMAMS

There are five hammams (Turkish baths) in the old city, although only one is still functioning. Unfortunately, the Sidon's grandest bathhouse, **Hammam al-Mir**, was partially destroyed by the Israelis, along with its mosaic-covered dome and marble floors. **Hammam al-Ward**, beside the Grand Mosque, was built in 1721 in an Italian-Ottoman style. Although in poor shape, it's still open for business. Hours and prices appear to be flexible. You may have to hunt for the custodian, but the adjacent shopkeepers will help.

Sleeping

Hotel d'Orient (☎ 720 364; Rue Shakrieh; s/d US$15/20) This small place has six rooms and basic bathroom facilities but only gets a mention because it's the only hotel in town. It is above a tiny baggage shop not far from the Muslim cemetery, and near the Soap Museum. It's hard to spot, so look for the red 'Orient Hotel' banner on a 1st-floor balcony across the road from Pizza Abu al-Ezz.

Katia's (☎ 03-442 141; Souq; per person US$15) Thankfully there's now another accommodation option in town: a former convent run by the friendly Katia. The rooms are very basic (it *was* a convent), but it's clean and your best bet for an overnight stay in Sidon. Located behind Khan al-Franj, it can be hard to find – look for the sign saying 'Couvent de Terre Sainte et Paroisse'. Failing this, phone, or ask the staff at the Soap Museum who'll point you in the right direction.

Eating

Foodwise, there are lots of sandwich stalls and cheap cafés around Saahat en-Nejmeh and the harbour. A good choice is Abou Ramy, a felafel shop opposite the Sea Castle.

Next to Bab al-Saray Mosque is an atmospheric café that serves large glasses of fresh juice for LL2000.

To sample *sanioura*, a speciality of Sidon, try **Patisserie Kanaan** (☎ 729 104; Saahat en-Nejmeh; ⊗ 6am-11pm). It's a good place for a rest and a cup of coffee.

Sidon's culinary highlight is **The Rest House** (☎ 722 469; mezze LL4000, grills LL9000; ⊗ 11am-11pm), overlooking the Sea Castle. It's a beautifully restored Ottoman khan, complete with vaulted ceilings and fine inlaid marble and stonework. The shaded garden terrace is on the edge of the sea and has a panoramic view of Sidon's seafront. Food here is traditional Lebanese, with good mezze, seafood, and Lebanese wine.

Getting There & Away

Buses and service taxis from Beirut to Sidon leave from the Cola bus station (see Bus p264 for details). To Sidon, OCFTC buses (LL750, one hour, every 10 minutes from 6am to 8pm daily) leave from the southwest side of the Cola roundabout. There is also an express bus service to Sidon (LL1500, 40 minutes, every 20 minutes from 7am to 8pm daily). Minibuses to Sidon cost LL1000 and service taxis, which congregate near the buses, cost LL2500.

Coaches leave Sidon for Beirut (LL1500, 40 minutes, every 20 minutes from 6am to 6.30pm daily) from the Lebanese Transport Office on Saahat en-Nejmeh; OCFTC buses (LL750, one hour, every 10 minutes from 5am to 6.30pm) also leave from here.

The bus from Sidon to Tyre (LL750, one hour, every 20 to 30 minutes from 6am to 6pm daily) leaves Saahat en-Nejmeh on Rue Fakhreddine, the continuation of Rue Riad as-Solh, near the Castle of St Louis. A service taxi from Sidon to Tyre costs LL3000 and a minibus (leaving from Saahat en-Nejmeh) costs LL1000.

AROUND SIDON
Temple of Echmoun   معبد أشمون

This Phoenician **temple** (🕐 7.30am-sunset) is about 2km northeast of Sidon on the Nahr al-Awali. The whole area is filled with citrus orchards and the riverbanks are a favourite summer picnic spot with locals. The region has long been a fruit-growing area and the site of the temple is known as Boustan al-Sheikh (Garden of the Sheikh).

Echmoun was the principal god of the city of Sidon and was associated with healing. This is the only Phoenician site in Lebanon retaining more than its foundation walls and it requires a little imagination to picture it in its prime. Brochures are available at the site.

The temple complex was begun in the 7th century BC and the following centuries saw numerous additions to the basic building. Some of the ruined buildings, such as the Roman colonnade and the Byzantine church and mosaics, are far later than the original Phoenician temple and are an indication of how long the site retained its importance as a place of pilgrimage.

The legendary story of Echmoun closely follows that of Tammuz and Adonis. Echmoun began as a mortal youth from Berytus (Beirut). The goddess Astarte fell in love with him; to escape from her, he mutilated himself and died. Not to be thwarted she brought him back to life in the form of a god, hence his story was linked to fertility and rebirth. He was still primarily a god of healing and is identified with the Greek Asklepios, the god of medicine, and the Roman Aesculapius. It is from the snake motif of Echmoun that we get the serpentine symbol of the medical profession. The idea of a serpent coiled around a staff was found on a gold plaque at Echmoun.

The temple complex has a nearby water source for ritual ablutions. It was customary for people coming to the temple to ask for the god's help to bring a small statue with the name of the person who needed healing. Many of these votive statues depicted children and wonderful examples can be seen at the National Museum in Beirut.

Between the 6th and 4th centuries BC Sidon was known for its opulence, culture and industry. During this era, one of the rulers was Echmounazar II. His sarcophagus, discovered in 1858, had inscriptions on it relating that he, and his mother, Amashtarte, built temples to the gods at Sidon, including the Temple of Echmoun. The sarcophagus is now in the Louvre in Paris.

Archaeologists rediscovered the temple built by Echmounazar II during the excavation of Boustan al-Sheikh earlier this century. It was destroyed by an earthquake around the middle of the 4th century BC. Although never rebuilt, the site retained its reputation as a place of healing and was used by both pagan and Christian pilgrims. The site remained popular until the 3rd century AD, though it was by that time in ruins.

As you enter the site, there is a **colonnade of shops** on the right that probably did a roaring trade selling souvenirs to pilgrims. On the left are the remains of a **Byzantine church** just past what was a large courtyard with some very faded 3rd-century-BC **mosaics** showing the seasons. On the right is a **Roman processional stairway**, which leads to the upper levels of the site. The stairway was added in the 1st century AD. Also on the right is a **nymphaeum** with a fountain and niches containing statues of the nymphs.

Further along on the right is one of the most interesting artefacts, the **Throne of**

THE SOUTH

Astarte, which is flanked by two sphinxes. The throne is carved from a solid block of granite and is in the Egyptian style. There is also a very worn **frieze** depicting a hunting scene.

GETTING THERE & AWAY

From Sidon you can take a taxi to the site (LL5000) or get a service taxi (LL1000) or minibus (LL500) to the turn-off on the highway at the funfair and then walk the 1.5km past orchards to the ruins.

Joun   جون

Joun is a large village in the midst of olive plantations above the river, Nahr al-Awali. Its main claim to fame is that it was the home for many years of the famous traveller Lady Hester Stanhope (see boxed text). Before the war there was even a café named after her in the main square.

To reach her home, pass through the village and after about 2km turn left at the sign for the 'Stanhope Tyre Factory'(!). Follow the road, bearing right at any forks, and eventually you will find yourself at the ruins of her once-substantial house. Fifty metres to the southwest was her tomb, which lay in the shade of an olive grove. However, the once simple step-pyramid grave was a casualty of the civil war and is now a hole in the ground with rubble strewn around. Still, her final resting place remains a picturesque spot and is ideal for picnicking.

GETTING THERE & AWAY

Joun is about 15km northeast of Sidon and can be reached by taxi or private car. Deir Moukhalles is about 3km further east of Joun, so it's recommended combining these two. The taxi fare is around US$12 one way. There is little other traffic on this road so

---

LADY HESTER STANHOPE

The Middle East has always attracted intrepid women explorers and adventurers. Lady Hester Stanhope was one of the more extreme examples. She was born into an affluent but eccentric life in London in 1776, the daughter of the domineering Earl of Stanhope and Hester Pitt, sister of William Pitt, the future prime minister of England.

She grew up without a governess and later on a tutor engaged by her father was charged with high treason. She became close to her uncle, William Pitt, and when he became prime minister she moved into 10 Downing Street and played political hostess. Her first love was Sir John Moore, who took her favourite brother, James, to serve with him in Salamanca. They were both killed and when her uncle also died, Hester was homeless and brokenhearted.

To forget her grief, Hester decided to travel abroad and took her personal physician, Dr Meryon, with her. He remained in her service for 28 years, even while she had a notorious affair with Ian Bruce. In typical colonial fashion, she and her retinue travelled the Middle East, being treated like royalty. Her greatest moment of glory was riding into Palmyra in Syria on an Arab stallion at the head of her travelling procession. For more on Lady Hester and Palmyra, see the boxed text An Expensive Precedent (p209).

Her name was known all over the Arab world by the time she came to Joun (northeast of Sidon). Having installed herself as a guest in the house of a Christian merchant, she announced that she liked the house so much that she would stay for the remainder of her days. When it became clear that she meant this literally, the merchant protested to the local emir; Hester wrote directly to the sultan in Constantinople, who wrote back 'Obey the Princess of Europe in everything'.

Once she possessed the Joun house, Lady Hester became increasingly eccentric, reportedly forsaking books for communing with the stars. Although greatly respected by local people, among whom she liberally distributed money until she bankrupted herself, she gradually became a recluse, only receiving a few European visitors who would wait at Sidon for word of whether she would see them. The poet Lamartine was one such visitor, as was the son of a childhood friend, Kinglake (author of Eothen). He reported that she was wearing a large turban of cashmere shawls and a flowing white robe and seemed to be quite alone in her oriental sitting rooms.

When she died in 1839 she was totally alone and in debt. The British consul had to be sent to take care of her burial and her remains were hurriedly placed alongside those of a young officer in Napoleon's Imperial Guard – reputedly a former lover – in a grave behind her house.

you will need to have the taxi wait or arrange to be collected.

Deir Moukhalles (Saint Saviour's Monastery)   دير المخلص

Local legend has it that this 18th-century Greek Catholic **monastery** was built on the site of a miracle. As the story goes, a bishop was passing through the area when one of the priests in his entourage was accidentally shot in the stomach. The alarmed bishop reportedly exclaimed 'holy saviour', at which the victim stood up and was found to be unhurt; the offending bullet had melted into a harmless flat disk. The bishop ordered that a monastery be built on the site. After being badly damaged in an earthquake in 1956, and abandoned during the civil war, the monastery was recently restored and houses some fine icons.

Deir Moukhalles is about 3km further east of Joun. See p344 for information on travelling there.

Jezzine   جزّين

One of the South's most famous summer resorts, Jezzine sits 950m up on the western slopes of Jebel Niha, below one of the eastern Mediterranean's largest pine forests.

Known for its 40m-high waterfalls and cool summer temperatures, the town has a long history, although most architectural remains have gone. One monument worth visiting is the **Farid Serhal Palace**, an Ottoman-style building with lavish interiors and displays of antiquities.

In the valley below Jezzine is **Fakhreddine's Cave**, where Fakhreddine, like his father before him, hid from the Ottomans. His father eventually died there but Fakhreddine was found and taken to İstanbul.

Take a service taxi (LL3000) or taxi (LL8000) from Sidon.

Sarafand   الصرفند

Sarafand is the biblical Zarephath (also later known as Sarepta), which is famous for the miracle of Elijah, who raised the widow's son from the dead and multiplied her olive oil and grain supplies (Kings 1:17). The ancient town was also mentioned in Egyptian and Assyrian texts. Apart from miracles, Sarafand was famed in ancient times for its glass-making (the word seraph means 'to melt' in Hebrew). Archaeological excava-

tion before the civil war revealed that the site was first occupied in the middle of the 2nd millennium BC, eventually becoming an important trading town. The original port extended for over 1km and enclosed three small bays, which are still used by local anglers as anchorages.

During the Crusades, Sarepta, as it was then called, was a large, fortified town. It was the seat of a bishopric and home to a Carmelite order. There was a church commemorating St Elijah in the centre of town, probably beneath the site of the Wadi al-Khader.

Modern Sarafand is 19km south of Sidon and is no longer a vital trading town, but a featureless village with a few restaurants built on the inland side of the main coastal road. Illegal construction and looting during the civil war have unfortunately destroyed many of the archaeological remains that were described by 19th-century travellers in the vicinity. To see the traces of the old port, head down to the fishing harbour.

SLEEPING & EATING

One of the few hotels in the South is in Sarafand. The **Mounis Hotel** (☎ 03-666 657, 07-390 667; d US$50) is built out on the water and is connected to the mainland by a causeway. It is clean, modern and bland. It's in a great position, however, and lunch and dinner are available in the hotel restaurant for about US$12.

Sarafand has spawned a collection of fish restaurants along the coast road, supplied by the local fishing industry. The fish is chosen by the customer and sold by weight. Allow from US$15 to US$20 per person for grilled fish and side dishes. A popular local favourite is **Fouad Ville** (☎ 07-722 442), on the Sidon side of town.

GETTING THERE & AWAY

Sarafand is on the main north–south highway and service taxis or buses can drop you here from either Beirut or Sidon. The service-taxi fare from Sidon is LL2000.

TYRE (SOUR)   صور

☎ 07

Tyre, 81km from Beirut, has a long and colourful history. Suffering dreadfully during the civil war and from Israeli incursions, the city is now on the threshold of renewal. Predominantly Shiite like most of the South, Tyre has traditionally suffered neglect at the hands of Beirut's Maronite power brokers. Practise saying 'salaam 'alaykum' (peace be upon you) and your visit to the clean beaches, extraordinary Roman sites, picturesque harbours and wonderful souqs will be made all the more pleasurable by the locals' response. Tyre makes a good base from which to explore the other attractions of the South.

History

Tyre's origins date back to around the 3rd millennium BC, when the original founders are thought to have come from Sidon to establish a new city port. Tyre fell under the supremacy of the pharaohs under the 18th Egyptian dynasty. From the 17th to 13th centuries BC it benefited from Egypt's protection and prospered commercially.

Toward the end of the 2nd millennium BC, Tyre became a kingdom ruled by Abibaal. His son, Hiram I, ascended the throne in 969 BC and forged close relations with the Hebrew kings Solomon and David. Hiram sent cedar wood and skilled workers to help construct the famed temple in Jerusalem, as well as large amounts of gold. In return he received a district in Galilee that included 20 towns.

Under Hiram's reign, Tyre flourished. Hiram changed the layout of the city – he joined the offshore island (the older part of the city) with another small island and linked it to the mainland via a narrow causeway. Hiram's ties with King Solomon helped develop trade with Arabia and North and East Africa. During his reign, the Phoenicians colonised Sicily and North Africa, which later became the offshoot Carthaginian empire. Such was Hiram's success that the Mediterranean Sea became known as 'the Tyrian Sea', and Tyre its most important city.

After Hiram's 34-year reign ended, Tyre fell into bloody revolution, even as it continued to expand its trading links. The city paid tribute to the Assyrians but remained close to the Israelites and was ruled by a succession of kings. The most famous woman of ancient Tyrian legend was Princess Elissa, also known as Dido. She was embroiled in a plot to take power and, when it became clear that she'd failed, seized a fleet of ships and sailed for North Africa. She founded a new port on the ruins of Kambeh, which became known in time as Carthage, near modern-day Tunis. This became the seat of the Carthaginian empire.

The rise of Carthage gradually saw a corresponding fall in Tyre's fortunes. Weakened as a power, the Tyrians sued for peace when the Assyrians conquered the Levant and became their vassal state. When Assyria's power weakened, Tyre ceased to pay tribute and rebelled against their overlords. Assyrian attempts to keep their rebellious vassal in line led to periods of war throughout the 7th and 6th centuries BC.

With the fall of the Assyrians in 612 BC, Tyre was peaceably controlled by the Neo-Babylonians until 586 BC, when it once again rebelled, leading to a 13-year siege by the Babylonian king, Nebuchadnezzar. The inhabitants stood firm behind the high walls of the island-city and the siege failed.

More successful however, was Alexander the Great. In 332 BC he marched along coastal Phoenicia exacting tribute from all its city-states. Tyre, in its time-honoured tradition, resisted and prepared for a long siege. The city was considered impregnable, but Alexander began building a land bridge in the sea to reach the city. This impressive feat was carried out under a constant hail of missiles from the Tyrians. Meanwhile, on the mainland, Alexander's engineers were constructing 20-storey siege towers, the tallest ever used in the history of war. After several months these great war machines lumbered across the land bridge and the battle for Tyre began in earnest.

Running low on supplies and morale, Tyre finally fell after seven months and Alexander, enraged at the dogged resistance of the Tyrians, allowed his troops to sack the city. The city's 30,000 citizens were massacred or sold into slavery. This destruction heralded the domination of the Greeks in the Mediterranean. Alexander's legacy lives on in Tyre as the land bridge he created became the permanent link between the old city and the mainland, and Tyre became a peninsula.

The city eventually recovered from its devastation and, after a period of Seleucid rule following Alexander's death, became autonomous in 126 BC. In 64 BC, Tyre became a Roman province, and later became the capital of the Roman province of Syria-Phoenicia.

Later Tyre became one of the first Lebanese towns to adopt Christianity and was the seat of an archbishopric, with 14 bishoprics under its control. In the Byzantine period, flourishing silk, glass and purple-dyeing industries allowed the city to prosper.

The Arabs took the city in 635, and its prosperity continued. The Umayyad caliph, Mu'awiyah, transformed the city into a naval base and it was from here that the first Arab fleet set sail to conquer Cyprus.

With the arrival of the Crusaders, Tyre's future was to become less assured. By paying tribute in 1099, the city avoided attack as the Crusaders marched on Jerusalem. It narrowly survived another Crusader encounter (1111–12), when King Baldwin placed it under siege for nearly five months, finally giving up after some 2000 of his men were killed. Twelve years later Tyre was not so lucky. People from other coastal cities had fled to Tyre when the Crusaders started to take the Middle East in 1124. After a siege of five and a half months, Tyre's defences collapsed and the Christian army occupied the city and the surrounding fertile land.

The Crusaders rebuilt the defensive walls and Tyre remained in Crusader hands for 167 years, until the Mamluk army of Al-Malik al-Ashraf retook the city in 1291. At the beginning of the 17th century Fakhreddine attempted to rebuild and revitalise Tyre, but without much success. Following the fall of the Ottoman Empire, Tyre was included in the French Mandate of Greater Lebanon, and then incorporated into the Lebanese republic.

Once the State of Israel was established in 1948, its position next to the closed border further marginalised the city, which was already sidelined by Beirut and Sidon. Along with the rest of the South it suffered greatly during the civil war, and Israel's long occupation of the adjacent border area left the city depressed long after the 1991 cease-fire.

Orientation

The old part of Tyre is on the peninsula jutting out into the sea and covers a relatively small area. The modern town is on the left-hand side as you arrive from the north. The coastal route goes all the way to Tyre's picturesque old port, around which are a few cafés and restaurants. Behind the port is the Christian quarter, with its tiny alleys and old houses around shaded courtyards.

To the left of the port the road forks southwards and goes around the excavation site of one of the Roman archaeological sites. There are several streets running parallel between the northern and southern coastal roads, and that's where you'll find banks, moneychangers, sandwich stalls, travel agencies and the souq.

Information

INTERNET ACCESS
Alpha Net (per hr LL2000)
Swiss Net (Rue Abu Deeb; per hr LL1500) Just north of the main roundabout and handy to waterfront accommodation.

MONEY
There are banks and ATMs scattered through the centre of the town as well as at the bus stop for Sidon. In the old souqs are several moneychangers offering reasonable rates.

POST
Post office (☎ 740 565; ◷ 7.30am-5pm Mon-Fri, 8am-1pm Sat) At the western end of the harbour.

TELEPHONE
Telephone Bureau At the post office.
Western Union Office (Rue Riad as-Solh; ◷ 9am-midnight) Has a private telephone office for overseas calls (LL3000 per minute).

Sights
ARCHAEOLOGICAL SITES
In 1984 Tyre was declared a World Heritage site, by Unesco, in the hope of halting the damage being done to archaeological remains by anarchic urban development and conflict. There are three sites within the city: Al-Mina (Areas 1 and 2), on the south side of the city, Al-Bass (Area 3), on the original

---

HIRAM VERSUS SOLOMON

Relations between King Hiram of Tyre and King Solomon of Israel were cordial but competitive. According to the annals of Tyre, there was a contest of wisdom between the two kings. They would each set riddles for the other. Whoever failed to guess correctly had to pay a fine. Wrong answers cost Hiram a fortune, but he eventually sharpened his wits and turned the tables on Solomon, winning back all he had lost and more.

---

mainland section, and a medieval site in the centre of town.

Al-Mina Archaeological Site

In an impressive setting leading down to the ancient Egyptian (south) harbour, **Al-Mina excavations** (Areas 1 & 2; adult/student & child LL6000/3500; ⊙ 8.30am-30 min before sunset) incorporate remains of Roman and Byzantine Tyre. Upon entering, a double line of columns to the right is thought to be part of the **agora** (market place). Further down is a long **colonnaded road** leading directly to what was the southern harbour. The marble sections of the pavement date back to the Roman era, while the black-and-white mosaics are Byzantine. To the right of the road, below a modern cemetery, are the remains of an unusual, rectangular **arena**, with five rows of terraced seating cut in to limestone. In the centre was a pool that may have been used for some kind of spectator water sport.

Beside the arena, and covering the area heading south towards the harbour, was the settlement's residential quarter. The remains are of small rooms, some of which have mosaic paving.

Across the colonnaded main road is the ruin of an extensive **Roman bathhouse**. Measuring some 40m by 30m, the complex did not fare well during the civil war. However, you can still see the vaulted mud-brick basement and several rows of stone disks, which were used to support a hypocaust (raised floor heated by hot air flowing underneath).

Crusader Cathedral

About a five-minute walk to the north of Al-Mina site, the remains of the **Holy Cross Cathedral** are unfortunately fenced off and closed to the public. However, you can see the ruins from the road. Foundations and granite columns are all that remain of the 12th-century building, giving scant indication of its importance in Crusader times. Beneath and around the cathedral is a network of Roman and Byzantine roads and other buildings, one of which may have been the original temple of Melkart, the ancient god of the city.

Al-Bass Archaeological Site

On the landward side of Tyre, about 20 minutes on foot from the other sites, is the enormous **Al-Bass site** (Area 3; adult/student & child LL6000/3500; ⊙ 8.30am-30 min before sunset). A colonnaded east–west road, possibly a continuation of the road at Al-Mina site, takes you through a vast **Roman necropolis** containing dozens of highly decorated marble and stone sarcophagi. The more elaborate have reliefs depicting scenes from Greek mythology and Homeric epics. Most are from the 2nd and 3rd century AD, but some date back as far as the 2nd century BC, and there are Byzantine coffins from as late as the 6th century.

A huge, triple-bay **triumphal arch** stands further along the colonnaded street. Originally the gateway to the Roman town, it dates to the 2nd century AD. Behind it, to the south of the road, are traces of the city's old **aqueduct**, which brought water from Ras al-Ain, 6km south of Tyre. According to travellers' accounts, it was almost intact during the 19th century but it did not fare so well in the 20th century.

Beyond the arch is the largest and best-preserved **Roman hippodrome** in the world. The partly reconstructed hippodrome is 480m long and once seated some 20,000 spectators. It was used for very popular and dangerous chariot races. A *metae* (turning stone), which you can still see, marked each end of the long, narrow course. The tight, high-speed turns at the *metae* were the most exciting part of the race and often produced dramatic spills and collisions.

FISHING HARBOUR & SOUQS

Small, but bustling with activity, the **fishing harbour** is the most picturesque part of Tyre, with its brightly coloured wooden boats and old-fashioned boat repair shops. There are also a couple of fish restaurants and cafés that overlook the water and make a good vantage point for watching the scene.

Behind them, running from east to west, lie Tyre's Ottoman-era **souqs**, which aren't as extensive as those of Sidon and Tripoli, but are still lively and interesting to explore.

As you walk around the northern side of the harbour, you come to the city's **Christian quarter**, where there are six churches (one ruined), reflecting Lebanon's multitude of Christian denominations. They are surrounded by narrow, winding residential streets, some lined with old houses, and make for a pleasant wander. Heading south, past the lighthouse, there are fantastic views of the sea.

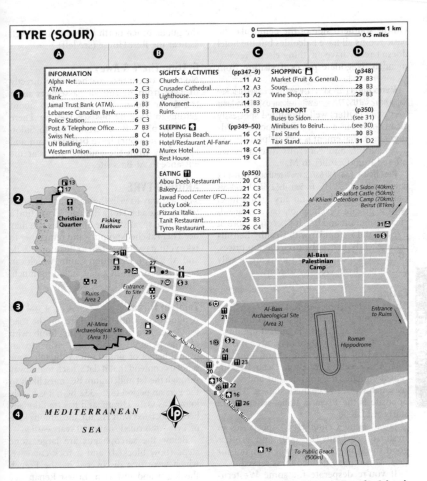

TYRE (SOUR)

INFORMATION		
Alpha Net	1	C3
ATM	2	C3
Bank	3	B3
Jamal Trust Bank (ATM)	4	B3
Lebanese Canadian Bank	5	B3
Police Station	6	C3
Post & Telephone Office	7	B3
Swiss Net	8	C4
UN Building	9	B3
Western Union	10	D2

SIGHTS & ACTIVITIES	(pp347–9)	
Church	11	A2
Crusader Cathedral	12	A3
Lighthouse	13	A2
Monument	14	B3
Ruins	15	B3

SLEEPING	(pp349–50)	
Hotel Elyssa Beach	16	C4
Hotel/Restaurant Al-Fanar	17	A2
Murex Hotel	18	C4
Rest House	19	C4

EATING	(p350)	
Abou Deeb Restaurant	20	C4
Bakery	21	C3
Jawad Food Center (JFC)	22	C4
Lucky Look	23	C4
Pizzaria Italia	24	C3
Tanit Restaurant	25	B3
Tyros Restaurant	26	C4

SHOPPING	(p348)	
Market (Fruit & General)	27	B3
Souqs	28	B3
Wine Shop	29	B3

TRANSPORT	(p350)	
Buses to Sidon	(see 31)	
Minibuses to Beirut	(see 30)	
Taxi Stand	30	B3
Taxi Stand	31	D2

Christian Quarter

Fishing Harbour

To Sidon (40km);
Beaufort Castle (50km);
Al-Khiam Detention Camp (70km);
Beirut (81km)

Al-Bass Palestinian Camp

Ruins Area 2

Entrance to Site

Al-Mina Archaeological Site (Area 1)

Rue Abu Deeb

Al-Bass Archaeological Site (Area 3)

Entrance to Ruins

Roman Hippodrome

MEDITERRANEAN SEA

Rue Nabih Berri

To Public Beach (500m)

Activities

SWIMMING

Just south of Tyre is a Lebanon rarity – a clean public beach. It's lined with trees and there are tented restaurants serving fish during the warmer months. Just take the road that heads south past the Rest House (p350) and you will see the beach to your right.

Festivals & Events

The annual **Tyre Festival** (☎ 03-816 992) is held in late July/early August at Al-Bass archaeological site and includes a mix of local and international singers, artists and musicians. For more specific details, contact the **tourist office** (☎ 01-343 073; www.lebanon-tourism.gov.lb) in Beirut or the festival organisers. If you're in Tyre at

the beginning of the Islamic year for **Ashurah** (see Islamic Religious Holidays p365) you can witness the Shiites mourning the death of Imam Hussein ibn Ali over a 10-day period that culminates in a procession.

Sleeping

Hotel/Restaurant Al-Fanar (☎ 741 111; alfanar@ville-tyr .com; d US$40, with sea views US$50, includes breakfast) One of the cheaper options is right by the lighthouse (*al-fanar* is Arabic for lighthouse) in the Christian quarter. The best thing about this place is the basement bar that looks right out onto the sea. Prices are US$10 cheaper from October to May.

Hotel Elyssa Beach (☎ 347 551; Rue Nabih Berri; s/d US$45/50, with private bathroom & TV US$55/60; ❄)

On the southern side of the peninsula, the basic rooms all have balconies but the hotel doesn't really have anything else to recommend it. Negotiate prices if visiting from October to May.

Murex Hotel (☎ 347 111; www.murexhotel.com; Rue Nabih Berri; s/d US$77/94, ste with balcony US$143, includes breakfast; ✷) Offers well-appointed spotlessly clean rooms in a newly constructed building. The management is very helpful, there's a restaurant, and generous discounts are offered from October to May.

Rest House (☎ 740 667/8; www.resthouse-tyr.com.lb; d/ste Mon-Thu US$98/135, Fri-Sun US$256/311, includes breakfast; ✷ ☒) A light and airy luxury hotel with a private beach, pool, bakery, health club, restaurant and bar. It's become more of a resort and is popular with wealthy Beirutis on weekends, hence the over-the-top prices. Breakfast is included and rooms are heavily discounted from October to May.

Eating

There is a fair choice of restaurants in Tyre and, despite its large Shiite population, alcohol is served at all but the budget options.

Tyre's cheap restaurants are mostly clustered on or near the roundabout on Rue Abu Deeb. The Abou Deeb Restaurant dominates the roundabout and serves reasonably priced Lebanese staples. Almost opposite is the Pizzaria Italia, where pizza starts at LL4000.

Jawad Food Center (JFC) specialises in fresh fruit cocktails (LL2000), and also has good shwarma. It's a favourite hangout for local Muslims, so no alcohol is served.

If you're desperate for some Western-style food, you could try **Lucky Look** (☎ 03-367 432), which serves steaks, seafood and burgers (LL2500) as well as kids plates.

Tyros Restaurant (☎ 741 027; Rue Nabih Berri; mezze LL4000, grills LL6000; ☻ 24hr) is an enormous place that's extremely popular with locals, especially on weekends when you need to book. It has a great atmosphere and the food is good.

Tanit Restaurant (☎ 740 987; mezze LL4000, grills LL15,000; ☻ 24hr) serves the best food in town, including some Chinese-style dishes. It's a small, friendly place that's very popular with the local United Nations Interim Force in Lebanon (Unifil) staff.

If you visit Tyre during the summer months there are restaurants that open on

the public beach north of the town, as well as near the Rest House (see left).

Getting There & Away

No buses or express coaches travel directly to Tyre from Beirut; all passengers must travel via Sidon. For information about getting to Tyre by bus see Getting There & Away p343. Buses from Tyre to Sidon (LL750, one hour) leave between 6am and 8pm daily from the roundabout near the entrance to Al-Bass site.

AROUND TYRE

The best way to visit the sights listed here is to negotiate a taxi for a day trip. Try to find a driver that speaks a little English, as you may need help at checkpoints – and remember to take your passport. A trip to Beaufort Castle and Al-Khiam Detention Camp, which can take the best part of a day including lunch, should cost around US$50.

Tomb of Hiram   قبر أحيرام

Around 6km southeast of Tyre, on the road to Qana, is a huge limestone tomb with a large pyramid-shaped top, rising to an overall height of almost 6m. Although some scholars contend that it dates back to midway through the 1st millennium BC, most likely to the Persian period (525–332 BC), it is locally known as Qabr Hiram, and has traditionally been associated with Hiram, the famous king of Tyre, who ruled some 500 years earlier.

Below the sarcophagus are large stone steps (now blocked) and a rock-cut cave, which were first discovered by the French theologist and historian, Ernest Renan; see the boxed text Ernest Renan (1823–92), on p287, for more information. When he started excavations at the foot of the tomb in the mid-19th century, he found an even earlier staircase connected to the mausoleum's foundations. There are other signs of tombs in the area as well as a sanctuary.

Qana   قانا

This small **Shiite village**, 14km southeast of Tyre, was tragically catapulted into international consciousness in 1996 for the massacre, by Israel, of civilians and UN soldiers sheltering at a base here (see the boxed text Bitter Wine from Grapes of Wrath, p352).

The village is at the centre of a scholarly debate whether it's in fact the biblical Cana,

CHECKPOINT ETIQUETTE

Israeli soldiers may finally have left the South, but that doesn't mean that Lebanon's ubiquitous checkpoints have disappeared. If you find the guns and tanks a little intimidating, remember that the days of kidnapping foreigners are long gone. Unless you're an undercover agent for Mossad or a draft-dodging local, you're not who they're looking for. Remember to wear your seatbelt; there are new laws and fines apply. Following are a few tips to help you negotiate the unfamiliar with humour.

Know Your Checkpoints

Syrian checkpoints are distinguishable by their general shabbiness, the iconic pictures of late Syrian President Assad and his son Bashar, and, of course, the Syrian flag. Lebanese checkpoints are neater, the soldiers wear cool sunglasses and natty uniforms, and there's a strong chance that at least one will be talking on a mobile phone. If you still can't tell, look for the cedar emblem.

Driving Through

Knowing how to get through a checkpoint with your cool intact will distinguish you from other tourists and help you blend in with locals. Keep in mind the following:

- Try not to stare in horror at the automatic weaponry
- Do not look nervous; an alert nonchalance is advisable
- Under no circumstances take photographs in the vicinity of a checkpoint
- Switch on the car's interior light at night, particularly if there are no street lights

Slow down to a gentle roll and act as if you're going to stop, but don't actually stop unless you're told to. How will you know? The word 'yameen' (right) is a sure sign to pull over; however, there are a number of other phrases the soldier could use. The signal to pass through could be a wave, a raised eyebrow, an almost imperceptible movement of the head, a slight twitch, or simply disinterest. It depends on the mood of the soldier.

When in doubt, creep forward slowly, keeping an eye on the rear-vision mirror. If there's any sign of excitement or raised voices behind you, pull over.

With thanks to Nate Scholz

where Jesus performed his first miracle of turning water into wine. Until recently it was assumed that the Israeli village of Kefr Kenna was the site of biblical Cana, but the 4th-century historian Eusebius seems to support that Cana was near Sidon, as do the 3rd-century writings of St Jerome. Further proof for the claim is centred on early Christian **rock carvings** and a grotto 1km outside the village. The worn carvings depict 13 figures, said by proponents of the Qana-as-Cana position to be Jesus and his disciples. The cave, just below the carvings, could possibly be where he and his followers hid from persecution. Elsewhere in the village large basins have been excavated and are said to have contained the water that was transformed into wine. Without more definitive proof no doubt the debate will continue, but the site is worth a visit.

To reach the carvings, go down the steep path next to the school, about 1km before the village (if you're coming from the Tomb of Hiram). The spot is marked by a modern, white-marble stone with black Arabic script. The track leads into a deep valley and it is a five-minute walk down to the grotto and carvings. The site is not supervised, so you can visit any time. The stone basins are between two back gardens of village houses, and you will need to ask the villagers (who are usually only too happy to help) for directions, or get your taxi driver to show you.

GETTING THERE & AWAY

You can take a service taxi from Tyre to Qana (LL2000) but they aren't frequent. A taxi from Tyre is about LL7500; LL10,000 for a return trip. The memorial to the massacre victims is at the UN base, 2km beyond the town.

Tibnin تبنين

Twelve kilometres northwest of the town of Bint Jbayl (and 30km from Tyre) is the town of Tibnin, famous in recent history as the birthplace of Amal leader Nabih Berri. Delving back slightly deeper into history, however, the town derives its fame for the **Crusader castle** that dominates the landscape. Built in 1104 by Hugues de Sain Omer, the governor of Tiberias, in preparation for the siege of Tyre, it was given the old French name of Le Toron, meaning high or isolated place. It fell to Saladin after the battle of Hittin in 1187, but was taken back by the Franks in 1229. The Mamluk sultan, Beybars, recaptured it again in 1266. The structure was added to and modified during Mamluk and Ottoman times, in particular by the 17th-century governor of Acre, Zaher al-Omar. Ahmed al-Jazzar later destroyed much of the building and the interior is still in ruins. Nevertheless, the castle still extends over an area of 2000 sq m and retains its outer fortified walls, to which extensive restoration work has been carried out in recent years. It affords spectacular views of the surrounding area.

Beaufort Castle قلعة الشقيف

This isolated and windswept military outpost, perched atop one of the highest ridges in the area, can be seen from miles around. **Qala'at ash-Shaqif** (قلعة الشقيف), as it's known in Arabic, has been fought over by almost every invader to have passed through the area over the past 1000 years. Its commanding hilltop location,

some 710m above sea level, gives superb panoramic views of the coast, northern Israel, Syria and the mountains to the north. The origins of the fortress are uncertain; some scholars argue that it was built in the Byzantine period, and restored and added to by the Arabs, and later by the Crusaders. It was captured from a local prince, Shehab ed-Din, in 1138 by the Fulk of Anjou, King of Jerusalem, who gave it to Sidon's Crusader overlords.

In the 17th century, Fakhreddine saw the advantage of such a fortress in his revolt against the Ottomans, and restored the structure. It was besieged and partially destroyed, however, when the pashas of Acre and Damascus sent forces against him.

Beaufort's strategic worth came into play again in the 1970s, when it was occupied by Palestinian guerrillas. It was then attacked and badly damaged by Israeli jets during the 1982 invasion. In one of those historical ironies that seem to be a Lebanese speciality, the Israelis (modern Crusaders who, with their Christian allies, were surrounded by a hostile, largely Muslim local population) proceeded to occupy the fortress for 20 years. The historical parallels continued with their ultimate defeat by Hezbollah.

In its retreat in May 2000 the Israeli army blew up parts of the castle to destroy traces of its occupation, despite a specific request by the Lebanese government that it respect the integrity of the already ravaged historic site.

BITTER WINE FROM GRAPES OF WRATH

By 1996 Israel had already occupied Lebanon for more than a decade with no appreciable gain. Hezbollah guerrillas continued their hit-and-run attacks on the occupying army, as well as launching sporadic rocket attacks into northern Israel. On 11 April of that year, Prime Minister Shimon Peres, under pressure to end the peace process after a wave of suicide bombings inside Israel, launched a 16-day air, artillery and naval attack dubbed 'Operation Grapes of Wrath'. Its stated objective was to wipe out Hezbollah bases throughout Lebanon. The intensity of the attack was such that an estimated 35,000 shells fell on Lebanese land, destroying infrastructure and damaging thousands of buildings.

On 18 April an estimated 800 people were sheltering from the fighting at the UN peacekeeping base in Qana. Nevertheless the base was shelled, with several direct hits on an underground shelter that left 102 dead and a further 120 wounded. At the time, Israel maintained that Hezbollah guerrillas had entered the base and that it hadn't known that there were civilians sheltering there. A UN investigation subsequently provided substantial evidence that this was unlikely.

There is now an official day of mourning on 18 April throughout Lebanon. The site of the massacre, including the twisted wreckage of the shelter, has been turned into a memorial to the victims.

THE SCARS OF WAR

The withdrawal of the Israeli armed forces and their Lebanese militia, the South Lebanon Army (SLA), from the south of Lebanon on 25 May 2000 was occasion for great rejoicing throughout Lebanon. Indeed, the government declared a public holiday – the Day of Resistance and Liberation – to mark its significance. A visit to the area formerly occupied by the Israelis will make all travellers appreciate just how great a cause for celebration the withdrawal was for the Lebanese people, particularly those living in the South, and is one of the most rewarding – if upsetting – experiences to be had during a visit to Lebanon.

A drive through the area's innumerable small villages is a sobering experience due to the presence of myriad multicoloured billboards featuring portraits of local young men 'martyred' during the occupation. The landscape itself is spectacular, and the two highlights of the region are undoubtedly Al-Khiam Detention Camp and Beaufort Castle. Don't miss either.

GETTING THERE & AWAY

Beaufort is above the village of Arnun, 7km southeast of Nabatiye. If you wish to visit from Sidon, service taxis to Nabatiye cost LL2000. From here your best bet is to hire a taxi (return around LL20,000). Try to negotiate a trip to Al-Khiam Detention Camp and Fatima Gate as well.

Al-Khiam Detention Camp   معتقل الخيام

The notorious hilltop prison that was run by the South Lebanon Army (SLA) during the occupation is **Al-Khiam Detention Camp**. Holding prisoners – who were held without

being charged – was an attempt to keep the rest of the local villagers in check. When the Israeli army withdrew in May 2000, the SLA guards fled and the local population flooded in to rescue the remaining 140 prisoners. The prison is now run as a museum by Hezbollah (Party of God), to which a visit is a truly shocking experience. The appalling conditions provide a stark reminder of the horror of the invasion – the conditions before the Red Cross was finally allowed to inspect the centre in 1995 were shocking – and the minimal but eloquent interpretation (innumerable signs denoting where prisoners were 'martyred') is extremely moving. This place redefines one's understanding of what a museum can be. There's no admission price, but there's a donation box at the front gate, as well as a Hezbollah souvenir shop, where you can buy kitsch key rings, perfumes and cassette tapes.

Fatima Gate   بوابة فاطمة

Adjacent to the town of Kfar Kila, Fatima Gate was a border crossing during the war. When Israel withdrew from Lebanon, Fatima Gate became a focal point of Lebanese celebration and also offered an opportunity for the population to vent their anger at Israel by throwing rocks towards the border. These days, however it's a minor tourist attraction, very popular with Lebanese families enjoying the views across to Israel, while the Hezbollah proudly fly their flag and sell souvenirs.

If you've not organised your visit here as part of a day trip, you can take a service taxi from Nabatiye for around LL4000. Occasionally vehicles will be stopped and you may not be allowed through; make sure there aren't any ongoing problems at the time of your visit by checking the *Daily Star* before you set off.

THE SOUTH

Directory

CONTENTS

ACCOMMODATION

Throughout this book we've listed accommodation prices for Syria using both the Syrian pound (S£) and US dollars (US$), and, with the devaluing of Lebanon's local currency during the 1980s, accommodation prices in Lebanon are now indicated only in US dollars.

Throughout this book we have divided accommodation into budget, mid-range and top-end categories; the corresponding price ranges are detailed below.

In Syria, you can get a bed for less than S£150 (US$3) and about S£250/400 (US$3/8) per single/double room. Some of the better-value cheapies charge up to about S£350/700

(US$7/14) for singles/doubles. In mid-range hotels expect to pay US$15 to US$30 for a single and US$20 to US$40 for a double. Top-end hotel accommodation starts at around US$80/100 per single/double.

In Lebanon, dorm beds/singles start at around US$5/8, doubles are US$10 to US$12. For mid-range accommodation expect to pay at least US$30/40 for singles/doubles. Top-end hotels start from US$80/100 for singles/doubles.

Rooms in cheap hotels are often let on a share basis and will have two to four beds. If you want the room to yourself you may have to pay for all beds, or an intermediate sum. Where there are no single rooms available solo females would be advised to take a room to themselves, ie pay for all beds in that room (for more information on women travellers in the region see p377).

It's worth knowing that during the low season (December to March) and outside the peak holiday seasons (around major religious festivals, such as Eid al-Adha), big discounts are frequently available at the region's hotels, including top-end establishments – it's always worth asking about special offers. For those generally staying at mid-range accommodation, you can find yourself in a top-end hotel for only slightly more than you budgeted. During the high-season months (May to September), it can be extremely difficult to get a room if you don't book well in advance. Prices in some mid-range and top-end hotels also go up by as much as 40% during the Islamic religious holidays due to an influx of Gulf Arabs. See Holidays for more details (p365).

In Lebanon summer destinations basically shut up shop during winter and offer only limited accommodation. It's worth being flexible and doing as the locals do, for instance, Zahlé (p321) in summer and Faraya (p273) in winter.

For more details on planning your trip see Itineraries, p13.

Camping

Official camping opportunities in both Syria and Lebanon are limited. Camping is allowed at only a few places around Syria, such as Damascus Camping (p102) near Damascus.

A few private hotels allow campers to set up in their backyard, such as the Zenobia (p214) at Palmyra. Camping facilities at most of these places are pretty basic.

The idea of camping is starting to grow in popularity in Lebanon, although there are currently only two official camp sites: Camping Amchit Les Colombes (p285) is just north of Byblos on a beautiful promontory overlooking the sea; and the other is La Reserve (p290), a tented resort in a stunning location high above the Adonis Valley, close to the Afqa Grotto.

Hotels

BUDGET

The spread of budget hotel options is uneven across both countries. Some cities have numerous budget lodgings, such as Aleppo, while others such as Tyre have none. This is certainly worth taking into account when planning your itinerary. Given this, it's worth planning day trips to sights both from Damascus and Beirut where budget accommodation is lacking. For some day trips where public transport is an option, consider saving on taxi plus driver costs and use the savings to upgrade to mid-range accommodation at your destination instead.

The biggest drawback with cheap hotels is that they are generally noisy. Rooms often open onto common TV lounges, or overlook busy streets. Earplugs can make all the difference. With a handful of exceptions in both countries, the bottom-level hotels are basic. Beds come with a sheet, sometimes two, and, in winter, a blanket. Sheets often haven't been changed from the previous guest but if you ask you'll be provided with a fresh set. Sometimes there's a ceiling fan, which you'll welcome in the hotter months.

MID-RANGE

Damascus has innumerable mid-range options, while Tripoli has no mid-range accommodation worth reviewing. Prices at Syria's mid-range hotels are often overblown – the places are frequently old with antiquated fittings and poor facilities and you may well find yourself aggrieved at the amount you're being asked to pay. In Beirut travellers can quite often get a room at a mid-range hotel at prices not too far above budget. Outside of Beirut mid-range options are not very good value, much the same as in Syria.

Across both countries, mid-range hotels vary wildly in terms of facilities; some extras to look for include air-con, satellite television and a fridge (handy if you're self-catering).

TOP END

In Syria the countrywide chain of state-owned five-stars, the Cham Palaces (pronounced sham) often lack character and are also usually a taxi ride away from the action. The notable exception is the Cham Palace (p103) in Damascus in that it's significantly better than its siblings in that it's well situated and well run.

Unfortunately, in Syria there are only a few alternatives to the Chams, and standards are below par in terms of level of facilities when compared with elsewhere in the world. Also, you'll find many Syrian top-end hotels are poorly situated away from the heart of the city.

Another option includes a new breed of private boutique hotels. These are in converted historical residences and are wonderful places, providing uniquely Syrian (there's something about the buildings with their narrow passages, beautiful carved wood and hidden cellars that makes them so memorable), and world-class, accommodation.

In Lebanon, sadly, there isn't the same standard of private boutique hotels, but the top-end hotels are significantly better than their Syrian counterparts.

Top-end hotels generally have air-con, satellite television, minibar, and a restaurant or hotel bar. Many have health clubs and swimming pools, but the outdoor pools are generally drained in winter.

Credit cards are accepted at all top-end hotels.

Rental Accommodation
Long-term rental apartments are available in Beirut. Grab a copy of the Ministry of Tourism's *Hotels in Lebanon* guide, which has furnished-apartment listings. These fill up quickly at the beginning of university semesters (February and October) and are usually rented for the duration of the semester. Long-term apartments are also available at coastal towns north of Beirut, but are usually booked well in advance of every summer; similarly, long-term rentals are usually booked out for the ski season, particularly for places such as The Cedars (p314) and Faraya Mzaar (p273).

ACTIVITIES
If you decide to go it alone, particularly with regards to any land-based activity, remember that there is a very real danger of land mines in parts of Lebanon (for more information see Dangers & Annoyances, p361). Always seek local advice about the safety of your intended route.

Caving
The best place for caving is Lebanon. The Jeita Grotto (p277) and Afqa Grotto (p289) may be Lebanon's most famous caverns but there are more than 400 explored cavities throughout the country, including some holes with depths of up to 602m – among the deepest in the Middle East. From small chambers in the rock to huge caverns, Lebanon's rugged mountains have enough crags and holes to keep most spelunkers happy for a very long time.

There are a few spelunking clubs in Lebanon and they organise trips throughout the country. If you don't speak French, don't worry: the clubs organise events with English as well as Swiss and French spelunkers.

Association Libanaise d'Etudes Speleologique (ALES; badrjg@hotmail.com) Run by Badr Gedeon.

Groupe d'Etudes et de Recherches Souterraines au Liban (GERSL; in Lebanon ☎ 03-293 210) The contact for this group is Pierre Abioun, who is also president of Wild Expeditions ecotourism.

Groupe Speleo de Wadi al-Arayech (in Lebanon ☎ 03-608 632) Founded in Zahlé in 1966. It is run by Charbel Abou Chebil.

Cycling
While the streets of both countries are filled with anarchic traffic, poor surfaces and high noise levels, away from the cities the mountains and national parks are great for mountain biking. In Syria, the Dead Cities (p200) and the areas around Palmyra (p204) and Krak des Chevaliers (p132) are super for cycling.

In Lebanon, the Horsh Ehden Forest Nature Reserve (p312) and Chouf Cedar Reserve (p297), Al-Jord (near Hermel in the Bekaa, p334) and The Cedars (p314) are just some of the areas that are ideal for mountain biking.

A couple of organisations run mountain-biking treks.

Lebanese Adventure (☎ /fax 01-398 982, ☎ 03-360 027; www.lebanese-adventure.com; Sioufi, Achrafiye, Beirut) Arranges cycling trips each week throughout Lebanon. It also tailors excursions for groups (minimum five people).

Thermique (☎ /fax 09-953 756, 03-288 193) In Ajaltoun, just outside Beirut, runs day-long guided bicycle tours in Qornet as-Sawda (p272), Lebanon's highest peak, among other destinations.

If you decide to bring your own bicycle or head off without a guide, remember that as well as being reckless, Syrian and Lebanese drivers are not used to bicycles. If you're on mountain roads this means that you could find yourself perilously close to drop-offs as a car speeds into your path around a blind curve. If you must use the roads, be extremely careful and don't assume that you have been seen; mirrors are rarely used. Also keep in mind that bicycle shops are almost nonexistent outside the capital cities, so you need to bring everything you are likely to need, including spare spokes, chain, cables, tubes and tyres. For further information, read *Cycling the Mediterranean* by Kameel B Nasr.

Paragliding

With its dramatic mountain scenery, Lebanon is prime paragliding territory and the sport is gradually being established here. The season is usually from May to October, depending on the weather, and the prime areas are The Cedars (p314), Faraya Mzaar (p273), Harissa (p280) and Qanat Bakiche (p273).

The following outfit offers paragliding courses in Lebanon.

Thermique (☎ /fax 09-953 756, 03-288 193) The Lebanese branch of a French paragliding school, Thermique is based in Ajaltoun and offers courses ranging from one to seven days, as well as equipment rental. Current prices range from US$500 to US$700 for a week-long course, including accommodation and insurance.

Skiing

Most of Lebanon's resorts are accessible on a day trip from Beirut and the ever fun-loving Lebanese make sure that the après-ski scene is worth sampling. The season lasts from early December to April, depending on the snow. The mountains are relatively close to the sea, so the air around the slopes is humid. In the morning, when the air is coldest, this can mean icy conditions; by the afternoon, with the rise in temperature, the snow becomes wetter. If you're looking for good powder skiing, head straight for The Cedars (p314), otherwise Faraya Mzaar (p273) is your best bet.

You can take a short, package ski holiday from Beirut arranged by some of the local tour operators. These include transfers to and from Beirut and full board at one of the ski hotels. Depending on the package chosen, and the class of hotel, the average costs are around US$80 per day inclusive, although this doesn't include ski and lift passes. The cost of hiring ski equipment is very reasonable and available at all resorts – a full kit will cost about US$15 per day, but remember this never includes gloves.

Cross-country skiing and snow-shoeing are growing in popularity and equipment can be rented at resorts. Most of Lebanon's trekking clubs also organise snow-shoeing day trips in winter. See Trekking (right) for more information.

For up-to-date information on the resorts, snow conditions and snow-cams, check www.skileb.com. For more details on ski resorts in Lebanon see the individual boxed texts for Ski Facts: Qanat Bakiche & Zaarour (p273); Faraya Mzaar (p274); Laklouk (p291); and The Cedars (p314).

Trekking

There are wonderful trekking opportunities in Syria, but currently little in the way of organised trips. The Dead Cities (p200) and the areas around Palmyra (p204) and Krak des Chevaliers (p132) are fantastic for trekking. For an organised trip, you could try **Jasmin Tours** (www.jasmintours.com); see p388 for more information.

Lebanon has fabulous trekking opportunities scattered through its mountains and gorges. There are well-maintained trails in Horsh Ehden Forest Nature Reserve (p312), near Tripoli, and in the Chouf Cedar Reserve (p297). Other popular areas include the Qadisha Valley (p310) and the Adonis Valley (p289).

There are a number of organisations that arrange treks and hikes throughout Lebanon.

Destination Liban (☎ 03-497 762; lucien@intracom.net .lb; 2nd fl, Safi Bldg, Rue Yared, near Rue Monot, Beirut) A travel agency that also arranges trekking and other outdoor activities.

Esprit-Nomade (☎ 03-223 552; www.esprit-nomade .com) Offers trekking, hiking and snow-shoeing, and promotes responsible ecotourism.

Greenline (☎ /fax 01-746 215; www.greenline.org.lb) One of Lebanon's most active environmental organisations, it arranges treks and day trips into the mountains and countryside of Lebanon.

Lebanese Adventure (☎ /fax 01-398 982, 03-360 027; www.lebanese-adventure.com; Sioufi, Achrafiye, Beirut) Arranges different outdoor activities throughout the country each weekend. It also tailors trips for groups (minimum five people).

Liban Trek (☎ 01-329 975; www.libantrek.com; 7th fl, Yazbek B, Rue Adib Ishac, Achrafiye, Beirut) A well-established trekking club that arranges weekend treks throughout Lebanon. It also organises other mountain sports.

Water Sports

Your best bet for water sports in Syria is Lattakia (p143), where the Shaati al-Azraq (Blue Beach) passes for Syria's premier coastal resort. Access to the best stretches of beach is controlled by the Le Meridien and Cham hotels. Both chains hire out pedal boats, jet skis and sailboards.

While much of Lebanon's swimming is from rocks or artificial platforms built out on jetties, there are one or two very pleasant public, sandy beaches. The best can be found in the far south of the country, just south of Tyre (p349) and near Byblos (p284). There is also a public sandy beach in Beirut, Ramlet al-Bayda (p250), but the cleanliness of the water is questionable. All public beaches get crowded on weekends during summer.

The rocky beaches make for good snorkelling and there are often water-sports facilities at the private beach resorts. Water-skiing and sailing are popular during summer and equipment can be rented from most resorts. There are good swimming pools at almost all the larger top-end hotels and resorts. Expect to pay between US$5 and US$25 per person per day, depending on the level of luxury.

For surfers, Batroun (p287) is where you'll find the closest thing to a community of like-minded individuals. Surfers should check out www.wannasurf.com/spot/Middle_East/Lebanon/ for more information on surfing spots around the country, and windsurfers can log on to www.batrounwindsurfers.cjb.net/ for details. Unfortunately, the best time of year (for the best waves) is also the coldest and most board-sports enthusiasts' thoughts are turning towards the snow.

BUSINESS HOURS
Syria

Government offices are generally open 8am to 2pm Saturday to Thursday, give or take an hour, and embassies and consulates are closed Saturday. Other offices and shops keep similar hours in the morning and often open again 4pm to 6pm or 7pm. Most restaurants but only a few small traders will stay open on Friday. Banks generally follow the government office hours, but there are quite a few exceptions; some branches keep their doors open 9am to noon, while some exchange booths are open as late as 7pm.

OPEN SESAME

Where possible, we've indicated throughout this book opening times of places of interest. However, often the reality on the ground is that sites open when the ticket office or guardian feels like it. On a good day they will be there an hour early, on a bad day they won't turn up at all. All opening hours must be prefaced, therefore, with a hopeful *in sha' Allah*.

Post offices close at 8pm in Damascus and Aleppo (where they are open on Friday, too); in smaller cities post offices close at 2pm. As a rule, telephone offices are open much longer hours (eg 24 hours in Damascus). Principal museums and monuments are open 9am to 6pm in summer, to 4pm from October to the end of March, while others are generally open 8am to 2pm. Most are closed on Tuesday.

Lebanon

Government offices, including post offices, are open 8am to 2pm Monday to Saturday, except Friday when the opening hours are 8am to 11am (however, you'll rarely find anyone at work before 9.30am). Banks are open 8.30am to 12.30pm Monday to Saturday. Shops and private businesses open 9am to 6pm Monday to Saturday. Many grocery stores keep later hours and open on Sunday, too. In summer many places close around 3pm. Most museums and monuments generally close Monday. There are no set restaurant hours. We've indicated these throughout the book where possible.

CHILDREN

Children are much-loved and fussed over in the Middle East and bringing along kids will open doors and guarantee you make new friends. For babies and young children, major brands of disposable nappies, baby foods and powdered milk are easily available, as is bottled water. It is a good idea to avoid travel at the height of summer (July and August) or in the middle of winter (late December to early February), as the extremes of heat and cold could make your family journey unpleasant. For the heat in summer, sunhats and maximum protection sun block are an absolute must. For winter, keeping kids warm and dry can be a challenge. See When to Go (p9) for details on the best times to visit.

Kids already eating solids shouldn't have many problems. Cooked meat dishes, the various dips (eg hummus), rice and the occasional Western-style burger or pizza, along with fruit (washed and peeled) should all be OK as a nutritional basis. Nuts are also a good, safe source of protein.

A potential worry is the high incidence of diarrhoea and stomach problems that travellers experience in the Middle East. If your kids get sick, keep in mind that children dehydrate far more quickly than adults and it is crucial to keep giving them liquids even if they just throw them up again. It's worth having some rehydration salts on hand just in case (they do double duty as an effective hangover cure). For more advice on health matters when travelling with children in the region, see p401.

For more comprehensive advice on the dos and don'ts of taking the kids away with you, see Lonely Planet's *Travel with Children* by Cathy Lanigan (foreword by Maureen Wheeler).

Practicalities

The larger chain hotels in both countries are well used to catering for families. Cots can be booked in these hotels, and baby-sitting facilities are available. Safety seats are available when hiring cars but generally not for taxis. Most good restaurants have high chairs, but dedicated nappy-changing facilities are scarce.

Sights & Activities

The open spaces of tourist sights can provide ample opportunities for children to expend some of that boundless energy.

While in Syria, outside of Damascus, the hotels and beaches of Lattakia (p143) are notable for water-based children's activities. See also Damascus for Children (p101) for other details on keeping the kids entertained.

While in Beirut, finding space for children to run is something of a challenge, but not impossible – see Beirut for Children (p252) for details.

Away from town, **Animal Encounter** (☎ 05-558 724, 03-667 355) in Aley, on the road to the Bekaa, is a nonprofit shelter for injured and orphaned wild animals and birds. It aims to educate adults and children about Lebanon's fauna and the importance of preserving its natural habitat. Whenever possible the rehabilitated animals are released back into the wild. The centre gets more than 40,000 visitors a year and more than half are school-age children. Contact founders Mounir or Diana Abi-Said for more information. The child-friendly Jeita Grotto (p277) also makes for a good excursion with children. If it's hot, you can take the kids to Splash Mountain in Beit Mery (p269), which has water slides and other water games.

If you want to get rid of your little darlings for a few days, La Reserve (p290), near the

Afqa Grotto, runs 12-day summer camps for children aged six to 15. Children participate in a wide variety of activities, including learning about the environment, visiting local archaeological sites and, of course, fun stuff like making mud sculptures, playing games and watching films.

CLIMATE CHARTS

Syria

Temperatures range widely from blistering summer peaks to snow-laden winter troughs. During summer proper (June to August) daily highs average around 35°C on the coast and inland in the fertile hinterland where most of the population lives. However, get out east into the desert and that rises to an average 40°C and highs of 46°C are not uncommon. In Damascus, the winter (December to February) daily average temperature might be 10°C, although it can get colder

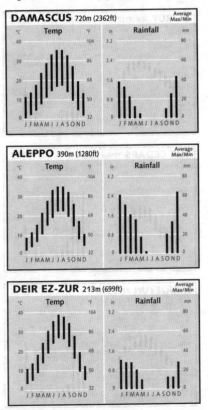

and snow is not uncommon. You certainly get snow on the higher peaks and it's even been known to fall as far east as Palmyra.

Lebanon

It's not surprising that the weather here varies quite considerably from region to region given its diverse topography. Broadly speaking, Lebanon has three different climate zones – the coastal strip, the mountains and the Bekaa Valley.

The coastal strip has cool, rainy winters (mid-December to February) and hot Mediterranean summers (June to September). The Mt Lebanon Range can concentrate the summer heat and humidity on the coast to a stifling degree. During the spring (March to May) and autumn (October until mid-December) the weather on the coast is warm and dry with occasional showers. October and April can see very heavy rainfall.

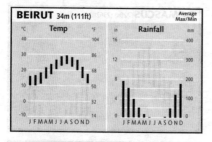

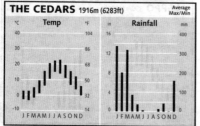

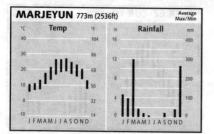

The mountains have a typical alpine climate; fresh breezes keep the summer heat comfortable, which is why many people head to the mountains to escape the oppressive heat during the summer months. There is heavy winter snow, which lasts from December to May on the higher peaks. At certain times of year you can stand on the warm coast and look inland at snow-covered peaks. The brochure clichés are true: it is indeed possible to go skiing in the morning and swimming in the afternoon, although few people actually do it. The Bekaa Valley has hot, dry summers and cold, dry winters with snow and frost. The valley is set between two parallel mountain ranges and the wind can blow fiercely, especially in winter.

COURSES

Language courses are the most popular courses given in both countries, but keep in mind these are generally geared to those intending to live and study in Syria or Lebanon. For details on courses in Damascus see p101, and for Beirut and other cities in Lebanon see p252.

CUSTOMS
Syria

Customs officials seem very interested in hi-tech electronic gear. Items such as video cameras and laptop computers may incur heavy taxes, or they may be written into your passport to ensure they leave the country with you and are not sold. Video (and even audio) cassettes or discs may also come under scrutiny. If you are carrying this sort of thing it's better not to be too obvious about it.

The duty-free allowance is 200 cigarettes and 1L of wine or spirits, or 100 cigarettes and 2L of wine or spirits.

Lebanon

There is no problem bringing most items into Lebanon, such as cameras, videos or computers, and there is no censorship of books and magazines. Duty-free allowances are 400 cigarettes and one bottle of spirits or 200 cigarettes and two bottles of spirits.

DANGERS & ANNOYANCES

The main danger and annoyance common to both countries is the driving style. Those arriving from a country where the act of changing lanes dangerously can be the start of a road-rage incident will find the chaos coupled with courtesy either refreshing or life-threatening. In Lebanon particularly, little things like lane markers and traffic lights are treated with derision – akin to advice from someone you don't particularly trust. If you are driving, try to relax and get into the swing of it. If you're a pedestrian, never relax – you're the last thing most drivers are thinking about.

Syria

Despite being depicted by the US administration and Western media as a terrorist training ground, Syria is an extremely safe country in which to travel. You can walk around virtually anywhere, at any time of the day or night without any problems. Syrians are friendly and hospitable and if someone invites you to their village or home you should accept their offer.

The general absence of theft is one of the most refreshing things about travelling in Syria. This is no excuse for inviting trouble through carelessness, but at least you don't have to keep a hawk-like watch over your stuff as you do in other parts of the world.

The one niggle is overcharging. Independent travellers who have found their feet and at least look as though they know what they are doing will usually pay the standard price for transport, food etc, but in the end, few completely avoid the odd petty rip-off – a sad and perhaps inevitable by-product of increasing tourist traffic. Remember to keep in perspective the amount that you have been cheated out of and keep in mind that it doesn't matter if you're a sandal-wearing kid on a gap-year trek with one change of clothes and S£200 in your pocket. By comparison, you're rich.

Lebanon

For a country that was lost in violent anarchy little more than a decade ago, it is amazing how safe Lebanon has become. Since the disarming and disbanding of the militias in the early 1990s, it has become possible to travel anywhere day or night without worries about security. There are frequent Lebanese and less frequent Syrian army checkpoints on the roads and occasionally you may be required to show your passport. This is usually just a formality but make sure you always carry it with you.

Currently, the main dangers to visitors wandering through the Lebanese countryside are land mines and unexploded ordnance. UN experts estimate that there are more than 100,000 and other explosive devices scattered over the area that was occupied by the Israelis for over 20 years (see the boxed text Warning, p339). Do not wander off tracks, particularly in remote areas, and check with locals if you're unsure.

Theft is a minor problem, but random crime is far lower than in most Western cities, although there has been a spate of motor-scooter bag snatchings. Power outages still occur occasionally in Beirut, but the duration of the outages is generally only a couple of minutes or so.

DISABLED TRAVELLERS
Syria

Generally speaking, scant regard is paid to the needs of disabled travellers in Syria. Steps, high kerbs and other assorted obstacles are everywhere, streets are often badly rutted and uneven, roads are made virtually uncrossable by heavy traffic, while many doorways are low and narrow. Ramps and specially equipped lodgings and toilets are an extreme rarity. You will have to plan your trip carefully and will probably be obliged to restrict yourself to luxury-level hotels and private, hired transport.

Lebanon

Considering the number of people who were disabled during the civil war, it is curious that Lebanon is not more disabled-friendly. Disabled people are rarely seen on the street, which is not surprising given the difficulties of navigating the potholes, rubble and anarchic traffic. Buildings and archaeological sites do not have wheelchair ramps and bathrooms are generally not modified for access. The exception is the newly constructed inner city, which has Braille in lifts (elevators) and wide-access doors.

DISCOUNT CARDS

There are no discount cards for seniors in either country.

Student Cards
SYRIA

Student cards get huge reductions on site fees which, after accommodation, are the major expense when travelling in Syria. The standard admission fee for museums and archaeological sites is S£300 (about US$6) but with a student card this drops to S£15 (US$0.30). Ticket officials are getting increasingly fussy about which kinds of cards they will accept. Student IDs issued by your college or university have a good chance of being rebuffed; you really need an International Student Identification Card (ISIC), or something similar that carries a photo and signature.

LEBANON
ISICs are of little use in Lebanon. Student discounts at archaeological sites and museums are only available to Lebanese students or children under 12.

EMBASSIES & CONSULATES
It's important to realise what your own embassy – the embassy of the country of which you are a citizen – can and can't do to help you if you get into trouble. Generally speaking, it won't be much help in emergencies if the trouble you're in is remotely your own fault. Remember that you are bound by the laws of the country you are in. Your embassy will not be sympathetic if you end up in jail after committing a crime locally, even if such actions are legal in your own country.

In genuine emergencies you might get some assistance, but only if other channels have been exhausted. For example, if you need to get home urgently, a free ticket home is unlikely – the embassy would expect you to have insurance. If you have all your money and documents stolen, it might assist with getting a new passport, but a loan for onward travel is out of the question.

Some embassies used to keep letters for travellers or have a small reading room with home newspapers, but these days the mail holding service has usually been stopped and even newspapers tend to be out of date.

Syria
SYRIAN EMBASSIES & CONSULATES
Following are Syrian embassies and consulates in major cities around the world.

Australia Melbourne (☎ 03-9347 8445, fax 9347 8447; 57 Cardigan St, Carlton, Melbourne, Vic 3053); Sydney (☎ 02-9597 7714, fax 9597 2226; 10 Belmore St, Arncliffe, Sydney, NSW 2205)

Canada Ottawa (☎ 613-569 5556, fax 569 3800; 151 Slater St, Suite 1000, Ottawa, Ontario K1P 5H3)

Egypt Cairo (☎ 02-337 7020, fax 335 8232; 18 Abdel Rahim Sabry, Doqqi, Cairo, Egypt; ⊙ 8am-1pm Sat-Thu)

France Paris (☎ 01 40 62 61 00) 20 Rue Vaneau, 75007 Paris)

Germany Berlin (☎ 030-220 20 46; Otto Grotewohl Str 3, Berlin); Bonn (☎ 0228-81 99 20, fax 81 92 99; Andreas Hermes Str 5, D-53175 Bonn); Hamburg (☎ 040-30 90 54 14, fax 30 90 52 33; Brooktor 11, 20457 Hamburg)

Jordan Amman (☎ 06-641392; Sharia Afghani, Jebel Amman)

Netherlands The Hague (☎ 070-346 9795; Laan van Meerdervoort 53d, 2517 AE Den Haag)

Turkey Ankara (☎ 312-440 9658; 40 Sedat Simari Sokak, Cankaya, Ankara); İstanbul (☎ 212-248 2735; 3 Silahhane Caddesi [aka Maçka Caddesi], Ralli Apt 59, İstanbul)

UK London (☎ 020-7245 9012, fax 7235 4621; 8 Belgrave Square, London SW1 8PH)

USA Washington (☎ 202-232 6313; 2215 Wyoming Ave NW, Washington DC 20008); New York (☎ 212-661 1313; 820 2nd Ave, New York, NY 10017); Newport Beach (☎ 949-640 9888; Newport Beach, CA)

EMBASSIES & CONSULATES IN SYRIA
Note: at present the Canadian embassy provides consular services to Australian citizens in case of emergency, while citizens from Ireland and New Zealand are looked after by the UK. All the following countries are represented in Damascus.

Belgium (Map p78; ☎ 011-333 2821, fax 333 0426; Sharia al-Jalaa, Abu Roumana)

Canada (☎ 011-611 6692, fax 611 4000; www.canembdam .org; Block 12, Autostraad al-Mezze) About 4km west of city centre.

Egypt (Map pp80-1; ☎ 011-333 3561, fax 333 7961; Sharia al-Jalaa, Abu Roumana)

France (Map p97; ☎ 011-332 7992; Sharia Ata Ayyubi, Salihiyya)

Germany (Map p78; ☎ 011-332 3800/1, fax 332 3812; 53 Sharia Ibrahim Hanano)

Iran (☎ 011-222 6459, fax 222 0997; Autostraad al-Mezze) About 4km west of city centre.

Jordan (Map pp80-1; ☎ 011-333 4642, fax 333 6741; Sharia al-Jalaa, Abu Roumana)

Netherlands (Map p78; ☎ 011-333 6871, fax 333 9369; Sharia al-Jalaa, Abu Roumana)

Turkey (Map pp80-1; ☎ 011-333 1411; 58 Sharia Ziad bin Abi Soufian)

UK (Map pp80-1; ☎ 011-373 9241/2/3/7, fax 373 1600; www.fco.gov.uk; 11 Sharia Mohammed Kurd Ali, Malki)

USA (Map pp80-1; ☎ 011-333 1342, fax 224 7938; www .usembassy.state.gov/damascus; 2 Sharia al-Mansour, Abu Roumana)

Lebanon

LEBANESE EMBASSIES & CONSULATES

Visas are available at all Lebanese foreign missions.

Australia Canberra (☎ 02-6295 7378, fax 6239 7024; 27 Endeavour St, Red Hill, ACT 2603); Sydney (☎ 02-9361 5449, fax 9360 7657; Level 5, 70 William St, Sydney, NSW 2000) Issues visas to NSW residents only; Melbourne (☎ 03-9529 4588; 117 Wellington St, Windsor, Melbourne, Vic 3181) Issues visas to Victorian residents only.

Canada Ottawa (☎ 613-236 5825, fax 232 1609; 640 Lyon St, KIS 3Z5 Ottawa, Ontario); Montreal (☎ 514-276 2638, fax 276 0090; 40 Chemin Côte Ste Catherine, H2V-2A2-PQ, Montreal 153)

Egypt Cairo (☎ 02-738 2823/5, fax 738 2818; 22 Mansour Mohamed St, Zamalek, Cairo) Alexandria (☎ 03-484 6589; 64 Rue de la Liberté, Alexandria)

France Paris (☎ 01 40 67 75 75, fax 01 40 67 16 42; 3 Villa Copernic, Paris 75016); Marseille (☎ 04 91 71 50 60, fax 04 91 77 26 75; 424 Rue Paradis, Marseille 13008)

Germany Berlin (☎ 4930-474 9860, fax 474 9866; Berlinerstrasse 126-127, 13187 Berlin)

Italy Rome (☎ 06-844 05 21, fax 841 17 94; Via Giacomo Carissimi 38, Rome 00198); Milan (☎ 02-86 45 45 40, fax 72 00 04 68; 26 Via Larga, Milan 20122)

Jordan Amman (☎ 592 9111/4, fax 592 2333; Sharia Mohammed Ali Bdeir, Abdoun, Amman)

Netherlands The Hague (☎ 070-365 8906, fax 362 0779; 2 Frederick St, The Hague 2514)

Spain Madrid (☎ 01-345 1370, fax 345 5631; 178 Paseo de la Castellana, 28046 Madrid)

Turkey Ankara (☎ 312-446 7487, fax 446 1033; 44 Kizculesi Sokak, Çankaya, Ankara); İstanbul (☎ 212-236 1365, fax 227 3373; Tesvikiye Caddesi, Sary Apt 134/1, 80200 Tesvikiye, İstanbul)

UK London (☎ 020-7229 7265/6, fax 7243 1699; 21 Palace Gardens Mews, London W8 4RA) Consular Section (☎ 020-7727 6696; 15 Palace Gardens Mews)

USA Washington (☎ 202-939 6300, fax 939 6324; 2560 28th St NW, Washington, DC 20008); Los Angeles (☎ 213-467 1253, fax 467 2935; Ste 510, 7060 Hollywood Blvd, Los Angeles, CA 90028); New York (☎ 212-744 7905/6, fax 794 1510; 9 East 76th St, NYC, New York 10021)

EMBASSIES & CONSULATES IN LEBANON

Nationals of New Zealand should contact the UK embassy. Embassies and consulates in Lebanon include:

Australia (Map pp244-5; ☎ 01-374 701, fax 374 709; Farra Bldg, Rue Bliss, Ras Beirut)

Canada (☎ 04-521 163/4/5; Coolrite Bldg, Jal al-Dib)

Egypt (Map p238; ☎ 01-862 932, 867 917; Rue Thomas Edison, Ramlet al-Bayda, Beirut)

France (Map p238; ☎ 01-616 730/5; Mar Takla, Hazmieh, Beirut)

Germany (☎ 04-914 444; Mataileb, Rabieh)

Italy (Map p248; ☎ 01-340 225/6/7; Cosmides Bldg, Rue Makdissi, Hamra, Beirut)

Jordan (☎ 05-922 500/1; Rue Elias Helou, Baabda)

Netherlands (Map p251; ☎ 01-204 663; 9th fl, ABM Amro Bldg, Achrafiye, Beirut)

Spain (☎ 05-464 120/1, fax 352 448; Palace Chehab, Hadath)

Turkey (☎ 04-520 929; Tobi Bldg, Rue 3, Zone II, Rabieh)

UK (Map p248; ☎ 01-990400, Serail Hill, Downtown, Beirut)

USA (☎ 04-417 774, 403 300, fax 407 112; Awkar, facing the Municipality, PO Box 70-840 Antelias)

FESTIVALS & EVENTS

Syria

APRIL & MAY

Spring Flower Festival Held in Hama during the last two weeks of April; expect lots of colour, people promenading through into the early hours of the morning, temporary markets, and the sluices open so that the fast-flowing Orontes gets the huge waterwheels turning.

Palmyra Festival Held around the end of April or early May, the desert ruins are the venue for a popular annual folk festival with horse and camel racing during the day, and music and dance performances in the ancient theatre (part of the civic centre) by night. For more information see the boxed text Palmyra Festival, p211.

International Flower Show Held in Damascus.

JULY

Cotton Festival Held in Aleppo, this festival celebrates the cotton harvest.

SEPTEMBER

Bosra Festival Held every odd-numbered year, it's a festival of music and theatre, noteworthy for the chance of being part of an audience in the town's spectacular Roman theatre-cum-Citadel.

Silk Road Festival Held late September, it celebrates Syria's long cultural history with events in Aleppo, Damascus and Palmyra.

Suweida Apple & Vine Festival Held in late September, this festival celebrates the annual harvest.

NOVEMBER & DECEMBER

Damascus International Film Festival Held every odd-numbered year, it shows an eclectic range of films, including many pan-Arab productions. There's also a theatre festival.

Lebanon

These days it seems that no large town in Lebanon is worth its salt without some sort of festival in one of its floodlit ancient sites. All of which is very good news for music and dance lovers. Many towns and villages have their own small festivals, which can be anything from local fairs to folkloric performances.

FEBRUARY

Al Bustan Festival (www.albustanfestival.com) An annual event held for five weeks in Beit Mery. Daily events feature opera, chamber music, and orchestral concerts.

JULY & AUGUST

Baalbek Festival (www.baalbeck.org.lb) Annual artistic event held in the historical Roman ruins in Baalbek in the Bekaa Valley. Features opera, jazz, poetry and pop, and stages theatre productions.

Beiteddine Festival (www.beiteddine.org.lb) Music, dance and theatre held in the beautiful courtyard of the Beiteddine Palace.

Byblos International Festival (www.byblosfestival.org) Held in August among the wonderful ruins of Byblos' ancient harbour – includes jazz pop, classic and world music, and opera.

OCTOBER

Beirut International Marathon (www.beirutmarathon .org) Held in early October, it includes wheelchair events, a 10km-long run, a minimarathon, and other marathon events.

Mid East Film Festival Beirut (www.beirutfilmfound ation.org) This festival showcases films from Lebanon and the Middle East, and aims to encourage co-productions between the Arab and international communities.

FOOD

Eating in Syria and Lebanon is a real treat and exceptionally good food is available all the way from the street stall to the very best restaurant. Street food is excellent, and very cheap; there is an abundance of snack bars selling chicken or meat *shwarma* (seasoned and spit-roasted meat) or felafel made up into delicious sandwiches. In Syria, a street *shwarma* costs around S£25 and fresh juices cost between S£35 and S£50. In Lebanon you can expect to pay around LL2000 for a medium-sized *shwarma* and about LL3000 for a fresh juice.

A traditional restaurant meal starts with mezze, which usually constitutes a selection of hot and cold starters. These can be quite simple or very elaborate. Some are so filling that you could easily forgo a main course altogether. There are enough meatless dishes to satisfy vegetarians; there are usually aubergine or cheese dishes and often pulses or beans. In Syria a mezze dish costs between S£20 and S£30 at all but the

best restaurants. In Lebanon, expect to pay between LL2000 and LL3000 for a mezze.

Main courses are usually chicken, lamb or fish grilled with rice and salad (or the ubiquitous French fries) served with flat bread. In Syria, expect to pay around S£60 to S£100 for a decent grill – sometimes more at a top-end restaurant. In Lebanon, LL6000 to LL8000 gets you a good grill in all but the most expensive places.

When eating out in both countries, you may order as many or as few dishes as you choose. It is quite acceptable to just order a range of mezze. As a general rule, three or four mezze dishes per person should be plenty for a good lunch or dinner; two mezze dishes each is usually enough if you are ordering a main course as well.

For more details on the cuisines of Syria and Lebanon, see Food & Drink, p62.

GAY & LESBIAN TRAVELLERS
Syria

Homosexuality is prohibited in Syria and conviction can result in imprisonment. In fact, the public position is that homosexuality doesn't exist in Syria, but of course it's no less prevalent than anywhere else in the world. However, discretion is advised.

That said, in his travelogue *Cleopatra's Wedding Present* (2003) the late Robert Tewdwr Moss describes a few months in Syria during which time he was anything but discreet about his homosexuality, and neither were many Syrians he met (for more information see also p10).

Lebanon

There is a thriving, if clandestine, gay and lesbian scene in Lebanon, largely concentrated in Beirut. It's the most open capital in the Middle East. For more information see Gay & Lesbian Beirut, p254.

However, homosexuality is illegal under Lebanese law so discretion is advised. It also pays to be discreet when checking into a double hotel room. As a basic rule, the Muslim areas tend to be more conservative than the Christian ones. Tripoli, is perhaps the exception as there is a flourishing 'underground' scene there. Openly gay venues tend to be shut down if they advertise as such, but a number of clubs are gay-friendly. The beaches near Byblos (p284) are also popular gay hang-outs.

HOLIDAYS
Islamic Religious Holidays

All Islamic holidays throughout the region are celebrated within the framework of the Muslim calendar, while secular activities are planned according to the Christian system.

The Muslim year is based on the lunar cycle and is divided into 12 lunar months, each with 29 or 30 days. Consequently, the Muslim year is 10 or 11 days shorter than the Christian solar year, and the Muslim festivals gradually move around the Western year, completing the cycle in roughly 33 years.

Year zero in the Muslim calendar was when Mohammed and his followers fled from Mecca to Medina (AD 622 in the Christian calendar). This Hejira, or migration, is taken to mark the start of the new Muslim era, much as Christ's birth marks year zero in the Christian calendar.

Eid al-Adha Also known as Eid al-Kebir, the 'great feast', this marks the time of the haj, the pilgrimage to Mecca. The haj culminates in the ritual slaughter of a lamb (in commemoration of Ibrahim's sacrifice) at Mina. This marks the end of the pilgrimage and the beginning of Eid al-Adha, or Feast of Sacrifice. Those who can afford to, buy a sheep to slaughter on the day of the feast, which lasts for three days (although many businesses reopen on the second day). Many families also head out of town, so if you intend travelling at this time secure your tickets well in advance.

Ras as-Sana Islamic New Year's Day (literally 'head of the year'). This day is celebrated on the first day of the Hejira calendar year, 1 Moharram. The whole country has the day off but celebrations are low-key.

Ashura This is the day of public mourning observed by the Shiites on 10 Moharram. It commemorates the assassination of Imam Hussein ibn Ali, grandson of the Prophet Mohammed, which led to the permanent schism between Sunnis and Shiites.

Moulid an-Nabi Feast celebrating the birthday of the Prophet Mohammed on 12 Rabi' al-Awal. One of the major holidays of the year – the streets are a feast of lights. For a long time this was not celebrated at all in the Arab world.

Ramadan The ninth month of the Muslim calendar, the month in which the Quran was first revealed. From dawn until dusk, Muslims are expected to abstain from eating, drinking, smoking and sexual activity. Those who are engaged in heavy physical work, travellers or nursing mothers are considered exempt, although they are expected to make up the fast at a later time. Although many Muslims do not follow the injunctions to the letter, most conform to some extent. Non-Muslims are not expected to observe the fast, but it is good manners not to eat and smoke in public. At sunset there is the *iftar*, or breaking of the fast, which is always a bit of a celebration. In some parts of town, tables are laid out in the street as charitable acts by the wealthy to provide food for the less fortunate. Evenings are imbued with a party atmosphere and there's plenty of street entertainment which often goes throughout the night until sunrise. Although there are no public holidays until Eid al-Fitr, it is difficult to get anything done because of erratic hours. Almost everything closes in the afternoon or has shorter daytime hours; this does not apply to businesses that cater to foreign tourists, but some restaurants and hotels may be closed for the entire month.

Eid al-Fitr A three-day feast (often longer) that marks the end of Ramadan. Similar in nature to Eid al-Adha. Generally, everything shuts down during this holiday.

Public Holidays

The Islamic holidays (and Christian Easter) change each year. Below are the fixed public holidays.

SYRIA

Most holidays are either religious (Islamic and Christian) or celebrations of important dates in the formation of modern Syria.

New Year's Day (1 January) Official national holiday but many businesses stay open.

Orthodox Christmas (7 January) A fairly low-key affair and only Orthodox businesses are closed for the day.

Commemoration of the Revolution (8 March) Celebrates the coming to power of the Arab Ba'ath Socialist Party.

Easter (March/April) Different dates each year. The most important date on the Christian calendar.

Commemoration of the Evacuation (17 April) Celebrates the end of French occupation in Syria.

May Day (1 May) Official national holiday.

Martyrs' Day (6 May) Celebrates all political martyrs who died for Syria.

ISLAMIC HOLIDAYS					
Hejira Year	**New Year**	**Prophet's Birthday**	**Ramadan**	**Eid al-Fitr**	**Eid al-Adha**
1425	22 Feb 04	2 May 04	15 Oct 04	14 Nov 04	21 Jan 05
1426	10 Feb 05	21 Apr 05	4 Oct 05	3 Nov 05	10 Jan 06
1427	31 Jan 06	11 Apr 06	24 Sep 06	24 Oct 06	31 Dec 06
1428	20 Jan 07	31 Mar 07	13 Sep 07	13 Oct 07	20 Dec 07

THE HAJ

The haj, or pilgrimage to Mecca, is the fifth pillar of Islam (see also the boxed text The Five Pillars of Islam, p44) and it is the duty of all Muslims to perform at least one haj in their lifetime. The traditional time for the haj is during the month of Zuul-Hijja, the 12th month of the Muslim year.

The high point of the pilgrimage is the visit to the Kaaba, the construction housing the stone of Ibrahim in the centre of the haram, the sacred area into which non-Muslims are forbidden to enter. The pilgrims, dressed only in a plain white robe, circle the Kaaba seven times and kiss the black stone. This is only one of a series of acts of devotion carried out by pilgrims.

The haj culminates in the ritual slaughter of a lamb (in commemoration of Ibrahim's sacrifice) at Mina. This marks the end of the pilgrimage and the beginning of Eid al-Adha, or Feast of Sacrifice. Throughout the Islamic world the act of sacrifice is repeated and the streets of towns and cities seem to run with the blood of slaughtered sheep. It is customary to give part of the sheep to the poor. The holiday runs from 10 to 13 Zuul-Hijja. The returned pilgrim can then be addressed as *haji*.

LEBANON

New Year's Day (1 January)
Feast of Mar Maroun (9 February)
Easter (March/April) Different dates each year. The most important date on the Christian calendar.
Qana Day (18 April)
Labour Day (1 May)
Martyrs' Day (6 May)
Assumption (15 August)
All Saints' Day (1 November)
Independence Day (22 November)
Christmas Day (25 December)

INSURANCE

Whichever way you're travelling, make sure you take out a comprehensive travel insurance policy that covers you for medical expenses and luggage theft or loss, and for cancellation of (or delays in) your travel arrangements. Ticket loss should also be included, but make sure you have a separate record of all the details, or better still, a photocopy of the ticket.

Travel insurance to cover theft, loss and medical is a good idea. Some policies specifically exclude dangerous activities, which can include scuba diving, motorcycling, snow-sports and even trekking. If you plan on doing any of these things, make sure the policy you choose fully covers you for your activity of choice.

You may prefer a policy that pays doctors or hospitals direct rather than you having to pay on the spot and claim later. If you have to claim later make sure you keep all documentation. Check that the policy covers ambulances or an emergency flight home.

For information on insurance matters relating to cars, see p384. The international student travel policies handled by **STA Travel** (www.statravel.com) and other student travel organisations are usually good value.

INTERNET ACCESS

Email and Internet addicts will find it possible to get connected while in Syria or Lebanon. For a list of useful websites, see p12.

Syria

Thanks to president Bashir al-Assad, the Internet flood gates have been opened and allowed Syrians access to the Internet (for details see the boxed text Internet for Everybody, opposite). Online activity has taken off in a huge way and every major town has at least two or three Internet cafés, with more on the way. Bear in mind that many of these places are recently established and some of them are bound to fail and disappear.

To date there are only a few national Internet Service Providers (ISPs), meaning information transfer is painfully slow. Costs are typically S£100 (US$2) per hour. If you are travelling around with your own laptop then you can get connected in some of the better hotels by using an RJ-11 standard telephone plug connector. At the time of writing there was no wireless Internet available in Syria.

Lebanon

There are Internet cafés in all Lebanese cities and in many smaller towns. Most charge between LL2000 and LL6000 per hour. If you don't have a Web-based service, remember that you'll need your incoming (POP or IMAP) mail server name, your account name and your password. Your ISP or network supervisor will be able to give you these. It pays to become familiar with the process of doing this before you leave home. One option is to open a free ekno Web-based account online at www.e kno.lonelyplanet.com. You can then access your mail from anywhere in the world from any Internet-connected machine running a standard Web browser.

If you're staying long-term, the country now has more than a dozen ISPs; here are three reputable ones:

Cyberia (☎ 01-744 101; www.thisiscyberia.com)
Libancom (☎ 01-877 202; www.libancom.com.lb)
Terranet (☎ 01-577 511; www.terra.net.lb)

If you plan to carry a laptop computer with you, remember that Lebanon's electricity supply is unstable, and power surges pose a real risk to your equipment. Most Lebanese run their equipment off voltage regulators, which are far too cumbersome for travelling. Ensure that your adaptor can handle higher than 220 volts (most laptop adaptors can take up to 240 volts) and don't leave the computer plugged in any longer than necessary.

Also, keep in mind that your PC-card modem may or may not work once you leave your home country – and you won't know for sure until you try. If you're not sure, the safest option is to buy a reputable 'global' modem before you leave home. Lebanon tends to have US-style phone sockets so check to see if you need an adaptor. For more information

on travelling with a portable computer, check out the website www.teleadapt.com. Wireless Internet cafés may start to flourish – try **Casper & Gambini** (Map p248; ☎ 01-983 666, 03 423 777; Rue al Maarad, Downtown; ◷ 9am-1am) in Beirut. Note as well that if you have a network card in your laptop, most listed Internet cafés in Beirut will let you use it to surf the Net at no extra charge than the hourly rate.

LEGAL MATTERS

Tourists should have few opportunities to get to know the legal system personally. Drug smuggling, long a problem in Lebanon, has been heavily clamped down on and carrying any kind of narcotics (including marijuana/hash) is a foolish undertaking. If you are caught in possession in either country, you could well wind up doing a heavy jail sentence. If you do cross the law in any way, remember that your embassy can do little to help other than contacting your relatives and recommending local lawyers.

MAPS

The best map is one produced by Freytag & Berndt – distinguished by its red and green cover. It covers the country at a scale of 1: 800,000 but also carries very good city plans of Damascus and Aleppo. It's widely available in Syria where it's published under licence by **Librairie Avicenne** (Map pp84-5; ☎ 011-224 4477; 4 Sharia Attuhami, Damascus; ◷ 9am-2pm & 4.30-8.30pm Sat-Thu) and costs S£250 (roughly US$5). There's also another, less-good sheet map put

---

INTERNET FOR EVERYBODY

Before the year 2000, Syria was steadfastly skirting the information superhighway. It was one of the few countries in the world without Internet connections – or for that matter, a mobile-phone network. All that has changed with the accession to power of Bashir al-Assad. Before stepping up to be president he was already using his position as head of the Syrian Computer Society to push for the introduction of computer training in the country. Now that he's the man at the top his ambitions have grown accordingly and he wants – in the words of an official statement – 'Internet for everyone in Syria'.

Consequently, in what can only be good news for travellers, as well as Internet-deprived locals, the government is in the process of expanding connections. The stated aim is for everyone to have access to email and to the full spectrum of international websites, except of course, to any that the government deems unethical or immoral. This being Syria, 'unethical' is a wide category that currently embraces all kinds of sites including those pernicious American 'mindwarpers' Yahoo! and MSN Hotmail. But don't worry, the kids have already found myriad ways around this – visit any Internet café and they can hook you up to any mail server you like. Several even have Hotmail as their home page.

out by GEO Projects, based in Beirut, on a scale of 1:1,000,000, also with city plans.

The tourist offices throughout Syria have free city and regional maps but these are generally way out of date and of very little use.

The best map of Beirut is published by GEO Projects. It publishes two different maps: a dedicated Beirut map and a larger Lebanon map with one side featuring Beirut. There is also a commercial map, published by **All Prints** (Map pp244-5; ☎ 01-342 009; Rue Jeanne d'Arc, Hamra, Beirut), which has a good city map of Beirut on the reverse. English and French versions are available.

MONEY
Lebanon

The currency in Lebanon is the Lebanese lira (LL), known locally as the Lebanese pound. The currency suffered from galloping inflation during the civil war and low denomination coins (piastres) are now virtually worthless. There are LL250 and LL500 coins still in circulation.

The notes are of the following denominations: 50, 100, 250, 500, 1000, 5000, 10,000, 20,000, 50,000 and 100,000, but you will rarely need anything smaller than 1000. US dollars are accepted virtually everywhere and the two are virtually interchangeable (for this reason both US$ and LL prices are given in this book). Many shops and restaurants display prices only in US dollars, however they will give you your change in either currency.

For details of exchange rates see the inside front cover of this guide.

ATMS

There are ATMs throughout the country and all dispense cash in either US dollars or Lebanese pounds. As always, though, keep some extra cash with you as insurance.

CASH

If you're travelling with US dollars you only need to exchange a small amount into lira for tipping, service taxis etc. Stick to US$50 and US$20, and also US$1 bills for tipping and small items. Note that worn or torn US notes may not be accepted.

Most banks will exchange cash if it is in British pounds or US dollars. There are many banks in the capital and all but the smallest village has at least one bank.

There is no black market in Lebanon.

CREDIT CARDS

Credit cards are accepted by almost all hotels with two or more stars, mid-range restaurants and many shops. They will not be accepted by budget hotels and restaurants. Cash advances are easily available in most banks, although transactions are far quicker at ATMs. If you are planning on hiring a car remember that almost all reputable companies will insist on a credit-card deposit.

INTERNATIONAL TRANSFERS

There are **Western Union offices** (in Beirut ☎ 01-391 000) in almost all major towns in Lebanon and they can arrange international transfers. For more information, contact them at their headquarters in Beirut.

MONEYCHANGERS

There are many private exchanges on and around Rue Hamra in Beirut, and all the smaller towns have at least one exchange shop. You may find it a problem changing money in some of the smaller places.

Before using moneychangers try to find out what the current exchange rates are. Either ask at a bank or check the previous day's closing exchange rates in the local newspapers. The rate you'll be offered will never be the same as the published rate, as it includes the moneychanger's commission, but you can always try to bargain with them to bring the rate closer to the published rate. If you're not happy with the rate offered by one moneychanger, try another. The commission varies from 3% to 5% for changing currency.

TIPPING

The general rule is, the more expensive the place the more likely a tip is expected. Waiters in better restaurants generally expect a tip, 10% of the bill is a good benchmark. At four- and five-star hotels it's generally expected that having your luggage taken to your room, for example, will set you back LL1000.

TRAVELLERS CHEQUES

Travellers cheques may be a smart way to change money, but they can be time-consuming, depending on the bank or currency exchange shop you find yourself in. Fees are US$1 per US$50, US$2 per US$100 and US$3 per US$1000 and so on.

Syria

The official currency is the Syrian pound (S£), also called the *lira*. There are 100 piastres (*qirsh*) to a pound but this is redundant because the smallest coin you'll find now is S£1. Other coins come in denominations of two, five, 10 and 25. Notes come in denominations of 50, 100, 200, 500 and 1000.

Common exchange rates are listed on the inside front cover. For information about costs for your trip, see p10.

ATMS

There is now an ATM at the arrivals hall at Damascus airport, one at the Cham Palace in Damascus, several in the centre of Damascus and one in the gold souq. See p83 for details.

Cash advances are officially not possible as the Commercial Bank of Syria (CBS) has no links with international credit-card companies. However, a few individual entrepreneurs carry out transactions via Jordanian or Lebanese banks. Bear in mind that the rate they offer may not be too great. If you do need cash advances ask at any shop displaying a Visa or Amex sign and chances are you'll be pointed in the right direction.

BLACK MARKET

The black market has all but disappeared and when you do encounter people on the street wanting to change money, they offer the same rate as the banks, so what's the point? Out of banking hours, hotel receptions are often willing to change cash or travellers cheques at the going bank rates.

CASH

Bring as much in cash dollars as you're comfortable with. Many mid-range hotels only take US$, ie no local currency, although some will take US$ travellers cheques at a push. Don't forget that if you're flying out, you'll have to pay the departure tax of S£200, so keep just enough tucked away.

CREDIT CARDS

Major credit cards such as Amex, Visa, MasterCard and Diners Club are accepted by top-end hotels, the swishest restaurants and stores, particularly those that enjoy the custom of foreigners. Credit cards are also handy for buying air tickets (as the only alternative is hard currency) and for some car-rental companies (it will save you having to leave a large cash deposit).

MONEYCHANGERS

The banking system in Syria was mostly state-owned, although this is changing now, and its public face is the CBS with at least one branch in every major town. The majority of branches will change cash and travellers cheques in most major currencies but each branch has its own quirks – some charge commission, some don't; some require the bank manager's signature to authorise transactions, some just hand over the cash without any form filling whatsoever. Generally speaking, the smaller the town, the less hassle.

There are also a number of officially sanctioned private exchange offices. These change cash, and sometimes travellers cheques, at official bank rates but generally don't charge commission. The other advantage is that whereas banks usually close for the day at 12.30pm or 2pm, the exchange offices are often open until 7pm.

TIPPING

Baksheesh, or tipping, is not as big a deal in Syria as it is in Egypt or Turkey. Waiters in better restaurants generally expect a tip, and some will help themselves by short-changing you a little, but otherwise a standard 10% of the bill is a good benchmark. Other services are also carried out with a view to being tipped – everything from having your luggage taken to your room to having doors opened for you. In most cases a tip of S£25 is considered more than fair.

TRAVELLERS CHEQUES

While cash is definitely king in Syria, travellers cheques are widely accepted and are obviously the safer alternative. Most major brands of cheque are accepted by the CBS, but you're much safer with widely known types, such as Thomas Cook, Eurocheque or Amex. Some branches of the CBS will charge a minimum one-off commission of S£25 per transaction, whether you change one or several cheques. Occasionally (most notably in Aleppo) you'll be asked to present sales receipts when changing travellers cheques, which of course you are not supposed to have together with the cheques.

PHOTOGRAPHY & VIDEO

Both Syria and Lebanon are photogenic countries with dramatic landscapes and clear Mediterranean light. Dust can be a problem in both countries and it is a good idea to keep your equipment wrapped in a plastic bag, even inside a camera bag. Take a soft lens brush and some camera wipes with you to prevent grit and dust getting inside the works. A flash gun is useful if you want to photograph the dark interiors of churches and mosques.

The best times to shoot are in the morning until 10am and the afternoon between 4pm and sunset (during the rest of the day the sunlight can be too bright and the sky too hazy, causing your photos to look washed out). If you can't avoid noon, use a warm filter and avoid unflattering shadows by shooting people in the shade, perhaps with a white reflector (a T-shirt will do) bouncing the light back onto their faces.

If in need of further help, *Travel Photography: A Guide to Taking Better Pictures* is written by internationally renowned travel photographer, Richard I'Anson. It's full colour throughout and designed to take on the road.

Syria
FILM & EQUIPMENT
In Damascus and Aleppo there's a wide choice of film available, including Elite, Kodak Gold, Ektachrome and K-Max film, sold at specialist photo shops that seem to take good care of their stock. Film generally costs as much as it does in the West. There are also shops selling memory cards for digital cameras, however the prices are higher than average.

Colour print processing costs vary depending where you go, but in Damascus you can pay as little as S£25 for processing plus S£10 per print.

You also shouldn't have too much trouble finding spare parts for the main makes of camera, such as Nikon, Pentax, Olympus and Canon. Nor is there a problem buying batteries.

RESTRICTIONS
Be careful when taking photos of anything other than tourist sites. It is forbidden to photograph bridges, train stations, anything military, airports and any other public works. If anyone kicks up a fuss when you point

your camera apologise and get the message across that you're just a 'dumb tourist' who doesn't know any better.

As a matter of courtesy, don't photograph people without asking their permission first. Also, some people are sensitive about the negative aspects of their country. It is not uncommon for someone to yell at you when you're trying to take photos of things like a crowded bus, a dilapidated building, or a donkey cart full of garbage, so exercise discretion.

Unless there are signs indicating otherwise, photography is usually allowed inside archaeological sites, as a rule; however, do not photograph inside a mosque during a service.

Lebanon
FILM & EQUIPMENT
You won't have any trouble buying film or video tapes in Lebanon; Kodak, Agfa and Fuji are the most widely available brands. Good-quality colour transparency films are available in Beirut and the larger towns, and occasionally in tourist shops at historical sites (check the expiry date). The cost -of processing in Lebanon is about LL4000 for negative film and about LL16,000 for transparency film. There are plenty of shops selling memory cards for digital cameras, however the prices are higher than average.

The cost of film and video tape is reasonable. A regular 36-exposure print film costs from LL6500 to LL8500 and a slide film is LL15,000 (which sometimes includes processing). Black-and-white film is harder to find and to process outside Beirut, so it is better to bring your own and have it processed when you return home.

You shouldn't have too much trouble finding spare parts for the main makes of camera, such as Nikon, Pentax, Olympus and Canon.

RESTRICTIONS
You shouldn't have any problems taking photographs in Lebanon, with the exception of military areas. As always, when people are going to be featured in your photo, it's polite to ask first; when it comes to conservative Muslim areas this is particularly important. Also, it's far easier for women to photograph women than it is for men. If you happen to be near an army checkpoint, go up to the

soldiers first and explain to them what it is you want to photograph – they usually won't object. Do not, however, try to take photos of the soldiers themselves, nor should you point your camera at buildings occupied by Syrian soldiers or any other military installations unless you've been given permission. If you offend they will not hesitate to ask you to remove your film.

POST
Syria

The Syrian postal service is slow but effective. Letters mailed from the main cities take about a week to reach Europe and anything up to a month to reach Australia or the USA. Mailing letters to the UK and Europe costs S£17, while to the USA and Australia it's S£18; stamps for postcards to the UK and Europe cost S£10, while to Australia and the USA they're S£13. You can also buy *tawaabi* (stamps) from most tobacconists, as well as at post offices.

The **poste restante counter** (Map pp80-1; Sharia Said al-Jabri; ☺ 8am-5pm, closed Fri) in the central post office in Damascus is more or less reliable. Take your passport as identification and be prepared to pay a S£10 pick-up fee.

To send a parcel from Damascus or Aleppo, take it (unwrapped) to the parcel post office for inspection. After it has been cleared it has to be wrapped and covered with cotton material, which will cost you about S£30 (ie you have to buy the material from one guy, pay another to give you some cardboard tags for the address, and yet another to wrap it). For all that, the process usually takes up to about half an hour.

Lebanon

Lebanon's postal service, LibanPost, has recently been privatised. For the moment, though, few Lebanese use it unless they have no other choice. There are hardly any public post boxes in Lebanon, and you have to go to a post office to buy stamps or send anything. It is recommended that you send your mail from Beirut to avoid delays. Some people claim that the post office at the American University of Beirut (AUB) is the most reliable for sending mail, if you can get access (for more details see p241). It's the same price to send a postcard or letter. To Europe it costs LL1250 and to Australia and the USA it's LL1500. Parcels to Europe and the USA cost LL30,000/65,000 per 1/5kg;

to Australia it costs LL35,000/100,000 per 1/5kg.

Letters can take anything from five to 21 days to reach Europe, North America or Australia – if they arrive at all. Most Lebanese use courier services for sending parcels: **DHL** (Map p248; Rue Emir Bechir, Downtown) has an office in Beirut; and its counterpart is **Federal Express** (Map p248; ☎ 01-345 385; Chaker Oueni Bldg, Riad El Solh Square, Downtown, Beirut).

Receiving mail from around the world generally takes several weeks, but Beirut's **LibanPost office** (Map pp244-5; 2nd fl, Matta Bldg, Rue Makdissi, Hamra, Beirut; ☺ 8am-5pm Mon-Fri, 8am-1pm Sat) has a poste restante facility. Amex provides a mail-holding service for people using its travellers cheques; letters can be sent to **Amex** (Map pp244-5; ☎ 01-749 574/5/6; 1st fl, Block C, Gefinor Center, Rue Maamari, Hamra, Beirut; ☎ 9am-4pm Mon-Fri, 8.30am-1.30pm Sat). If you know the hotel in which you'll be staying, the staff will keep your incoming mail for you if you let them know that you are expecting letters.

SHOPPING

While Syria doesn't have much in the way of high street shopping, it more than compensates with its souqs. Every town and village has a souq of some sort, although by far the best are in Damascus and Aleppo.

Carpets, rugs and kilims are best found in the markets of Damascus and Aleppo in Syria, and in Beirut. You can find gold shops scattered about the bigger cities of Syria, but they are at their most concentrated in parts of the Damascus and Aleppo souqs. As a rule, gold is sold by weight, and all pieces should have a hallmark guaranteeing quality. Silver is the most common material used by Bedouin women to make up often striking jewellery.

For centuries Damascus was, along with Toledo in Spain, one of the greatest centres for the production of quality swords. Tamerlane forcefully transferred the Damascene sword-makers to Samarkand in the 15th century, but something of the tradition stuck. There is little use for such things these days, but several shops in Damascus still produce them for sale as souvenirs.

From Morocco to Baghdad you will find much the same sorts of brass and chased copper objects for sale. Most common are the very large decorative trays and tabletops, but other items typical of the Middle East include

Arabic coffeepots and even complete coffee sets with small cups (the little traditional cups without handles should preferably be ceramic, however). Incense-burners and teapots are among other possible buys.

A local speciality is *ad-dahiri* (the ancient art of brass and copper engraving and gold and silver inlaying), which in the past was the preserve Damascene Jews. They've all left but others carry on the work.

Quite a few souq stalls sell either ouds (Arabic lutes) or *darbukkas*, the standard Middle Eastern-style drum. The latter can go quite cheaply, and even the ouds are hardly expensive at around US$40 for a typical model.

Damascus, in particular, is known for its textiles, and has been since antiquity. This has to be one of the best places in the world to look for tablecloths and the like. They are generally made of fine cotton and handsomely adorned with silk. The heavy Damascene tablecloths are about the most beautiful things to buy in Syria. Made from fine lustrous cotton they come in deep reds, burgundies, azure blues and emerald greens, patterned with geometric or paisley-style designs. The best have traditionally been made in Damascus but these are becoming much more difficult to find as far fewer are produced these days.

Brocade is another speciality, and the Bedouin-style vests on sale in some of the more reputable shops in the Damascus souqs are very popular. Good ones will go for around US$10. Along the same line are jalabiyyas, the long and loose robes that you'll see many men and women getting around in. The men's version tends to be fairly sober in colouring, while this kind of women's clothing can be almost blindingly gawdy.

A popular buy with foreigners are the woodwork items. They range from simple jewellery boxes to elaborate chess sets and backgammon boards. The better-quality stuff tends to be of walnut and inlaid with mother-of-pearl. If the mother-of-pearl gives off a strong rainbow-colour effect, you can be almost sure it is the real McCoy. Otherwise it is more likely to be cheap plastic. The actual woodwork on many of these items tends to be a little shoddy, even on the better-quality items, so inspect the joints and inlay carefully.

The ubiquitous nargileh are about as vivid a reminder of a visit to the Middle East as one can imagine. Some of the smaller, simpler ones can start from as low as US$2 to US$3, but ornate ones will cost considerably more. Remember to buy a supply of charcoal to get you going if you intend to use the thing when you return home. Of all the souvenirs you could buy, this has to be about the most awkward to cart around with you – and its chances of surviving the post are not good.

Another simple idea (and much easier to carry around) is the traditional Arab

THE ART OF BARGAINING

Almost all prices are negotiable in the souq, where there is no such thing as a correct price. Bargaining is a process to establish how much the customer is willing to pay. It can be a hassle, but keep your cool and remember it's a game, not a fight.

The first rule is never to show too much interest in the item you want to buy. Secondly, don't buy the first item that takes your fancy. Wander around and price things, but don't make it obvious otherwise when you return to the first shop the vendor will know it's because they are the cheapest.

Decide how much you would be happy paying and then express a casual interest in buying. The vendor will state their price, grossly inflated, doubly so if it's a foreigner doing the buying. Respond with a figure somewhat lower than the one you have fixed in your mind. So the bargaining begins. The shopkeeper will inevitably huff about how absurd your offer is and then tell you the 'lowest' price. If it is still not low enough, be insistent and keep smiling. Tea or coffee might be served as part of the bargaining ritual but accepting it doesn't place you under any obligation to buy. If you still can't get your price, then walk away. This often has the effect of closing the sale in your favour. If not, there are thousands more shops in the souq.

If you do get your price or lower, never feel guilty. No vendor, no matter what they say, ever sells below cost.

headcloth, or *kufeyya*, and *iqal* (the black cord used to keep it on your head) so characteristic of the region. Be aware that the quality of *kufeyya* varies considerably, with some being very bare strips of white cotton and others densely sewn in red or black patterns. Compare before you buy. Even the quality of the *iqal* can vary. A good set should not cost more than about US$4 to US$5 at the most.

SOLO TRAVELLERS

Solo travellers will have no problems travelling in Syria and Lebanon – apart from answering the obvious question, why *are* you alone? In the Middle East, family and friends are essential ingredients in a happy life, and many people you meet won't understand why you would choose to travel alone. There are advantages however; touts and postcard sellers will leave you alone when there are groups to chase and waiters will be more willing to strike up a conversation with someone eating alone.

If you're travelling solo and want to make friends, plenty of young Syrians and Lebanese are keen to practise their English – many of them are learning it at school or university. Cafés are great places to meet young locals and get an insight into their lives; they'll probably invite you back to their place for more coffee, tea and conversation. Keep in mind that most young Lebanese and Syrians are living at home with their parents and it's a perfectly customary offer. Of course, if you in any way feel uncomfortable about it, politely refuse, but do make up a good excuse!

To meet other travellers, the best thing to do is to stay at *the* backpacker hang-outs in each town. Meeting new people this way is great; it's also a great way to do day trips – often people are happy to have an extra person on board to share the cost.

Women travelling on their own should exercise caution; see Women Travellers for (p377) for more information.

Above all, remember the best thing about travelling alone is that you don't have to argue with anyone about the itinerary!

TELEPHONE & FAX

For details on individual telephone codes for Syria and Lebanon, see the inside front cover.

Syria
FAX
It is possible to send telexes, telegrams and faxes from telephone offices or sometimes from main post offices but they are very expensive. For instance, from the main telephone office in Damascus to fax the UK costs S£180 for the first minute and S£90 for each further minute. As there's a two-minute minimum charge that means that at the least your fax will cost S£270. To Australia it's S£220 for the first minute and S£110 per minute beyond that.

PHONECARDS
Calling from Damascus, Aleppo and Hama is straightforward – you just use one of the direct-dial Easycomm card phones dotted about town (plentiful in Damascus, less so in Aleppo and Hama). Phonecards are bought from shops – just ask at the nearest shop, no matter what kind of shop it is, and if they don't have them, they'll point you to someone who does. The cards come in denominations of S£200 (local and national calls only), S£350, S£500 and S£1000. For cheaper rates to Australia call from 2pm to 7pm; to the USA from 3am to 8am; and to Europe from 1am to 7am.

Elsewhere in the country international calls have to be made from card phones located inside or just outside the local telephone office. You buy the necessary card either from a booth within the office or from a vendor who'll be hovering around the phones. Cards bought in Damascus, Aleppo or Hama will not work in phones anywhere else and vice versa.

PHONE CODES
The country code for Syria is ☎ 963, followed by the local area code (minus the zero), then the subscriber number. Local area codes are given at the start of each city or town section. The international access code (to call abroad from Syria) is ☎ 00. Reverse-charge calls cannot be made from Syria; to get the operator dial ☎ 143/144.

MOBILE PHONES
You should now be able to use your mobile (cellular) phone in Damascus and Aleppo. Travellers from most countries can use their mobile Global System for Mobile (GSM) phones in Syria. Coverage is not complete

across the country but it's reliable in most cities. Check with your GSM service company for details as to whether they have an agreement with one of the two operators in Syria.

Lebanon

While the state telephone system works well enough these days, there are few pay phones. When you do locate one, local calls cost LL250 or LL500 depending on the length of the call (whereas local calls from a private phone within the same area code cost LL30 for the first minute and then LL20 per subsequent minute). Local phone calls from corner shops and private offices can cost as much as LL1000, or LL2000 if you're dialling long-distance within Lebanon.

FAX

Fax machines are quite widely used and most hotels, except for the very smallest, seem to have one. Many of the private telephone bureaus also have fax machines. You can often get a hotel to send a fax for you even if you are not staying there. They charge commercial rates but they are not too exorbitant. From a hotel, faxes are charged at the same rate as phone calls.

INTERNATIONAL CALLS

International calls are expensive and are usually made through private phone offices, large hotels or *centrales* (government-run phone offices). The latter is the cheapest option but they are often crowded. To make a call you must fill out a slip of paper with the number(s) you require and wait until you are called. You pay at the desk when your calls are complete. The minimum charge for an international call is for three minutes. From the *centrale*, calls cost LL2100 per minute to the UK, the USA and Europe. Peak time in Lebanon is from 7am to 10pm, and tariffs drop by about one-third outside these hours.

Despite the government's objections that it is undercutting its phone system, many Internet cafés offer **Net2phone** (www.net2phone .com), telephone calls via the Internet, which is a far cheaper way of making international calls.

MOBILE PHONES

Mobile phone numbers in Lebanon start with 03. Most Lebanese, if they can afford

it, use mobile phones, and have the dubious distinction of clocking up more minutes per month than almost any other country in the world. Mobile-phone coverage extends throughout the country, with only one or two remote areas falling outside the network area. Calling to or from a mobile phone costs about US$0.06 per minute. Getting a mobile phone costs at least US$250 to US$300 but you can rent them through the larger car-rental agencies for about US$6 per day, plus a deposit and call charges. For details of car-rental companies see p391. If you have your own GSM phone, you can get a chip with a prepaid line of 220 units for about US$60 from any of the hundreds of mobile-phone dealers throughout the country. There are two companies, LibanCell and Cellis, and both offer the same service for around the same price. Service lasts for 30 days, although you can receive calls for a further five days. If you want extra call units you can buy cards for US$22, US$33 and US$44 (SMS is a hidden extra at US$10 and you need to purchase an extra card). Note: during research of this book these prices nearly doubled and then went back down again – the mobile-phone industry was still in a state of flux at the time of writing.

TIME

Both Syria and Lebanon are two hours ahead of GMT/UTC in winter (October to March) and three hours ahead in summer (April to September), when daylight saving is used. For more on international timing, see the map of the world time zones (p402) at the back of this book.

One important thing to bear in mind regarding time is that Syrians and Lebanese always seem to have plenty of it – something that should take five minutes will invariably take an hour. Trying to speed things up will only lead to frustration. Take it philosophically and don't try to fight it – a bit of patience goes a long way here.

TOILETS

Travellers who have experienced some Middle Eastern toilets need fear not – Syrian and Lebanese toilets are generally very clean. You will find a mixture of Western-style upright toilets and the squat hole-in-the-floor variety, although the latter are usually only found at very cheap hotels and restaurants or in public conveniences (which should be avoided except in dire emergency). In both Syria and Lebanon you are almost always close enough to a decent hotel or restaurant that will let you use their facilities. Remember toilet paper is not always available so it's a good idea to carry tissues.

VISAS
Syria
All foreigners entering Syria must must obtain visas from Syrian consulates abroad, but if there is no Syrian representation in your home country, then *in theory* you should be able to get a visa at the border or on arrival at the airport (for details on obtaining visas at the border see below). Some travel companies (tourism operators) in Syria claim to be able to organise your visa by faxing them copies of your passports and associated documents.

The easiest and surest way to get your visa is to apply for it in your home country. Try to avoid applying in a country that is not your own or where you don't hold residency as the Syrians don't like this. At best they will ask you for a letter of recommendation from your own embassy (which is often an expensive proposition), at worst they'll turn you down flat. In fact, US citizens must get their visas at home as US embassies abroad have a policy of not issuing letters of recommendation – the only place you can get around this is at the Syrian embassy in Cairo (see p362 for contact details), which, at the time of writing, didn't ask for a letter. If your home country doesn't have a Syrian embassy or consulate, then there's no problem with you applying anywhere else.

At most embassies and consulates you can apply in person or by post and the visa takes from four days to two weeks to issue. There are rarely any problems with getting the visa; however, if there is any evidence of a visit to Israel & the Palestinian Territories (I&PT) in your passport, your application will be refused (for more details regarding passports and visiting I&PT, see p380). There are two types of visa issued – single- and multiple-entry – but both are valid only for 15 days inside Syria and must be used within three months of the date of issue (six months for multiple-entry visas). Don't be misled by the words on the visa stating a validity of three months – this simply means

the visa is valid for presentation for three months. Once in Syria it is easy to get your visa extended (see p376).

On entry, you will fill out a yellow or white entry card (in English); keep this, as you'll need it to get visa extensions and to exit the country.

Lebanon
All nationalities need a visa to enter Lebanon. Visas can be obtained in advance at any Lebanese embassy or consulate; you'll need two passport-sized photographs and usually a letter of recommendation from your employer to say that you are returning to your job. Visas are usually issued the next day but can sometimes take longer.

When planning your trip, keep in mind Lebanese visas are not available in Damascus, Syria; however, visas are now available at all points of entry into Lebanon, so if you come from Syria it is now possible to get a visa at the border (for more information see below). Note that you cannot get a visa to enter Syria from Lebanon. Only passport-holders from countries that have no Syrian consulate may obtain visas at the Syrian border, so if you want to travel overland, make sure you have a valid Syrian visa before you go to Lebanon. If you have an Israeli stamp in your passport, or have stamps from Egyptian or Jordanian crossing points, you will be refused entry into Lebanon. For more information on entering Lebanon see p380.

Visas at the Border
SYRIA
The official line is that if there is no Syrian representation in your country, you are entitled to be issued a visa on arrival at the border, airport or port. Conversely, there are multiple Syrian consulates in Australia but there have been plenty of emails from Aussie travellers who managed to get a visa at the Turkey-Syria border with no problems. It's a situation that seems largely governed by the whims of the individual immigration official. Because of this, our advice is get your visa in advance. If that's not possible in your own country then consider picking up the visa en route on your travels.

LEBANON
Nationals of the following countries – Australia, Austria, Belgium, Canada, Denmark,

Finland, France, Germany, Greece, Ireland, Italy, Japan, Luxembourg, Netherlands, Norway, Portugal, South Korea, Spain, Sweden, Switzerland, the USA, and members of the Gulf Cooperation Council (GCC) can get a tourist or business visa upon arrival at the Beirut airport.

Getting Your Visa in the Middle East

The Syrian embassy in Amman issues visas only to nationals and residents of Jordan and to nationals of countries that have no Syrian representation. So, if you are from a country such as the UK, the USA or France that has a Syrian embassy then you cannot get a Syrian visa in Jordan. In Cairo, the Syrian embassy issues visas to *all nationalities* on the same or next day depending on how early in the morning you get your application in (for contact details see p362). For Australians and Canadians the visa is free, Americans pay US$34, UK citizens pay US$60 and most other nationalities pay US$54.

In Turkey, you can get Syrian visas in both Ankara and İstanbul without too much of a problem. Australians and Canadians pay nothing, while New Zealanders pay about US$6. German, French and US citizens pay more, while Brits take all the prizes, paying about US$60. Nonresidents in Turkey need a letter of recommendation from their embassy, for which they may be charged. UK citizens, for example, have to pay UK£35 for this service. Visas in Turkey take one working day to issue. Note that the Syrian consulate in İstanbul (for contact details see p362) is only open for applications from 9.30am to 11am, and for pick-up from 2pm to 2.30pm the next working day.

We've had reports that visas issued in Cairo and Turkey are only valid for presentation within one month; ask for more details when collecting.

Visa Costs
SYRIA

The cost of visas varies according to nationality and where you get them. There seems to be little rhyme or reason in deciding which nationalities pay what, except in the case of UK passport-holders, who always pay a lot. New Zealanders need to apply to Melbourne or Sydney because there's no Syrian representation in New Zealand (the same costs apply).

country	single-entry visa	multiple-entry visa
Australia	A$35*	A$45*
	A$75**	A$100**
Canada	US$56	US$108
France	€26	€49
Germany	€30	€49
Ireland	UK£37	UK£70
UK	UK£37	UK£57***
USA	US$61****	

* If applying in the Melbourne consular office.

** If applying in the Sydney consular office.

*** British citizens looking for a multiple-entry visa should be aware that visas are not currently issued at a point of entry into Lebanon.

**** In the USA the visa cost is the same for single or 'double' entry. The latter allows you to enter twice – useful if you wish to enter Lebanon and return to Syria. Note that the cost includes a US$16 visa fee and a US$45 nonrefundable application fee.

For contact details of Syrian and Lebanese diplomatic representations abroad see p362.

LEBANON

The visas are valid for three months and cost about US$20/40 for a single-/multiple-entry visa (the multi-entry visa is useful if you're planning to visit Syria from Lebanon and return to Beirut). Once you've arrived at Beirut airport you'll find visa stamps are sold at a window on the left, just before you reach passport control. A stamp for a two-week/three-month visa costs US$15/37. This 'three-month' visa requires you to extend this before the end of your first month – see opposite for more information.

Visa Extensions
SYRIA

If your stay in Syria is going to be more than 15 days you have to get a visa extension while in the country. This is done at an immigration office, which you'll find in all main towns and cities. You can get more than one extension and their length appears to depend on a combination of what you're willing to ask for and the mood of the official you deal with – it's usually one month.

Extensions are usually only granted on the 14th or 15th day of your stay, so if you apply earlier expect to be knocked back. If, as occasionally happens, you are allowed to extend your visa earlier than this, check that the extension is from the last day of your visa or previous extension and not from the day of your application.

The specifics vary from place to place but there are always several forms to fill in, in French, usually containing questions repeated several times in slightly different ways. You need from three to six passport photos. The cost is never more than US$1. Processing time varies from on-the-spot to come back the following day. Damascus and Aleppo are about the most tedious places to extend your visa, while small towns like Deir ez-Zur or Tartus are the most straight-forward.

LEBANON

To make your 'three-month' visa actually valid for three months, you must go to the **General Security office** (Map pp244-5; Rue Spears; ☾ 8am-1pm Mon-Thu, 8-10am Fri, 8am-noon Sat, closed Sun) in Beirut, at least a few days before the end of the first month, taking with you a passport-sized photo and a photocopy of the front page of your passport, the page where the initial visa was stamped. As always, it's best to make separate copies of these for yourself. Go to the 2nd floor of the building and work your way to one of the windows of the main office – there are usu-ally a couple of officers there who speak English. After the paperwork is filled out ask the officer to point you to your next destina-tion where you hand over your passport and forms. All you will take away from the office is a green form which has the details of your passport on it plus details of the date/day to come back (it usually takes a week) and pick up your passport. Obviously it's a good idea not to lose this form! When you go back to the office on the indicated date, proceed to the 1st floor, where you pick up your passport. It's also not a good idea to travel too far from Beirut during this time, as not having a passport at a checkpoint can be problematic, to say the least.

WOMEN TRAVELLERS
Syria

As a woman traveller in Syria you can expect a little verbal harassment, unless you're with a male companion. This usu-ally goes no further than irritating banter, proposals of marriage or even declarations of undying love, but harassment can also take the form of leering and sometimes of being followed.

If you are finding that you are being harassed, if you're in a crowded area, a decent, loud *'halas!'* (which means 'enough') should attract enough attention to embar-rass the perpetrator and have him scolded by local onlookers. Otherwise, the best bet is to simply ignore it (see also the boxed text Tips for Women Travellers, p378, for more information). Keep in mind that plenty of women travel through Syria, often alone, and never encounter any serious problems. Use common sense.

The majority of Syrians are, to a greater or lesser degree, quite conservative about dress. The woman wearing short pants and a tight T-shirt on the street is, in some people's eyes, confirmation of the worst views held of Western women.

As hot as it gets in Syria you'll have fewer hassles if you don't dress for hot weather in the same way you might at home. Baggy T-shirts and loose cotton trousers or long skirts won't make you sweat as much as you think and will protect your skin from the sun as well as from unwanted comments.

As with anywhere, take your cues from those around you: if you're in a rural area and all the women are in long, concealing dresses, you should dress conservatively. If you're going to an upmarket Damascus restaurant, you're likely to see some middle- and upper-class Syrian women in slinky designer outfits and you can dress accord-ingly – but avoid walking to the restaurant if possible.

Unfortunately, although dressing con-servatively should reduce the incidence of such harassment, it by no means guarantees you'll be left alone.

Some activities, such as sitting in coffee-houses, are usually seen as a male preserve and although it's OK for Western women to enter, in some places the stares may cause discomfort. Quite a few restaurants have a 'family area' set aside for women; you can sit wherever you want though, and if you are travelling without male company you might feel more comfortable in these sections. As a rule, mixed foreign groups have no trouble wherever they sit, including coffeehouses and bars. In some of the local bars and cafés there is only one toilet – since generally

TIPS FOR WOMEN TRAVELLERS

There are a number of things that you can do to lessen the likelihood of harassment, but top of the list is to dress modestly. Other helpful tips:

- Wear a wedding band. Generally, Middle Eastern males seem to have more respect for a married woman.
- If you are unmarried but travelling in male company say you are married rather than girlfriend/boyfriend or just friends.
- Don't say that you are travelling alone or just in the company of another female friend – always say that you are with a group.
- Avoid direct eye contact with local men; wearing dark sunglasses could help.
- On public transport, sit next to a woman if possible.
- Be very careful about behaving in a flirtatious or suggestive manner, it could create more problems than you bargained for.
- If you need help for any reason (directions etc), ask a woman first.
- If dining alone, be aware that some places are almost strictly male preserves, such as the local coffeehouse.
- It is perfectly acceptable for a woman to go straight to the front of a queue or to ask to be served first before any men that may be waiting.
- Women should not get into an unlicensed service taxi if there are no other passengers, especially at night.
- Don't respond to any obnoxious comments – act as if you didn't hear them. If they persist, an easy Arabic word to learn is to tell them loudly *'Halas!'* ('Enough!'). This should attract enough attention for local onlookers to scold the perpetrator(s).
- Going to the nearest public place, such as the lobby of a hotel, usually works in getting rid of any 'admirers'. If they still persist, however, then ask the receptionist to call the police. This will usually frighten them off.

only men frequent these places. This does not necessarily mean women can't use them but you should be aware of this unwitting unisex situation before settling in for a few drinks.

Staying in budget hotels can sometimes be problematic if you're alone. You may have to take a room for yourself if there are no other travellers to share with.

Lebanon

Women travelling in Lebanon will notice a huge difference in the attitude towards them compared with most other parts of the Middle East, including Syria. In Beirut it is common to see Lebanese women in the tightest and tiniest of outfits, including micro miniskirts, tight trousers and tiny tank tops. However, if you are travelling alone, you may want to be a little more restrained than your Lebanese sisters. As a

foreign woman you are perceived by some as outside the protection of male relatives and therefore as fair game for the odd leer and comment.

Having said that, you can usually wear more or less whatever you want, particularly when you're in Beirut. In the coastal resorts the dress code is also relaxed and bikinis are *de rigueur* on the beach. Going topless, however, is out.

Away from Beirut and the resorts, and particularly in predominantly Muslim areas, it is sensible to adopt a more conservative style of dress to avoid unwelcome attention. If you are planning to visit any mosques, be sure that your arms and legs are covered and that you take a headscarf with you. Some mosques provide women visitors with a black cloak at the door.

In the mid-range and top-end hotels the security is usually very good and women need not worry about being hassled. In budget hotels it might be more of a problem. As a rule, do not open your hotel room door unless you know who is there, and when you are alone in your room keep the door locked.

Also, see the boxed text Tips for Women Travellers, opposite.

WORK
Syria

Possibilities are severely limited. About the only work available might be as a language teacher. The **American Language Center** (ALC; ☎ 011-332 7236) is probably the best place to try your luck, followed by the **British Council** (Map p78; ☎ 011-333 0631, fax 332 1467; www.britishcouncil.org/syria; Sharia Karim al-Khalil, off Sharia Maysaloun; ◷ 9am-8pm Sun-Thu, 10am-5pm Sat), both of which are in Damascus.

Because the British Council is smaller and tends to recruit directly from the UK rather than locally, the ALC should be your first port of call. The ALC prefers people with a Bachelor's degree and some form of teaching experience. Pay is calculated on a points system, so the better your qualifications, the better your chances of getting a job and the higher the income. A Certificate in English Language Teaching to Adults (Celta), or second language qualification, knowledge of Arabic, postgraduate studies and prior experience in teaching improve your chances.

French travellers could try their luck at the **Centre Culturel Français** (Map pp80-1; ☎ 011-231 6181, fax 231 6194; off Sharia Yousef al-Azmeh, Bahsa; ◷ 9am-9pm Mon-Sat) in Damascus.

Lebanon

With the economy still not in great shape, this is not the best time to look for work. Lebanese are highly educated and most speak at least two or three languages fluently, so competition is stiff. The tourism industry is expanding and resorts may need people for seasonal work but, unless you're fluent in both French and Arabic, you're at a distinct disadvantage. English-language publications often need writers and copy editors. Lebanon is a great place to live but the pay is usually low.

Another option for those men and women of Letters, is the **American University of Beirut** (AUB; Map pp244-5; ☎ 01-340 460, fax 351 706; www.aub.edu; Rue Bliss, Beirut) as the language of instruction is English. For most faculty positions you need a PhD.

If you do have a job, work permits are not difficult to get, although your employer must prove that there is no Lebanese capable of doing the job. The salary varies according to nationality and profession. You need a health insurance policy that guarantees repatriation of your corpse should you die in Lebanon (presumably a war-time hangover), a letter from your employer (either here or abroad) and roughly US$667 per year for both work and residency permit.

Other options include coming in on a tourist visa and renewing it every three months, up to a maximum of four times. However, there are periodic crackdowns during which renewals are no longer issued, and customs and passport control check the number of stamps in your passport carefully upon arrival in the country.

Transport

CONTENTS

GETTING THERE & AWAY

Heading to Syria and Lebanon is fairly straightforward, especially if you are coming from Europe or the Middle East where there are a range of airlines and a number of direct flights to both Damascus and Beirut. From other regions, flights again are fairly straightforward, just expect a couple of stops on the way. There is also the option, for those with a bit of time, of travelling overland.

ENTERING SYRIA & LEBANON

Entering both countries is very easy from a bureaucratic standpoint: all you need is a non-Israeli stamped valid passport and a valid visa.

Syria and Lebanon refuse to admit anyone who has ever visited their neighbour, Israel & the Palestinian Territories (I&PT). The evidence immigration officials will be looking for is any kind of incriminating stamp in your passport. This can include arrival/departure stamps from I&PT's Ben-Gurion Airport, or similar stamps from border crossing points, such as Rafah and Taba on the Egyptian border or any of the crossings with Jordan.

There's also a question on some visa application forms that asks, 'Have you ever visited Occupied Palestine'? to which a yes response will see your application turned down flat. And should you plan on going to

I&PT after Syria, keep it to yourself. If you are doing a trip right through the Middle East, you can save yourself some potential trouble and leave I&PT as the last stop on your itinerary.

Immigration at the airports in both countries is quite efficient, but the customs staff at Beirut often check travellers' luggage.

The level of attention you receive entering either country by road is purely at the whim and boredom or stress level of the staff working at the border point. Regardless of their attitude, be unfailingly polite – despite the journey you've endured to get there.

See also the boxed text Departure Tax (p384) for information regarding taxes.

Passport

Make sure that your passport is valid well beyond the period of your intended stay. If your passport is just about to expire, immigration may not let you into the country. Also, make sure it has sufficient space for any new visa stamps that you're liable to pick up.

You should get into the habit of carrying your passport at all times while in Syria and Lebanon as you often need to present it to change money, cash travellers cheques, buy long-distance bus tickets and, in some destinations, even to make telephone calls. In Lebanon there are still many Lebanese and Syrian army checkpoints, although the officials rarely ask to see your ID these days. However, if you are stopped and you don't have any ID, it will create delays and hassles.

THINGS CHANGE...

The information in this chapter is particularly vulnerable to change. Check directly with the airline or a travel agent to make sure you understand how a fare (and ticket you may buy) works and be aware of the security requirements for international travel. Shop carefully. The details given in this chapter should be regarded as pointers and are not a substitute for your own careful, up-to-date research.

AIR
Airports & Airlines
SYRIA
Syria has two international airports, one in Damascus and the other in Aleppo, plus a third, in Lattakia, which is international in name only. Both Damascus (DAM) and Aleppo (ALP) have regular connections to Europe, Africa, Asia and other cities in the Middle East, while Aleppo has more limited services. Most air travellers arrive in Damascus but there are some direct flights from Europe and other Middle Eastern destinations to Aleppo.

The **Damascus airport** (DAM; ☎ 011-543 0201/9) is 26km southwest of the city centre. There's a branch of the Commercial Bank of Syria (CBS) and a tourist office, plus desks for the major car-hire companies. Note, the bank will *not* change Syrian pounds back into dollars or any other hard currency. On the plus side, there is a duty-free store that takes Syrian pounds and US dollars, and is amazingly cheap.

For information on how to get to and from the airport, see p114 , including the boxed text Arriving in Damascus by Air (p112). Syria's national carrier **SyrianAir** (Syrian Arab Airlines; www.syrian-airlines.com) flies to Europe, Delhi, Mumbai and Karachi in Asia, many Middle Eastern destinations and North Africa, and it's not a bad airline for short-haul travel.

Major airlines offering services to and from Damascus.

Air France (in Damascus ☎ 011-221 8990; www.airfrance .com; airline code AF; hub Charles de Gaulle Airport, Paris)
British Airways (in Damascus ☎ 011-331 0000; www .britishairways.com; airline code BA; hub Heathrow Airport, London)
Cyprus Airways (in Damascus ☎ 011-222 5630; www .cyprusairways.com; airline code CY; Larnaca Airport, Larnaca; LCA)
EgyptAir (in Damascus ☎ 011-223 2158; www.egyptair .com.eg; airline code MS; hub Cairo International Airport, Cairo)
Emirates (in Damascus ☎ 011-231 3450; www.emirates .com; airline code EK; Dubai Airport, Dubai; DXB)
Gulf Air (in Damascus ☎ 011-222 1209; www.gulfairco .com; airline code GF; Bahrain Airport, Bahrain; BAH)
Lufthansa (in Damascus ☎ 011-221 1165; www.lufthansa .com; airline code LH; Frankfurt Airport, Frankfurt; FRA)
Royal Jordanian Airline (in Damascus ☎ 011-231 5577; www.rja.com.jo; airline code RJ; Queen Alia Airport, Amman; AMM)

SyrianAir (Airport office ☎ 222 9001; www.syrian-airlines .com; airline code RB; Damascus airport, Damascus; DAM)
Turkish Airlines (in Damascus ☎ 011-223 9770; www .turkishairlines.com; airline code TK; Ataturk Airport, İstanbul; IST)

LEBANON
There is only one international airport in Lebanon, **Beirut International Airport** (BEY; ☎ 01-628 000; www.beirutairport.gov.lb), which is also Lebanon's only airport. Despite rumours, it's unlikely that another will be opened, mainly due to the short travelling times within Lebanon. There are no direct flights to the USA; though connections to Europe, Africa and Asia are frequent. The arrivals hall is well organised, and immigration procedures are reasonably straightforward, although customs can be slow if luggage is being checked. Facilities inside the airport are still thin on the ground, but some car-rental agencies and exchange places are open. For details on getting to and from the airport, see p265.

The national carrier, **Middle East Airlines** (MEA; in Beirut ☎ 01-737 000; www.mea.com.lb; Beirut International Airport, Beirut) has an extensive network, including flights to and from Australia, Europe and the Arab world. The airline has a pretty good safety record, and is serviceable enough, and good for regional connections.

Airlines that fly to and from Lebanon:
Air France (in Beirut ☎ 01-200 700; www.airfrance.com; airline code AF; hub Charles de Gaulle Airport, Paris)
British Airways (in Beirut ☎ 01-747 777; www.british airways.com; airline code BA; hub Heathrow Airport, London)
Cyprus Airways (in Beirut ☎ 01-200 886; www.cyprus airways.com; airline code CY; Larnaca Airport, Larnaca; LCA)
EgyptAir (in Beirut ☎ 01-980 165; www.egyptair.com.eg; airline code MS; hub Cairo International Airport, Cairo)
Emirates (in Beirut ☎ 01-739 042; www.emirates.com; airline code EK; Dubai Airport, Dubai; DXB)
Gulf Air (in Beirut ☎ 01-323 332; www.gulfairco.com; airline code GF; Bahrain Airport, Bahrain; BAH)
Lufthansa (in Beirut ☎ 01-347 006; www.lufthansa.com; airline code LH; Frankfurt Airport, Frankfurt; FRA)
Malaysia Airlines (in Beirut ☎ 01-741 344; www.mas .com.my; airline code MH; Sepang International, Kuala Lumpur; KUL)
Middle East Airlines (in Beirut ☎ 01-737 000; www.mea .com.lb; airline code ME; Beirut International Airport, Beirut; BEY)
Royal Jordanian Airline (in Beirut ☎ 01-379 990; www .rja.com.jo; airline code RJ; Queen Alia Airport, Amman; AMM)

Syrian Arab Airlines (in Beirut ☎ 01-375 632; www
.syrian-airlines.com; airline code RB; Damascus Airport,
Damascus; DAM)
Turkish Airlines (in Beirut ☎ 01-741 391; www.turkish
airlines.com; airline code TK; Ataturk Airport, İstanbul; IST)

Tickets

As Syria is one of the more popular Middle
East destinations you will probably find discounted fares, particularly from Europe.
Prices vary from one agency to the other, so
take the time to call around. If you're planning to tour either Jordan or Turkey as well as
Syria, you should consider flying to Amman
or İstanbul, as a greater range of airlines serve
those cities with a wider spread of fares.

For Beirut, it really depends where you're
coming from. Online agencies will give a reasonable discount, but to save money you'll be
taking a connecting flight or sometimes two.

BUYING TICKETS

An air ticket alone can eat into anyone's
budget, but you can reduce the cost of your
ticket by finding discounted fares. For long-
term travel, discount tickets are usually valid
for 12 months, allowing travellers multiple
stopovers with open dates.

Consider online booking: many airlines
offer excellent fares to Web surfers. Many
travel agents have websites, which can
make the Internet a quick and easy way to
compare prices (see the boxed text Online
Tickets for a list of online booking services).
Online ticket sales work well if you are doing
a simple one-way or return trip on specified
dates. If you purchase a ticket and later
want to make changes to your route or get
a refund, you need to contact the original
travel agent. Airlines only issue refunds to
the purchaser of a ticket – usually the travel
agent who bought the ticket on your behalf.

ONLINE TICKETS

To research and buy tickets on the Internet,
try these online booking services.
www.travelocity.com Can give you airfares
originating from anywhere in the world, not only
from the US.
www.expedia.com It has localised sites for
several countries.
www.lastminute.com It also goes worldwide,
and offers accommodation and car-rental deals.

Think carefully before you buy a ticket that
cannot be easily refunded.

STUDENT & YOUTH FARES

Full-time students and people under 26 have
access to better deals than other travellers.
The better deals may not always be cheaper
fares but can include more flexibility to
change flights and/or routes. You have to
show a document proving your date of birth
or a valid International Student Identity Card
(ISIC) when buying your ticket and boarding
the plane.

Most airlines offer frequent-flier deals
that can earn you a free air ticket or up-
grades. To qualify, you have to accumulate
sufficient mileage with the same airline or
airline alliance. Many airlines have 'blackout
periods', or times when you cannot fly for
free on your frequent-flier points.

From Asia

For both Damascus and Beirut, flights gen-
erally land in Dubai first. Saudi Arabian,
Emirates, Gulf Air and Qatar Airways all
offer connecting flights that add about
US$100 to the return flight to Dubai. For
Beirut it's about the same, with Gulf Air,
Malaysia and Emirates offering the best
deals. Return flights from Kuala Lumpur to
both Damascus and Beirut start at around
US$800 from online agencies.

From Australia & New Zealand

From Australia, low-season fares to Damas-
cus and Beirut start at about A$1700 return
with Thai International/Royal Jordanian,
Gulf Air and Qantas. From New Zealand,
return low-season fares with Emirates
or Malaysian Airlines start from around
NZ$2300. Middle East Airlines flights from
Australia and New Zealand are operated by
Malaysian Airlines. From both Australia and
New Zealand, expect a couple of stopovers
on the way. Depending on the airline, the
stopovers in Asia are usually Singapore or
Kuala Lumpur and Bahrain or Dubai in the
Middle East. Round-the-world tickets start
from A$2420 from Australia or NZ$2880
from New Zealand.

For the location of STA Travel branches
call ☎ 1300 733 035 or visit www.statravel
.com.au. **Flight Centre** (☎ 133 133; www.flightcentre
.com.au) has offices throughout Australia. For
online bookings, try www.travel.com.au. Both

Flight Centre (☎ 0800 243 544; www.flightcentre.co.nz) and **STA Travel** (☎ 0508 782 872; www.statravel.co.nz) have branches throughout the country. The site www.travel.co.nz is recommended for online bookings.

From Canada

From Canada, flights are via one of the European capitals and depending on the airline, sometimes via the USA as well. Return flights to either Damascus or Beirut with Air Canada and British Airways start from around C\$1850 from Vancouver or C\$1680 from Toronto.

Travel Cuts (☎ 800-667-2887; www.travelcuts.com) is Canada's national student travel agency. For online bookings try www.expedia.ca and www.travelocity.ca.

From Continental Europe

Airlines including Air France, Austrian Airlines, Alitalia, KLM, Royal Jordanian, Gulf Air, Middle East Airlines and SyrianAir offer regular flights to Damascus and/or Beirut from most European cities. KLM and Air France have direct flights to Beirut from Amsterdam and Air France and Austrian Airlines offer direct services to Damascus from Amsterdam. From Paris, Air France offers direct flights to Beirut and Damascus. Alitalia also has direct flights to both these cities from Milan as does Lufthansa from Frankfurt.

Depending on the airline and number of stops (direct flights are generally more expensive) return flights from these cities to either Damascus or Beirut are around €400 to €500.

FROM FRANCE

Recommended agencies:

Anyway (☎ 0892 893 892; www.anyway.fr)

Lastminute (☎ 0892 705 000; www.lastminute.fr)

Nouvelles Frontières (☎ 0825 000 747; www.nouvelles-frontieres.fr)

OTU Voyages (www.otu.fr) Specialises in student and youth travellers.

Voyageurs du Monde (☎ 01 40 15 11 15; www.vdm.com)

FROM GERMANY

Recommended agencies:

Expedia (www.expedia.de)

Just Travel (☎ 089 747 3330; www.justtravel.de)

Lastminute (☎ 01805 284 366; www.lastminute.de)

STA Travel (☎ 01805 456 422; www.statravel.de) For travellers under the age of 26.

FROM ITALY

One recommended agent is **CTS Viaggi** (☎ 06-462 0431; www.cts.it), specialising in student and youth travel.

FROM THE NETHERLANDS

Recommended agencies are **Airfair** (☎ 020 620 5121; www.airfair.nl) or **Mytravel** (☎ 099 10 20 300; wwwmytravel.nl).

From the Middle East & North Africa

Middle East Airlines has regular flights to Beirut from the Middle East capitals of Amman, Abu Dhabi, Kuwait and Dubai. As well it offers flights to Beirut from the African cities of Cairo, Abidjan (Ivory Coast), Accra (Ghana) and Kano (Nigeria).

SyrianAir has regular connections to Beirut from many Middle East and North African cities including Amman, Abu Dhabi, Algiers, Bahrain, Cairo, Dhahran, Doha, Dubai, Jeddah, Khartoum, Kuwait, Muscat, San'a, Sharjah, Riyadh, Tehrān and Tunis.

Both Turkish Airlines and Middle East Airlines have direct flights from İstanbul to Beirut. Turkish Airlines also offers direct services from İstanbul to Damascus. Check the airlines websites for an idea of fares between cities.

Recommended agencies:

Al-Rais Travels (www.alrais.com) In Dubai.

Egypt Panorama Tours (☎ 2-359 0200; www.eptours.com) In Cairo.

The Israel Student Travel Association (ISTA; ☎ 02-625 7257) In Jerusalem.

From the UK

From the UK there are a number of airlines offering flights to both Syria and Lebanon. British Airways (flights are operated by British Mediterranean Airways) and Middle East Airlines operate direct flights to Beirut, while British Airways, again operated by British Mediterranean, and SyrianAir have direct flights to Damascus. British Mediterranean also offers direct flights to Aleppo. Other flight options from London to Damascus include KLM via Amsterdam, Alitalia via Milan or Air France via Paris.

At the time of writing return flights from London to Damascus or Beirut were around £300.

DEPARTURE TAX

When heading for the airport in Syria, make sure that you keep enough Syrian currency for the departure tax: S£200, paid after check-in. There is no tax to be paid when departing by a land border.

Airline passengers departing from Beirut International Airport must pay a steep US$33/49 if travelling economy/business class. The tax is usually included in your ticket price – ask your agent.

Discount air travel is big business in London. Advertisements for many travel agencies appear in the travel pages of the weekend broadsheet newspapers, in *Time Out*, the *Evening Standard* and in the free magazine *TNT*.

Recommended travel agencies:

Bridge the World (☎ 0870 444 7474; www.b-t-w.co.uk)
Flightbookers (☎ 0870 010 7000; www.ebookers.com)
Flight Centre (☎ 0870 890 8099; flightcentre.co.uk)
Quest Travel (☎ 0870 442 3542; www.questtravel.com)
STA Travel (☎ 0870 160 0599; www.statravel.co.uk) For travellers under the age of 26.
Trailfinders (www.trailfinders.co.uk)

From the USA

Although there are no direct flights from the USA, there are quite a few options for getting to either Syria or Lebanon. Flights to Damascus and Beirut are via one, sometimes two, European capitals, usually London or Paris or another Middle East capital. Return fares from New York with airlines including British Airways, Royal Jordanian and Air France start from around US$1100 while return fares from Los Angeles start from US$1700. Another option from the USA is to buy a return to London and from there, a cheap fare to either Damascus or Beirut. If you are travelling to Syria or Lebanon as part of a bigger trip, expect to pay around US$2500 for a round-the-world ticket that takes in Beirut or Damascus.

Discount travel agents in the USA are known as consolidators (although you won't see a sign on the door saying 'Consolidator'). San Francisco is the ticket consolidator capital of America, although some good deals can be found in Los Angeles, New York and other big cities.

The following agencies are recommended for online bookings.

- www.cheaptickets.com
- www.expedia.com
- www.lowestfare.com
- www.sta.com (for travellers under the age of 26)
- www.travelocity.com

LAND
Border Crossings

The only land borders open to Lebanon at the moment are those with Syria. Despite the Israeli withdrawal, the southern border is closed with no immediate sign of opening.

Whether leaving by land (or air), have your yellow entry card, or the equivalent you received on getting a visa extension, ready to hand in. There may be a small fine to pay if you don't have it – which could be awkward if you have made sure to spend your last Syrian pounds before crossing the frontier.

If you've overstayed your 15-day limit without getting the required visa extension, reports indicate you can get away with being a day or two over, but for anything more you must get an exit visa from an immigration office. If you don't, you risk being turned back.

BRINGING YOUR OWN VEHICLE

It's no problem to bring your own vehicle to Syria. A *carnet de passage en douane* is apparently no longer needed. Instead, drivers arriving with vehicles have to buy what amounts to a temporary customs waiver at the border. This costs about US$50, plus possible bribes to grumpy customs officials. Third-party insurance must also be bought at the border, costing US$36 a month. This supposedly also covers you for Lebanon, but double-check. The real value of these compulsory insurance deals is questionable, so make sure your own insurance company will cover you for Syria.

If you are bringing a foreign-registered vehicle into Lebanon, there is a hefty charge levied at the border (refundable when you leave). This is calculated on a sliding scale depending on the value of the vehicle. Unless you have large amounts of cash to leave as a deposit, this ruling effectively makes it unfeasible to bring your own car into Lebanon. A better plan would be to arrive by bus or service taxi and then rent a car locally.

Also see Car & Motorcycle for Syria (p390) and Lebanon (p394) for more specific details.

Iran

In March 2001, the Syrians and Iranians, with a bit of cooperation from the Turks, got it together to launch a new service connecting Damascus and Tehrān by rail. The route is Damascus, Aleppo, then into Turkey – Malatya, Van – and on into Iran – Tabriz, Tehrān. The departure from Tehrān is 8.15pm Saturday, arriving Damascus 7.20am Tuesday; the reverse journey departs Damascus 7.21am Saturday, arriving Tehrān 6.45pm Monday. The first-class fare is €34. For departures from Aleppo, see p195.

Jordan

The main border crossing between Syria and Jordan is just southeast of Der'a on a new highway that connects the two country capitals. This is the express route taken by all direct bus and service taxis. There's also a second older and little-used crossing due south of Der'a connecting with the Jordanian town of Ramtha. For details see the boxed text Crossing Into Jordan (p123).

BUS

There is one air-con Karnak bus and one JETT bus daily in each direction between Amman and Damascus. You need to book in advance as demand for seats is high. For details of departure times and prices from Damascus see (p112).

SERVICE TAXI

Service taxis are faster than the buses and depart much more frequently. Damascus to Amman costs JD5.500 (S£385) either way. Service taxis run between Damascus and Irbid for JD4 (S£300).

TRAIN

The Hejaz Railway, a narrow-gauge line that was meant to link Damascus to Medina for the annual pilgrimage (see the boxed text The Hejaz Railway), is alive and kicking feebly on the stretch between Damascus and Amman (see p114 for departure times and costs). Train-watchers and nostalgics should be warned that the locomotive is generally a Romanian diesel-run machine, not a romantic, sooty steam

---

THE HEJAZ RAILWAY

Begun in 1907, the Hejaz Railway was the last grand vision of the dying Ottoman Empire. It was an ambitious scheme to connect Damascus to Medina in Saudi Arabia by rail. Ostensibly, this was to facilitate the annual pilgrimage to Mecca but, perhaps more importantly, it was a way of consolidating Constantinople's hold on the region – the trains were as useful for troops as pilgrims.

This underlying military significance very quickly proved the undoing of the line. When war broke out in 1914 the Hejaz became a strategic target and it was this railway that was repeatedly blown up by Lawrence of Arabia.

The line never, in fact, reached Medina and with the dissolution of the Ottoman Empire that followed the Allied victory, there was never any need for it to be completed. In recent times desultory talks on the possibility of resurrecting the Hejaz Railway in its full glory have concluded that such a project would only be viable if the line were reconnected to the European rail network – a long-term goal of more visionary thinkers in the Middle East, but some way from becoming reality.

---

job, although some travellers have had the luck to get the sooty version on the Syria leg.

Saudi Arabia & Kuwait

It is possible to go direct from Syria to Saudi Arabia by bus, via Jordan. There are also irregular services all the way to Kuwait. For details inquire at the Karnak office at the Baramke terminal in Damascus.

Turkey
BUS

You can buy tickets in İstanbul for buses to Aleppo (approximately 24 hours) or Damascus (30 hours), costing US$24 to US$30, depending on which company you travel with and regardless of whether you are going to Aleppo or Damascus. Buses leave daily, usually with five or six departures between about 11am and early evening. The journey usually involves a change of bus at Antakya, the last major Turkish city before the border.

The buses cross at Bab al-Hawa, the most convenient and busiest border post between the two neighbours. The volume of traffic means delays are frequent with waits of up to a couple of hours. One way to side step this is to in İstanbul buy a bus ticket only as far as Antakya, and from there make your own way to Syria. Take a local bus from Antakya to Reyhanli from where you can catch a dolmuš (shared taxi; can be a minibus or sedan) to the border; after crossing on foot (a long and sweaty 2km in summer) you can try to pick up a lift on the Syrian side.

Alternatively, from Antakya you also have the option of catching a dolmuš south to Yayladaği (these go from beside the Etibank, opposite the entrance to the bus station), from where you pick up a taxi or hitch the few kilometres further to the border. Once across (crossing takes just 15 minutes), you're only 2km from the Syrian mountain village of Kassab, from where regular microbuses make the 45-minute run to Lattakia on the Mediterranean coast. To get to Kassab from the border, walk about 10 minutes to the main road at the point where it curves sharply to your right, and then flag down any northbound microbus. (Southbound microbuses will be heading from Kassab to Lattakia, but they'll probably be already full and won't pick you up here.)

You can also cross from Gaziantep: take a dolmuš to Kilis, then another to the border, walk across then take a taxi for around US$2 to Azaz in Syria from where a bus to Aleppo is just S£20.

From northeast Syria it's also possible to cross into Turkey at Qamishle (see p227. From Damascus and Aleppo, there are direct buses to İstanbul and several other Turkish destinations, including Ankara. Fares are considerably cheaper from Aleppo: S£950 to İstanbul as opposed to S£1500 from Damascus.

TRAIN

Syria used to be the terminus for the *Tarsus Express*, the eastward extension of the famed *Orient Express*. The *Tarsus* set off from İstanbul's Haydarpaşa station and terminated at Aleppo, where travellers could then change trains and catch a service that went via Lattakia down through Beirut and to Haifa in I&PT. Aleppo was also the starting point for services to Baghdad and through to Tehrān.

Sadly, that sort of rail travel came to an end in the Middle East soon after WWII when poor relations between the newly emerging states of the region meant minimal cooperation and locked down borders.

However, a limited form of rail travel between Turkey and Syria has persisted, and there is one weekly service that continues to run between İstanbul and Aleppo/Damascus. It departs Haydarpaşa station at 8.55am Thursday morning, arriving 2.34pm in Aleppo (£19) the following day, terminating at Damascus at 8.06pm (£24). The sleeper supplement is £17/17 (Aleppo/Damascus) for a single or £11/11 per person in a double. For further details you could check the website for **Turkish Railways** (www.tcdd.gov.tr), but the English version was being redeveloped and it was in Turkish only at the time of writing.

For details of train services from the Syrian side, see the Getting There & Away sections for Damascus (p112) and Aleppo (p194).

Also see the website http://www.seat61.com for other useful travel information.

OVERLAND TOURS

For people with time to indulge, Syria can be visited as part of an overland trip taking in a combination of three, four or more countries – typically Turkey, Syria, Jordan and Egypt. You travel in a specially adapted 'overland truck' with anywhere between 16 and 24 other passengers and your group leader. Accommodation is usually a mix of camping and budget hotels and everyone is expected to pitch in.

Travelling in such a self-contained bubble, the success of the trip very much depends on the group chemistry. It could be one long party on wheels or six endless weeks of grin and bear it. And no, you don't get to vote anyone off.

Following is a list of tour operators.

Dragoman (☎ 01728 862 222; www.dragoman.com) İstanbul to Cairo (or vice versa) through Turkey, Syria, Jordan and Egypt in four to 6½ weeks.

Exodus (☎ 020-8675 5550; www.exodus.co.uk) Trips include a 'Middle East Explorer' – seven weeks through Turkey, Syria, Jordan and Egypt.

Kumuka (☎ 0800 068 8855; www.kumuka.co.uk) Masses of routes offered including dedicated explorations of Egypt, Jordan or Syria.

Oasis Overland (☎ 01258 471 155; www.oasisoverland.co.uk) Turkey, Syria, Jordan and Egypt in 21 or 35 days.

GETTING AROUND

TRAVEL BETWEEN SYRIA & LEBANON

You cannot get a Syrian visa in Lebanon, but you can now get a Lebanese visa at the border when entering from Syria. For more details, see Visas (p375).

There are four different crossing points from Lebanon into Syria: Masnaa, on the Beirut-Damascus Hwy, Al-Qaa, at the northern end of the Bekaa Valley, Aarida on the coastal road from Tripoli to Lattakia and Aabboudiye on the Tripoli to Homs route.

Air

For information on flying in and out of Syria, see p112, and for Lebanon, see p381.

Bus

Buses to Syria from Beirut leave from Charles Helou bus station, just east of the restored downtown area. You must go in person to buy your ticket and, if possible, it's best to book a seat the day before you travel. The first bus to Damascus leaves at 5.30am, and they run every half-hour until 7am, after which they leave hourly. Buses to Aleppo (ask for Halab) start at 7.30am and leave at half-hourly intervals until midday. There are also three buses a day (10.30am, 2pm and 5.30pm) to Lattakia, six to Homs (7.30am, 9.30am, 1.30pm, 5pm, 7pm and 9.30pm) and four to Hama (9.30am, 5pm, 7pm and 9.30pm).

Tripoli also has extensive bus services to Syria. A number of bus companies cluster around Jamal Abdel Nasser Square in the city centre, many offering air-con and on-board videos. There are frequent departures to Homs, Hama and Aleppo in the morning, starting at around 9am until midday; there are not as many buses in the afternoon. Buses travelling to Lattakia and Damascus are fewer in number and tend to depart in the afternoon. For average prices and travel times, see the boxed text Fares Between Syria & Lebanon.

From Damascus, private and Karnak (government-run) buses travel to Lebanon. Both types of buses leave from the Baramke terminal, which is about a 15-minute walk to the west of Martyrs Square. The prices quoted in the table are for the privately operated buses; Karnak bus fares tend to be a bit cheaper.

From Aleppo, the buses leave from the bus station tucked away just behind Baron St, not two minutes from the Baron Hotel. Again the services to Beirut are mainly privately operated buses.

Service Taxi & Taxi

If you do prefer to take a taxi, either service or private, in Beirut they depart from the Cola bus station and taxi stand or from Charles Helou bus station. In Tripoli they depart from Jamal Abdel Nasser Square. The service taxis leave when they are full but there is seldom a wait of more than 20 minutes or so. Service and private taxis travel to and from Damascus, where you can change to continue on to Jordan. A private taxi from Beirut to Damascus costs about US$50.

TRANSPORT

FARES BETWEEN SYRIA & LEBANON

Bus

route	cost (LL/S£)	duration
Beirut–Aleppo	LL10,500/S£250	6hr
Beirut–Damascus	LL7000/S£175	3hr
Beirut–Hama	LL9000/S£250	6hr
Beirut–Homs	LL8500/S£250	4hr
Beirut–Lattakia	LL9000	4hr
Tripoli–Aleppo	LL8000/S£175	4hr
Tripoli–Hama	LL6500	2hr
Tripoli–Homs	LL6000/S£150	1½hr
Tripoli–Lattakia	LL6000	2hr

Service Taxi

route	cost	duration
Baalbek–Damascus	LL9000/S£300	1½hr
Baalbek–Homs	LL9000	1½-2½hr
Beirut–Aleppo	LL21,000/S£300	5hr
Beirut–Damascus	LL15,000	3hr
Beirut–Hama	LL15,000	4hr
Beirut–Homs	LL15,000	3hr
Beirut–Lattakia	LL15,000	3hr
Beirut–Tartus	LL12,000	2hr
Tripoli–Hama	LL9000	2hr
Tripoli–Homs	LL7000	1½hr
Tripoli–Lattakia	LL9000	2hr

Note: Travel times do not include the border crossings, which depend on the traffic.

TRANSPORT

Tours

See the Tours sections under Damascus (p101) and Beirut (p253) for details of tours around each individual city.

LOCAL TOUR OPERATORS

Local tour operators offer a variety of tours – most (with a couple of exceptions) offer one-day excursions starting and ending in Beirut. There are some longer tours available which include Syria and/or Jordan.

Adonis Travel (www.adonistravel.com)

Campus Travel (☎ 01-744 588; www.campus-travel.net; Maktabi Bldg, Rue Makhoul, Hamra, Beirut) Travel agency focusing on student travel. Arranges skiing trips, tours in Lebanon and to neighbouring countries such as Syria and Jordan.

Destination Liban (☎ 03-497 762; lucien@intracom.net.lb; 2nd fl, Safi Bldg, Rue Yared, near Rue Monot, Achrafiye, Beirut) Specialising in youth and budget travel, Destination Liban arranges cheap accommodation, gives information on places to eat and offers small tours of archaeological sites (usually guided by archaeology students) for about US$30 to US$45 per day, all inclusive. Also arranges outdoor activities such as rafting and hiking.

Esprit-Nomade (☎ 03-223 552; www.esprit-nomade.com) Offers hiking, rural tourism and responsible ecotourism with innovative programming.

Greenline (☎ /fax 01-746 215; www.greenline.org.lb) One of Lebanon's most active environmental organisations, it arranges treks and day trips into the mountains and countryside of Lebanon.

Jasmin Tours (www.jasmintours.com) Based in Damascus, this company offers a variety of Syrian tours, including hiking, culture and nature tours. It also offers tours of Lebanon, Jordan and Iran.

Lebanese Adventure (☎ /fax 01-398 982, 03-360 027; www.lebanese-adventure.com; Sioufi, Achrafiye, Beirut) Different outdoor activities throughout the country are arranged each weekend. It can also tailor-make excursions for a minimum of five people.

Liban Trek (☎ 01-329 975; www.libantrek.com; 7th fl, Yazbek B, Rue Adib Ishac, Achrafiye, Beirut) A well-established trekking club that arranges weekend treks throughout Lebanon. It also organises trips to Syria, Jordan, Egypt and Turkey, as well as other mountain sports.

Mosaic Travel (www.mosaic-travel.com)

Nakhal & Co (☎ 01-389 389; www.nakhal.com.lb; Ghorayeb Bldg, Rue Sami al-Solh, Badaro) Its local tours cover Aanjar, Baalbek, Beiteddine, Byblos, The Cedars, Sidon, Tripoli and Tyre. It also organises tours from Lebanon to Syria.

Saad Tours (☎ 01-429 429, 427 427; www.saadtours.com; 8th fl, George Haddad Bldg, Rue Amin Gemayel, Sioufi, Achrafiye, Beirut) A consortium of tour operators that offers local sightseeing trips and tours to Syria and Jordan.

Safir Travel (www.safir-travel.com/program.htm)

Tania Travel (☎ 01-739 682/3/4; www.taniatravel.com; 1st fl, Shames Bldg, Rue Sidani, opposite Jeanne d'Arc theatre, Hamra, Beirut) Has tours to Aanjar, Baalbek, Bcharré, Beiteddine, Byblos, The Cedars, Deir al-Qamar, Sidon, Tyre and one-day trips to Damascus.

Thermique (☎ /fax 09-953 756, 03-288 193) In Ajaltoun, just outside Beirut, runs day-long guided bicycle tours in Qornet as-Sawda (p273), Lebanon's highest peak, among other destinations. It also arranges paragliding expeditions p357.

ORGANISED IN YOUR HOME COUNTRY

The companies listed here offer trips to the Middle East of one kind or another. It does pay to do some research yourself, including checking travel magazines and travel supplements in the national newspapers.

Australia

Most of the companies act as agents for the UK packages, though there are a few interesting home-grown outfits:

Adventure World (☎ 1800 133 322, 02-9956 7766) Agents for the UK's Explore Worldwide and Exodus.

Passport Travel (☎ 03-9867 3888; www.travelcentre.com.au) Middle East specialist with no packages, no brochures; instead Passport assists in arranging itineraries for individuals or groups.

Peregrine (☎ 03-663 8611; www.peregrine.net.au) Agents for the UK's Dragoman and The Imaginative Traveller.

Yalla (☎ 03-9510 2844; www.yallatours.com.au) Wide variety of pick 'n' mix package tours and private arrangement tours including Syria.

UK

Exodus (☎ 0870 240 5550; www.exodus.co.uk; 9 Weir Rd, London SW12 0LT) Well-regarded adventure specialists whose itineraries include 'A Week in Syria'.

Explore Worldwide (www.exploreworldwide.com) Offers numerous tours of Syria and Lebanon, catering for family groups to those requiring more adventurous journeys.

Martin Randall Travel Ltd (☎ 020-8742 3355; www.martinrandall.com) Cultural tours led by academics. Includes Syria and Lebanon.

Travelbag Adventures (☎ 01420 541 007; www.travelbag-adventures.com) Small group adventure tours including 'Castles & Caravans' excursion.

USA & Canada

Adventure Center (☎ 1 800-227 8747; www.adventure-center.com) Agents for the UK's Dragoman and Explore Worldwide.

Bestway Tours & Safaris (☎ 1 800-663 0844; www.bestway.com) Small Canadian-based group tours including nine- and 15-day packages combining Syria and Lebanon.

Geographic Expeditions (☎ 1 800-777 8183; www
.geoex.com) Offers a 22-day crammed tour taking in some of
the highlights of Lebanon, Syria and Jordan – quickly.

SYRIA
Air
The national carrier, SyrianAir, operates a
very reasonable internal air service and flights
are cheap by international standards. Unless
you're on a 'cash rich–time poor' itinerary it
may make more sense to catch the bus; the
Damascus–Qamishle flight is perhaps the
only exception to this.

Sample one-way fares (return fares are
double):

Aleppo S£900
Deir ez-Zur S£742
Lattakia S£532
Qamishle S£1200

Bicycle
A growing number of independent travellers
are choosing to cycle Syria, both as a destination in itself or as part of a wider bike tour
around the Mediterranean, Middle East,
or indeed overland from Europe to Asia.
Cycling Syria can be hard work for several
reasons: Syrians are not used to long-distance
cyclists, which means you need to pay extra
attention on the roads; the extreme temperatures, especially in summer, need to be taken
into account; plus, you need to carry a fairly
hefty amount of kit, including complete
tools and spares, because you cannot rely on
finding what you need on the way.

On the plus side, cyclists manage to meet
more people and therefore are the recipients
of wonderful Syrian hospitality – receiving
fantastic welcomes everywhere they go,
showered with invitations to stop and eat or
drink and frequently offered accommodation
for the night.

PRACTICALITIES
Carry a couple of extra chain links, a chain
breaker, spokes, a spoke key, two inner tubes,
tyre levers and a repair kit, a flat-head and
Phillips screwdriver, and Allen keys and span-
ners to fit all the bolts on your bike. Check the
bolts daily and carry spares. Fit as many water
bottles to your bike as you can – it gets hot.

Make sure the bike's gearing will get you
over the hills, and confine your panniers
to 15kg maximum. May to mid-June and
September to October are the best times for

cycling; in between, bring lots of extra water.
In your panniers include: a two-person tent
(weighing about 1.8kg) that can also accommodate the bike where security is a concern;
a sleeping bag rated to 0°C and a Therm-a-
Rest; small camping stove with gas canisters;
MSR cooking pot; utensils; Katadyn water
filter (2 microns) and Maglite. Wear cycling
shorts with chamois bum and cleated cycling
shoes. Don't fill the panniers with food as it
is plentiful and fresh along the route.

It's also a good idea to carry a **Dog Dazer**
(www.ctcshop.co.uk) or something similar. Wild,
biting mutts are a big problem, particularly
on the Desert Hwy out to Palmyra and Deir
ez-Zur. If nothing else, carry a big stick or a
pouch of stones.

Throughout this guide there are addresses
and locations of bicycle repairs and spares
workshops; look for them in the Getting
Around section of each town and city entry.

Bus
Syria has a well-developed road network
and, partly because private car ownership is
comparatively low level, public transport is
frequent and very cheap. Distances are short,
so journeys are rarely more than a few hours.
About the longest single bus ride you can
take is the nine-hour trip from Damascus
to Qamishle in the northeast.

Several kinds of buses ply the same routes,
the best being the 'luxury' buses, then Karnak,
then the Pullmans.

KARNAK & OTHER BUSES
The orange-and-white buses of the state-
run Karnak company were once the deluxe
carriers on the Syrian highways. However,
with so many rival companies now employing faster, sleeker vehicles, they look a poor
cousin today – but they are usually 20% to
30% cheaper. For this reason – and because
the services are few – it's always wise to book
at least a day in advance.

There's also a third, even cheaper category
of buses, sometimes referred to as 'Pullmans'. These are old, battered stock – in the
more extreme cases, genuine rust buckets for
which a punt on a ticket is akin to a gamble
on whether the vehicle's going to make it or
not. This is the cheapest way of covering
long distances between towns. These vehicles have their own 'garages', quarantined
well away from those of the luxury buses. At

BUS STATIONS & TICKETING

Most Syrian towns and cities have a central or main bus station, which is home base for the various 'luxury' companies. There's often a second or third station too, devoted to second and third ranks of buses. These stations, known locally as *karaj*, ie garages, are basic affairs, no more than an asphalt lot with a row of prefab huts serving as booking offices for the various companies. Annoyingly, there's no central source of information giving departure times or prices so it's simply a case of walking around and finding out which company has the next bus to your desired destination.

With so many companies, departures are frequent, and it's rarely necessary to book in advance. Just show up at the station and something will be heading off your way sometime usually about right now.

Beware the touts – particularly persistent at Aleppo, Damascus and Homs – who will attempt to steer you to the bus company paying the greatest commission, irrespective of the time of the next bus. Start by heading straight for the Qadmous or Al-Ahliah office, and if they don't have a bus departing any time soon, then walk around and start asking the times of the other companies' buses.

Buying tickets is straightforward, but you need your passport so the ticketing person can enter your details in the log. It's always wise to carry your passport at all times anyway in case of random ID checks. Seats are assigned.

---

the same 'old bus' stations you'll usually find boxy minibuses, which run the same long-distance routes offering a bare minimum of comfort at an even cheaper price.

LUXURY BUS

At one time the state-owned bus company, Karnak, had a monopoly on the road, but since the early 1990s a crop of private companies, running what are commonly referred to as 'luxury' buses, has overtaken it. Routes are few and the many operators are all in fierce competition. Consequently, fares vary little and the buses are all pretty much the same: large, newish, air-con – comfortable. Travelling with Qadmous, Al-Ahliah and Al-Rayan is recommended.

MINIBUS & MICROBUS

While buses – of whatever vintage – connect the major towns and cities, short hops and out-of-the-way places are serviced by fleets of minibuses and microbuses.

The term microbus (pronounced '*mee-crobaas*' or just '*mee-cro*') is a little blurred, it typically refers to those modern (mostly Japanese) little vans that are white with a sliding side door, and squeeze in about 12. These have set routes but no schedules, leaving when full. Passengers are picked up/set down anywhere along the route; just yell out for the driver to stop or flag him down from the roadside. Destinations may be written in Arabic on the front of the bus. At the micro-

bus station just listen out for somebody shouting the name of your destination.

SERVICE TAXI

Share taxis, which are also called service taxis (ser-*vees*), are usually old American Desotos and Dodges from the 1950s and '60s. There's a chronic shortage of spare parts but ingenuity and improvisation keep them running. Although more modern vehicles have begun to appear, most drivers persist with their old favourites – largely for their robustness and size (good for squeezing people in) – although they're fast disappearing.

Share taxis only operate on some major routes and in some cases seem to have succumbed to competition from microbuses. They can cost a lot more than the buses. Unless you're in a hurry, or you find yourself stuck on a highway and it's getting late, there's really no need to use them.

Car & Motorcycle
DRIVING LICENCE

Theoretically, you do require an International Driving Permit (IDP), but on the ground your own national licence should generally be sufficient. If you do decide to drive into Lebanon, you will need an IDP, the vehicle's registration papers and liability insurance. It is possible to service most common makes of vehicle in Lebanon. Petrol, available in the usual range of octanes and lead-free, is sold at most petrol stations.

HOSTAGE TO HOSPITALITY

The number one rule of travel in Syria is: be flexible. It's not that the transport system is bad – on the contrary, all manner of four-wheeled vehicles go wherever you need to go, frequently, and for very little money. But you share your journey with local Syrians and that adds an element of unpredictability. As a foreigner you're viewed as a 'guest in Syria' so you can expect to receive frequent invitations to talk, share in food, and often to come back home or accompany your fellow passenger to wherever it is they're going. Depending on how open you are to this proffered hospitality, you can find yourself alighting from the bus several stops earlier than anticipated in the company of a new companion heading off to go for tea, meet the family, look at some photos, watch some TV.

All of this is wonderful as long as you're not in any kind of hurry. Anyone with a relaxed attitude to sightseeing should take the locals up on their offers – it's a fine way to experience the country through its people rather than just its old stones. If refusing, be very polite.

FUEL & SPARE PARTS

If you are driving a car in Syria you'll be better off if it runs on diesel (mazout), which is widely available and dirt cheap at S£2.66 per litre. Regular petrol (benzin) costs S£6.85 a litre and super (sometimes referred to as *mumtaz*) costs S£20.40 a litre. The latter is fairly widely available, but you can forget about lead-free petrol.

Bring a good set of spare parts and some mechanical knowledge, as you will not always be able to get the help you may need. This is especially the case for motorcycles; there are precious few decent bike mechanics in Syria.

HIRE & INSURANCE

For a long time Europcar was the only car-hire firm in Syria, but Hertz now operates through Chamcar.

Rental rates are not cheap – far more expensive in fact than in Europe and America. Europcar's cheapest standard rate, for example, is US$62 a day for a Peugeot 106, unlimited kilometres, or US$35 for up to 100km then US$3.50 for every 10km thereafter. There's also a minimum rental of two/three days for limited kilometres/unlimited kilometres, which is standard with rental companies in Syria. Europcar also charges an additional fee of 75% of the daily rate if the car is returned to another town other than where it was rented.

A plethora of local companies has appeared since the early 1990s but many don't offer full insurance. Another problem with local agencies is maintenance. Vehicles are prone to breakdowns and poor back-up service translates to you hanging around for a day or two waiting for your hire car to be fixed or replaced.

You need to be at least 21 years old to rent a car in Syria, although some places require that you be 23. Most companies will require a deposit in cash of up to US$1000, or you can leave your credit card details. The following is a selection of car-rental companies:

Europcar Has hire desks in the Sheraton (☎ 011-222 9300) and Le Meridien (☎ 011-222 9200) hotels in Damascus.

Hertz (in Damascus ☎ 011-223 2300) This outfit operates through Chamcar.

Marmou (☎ 011-333 5787)

Cars & Drivers

An alternative option is to hire a car and driver for a day. Europcar charges US$87 a day for this, but you can usually manage to get a big old Mercedes taxi to ferry you around for a full day – and no insurance necessary and no deposit. You should be able to arrange something similar through your hotel but make it clear how many hours you want to be out and where you wish to go, and get a firm agreement on this and the price beforehand.

ROAD RULES

Traffic runs on the right-hand side of the road, while the speed limit is generally 60km/h in built-up areas, 70km/h on the open road and 110km/h on major highways.

The roads are generally quite reasonable in Syria, but in the backblocks you will find that most signposting is in Arabic only. Always take care when driving into villages and other built-up areas, as cars, people and animals all jostle for the same space.

TRANSPORT

SYRIA: ROAD DISTANCES (KM)

Damascus to Beirut = 127km

	Aleppo	Ath-Thaura	Bosra	Damascus	Deir ez-Zur	Hama	Homs	Lattakia	Maalula	Palmyra	Qala'at al-Hosn	Safita	Seidnayya	Suweida	Tartus
Aleppo	---														
Ath-Thaura	150	---													
Bosra	501	651	---												
Damascus	355	505	146	---											
Deir ez-Zur	321	201	567	421	---										
Hama	146	296	355	209	401	---									
Homs	193	343	308	162	354	47	---								
Lattakia	187	337	494	348	508	147	186	---							
Maalula	311	466	204	58	420	167	120	306	---						
Palmyra	353	194	366	220	201	207	160	346	230	---					
Qala'at al-Hosn	252	402	367	221	414	106	156	179	179	219	---				
Safita	261	421	386	240	432	125	78	120	120	238	32	---			
Seidnayya	339	489	176	30	420	196	149	335	335	250	208	227	---		
Suweida	462	614	39	107	528	316	269	455	167	327	328	347	137	---	
Tartus	287	437	404	258	450	143	96	90	90	256	73	31	245	365	---

Long-distance night driving can be just a little hairy, as not all drivers believe in using headlights, and general lighting is poor. Beware also of the mad overtaking. Some people appear to consider it a test of their courage to overtake in the most impossible situations.

Hitching

Although generally speaking Lonely Planet does not advocate hitching because of the small but potentially serious risk it involves, unless you have your own transport hitching cannot be avoided if you want to see some of Syria's more remote sites. In fact, as so many locals don't own cars, it is an accepted means of getting around. National courtesy dictates that often the first vehicle along will stop. Money is never expected and any attempt to pay is unequivocally refused.

However, despite the hospitality of many Syrians, people who choose to hitch will be safer if they travel in pairs and let someone know where they are planning to go. Women should never hitch alone.

Local Transport
BUS

All the major cities have a local bus and/or microbus system but, as the city centres are compact, you can usually get around on foot. This is just as well because neither the buses nor the microbuses have signs in English (and often no signs in Arabic), though they can be useful (and cheap) for getting out to distant microbus or train stations, especially in Damascus.

SERVICE TAXI & TAXI

Taxis in most cities are plentiful and cheap. In Damascus they have meters, although most drivers are unaware of their existence. Despite this, if you get into a taxi and ask how much it is to the bus station (or wherever) you will often be told the correct fare and bargaining will get you nowhere.

Although they are not in evidence in Damascus, some other cities, notably Aleppo, are served by local service taxis that run a set route, picking up, and dropping off passengers along the way for a set price. For the outsider, there is no obvious way to distinguish them from the normal taxis. If you can read Arabic, it's easy. Regular taxis have a sign on the doors reading 'Ujra medinat Halab, raqm...' (City of Aleppo Taxi, Number ...), while service taxis have a similar-looking sign reading 'Khidma Medinat Halab' (City of Aleppo Service) followed by the route name.

Should you end up sharing with other people and the taxi doesn't take you exactly where you want to go, you're probably in a service taxi.

Train

Syria has potentially an excellent railway network with more than 2000km of track connecting most main centres. The main line snakes its way from Damascus north to Aleppo via Homs and Hama before swinging southeast for Deir ez-Zur via Raqqa. At that point it turns northeast to Hassake and finally to Qamishle. Trains also operate on a couple of secondary lines, one of which runs from Aleppo to Lattakia, and then down the coast to Tartus and on to Homs to connect with the Damascus line.

However, the reality is that train travel is rarely an attractive option. The first drawback is that there are never more than three or four services a day between any given destinations (and often fewer) and some arrive and depart in the dead hours of morning. Not only does this disrupt your sleep but also most journeys are made in complete darkness so you don't see any scenery. Rolling stock is 1970s Russian with all the levels of comfort that implies. To compound matters, the stations are often awkwardly located a few kilometres from the centre of town and are poorly catered to, with little or no public transport (Aleppo and Lattakia, to name two, are exceptions).

Nevertheless, there are exceptions. The line between Aleppo and Lattakia passes through, under and over some beautiful scenery as it snakes its way across the barrier of the Jebel an-Ansariyya and down to the coast. There are four services a day, all travelling during daylight hours. Readers have also commended the overnight service from Aleppo down to Damascus, which seems a sensible way to cover ground if you're short on time (it saves wasting a day on a bus), plus it saves on at least one night's hotel bill.

Steam train buffs might appreciate the summer service up the Barada Gorge to Zabadani – see p121. It goes nowhere in particular but there's fun in getting there.

LEBANON

Lebanon is a tiny country, and although there are no internal air services, you don't really need them. You can drive from one end of the country to the other in half a day, depending on traffic congestion. Most visitors use the ever-useful service taxis (servees) to get around. A huge number run on set routes around the country, although you may have to use more than one to get to where you want to go. If you're going to less-travelled areas, taxis can add up and it could be worth your while to rent a car, which can be done very reasonably in Beirut.

Buses and minibuses also link the larger Lebanese towns, and there are two bus companies with extensive routes throughout Beirut and the outlying areas.

Bus

Buses travel between Beirut and Lebanon's major towns. There are three main bus pick-up and drop-off points in Beirut:

Charles Helou bus station (Map p251) Just east of downtown, for destinations north of Beirut (including Syria).

Cola transport hub (Map p238) This is in fact a confused intersection that is sometimes called Mazraa. It is generally for destinations south of Beirut.

Dawra transport hub East of Beirut, and covering the same destinations as Charles Helou, it is usually a port of call on the way in and out of the city.

Charles Helou is the only formal station and is systematically divided into three signposted zones:

Zone A For buses to Syria.

Zone B For buses servicing Beirut (where the route starts or finishes at Charles Helou).

Zone C For express buses to Jounieh, Byblos and Tripoli.

Zones A and C have ticket offices where you can buy tickets for your journey.

Cola is not as well organised as Charles Helou but if someone doesn't find you first (which is what usually happens) ask any driver where the next bus to your destination is leaving from. Buses usually have the destination displayed on the front window or above it in Arabic only. There's also a growing number of independently owned microbuses covering the same routes, which are slightly more expensive than regular buses, but a lot cheaper than service taxis. They are small, comfortable and frequent, but you take your chances regarding the driver's ability. You pay for your ticket on the microbus, at either the start or the end of your journey.

Car & Motorcycle
DRIVING LICENCE
Theoretically, you do require an International Driving Permit (IDP) to hire a car, but on the ground your own national licence should generally be sufficient. If you do decide to drive into Lebanon, you will need an IDP.

FUEL & SPARE PARTS
Petrol, including unleaded, are easily available and reasonably priced (about LL1100 per litre for unleaded).

HIRE & INSURANCE
If your budget can cover renting a car, it is the best way to see the most beautiful areas of Lebanon. Cars can easily be rented in Lebanon and, if you shop around, for surprisingly reasonable prices. If there are three or four of you, it becomes a very feasible way to travel, even if you're on a tight budget. Most of the big rental agencies are in Beirut (see p265 for a selection of car-rental companies), although a few can be found in other cities. If you shop around, you can find a small two- or three-door car for as little as US$25 per day with unlimited kilometres. A more luxurious model (Mercedes, for example) will be more like US$250 per day. If you want a local driver, it will set you back an additional US$25 to US$50 per day.

All companies require a refundable deposit from all except credit-card holders, and offer free delivery and collection during working hours. The minimum age for drivers is 21 years, but some rental agencies will charge extra if you are under 25. You cannot take hire cars over the border into Syria.

ROAD RULES
The first rule of driving in Lebanon is: forget rules. Driving is on the right side of the road, unless the vehicles in front are not fast enough, in which case one drives on the left. The horn is used liberally because nobody uses their mirrors. In other words, anarchy rules and if you like aggressive driving, you'll

do just fine. If you're a nervous driver, you might be too intimidated to nose your way out of the car-rental garage. If you do take the plunge (and it's surprisingly easy to unlearn the rules of the road), stay extremely alert, particularly on mountain roads, where cars hurtle around hairpin bends without a thought to oncoming traffic. The only other thing to remember is that you must stop at ALL military checkpoints. See the boxed text Checkpoint Etiquette (p351) for tips on getting through them with your dignity intact.

Hitching
Hitching is not very common in Lebanon – the tourists who venture off the service-taxi routes tend to either rent cars or private taxis. This may be to your advantage if you decide to try hitching a lift. The novelty of foreigners increases your chances of a lift – it helps if you look foreign. The usual precautions apply, though: never hitch alone if you are a woman, and even two women travelling together are vulnerable. With the habit of private cars turning into taxis at will, there is a chance that the driver will expect payment. There does not seem to be a very polite way out of this situation, except to ask first if the driver is going to charge you for the ride. Travellers who decide to hitch should understand that they are taking a small but potentially serious risk. People who do choose to hitch will be safer if they travel in pairs and let someone know where they are planning to go.

Local Transport
BICYCLE
The terrain in Lebanon is extremely steep once you leave the coastal strip and it really suits a mountain bike. The state of some of the urban roads also demand a rugged all-terrain type bike. Keep in mind that the traffic problems described earlier under Road Rules will also present a hazard to the cyclist and extreme care should be taken when riding anywhere in Lebanon. Having said that, the scenery is beautiful and the air in the mountains clear, although it would be best to avoid the summer months when heat exhaustion can be a real hazard.

BUS
Beirut and its environs now have two bus services, one operated by the privately owned

LEBANON: ROAD DISTANCES (KM)

Beirut to Damascus = 127km

	Amioun	Baalbek	Batroun	Bcharré	Beirut	Beiteddine	Byblos	Hermel	Jezzine	Jounieh	Marjeyun	Sidon	Tripoli	Tyre	Zahlé
Amioun	---														
Baalbek	97	---													
Batroun	24	113	---												
Bcharré	37	60	53	---											
Beirut	82	83	58	111	---										
Beiteddine	125	88	97	154	43	---									
Byblos	47	119	223	75	36	78	---								
Hermel	117	62	133	80	146	150	155	---							
Jezzine	153	109	129	182	71	29	107	179	---						
Jounieh	61	101	37	90	21	64	14	167	92	---					
Marjeyun	185	115	160	175	102	85	138	185	56	124	---				
Sidon	123	124	99	152	41	42	77	187	30	62	61	---			
Tripoli	222	109	33	49	91	134	55	102	162	70	193	132	---		
Tyre	161	163	137	190	79	80	115	225	48	101	79	38	170	---	
Zahlé	133	36	105	96	47	52	79	99	73	65	78	88	138	126	---

Lebanese Commuting Company (LCC), the other by the state-owned OCFTC. They both operate a hail and ride system and have a fare of LL500 for all except the most distant destinations (such as Byblos and far-off suburbs). For route details, see Public Transport (p265).

SERVICE TAXI & TAXI

Most routes around towns and cities are covered by service taxi and you can hail one at any point on the route. The only way to find out if the driver is going where you want is to hail him and ask. If the driver is not going where you want he'll (and it's nearly always a 'he') respond by driving off. If he's going in your direction the acknowledgment to get in may be as imperceptible as a head gesture. You can get out at any point along their route by saying 'anzil huun' (I get out here), to the driver. Occasionally when the drivers have an empty car they will try and charge you a private taxi fare. To let him know that you want to take the taxi as a service taxi, be sure to ask him 'servees?'. Taxis are usually

an elderly Mercedes with red licence plates, generally with a taxi sign on the roof and smoke belching from both the interior and the exhaust. The fixed fare for all routes around towns is LL1000. The fare to outlying parts of towns is LL2000. Try and pay at the earliest opportunity during your trip. It's a good idea to keep a few LL1000 notes handy for these trips.

If you do wish to take a service taxi as a private taxi, make sure the driver understands exactly where you are going and negotiate a price before you get in. Prices vary according to destination, and the typical fares are listed in the Getting There and Away section of each destination. If you have a lot of sightseeing to do in out-of-the-way places, you can hire a taxi and driver by the day. Haggling skills come to the fore here, but expect to pay at least US$50 per day plus tip.

You can order taxis by phone from a number of private companies; they'll take you anywhere in Lebanon and some also have services to Syria and Jordan. See p265 for contact numbers.

Health Dr Caroline Evans

Prevention is the key to staying healthy while travelling in the Middle East. Infectious diseases can and do occur in the region, but these are usually associated with poor living conditions and poverty and can be avoided with a few precautions. The most common reason for travellers needing medical help is as a result of accidents – cars are not always well maintained and poorly lit roads are littered with potholes. Medical facilities can be excellent in large cities, but in remoter areas they may be more basic.

BEFORE YOU GO

A little planning before departure, particularly for pre-existing illnesses, will save you a lot of trouble later. See your dentist before a long trip; carry a spare pair of contact lenses and glasses (and take your optical prescription with you); and carry a first-aid kit.

It's tempting to leave it all to the last minute – don't! Many vaccines don't ensure immunity for two weeks, so visit a doctor four to eight weeks before departure. Ask your doctor for an International Certificate of Vaccination (otherwise known as the yellow booklet), which will list all the vaccinations you've received. This is mandatory for countries that require proof of yellow fever vaccination upon entry, but it's a good idea to carry it wherever you travel.

Travellers can register with the International Association for Medical Advice to Travellers (IMAT; www.iamat.org). Its website can help travellers to find a doctor with recognised training. Those heading off to very remote areas may like to do a first-aid course (Red Cross and St John Ambulance can help) or attend a remote medicine first-aid course such as the one offered by the Royal Geographical Society (www.rgs.org).

Bring medications in their original, clearly labelled, containers. A signed and dated letter from your physician describing your medical conditions and medications, including generic names, is also a good idea. If carrying syringes or needles, be sure to have a physician's letter documenting their medical necessity.

INSURANCE

Find out in advance if your insurance plan will make payments directly to providers or reimburse you later for overseas health expenditures (in many countries doctors expect payment in cash); it's also worth checking that your travel insurance will cover repatriation home or to better medical facilities elsewhere. Your insurance company may be able to locate the nearest source of medical help, or you can ask at your hotel. In an emergency contact your embassy or consulate. Your travel insurance will not usually cover you for anything other than emergency dental treatment. Not all insurance covers emergency air evacuation home or to a hospital in a major city, which may be the only way to get medical attention for a serious emergency.

RECOMMENDED VACCINATIONS

The World Health Organization recommends that all travellers, regardless of the region they are travelling in, should be covered for diphtheria, tetanus, measles, mumps, rubella and polio, as well as hepatitis B. While making preparations to travel, take the opportunity to ensure that all of your routine vaccination cover is complete. The consequences of these diseases can be severe and outbreaks do occur in the Middle East.

MEDICAL CHECKLIST

Following is a list of items you should consider packing in your medical kit.

- Antibiotics (if travelling off the beaten track)
- Antidiarrhoeal drugs (eg loperamide)
- Acetaminophen/paracetamol (Tylenol) or aspirin
- Anti-inflammatory drugs (eg ibuprofen)
- Antihistamines (for hay fever and allergic reactions)
- Antibacterial ointment (eg Bactroban) for cuts and abrasions
- Steroid cream or cortisone (for allergic rashes)
- Bandages, gauze and gauze rolls
- Adhesive or paper tape
- Scissors, safety pins and tweezers
- Thermometer
- Pocket knife
- DEET-containing insect repellent for the skin
- Permethrin-containing insect spray for clothing, tents and bed nets
- Sun block
- Oral rehydration salts
- Iodine tablets (for water purification)
- Syringes and sterile needles (if travelling to remote areas)

INTERNET RESOURCES

There is a wealth of travel health advice on the Internet. For further information, the Lonely Planet website (www.lonelyplanet.com) is a good place to start. The World Health Organization (www.who.int/ith) publishes a superb book, *International Travel and Health*, which is revised annually and is available online at no cost. Another website of general interest is MD Travel Health (www.mdtravelhealth.com), which provides complete travel health recommendations for every country, updated daily, also at no cost. The Centers for Disease Control and Prevention website (www.cdc.gov) is a very useful source of traveller's health information.

FURTHER READING

Lonely Planet's *Travel With Children* is packed with useful information including pretrip planning, emergency first aid, immunisation and disease information, and

---

TRAVEL HEALTH WEBSITES

It's usually a good idea to consult your government's travel health website before departure, if one is available.

Australia (www.dfat.gov.au/travel)
Canada (www.travelhealth.gc.ca)
United Kingdom (www.doh.gov.uk/traveladvice)
United States (www.cdc.gov/travel)

---

what to do if you get sick on the road. Other recommended references include *Traveller's Health* by Dr Richard Dawood (Oxford University Press), *International Travel Health Guide* by Stuart R Rose MD (Travel Medicine Inc) and *The Travellers' Good Health Guide* by Ted Lankester (Sheldon Press), an especially useful health guide for volunteers and long-term expatriates working in the Middle East.

IN TRANSIT

DEEP VEIN THROMBOSIS (DVT)

Deep vein thrombosis occurs when blood clots form in the legs during plane flights, chiefly because of prolonged immobility. The longer the flight, the greater the risk. Though most blood clots are reabsorbed uneventfully, some may break off and travel through the blood vessels to the lungs, where they may cause life-threatening complications.

The chief symptom of deep vein thrombosis is swelling or pain in the foot, ankle or calf, usually but not always on just one side. When a blood clot travels to the lungs, the clot may cause chest pain and difficulty breathing. Travellers with any of these symptoms should immediately seek medical attention.

To prevent the development of deep vein thrombosis on long flights you should walk about the cabin, perform isometric compressions of the leg muscles (ie contract the leg muscles while sitting), drink plenty of fluids, and avoid alcohol and tobacco.

JET LAG & MOTION SICKNESS

Jet lag is common when crossing more than five time zones; it results in insomnia, fatigue, malaise or nausea. To avoid jet lag try drinking plenty of fluids (nonalcoholic) and eating light meals. Upon arrival, seek exposure to natural sunlight and readjust your schedule (for meals, sleep etc) as soon as possible.

Antihistamines such as dimenhydrinate (Dramamine) and meclizine (Antivert, Bonine) are usually the first choice for treating motion sickness. Their main side-effect is drowsiness. A herbal alternative is ginger, which works like a charm for some people.

IN SYRIA & LEBANON

AVAILABILITY & COST OF HEALTH CARE

The health-care systems in the Middle East are varied. Reciprocal arrangements with countries rarely exist and you should be prepared to pay for all medical and dental treatment.

Medical care is not always readily available outside major cities. Medicine, and even sterile dressings or intravenous fluids, may need to be bought from a local pharmacy. Nursing care may be limited or rudimentary as this is something families and friends are expected to provide. The travel assistance provided by your insurance may be able to locate the nearest source of medical help, otherwise ask at your hotel. In an emergency contact your embassy or consulate.

Standards of dental care are variable and there is an increased risk of hepatitis B and HIV transmission via poorly sterilised equipment. Keep in mind that your travel insurance will not usually cover you for anything other than emergency dental treatment.

For minor illnesses such as diarrhoea, pharmacists can often provide valuable advice and sell over-the-counter medication. They can also offer advice on when more specialised help is needed.

INFECTIOUS DISEASES
Diphtheria

Diphtheria is spread through close respiratory contact. It causes a high temperature and severe sore throat. Sometimes a membrane forms across the throat requiring a tracheostomy to prevent suffocation. Vaccination is recommended for those likely to be in close contact with the local population in infected areas. The vaccine is given as an injection alone, or with tetanus, and lasts 10 years.

Hepatitis A

Hepatitis A is spread through contaminated food (particularly shellfish) and water. It causes jaundice, and although it is rarely fatal, can cause prolonged lethargy and delayed recovery. Symptoms include dark urine, a yellow colour to the whites of the eyes, fever and abdominal pain. Hepatitis A vaccine (Avaxim, VAQTA, Havrix) is given as an injection: a single dose will give protection for up to a year while a booster 12 months later will provide a subsequent 10 years of protection. Hepatitis A and typhoid vaccines can also be given as a single dose vaccine, hepatyrix or viatim.

Hepatitis B

Infected blood, contaminated needles and sexual intercourse can all transmit hepatitis B. It can cause jaundice, and affects the liver, occasionally causing liver failure. All travellers should make this a routine vaccination. (Many countries now give hepatitis B vaccination as part of routine childhood vaccination.) The vaccine is given singly, or at the same time as the hepatitis A vaccine (hepatyrix). A course will give protection for at least five years. It can be given over four weeks, or six months.

HIV

HIV is spread via infected blood and blood products, sexual intercourse with an infected partner and from an infected mother to her newborn child. It can be spread through 'blood to blood' contacts such as contaminated instruments during medical, dental, acupuncture and other body piercing procedures and sharing used intravenous needles.

Countries in the region that require a negative HIV test as a visa requirement for some categories of visas include the United Arab Emirates, Egypt, Iran, Iraq, Jordan, Kuwait, Lebanon, Libya, Qatar and Saudi Arabia.

Leishmaniasis

Spread through the bite of an infected sand fly, leishmaniasis, in its cutaneous form, can cause a slowly growing skin lump or ulcer. In its visceral form it may develop into a serious life-threatening fever usually accompanied by anaemia and weight loss. Infected dogs are also carriers of the infection. Sand fly bites should be avoided whenever possible by using DEET-based repellents.

Malaria

The prevalence of malaria varies throughout the Middle East. Many areas are considered to be malaria-free, while others have seasonal risks. The risk of malaria is minimal in most cities, however check with your doctor if you are considering travelling to any rural areas. It is important to take antimalarial tablets if the risk is significant. For up-to-date information about the risk of contracting malaria in a specific country, contact your local travel-health clinic.

Anyone who has travelled in a country where malaria is present should be aware of the symptoms of malaria. It is possible to contract malaria from a single bite from an infected mosquito. Malaria almost always starts with marked shivering, fever and sweating. Muscle pains, headache and vomiting are common. Symptoms may occur anywhere from a few days to three weeks after the infected mosquito bite. The illness can start while you are taking preventative tablets if they are not fully effective, and may also occur after you have finished taking your tablets.

Poliomyelitis

Polio is generally spread through contaminated food and water. It is one of the vaccines given in childhood and should be boosted every 10 years, either orally (a drop on the tongue) or as an injection. Polio may be carried without symptoms, although it can cause a transient fever and, in rare cases, potentially permanent muscle weakness or paralysis.

Rabies

Spread through bites or licks on broken skin from an infected animal, rabies is fatal. Animal handlers should be vaccinated, as should those travelling to remote areas where a reliable source of post-bite vaccine is not available within 24 hours. Three injections are needed over a month. If you are infected and you have not been vaccinated, you will need a course of five injections starting within 24 hours or as soon as possible after the injury. Vaccination does not provide you with immunity, it merely buys you more time to seek appropriate medical help.

Rift Valley Fever

This haemorrhagic fever is spread through blood or blood products, including those from infected animals. It causes a 'flu-like' illness with fever, joint pains and occasionally more serious complications. Complete recovery is possible.

Schistosomiasis

Otherwise known as bilharzia, this is spread through the fresh water snail. It causes infection of the bowel and bladder, often with bleeding. It is caused by a fluke and is contracted through the skin from water contaminated with human urine or faeces. Paddling or swimming in suspect fresh water lakes or slow-running rivers should be avoided. There may be no symptoms. Possible symptoms include a transient fever and rash, and advanced cases of bilharzia may cause blood in the stool or in the urine. A blood test can detect antibodies if you have been exposed and treatment is then possible in specialist travel or infectious disease clinics.

Tuberculosis

Tuberculosis (TB) is spread through close respiratory contact and occasionally through infected milk or milk products. BCG vaccine is recommended for those likely to be mixing closely with the local population. It is more important for those visiting family or planning on a long stay, and those employed as teachers and health-care workers. TB can be asymptomatic, although symptoms can include a cough, weight loss or fever months or even years after exposure. An X-ray is the best way to confirm if you have TB. BCG gives a moderate degree of protection against TB. It causes a small permanent scar at the site of injection, and is usually only given in specialised chest clinics. As it's a live vaccine it should not be given to pregnant women or immunocompromised individuals. The BCG vaccine is not available in all countries.

Typhoid

This is spread through food or water that has been contaminated by infected human faeces. The first symptom is usually fever or a pink rash on the abdomen. Septicaemia (blood poisoning) may also occur. Typhoid vaccine (typhim Vi, typherix) will give protection for three years. In some countries, the oral vaccine Vivotif is also available.

HEALTH

Yellow Fever

A yellow fever vaccination is not required for any areas of the Middle East. However, the mosquito that spreads yellow fever has been known to be present in some parts of the Middle East. It is important to consult your local travel-health clinic as part of your predeparture plans for the latest details. Any travellers from a yellow fever endemic area *will* need to show proof of vaccination against yellow fever before entry into Syria and Lebanon. This normally applies to travellers arriving directly from an infected country, or travellers who have been in an infected country during the last 10 days. However it's a good idea to carry a certificate if you have been in an infected country any time in the last month, to avoid any possible difficulties with immigration. There is always the possibility that without an up-to-date certificate you will be vaccinated and detained in isolation at your port of arrival for up to 10 days, or even repatriated. The yellow fever vaccination must be given at a designated clinic, and is valid for 10 years. It is a live vaccine and must not be given to immunocompromised or pregnant travellers.

TRAVELLER'S DIARRHOEA

To prevent diarrhoea, avoid tap water unless it has been boiled, filtered or chemically disinfected (iodine tablets). Eat only fresh fruits or vegetables if cooked, or if you have peeled them yourself, and avoid dairy products that might contain unpasteurised milk. Buffet meals are risky – food should be piping hot; meals freshly cooked in front of you in a busy restaurant are more likely to be safe.

If you develop diarrhoea, be sure to drink plenty of fluids, preferably an oral rehydration solution containing lots of salt and sugar. A few loose stools don't require treatment but, if you start having more than four or five loose stools a day, you should start taking an antibiotic (usually a quinolone drug) and an antidiarrhoeal agent (such as loperamide). If diarrhoea is bloody, persists for more than 72 hours, or is accompanied by fever, shaking chills or severe abdominal pain, you should seek medical attention.

ENVIRONMENTAL HAZARDS
Heat Illness

Heat exhaustion occurs following heavy sweating and excessive fluid loss with inadequate replacement of fluids and salt. This is particularly common in hot climates when taking unaccustomed exercise before full acclimatisation. Symptoms include headache, dizziness and tiredness. Dehydration is already happening by the time you feel thirsty. A good indicator is the colour of your urine – aim to drink enough water to keep it pale and diluted. The treatment for heat exhaustion is fluid replacement with water or fruit juice or both, and cooling by cold water and fans. Treat salt loss with salty fluids such as soup or broth, and add a little more table salt to foods than usual.

Heatstroke is much more serious than heat exhaustion. This occurs when the body's heat-regulating mechanism breaks down. An excessive rise in body temperature leads to sweating ceasing, irrational and hyperactive behaviour and eventually loss of consciousness and death. Rapid cooling by spraying the body with water and fanning is an ideal treatment. Emergency fluid and electrolyte replacement by intravenous drip is usually also required.

Insect Bites & Stings

Mosquitoes may not carry malaria but can cause irritation and infected bites. Using DEET-based insect repellents will prevent bites. Mosquitoes also spread dengue fever.

Bees and wasps only cause real problems to those with a severe allergy (anaphylaxis). If you have a severe allergy to bee or wasp stings you should carry an adrenaline injection or something similar.

Sand flies are located around Mediterranean beaches. They usually only cause a nasty itchy bite but can carry a rare skin disorder called cutaneous leishmaniasis (see p398). Bites may be prevented by using DEET-based repellents.

Scorpions are frequently found in arid or dry climates. They can cause a painful bite which is rarely life threatening.

Bed bugs are often found in hostels and cheap hotels. They lead to very itchy, lumpy bites. Spraying the mattress with an appropriate insect killer will do a good job of getting rid of them.

Scabies are also frequently found in cheap accommodation. These tiny mites live in the skin, particularly between the fingers. They cause an intensely itchy rash. Scabies is easily treated with lotion available from pharmacies;

people you come into contact with also need treating to avoid spreading scabies.

Snake Bites

Do not walk barefoot or stick your hand into holes or cracks. Half of those bitten by venomous snakes are not actually injected with poison (envenomed). If bitten by a snake, do not panic. Immobilise the bitten limb with a splint (eg a stick) and apply a bandage over the site, firm pressure, similar to a bandage over a sprain. Do not apply a tourniquet, or cut or suck the bite. Get the victim to medical help as soon as possible so that antivenin can be given if necessary.

Water

Tap water is not safe to drink in the Middle East. Stick to bottled water or boil water for 10 minutes, or use water purification tablets or a filter. Do not drink water from rivers or lakes, this may contain bacteria or viruses that can cause diarrhoea or vomiting.

TRAVELLING WITH CHILDREN

All travellers with children should know how to treat minor ailments and when to seek medical treatment. Make sure the children are up to date with routine vaccinations, and discuss possible travel vaccines well before departure as some vaccines are not suitable for children aged under one year old.

In hot, moist climates any wound or break in the skin may lead to infection. The area should be cleaned and then kept dry and clean. Remember to avoid contaminated food and water. If your child is vomiting or experiencing diarrhoea, lost fluid and salts must be replaced. It may be helpful to take rehydration powders for reconstituting with boiled water. Ask your doctor about this.

Encourage children to avoid dogs or other mammals because of the risk of rabies and other diseases. Any bite, scratch or lick from a warm-blooded, furry animal should immediately be thoroughly cleaned. If there is any possibility that the animal is infected with rabies, seek immediate medical assistance.

WOMEN'S HEALTH

Emotional stress, exhaustion and travelling through different time zones can all contribute to an upset in the menstrual pattern. If using oral contraceptives, remember some antibiotics, diarrhoea and vomiting can stop the pill from working and lead to the risk of pregnancy – remember to take condoms with you just in case. Condoms should be kept in a cool dry place or they may crack.

Emergency contraception is most effective if taken within 24 hours of unprotected sex. The International Planned Parent Federation (www.ippf.org) can advise you on the availability of contraception in different countries. Tampons and sanitary towels are not always available outside major cities in the Middle East.

Travelling during pregnancy is usually possible but there are important things to consider. Have a medical check-up before embarking on your trip. The most risky times for travel are during the first 12 weeks of pregnancy, when miscarriage is most likely, and after 30 weeks, when complications such as high blood pressure and premature delivery can occur. Most airlines will not accept a traveller after 28 to 32 weeks of pregnancy, and long-haul flights in the later stages can be very uncomfortable. Antenatal facilities vary greatly between countries in the Middle East and you should think carefully before travelling to a country with poor medical facilities or where there are major cultural and language differences from home. Take written records of the pregnancy including details of your blood group in case you need medical attention while away. Ensure your insurance policy covers pregnancy, delivery and postnatal care, but remember insurance policies are only as good as the facilities available.

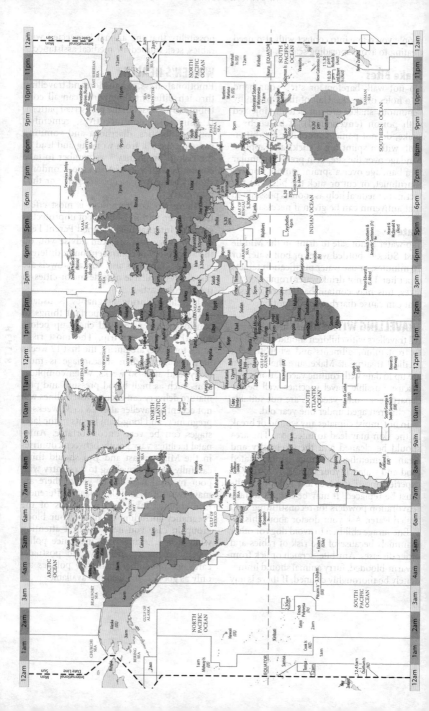

Language

CONTENTS

Arabic is the official language of both Syria and Lebanon. Though French is also widely spoken, and English is rapidly gaining ground, any effort to communicate in Arabic will be well rewarded. No matter how bad your pronunciation or grammar might be, you'll often get the response (usually with a big smile): 'Ah, you speak Arabic very well!'. Greeting officials, who are often less than helpful, with *salaam alaykum* (peace be upon you), often works wonders.

Learning a few basics for day-to-day travelling doesn't take long at all, but to master the complexities of Arabic would take years of consistent study. The whole issue is complicated by the differences between Classical Arabic (*fus-ha*), its modern descendant MSA (Modern Standard Arabic) and regional dialects. The classical tongue is the language of the Quran and Arabic poetry of centuries past. For long it remained static, but in order to survive it had to adapt to change, and the result is more or less MSA, the common language of the press, radio and educated discourse. It is as close to a *lingua franca* (common language) as the Arab world comes, and is generally understood – if not always well spoken – across the Arab world.

For most foreigners trying to learn Arabic, the most frustrating aspect remains understanding the spoken language (wherever you are), as there is virtually no written material to refer to for back up. Acquisition of MSA is a long-term investment, and an esoteric argument flows back and forth about the relative merits of learning MSA first (and so perhaps having to wait some time before being able to communicate adequately with people in the street) or learning a dialect. All this will give you an inkling of why so few non-Arabs, or non-Muslims, develop the urge to embark on a study of the language.

As it happens, the spoken dialects of Syria and Lebanon are not too distant from MSA. Significant differences between the Lebanese and Syrian varieties are covered in the words and phrases in this language guide, marked either (Leb) or (Syr).

PRONUNCIATION

Pronunciation of Arabic in any of its guises can be tongue-tying for someone unfamiliar with the intonation and combination of sounds. Pronounce the transliterated words slowly and clearly.

This language guide should help, but bear in mind that the myriad rules governing pronunciation and vowel use are too extensive to be covered here.

Vowels

Technically, there are three long and three short vowels in Arabic. The reality is a little different, with local dialect and varying consonant combinations affecting their pronunciation. This is the case throughout the Arabic-speaking world. More like five short and five long vowels can be identified; in this guide we use all but the long 'o' (as in 'or').

a	as in 'had'
aa	as the 'a' in 'father'
e	short, as in 'bet'; long, as in 'there'
i	as in 'hit'
ee	as in 'beer', only softer
o	as in 'hot'
u	as in 'put'
oo	as in 'food'

THE STANDARD ARABIC ALPHABET

Final	Medial	Initial	Alone	Transliteration	Pronunciation
ﺎ			ا	**aa**	as in 'father'
ﺐ	ﺒ	ﺑ	ب	**b**	as in 'bet'
ﺖ	ﺘ	ﺗ	ت	**t**	as in 'ten'
ﺚ	ﺜ	ﺛ	ث	**th**	as in 'thin'
ﺞ	ﺠ	ﺟ	ج	**j**	as in 'jet'
ﺢ	ﺤ	ﺣ	ح	**H**	a strongly whispered 'h', like a sigh of relief
ﺦ	ﺨ	ﺧ	خ	**kh**	as the 'ch' in Scottish *loch*
ﺪ			د	**d**	as in 'dim'
ﺬ			ذ	**dh**	as the 'th' in 'this'; also as **d** or **z**
ﺮ			ر	**r**	a rolled 'r', as in the Spanish word *caro*
ﺰ			ز	**z**	as in 'zip'
ﺲ	ﺴ	ﺳ	س	**s**	as in 'so', never as in 'wisdom'
ﺶ	ﺸ	ﺷ	ش	**sh**	as in 'ship'
ﺺ	ﺼ	ﺻ	ص	**ş**	emphatic 's'
ﺾ	ﻀ	ﺿ	ض	**ḍ**	emphatic 'd'
ﻂ	ﻄ	ﻃ	ط	**ţ**	emphatic 't'
ﻆ	ﻈ	ﻇ	ظ	**ẓ**	emphatic 'z'
ﻊ	ﻌ	ﻋ	ع	**'**	the Arabic letter *'ayn*; pronounce as a glottal stop – like the closing of the throat before saying 'Oh-oh!' (see Other Sounds on p405)
ﻎ	ﻐ	ﻏ	غ	**gh**	a guttural sound like Parisian 'r'
ﻒ	ﻔ	ﻓ	ف	**f**	as in 'far'
ﻖ	ﻘ	ﻗ	ق	**q**	a strongly guttural 'k' sound; also often pronounced as a glottal stop
ﻚ	ﻜ	ﻛ	ك	**k**	as in 'king'
ﻞ	ﻠ	ﻟ	ل	**l**	as in 'lamb'
ﻢ	ﻤ	ﻣ	م	**m**	as in 'me'
ﻦ	ﻨ	ﻧ	ن	**n**	as in 'name'
ﻪ	ﻬ	ﻫ	ه	**h**	as in 'ham'
ﻮ			و	**w**	as in 'wet'; or
				oo	long, as in 'food'; or
				ow	as in 'how'
ﻲ	ﻴ	ﻳ	ي	**y**	as in 'yes'; or
				ee	as in 'beer', only softer; or
				ai/ay	as in 'aisle'/as the 'ay' in 'day'

Vowels Not all Arabic vowel sounds are represented in the alphabet. For more information on the vowel sounds used in this language guide, see Pronunciation on p403.

Emphatic Consonants To simplify the transliteration system used in this book, the emphatic consonants have not been included.

Consonants

Pronunciation for all Arabic consonants is covered in the alphabet table on p404. Note that when double consonants occur in transliterations, both are pronounced. For example, *al-hammam* (toilet), is pronounced 'al-ham-mam'.

TRICKY SOUNDS

Arabic has two sounds that are very tricky for non-Arabs to produce: the 'ayn and the glottal stop. The letter 'ayn represents a sound with no English equivalent that comes even close. It is similar to the glottal stop (which is not actually represented in the alphabet), but the muscles at the back of the throat are gagged more forcefully and air is released – it has been described as the sound of someone being strangled. In many transliteration systems 'ayn is represented by an opening quotation mark, and the glottal stop by a closing quotation mark. To make the transliterations in this language guide (and throughout the rest of the book) easier to use, we have not distinguished between the glottal stop and the 'ayn, using the closing quotation mark to represent both sounds. You should find that Arabic speakers will still understand you.

TRANSLITERATION

It's worth noting here that transliteration from the Arabic script into English – or any other language for that matter – is at best an approximate science.

The presence of sounds unknown in European languages and the fact that the script is 'incomplete' (most vowels are not written) combine to make it nearly impossible to settle on one universally accepted method of transliteration. A wide variety of spellings is therefore possible for words when they appear in Latin script – and that goes for places and people's names as well.

The whole thing is further complicated by the wide variety of dialects and the imaginative ideas Arabs themselves often have on appropriate spelling in, say, English (words spelt one way in Jordan may look very different again in Lebanon and Syria, with strong French influences); not even the most venerable of western Arabists have been able to come up with a satisfactory solution.

While striving to reflect the language as closely as possible and aiming at consistency, this book generally anglicises place, street and hotel names and the like as the locals have done. Don't be surprised if you come across several versions of the same thing.

ACCOMMODATION

I'd like to book a ...	*biddee ehjuz ...*
Do you have a ...?	*fi ...?*
(cheap) room	*ghurfa (rkheesa)*
single room	*ghurfa mufrada*
double room	*ghurfa bi sareerayn*
for one night	*li layli waHde*
for two nights	*layltayn*
May I see it?	*mumkin shoofa?*
It's very noisy/dirty.	*kteer dajeh/wuskha*
How much is it per person?	*'addaysh li kul waHid?*
How much is it per night?	*'addaysh bel layli?*
Where is the bathroom?	*wayn al-Hammam?*
We're leaving today.	*niHna musafireen al-youm*
address	*al-'anwaan*
air-conditioning	*kondishon/mookayif*
blanket	*al-bataaniyya/al-Hrem*
camp site	*mukhayam*
electricity	*kahraba*
hotel	*funduq/otel*
hot water	*mai sukhni* (Leb)
	mai saakhina (Syr)
key	*al-miftaH*
manager	*al-mudeer*
shower	*doosh*
soap	*saboon*
toilet	*twalet* (also *bet al-mai* in Syria)

CONVERSATION & ESSENTIALS

Arabs place great importance on civility and it's rare to see any interaction between people that doesn't begin with profuse greetings, enquiries into the other's health and other niceties.

Arabic greetings are more formal than in English and there is a reciprocal response to each. These sometimes vary slightly, depending on whether you're addressing a man or a woman. A simple encounter can become a drawn-out affair, with neither side wanting to be the one to put a halt to the stream of greetings and well-wishing. As an *ajnabi* (foreigner), you're not expected to know all the ins and outs, but if you come up with the right expression at the appropriate moment they'll love it.

The most common greeting is *salaam alaykum* (peace be upon you), to which the correct reply is *wa alaykum as-salaam* (and upon you be peace). If you get invited to a birthday celebration or are around for any of the big holidays, the common greeting is *kul sana wa intum bikher* (I wish you well for the coming year).

After having a bath or shower, you will often hear people say to you *na'iman*, which roughly means 'heavenly' and boils down to an observation along the lines of 'nice and clean now, eh'.

Arrival in one piece is always something to be grateful for. Passengers will often be greeted with *il-Hamdu lillah al as-salaama* – 'thank God for your safe arrival'.

Hi.	marHaba
Hi. (response)	marHabtain
Hello.	ahlan wa sahlan or just ahlan (Welcome)
Hello. (response)	ahlan beek/i (m/f)

It's an important custom in Lebanon and Syria to ask after a person's or their family's health when greeting, eg *kayf es-saHa?* (How is your health?), *kayf il'ayli?* (How is the family?). The response is *bikher il-Hamdu lillah*, (Fine, thank you).

Goodbye.	ma'a salaama/Allah ma'ak
Good morning.	sabaH al-khayr
Good morning. (response)	sabaH 'an-noor
Good evening.	masa' al-khayr
Good evening. (response)	masa 'an-noor
Good night.	tisbaH 'ala khayr
Good night. (response)	wa inta min ahlu

Yes.	aiwa/na'am
Yeah.	ay
No.	la
Please. (request)	min fadlak/fadleek (m/f) or iza bitreed/bitreedi (m/f) (Leb)
Please. (polite)	law samaHt/samaHti (m/f)
Please. (come in)	tafaddal/tafaddali (m/f)/ tafaddaloo (pl)
Thank you.	shukran
Thank you very much.	shukran kteer/shukran jazeelan

You're welcome.	'afwan or tikram/tikrami (m/f)
One moment, please.	lahza min fadlak/i (m/f)
Pardon/Excuse me.	'afwan
Sorry!	aasif/aasifa! (m/f)
No problem.	mafi mushkili/moo mushkila
Never mind.	ma'alesh
Just a moment.	laHza
Congratulations!	mabrouk!

Questions like 'Is the bus coming?' or 'Will the bank be open later?' generally elicit the response: *in sha' Allah* – 'God willing' – an expression you'll hear over and over again. Another common one is *ma sha' Allah* – 'God's will be done' – sometimes a useful answer to probing questions about why you're not married yet.

How are you?	kayf Haalak/Haalik? (m/f)
How're you doing?	kayfak/kayfik? (m/f)
Fine thank you.	bikher il-Hamdu lillah
What's your name?	shu-ismak/shu-ismik? (m/f)
My name is ...	ismi ...
Pleased to meet you. (when departing)	tsharrafna/fursa sa'ida (Leb/Syr)
Nice to meet you. (lit: you honour us)	tasharrafna
Where are you from?	min wayn inta/inti? (m/f)
I'm from ...	ana min ...
Do you like ...?	inta/inti bitHeb ...? (m/f)
I like ...	ana bHeb ...
I don't like ...	ana ma bHeb ...

I	ana
you	inta/inti (m/f)
he	huwa
she	hiyya
we	niHna
you	into
they	homm

DIRECTIONS

How do I get to ...?	keef boosal ala ...?
Can you show me (on the map)?	mumkin tfarjeeni ('ala al-khareeta)?
How many kilometres?	kam kilometre?
What street is this?	shoo Hash-shari hayda? (Leb) shoo Hal shanki had? (Syr)
on the left	'ala yasaar/shimaal
on the right	'ala yameen
opposite	muqaabil
straight ahead	dughri
at the next corner	tanee mafraq

SIGNS

Entrance	مدخل
Exit	خروج
Information	معلومات
Open	مفتوح
Closed	مغلق
Prohibited	ممنوع
Police	شرطة
Men's Toilet	حمام للرجال
Women's Toilet	حمام للنساء
Hospital	مستشفى

this way	min hon
here/there	hon/honeek
in front of	amaam/iddaam
near	qareeb
far	ba'eed
north	shimaal
south	janub
east	sharq
west	gharb

EMERGENCIES

Help me!	saa'idoonee!
I'm sick.	ana mareed/mareeda (m/f)
Call the police!	ittusil bil polees! (Leb)
	ittusil bil shurta! (Syr)
doctor	duktoor/tabeeb
hospital	al-mustash-fa
police	al-polees/ash-shurta (Leb/Syr)
Go away!	imshee!/rouh min hoon!
Shame (on you)!	aayb!
(said by woman)	

HEALTH

I'm ill.	ana mareed/a (m/f)
My friend is ill.	sadeeqi mareed (m)
	sadeeqati maareeda (f)
It hurts here.	beeyujani hon

I'm ...	andee ...
asthmatic	azmitrabo
diabetic	sukkari
epileptic	saraa/alsaa'a

I'm allergic ...	andee Hasasiyya ...
to antibiotics	min al-mudad alHayawi
to aspirin	min al-aspireen
to penicillin	min al-binisileen
to bees	min al-naHl
to nuts	min al-mukassarat

antiseptic	mutahhi
aspirin	aspireen/aspro (brand name)
Band-Aids	plaster
chemist/pharmacy	al-farmashiya (Leb)
	as-sayidiliyya (Syr)
condoms	kaboot
contraceptive	waseela lee mana' al-Ham
diarrhoea	is-haal
fever	Harara
headache	wajaa-ras
hospital	mustashfa
medicine	dawa
pregnant	Hamel
prescription	wasfa/rashetta
sanitary napkins	fuwat saHiyya
stomachache	wajaa fil battu
sunblock cream	krem waki min ashilt al-shams
tampons	kotex (brand name)

LANGUAGE DIFFICULTIES

Do you speak English?	bitiHki ingleezi?
I understand.	ana afham
I don't understand.	ana ma bifham

I speak ...	ana baHki ...
English	ingleezi
French	faransi
German	almaani

I speak a little Arabic.	ana baHki arabi shway
I don't speak Arabic.	ana ma beHki arabi
I want an interpreter.	biddee mutarjem
Could you write it down, please?	mumkin tiktabhu, min fadlak?
How do you say ... in Arabic?	kayf t'ul ... bil'arabi?

NUMBERS

0	sifr
1	waHid
2	itnayn/tintayn
3	talaata
4	arba'a
5	khamsa
6	sitta
7	saba'a
8	tamanya
9	tis'a
10	'ashara
11	yeedaa'sh

12	yeetnaa'sh
13	talaatash
14	arbatash
15	khamastash
16	sittash
17	sabatash
18	tamantash
19	tasatash
20	'ashreen
21	wäHid wa 'ashreen
22	itnayn wa 'ashreen
30	talaateen
40	arba'een
50	khamseen
60	sitteen
70	saba'een
80	tamaneen
90	tis'een
100	miyya (meet before a noun)
200	miyyatayn
1000	'alf
2000	'alfayn
3000	talaat-alaf

PAPERWORK

date of birth	tareekh al-meelad/-wilaada
name	al-ism
nationality	al-jenseeya
passport	jawaz al-safar (or simply paspor)
permit	tasriH
place of birth	makan al-meelad/-wilaada
visa	visa/ta'shira

SHOPPING & SERVICES

I'm looking for ...	ana abHath ... aa'n
Where is the ...?	wayn/fayn ...?
bank	al-bank
beach	ash-shaati'/al-plaaj/al-baHr
chemist/pharmacy	as-sayidiliyya (Syr)
	al-farmashiya (Leb)
city/town	al-medeena
city centre	markaz al-medeena
customs	al-jumruk
entrance	al-dukhool/al-madkhal
exchange office	al-masref/al-saraf
exit	al-khurooj
hotel	al-funduq/al-otel
information desk	isti'laamaat
laundry	al ghaseel
market	al-sooq
mosque	al-jaami'/al-masjid
museum	al-matHaf
newsagents	al-maktaba

old city	al-medeena al-qadeema/
	al-medeena l'ateeqa
passport &	maktab al-jawazaat wa al-hijra
immigration office	
police	ash-shurta
post office	maktab al-bareed
restaurant	al-mata'am
telephone office	maktab at-telefon/
	maktab al-haalef
temple	al-ma'abad
tourist office	maktab al-siyaHa
I want to change ...	baddee sarref ...
money	masaari
travellers cheques	sheeket siyaHiyya

What time does it open?	emta byeftaH?
What time does it close?	emta bi sakkir?
I'd like to make a telephone call.	fini talfen 'omol maaroof (Leb)
	mumkin talfen min fadlak(Syr)
Where can I buy ...?	wayn/fayn feeni eshtiree ...?
What is this?	shu hayda/hada? (Leb/Syr)
How much?	addaysh? (also bikam in Syr)
How many?	kim waHid?
How much is it?	bi addaysh?
That's too expensive.	hayda kteer ghaalee (Leb)
	hada ghalee kheteer (Syr)
Is there ...?	fee ...?
There isn't (any).	ma fee
May I look at it?	feeni etallaa 'alaya? (Leb)
	mumkin shoof? (Syr)
big/bigger	kbeer/akbar
cheap	rkhees
cheaper	arkhas
closed	msakkar
expensive	ghaali
money	al-fuloos/al-masaari
open	maftuH
small/smaller	sagheer/asghar

TIME & DATE

What's the time?	addaysh essa'aa?
When?	emta?
now	halla
after	b'adayn
on time	al waket
early	bakkeer
late	ma'qar
daily	kil youm
today	al-youm
tomorrow	bukra

day after tomorrow	ba'ad bukra
yesterday	imbaarih
minute	daqeeqa
hour	saa'a
day	youm
week	usboo'
month	shahr
year	sana
morning	soubeH
afternoon	ba'ad deher
evening	massa
night	layl

Monday	al-tenayn
Tuesday	at-talaata
Wednesday	al-arba'a
Thursday	al-khamees
Friday	al-jum'a
Saturday	as-sabt
Sunday	al-aHad

The Western Calendar Months

The Islamic year has 12 lunar months and is 11 days shorter than the Western (Gregorian) calendar, so important Muslim dates will occur 11 days earlier each (Western) year.

There are two Gregorian calendars in use in the Arab world. In Egypt and westwards, the months have virtually the same names as in English (January is *yanaayir*, October is *octobir* and so on), but in Lebanon and eastwards, the names are quite different. Talking about, say, June as 'month six' is the easiest solution, but for the sake of completeness, the months from January are:

January	kanoon ath-thani
February	shubaat
March	azaar
April	nisaan
May	ayyaar
June	Huzayraan
July	tammooz
August	'aab
September	aylool
October	tishreen al-awal
November	tishreen ath-thani
December	kaanoon al-awal

The Hejira Calendar Months

1st	MoHarram
2nd	Safar
3rd	Rabi' al-Awal
4th	Rabay ath-Thaani
5th	Jumaada al-Awal
6th	Jumaada al-Akhira
7th	Rajab
8th	Shaban
9th	Ramadan
10th	Shawwal
11th	Zuul-Qeda
12th	Zuul-Hijja

TRANSPORT
Public Transport

Where is ...?	wayn/fayn ...?
airport	al-mataar
bus station	maHattat al-baas/ maHattat al-karaj
ticket office	maktab at-tazaakar
train station	maHattat al-qitaar

What time does ... leave/arrive?	ay saa'a biyitla'/biyusal ...?
boat/ferry	al-markib/as-safeena
(small) boat	ash-shakhtura
bus	al-baas
plane	al-teeyara
train	al-qitaar

Which bus goes to ...?	aya baas biyruH 'ala ...?
I want to go to ...	ana badeh ruH ala ...
Does this bus go to ...?	hal-baas biyruH 'ala ...?
How many buses per day go to ...?	kam baas biyruH ben nahar ...?
How long does the trip take?	kam sa'a ar-riHla?
Please tell me when we get to ...	'umal ma'aroof illee lamma noosal la ...
Stop here, please.	wa'if hoon 'umal ma'aroof
Please wait for me.	'umal ma'aroof unturnee (Leb) 'umal ma'aroof istanna (Syr)
May I sit here?	mumkin a'ood hoon?
May we sit here?	mumkin ni'ood hoon?

1st class	daraja oola
2nd class	daraja taaniya
ticket	at-tazaakar
to/from	ila/min

Private Transport

I'd like to hire a ...	biddee esta'jer ...
Where can I hire a ...?	wayn/fayn feeni esta'jer ...?
bicycle	bisklet
camel	jamal
car	sayyaara
donkey	Hmaar
4WD	jeep

horse	Hsaan
motorcycle	motosikl
tour guide	al-dalee as-siyaaHi/
	al-murshid as-siyaaHi

Is this the road to ...?
Hal Haza al-tareeq eela ...?
Where's a service station?
wayn/fayn maHaltet al-benzeen?
Please fill it up.
min fadlak (emla/abee) Ha
I'd like (30) litres.
biddee talaateen leeter

ROAD SIGNS

Stop	قف
No Entry	ممنوع الدخول
No Parking	ممنوع الوقوف
Danger	خطر
Slow Down	هادي السرعة
One Way	إتجاه واحد

diesel	deezel
leaded petrol	benzeen bee rasa
unleaded petrol	benzeen beedoon rasas

(How long) Can I park here?
(kam sa'a) mumkin aas-f hon?

Where do I pay?
fayn/wayn mumkin an addf'aa?
I need a mechanic.
bidee mekaneesyan
The car/motorbike has broken down (at ...)
al-sayyaara/-mutusikl it'atlit ('an ...)
The car/motorbike won't start.
al-sayyaara/-mutusikl ma bit door
I have a flat tyre.
nzel al-doolab
I've run out of petrol.
mafi benzeen or al-benzeen khalas
I've had an accident.
aamalt hads

TRAVEL WITH CHILDREN

Is there a/an ...? fee ...?
I need a/an .... biddee ...

car baby seat	kursee sayyaara leel bebe'
disposable nappies	pamperz (brand name)
nappies (diapers)	Ha fa daat
formula (baby's milk)	Haleeb bebe'
highchair	kursee atfaal
potty	muneeyai
stroller	arabeyet atfaal

Do you mind if I breastfeed here?
mumkin aradda hon?
Are children allowed?
Hal yousmah leel atfaal?

Glossary

Abbasids – Baghdad-based successor dynasty to the *Umayyads*. It ruled from AD 750 until the sacking of Baghdad by the Mongols in 1258.

abd – servant of

abeyya – women's cloak

ablaq – alternating courses of coloured stone

abu – father, saint

acropolis – citadel of an ancient city (usually Greek)

ain – well, spring

al-muderiyya – town hall

Amal – Shiite militia turned political party

Amorites – Western Semitic people who emerged from the Syrian deserts around 2000 BC and influenced life in the cities of Mesopotamia and Phoenicia until 1600 BC

apse – semicircular recess for the altar in a church

Arab League – league of 22 independent Arab states, formed in 1945, to further cultural, economic, military, political and social cooperation between the states

architrave – the lowest division of the *entablature*, extending from column to column. Also the moulded frame around a door or window.

Arz ar-Rab – 'Cedars of the Lord'. The local name for a small remaining group of cedar trees near Bcharré.

AUB – American University of Beirut

Ayyubids – an Egyptian-based dynasty founded by *Saladin*

bab (s), abwab (pl) – gate, door

bahr – river

baksheesh – tipping

baladi – local, rural

beit – house

bey – term of respect

Bilad ish-Sham – the area of modern Syria, Lebanon and Palestine

bir – spring, well

birket – lake

burj – tower

caliph – Islamic ruler. The spiritual and temporal leader of the Sunni Muslim community, or 'umma' (note the institution of the caliphate was abolished in 1924). Also spelt 'khalif'.

capital – the top, decorated part of a column

caravanserai – see *khan*

cardo maximus – the main north-south street of a Roman-era town

cella – inner part of temple that houses the statue of a god or goddess

centrale – government phone office

chador – one-piece head-to-toe black garment worn by Muslim women

chai – tea

Chalcolithic – period between the Neolithic and Bronze Ages, in which there was an increase in urbanisation and trade and the occasional use of copper

cornice – the upper portion of the *entablature* in classical or Renaissance architecture

cornice, the – seashore

cuneiform – wedge-shaped characters of several different languages, including Babylonian

dabke – an energetic folk dance that is the national Lebanese dance

decumanus maximus – the main east-west street of a Roman-era town

deir – monastery, convent

donjon – castle keep or great tower

Druze – a religious sect based on Islamic teachings. Its followers are found mainly in Lebanon, with some in Syria and in Israel & the Palestinian Territories.

eid – Islamic feast

Eid al-Adha – Feast of Sacrifice, which marks the end of the pilgrimage to Mecca

Eid al-Fitr – Festival of Breaking the Fast, which is celebrated at the end of *Ramadan*

emir – Islamic ruler, military commander or governor

entablature – upper part of the classical temple, comprising the *architrave, frieze* and *cornice,* supported by the colonnade

exedra – a room or outdoor area with seats for discussions

ezan – call to prayer

Fakhreddine – a Lebanese nationalist hero. Appointed by the Ottomans in 1590 to pacify the Druze, he unified the Mt Lebanon area. Also spelt Fakhr ad-Din.

Fatimids – a Shiite dynasty from North Africa that claimed to be descended from Fatima, daughter of the Prophet Mohammed, and her husband Ali ibn Abi Taleb

frieze – central part of the *entablature*

funduq – hotel

furn – oven

Green Line – line that divided Beirut's eastern (Christian) half from its western (Muslim) half

haj – pilgrimage to Mecca

hakawati – storyteller

halawat al-jibn – a soft cheese-based, doughy delicacy drenched in honey or syrup and often topped with ice cream

hamam – pigeon

hammam – bathhouse

hara – small lane, alley

haram – the sacred area inside a mosque

haramlek – family quarters

haramlik – women's quarters

hejab – woman's headscarf

Hejira – migration. Usually refers to Mohammed's flight from Mecca in AD 622. Also the name of the Islamic calendar.

Hezbollah – Party of God, radical Shiite political party based in Lebanon. Its guerilla arm, *Islamic Jihad*, was largely responsible for expelling Israel from the south of Lebanon.

Hyksos – Semitic invaders from Western Asia, probably from Asia Minor (ie Anatolia) famed for their horsemanship. They introduced the horse to Pharaonic Egypt and ruled there from 1720 to 1560 BC.

hypocaust – raised floor in Roman bathhouses, heated by circulating hot air beneath it

hypogeum – underground burial chamber

iconostasis – screen with doors and icons set in tiers, used in eastern Christian churches

iftar – breaking of the day's fast during *Ramadan*

imam – a man schooled in Islam and who often doubles as the *muezzin*

Islamic Jihad – armed wing of *Hezbollah*

iwan – vaulted hall, opening into a central court, in the *madrassa* of a mosque

jalabiyya – full-length robe worn by men and women

jebel – mountain or mountain range

jezira – island

jihad – literally 'striving in the way of the faith'; holy war

Kaaba – the rectangular structure at the centre of the grand mosque in Mecca (containing the black stone) around which pilgrims walk

kalybe – open-fronted shrine

kanjar – dagger

karaj/karajat – garage/garage of

Karnak – Syrian government-run buses

khan – a merchant's inn

kineesa – church

kiyaas hammam – goat-hair bags used as loofahs

kubri – bridge

kufeyya – distinctive black-and-white or red-and-white headdress worn by traditional Muslim and Bedu Arabs

kursi – a wooden stand for holding the Quran

kuttab – Quranic school

Levant – literally 'where the sun rises'. Region of the Eastern Mediterranean from Egypt to Greece.

loggia – colonnaded arcade providing a sheltered extension of a hall

madrassa – school where Islamic law is taught

mahatta – station

maktab amn al-aam – general security office

Mamluks – military class of ex-Turkish slaves, established about AD 1250, that ruled much of Syria and Lebanon from Egypt and remained in power in the latter until 1805

manakeesh – a type of flat bread

mar – saint

maristan – hospital

Maronite – Lebanese Christians who embrace the Monothelite Doctrine that Christ had two natures but only a single divine will

mashrabiyya – ornately carved wooden panel or screen

matar – airport

medina – old walled centre of any Islamic city

meghazils – spindles

mezze – starters, appetisers

mihrab – niche in the wall of a mosque that indicates the direction of Mecca

minaret – tower of a mosque from which *ezan* is made

minbar – pulpit in a mosque

muezzin – mosque official who calls the faithful to prayer five times a day from the *minaret*

muqarnas – stalactite-type stone carving used to decorate doorways and window recesses

murex – a kind of mollusc from which the famous purple dye of Tyre comes

mutasarrifa – an Ottoman administrative unit, eg Mt Lebanon

nahr – river

nargileh – water pipe

nave – central part of a church

nebaa – spring

Neolithic – literally 'new stone' age. Period, based on the development of stone tools, which witnessed the beginnings of domestication and urbanisation.

nymphaeum – monumental fountain

oud – literally 'wood'. Used for both a kind of lute and wood burned on an incense burner.

pasha – lord. Also a term used more generally to denote a person of standing.

Phalangist – member of the Lebanese Christian paramilitary organisation, founded in 1936

PLO – Palestine Liberation Organisation

propylaeum – a portico, especially one that forms the monumental entrance to a temple, a gateway

qa'a – reception room

qahwa – coffee or coffeehouse

qala'at – fortress

qasr – palace

rais – waiter

rakats – cycles of prayer during which the Quran is read and bows and prostrations are performed

Ramadan – ninth month of the lunar Islamic calendar, during which Muslims fast from sunrise to sunset

ras – headland

saahat – square

sabil – public drinking fountain

Saladin – warlord who retook Jerusalem from the Crusaders and founder of the Ayyubid dynasty. Also spelt Salah ad-Din.

saray – palace

Seleucids – royal dynasty (312–64 BC) whose rule extended from Thrace to India at its peak. Founded by Seleucus, a Macedonian general in Alexander the Great's army.

serail – Ottoman palace. Also spelt 'seraglio'.

servees – service taxi

sharia – road, way

Sharia'a – Islamic law, the body of doctrine that regulates the lives of Muslims

Shiism – a branch of Islam that regards the prophet Mohammed's cousin Ali and his successors as the true leaders

shwarma – meat sliced off a spit and stuffed in a pocket of pita-type bread with chopped tomatoes and garnish. Equivalent to the Turkish döner kebab.

SLA – South Lebanon Army

souq – bazaar, market

speos – rock-cut tomb or chapel

stele (s), stelae (pl) – stone or wooden commemorative slab or column decorated with inscriptions or figures

Sufi – follower of the Islamic mystical orders, which emphasise dancing, chanting and trances in order to attain unity with God

sultan – the absolute ruler of a Muslim state

sumac – reddish, lemony dried herb, delicious in salad

Sunni – main branch of Islam. Based on the words and acts of the Prophet Mohammed, with the *caliph* seen as the true successor.

tabla – small hand-held drum

tell – artificial mound

tetrapylon – four-columned structure

ulema – group of Muslim scholars or religious leaders, a member of this group

Umayyads – first great dynasty of Arab Muslim rulers, based in Damascus

umm – mother of

Unifil – United Nations Interim Force in Lebanon

wadi – desert watercourse, dry except in the rainy season

waha – oasis

waqf – religious endowment

zaatar – thyme-like herb

zawiya – hospice and religious school

zikr – long sessions of dancing, chanting and swaying carried out by Sufis to achieve oneness with God

Behind the Scenes

This book is an amalgamation of Lonely Planet's *Syria* and *Lebanon* titles. *Syria*, researched and written by Andrew Humphreys and Damien Simonis, was first published in 1999. The first edition of *Lebanon*, published in 1998, was written by Ann Jousiffe; the second edition of *Lebanon* was revised and updated by Siona Jenkins.

THIS BOOK

For this book Andrew Humphreys conducted preliminary research in Syria, while Terry Carter and Lara Dunston researched and wrote the Lebanon section, did some extra research in Syria and compiled and wrote the preliminary and end chapters. Greg and Geoff Malouf wrote the Food & Drink chapter and Dr Caroline Evans wrote the Health chapter.

THANKS from the Authors

Terry Carter & Lara Dunston A very special thanks to Samar for her help and advice. Nate Scholz for his help with the streets of Tyre. Rania al-Souki for her years of little insights into the Lebanese way of life. Thanks to the Mid East Film Festival people; Nadia, Nathalie and Colette and, in a strange way, Todd S. Much thanks to foodies Janina and Tutu for Beirut eating tips. Chris Walley for his geological advice. Bassam and Wissam for their hospitality and long conversations. Thanks to Munir Bashir, Outkast, and The Thrills for providing the soundtrack to the write-up. Finally, a big thank you to all the friendly people we met on our travels through Lebanon and Syria.

CREDITS

Coordinating the production of this guide were Gina Tsarouhas (editorial), Julie Sheridan (cartography) and Katherine Marsh (layout). Overseeing production was Chris Love (project manager). This title was commissioned in Lonely Planet's Melbourne office by Lynne Preston. Will Gourlay wrote the brief with assistance from Julia Taylor and Kalya Ryan; Evan Jones and Will completed the manuscript assessment. Cartography for this guide was developed by Shahara Ahmed. The cover and artwork were done by James Hardy, Quentin Frayne compiled the Language chapter (with assistance from Mohamed al-Samsam who provided Arabic translations and useful language advice), and Emma Koch and Diana Saad assisted with script.

Assisting were a talented group of editors, proofers and cartographers: Andrea Baster, Dan Caleo, Monique Choy, Barbara Delissen, Tony Fankhauser, Victoria Harrison, Samantha McCrow, Lucy Monie, Anne Mulvaney and Sally O'Brien. Many thanks to Kristin Odijk and Tamsin Wilson for helping with the index!

THANKS from Lonely Planet

Many thanks to the travellers who used the last edition and wrote to us with helpful hints, useful advice and interesting anecdotes:

A Atef Abbas, Rob Abbott, Zaher Aboultaif, Susan Al-Baghdadi, Elias al-Ward, Ann Marie Aoki, Kazuya Ayani, Kagan Aybudak **B** Peter & Rosemary Balmford, David Barr, Geoff Barton, Cliff & Jenny Batley, Taher Bazerbashi, Tony Bazouni, John Bedford, Luca Belis, Melanie Bell, Alain Bertallo, Laurent Bianchi, Julia

THE LONELY PLANET STORY

The story begins with a classic travel adventure: Tony and Maureen Wheeler's 1972 journey across Europe and Asia to Australia. There was no useful information about the overland trail then, so Tony and Maureen published the first Lonely Planet guidebook to meet a growing need.

From a kitchen table, Lonely Planet has grown to become the largest independent travel publisher in the world, with offices in Melbourne (Australia), Oakland (USA), London (UK) and Paris (France).

Today Lonely Planet guidebooks cover the globe. There is an ever-growing list of books and information in a variety of media. Some things haven't changed. The main aim is still to make it possible for adventurous travellers to get out there – to explore and better understand the world.

At Lonely Planet we believe travellers can make a positive contribution to the countries they visit – if they respect their host communities and spend their money wisely.

Bishop, Mario Bofondi, Rachel Borer, Kenneth Brazier, Gerbert Brendtner, Sophia Brittan, Marie Brodeur Gelinas, Richard Brooks, Eric Brouwer, Douglas Buchanan, Hans J Buhrmester, Steffan Bush, Holly Byrne **C** Maria Calleja, Elizabeth Campbell, Jack Campbell, Michelle Carlile, Lucienne Cermann, Gideon Charlap, Fitz Charlie, Arthur Ciastoch, Caroline Cloutier, Phillipe Cook, Geoff Cosson, Dale Cottam, Michael Counsell, Andrew Craig, Linton Cull **D** Rukia Daaboul, Fernando De La Puente, Judy & Martin Dean, Jan Defleyt, Jacqueline Diffey, Brian Donnolley, Els Drent **E** Rachel Edwards, Bruce Elliott, Paul England, Rob & Brenda Epps, **F** Harold Fairfull, Lyndon Ferguson, Mike & Gill Finnie, Uli Flechner, Diana Fletcher, Mark Forkgen, Art Fox, Franca Franceschini, Jonathan Freeman, Ludek Frybort, Ralph Fuchs, Richard Fullerton, Sana Fullerton, Tammo Funke **G** V K Gadman, Luis Garcia Marco, Ben Gazzal, Johannes Gehringer, Bernhard Gerber, Nidal Ghorayeb, Kathleen Gilbert, Declan Gilmurray, David Gips, Olga Gora, Johann Groll, Don & Marlene Gunther, Peder Gustafsson **H** Oskar Habjanic, Pamela Hagedorn, Georg Hamacher, Annika Hampson, Mary Harawi, John Harris, Jim Hartley, Zeid Hashim, Kevin Hassett, Chris Havre, Janice Hazlehurst, Martin Helmantel, Saskia Helmantel, Marj Henningsen, Simon Heuking, John & Rosemary Hillard, Suzie Hinson, Peter Hitchcock, Liv Hjelle, Christoph Hofmann, Danielle Houbrechts, Nancy Hourani, Matt Howes, Steuart Hutchinson Blue, Ruth Hutson **I** Alison Icer **J** Miki Jablkowska, Mary Jackson, Steven Jacobs, Melody Jeannin, Juliette Jeffries, Eric & R. Jensen, Fritz Jensen, Jacques Julien **K** Nazima Kadir, A Kamberg, Viktor Kaposi, Estaphan Kareh, Gina Kattenberg, Mark-Matthijs Kattenberg, Karen Killalea, Juergen Kirst, Tetsuo & Mariko Kitadai, Sabine Klahr, Marnix Koets, Paul Koetsawang, Kiros Kokkas, Andrzej Komorowski, Peter Koutsoukos, Franz Kramer, Krijn Kramer, Sarah Kwiatkowski **L** Norma Lammont, Donna Landry, Espen Lauritzen, Al Lawrence, Valerie & Christophe Lefebvre, Dieter Lehmann, Jean Francois Lemay, Rob Leutheuser, Hajek Libor, Rolf Lienekogel, Zhiyu Liu, Richard Lombaert, Thomas Loughlin, Panos Loupasis, Roger Low Puay Hwa, Janine Lucas, Marc Luetolf, Helen Lundgaard, Graziella Lunetta **M** Glenn McAllister, Derek McDermott, Sarah McElwain, Gerald MacLean, Peter McLennan, E Maud McLeod, Jurgen Maerschand, Attila Mag, Alessandra Manca, Michael Manser, Sylvia M Maresca, Humberto Martin, Nuno Martins, Bob Maysmor, Janet Miller, Tsevi Minister, Galder Mitxelena, Jean-Marc Mojon, Ben Moloney, Ray Mondo, Anita Montvajszki, Marcel Mooij, Edward Moore, Charmaine Morgan, Edan Mumford, Andrea Mussi **N** Georges Nasr, Alexander Nitzsche, Julie Norton **O** Pol O'Gradaigh, G O'Limann, Phil Oh, Irene Otto, Ben Owens **P** GL & MJ Palm, Neisha Parekh, Edwin & Barbara Parks, David Patel, Chris Patterson, TL Peirce, Davide Perdomo, Erika Peron, Richard & Alison Perruso, Wendy Pickness, Wayne Pitard, Imma Plana, Leo Planken, Susan Polk, Litl Porto, Guillermo Pascual Pouteau, Marcelo Horacio Pozzo, Lyndee Prickitt, Marc Proksch, Luca Provenzano **Q** Therese Quin, Lucas A Quiroga **R** Loretta Rafter, Patrick Raiman, Svea Rathje, Rachad Rayess, Manuel Rincon, Kate Rizk, Katherine Rizk, Jacob Robson, Jennifer Rooke,

SEND US YOUR FEEDBACK

We love to hear from travellers – your comments keep us on our toes and help make our books better. Our well-travelled team reads every word on what you loved or loathed about this book. Although we cannot reply individually to postal submissions, we always guarantee that your feedback goes straight to the appropriate authors, in time for the next edition. Each person who sends us information is thanked in the next edition – and the most useful submissions are rewarded with a free book.

To send us your updates – and find out about LP events, newsletters and travel news – visit our award-winning website: **www.lonelyplanet.com**.

Note: We may edit, reproduce and incorporate your comments in Lonely Planet products such as guidebooks, websites and digital products, so let us know if you don't want your comments reproduced or your name acknowledged. For a copy of our privacy policy visit www.lonelyplanet.com/privacy.

Skip Roothans, Auri Roque, Randy Rossit, Frank Ruhe, Andy Ryan, Krysztof Rybak **S** Will Saab, H Sabathy, Sam Sale, Sebastien Sam, Sibel Samaha, Joan Schlegel, Katya Schodts, E Schotman, Sasa Schram, James Scott, Nicola Seu, Trevor Sewell, Sammy Shamoon, Family Shirvill, Philippe Sibelly, Olga Simkova, Rainer Sittenthaler, Stephen Smith, Nora Soliman, Joseph T Stanik, Arne Stapnes, Donald Stewart, Timo Stewart, Knut Arne Stromme, Imre Szucs **T** Andrei Tchijov, Carl Thalbitzer, Christina Themar, B Theroux, Dennis Thomas, Michel Thomas, Bruce Thompson, Ippolita Tolja, Eleana Tsocas, Max & Eva Tsolakis, Andrew Turner **V** Franco Valdes, Desiree van der Mei, Jan van Es, Diana van Geffen, Joeri van Meenen, Linda van Schel, Agnes van Veen, Sandra Vanseveren, Tamara Veenendaal, Hendrik Joris Verboomen, Gregory Viscusi, Tommaso Vistosi, Eric Voinot **W** Arno Waal, David Walker, Joan Wardle, Sylvie & Matt Waudby Yang, Dirk Weber, Ben White, Michael Whitehouse, Jorien Wiersum, Helena Wilde, Chris Willcox, Frank Windels, Tanja Wohlleber, Moritz Worner **Y** Mong Yang Loh, Hau Yen Tsen **Z** Andreas Zahner, Adrian Zaugg, Petr Zavrel, Mohammad Ziadeh and Beate Ziegler

ACKNOWLEDGMENTS

Many thanks to the following for the use of their content:
Globe on back cover © Mountain High Maps 1993 Digital Wisdom, Inc.

SEND US YOUR FEEDBACK

ACKNOWLEDGMENTS

Index

000 Map pages
000 Location of colour photographs

MAP LEGEND

ROUTES

Freeway	Unsealed Road
Primary Road	Street Mall/Steps
Secondary Road	Tunnel
Tertiary Road	Walking Tour
Lane	Walking Tour Detour
One-Way Street	Walking Trail

TRANSPORT

Ferry	Rail
Cable Car, Funicular	Rail (Underground)

HYDROGRAPHY

River, Creek	Water
Intermittent River	Lake (Dry)
Swamp	Lake (Salt)

BOUNDARIES

International	Ancient Wall
State, Provincial	Cliff
Disputed	

AREA FEATURES

Airport	Cemetery, Christian
Area of Interest	Cemetery, Other
Beach, Desert	Park
Building	Sports
Campus	Urban

POPULATION

○ CAPITAL (NATIONAL)	● Small City
● Large City	● Town, Village
● Medium City	

SYMBOLS

Sights/Activities
- Beach
- Buddhist
- Castle, Fortress
- Christian
- Islamic
- Jewish
- Monument
- Museum, Gallery
- Point of Interest
- Pool/Swimming
- Ruin/Tomb
- Skiing

Eating
- Eating

Drinking
- Drinking
- Café

Entertainment
- Entertainment

Shopping
- Shopping

Sleeping
- Sleeping
- Camping

Transport
- Airport, Airfield
- Border Crossing
- Bus Station
- Taxi Rank

Information
- Bank, ATM
- Embassy/Consulate
- Hospital, Medical
- Information
- Internet Facilities
- Parking Area
- Petrol Station
- Police Station
- Post Office, GPO
- Telephone
- Toilets

Geographic
- Hazard
- Lighthouse
- Mountain, Volcano
- Oasis
- Waterfall

LONELY PLANET OFFICES

Australia
Head Office
Locked Bag 1, Footscray, Victoria 3011
☎ 03 8379 8000, fax 03 8379 8111
talk2us@lonelyplanet.com.au

USA
150 Linden St, Oakland, CA 94607
☎ 510 893 8555, toll free 800 275 8555
fax 510 893 8572, info@lonelyplanet.com

UK
72–82 Rosebery Ave,
Clerkenwell, London EC1R 4RW
☎ 020 7841 9000, fax 020 7841 9001
go@lonelyplanet.co.uk

France
1 rue du Dahomey, 75011 Paris
☎ 01 55 25 33 00, fax 01 55 25 33 01
bip@lonelyplanet.fr, www.lonelyplanet.fr

Published by Lonely Planet Publications Pty Ltd
ABN 36 005 607 983

© Lonely Planet 2004

© photographers as indicated 2004

Cover photographs by Lonely Planet Images: Pillars and entablature ruins at the site of the ancient city of Baalbek, Eric L Wheater (front); Sweet tea from the Old City citadel in the Souq al Hamidiyya, Damascus, John Elk III (back). Many of the images in this guide are available for licensing from Lonely Planet Images: www.lonely planetimages.com.

Printed through The Bookmaker International Ltd
Printed in China